Handbook of Mobile Learning

This handbook provides a comprehensive compendium of research in all aspects of mobile learning, one of the most significant ongoing global developments in the entire field of education. Rather than focus on specific technologies, expert authors discuss how best to utilize technology in the service of improving teaching and learning.

For more than a decade, researchers and practitioners have been exploring this area of study as the growing popularity of smartphones, tablets, and other such devices—as well as the increasingly sophisticated applications they use—has allowed educators to accommodate and support an increasingly mobile society. This handbook provides the first authoritative account of the theory and research that underlies mobile learning, while also exemplifying models of current and future practice.

Zane L. Berge is Professor of Education at the University of Maryland, Baltimore County.

Lin Y. Muilenburg is Assistant Professor of Educational Studies at St. Mary's College of Maryland.

Handbook of Mobile Learning

Edited by Zane L. Berge and Lin Y. Muilenburg

NEW YORK AND LONDON

First published 2013
by Routledge
711 Third Avenue, New York, NY 10017

Simultaneously published in the UK
by Routledge
2 Park Square, Milton Park, Abingdon, Oxon OX14 4RN

Routledge is an imprint of the Taylor & Francis Group, an informa business

© 2013 Taylor & Francis

Library of Congress Cataloging in Publication Data
Handbook of mobile learning/edited by Zane L. Berge and Lin Y. Muilenburg.
   p. cm.
   Includes bibliographical references and index.
   1. Mobile communication systems in education. I. Berge, Zane L., editor of compilation.
II. Muilenburg, Lin Y., editor of compilation. III. Crompton, Helen. Historical overview of mLearning.
   LB1044.84.H36 2013
   371.33—dc23   2012041546

ISBN: 978–0–415–50369–3 (hbk)
ISBN: 978–0–203–11876–4 (ebk)

Typeset in Minion
by Florence Production Ltd, Stoodleigh, Devon, UK

Printed and bound in the United States of America by Sheridan Books, Inc. (a Sheridan Group Company).

CONTENTS

Helen Crompton

Through the study of recent histories, this chapter provides a historical
view of the field of electronic learning. The chapter begins by explicating
the philosophical, pedagogical, and conceptual underpinnings regarding
learning, particularly toward learner-centered pedagogies. This is followed
by a discussion of the technology, covering the evolution of the hardware/
software, its adoption into society, and how these technological
advancements have led to today's new affordances for learning.

William C. Diehl

The use of mobile devices for educational purposes is increasing, and
m-learning has the potential to revolutionize the way that people learn,
but the use of technology to connect learners with content and with
teachers at a distance is not new. Like mobile devices, technologies such
as the printing press, radio, and television—and systems such as the
postal service—have also increased the opportunities for both planned
and spontaneous individual informal learning. This chapter provides
historical context, presents m-learning as a subfield of distance education,
and focuses on early technologies and social movements within the field.

Thomas Cochrane

This chapter overviews a short, recent history and critique of mobile-
learning research, indicating the research gaps that future m-learning

v

research needs to fill, and situates the research literature within the context of current mobile-learning practice. Although still a relatively young field of academic research, the first decade of mobile-learning research has established a solid foundation on which to build as we move into a second decade of research that can provide the basis for the development of theoretical frameworks as we reflect upon an increasing body of longitudinal research. Rather than continually reinventing the wheel with a series of short-term case studies, mobile-learning research needs to take a more strategic approach that focuses upon how pedagogy can be reinvented using mobile devices as a catalyst for change.

construction of knowledge through interaction with peers and on ill-structured problems. What is often missing as we seek to transition face-to-face educational experiences to mobile ones is theory that recognizes the importance of human communication as the center of teaching and learning experiences. The goal of this chapter is to introduce learning and teaching as communicative-actions theory, which is here offered as one theoretical support structure for using mobile devices and applications to support learning. This theory expands upon the pragmatic communication and social works of Jürgen Habermas. This chapter further connects this theory to how social-media tools may be understood to act in the service of instruction and learning.

Mindtools and expert system-oriented Mindtools. The former are used to help students organize and visualize their knowledge by linking the new experiences with their prior knowledge, and the latter have been employed to help students identify and differentiate a set of learning targets based on the common and distinct features of those targets.

triggers this collaboration have so far been made. However, *social flow*, which extends Csikszentmihalyi's flow theory, may help partially explain the triggering mechanism of collaborative m-learning. This chapter discusses how the concept of social flow in a collaborative learning space might sketch out what triggers an optimal learning experience in collaboration, and what can be additionally achieved.

The study has been conducted over an 18-month period, from December 2010 to June 2012. This chapter identifies an important gap in both the literature and practice, as little research has been conducted into the lecturer's use of mobile technologies in the classroom. The chapter concludes by presenting seven principles for successfully managing the introduction of mobile technology into an organization.

the relevant world literature regarding mobile devices-based assessment. It describes the progress made in the field of mobile assessment (m-assessment), explaining current practices and addressing different aspects associated with design and implementation issues, as well as the affordances and constraints of this emerging field.

smartphones, laptops, cameras, and e-readers all have a place in a
learning environment. Although specialized functions (feature-length
video production, probe-based science labs, digital music creation, etc.)
will still be maintained in a traditional lab format, basic technology
integration such as Internet research, writing, e-mail, and other uses
will be conducted on the device in each student's personal control.
The model empowers students. They evaluate the goal of the assignment,
choose the proper tools for their learning style, use tools with which
they are familiar, and develop personal responsibility. Moreover,
students, teachers, and technology staff together focus on learning
objectives, rather than the maintenance of uniform carts of technology
that may or may not fit the learning needs of any particular student or
class.

component of the American Council on the Teaching of Foreign Languages' communication learning goal. Furthermore, with m-learning, the students can talk about up-to-moment, real-world situations (culture) in the target language. The author identifies many different mobile-assisted language learning activities for student speaking, speaking about culture, and assessing speaking.

distributed locations to deliver a service that would be free to the end user.

        Matthew Kam
        The cell phone's ubiquity in developing countries has made it widely
        hyped as a highly appropriate e-learning device in these regions.
        However, the evidence base remains scant. This chapter summarizes 5
        years of research on designing and evaluating mobile-learning games with
        low-income children in the urban slums and villages in India, based on
        research that I carried out when I was at the University of California,
        Berkeley, and Carnegie Mellon University. The chapter next reports that
        children experienced significant post-test gains associated with the
        mobile-learning games designed by my research team. Furthermore, even
        in the absence of supervision from adults, rural children were expected to
        voluntarily cover nearly one-third of the vocabulary that they should
        acquire under ideal "industrialized country" conditions.

ABOUT THE AUTHORS

Zoraini Wati Abas is a Professor and Program Coordinator of the Doctor of Education program at the Open University Malaysia. Her interests are in instructional design and emerging learning technologies.

Trish Andrews is a Senior Lecturer in Higher Education at the University of Queensland and a member of the anzMLearn executive. Dr. Andrews's interests include m-learning for distance learners and the adoption of m-learning.

Patricia Aufderheide is University Professor in the School of Communication at American University in Washington, DC, and founder–director of the Center for Social Media there. She is the co-author with Peter Jaszi of *Reclaiming Fair Use: How to Put Balance Back in Copyright* (University of Chicago Press, July 2011) and author of, among others, *Documentary: A Very Short Introduction* (Oxford University Press, 2007), *The Daily Planet* (University of Minnesota Press, 2000), and *Communications Policy and the Public Interest* (Guilford Press, 1999). She heads the Fair Use and Free Speech research project at the Center, in conjunction with Professor Peter Jaszi, in American University's Washington College of Law.

Ben Bachmair was Professor of Pedagogy, Media Education, and Instructional Technology at the University of Kassel, Germany, until his retirement in 2008. His specialisms include: mass communication and education, media and learning, media socialization and media reception, and media within cultural development.

Stephen Baldridge currently serves on the Social Work faculty of Abilene Christian University, where he directs the undergraduate social work program. His research interests include family dynamics, childhood behavior, and using technology in higher-education classes. Stephen consults with school districts around the nation, helping them implement mobile technology in the tracking and treating of student behavior.

Michael K. Barbour is an Assistant Professor in Instructional Technology and Educational Evaluation and Research at Wayne State University. He has been involved with K–12 online learning in Canada, the United States, and New Zealand for over a decade, as a researcher, teacher, course designer, and administrator. His research focuses on the effective design, delivery, and support of K–12 online learning, particularly for students located in rural jurisdictions.

George Baroudi is Vice President for Information Technology, CIO, and Chief Business Process Improvement Officer for Long Island University, Brookville, NY, USA. Mr. Baroudi is an electrical engineer by training. He entered the IT field at the time of the desktop revolution, when desktops began replacing mainframe systems. The mobile revolution, as mobility replaces desktop computing, extends the continuum.

Siew Mee Barton is a Lecturer in the School of Marketing and Management at Deakin University and is the joint Unit Chair for Business Communications.

Elizabeth A. Beckmann is Senior Lecturer at the Centre for Higher Education, Learning and Teaching at the Australian National University. Dr. Beckmann's teaching and research are related to the professional development of academics as teachers, and student responses to technology-enhanced learning.

Terese Bird is Learning Technologist at Beyond Distance Research Alliance, University of Leicester, UK. Her work involves supporting academics to use technology in their teaching.

Adele Botha is a principal researcher at the CSIR Meraka Institute and research associate at the University of South Africa. Her research is in the use of mobile technologies for goal-oriented interactions in a developing context.

Beverly B. Bowers is Associate Professor and Assistant Dean for the Center for Educational Excellence at the OU College of Nursing, where she promotes faculty development and integration of technology into teaching and online learning.

Richard Brandt, PA-C, MPAS, is a Physician Assistant with over 12 years of clinical experience in medical and surgical dermatology. He has served as a sub-investigator (Sub-I) on multiple clinical-research studies, an adjunct faculty member in Physician Assistant Studies, a moderator for Dermatology PA meetings, and an educator while performing P2P and student lecturing. Additionally, he is a doctoral student in Texas Tech University's Technical Communication and Rhetoric program, studying new media and m-learning in medicine.

Denise M. Bressler, having been a museum professional for over six years, is now a graduate student at Lehigh University, USA. Bressler's doctoral work focuses on mobile technologies and science education.

Laurie Butgereit is the technical lead behind the Dr Math tutoring project. She is a principal technologist at the CSIR Meraka Institute in South Africa.

Colleen Carmean serves as UWT's strategist for e-learning and emerging technologies. Her work lies in the research and design of shared-knowledge systems, including environments for new, mobile, and social media. She teaches critical thinking and applied computing, and is currently doing research on engagement practices in e-learning.

Ana Amélia Carvalho is Professor of the Faculty of Psychology and Education, University of Coimbra, Portugal. Dr. Carvalho's teaching and scholarship involve educational technology in Masters and PhD programs, in face-to-face and distance-education courses.

Baiyun Chen is an instructional designer for the Center for Distributed Learning at UCF. Her current research interests mainly focus on the use of social-media technologies, their impact on teaching and learning, and design and evaluation of e-learning systems.

Andreas Christ is Professor and, since 2007, Vice President of the Offenburg University of Applied Sciences. Also, as Head of the Information Center, he is responsible for the deployment of, and support for, e-learning and electronic media for education and research purposes. His professional interests include technologies for mobile Internet.

Maria Cinque works in the Department of Educational Research of Fondazione Rui and teaches learning and communication skills at Campus Bio-Medico University in Rome. Her main research interests focus on m-learning, technology-enhanced learning and creativity, and talent management and development.

Thomas Cochrane is Academic Advisor in eLearning and Learning Technologies at the Centre for Learning and Teaching at AUT. Dr. Cochrane's PhD thesis was titled, "Mobilizing Learning: Transforming pedagogy with mobile web 2.0."

John Cook is Professor of Technology-Enhanced Learning. He has an interest in five related areas: informal learning, m-learning in all sectors, augmented contexts for development, user-generated contexts, and work-based learning.

Helen Crompton is a graduate student at the University of North Carolina at Chapel Hill, USA. Crompton's PhD foci are educational technologies, specifically mobile technologies, and mathematics teacher preparation. Crompton is an officer in the SIG Mobile Learning for the International Society for Technology in Education.

Paul Davies is a lecturer in science education. His teaching is focused on initial teacher training, where he specializes in biology education. He has a particular interest in the development of teacher subject knowledge and pedagogic content knowledge.

Inge de Waard is e-learning coordinator and researcher at the Institute of Tropical Medicine in Antwerp, Belgium, and researcher at Athabasca University. Inge explores and embeds innovative, educational solutions fitting local infrastructure and learning contexts. She is an international speaker and collaborates with educational institutes in several developing regions to set up technology-enhanced learning.

William C. Diehl is an independent consultant, an instructor at The Pennsylvania State University, and the interviews editor for *The American Journal of Distance Education*. His work focuses on emerging technologies, historical foundations, and theory of open and distance education.

Laurel E. Dyson is a Senior Lecturer in Information Technology at the University of Technology, Sydney, Australia, and President of anzMLearn, the Australian and New Zealand Mobile Learning Group. Dr. Dyson's interests include m-learning and mobile technology use in indigenous communities.

Martin Ebner is Head of the Social Learning Department of the Computer and Information Services, as well as Senior Researcher at the Institute of Information Systems Computer Media.

Anastasios A. Economides is a Professor of Computer Networks and Telematics Applications, and Chairman of the Information Systems Postgraduate Program at the University of Macedonia, Greece. He is the director of CONTA (Computer Networks and Telematics Applications) Laboratory. He has published over 200 peer-reviewed papers on computer networks, e-learning, and other e-services.

Palitha Edirisingha is lecturer in learning technology at Beyond Distance Research Alliance, University of Leicester, UK. Dr. Edirisingha's teaching and research involve investigating the impact of technology on teaching and student experience.

William Farr is a Research Fellow in human–computer interaction, having trained in psychology and informatics for hard-to-reach user groups. His PhD work focused on using tangible user interfaces for children with autism, in collaboration with Massachusetts Institute of Technology and Swiss Federal Institute of Technology, Zurich.

J. D. Ferries-Rowe received his bachelor's degree from Bradley University. He has served in a number of roles, including English teacher, debate coach, Academic Assistant Principal, and the ambiguous Coordinator for Special Projects. He has been a presenter at a number of conferences, consults with public and private schools, and is currently the National Coordinator for Technology Specialists for the Jesuit Secondary Education Association. Areas of interest and research include: flipped classrooms, social media, strategic planning for schools, and comic books. Follow him @jdferries.

Jill L. Frankfort is a co-founder of Persistence Plus. Forging connections among behavioral psychology, mobile technology, and student success, she is working to transform student support systems and college completion strategies. Previously, she was a director at Jobs for the Future, where she worked with colleges and districts to improve the educational outcomes of students.

Xun Ge is Professor of Instructional Psychology and Technology and Chair of the Department of Educational Psychology at the University of Oklahoma. Dr. Ge's scholarship and teaching involve designing and developing advanced-learning technologies, inquiry-based learning environments, game-based learning environments, and virtual-learning communities to scaffold learners' ill-structured problem-solving and self-regulated learning.

Jackie Gerstein has been teaching face to face and online for several decades. Her background includes a strong focus on experiential and adventure learning, which she brings into her online teaching. You can learn more about her at http://jackiegerstein.weebly.com.

Michael M. Grant is an Associate Professor in Instructional Design and Technology at the University of Memphis. Dr. Grant has been working with elementary and secondary teachers across the south for over 10 years. His research considers how to best help teachers integrate technology and how students represent their learning with computer technologies, particularly within project-based learning.

Scott Hamm coordinates the mobile-learning research at Abilene Christian University. Currently working on his second doctorate, a PhD in computing technology, he is focusing his course work on mobile integration in learning environments. Scott presents and publishes in the area of m-learning and spirituality and technology. He teaches for the Sloan Consortium on mobile integration in online courses.

Dingchung Huang is an Instructional Designer at the Department of Forensic and Investigative Genetics, University of North Texas Health Science Center Campus. He graduated with a MEd degree from the Instructional Psychology and Technology Program at the University of Oklahoma. Mr. Huang's work involves developing online training programs related to DNA data interpretation and statistical evaluation for the forensic community.

Sabrina Huber is a student of computer science management and English (as a degree student in a teacher-training program) at the University of Technology of Graz and the University of Graz.

Raja Maznah Raja Hussain is a Professor at the Faculty of Education, University of Malaya and Director of the Academic Development Centre; he is interested in the design and development of personalized learning environments.

Gwo-Jen Hwang is currently Chair Professor of National Taiwan University of Science and Technology. His research interests include mobile and ubiquitous learning and digital game-based learning. Owing to the distinguished achievements in mobile and ubiquitous learning studies, in 2007, Dr. Hwang was elected as the Chair of the Special Interest Group of Mobile and Ubiquitous Learning of the National Science Council in Taiwan.

Sheila Jagannathan is Program Manager of the e-Institute for Development, and Senior Education Specialist at the World Bank Institute in Washington, DC. Her experience is in the blend of technology and learning. She has worked for over 25 years in private- and public-sector organizations, designing and managing distance-learning program and knowledge products in the US, East Asia, China, Middle East, and North Africa, and more recently in Africa and South Asia. She is passionate about e-learning and its opportunities for development; her current interests include pedagogy and technologies, including serious games, social technologies, open-source content and tools, collaborative platforms, and future e-learning trends. She has a Masters degree, Certificates of Advanced Graduate study in Educational Media and Technology from Boston University, and has completed all the requirements except for the dissertation toward a PhD on applying artificial-intelligence techniques to design intelligent tutoring systems.

Breana Jones is a research assistant in the Teaching, Learning and Technology Center at Abilene Christian University, where she does statistical analysis, writes, and presents research on behalf of the university.

Vani Kalloo has an MPhil in Computer Science and is currently pursuing a PhD in computer science at the University of the West Indies, St. Augustine, Trinidad and Tobago. She is currently doing research work in m-learning for mathematics with secondary-school students, game-based learning, and personalization. She is currently a teaching assistant at the University of the West Indies.

Matthew Kam is the senior specialist for Information and Communication Technologies at the American Institutes for Research's International Development Program (IDP). He leads IDP's research and implementation initiatives in the design, applications, and evaluations of appropriate computing technologies that aim to improve lives in the so-called developing world.

Mehmet Kesim is Professor at Anadolu University. His fields of interest include new communications technologies and distance-education technologies. He accomplished significant work conducting technical projects and applications in the field of distance education for Anadolu University's Open Education Faculty.

Ferial Khaddage is a Lecturer in I.T. Faculty of Science, Engineering and Built Environment at the School of Information Technology, Deakin University, Burwood Campus, Melbourne, Australia. Her research interests are in m-learning technologies and applications, and she has published widely in the area. She is an active member of AACE and an executive committee member and founder of Global Learn Asia Pacific.

Agnes Kukulska-Hulme is Professor of Learning Technology and Communication and Associate Director of the Open University's Institute of Educational Technology. She is President of the International Association for Mobile Learning.

Jennifer LaMaster is the Director of Faculty Development at Brebeuf Jesuit Preparatory School. She is a former classroom teacher (she has a BS in Theatre/Speech Education, from Bradley University), school media specialist (she has a Masters degree in Library Science, from Indiana University), and is certified via ISTE for Proficiency for Teaching with the National Educational Technology Standards—Teacher. Areas of interest and research include: re-visioning assessment, multichannel learners, technology trends in the classroom, and social media in education. Follow her @40ishoracle.

Christoph Lattemann is Professor of Business Administration and Information Management. His research interest is in social-media and mobile-technologies integration in the corporate context and in education. He has published seven books and more than 130 articles. He is a member of various review boards and professional associations.

Ah-reum Lee is a research associate at Hanyang University, who is interested in studying information design and practical issues in human–computer interaction.

Chee-Kit Looi is Professor of Education at the National Institute of Education, Nanyang Technological University, Singapore. Dr. Looi's teaching and scholarship include the field of m-learning and computer-supported collaborative learning.

Mpine Makoe is a senior researcher at the Institute for Open Distance Learning at the University of South Africa (UNISA). Her scholarship involves professional development in distance education and m-learning.

Nancy Marksbury is Deputy CIO for the Post campus of Long Island University. Ms. Marksbury is currently a graduate student at the Palmer School of Information Science at Long Island University. In addition to overseeing information technology for the campus, her PhD research focuses on technology and communication.

M. Daniel Martìn is Associate Professor in the School of Language Studies at the Australian National University. Dr. Martìn was responsible for the establishment of the university's Spanish program and has taught Spanish at all levels. His areas of research are social linguistics and the history of language teaching in Australia, and he also a creative writer in Spanish.

Patrick Meyrueis has been Professor at the University of Strasbourg since 1986. He is the founder and director of the Photonics Systems Laboratory, which is now one of the most advanced labs in the field of planar digital optics. His professional interests include, but are not limited to, 3D imaging, virtual reality, holography, and optics.

Marcelo Milrad is Professor of Media Technology at Linnaeus University, Sweden. His current research interest focuses on the design and development of mobile and wireless applications to support collaborative learning. He is one of the initiators of the IEEE international conference on Wireless, Mobile, and Ubiquitous Technologies in Education. He has published over 150 papers in international journals, and refereed conferences, books, and technical reports.

Plamen Miltenoff is Professor in the Department of Information Media at St. Cloud State University (SCSU), in Minnesota, USA. He has terminal degrees from the United States and several other European universities. Dr. Miltenoff had taught and worked at several European educational institutions and has taught educational technology at SCSU for more than 10 years.

Permanand Mohan is a Senior Lecturer in Computer Science in the Department of Computing and Information Technology at the University of the West Indies, St. Augustine Campus, in Trinidad and Tobago. He has a PhD in computer science. Dr. Mohan was a Fulbright Visiting Scholar to the School of Information Sciences at the University of Pittsburgh. He is currently working on several research projects investigating the use of mobile technology to provide ongoing education to diabetic patients and to support the learning of mathematics at the secondary level. He presently supervises several postgraduate students in the areas of mobile health, m-learning, e-learning, and games for learning. Dr. Mohan is also the Chief Examiner of the Caribbean's CXC CAPE examinations in computer science.

Adelina Moura is a lecturer in educational technology at Portucalense University. Dr. Moura has a vast teaching and scholarship experience. She teaches languages (Portuguese and French) in the K–12 classrooms. She also teaches educational technology in Masters programs. Furthermore, she offers online courses in Web 2.0 and Web 2.0 mobile tools for language teachers.

Diana J. Muir is the CEO and Director of both the Hawking Institute, an NGO of the UN, and the World Virtual School, in Davenport, IA, USA. Dr. Muir's emphasis in education is technology and social change, using instructional technology in the classroom, online, and through m-learning. Dr. Muir has been active in online learning since 1995 and is considered a pioneer in the field of distance learning. In 2010, she was named the Global Educator of the Year by CCLP Worldwide.

Leanne Ngo is a lecturer in e-learning in the Faculty of Business and Law at Deakin University.

Ming Nie is a research associate in learning technology at Beyond Distance Research Alliance, University of Leicester, UK. Dr. Nie's research investigates how to integrate technology into teaching and learning.

Stavros A. Nikou holds a physics degree from Aristotle University, Thessaloniki, Greece, and an MSc in computer science from the University of Houston–Clear Lake, USA. He is a PhD student in the field of m-learning at the University of Macedonia, Greece.

Cathleen A. Norris is a Regents Professor in the College of Information, where she is designing strategies for K–12 teachers to become comfortable and effective using mobile technologies and designing curricula that leverage the affordances of mobile technologies.

Andrew M. O'Loughlin is a Senior Lecturer in the School of Marketing and Management at Deakin University and is the Unit Chair for Business Communications.

Hiroaki Ogata is an Associate Professor at the Faculty of Engineering in the University of Tokushima, Japan. He received the BE, ME, and PhD degrees from the University of Tokushima in 1992, 1994, and 1998, respectively. His current research interests are in computer-supported, ubiquitous, and m-learning and learning analytics.

Ozlem Ozan is a research assistant at Eskisehir Osmangazi University Department of Computer Education and Instructional Technology. Her dissertation is about m-learning. Her fields of interest also include distance education, new communications technologies, and open educational resources.

Norbert Pachler is Professor of Education. He is the founder and convenor of the London Mobile Learning Group (www.londonmobilelearning.net). His research interests are in the fields of technology-enhanced learning, with a particular emphasis on m-learning and e-learning, teacher education and development, and foreign-language education.

Scott Perkins is Professor of Psychology at Abilene Christian University (ACU). Over the last four years, Dr. Perkins' research has focused on issues and outcomes related to ACU's connected m-learning initiative, including student engagement, learning outcomes, and utilization patterns related to the integration of m-learning devices in higher education. Perkins has played a leadership role in conducting and encouraging faculty research on mobility across the ACU campus for the last decade.

Sara Price is a Senior Lecturer in Technology-Enhanced Learning. Her work encompasses the educational application of pervasive, mobile, and tangible technologies, and the relationship between technology and educational practice. She was recently PI on the JISC-funded project GeoSciTeach.

Clark N. Quinn is Executive Director of Quinnovation and Senior Director of Interaction and Mobile for the Internet Time Alliance. Dr. Quinn consults, writes, and speaks on the strategic implementation of advanced learning and performance technology.

Rich Rice is Associate Professor of English at Texas Tech University, where he specializes in technical communication and rhetoric. He directs the TTU English Multiliteracy Lab, which explores intersections between new media composing and teaching, research, service, and grant writing. He teaches online, hybrid, and F2F courses in new media and rhetoric, grant writing, multimodal composing, and technical communication.

Jodi B. Roberts is the IRB Officer for the Human Research Protection Program at MSU. Dr. Roberts has 8 years of experience in distance learning and 13 years of experience in the field of disability studies.

Hokyoung Ryu is a human–computer-interaction and mobile-learning researcher with an interest in new information design; he is an Associate Professor in the Department of Industrial Engineering at Hanyang University, Korea.

Kenneth N. Salim is a co-founder of Persistence Plus. An expert on supporting students to and through college, he has served as a senior public-school district administrator and superintendent of schools in Massachusetts and has led initiatives to increase graduation rates.

George Saltsman is the Executive Director of the Taskforce on Innovation in Learning and Educational Technology at Abilene Christian University and leader of ACU's connected m-learning program. George is an Apple Distinguished Educator and the winner of multiple awards, including Campus Technology Innovator of the Year and the New Media Consortium's Center of Excellence award. He is co-author of *An Administrators Guide to Online Education* and multiple other works focused on the integration of technology in education.

Aaron J. Sams is a science teacher at Woodland Park High School, Woodland Park, CO, USA. Mr. Sams is an award-winning science teacher who co-chaired the committee to revise the Colorado state science standards in 2009. He is a pioneer in the flipped-classroom concept and conducts flipped-classroom training and workshops around the world.

Ryan M. Seilhamer is an instructional designer for the Center for Distributed Learning at UCF. Ryan's teaching and learning interests involve emerging technologies such as m-learning for higher education.

Mike Sharples is Professor of Educational Technology in the Institute of Educational Technology at the Open University, UK. His research involves human-centered design of new technologies for learning. He inaugurated the mLearn conference series and was Founding President of the International Association for Mobile Learning. He is the author of over 250 papers in the areas of educational technology, science education, human-centered design of personal technologies, artificial intelligence, and cognitive science.

Robyn Smith is an Associate Professor and Director of Learning and Teaching Support. Her research interests include synchronous communications technologies and innovating pedagogies in higher education.

Elliot M. Soloway is an Arthur F. Thurnau Professor in the College of Engineering, where he is developing end-to-end—handheld clients to cloud backends—mobile-learning platforms that support synchronous and asynchronous collaborative learning, 24/7.

Ioana A. Stănescu works as a project manager at Advanced Technology Systems, Romania. Her research focuses on decision-support systems, knowledge management, interoperability and semantics, mobile technologies, and game-based and creative learning.

Antoniu Ştefan is a software developer at Advanced Technology Systems, Romania. Mr. Ştefan designs Web- and Windows-based applications for electronic services such as m-learning, m-government, and m-business.

Sharon Stoerger is an instructional design consultant and adjunct instructor at the University of Wisconsin, Milwaukee, USA. Dr. Stoerger's teaching and scholarship are focused on social media, including virtual worlds, m-learning, and pedagogical practices in e-learning environments.

Amy B. Sugar is an instructional designer for the Center for Distributed Learning at the University of Central Florida, USA. Her teaching and learning research interests include social media, m-learning, and accessibility to online materials for individuals with disabilities.

Dustin C. Summey is an instructional designer and teaches for the instructional-technology graduate program at the University of Central Arkansas, USA. Mr. Summey's teaching and scholarship involve professional development, online teaching, and m-learning in both K–12 and higher education.

Razia Sultana is working as a research assistant in Offenburg University of Applied Sciences and is a doctoral student in the University of Strasbourg, France. Her thesis area involves device-independent communication and delivery of virtual-reality scenes in different devices, including mobile devices.

John M. Traxler is Professor of Mobile Learning, probably the world's first and a full UK professor, and Director of the Learning Lab at the University of Wolverhampton. He is a Founding Director of the International Association for Mobile Learning and Associate Editor of the *International Journal of Mobile and Blended Learning* and of *Interactive Learning Environments*. He is on the Research Board of the Association for Learning Technology and the Editorial Board of *Research in Learning Technology* and *IT in International Development*. He was Conference Chair of mLearn2008, the world's biggest and oldest mobile-learning research conference. John has co-written a guide to m-learning in developing countries and is co-editor of the definitive book, *Mobile Learning: A Handbook for Educators and Trainers*, with Professor Agnes Kukulska-Hulme.

Harry Grover Tuttle teaches Spanish at Onondaga Community College, Syracuse, NY. Dr. Tuttle focuses his research on improving student learning through formative assessment, m-learning, speaking, and culture.

Jenny S. Wakefield works as an instructional designer at the University of Texas at Dallas. She is a doctoral student and Teaching Fellow in the Department of Learning Technologies at the University of North Texas. Her work includes supporting higher-education learning through social media and with virtual worlds.

Ruth Wallace is Director of the Northern Institute, Charles Darwin University's research institute for social and public policy, education, and the humanities. Associate

Professor Wallace's particular interest is in research that improves outcomes for stakeholders in regional and remote Australia.

Scott J. Warren is an Associate Professor of Learning Technologies at the University of North Texas. His research examines the use of emerging online technologies such as immersive digital-learning environments and educational games and simulations in K-20 settings.

Rachel Wexelbaum is Collection Management Librarian at St. Cloud State University, in Minnesota, USA. Ms. Wexelbaum currently teaches a research-strategies course; her scholarship involves representation of underserved populations in collection development, the challenges of e-reader adoption in academic libraries, and advances in technology to deliver and promote library resources and services.

Julie A. Willems (http://wikieducator.org/user:julie_willems) is an e-learning designer/ educational developer in the School of Rural Health, Monash University, Australia. Dr. Willems' research foci include educational technology (particularly mobile technologies), social media for formal and informal learning, learning during emergencies and disasters, and educational diversity, equity, and access. Julie is on the National Executive of the Open and Distance Learning Association of Australia.

Lung-Hsiang Wong is a research scientist in the Learning Sciences Laboratory, National Institute of Education, Nanyang Technological University, Singapore. Dr. Wong's main research interests are in the areas of mobile and seamless learning, and technology-enhanced language learning.

Huimin Zhang is a training specialist in the Inflight Services Training and Development Department of Cathay Pacific Airways Ltd. Huimin Zhang graduated with an MEd degree from the Instructional Psychology and Technology Program at the University of Oklahoma. Ms. Zhang is involved in training cabin crew through face-to-face and computer-based instruction.

PREFACE

Over the past decade and a half, the use of mobile devices has changed the landscape of communication in business and society generally. When technology makes sweeping changes such as this, it is little wonder that educators explore and experiment with how those technologies might help solve educational problems or increase student performance.

A lot of time and intellectual effort has been expended trying to define what mobile learning (m-learning) is and how it differs from other types of educational delivery, and in describing the salient elements of m-learning regarding teaching and learning. M-learning uses the same mobile devices that are used throughout our daily lives for friendly communication in the variety of venues a person finds him/herself. These are ubiquitous, personal, mobile devices that are relatively inexpensive and easy to carry and provide immediate access to people and information that helps an individual solve his/her problems whenever and wherever that individual is located. To the extent education can integrate an individual's learning with the other aspects of his/her life, m-learning may be successful for improving education or training.

There are several components of m-learning used for educational purposes that are important, especially when combined. Wireless, easy-to-carry, mobile devices lead to the learner's mobility, untethering that individual from a particular place. This also allows learners to converse and explore information across the many locations and contexts in which they find themselves throughout the day. As the learner faces the need for information or problem-solving, the need is for personal, just-in-time performance support, information, or learning to meet these individual challenges. To a large extent, m-learning can be thought of as *communication in context*. Many of the chapters in this *Handbook* speak to such mobile educational practices as using mobile devices within in-person classrooms, using the applications built specifically for use in these more traditional classes, and the tools built into mobile devices (e.g., video and still camera, audio recorder, GPS) that promote interesting, hands-on projects. Other chapters in this *Handbook*, such as the ones set in developing countries, point out the value of mobile phones as the only practical technology available for delivery of distance education.

However, for many teachers and scholars, when thinking of m-learning, the first thing that comes to their minds is not the delivery of courses, as is done in a traditional school, university, or training classroom. Rather, m-learning's main strength is more about learning that occurs *outside* of these formal learning environments. Performance support, informal learning, and learning that is driven solely by the curiosity of the learner are some of the first thoughts that enter their minds when the concept of m-learning is mentioned. For them, the central position in m-learning is the learner, rather than the teacher. M-learning is all about what learners do with mobile devices, rather than how educators want learners to use mobile devices.

In-person education is based on interpersonal communication between the teacher and students in the classroom. For educators who believe m-learning needs to focus on learning, m-learning doesn't fit so well with in-person education and training. The technology that is used in traditional classrooms *supplements* the teacher. So, m-learning *can* be used for in-person education, but is it built for it? In many ways, these educators are excited about m-learning as the *rejection* of technology-enhanced education and see m-learning as a possible way of transforming the educational enterprise. Although m-learning shares elements of distance education and e-learning, such as the separation of teacher and learner and the substitution of the teacher in the classroom with technology for the delivery of instruction, all these forms of education generally focus on teaching rather than learning. In other words, to some educators, m-learning doesn't fit so well into *any* education. It is because of these ideological differences, how educators differ in their beliefs about *education* and the *purposes of education*, that defining educational technology, including m-learning, continues to be troublesome.

This *Handbook* is organized into five parts. Following is a brief outline of the contents.

PART I

Part I lays the theoretical groundwork for the remainder of the book. It begins with historical perspectives and an overview of mobile-learning literature, then presents new learning theories specific to m-learning, and ends with predictions about the future of this budding field. In Chapter 1, Crompton presents a historical overview of the field of electronic learning and the recent development of the field of m-learning. Diehl (Chapter 2) provides historical context and presents m-learning as a subfield of distance education, and then focuses on early technologies and social movements within the field of m-learning. Cochrane (Chapter 3) provides an overview and critique of m-learning research, suggesting gaps in the literature and a more strategic approach to research in the future.

Because m-learning is a relatively young field, researchers are keen on articulating learning theories that can guide the work of practitioners and researchers alike. Several of our authors offer theories for m-learning. Pachler, Bachmair, and Cook (Chapter 4) examine m-learning through a sociocultural lens and consider the mobile complex— the specific structures, agency, and cultural practices—as it relates to the field of education. In Chapter 5, Crompton makes a case that m-learning, being uniquely different from conventional tethered electronic learning and traditional learning, requires a new theory based on the themes of context, connectivity, time, and personalization. Moura and Carvalho (Chapter 6) present their framework for the integration of mobile technologies in education, which is based on constructivist approaches, activity theory, and the ARCS model. Warren and Wakefield (Chapter 7) base their theory of learning and teaching as communicative action on the importance of human communication as the center of teaching and learning experiences.

The next group of authors take a forward-looking view of m-learning, boldly predicting where this rapidly evolving field may be headed. Quinn (Chapter 8) explores how new devices, trends, and emerging capabilities will augment performance support and formal learning, support contextual learning, make thinking visible, and make learning more engaging. Milrad et al. (Chapter 9) consider how mobile and ubiquitous technology enhances learning, offering the opportunity for seamless learning, which may help educational institutions overcome challenges in implementing innovative practices, instituting m-learning in classroom settings, and attaining sustainability. Norris and Soloway (Chapter 10) present their optimistic and empowering view that mobile technology (and bring-your-own-device initiatives) will transform the pedagogy and curriculum of K–12 schools, empowering students who will learn by doing. In Chapter 11, Khaddage and Lattemann discuss the future of mobile apps for teaching and learning in higher education and identify the organizational and social barriers to their adoption. To wrap up Part I, Traxler (Chapter 12) analyzes a decade's worth of mobile-learning programs and projects that address issues of access, inclusion, and equity, in both the developed and the developing world, to determine the factors that support such complex efforts.

PART II

Part II of the book focuses on the learner and learning. Authors in this part explore how to improve the mobile-learning experience through effective learner support. Kukulska-Hulme (Chapter 13) sets the stage by sharing her findings from a review of 10 years of mobile-learning conference proceedings, in which she identifies the groups of learners most often targeted in mobile-learning literature and groups who have thus far been largely overlooked. Next, Hwang (Chapter 14) discusses how mobile devices can be used to provide learning support, and describes mobile-learning projects that utilized specific Mindtools such as concept maps and expert systems, which simulate expert reasoning using artificial intelligence. In Chapter 15, Ozan and Kesim continue with the idea of learner support by explicating four types of scaffolding for m-learning: instructional, social, technical, and managerial. Stemming from their experiences with the campus-wide mobile-learning implementation at Abilene Christian University, Hamm, Saltsman, Jones, Baldridge, and Perkins (Chapter 16) build a case for a more student-centric mobile-learning model, based on the themes of increased learner engagement, learner independence, and communication.

One of the purported strengths of m-learning is the provision of personalized learning experiences; however, this potential is not often fully exploited. Presenting a truly unique approach to learner support in Chapter 17, Carmean, Frankfort, and Salim share how real-time, personalized support focused on goal setting, time management, and dealing with academic setbacks has enhanced the resiliency, persistence, and success of college students. A second strength of m-learning is that it supports collaborative and con-nectivist learning environments. In Chapter 18, Lee and Ryu discuss how highly collaborative mobile-learning experiences trigger social flow, creating an optimal learning environment in which learners are willing to take greater risks and can achieve more than when working independently.

A major advantage of mobile devices is their portability, which allows for use anytime and anywhere. People can learn while situated in real-world contexts and activities, and thus m-learning supports authentic learning opportunities. Chapters 19 through 21 exemplify authentic, situated m-learning. Cinque (Chapter 19) describes two projects in which learners used mobile devices seamlessly for a variety of purposes during on-the-job training in a medical school and a cooking school. Interestingly, the uptake of m-learning differed between these diverse settings. In Chapter 20, Bressler describes how the affordances of m-learning are changing the face of museum education. Museums are more actively engaging learners with their content, using such technologies as geo-referenced data and augmented reality—all of which is leading to a more participatory culture. Finally, Nie, Bird, and Edirisingha continue the examination of the use of mobile devices to support work-based learning. In Chapter 21, they focus on the impact e-book readers and PDAs had on learners' mobility, learner support, learning time and cost, and learning design.

PART III

The focus shifts in Part III to an examination of teaching with mobile devices and instructional design for m-learning. Cochrane (Chapter 22) leads off this part by making a strong case that m-learning can serve as a catalyst for pedagogical change. He considers how m-learning transformed pedagogy in four different higher-education contexts and outlines a framework for supporting the pedagogical change enabled by m-learning. The next four chapters explore teacher experiences when integrating m-learning and offer suggested approaches for effective teaching and learning with mobiles. In Chapter 23, Sams explains how mobile technologies can be exploited to support a flipped classroom, thereby making the best use of class time, and to provide more individualized instruction to learners. Gerstein (Chapter 24) shares an assortment of team-building and community-building activities that can be conducted using students' mobile devices. Grant and Barbour (Chapter 25) relate lessons learned from two pilot projects: the first, m-learning integrated into K–12 teacher professional development, and the second, utilized m-learning in an online advanced-placement course. Finally, O'Loughlin, Barton, and Ngo recount the experiences of five lecturers who were provided iPads to support their classroom teaching.

The remaining five chapters in this part consider aspects of instructional design for m-learning. Price, Davies, and Farr (Chapter 27) explore how participatory design affects teachers' understanding of geospatial science concepts, beliefs about the use of smartphone technologies, and ultimately the adoption of mobile-learning activities with their K–12 students. Huber and Ebner (Chapter 28) analyze the iPad Human Interface Guidelines to determine the relationship between good interface design and ease of use of learning applications. Based on their observations of learners using a variety of iPad apps, they provide excellent general guidelines for the use of tablets in the K–12 classroom. In Chapter 29, Ge, Huang, Zhang, and Bowers propose a conceptual framework, which includes pedagogical, design, and technological dimensions, to guide instructional design practices for m-learning. Nikou and Economides (Chapter 30) synthesize the research on mobile assessment, explaining current practices, affordances, and constraints of this emerging field. Rounding out this part, de Waard (Chapter 31) illustrates her model for the design of a mobile Massive Open Online Course (mMOOC).

PART IV

Many of the chapters in this book discuss the challenges faced when implementing an m-learning initiative. Without the proper administration, management, and policies in place, sustaining m-learning is difficult, if not impossible. Several authors in Part IV share lessons learned from undertaking mobile-learning initiatives at their institutions. Through the lens of change management, Baroudi and Marksbury (Chapter 32) analyze the technological and sociocultural challenges faced when their institution distributed 12,000 iPads to students, faculty, and staff, then offer suggestions for other large-scale deployments. Seilhamer, Chen, and Sugar (Chapter 33) introduce the Mobile Implementation Framework, which offers a systematic approach to a campus-wide mobile-technology implementation. They present lessons learned from the release of the Blackboard Mobile Learn product at a very large higher-education institution. LaMaster and Ferries-Rowe (Chapter 34) thoroughly describe the development, implementation, and evaluation of a bring-your-own-technology program utilizing cloud-based computing at an 800-student private preparatory high school. Pedagogy and student learning were the driving forces in decision-making for issues such as access, bandwidth, student safety, technical support, financial aid, and staff development.

Today's administrators, managers, designers, teachers, and learners must concern themselves with the legal and ethical issues surrounding the use of m-learning. Several authors help to demystify these complex topics. Dyson, Andrews, Smith, and Wallace (Chapter 35) examine a range of ethical issues in m-learning, offer a framework for an ethical approach to m-learning, and propose that educators, administrators, and students adopt an ethic of responsibility. Aufderheide (Chapter 36) shares her expertise and guidance on U.S. copyright policy and the right of fair use, as well as community-based codes of best practice in fair use, as they apply to m-learning. Roberts (Chapter 37) outlines accessibility laws, presents accessibility and universal design principles, and makes recommendations for accessible m-learning.

Considering the changes brought about by m-learning in areas such as ethics, accessibility, and copyright policy, and the organizational structures necessary to support mobile-learning initiatives, one stakeholder is uniquely poised to support mobile-learning initiatives. In Chapter 38, Wexelbaum and Miltenoff build a case that academic libraries should be considered an integral part of any mobile-learning initiative. Librarians have a highly relevant skill set and can provide invaluable resources and support to mobile learners.

PART V

M-learning offers broad opportunities for application in diverse settings with all sorts of learners. Part V comprises 15 chapters that explore m-learning projects and cases from around the world, situated in many different contexts. A common thread that runs through these cases is optimism about the promise of m-learning. Authors describe both the benefits and the challenges faced when implementing projects and learning activities using mobile devices, and offer insightful advice for your consideration.

Improving student and teacher performance in K–12 schools is a critical goal for countries around the world. The integration of technology is often seen as a promising path to help learners attain 21st-century learning goals, and many of this book's authors see potential in mobile-learning initiatives. Summey (Chapter 39) explores mobile-learning strategies that enhance various aspects of K–12 teacher professional development in the United States. Kalloo and Mohan (Chapter 40) discuss the use of a customized mobile math game to improve the motivation and performance of high-school algebra students in the Caribbean.

With more resources and latitude for experimentation, and a ready cadre of researchers and academic writers, initiatives at higher-education institutions are often presented in the mobile-learning literature. Stoerger (Chapter 41) discusses the potential of ubiquitous learning opportunities to transform education, sharing several mobile-learning projects at her U.S. institution of higher education. Yet there are many intriguing m-learning projects happening across a spectrum of contexts. In Chapter 42, Brandt and Rice explain how medical care and training are evolving in the United States through the praxis of mobile medicine. Mobile tools are also changing military education, as demonstrated by Stănescu and Ştefan (Chapter 43) in their development of a mobile knowledge management system, a virtual network that provides real-time access to knowledge and learning for the Romanian military. Willems (Chapter 44) outlines how mobile-learning initiatives in Australia are saving lives during emergencies, disasters, and catastrophes, when typical communications channels are either down or can't provide timely and accurate information.

Owing to the unique affordances of mobile devices, one area that appears ripe for mobile-learning implementation is in foreign-language learning. Tuttle (Chapter 45) explains why this is the case, and presents a broad array of mobile-assisted language learning activities to improve student speaking, speaking about culture, and assessing speaking of a foreign language. Beckmann and Martìn (Chapter 46) extend this discussion by analyzing their extensive experiences using m-learning to facilitate Spanish-language learning for university students in Australia. In Chapter 47, Christ, Meyrueis, and Sultana describe the architecture of a mobile collaborative language learning game developed in Germany that allows adult learners to practice the target language using a mobile device.

Educators and instructional designers in developed countries often struggle to effectively implement m-learning, perhaps because learners have so many options for access. If a mobile-learning experience is not better than the alternatives—more effective, efficient, convenient, or fun—users may not be motivated to persist. But what happens when mobile devices offer what is often the only access to electronic learning resources? Muir (Chapter 48) provides an enlightening description of the unique learner needs and some unexpected challenges in providing mobile-learning opportunities in former communist and developing countries. Yet she maintains an extremely positive message throughout by providing suggestions for overcoming these barriers. Jagannathan (Chapter 49) describes several innovative mobile-learning projects that are transforming the lives of poor people in developing countries, including the provision of: just-in-time notifications of the availability of drinking water, information on farming techniques, medical consultations, and communication channels for participatory government. As an interesting contrast, Abas and Raja Hussain (Chapter 50) describe the extraordinary investment the developing country Malaysia has made in information communication and technology to establish a knowledge-based economy. They then examine tablet-device usage among higher-education faculty in Malaysia. Makoe (Chapter 51) continues the examination of mobile-device use by educators, studying the attitudes and usage level of teachers in South African rural communities. Botha and Butgereit (Chapter 52) tell the story of the sustained development and incredible growth of a free mobile math-tutoring service for learners in South Africa. And finally, Kam (Chapter 53) shares the fascinating results of a multi-year project to develop mobile-learning games for low-income children in India.

Taken together, the 53 chapters in the *Handbook of Mobile Learning* provide a comprehensive, scholarly review of m-learning. Along with the many benefits of m-learning that are discussed throughout the book, such as accessibility, flexibility, and convenience, there are inhibitors, too, just as there are to any delivery system used for educational purposes. These barriers include technical, social, managerial, and pedagogical challenges to using m-learning. We hope that this *Handbook* helps its readers—educational administrators, teachers, support staff, students, and scholars—as they learn more about m-learning.

Lin Y. Muilenburg
Zane L. Berge
Maryland, October 2012

Part I

Foundations and Future

1

A HISTORICAL OVERVIEW OF M-LEARNING

Toward Learner-Centered Education

Helen Crompton

A consideration of all the various historical and cultural events that have led to mobile learning (m-learning) would trace back through history far beyond the invention of Gutenberg's printing press and the influence of the Industrial Revolution. Although it needs to be acknowledged that these events have enabled the mobile age to reach where it is today, this chapter looks more specifically into recent history, starting when the mobile technological epoch began to take shape. In order to explain the history, *mobile* and *learning* have been separated, before I explicitly detail the interconnections for what has now become this young field of m-learning. The chapter will begin by explicating the philosophical, pedagogical, and conceptual underpinnings regarding learning, particularly toward learner-centered pedagogies. This will be followed by a discussion of the technology, covering the evolution of the hardware/software, its adoption into society, and how these technological advancements have led to today's new affordances for learning.

DEFINING MOBILE LEARNING

At this time, there is no definitive definition of m-learning. If terms such as *distance education* are any indication, there probably will not be a lasting definition of *m-learning* for a long time to come. In January 2005, Laouris and Eteokleous (2005) reported receiving 1,240 items when searching Google for the terms + "mobile learning" + "definition"; remarkably, when they conducted the same search in June 2005, Google provided 22,700 items. So, it appears that 2005 was the year in which m-learning became a recognized term.

In m-learning's relatively short existence, scholars and practitioners have attempted to define it. An early definition of m-learning was simply the use of a palm as a learning device (Quinn, 2000; Soloway et al., 2001). Since then, deep debates have been ongoing as to which attributes should be included in a definition of m-learning (e.g., Laouris & Eteokleous, 2005; Sharples, Taylor, & Vavoula, 2007; Traxler, 2009), and, from a study of the literature, it appears that pedagogy, technological devices, context, and social interactions are the four central constructs. For example, O'Malley et al. (2003) defined m-learning as, "Any sort of learning that happens when the learner is not at a fixed, predetermined location, or learning that happens when the learner takes advantage of learning opportunities offered by mobile technologies." In O'Malley et al.'s definition, the initial focus is contextual, although closely followed by pedagogies and technologies.

Traxler's (2005) early definition, "any educational provision where the sole or dominant technologies are handheld or palmtop devices," was a good example of a definition centered on the technology. Many early definitions were criticized for taking a technocentric approach (Traxler, 2010). One issue that is agreed upon by academics and practitioners is that further research is necessary to better understand the field of m-learning (Goh & Kinshuk, 2006), which will undoubtedly lead to many further changes to the definition of m-learning.

Sharples et al. (2007) defined m-learning as, "The process of coming to know through conversations across multiple contexts amongst people and personal interactive technologies" (Sharples et al., 2007, p. 4). Although this definition included the four central constructs of m-learning (namely, pedagogy, technological devices, context, and social interactions), the definition is somewhat confusing and ambiguous. For example, the word *conversations* is used early in the definition, which highlights the importance of this word to the definition, and, yet, the definition of conversation is "Oral exchange of sentiments, observations, opinions or ideas" ("Conversation," *Merriam–Webster Dictionary*, 2011). Does this, then, mean that m-learning is centered round verbal communication? Sharples et al.'s definition was written for an article that highlighted conversational theory, and, although they may have intended for conversation to be interactions in general, a word has been chosen that connotes simply *oral interactions.*

Therefore, for the purpose of the chapter, and this book at large, the author of this chapter and the editors of this book (Crompton, Muilenburg, and Berge) have modified Sharples et al.'s (2007) definition. This new definition includes the four central constructs of m-learning, but the wording has been chosen to reduce ambiguity, and additional punctuation has also been included for clarity. Therefore, Crompton, Muilenburg, and Berge's definition for m-learning is "learning across multiple contexts, through social and content interactions, using personal electronic devices."

To be clear, the word "context" in this definition encompasses m-learning that is formal, self-directed, and spontaneous learning, as well as learning that is context aware and context neutral. In other words, the learning may be directed by others or by oneself, and it can be an unplanned, spontaneous learning experience; learning can happen in an academic setting, or any other non-academic setting; and the physical environment may or may not be involved in the learning experience.

Therefore, m-learning can occur inside or outside the classroom, participating in a formal lesson on a mobile device; it can be self-directed, as a person determines his or her own approach to satisfy a learning goal; or spontaneous learning, as a person can use the device to look up something that has just prompted an interest. The environment may be part of the learning experience (e.g., scanning codes to obtain further information about an exhibit in a museum), or the environment may have a neutral role in the learning experience (e.g., reading articles from the Web while traveling on the bus).

PEDAGOGICAL SHIFTS IN LEARNING

Throughout history, learning has been of paramount importance in all cultures. In simple terms, learning is essential to personal and professional survival, and a culture's pedagogical choice is often driven by social behavior, expectations, and values. For example, Western pedagogies during the 1930s did not encourage autonomy and self-direction. A student was to learn facts without question. Even into the 1950s, pedagogies typically emulated the *tabula rasa* approach, teaching the students as though they were empty vessels waiting for the teachers to impart knowledge.

Learners today are viewed very differently: students are encouraged to be active in their own learning, to be self-thinking and active consumers of knowledge. Historical components that form a background to this cultural and societal pedagogical shift include: reactions to behaviorism, linguistic pragmatism, minority rights movements, increased internationalism, and wider access to education (Gremmo & Riley, 1995). Shifts in educational philosophy have been led by calls for change toward active learnership. Piaget (1929) pioneered the transition from the *tabula rasa* view of young learners, to instead positing learners with complex cognitive structures, seeking environmental stimulation to promote intellectual development.

Building from Piaget's (1929) position toward cognitive theories of learning, Bruner (1966) added that learners use current and past knowledge during the active learning process. Soon afterward, the learner-centered pedagogical epoch commenced.

Discovery Learning in the 1970s

Learning the heuristics of discovery through active participation was Bruner's (1966) recipe for increasing intellectual potency. He believed students are more likely to remember concepts they deduce on their own. This philosophy led to the discovery-learning movement, with the focus on how students acquire, retain, and recall knowledge, a transition from the behaviorist stimulus–response approach. Unfortunately, technology in schools was generally lagging behind instructional pedagogies; the few schools that had computers in the 1970s utilized behavioristic computer-assisted learning programs (Lee, 2000). The World Wide Web (WWW) would have been a great learning support to discovery learning, although only a small number of people had Internet access until the 1990s.

Constructivist Learning in the 1980s

Constructivism is an epistemic belief about how students learn. Following Piaget's (1929), Bruner's (1966), and Jonassen's (1999) educational philosophies, constructivists proffer that knowledge acquisition develops through interactions with the environment. During the 1980s, the development and distribution of multimedia personal computers offered such an interactive method of learning. "The computer was no longer a conduit for the presentation of information: it was a tool for the active manipulation of that information" (Naismith, Lonsdale, Vavoula, & Sharples, 2004, p. 12).

Constructionist Learning in the 1980s

Constructionism differed from constructivism, as Papert (1980) posited an additional component to constructivism: students learned best when they were actively involved in *constructing* social objects. Using Taylor's (1980) tutor, tool, and tutee computer analogy, Papert's constructionism advocates the tutee position. For example, the computer-as-tutee approach would involve students using Logo to teach the computer to draw a picture (Papert, 1980). Another technology example would be using another, slightly more advanced, microworld to teach Karel the Robot to perform various tasks.

Problem-Based Learning in the 1990s

Although problem-based learning was developed in medical education in the 1950s, the methodology was not widely used in K–12 schools until the 1990s (Wilson, 1996). Problem-based learning involves students working on tasks and activities authentic to the environment in which those particular skills would be used. Students then learn by constructing their own knowledge from thinking critically and creatively to solve problems. This pedagogical practice caused a technological dilemma, in that desktop computers could not easily be transported around from place to place. Therefore, it is reasonable to claim that mobility became a desired attribute for technologies used with problem-based learning.

Learner-centered education, as the name implies, focuses on the role of the learner rather than the teacher; problem-based learning is a clear example of such a shift in the role of student and teacher. The teacher is the guide in the process, and no longer the main repository of knowledge (Hmelo-Silver, 2004). In the problem-based learning of the 1990s, students often worked in small groups of five or six to pool knowledge and resources to solve problems. This launched the start of the sociocultural revolution, focusing on learning in out-of-school contexts and the acquisition of knowledge through social interaction.

Socio-Constructivist Learning in the 1990s

The next logical step in the learner-centered evolution was toward socio-constructivist learning. Social constructivists believe that social and individual processes are interdependent in the co-construction of knowledge (Sullivan-Palincsar, 1998; Vygotsky, 1978). The tenet of socio-constructivism is that intellectual advancement occurs through interactions with a group.

The sociocultural revolution was not limited to education specifically. SixDegrees.com was the first public social-networking site, launched in 1997 (Boyd & Ellison, 2007). This initial site developed into the plethora of social-networking sites available today, including Facebook, LinkedIn, and Twitter. Social networking sites provide "latent ties" (Haythornthwaite, 2005), which are those with established offline connections, and there is also the opportunity to meet online with people one may never meet face to face.

Learner-Centered Developments

Thus far, a description has been given of the main learner-centered pedagogical developments from the 1970s to the end of the 1990s. There were other pedagogies/theories of learning during this time, such as discovery learning (Anthony, 1973), inquiry learning (Papert, 1980), and experiential learning (Kolb & Fry, 1975), which are similar to those described in this part. From studying the learning pedagogies and theories, it is clear that pedagogical practice since the 1970s has continually revised the model and theories behind learner-centered pedagogies. Table 1.1 provides a visual overview of this revision process.

Table 1.1 Overview of the Revision Process in Learner-Centered Pedagogies/Theories

Learner pedagogies/theories	Decade	Main tenets of the pedagogies/theories
Discovery learning	1970s	Knowledge is discovered through active participation in the learning process
Constructivist learning	1980s	Knowledge develops through interactions with the environment
Constructionist learning	1980s	Knowledge is gained through actively creating social objects
Problem-based learning	1990s	Knowledge is developed through working on tasks and skills authentic to the environment in which those particular skills would be used
Socio-constructivist learning	1990s	Knowledge is co-constructed interdependently between the social and the individual

The common evolving attributes listed in Table 1.1 are active involvement of the learner in the knowledge-making process and learner interaction with the environment and society. This is where we arrive at the learning pedagogies of the 2000s, with m-learning and context-aware ubiquitous learning providing new affordances for learners. M-learning and context-aware ubiquitous learning will be described later in this chapter.

Looking back at the brief descriptions of the technologies connected with the learning pedagogies of that time, it appears that technologies have had to play catch-up with pedagogical trends. However, there are those who believe that it is the technology leading pedagogical practice. Sharples (2005) proposed:

> Every era of technology has, to some extent, formed education in its own image. That is not to argue for the technological determinism of education, but rather that there is a mutually productive convergence between main technological influences on a culture and the contemporary educational theories and practices.
>
> (Sharples, 2005, p. 147)

The technological influence has also been reflected in educators and governments recently advocating for educational reforms to utilize technologies during teaching and learning (Common Core State Standards Initiative, 2010; Greenhow & Robelia, 2009; Jonassen, Howland, Marra, & Crismond, 2008). Teachers and students became increasingly aware of the potential to use the devices for differentiated, private, and self-directed learning.

Since the increase in technologies, such as the social adoption of the WWW and cell phones during the 1990s, the argument could be made that society's adoption and perceptions of technological hardware/software influence how people learn. The next section of this chapter gives a brief chronological overview of the technological underpinnings of technology relating to the development of m-learning.

ADVANCES IN TECHNOLOGY

1970s

The 1970s were a significant decade for the development of many hardware/software technologies such as the floppy disk, the microcomputer, the VHS videocassette recorder, and the first mobile phone. This was also the decade in which Kay (1972) created the concept model of the Dynabook, the first handheld multimedia computer intended as a learning device. As Kay conceptualized the Dynabook, he described some of the attributes the revolutionary device would hold:

> Imagine having your own self-contained knowledge manipulator in a portable package the size and shape of an ordinary notebook. Suppose it had enough power to outrace your senses of sight and hearing, enough capacity to store for later retrieval thousands of page-equivalents of reference materials, poems, letters, recipes, records, drawings, animations, musical scores, waveforms, dynamic simulations, and anything else you would like to remember and change.
>
> (Kay & Goldberg, 1977/2001, p. 167)

The Dynabook was never actually created, but the ripples of his ideas have continued through to the 21st century. Sharples (2002) believed that the actual device did not move beyond the conceptual phase because technologies were not advancing fast enough. It also conflicted with the drive for the incorporation of desktop computers in classroom teaching.

Although the Dynabook never reached fruition, Kay and Goldberg's research developed prototype desktop computers, described as "interim Dynabooks" (Kay & Goldberg, 1977/2001, p. 168), and a programming language called SmallTalk. SmallTalk was an object-oriented software language, responsible for the later invention of the graphical user interface (GUI) for use on computers, portable media players, gaming devices, and handheld devices. This was a significant event in the history of electronic technologies, as the GUI allowed users to command the device through clicking on icons, rather than having to type in command strings, making it simpler for the novice user.

The first mobile phone, developed in 1973, was the Motorola DynaTAC 8000X, although it was not until 1983 that the commercial version was on sale. Nevertheless, the Dynabook and the first mobile phones paved the way for the m-learning devices that are readily available today.

1980s

During this decade, numerous companies heralded the arrival of handheld computers. Table 1.2 lists a selection of the handheld devices introduced during the 1980s.

Other companies, such as Panasonic, Sharp, Texas Instruments, and Seiko Instruments, also produced commercial handheld computers in the 1980s. The handheld computers of the 1980s are still far from resembling the Dynabook conceived by Kay and Goldberg (1977/2001), and they were typically marketed and used in business settings, but a clear progression can be seen over the decade.

Technologies in general were becoming more personalized, moving from the shared desktop PCs to laptops and handheld personal computers, and from the fixed telephone to personal cell phones. During the early 1980s, the first commercial laptop computer was introduced to the market, and, during the late 1980s and 1990s, many schools and colleges began to allow students to bring laptops into schools and lecture halls. Cell phones also continued to evolve during the 1980s, becoming customizable, flexible, and increasingly smaller, with the phone connected to the person rather than the household (Goggin, 2006).

Table 1.2 Selection of the Commercial Handheld Computers Introduced During the 1980s

1980	TRS-80 Pocket Computer	Radio Shack	—24 × 1 text LCD display —1.5K RAM
1982	PHC-8000 Handheld Computer	Sanyo	—One-line LCD display —4kB RAM —Allows connection to video monitor
1982	Pasopia Mini	Toshiba	—One-line LCD display —4 kB RAM
1984	PB-700 Handheld Computer	Casio	—20 × 4 text LCD display —4 kB RAM
1989	Portfolio, Portable Computer	Atari	—40 × 8 text LCD display —128K, card slot for RAM —MS-DOS-compatible computer —Includes a speaker
1989	Poqet PC Computer	Poqet	—80 × 25 text LCD screen —512 kB RAM —Additional card slots for ROM or RAM

From this trend toward personal technologies, educational establishments looked for a way to connect with the learner-centered approach evolving since the 1970s. Classroom response systems (CRSs) were just one such technology developed in the late 1980s as a way to reach the individual students in the classroom, although CRSs did not achieve widespread use until the late 1990s.

1990s

During this decade, the learner-centered pedagogical movement was well established in schools, and, in a parallel development, technologies had become more advanced, personalized, and novice-friendly. Soloway, Guzdial, and Hay (1994) considered the direction in which technologies should progress, stating "Simply put, the HCI [Human Computer Interaction] community must make another transition: we must move from 'user-centered' design to 'learner-centered' design" (p. 38). Soloway et al. proposed that this should occur by considering three key questions: "Why support learners and learning? How might the interface support learners and learning? What are the issues involved in providing such support?" (p. 38). These were essential questions during a decade of significant technological adoption in the educational setting.

The 1990s were the decade in which the first digital camera, Web browser, and graphing calculator were developed. Many schools were using computer-assisted instruction programs on the multimedia computers. Palm Pilot personal digital assistants (PDAs) were the first multipurpose, handheld devices that could be utilized in the educational setting. The device ran basic programs, including calculator, tests, calendar, contacts, memos, photos, and notepad. In 1998, Sharples began an attempt at recreating the Dynabook. The Handheld Learning Resource (HandLeR) project studied the design of mobile devices in an attempt at creating an instrument to aid "lifelong learning," based on the tenets of experiential and collaborative learning (Sharples, Corlett, & Westmancott, 2001). Sharples et al. were also interested in learning contexts bridging formal and informal learning. The HandLeR was designed for use at any age or in any context, although the mentor character/animal interface was more suited for children than adults.

Portable digital devices have developed rapidly since they came onto the market in the latter part of the 1970s. From Kay's Dynabook concept in 1972, technologies have been progressing toward making Kay's dream a reality. Mobile devices have decreased in size and cost and increased in power, speed, memory, and functionality. The devices provide unique affordances for learner-centered pedagogies, which have further developed into the 21st century. The focus of this section has been directed toward the actual technological devices. One must also take into account the development of wireless wide-band technologies and application services—for example 3D phones, IEEE 802.11 (Wi-Fi) networks, 802.15.1 (Bluetooth) networks, active/passive radio-frequency identification, and global positioning system receivers—enabling an impressive system of networks for use on such devices (Caudill, 2007; Ding, 2010). Without such wireless technologies, m-learning would not exist. The next section of this chapter explicates the interconnectedness between the technologies and the learner pedagogies in the 21st century.

CONNECTING THE TECHNOLOGIES AND THE LEARNING

In this chapter, m-learning has often been dichotomized into learning and technology so that we can better understand the changes that have taken place historically. However, the essence of m-learning is not in the learning or in the technology, but in the marriage between the two entities. This section explains the history of learning and technology as they became recognized as interconnected theories/pedagogies, namely e-learning and m-learning, while briefly touching upon a subdivision of m-learning titled context-aware ubiquitous learning (u-learning).

The first two sections of this chapter provide an overview of how e-learning and m-learning emerged from both a drive in educational philosophy and practice toward learner-centered pedagogies, and through technologies that put the learner at the heart of learning. These new methods of learning provide opportunities such as flexibility, accessibility, and convenience (Benedek, 2007), and a pedagogy that is personalized, learner centered, contextualized, and cooperative (Ding, 2010).

E-Learning

Electronic learning appears to be the first recognized term to specifically connect learning with the technologies. Learning typically mimicked traditional teaching approaches, and early definitions describe e-learning as teaching and learning supported by electronic media and tools (e.g., Pinkwart, Hoppe, Milrad, & Perez, 2003). Researchers such as Keegan (2002) believed that e-learning was distance learning, which had been converted to e-learning through the use of technologies such as the WWW. As e-learning developed, along with the ever-expanding new technologies available for use, questions arose as to which electronic media and tools constituted e-learning; for example, did it matter if the learning took place through a networked technology, or was it simply learning with an electronic device? To clearly explain the technologies involved and to set e-learning apart from that of traditional learning, Tavangarian, Leypold, Nolting, and Voigt (2004) proposed that e-learning was:

> All forms of electronic supported learning and teaching, which are procedural in character and aim to effect the construction of knowledge with reference to individual

experience, practice and knowledge of the learning. Information and communication systems, whether networked or not, serve as specific media to implement the learning process.

(Tavangarian et al., 2004, p. 274)

The WWW made up a significant portion of the technological content fitting the category of e-learning during the 1990s and 2000s. Since society's adoption of the WWW in the 1990s, it has undergone radical changes. Websites have gone from static to dynamic and interactive, progressing from the read-only Web to the read–write Web (Richardson, 2005), which offered the users of the WWW more interaction and choice. In the past 20 years, a great many artifacts such as books, documents, and audiovisual materials were uploaded to the Web, as libraries and museums digitized collections, creating a bank of digital artifacts available to the public (Benedek, 2007). Those developing the content of the WWW utilized social theories of learning, offering social-networking sites and learning-management systems (LMSs) that were established and implemented in schools and universities across the Western world. LMS developed to mediate Web-based learning artifacts and communication between students and teachers.

Considering Table 1.1, which listed the tenets of learner-centered education, e-learning provides opportunities for learners to take advantage of many of the desirable learner-centered attributes. For example, students can be actively involved in the knowledge-making process, through writing a collaborative essay in Google Docs or defining a concept in a wiki. These examples show learners interacting with society, although the interactions are virtual, using computers based in a fixed location, with the learners shut off from the rest of the physical world. What e-learning lacked early on were physical interactions with the environment and society, without spatial and temporal limitations.

M-Learning

During 2005, m-learning became a recognized term. M-learning as defined in this chapter encapsulates the attributes identified in Table 1.1 for learner-centered pedagogies. M-learning makes not only a step, but a leap further into the realm of learner-centered pedagogies. Still, this did not happen all at once.

Early on, m-learning was typically used to channel e-learning methods and techniques, quickly exposing the limitations of cell phones and PDAs compared with desktop computers at the time (Traxler, 2011). Early mobile technologies lacked functionality, screen size, processor speed, and battery life. Many of the unique opportunities offered by the mobile devices were not utilized.

As the 2000s progressed, the interest in PDAs decreased, as smartphones offered the same application and Web functionalities, but with the added mobile-phone capability. Cell phones, which were once a symbol of financial prowess, became a companion for the masses. Although technology was often an expensive option in higher education, colleges found that the number of students owning devices cut or abolished additional school cost entirely. Tablet computers continued the trend toward greater mobility. To put it simply, the first devices to be called tablets were laptops with a rotating screen and touch-screen capabilities, such as the Microsoft Tablet PC, commercially available in 2001. Ultra-mobile PCs, such as the Wibrain B1, were quietly introduced on the market in 2006 as smaller, more mobile versions of a laptop/tablet, but were quickly supplanted by today's tablets, such as the iPad (2010) and Motorola Xoom (2011), which are overall more mobile that their initial counterparts.

As m-learning continued to develop, the multiple affordances the devices offered to further extend learner-centered pedagogies became evident. Traxler (2011) described five ways in which m-learning offers new learning opportunities: (1) contingent learning, allowing learners to respond and react to the environment and changing experiences; (2) situated learning, in which learning takes place in the surroundings applicable to the learning; (3) authentic learning, with the tasks directly related to the immediate learning goals; (4) context-aware learning, in which learning is informed by the history and the environment; and (5) personalized learning, customized for each unique learner in terms of abilities, interests, and preferences.

Technologies advanced to provide other forms of mobile technology, such as advanced tablets and laptops with many additional capabilities. Mobile phones now have the same capabilities as microcomputers, at a small fraction of the size. As m-learning is rapidly developing, offshoots of m-learning are being created. One such subdivision is context-aware ubiquitous learning, which describes learning that offers seamless services, adaptive services, and context-aware services (Yang, Zhang, & Chen, 2007), in which computing, communication, and sensor devices are integrated into the daily life of a learner. M-learning and the offshoot u-learning literally embody learner-centered education, in that learning will soon be omnipresent to the learner.

CONCLUSION

Although m-learning is a relatively young field, this chapter provides a diachronic overview of how the philosophical, pedagogical, and conceptual underpinnings of a learner-centered approach, as well as the technological accomplishments, have engendered m-learning as the field it is today. Although this chapter has covered historical events leading to the field of m-learning, one must remember that this is merely one chapter of a book. For all the details that have been given, there are probably many that have been missed. A message to take away from this chapter is that, in 1972, Kay had a vision of a mobile-learning technology, compact enough to easily transport, with the capacity to store multiple reference materials and enough power to outrace the senses. Although the Dynabook was beyond the capabilities of technologies at that time, technologies have now caught up with this vision, and Kay's ideas for an alternative learning paradigm are appearing throughout the world.

REFERENCES

Anthony, W. S. (1973). Learning to discover rules by discovery. *Journal of Educational Psychology, 64*, 325–8.

Benedek, A. (2007). Mobile learning and lifelong knowledge acquisition. In K. Nyiri (Ed.), *Mobile studies: Paradigms and perspectives. Communications in the 21st century* (pp. 35–44). Vienna: Passagen Verlag.

Boyd, D. M., & Ellison, N. B. (2007). Social network sites: Definition, history, and scholarship. *Journal of Computer-Mediated Communication, 13*(1), article 11.

Bruner, J. S. (1966). *Toward a theory of instruction.* Cambridge, MA: Harvard University Press.

Caudill, J. G. (2007). The growth of m-learning and the growth of mobile computing: Parallel developments. *International Review of Research in Open and Distance Learning, 8*(2), 1–13.

Common Core State Standards Initiative. (2010, June). *Reaching higher: The common core state standards validation committee.* A report from the National Governor's Association Center for Best Practices and the Council of Chief State School Officers. Retrieved from: www.corestandards.org/_assets/_CommonCoreReport_6.10.pdf

Ding, G. (2010). New theoretical approach to integrated education and technology. *Frontiers of Education in China, 5*(1), 26–36.

Goggin, G. (2006). *Cell phone culture: Mobile technology in everyday life.* New York: Routledge.

Goh, T., & Kinshuk, D. (2006). Getting ready for mobile learning-adaptation perspective. *Journal of Educational Multimedia and Hypermedia, 15*(2), 175–198.

Greenhow, C., & Robelia, B. (2009). Web 2.0 and classroom research: What path should we take now? *Educational Researchers, 38*(4), 246–259.

Gremmo, M. J., & Riley, P. (1995). Autonomy, self-direction and self-access in language teaching and learning: The history of an idea. *System, 23*(2), 151–164.

Haythornthwaite, C. (2005). Social networks and Internet connectivity effects. *Information, Communication, & Society, 8*(2), 125–147.

Hmelo-Silver, C. E. (2004). Problem-based learning: What and how do students learn? *Educational Psychology Review, 16*(3), 235–266.

Jonassen, D. (1999). Designing constructivist learning environments. In C. M. Reigeluth (Ed.), *Instructional-design theories and models: A new paradigm of instructional theory* (Vol. 2, pp. 217–239). Mahwah, NJ: Lawrence Erlbaum Associates.

Jonassen, D., Howland, J., Marra, R., & Crismond, D. (2008). *Meaningful learning with technology* (3rd ed.). Upper Saddle River, NJ: Pearson.

Kay, A. C. (1972, August). *A personal computer for children of all ages.* Proceedings of the ACM National Conference, Boston. DOI: 10.1145/800193.1971922

Kay, A. C., & Goldberg, A. (2001). Personal dynamic media. In R. Packer & J. Jordan (Eds.), *Multimedia: From Wagner to virtual reality* (pp. 167–178). London: W. W. Norton & Company. (Original work published 1977)

Keegan, D. (2002). *The future of learning: From elearning to mlearning.* Retrieved from: www.worldcat.org/title/future-of-learning-from-elearning-to-mlearning/oclc/77086825?referer=di&ht=edition

Kolb, D. A., & Fry, R. (1975). Toward an applied theory of experiential learning. In C. Cooper (Ed.), *Studies of group process* (pp. 33–57). New York: Wiley.

Laouris, Y., & Eteokleous, N. (2005). *We need an educationally relevant definition of mobile learning.* Paper presented at mLearn 2005, 4th World Conference on Mobile Learning, Cape Town, South Africa.

Lee, K. W. (2000). English teachers' barriers to the use of computer-assisted language learning. *The Internet Teachers of English as a Second Language Journal, 6.* Retrieved from the Internet TESL Journal website: http://202.194.48.102/englishonline/jxyj/iteslj/Lee-CALLbarriers.html

Merriam-Webster Dictionary (11th ed.) (2011). Conversation. Retrieved from: www.merriam-webster.com/_dictionary/_conversation

Naismith, L., Lonsdale, P., Vavoula, G., & Sharples, M. (2004). Literature review in mobile technologies and learning. *FutureLab Report, 11.*

O'Malley, C., Vavoula, G., Glew, J., Taylor, J., Sharples, M., & Lefrere, P. (2003). Guidelines for learning/teaching/tutoring in a mobile environment. *MOBIlearn Deliverable, 4.* Retrieved from: http://mobilearn.mobi/

Papert, S. (1980). *Mindstorms: Children, computers, and powerful ideas.* Brighton, UK: Harvester Press.

Piaget, J. (1929). *The child's conception of the world.* New York: Harcourt, Brace Jovanovich.

Pinkwart, N., Hoppe, H. U., Milrad, M., & Perez, J. (2003). Educational scenarios for the cooperative use of personal digital assistants. *Journal of Computer Assisted Learning, 19*(3), 383–391.

Quinn, C. (2000). mLearning: Mobile, wireless, in-your-pocket learning. *LiNE Zine.* Retrieved from: www.linezine.com/2.1/features/cqmmwiyp.htm

Richardson, W. (2005). The educator's guide to the read/write web. *Educational Leadership, 4,* 24–17.

Sharples, M. (2002). Disruptive devices: Mobile technology for conversational learning. *International Journal of Continuing Engineering Education and Life Long Learning, 12*(5/6), 504–520.

Sharples, M. (2005). Learning as conversation: Transforming education in the mobile age. In *Proceedings of Conference on Seeing, Understanding, Learning in the Mobile Age* (pp. 147–152). Budapest, Hungary.

Sharples, M., Corlett, D., & Westmancott, O. (2001). *A systems architecture for handheld learning resources.* Paper presented at the CAL2001 Conference, Warwick, UK.

Sharples, M., Taylor, J., & Vavoula, G. (2007). A theory of learning for the mobile age. In R. Andrews, & C. Haythornthwaite (Eds.), *The Sage handbook of e-learning research* (pp. 221–247). London: Sage.

Soloway, E., Guzdial, M., & Hay, K. E. (1994). Learner-centered design: The challenge for HCI in the 21st century. *Interactions, 1*(2), 36–48.

Soloway, E., Norris, C., Curtis, M., Jansen, R., Krajcik, J., Marx, R., Fishman, B., & Blumenfeld, P. (2001). Making palm-sized computers the PC of choice for K–12. *Learning and Leading with Technology, 28*(7), 32–57.

Sullivan-Palincsar, A. (1998). Social constructivist perspectives on teaching and learning. *Annual Review of Psychology, 49,* 345–375.

Tavangarian, D., Leypold, M. E., Nolting, K., & Voigt, D. (2004). Is e-Learning the solution for individual learning? *Electronic Journal of E-learning, 2*(2), 273–280.

Taylor, R. (Ed.) (1980). *The computer in the school: Tutor, tool, and tutee.* New York: Teachers College Press.

Traxler, J. (2005, June). *Defining mobile learning.* Paper presented at the IADIS International Conference Mobile Learning 2005, Qawra, Malta.

Traxler, J. (2009). Learning in a mobile age. *International Journal of Mobile and Blended Learning, 1*(1), 1–12.

Traxler, J. (2010). Distance education and mobile learning: Catching up, taking stock. *Distance Education and Mobile Learning, 31*(2), 129–138.

Traxler, J. (2011). Introduction. In J. Traxler & J. Wishart (Eds.), *Making mobile learning work: Case studies of practice* (pp. 4–12). Bristol, UK: ESCalate Education Subject Centre: advanced learning and teaching in education.

Vygotsky, L. S. (1978). *Mind in society: The development of higher psychological processes.* Cambridge, UK: Harvard University Press.

Wilson, B. G. (1996). *Constructivist learning environments: Case studies in instructional design.* Englewood Cliffs, NJ: Library of Congress.

Yang, S. J. H., Zhang, J., Chen, I. Y. L. (2007). Ubiquitous provision of context-aware web services. *International Journal of Web Service Research, 4*(4), 83–103.

2

M-LEARNING AS A SUBFIELD OF OPEN AND DISTANCE EDUCATION

William C. Diehl

Although it is clear that the use of mobile devices for educational purposes is increasing, and that m-learning has the potential to revolutionize the way that people learn, the use of technology to connect learners with content and with teachers at a distance is not new. Indeed, since the beginning of correspondence education, and throughout the evolution of open and distance education, new technologies have made it possible for teachers and organizations to systematically deliver educational materials, and for students and teachers to communicate with one another at a distance. Like mobile devices, technologies such as the printing press, radio, television, satellites, and the computer—and systems such as the postal service and the Internet—have also increased the opportunities for both planned and spontaneous individual informal learning.

The purpose of this chapter is to present m-learning in a historical context, in relation to the field of distance education, and to provide an overview of the rich history of the field that can be drawn upon as educators look to the future of m-learning. This chapter will address the following topics: (1) united aims in a fractured field, and (2) social and technological foundations of distance education.

UNITED AIMS IN A FRACTURED FIELD

As Crompton (2013, p. 4) stated in a previous chapter in this handbook, the definition of m-learning is likely to evolve, just as the definition of distance education has throughout the decades. Distance education has been referred to in a variety of ways, including home study, independent study, correspondence study, external learning, self-directed learning, telelearning, cyber-learning, e-learning, and distributed learning (and many others). As distance-education pioneer Charles Wedemeyer (1981) noted decades ago, "the people who work within these separate but basically similar programs perceive themselves as in some way different from their colleagues in the other programs, as though the recent labels represent genuinely different aims, methods and programs in education" (p. 55).

There are myriad methods of development, design, and delivery in the thousands of distance-education systems operating today, and they range from the use of more traditional methods of correspondence, to television, to Internet-based methods. Course design also varies from system to system and ranges widely, incorporating course teams in some instances and, in others, relying on the instructor for the individual course design and development. The field of distance education, in many ways, is fractured. Saba (2005) sees different cultures (premodern faculty, modern administration, and postmodern distance educators) attempting to evolve and survive in the technology-driven academic environment. The fractures are also caused by conceptual confusion, as new terms arise and as new technologies are applied to the field (e.g., terms such as e-learning, m-learning, distributed learning, blended learning, Education 2.0, Web 2.0, flexible learning) (W. Diehl, 2007; Moore & Kearsley, 2005; Saba, 2005; Thompson, 2007).

Crompton, Muilenburg, and Berge's (Crompton, 2013, p. 4) definition of m-learning that has been established for this handbook includes formal and informal learning and is student centered and self-directed. Forty years ago, Wedemeyer developed a systems approach in the changing field as a way of providing access to education for nontraditional adult students (Wedemeyer, 1981). Contrasted to the popular behaviorism that was prevalent during his career, he applied technology to reach for humanistic educational results in a student-centered, interactive learning process. Wedemeyer believed that developing skills that allow students to become independent learners was necessary so that effective lifelong learning could take place.

Wedemeyer (1971) developed a definition of independent study, defined as:

> various forms of teaching–learning arrangements in which teachers and learners carry out their essential tasks and responsibilities apart from one another, communicating in a variety of ways, for the purposes of freeing internal learners from inappropriate class pacings or patterns, or providing external learners opportunity to continue learning in their own environments, and developing in all learners the capacity to carry on self-directed learning, the ultimate maturity required of the educated person. Independent Study programs offer learners varying degrees of freedom in the self-determination of goals and activities, and in starting, stopping and pacing individualized learning programs which are carried on to the greatest extent possible at the convenience of the learners.
>
> (p. 148)

Wedemeyer's definition of independent study emphasized student-centered learning and the distance between teachers and learners, which is a defining characteristic of distance education. Moore and Kearsley (2012) incorporate this concept of distance into one of the most widely accepted definitions of distance education, describing it as "planned learning that normally occurs in a different place from teaching, requiring special course design and instruction techniques, communication through various technologies, and special organizational and administrative arrangements" (p. 2).

Moore and Kearsley (2012) echo Wedemeyer regarding the confusion that is created "when people define education by the technology used" (p. 3). Early pioneers and colleagues of Wedemeyer—Börje Holmberg, Otto Peters, and Michael G. Moore—worked individually to develop theories that could provide a framework for what takes place in the systems and processes related to distance education. Moore went on to develop theory related to independent learning and teaching (Moore, 1972, 1973a, 1973b) and, later, the theory of transactional distance (Moore, 1997, 2007, 2013). Moore also introduced the idea of different types of interaction in distance education (learner–learner, learner–teacher, learner–content). Holmberg's theory, which is based on learner–teacher interaction, stresses that the personal relationship and feelings of empathy will improve learning in a distance-education setting (Bernath & Vidal, 2007; W. C. Diehl, 2011b; Holmberg, 1960, 1961, 2003, 2007). Otto Peters' theory developed from his recognition that distance-education systems resembled and contained the characteristics of industrialized systems that existed in a postindustrial society (Bernath & Vidal, 2007; Peters, 2007; Peters & Keegan, 1994).

With the development of the now ubiquitous World Wide Web, there are "a large— and seemingly ever-growing—set of communication and information management tools which can be harnessed for education provision" (Anderson, 2008, pp. 52–53). Theory building in distance education, which began with Wedemeyer, continues. Scholars continue to build models upon the work of Holmberg, Moore, and Peters, the goal being a deeper "understanding of this complex educational context" that will "lead us to hypotheses, predictions, and most importantly, improvements in our professional practice" (Anderson, 2008, p. 68).

SOCIAL AND TECHNOLOGICAL FOUNDATIONS OF DISTANCE EDUCATION

In a previous chapter, Crompton (2013) covered advances in mobile technologies since the 1970s and has noted that, although technology has driven the field, there is a reflexive societal aspect that must also be considered. Social movements and the growing philosophy of access to education for all have also played a major role. The following section provides an overview of early social movements and technologies that have played a part in the evolution of distance education.

Early Social Movements and the Opening of Educational Access

Generally, the roots of education in England were deeply grounded in "the dissemination of religious truth" (Hudson, 1851, p. 1), and government funding and participation were minimal until universal elementary education came about in the late 1800s (Halls, 1995). In circulating schools in the mid 1750s and for the next quarter of a century in western England, it was estimated that 100,000 adults learned to read, along with some 50,000 children who also attended the lessons. Although the numbers of people learning to read was growing, the vast majority of the population could not read or write, and also, in the 1780s in England, less than 3 percent of the 8 million citizens had the right to vote (TNA, 2009).

The Reform Act of 1832 in England granted "such privilege to large populous and wealthy towns to increase the number of knights of the shire to extend the elective franchise to many of his majesty's subjects who have not heretofore enjoyed the same and to diminish the expense of elections" (TNA, 1832). Later, in 1867, the Second Reform Act gave skilled workers the right to vote, and, beginning in the 1870s, adults from the working classes could attend extension classes, which were associated with Oxford and Cambridge (Goldman, 1999).

Educational opportunities that were established also had political motivations. As more and more working-class people became interested in learning, various political groups (which merged and evolved to become the Labour party) became especially active in establishing classes that taught about democracy and socialism—in order to "integrate the working classes, train them for power and lead them to political victory" (Goldman, 1999, p. 95). Later, in 1884, manual workers gained the vote, further increasing the numbers of eligible voters. During this 54-year period (between 1831 and 1885), the number of men who were eligible to vote rose from 366,000 to approximately 8 million. The right to vote, however, still excluded women and the lower classes.

Improvement societies such as the Wigan Instructive and Philanthropic Society continued to be established around England. Mechanics' Institutes remained popular until after 1870, when the government became involved in education, and public libraries began to proliferate (Verity, 1995).

Early Technologies and the Opening of Educational Access
The Penny Black Stamp and Postal Service

The widespread use of correspondence education was fueled by technological innovations such as the steam-powered printing press, the Penny Black stamp and postal services, as well as improvements to transportation systems that opened up the flow of information on a scale heretofore not seen. With improvements to the transportation system, it became possible to carry letters and information to people in rural areas that had previously been extremely isolated. In the American colonies, the British owned the postal service until 1785, and the citizenry in the American colonies continued to improve their roads and postal delivery system as the colonies expanded. Between 1790 and 1860, the U.S. population grew from about 3.9 million to 31.4 million, and the number of post offices grew from 75 to 28,498. In 1828, there were 7,530 post offices and 29,956 postal employees, and, by 1831, postal employees accounted for 76 percent of the civilian federal workforce. During Andrew Jackson's presidency, postmasters outnumbered soldiers 8,764 to 6,332 and were the most widespread representatives of the federal government. The Act of March 3, 1863 (12 Stat. 704) eliminated the letter's postage rate relationship based on distance, and the result was that customers could now send letters to and from wherever they wanted within the growing country (USPS, 2007).

Lyceums and the Extension Movement

In the early 1830s in the United States, a national lyceum educational movement that included lectures and debates were attended by large numbers of people. In Millbury, Massachusetts, the first lyceum was organized, and "By the end of 1834 there were 3,000 town lyceums spread throughout the country from Boston to Detroit and Maine to Florida" (Noffsinger, 1926, p. 102). In Boston, in 1873, following the Civil War, Anna Eliot Ticknor, inspired by the British, started the Society to Encourage Studies at Home, and, by 1882, about 1,000 students, mostly women, were exchanging letters and studying history, science, art, literature, French, and German. In all, 24 subjects were offered. Also in 1873, Illinois Wesleyan began to offer nonresident courses to its students (MacKenzie et al., 1968).

The British extension movement began in 1873 at Cambridge University, followed by programs at London University in 1876 and then Oxford in 1878. In 1887, Professor Herbert B. Adams from Johns Hopkins University spoke to an American audience about the British extension movement, and, only four years later, there were over 200 extension programs organized. The First Annual Meeting of the National Conferences on University Extension was held in Philadelphia on December 29 (Hall-Quest, 1926), with the goal of cooperation between organizations stressed in the proceedings. In attendance were representatives from about 19 U.S. states, including Bishop John H. Vincent, founder of the Chautauqua Institute.

Vincent's Chautauqua Institute extended opportunities to adults in the late 1800s through a "system of correspondence with professors of departments" (Vincent & Miller, 1886, p. 87) that expanded their face-to-face lectures. Chautauqua's mission reflected a growing belief in democratic ideals in education, one that exalted "education—the mental, social, moral, and religious culture of all who have mental, social, moral, and religious faculties; of all, everywhere, without exception" (Vincent & Miller, 1886, p. 4). The Chautauqua idea continued to spread, and it is widely cited today in books and articles as a major influence on distance and adult education (Kang, 2009; Milam, 1934; Moore, 2003; Moore, Pittman, Anderson, & Kramarae, 2003).

Individuals such as William Rainey Harper were recruited by John Vincent. Harper, who gained experience at Chautauqua, using correspondence education to teach Hebrew to his students as early as 1881, was also named principal of the Chautauqua College of Liberal Arts. Harper went on to establish a university extension program at the University of Chicago in 1892, and correspondence education was an important part of this division. Under Harper's leadership as president, the University of Chicago became a leader in extending opportunities to adults through correspondence study. Other schools, such as Penn State, Baylor, and University of Wisconsin, soon followed with their own programs.

In the next few decades, the University of Wisconsin in Madison became one of the leading universities in the country, and, in 1903, Charles Van Hise took over as president and vowed that the university should reach and benefit every citizen in the state. Van Hise went on to preside over the first annual National University Extension Association (NUEA) conference in 1915. A decade later, the National Home Study Council was established, and efforts were made to reform the standards in proprietary correspondence schools. Correspondence education, during the early part of the 20th century, however, was dominated by poor standards in proprietary schools and suffered generally from a poor reputation, but, beginning in the 1950s, Charles Wedemeyer and Gayle Childs worked at their respective universities and as leaders at the NUEA to establish best practices, based on research. By 1959, the U.S. Department of Education approved the National Home Study Council's (NHSC) Accrediting Commission as an accrediting agency for correspondence schools, and, a few years later, NUEA adopted standards based on NHSC criteria (Feasley & Bunker, 2007).

On the global scene, the International Council for Correspondence Education (ICCE) became an official organization in 1948. The organization, which became the International Council for Open and Distance Education (ICDE) in 1982, has always maintained an "unremitting allegiance to the belief in the value of providing access to all learners, no matter how dispersed or disadvantaged by economic, personal, or political situation" (Feasley & Bunker, 2007, p. 24). The organization has focused on international collaboration, ICT-enabled education, quality and accreditation, globalization, culture and open and distance learning, and distance education for development (Feasley & Bunker, 2007).

International collaboration led to increased research, improved practice, and development of theory. Charles Wedemeyer, who was president of ICCE from 1969 to 1972, played a key role in encouraging the development of theory; he also became a major influence upon three of distance education's earliest theorists, Börje Holmberg, Otto Peters, and Michael G. Moore (Black, 2004, 2007, 2013; W. C. Diehl, 2013). Another Wedemeyer achievement was developing systems that could serve learners throughout their lifetime, whenever they needed it, and his experimental Articulated Instructional Media (AIM) program at the University of Wisconsin became a model for the Open University of the United Kingdom (W. C. Diehl, 2009, 2011a, 2013; Moore & Kearsley, 2005, 2012).

The Emergence of Radio

Experimentation with what would eventually be known as radio technology was widespread at U.S. colleges and universities as early as 1909, but what was referred to then as wireless telegraphy was introduced to the community at the University of Wisconsin at Madison in March 1915 as part of an exhibit by the electrical engineering department. The technology grew out of the invention of the telegraph and the telephone. As early as 1883, a Buenos Aires' telephone company sent messages to multiple customers at one time, and, in the early 1890s, the Budapest Telephone Service transmitted news and entertainment to subscribers (Davidson, 2006).

Early research by Scottish researcher James Clark Maxwell and German researcher Heinrich Hertz led to the development of a device by Italian Guglielmo Marconi that could transmit Morse code via waves. In 1899, Marconi interested the U.S. Navy in the technology and incorporated the Marconi Wireless Company of America. By 1900, former Edison employee Reginal Fessenden had made sufficient advances in the technology and actually transmitted his voice via a "continuous wave," from Western University in Pittsburgh, Pennsylvania (Davidson, 2006, p. 5). Six years later, with the assistance of Swedish-born Ernst F. W. Alexanderson, Fessenden developed a system that enabled him to broadcast his voice from Brant Rock, Massachusetts, over a distance of 10 miles.

Eight years later, a former Fessenden staff member named Edward Bennett, a professor at the University of Wisconsin at Madison, set up the same type of system on campus and, in compliance with the federal Radio Act of 1912, applied and received an experimental license for the use of wireless transmission with the call letters 9XM. On January 13, 1922, WHA radio in Madison received its license for "limited commercial" broadcasting. Only 28 stations existed at the beginning of 1922, but, by the end of the year, there were almost 600 in all 48 states. That same year, WHA demonstrated a broadcast of market reports to farmers in Wisconsin, and, a month later, *The Milwaukee Journal* expressed an interest in developing a relationship with the station (Davidson, 2006).

William H. Lighty, who was then the program manager of the station in Madison, saw the potential of this technology and introduced weather, market reports, concerts, talks, university news, activities, and information that would be broadcast on a regular schedule. WHA received letters from listeners around the country in response to broadcasts (Davidson, 2006).

In March 1922, a professor from the University of Wisconsin, Alfred Haake, was unable to attend a conference in person and instead broadcast his talk to his audience, who were 80 miles away. The next morning, the *Wisconsin State Journal* ran a front-page story on the event. This kind of publicity helped the station to increase its audience, and, in the early stages of the use of the station, Lighty was sure to forward letters from listeners to university president Birge. Birge approved a $500 budget increase for the upcoming school year. Lighty pushed to develop "an on-air correspondence course in building and maintaining radio sets," and "by early October more than one hundred people had signed up" (Davidson, 2006, p. 69). Another technological development increased the exposure and appeal of radio—the demonstration in Madison of a car radio, by B. B. Jones and Max Littleton. Jones and Littleton used the car battery to power a radio receiver and loudspeaker, and residents in downtown Madison were able to hear broadcasts, not only from WHA, but also from as far away as Detroit, Pittsburgh, and Newark.

By the 1940s, commercial stations could be found all over the United States. The events in Europe and the use of radio for control of the public mindset in Germany and Italy were well known—and debate centered on who should control the airwaves in the United States. Battles centered around public vs. commercial control, and, during this time period, there were only about two dozen educational radio stations out of the over 400 total stations nationwide (Davidson, 2006).

Educational Television

Television is another technology that emerged and initially was seen as having great potential for educational benefits. Similar to radio, the debate over commercial and public stations raged. Following World War II, the Federal Communications Commission (FCC) froze its broadcast licensing process in order to reorganize its licensing system, and the Joint Committee for Educational Television and Ford Foundation, led by FCC Commissioner Frieda Hennock, eventually and successfully lobbied the FCC to set aside 242 channels for education (Zechowski, 2010).

Universities such as the University of Iowa experimented with educational broadcasting as early as 1934. Once World War II began, television was primarily used for education of air-raid wardens and of the general public on air raids and first aid. In the post-war period, the Chicago Public Schools and WBDB experimented with educational broadcasts, and CBS and the New York City Schools conducted two shows a month for two years. NBC studios provided science shows to junior-high students, and research they conducted showed promise that educational television could be effective (Levenson & Stasheff, 1952). In the mid 1940s, there were only six television stations and 10,000 televisions operating in the United States, but, by 1950, approximately 6 million families owned televisions. Still, few if any commercial television stations were profitable, and few educational shows were produced (mainly because of infrastructure and television costs). A few schools in Chicago, Philadelphia, and Baltimore experimented with educational broadcasting, but, throughout the country, there was minimal use in schools (Levenson & Stasheff, 1952).

CONCLUSION

Ever since the first system was developed that enabled a student to learn at a distance, technologies have been used to mediate the educational experience. As each new technology emerges, distance educators and technologists experiment and research the potential of the new tool, and thus another subfield of distance education is born. Although each of these new technologies has been hailed as holding the promise of educational breakthroughs, pedagogical approaches (e.g., teacher centered, behaviorist) remained relatively consistent and limited for many decades. Additionally, research on the effectiveness of these approaches was almost nonexistent, and educators who used these new innovations have often remained isolated within their own technological and educational silos.

Similarly, personal mobile devices such as smartphones and tablets are at the center of m-learning, the exciting new subfield of distance education, and they are the latest technologies to be used in an effort to bridge the geographical and psychological gaps that are part of the distance-learning experience. As an area of study, m-learning perhaps provides and represents the most geographically fluid and flexible extension of access to learning materials and communication opportunities that the world has known. This handbook lays the groundwork for the work that lies ahead and that will determine whether or not m-learning professionals will innovate and succeed in using the latest technologies (for learning) to their fullest potential.

This chapter is a reminder to m-learning professionals that they are a part of the larger field of distance education, and that they can build upon the lessons learned through the efforts of those who have laid the groundwork before them. A better understanding of the evolution of the major field of distance education provides us with insights and a foundation to build upon in practice and theory, as we venture into the future of m-learning.

REFERENCES

Anderson, T. (2008). Towards a theory of online learning. In T. Anderson (Ed.), *The theory and practice of online learning* (1st ed.). Edmonton, AB: AU Press.

Bernath, U., & Vidal, M. (2007). The theories and the theorists: Why theory is important for research. *Distances et savoirs, 5*(3), 427–458.

Black, L. (2004). A living story of the origins and development of scholarship in the field of distance education. DEd dissertation, The Pennsylvania State University, University Park.

Black, L. (2007). A history of scholarship. In M. G. Moore (Ed.), *Handbook of distance education* (2nd ed., pp. 3–14). Mahwah, NJ: Lawrence Erlbaum Associates.

Black, L. (2013). A history of scholarship. In M. G. Moore (Ed.), *Handbook of distance education*.

Crompton, H. (2013). A historical overview of mobile learning: Toward learner-centered education (pp. 3–14). In Z. Berge, & L. Muilenburg (Eds.), *Handbook of mobile learning*. New York: Routledge.

Davidson, R. (2006). *9XM talking: WHA radio and the Wisconsin idea*. Madison, WI: University of Wisconsin Press, Terrace Books.

Diehl, W. C. (2007). *The new social networking technologies: Educators get a Second Life*. Paper presented at the the Cambridge International Conference on Open and Distance Learning, Cambridge, UK.

Diehl, W. C. (2009). A glance back at Charles Wedemeyer: Excerpts from an interview with Michael G. Moore [Video]. PhD.

Diehl, W. C. (2011a). *Learning at the back door: Charles A. Wedemeyer and the evolution of open and distance learning*. PhD dissertation, The Pennsylvania State University.

Diehl, W. C. (2011b). Speaking personally—with Börje Holmberg. *The American Journal of Distance Education, 25*(1), 64–71.

Diehl, W. C. (2013). *Charles A. Wedemeyer: Pioneer of distance education*. In M. G. Moore, *Handbook of distance education* (3rd ed., pp. 38–48). New York: Routlege.

Feasley, C., & Bunker, E. (2007). A history of national and regional organizations and the ICDE. In M. G. Moore (Ed.), *Handbook of distance education* (2nd ed., pp. 15–29). Mahwah, NJ: Lawrence Erlbaum Associates.

Goldman, L. (1999). Education as politics: University adult education in England since 1870. *Oxford Review of Education, 25*(1 & 2), 89–101.

Hall-Quest, A. L. (1926). *The university afield*. New York: The Macmillan Company.

Halls, W. (1995). United Kingdom. In T. N. Postlethwaite (Ed.), *International encyclopedia of national systems of education* (2nd ed.). Oxford, UK, Tarrytown, NY: Pergamon.

Holmberg, B. (1960). *On the methods of teaching by correspondence.* Lund: C.W.K. Gleerup.

Holmberg, B. (1961). On the methods of teaching by correspondence. *The Home Study Review, 2*(Spring).

Holmberg, B. (2003). A theory of distance education based on empathy. In M. G. Moore & W. G. Anderson (Eds.), *Handbook of distance education* (1st ed., pp. 79–86). Mahwah, NJ: Lawrence Erlbaum Associates.

Holmberg, B. (2007). A theory of teaching–learning conversations. In M. G. Moore (Ed.), *Handbook of distance education* (2nd ed., pp. 69–75). Mahwah, NJ: Lawrence Erlbaum Associates.

Hudson, J. W. (1851). *The history of adult education.* London: Longman, Brown, Green & Longman's Row.

Kang, H. (2009). *A comparative study of the distance education history in China and the United States: A socio-historical perspective.* PhD dissertation, The Pennsylvania State University, University Park.

Levenson, W. B., & Stasheff, E. (1952). *Teaching through radio and television* (Rev. ed.). New York: Rinehart.

MacKenzie, O., Christensen, E. L., Rigby, P. H., American Council on Education, & National Commission on Accrediting (1968). *Correspondence instruction in the United States: A study of what it is, how it functions, and what its potential may be.* New York: McGraw-Hill.

Milam, C. (1934). American Association for Adult Education. In D. Rowden (Ed.), *Handbook of adult education in the United States 1934* (pp. 98–100). New York: AAAE.

Moore, M. G. (1972). Learner autonomy: The second dimension of independent learning. *Convergence, 5*(2), 76–88.

Moore, M. G. (1973a). *Some speculations on a definition of independent study.* Paper presented at the Kellogg Seminar on Independent Learning in the Health Sciences, University of British Columbia, Vancouver, Canada.

Moore, M. G. (1973b). Towards a theory of independent learning and teaching. *Journal of Higher Education,* (44), 661–679.

Moore, M. G. (1997). Theory of transactional distance. In D. Keegan (Ed.), *Theoretical principles of distance education* (pp. 22–38). London: Routledge.

Moore, M. G. (2003). *From Chautauqua to the virtual university: A century of distance education in the United States. Information Series.* Columbus, OH: Center on Education and Training for Employment.

Moore, M. G. (2007). The theory of transactional distance. In M. G. Moore (Ed.), *Handbook of distance education* (2nd ed., pp. 89–105). Mahwah, NJ: Lawrence Erlbaum Associates.

Moore, M. G. (2013). Transactional distance. In M. G. Moore (Ed.), *Handbook of distance education* (3rd ed.). Mahwah, NJ: Lawrence Erlbaum Associates.

Moore, M. G., & Kearsley, G. (2005). *Distance education: A systems view* (2nd ed.). Belmont, CA: Thomson/Wadsworth.

Moore, M. G., & Kearsley, G. (2012). *Distance education: A systems view of online learning* (3rd ed.). Belmont, CA: Wadsworth.

Moore, M. G., Pittman, V. V., Anderson, T., & Kramarae, C. (2003). *From Chautauqua to the virtual university: A century of distance education in the United States.* Columbus, OH: Center on Education and Training for Employment, College of Education, Ohio State University.

Noffsinger, J. S. (1926). *Correspondence schools.* New York: Macmillan Publishing Company.

Peters, O. (2007). The most industrialized form of education. In M. G. Moore (Ed.), *Handbook of distance education* (2nd ed., pp. 57–68). Mahwah, NJ: Lawrence Erlbaum Associates.

Peters, O., & Keegan, D. (1994). *Otto Peters on distance education: The industrialization of teaching and learning.* London, New York: Routledge.

Saba, F. (2005). Critical issues in distance education: A report from the United States. *Distance Education, 26*(2), 255–272.

Thompson, M. M. (2007). *From distance educaton to e learning.* London: SAGE.

TNA. (1832). *Great Reform Act, 1832.* London: The National Archives (TNA). Retrieved from: www.national archives.gov.uk/pathways/citizenship/struggle_democracy/transcripts/great_reform.htm

TNA. (2009). The struggle for democracy. Retrieved from: www.nationalarchives.gov.uk/pathways/citizenship/struggle_democracy/getting_vote.htm

USPS. (2007). *The United States Postal Service: An American history.* Washington, DC: Government Relations, United States Postal Service.

Verity, D. (1995). History of the Bradford Mechanics' Institute Library. *Library Review, 44*(3), 8–11.

Vincent, J. H., & Miller, L. (1886). *The Chautauqua movement.* Boston, MA: Chautauqua Press.

Wedemeyer, C. (1971). Independent study. In L. C. Deighton (Ed.), *The encyclopedia of education* (Vol. 4, pp. 548–557). New York: Free Press.

Wedemeyer, C. (1981). *Learning at the back door: Reflections on non-traditional learning in the lifespan.* Madison, WI: University of Wisconsin Press.

Zechowski, S. (2010). Educational television. Retrieved from: www.museum.tv/eotvsection.php?entrycode=educationalt

3

A SUMMARY AND CRITIQUE OF M-LEARNING RESEARCH AND PRACTICE

Thomas Cochrane

In their summary of the scope of m-learning research, Traxler and Kukulska-Hulme's (2006) main critique of these early m-learning research projects was for a general lack of rigor in evaluation and epistemological underpinnings.

> M-learning is at a leading edge of learning technologies and is at present characterized by pilots and trials that allow mobile technologies to be tested out in a variety of learning contexts. The sustained deployment of m-learning will depend on these pilots and trials, especially their evaluation methodology and reporting. The majority of pilots and trials in our samples had no apparent epistemological or educational foundations
> (Traxler & Kukulska-Hulme, 2006, p. 143, 148).

OVERVIEW OF M-LEARNING RESEARCH

This section briefly overviews a short history and critique of m-learning research, indicating the research gaps within the context of current m-learning activity. The scope of the chapter is limited by its necessary briefness, and focuses upon several broad themes.

Phases of M-Learning Research

The 21st century has seen the consolidation and maturing of m-learning research (Traxler, 2008). Internationally, many early (pre-2005) m-learning studies were typically short-term pilot studies. M-learning research now spans the globe: for example, Africa (Vosloo, Walton, & Deumert, 2009), Asia (Ogata et al., 2010), North America (Metcalf, 2006), Europe (Seta et al., 2010; Unterfrauner & Marschalek, 2010), Scandinavia (Laine & Suhonen, 2008), Australia (J. Herrington, Herrington, Mantei, Olney, & Ferry, 2009; Litchfield, Dyson, Lawrence, & Zmijewska, 2007), and New Zealand (Chan, 2007; Cochrane, 2011).

According to Cook (2009a) and Sharples (2010), the development of m-learning research has been characterized by three general phases:

1. a focus upon devices (for example: handheld computers in schools (Perry, 2003));
2. a focus on learning outside the classroom (for example: MOBILearn (O'Malley et al., 2005));
3. a focus on the mobility of the learner (for example: MyArtSpace (Sharples, Lonsdale, Meek, Rudman, & Vavoula, 2007), CONTSENS (Cook, 2010)).

Since 2005, there has been a flurry of m-learning research and case studies, particularly from the United Kingdom (UK). M-learning and Web 2.0 technologies have been identified as emerging tools to enhance teaching and learning (Anderson, 2007; Becta, 2007; Johnson, Levine, & Smith, 2007, 2008, 2009; McFarlane, Roche, & Triggs, 2007; McLoughlin & Lee, 2008; Sharples, Milrad, Arnedillo-Sanchez, & Vavoula, 2009; Traxler, 2007; Trinder, Guiller, Marggaryan, Littlejohn, & Nicol, 2008), but are not usually explicitly linked together. The following all demonstrate an increase in mainstream interest in m-learning: the increase in m-learning-focused conferences (for example: MLearn, Handheld Learning, Multimedia and Information and Communication Technologies in Education, the International Association for Development of the Information Society m-learning conference, Wireless Mobile and Ubiquitous Technologies in Education); research projects and briefing papers from organizations such as the Joint Information Systems Committee (JISC) and the British Educational Communications and Technology Agency (Becta); articles in educational journals such as *Educause* and the *Journal of Computer Assisted Learning*; the establishment of several m-learning-focused journals (for example: *International Journal of Mobile Learning and Organization, International Journal of Mobile and Blended Learning, International Journal of Handheld Computing Research*); and books (Ally, 2009; Metcalf, 2006; Pachler, Bachmair, & Cook, 2010; Ryu & Parsons, 2009; Woodill, 2010).

M-Learning Research Approaches

Approaches to m-learning vary from a focus upon content delivery (McKinney, Dyck, & Luber, 2009), short message service (SMS) (Mellow, 2005), polling (Dyson, Litchfield, Lawrence, Raban, & Leijdekkers, 2009), and location awareness (EDUCAUSE Learning Initiative, 2009; Pachler et al., 2010), to facilitating student-generated-content sharing (Sharples, et al., 2007) and augmented reality (Priestnall, Brown, Sharples, & Polmear, 2009; Sharples, 2009). In their review of 102 innovative m-learning projects published between 2002 and 2007, Frohberg, Goth, and Schwabe (2009) found that only 5 percent of these projects focused upon social learning, and less than 4 percent required higher-level thinking, with 89 percent targeting novice learners and 10 percent facilitating user-generated content. Many m-learning studies focus upon content delivery for small-screen devices (Stead & Colley, 2008) and the PDA capabilities of mobile devices (Corlett, Sharples, Bull, & Chan, 2005), rather than leveraging the potential of mobile devices for collaborative learning, as recommended by Hoppe, Joiner, Milrad and Sharples (2003):

Content delivery to mobile devices may well have a useful place in m-learning, however, there is an imperative to move from a view of e- and m-learning as solely delivery mechanisms for content . . . Handheld devices are emerging as one of the most promising technologies for supporting learning and particularly collaborative learning scenarios.

(Hoppe et al., 2003, p. 1)

Informal m-learning case studies in museum-tour environments have been popularized by the work of Sharples, Lonsdale, et al. (2007). Other popular m-learning-project contexts include the use of podcasts (McKinney et al., 2009) or mobile devices for language learning (Thornton & Houser, 2005) and geolocation (Priestnall et al., 2009). Many recent m-learning research projects, while focusing on the informal learning environment, often presuppose "self-motivated learners" (Cook, Pachler, & Bradley, 2008, p. 4) such as pre-service teachers. Few studies have yet to explicitly bridge both the formal and informal learning contexts within "mainstream" tertiary education. One exception was the Advanced Mobile and Ubiquitous Learning Environments for Teachers and Students project (CeLeKT, 2009), which explored collaboration in a variety of contexts, bridging indoor and outdoor learning experiences using mobile and location-aware devices in both secondary and tertiary scenarios.

Large-Scale M-Learning Projects

Several larger m-learning projects have tended to focus on specific groups of learners, rather than developing pedagogical strategies for the integration of m-learning within tertiary education in general. For example, the "m-learning project" extended over four years, focusing on retention of at-risk learners by using cell-phone technologies (Attewell, 2005). The Remote Authoring of Mobile Blogs for Learning Environments m-learning project (Trafford, 2005) investigated the use of mobile devices for blogging and accessing a virtual learning environment (VLE). However, the mobile devices (Palm OS PDAs) were not wireless capable, relying upon desktop computers for synchronization to update the students' blogs. In comparison, Corlett et al. (2005) identified wireless connectivity as a key factor in the success of their implementation of an m-learning organizer. Other examples of large-scale m-learning projects include: MOBILearn (Europe; www.mobilearn.org/), MobilED (South Africa; http://mobiled.uiah.fi/), and the m-learning network MoLeNET (UK). MoLeNET is possibly the largest m-learning research project undertaken so far. MoLeNET was UK based, focused on further-education (FE) institutions, and funded by the Learning and Skills Council. In its initial phase (2007–2008), the MoLeNET project included 32 FE institutions undertaking a variety of m-learning implementations. In its third year, MoLeNET provided £12 million of funded investment in m-learning in the UK to 115 colleges and 29 schools, involving around 20,000 learners and 4,000 staff. MoLeNET funding has been directed towards wireless infrastructure and the purchase of mobile devices, and it is yet to be seen whether this approach can be sustainable or transferable to student-owned devices (Traxler, 2009, 2010) and newer mobile devices, as those purchased quickly become out of date. Many of the MoLeNET projects investigated the affordances of a variety of mobile devices loaned to students for accessing course-related content. The focus of these projects tended to be on the delivery of content for access on a range of mobile devices. As such, the MoLeNET project can be characterized as a step backwards to the first "phase" of m-learning, a focus upon devices. However, the MoLeNET project had a robust focus on developing a model of professional development and support for educators, and a rigorous evaluation process.

The funding available from LSC was ring fenced for spending on capital equipment, and evidence from previous initiatives over many years indicated that it is very difficult to achieve ongoing change with one-off capital funding, as there is a tendency for initiatives to die when external funding runs out. Therefore, it was necessary to develop sustainability strategies to maximize the likelihood of any introduction of m-learning continuing beyond the initial funded phase (Attewell, 2008, p 28).

M-Learning Research Funding

The level of government funding of m-learning projects in the UK has spawned a very active m-learning research community, and, as a consequence, the UK is regarded as "leading" the world in m-learning research (Sharples, 2009). The availability of m-learning research funding has sometimes led to the exploration of bizarre, overly complicated projects that push the boundaries of the current mobile technology but do not produce widespread adoption or pedagogical transformation. However, some of these projects have produced sustainable models, for example the development of OOKL (an anagram of LOOK) as a framework for interactive museum visits, facilitating links to reflective classroom presentations (Sharples, Vavoula, Meek, Lonsdale, & Rudman, 2007). The focus of much of this government funding has been on "at-risk" learners, accounting for the high percentage of m-learning projects in this context. In comparison, m-learning research projects in countries with smaller population sizes such as Australia and New Zealand are typically funded on a "shoe-string" budget. As a result, these m-learning projects are generally smaller in scale than the large-scale UK projects such as MoLeNET, and have tended to be more focused upon exploring cost-effective m-learning implementation strategies (Bell, Cockburn, Wingkvist, & Green, 2007; Chan, 2007; Clark, Sutton-Brady, Scott, & Taylor, 2007; J. Herrington et al., 2009; Mackay, 2007; Mellow, 2005; Nalder, Kendall, & Menzies, 2007).

M-Learning Project Contexts

A list of a range of up-to-date m-learning projects from around the world can be found on the International Association for Mobile Learning website (2012; www.iamlearn.org/projects). The listed projects encompass a wide variety of m-learning implementations. Many projects involve the development and use of proprietary software (and sometimes hardware) that is often platform specific (for example, Windows Mobile) or Java-based, and also often only has a limited "shelf-life," as the designed-for devices go out of date quickly. The software is also usually task specific and hard to customize. These projects balance investment in high levels of technology support and development against low levels of user training required (simple and task-specific interfaces). These projects require high technical expertise (specialist mobile-application programming knowledge) and are, therefore, often complicated and difficult to transfer to widespread adoption.

European m-learning research has focused upon the context affordances of mobile devices. In their summary of European m-learning research, Kukulska-Hulme, Sharples, Milrad, Arnedillo-Sanchez, and Vavoula (2009) concluded:

> While delivery of educational content to mobile devices may have specific uses in training and professional development, there are other approaches to mobile learning that can make better use of the distinctive properties of mobile technology, including context-based guidance, learning through conversation, and mobile media creation.
> (p. 19)

For example, Cook's (2010) m-learning research projects focused upon augmenting the learners experience in the field, and, in reflection, he asks, "How do we get beyond good and useful exemplars?" (Cook, 2009b, p. 35). He proposes that to get wide-scale practitioner and institutional uptake requires an institutional cultural change. Several criticisms can be leveled at these "exemplars": the projects do not demonstrate a focus upon student-generated content or contexts, as they are predefined; there is no long-term change in student learning paradigms, as these are short, day-long projects with no longitudinal scaffolding for students to personally appropriate the use of the mobile tools beyond the project; the students involved are self-motivated learners and in small numbers, minimizing transferability; and there is a high technical requirement for these projects, involving the development of project-specific and intricate augmented-reality multimedia.

Cochrane (2010) and Cochrane and Bateman (2010, 2011) propose an alternative approach to m-learning design to minimize the technical expertise required for m-learning implementation and maximize transferability, while explicitly using a social-constructivist pedagogical foundation, focusing upon the potential of Mobile Web 2.0. Mobile Web 2.0 enables learner-generated content and learner-generated contexts, as suggested by Cook, Bradley, Lance, Smith, and Haynes (2007) and Luckin et al. (2008), guided by the pedagogical integration of these into their courses, as emphasized by Herrington and Herrington (2007) and Laurillard (2007). Examples of m-learning projects with a focus on freely available Mobile Web 2.0 tools and a social-constructivist pedagogy include the work of Chan (2007), the JISC-funded Mobilising Remote Student Engagement (MORSE) project (Andrew, Hall, & Taylor, 2009), and the m-learning projects at the University of Wollongong (A. Herrington, 2008; J. Herrington et al., 2009; J. Herrington, Mantei, Herrington, Olney, & Ferry, 2008). Chan investigated the potential of moblogging to support work-based learning for apprentice bakery chefs. The MORSE project (November 2008 to October 2010) investigated the use of Mobile Web 2.0 tools to support students away from the institution during field trips and work placement (ranging from one day to two weeks' duration, up to 15 times per year). The University of Wollongong projects were a series of short-term (six-weeks long) m-learning projects based around the affordances of institutionally loaned Palm Treo smartphones and iPods in tertiary education.

M-Learning Research Methodologies

Chen, Millard, and Wills (2008) evaluated the 40 research papers submitted to MLearn2007, categorizing the 17 m-learning scenarios described according to a four-category framework (learning objective, learning environment, learning activity, and learning tools), to establish how student-directed these projects were. Only two papers demonstrated alignment with being student-directed in all four categories (see, for example, Cochrane, 2007). The authors, therefore, concluded that, "In essence m-learning researchers are reinventing the VLE on the mobile device, rather than looking at how we could use them to support more subtle aspects of informal learning, and thus the increasingly important PLE area" (Chen et al., 2008, p. 88).

This selection of the m-learning research literature therefore indicates that the majority of current research has focused upon delivery of content to mobile devices (teacher generated and controlled), rather than student-generated content and contexts.

Another review of MLearn2007 and 2008 papers (Wingkvist & Ericsson, 2009) classified and critiqued the research methodologies reported in these papers. All 76 full papers were classified according to eight research methodologies (case study, field study, action research, experiment studies, survey research, basic research, applied research, and normative research) and four research purposes (describing, developing, under-standing, and evaluating). The reviewers found that the representative m-learning research consisted predominantly of small-scale descriptive case studies, with little evaluation and reflection witnessed. An action-research methodology was used by only 5 percent of these papers. This indicates that there is a significant gap in the literature of m-learning research dealing with longitudinal action-research projects. With some notable exceptions (for example, MoLeNET), m-learning research has been predomi-nantly characterized by short-term case studies focused upon the implementation of rapidly changing technologies with early adopters but with little evaluation, reflection, or emphasis on mainstream tertiary-education integration.

Identifying the Gaps in M-Learning Research
The author's review of the m-learning literature indicates that, to date, there are several common shortcomings in the majority of m-learning research:

- a lack of explicit underlying pedagogical theory (Traxler & Kukulska-Hulme, 2005);
- a lack of transferable design frameworks (Armstrong et al., 2008; Sharples, Crook, et al., 2009);
- a general lack of evaluation of the projects (Kukulsa-Hulme & Traxler, 2005; Vavoula & Sharples, 2009);
- a lack of longitudinal studies (Traxler & Kukulska-Hulme, 2005);
- a lack of the importance of pedagogical integration (Laurillard, 2007);
- a lack of explicit student and lecturer support and scaffolding (Attwell, 2007; J. Herrington & Oliver, 2000);
- a lack of awareness of the ontological shifts (Chi & Hausmann, 2003) required for both the learners' conception of learning and the lecturers' conception of teaching. Often, "net generation" skills are assumed (Barbaux, 2006), and most of the case studies consist of lecturers who are early technology adopters (Armstrong et al., 2008).

However, the identified shortcomings can be addressed by the explicit planning and investigation of these issues within m-learning research-project design. Although the first four identified shortcomings of m-learning research have been signaled by several researchers, there has been little emphasis upon the last three shortcomings identified here. The author believes that this is the result of the focus of the three phases (see the following section) of m-learning research upon short-term projects that explore m-learning mainly within informal learning contexts, with little focus upon sustainable integration of m-learning into formal education contexts.

In summary, the literature indicates that there is a gap in m-learning research around the integration of Mobile Web 2.0 within longitudinal projects focused upon learner-generated content and learner-generated contexts.

FOCUSING ON THE FUTURE OF M-LEARNING RESEARCH

There is a wealth of research into the use of mobile devices in education that can be utilized for future research: for example, the JISC-produced guide to implementing m-learning within a tertiary institution (Joint Information Systems Committee, 2005), user evaluation surveys for implementation trials, and a manager's framework for implementing m-learning in higher education (Knight, 2005). More recently, JISC has produced a mobile review (Belshaw, 2010), and an m-learning info kit (Belshaw, 2011).

The unique potential impact of m-learning on education is founded upon the rise of mobile devices to almost ubiquitous ownership (International Telecommunications Union, 2009) and their primary functionality as ubiquitously connected communication devices. These two characteristics of wireless mobile devices enable their use as disruptive devices to act as catalysts for pedagogical change by mediating student-generated learning contexts and sharing student-generated content as key elements of social-constructivist learning, or Pedagogy 2.0 (McLoughlin & Lee, 2010). The 2010 JISC mobile review (Belshaw, 2010) concludes that m-learning presents the potential to drive innovation in education:

> Mobile learning may mean different things to different people, but it is the dialogue that an institution begins with itself, its staff, its learners, its community—that matters. It is certainly not time for "business as usual". It is time to define and start driving innovation.
>
> (p. 63)

This potential for innovation is both driven and hampered by the rate of change in mobile technologies. Although the rate of change of mobile technology is very high, the author argues that the choice of a pedagogical framework and foundational pedagogical theory can guide the appropriate pedagogical use of future m-learning developments.

CONCLUSION

As the field of m-learning research enters its second decade of intense publication, it is an appropriate point at which to take stock of where we have been and where we should head in the future. This chapter identifies gaps in the m-learning literature and research, predominantly around the immaturity of the research approaches and evaluation strategies taken. In order to realize the unique potential of m-learning as a catalyst for pedagogical change, researchers need to look beyond a continual series of short-term projects. We must become more critically reflective and look towards sustainable approaches, such as focusing upon student-owned devices for enabling student-generated content and student-generated learning contexts.

REFERENCES

Ally, M. (Ed.) (2009). *Mobile learning: Transforming the delivery of education and training.* Edmonton, AB: AU Press, Athabasca University.

Anderson, P. (2007). What is Web 2.0? Ideas, technologies and implications for education. *TechWatch: Horizon Scanning Reports, 63.* Retrieved from: http://www.jisc.ac.uk/whatwedo/services/techwatch/reports/horizon scanning/hs0701.aspx

Andrew, M., Hall, R., & Taylor, P. (2009). Mobilising remote student engagement (MORSE) using mobile and web2.0 technologies: Initial perspectives. In I. A. Sanchez & P. Isaias (Eds.), *IADIS International Conference on Mobile Learning 2009* (pp. 199–202). Barcelona, Spain: International Association for Development of the Information Society.

Armstrong, J., Franklin, T., McLoughlin, C., Westera, W., Schmidt, P., Kelly, B., et al. (2008). *A review of current and developing international practice in the use of social networking (Web 2.0) in higher education.* York, UK: Franklin Consulting.

Attewell, J. (2005, October). *From research and development to mobile learning: Tools for education and training providers and their learners.* Paper presented at the mLearn 2005: 4th World Conference on Mobile Learning, Cape Town.

Attewell, J. (2008). Towards sustainable large scale implementation of mobile learning: The mobile learning network (MoLeNET). In J. Traxler, B. Riordan, & C. Dennett (Eds.), *MLearn08: The bridge from text to context* (pp. 28–35). Ironbridge Gorge, Shropshire, UK: University of Wolverhampton, School of Computing and IT.

Attwell, G. (2007). The personal learning environments—the future of eLearning? *eLearning Papers, 2*(1), 1–8.

Barbaux, M.-T. (2006). From lifelong learning to m-learning. In D. Whitelock & S. Wheeler (Eds.), *Proceedings of the 13th Association for Learning Technology Conference (ALT-C 2006)* (pp. 132–141). Heriot-Watt University, Edinburgh, UK: Association for Learning Technology.

Becta. (2007, March). Emerging technologies for learning. Volume 2. Retrieved from: http://herkomer.wikispaces.com/file/view/emerging_technologies07.pdf

Bell, T., Cockburn, A., Wingkvist, A., & Green, R. (2007). Podcasts as a supplement in tertiary education: An experiment with two computer science courses. In D. Parsons & H. Ryu (Eds.), *Proceedings of the Conference on Mobile Learning Technologies and Applications (MOLTA)* (pp. 70–77). Massey University, Auckland, New Zealand.

Belshaw, D. (2010). *Mobile and wireless technologies review.* Newcastle upon Tyne, UK: JISC infoNet.

Belshaw, D. (2011). *Mobile learning infokit.* Newcastle upon Tyne, UK: JISC infoNet.

CeLeKT. (2009, July). *AMULETS. Advanced mobile and ubiquitous learning environments for teachers and students.* Retrieved from: www.celekt.info/projects/show/11

Chan, S. (2007). mLearning and the workplace learner: Integrating mlearning ePortfolios with Moodle. In D. Parsons & H. Ryu (Eds.), *Procedings of the Conference on Mobile Learning Technologies and Applications (MOLTA)* (pp. 55–62). Massey University, Auckland, New Zealand.

Chen, W. P., Millard, D. E., & Wills, G. B. (2008). Mobile VLE vs. mobile PLE: How informal is mobile learning? In J. Traxler, B. Riordan, & C. Dennett (Eds.), *Proceedings of MLearn08: The bridge from text to context* (pp. 82–88). Ironbridge Gorge, Shropshire, UK: University of Wolverhampton, School of Computing and IT.

Chi, M., & Hausmann, R. (2003). Do radical discoveries require ontological shifts? In L. Shavinina & R. Sternberg (Eds.), *International handbook on innovation* (Vol. 3, pp. 430–444). New York: Elsevier Science Ltd.

Clark, S., Sutton-Brady, C., Scott, K., & Taylor, L. (2007). Short podcasts: The impact on learning and teaching. In C. Oliver (Ed.), *Proceedings of MLearn 2007—Making the Connections 6th International Conference on Mobile Learning* (pp. 270–274). Melbourne, Australia: MLearn 2007.

Cochrane, T. (2007). Mobile blogging: A guide for educators. In C. Oliver (Ed.), *Proceedings of MLearn 2007—Making the Connections 6th International Conference on Mobile Learning* (pp. 26–34). Melbourne Exhibition Centre, Melbourne, Australia: MLearn 2007.

Cochrane, T. (2010). Beyond the Yellow Brick Road: Mobile web 2.0 informing a new institutional elearning strategy. *ALT-J, Research in Learning Technology, 18*(3), 221–231.

Cochrane, T. (2011). Reflections on 4 years of mlearning implementation (2007–2010). *International Journal of Mobile and Blended Learning, 3*(3), 1–22.

Cochrane, T., & Bateman, R. (2010). Smartphones give you wings: Pedagogical affordances of mobile web 2.0. *Australasian Journal of Educational Technology, 26*(1), 1–14.

Cochrane, T., & Bateman, R. (2011). Strategies for mlearning integration: Evaluating a case study of staging and scaffolding mlearning integration across a three-year bachelor's degree. *Waikato Journal of Education, 16*(1), 109–124.

Cook, J. (2009a). *Phases of mobile learning.* Paper presented at Joint European Summer School on Technology Enhanced Learning (May 30–June 6). Retrieved from: www.slideshare.net/johnnigelcook/cook-phases-of-mobile-learning

Cook, J. (2009b). *Scaffolding the mobile wave.* Paper presented at JISC Institutional Impact Programme online meeting (July 9). Retrieved from: www.slideshare.net/johnnigelcook/cook-1697245

Cook, J. (2010). *Mobile phones as mediating tools within augmented contexts for development.* Paper presented at the Education in the Wild, Alpine Rendez-Vous, within the framework of the STELLAR network of excellence. Retrieved from: www.slideshare.net/johnnigelcook/cook-mobile-phones-as-mediating-tools-within-augmented-contexts-for-development

Cook, J., Bradley, C., Lance, J., Smith, C., & Haynes, R. (2007). Generating learner contexts with mobile devices. In N. Pachler (Ed.), *Mobile learning: Towards a research agenda* (pp. 55–73). London: WLE Centre, Institute of Education.

Cook, J., Pachler, N., & Bradley, C. (2008). Bridging the gap? Mobile phones at the interface between informal and formal learning. *Journal of the Research Center for Educational Technology, 4*(1), 3–18.

Corlett, D., Sharples, M., Bull, S., & Chan, T. (2005). Evaluation of a mobile learning organiser for university students. *Journal of Computer Assisted Learning, 21*(3), 162–170.

Dyson, L. E., Litchfield, A., Lawrence, E., Raban, R., & Leijdekkers, P. (2009). Advancing the m-learning research agenda for active learning: Four case studies. *Australasian Journal of Educational Technology, 25*(2), 250–267.

EDUCAUSE Learning Initiative (2009). 7 things you should know about location-aware applications. *7 things you should know about . . . 2009* (March 16). Retrieved from: www.educause.edu/ELI/7ThingsYouShould KnowAboutLocat/163839

Frohberg, D., Goth, C., & Schwabe, G. (2009). Mobile learning projects—a critical analysis of the state of the art [Research article]. *Journal of Computer Assisted Learning, 25*(4), 307–331.

Herrington, A. (2008). Adult educators' authentic use of smartphones to create digital teaching resources. In A. Farley & D. Holt (Eds.), *Proceedings of ASCILITE 2008* (pp. 414–418). Deakin University, Melbourne, Australia: ASCILITE.

Herrington, A., & Herrington, J. (2007). *Authentic mobile learning in higher education.* Paper presented at the AARE 2007 International Educational Research Conference. Retrieved from: www.aare.edu.au/07pap/ abs07.htm

Herrington, J., Herrington, A., Mantei, J., Olney, I., & Ferry, B. (Eds.) (2009). *New technologies, new pedagogies: Mobile learning in higher education.* Wollongong, Australia: Faculty of Education, University of Wollongong.

Herrington, J., Mantei, J., Herrington, A., Olney, I., & Ferry, B. (2008). New technologies, new pedagogies: Mobile technologies and new ways of teaching and learning. In A. Farley & D. Holt (Eds.), *Proceedings of ASCILITE 2008* (pp. 419–427). Deakin University, Melbourne, Australia: ASCILITE.

Herrington, J., & Oliver, R. (2000). An instructional design framework for authentic learning environments. *Educational Technology Research and Development, 48*(3), 23–48.

Hoppe, H. U., Joiner, R., Milrad, M., & Sharples, M. (2003). Guest editorial: Wireless and mobile technologies in education. *Journal of Computer Assisted Learning, 19*(3), 255–259.

International Association for Mobile Learning. (2012). Mobile learning projects. Retrieved from: www.iamlearn.org/ projects

International Telecommunications Union. (2009). *The world in 2009: ICT facts and figures.* Geneva: International Telecommunications Union.

Joint Information Systems Committee. (2005). Innovative practice with e-learning: A good practice guide to embedding mobile and wireless technologies into everyday practice. Retrieved from: www.jisc.ac.uk/eli_ practice.html

Johnson, L., Levine, A., & Smith, R. (2007). *The horizon report: 2007 edition.* Retrieved from: http://www.nmc.org/ pdf/2007_Horizon_Report.pdf

Johnson, L., Levine, A., & Smith, R. (2008). *The horizon report: 2008 edition.* Retrieved from: http://horizon.nmc.org/ wiki/Main_Page

Johnson, L., Levine, A., & Smith, R. (2009). *The horizon report: 2009 edition.* Austin, TX: New Media Consortium.

Knight, S. (Ed.) (2005). *Innovative practice with e-learning: A manager's planning tool for use of mobile and wireless technologies* (Vol. 2005). Bristol, UK: JISC.

Kukulska-Hulme, A., & Traxler, J. (2005). *Mobile Learning.* Oxford, UK: Routledge.

Kukulska-Hulme, A., Sharples, M., Milrad, M., Arnedillo-Sanchez, I., & Vavoula, G. (2009). Innovation in mobile learning: A European perspective. *International Journal of Mobile and Blended Learning, 1*(1), 13–35.

Laine, T. H., & Suhonen, J. (2008). Establishing a mobile blog system in a distance education environment. *International Journal of Mobile Learning and Organisation, 2*(2), 149–165.

Laurillard, D. (2007). Pedagogical forms of mobile learning: Framing research questions. In N. Pachler (Ed.), *Mobile learning: Towards a research agenda* (pp. 33–54). London: WLE Centre, Institute of Education.

Litchfield, A., Dyson, L. E., Lawrence, E., & Zmijewska, A. (2007). Directions for m-learning research to enhance active learning. In R. J. Atkinson, C. McBeath, S. K. A. Song, & C. Cheers (Eds.), *Proceedings of Ascilite 2007, ICT: Providing choices for learners and learning* (pp. 587–596). Singapore: Centre for Educational Development, Nanyang Technological University.

Luckin, R., Clark, W., Garnett, F., Whitworth, A., Akass, J., Cook, J., et al. (2008). Learner generated contexts: A framework to support the effective use of technology to support learning. Retrieved from: http://knowledge illusion.files.wordpress.com/2012/03/bookchapterluckin2009learnergeneratedcontexts.pdf

Mackay, B. (2007). M-support for nursing students in primary health care nursing. In D. Parsons & H. Ryu (Eds.), *Proceedings of Mobile Learning Technologies and Applications (MOLTA)* (pp. 78–85). Massey University, Auckland, New Zealand.

McFarlane, A., Roche, N., & Triggs, P. (2007). *Mobile learning: Research findings.* Bristol, UK: University of Bristol.

McKinney, D., Dyck, J. L., & Luber, E. S. (2009). iTunes University and the classroom: Can podcasts replace professors? *Computers & Education, 52*(3), 617–623.

McLoughlin, C., & Lee, M. (2008). Future learning landscapes: Transforming pedagogy through social software. *Innovate: Journal of Online Education, 4*(5), 7.

McLoughlin, C., & Lee, M. (2010). Pedagogy 2.0: Critical challenges and responses to Web 2.0 and social software in tertiary teaching. In M. Lee & C. McLoughlin (Eds.), *Web 2.0-based e-learning: Applying social informatics for tertiary teaching* (pp. 46–69). Hershey, PA: IGI Global.

Mellow, P. (2005). The media generation: Maximise learning by getting mobile. In H. Goss (Ed.), *Proceedings of 22nd ASCILITE Conference: Balance, Fidelity, Mobility. Maintaining the Momentum?* (pp. 469–476). Brisbane, Australia: Queensland University of Technology.

Metcalf, D. (2006). *mLearning: mobile learning and performance in the palm of your hand.* Amherst, MA: HRD Press, Inc.

Nalder, G., Kendall, E., & Menzies, V. (2007). Self-organising m-learning communities: A case-study. In C. Oliver (Ed.), *Proceedings of MLearn 2007—Making the Connections 6th International Conference on Mobile Learning* (pp. 171–178). Melbourne, Australia: mlearn.

O'Malley, C., Vavoula, G., Glew, J., Taylor, J., Sharples, M., Lefrere, P., et al. (2005). MOBIlearn: D4.1 Guidelines for learning/teaching/tutoring in a mobile environment. Retrieved from: http://kn.open.ac.uk/public/document.cfm?docid=7232

Ogata, H., Li, M., Hou, B., Uosaki, N., El-Bishouty, M., & Yano, Y. (2010). SCROLL: Supporting to share and use ubiquitous learning log in the context of language learning. In M. Montebello, V. Camilleri, & A. Dingli (Eds.), *Proceedings of MLearn 2010: The 9th International Conference on Mobile Learning* (pp. 40–47). Valletta, Malta: University of Malta.

Pachler, N., Bachmair, B., & Cook, J. (2010). *Mobile learning: Structures, agency, practices.* London: Springer.

Perry, D. (2003). Handheld computers (PDAs) in schools. Retrieved from: http://dera.ioe.ac.uk/1644/1/becta_2003_handhelds_report.pdf

Priestnall, G., Brown, E., Sharples, M., & Polmear, G. (2009). A student-led comparison of techniques for augmenting the field experience. In D. Metcalf, A. Hamilton, & C. Graffeo (Eds.), *Proceedings of mLearn2009: 8th World Conference on Mobile and Contextual Learning* (pp. 195–198). Orlando, FL: University of Central Florida.

Ryu, H., & Parsons, D. (2009). *Innovative mobile learning: Techniques and technologies.* Hershey, PA: Information Science Reference.

Seta, L., Taibi, D., Fulantelli, G., Arrigo, M., Giuseppe, O. D., Gentile, M., et al. (2010). Mobile learning for lifelong learning projects in the Italian context. In M. Montebello, V. Camilleri, & A. Dingli (Eds.), *Proceedings of MLearn 2010: The 9th International Conference on Mobile Learning* (pp. 374–377). Valletta, Malta: University of Malta.

Sharples, M. (2009, October). *Learning at large.* Paper presented at MLearn 2009: The 8th World Conference on Mobile and Contextual Learning, University of Central Florida, Institute for Simulation and Training, Orlando, Florida.

Sharples, M. (2010). *Innovation in mlearning: An international perspective.* Paper presented at mLearnCon. Retrieved from: www.elearningguild.com/mLearnCon/concurrent-sessions/session-details.cfm?event=62&date=06/15/2010&time=10:45:00#2425

Sharples, M., Crook, C., Jones, I., Kay, D., Chowcat, I., Balmer, K., et al. (2009). *CAPITAL year one final report* (Draft), University of Nottingham, UK.

Sharples, M., Lonsdale, P., Meek, J., Rudman, P., & Vavoula, G. (2007, October). *An evaluation of MyArtSpace: A mobile learning service for school museum trips.* Paper presented at MLearn 2007—Making the Connections 6th International Conference on Mobile Learning, Melbourne, Australia.

Sharples, M., Milrad, M., Arnedillo-Sanchez, I., & Vavoula, G. (2009). Mobile learning: Small devices, big issues. In N. Balacheff, S. Ludvigsen, T. de Jong, A. Lazonder, S. Barnes, & L. Montandon (Eds.), *Technology enhanced learning: Principles and products* (pp. 233–249). Berlin: Springer-Verlag.

Sharples, M., Vavoula, G., Meek, J., Lonsdale, P., & Rudman, P. (2007). OOKL evaluation. 3. Retrieved from: http://ookl.files.wordpress.com/2008/10/u-of-birmingham-final-report-headlines.pdf

Stead, G., & Colley, J. (2008, October). *The power of me: Learning by making your own rich media mobile resources.* Paper presented at MLearn08: The Bridge From Text to Context, Ironbridge Gorge, Shropshire, UK.

Thornton, P., & Houser, C. (2005). Using mobile phones in English education in Japan. *Journal of Computer Assisted Learning, 21*(3), 217–228.

Trafford, P. (2005). Mobile blogs, personal reflections and learning environments. *Ariadne,* (44), 9. Retrieved from: www.ariadne.ac.uk/issue44/trafford

Traxler, J. (2007). Defining, discussing, and evaluating mobile learning: The moving finger writes and having writ . . . *International Review of Research in Open and Distance Learning, 8*(2), 12.

Traxler, J. (2008). From text to context. In J. Traxler, B. Riordan, & C. Dennett (Eds.), *Proceedings of mLearn2008* (pp. 9–11). Ironbridge Gorge, Shropshire, UK: University of Wolverhampton.

Traxler, J. (2009). Current state of mobile learning. In M. Ally (Ed.), *Mobile learning: Transforming the delivery of education and training* (pp. 9–24). Edmonton, AB: AU Press, Athabasca University.

Traxler, J. (2010). Will student devices deliver innovation, inclusion, and transformation? *Journal of the Research Center for Educational Technology, 6*(1), 3–15.

Traxler, J., & Kukulska-Hulme, A. (2005, October). *Evaluating mobile learning: Reflections on current practice.* Paper presented at mLearn 2005, Cape Town, South Africa.

Traxler, J., & Kukulska-Hulme, A. (2006). The evaluation of next generation learning technologies: The case of mobile learning. In D. Whitelock & S. Wheeler (Eds.), *13th Association for Learning Technology Conference* (pp. 143–152). Heriot-Watt University, Edinburgh, UK: Association for Learning Technology.

Trinder, K., Guiller, J., Marggaryan, N., Littlejohn, A., & Nicol, D. (2008). *Learning from digital natives: Bridging formal and informal learning.* Glasgow Caledonian University, UK: The Higher Education Academy.

Unterfrauner, E., & Marschalek, I. (2010). Appropriation of an online mobile community by marginalised young people: Experiences from an Austrian case study. In M. Montebello, V. Camilleri, & A. Dingli (Eds.), *Proceedings of MLearn 2010: The 9th International Conference on Mobile Learning* (pp. 276–281). Valletta, Malta: University of Malta.

Vavoula, G., & Sharples, M. (2009). Meeting the challenges in evaluating mobile learning: A 3-level evaluation framework. *International Journal of Mobile and Blended Learning, 1*(2), 54–75.

Vosloo, S., Walton, M., & Deumert, A. (2009). m4Lit: A teen m-novel project in South Africa. In D. Metcalf, A. Hamilton, & C. Graffeo (Eds.), *Proceedings of MLearn 2009: The 8th World Conference on Mobile and Contextual Learning* (pp. 207–211). Orlando, FL: University of Central Florida, Institute for Simulation and Training.

Wingkvist, A., & Ericsson, M. (2009). Current practice in mobile learning: A survey of research method and purpose. In D. Metcalf, A. Hamilton, & C. Graffeo (Eds.), *MLearn 2009: 8th World Conference on Mobile and Contextual Learning* (pp. 103–111). Orlando, FL: The University of Central Florida.

Woodill, G. (2010). The mobile learning edge: Tools and technologies for developing your teams. New York: McGraw-Hill Professional.

4

A SOCIOCULTURAL ECOLOGICAL FRAME FOR MOBILE LEARNING

Norbert Pachler, Ben Bachmair, and John Cook

The increasing normalization of mobile devices in everyday life, including the lifeworlds of young people, raises questions about their potential for learning. Attempts to appropriate media from the world of work, as well as everyday life, have a long tradition in education and tend to be discussed under the guise of 'technology-enhanced learning'. A certain degree of optimism has tended to surround new media resources – be they from mass communication, such as video, or from business, such as the computer – and their meaningful integration into teaching and learning in schools. Of course, the question of whether new media resources are appropriate for school has long been debated: do media really enhance learning, or, in view of their rootedness in entertainment, do they actually subdue the educational rationale for learning? It is not easy to formulate an answer, because there exist no general educational principles for media use, owing to the societal and cultural character of media, technology, learning and education. For this reason, we propose a line of argumentation that defines mobile devices such as mobile phones as cultural resources. Mobile cultural resources emerge within what we call a 'mobile complex', which consists of specific *structures*, *agency* and *cultural practices* (see Pachler, Bachmair and Cook, 2010). These specific structures, agency and cultural practices of the mobile complex are in perpetual flux. The mobile cultural resources of the mobile complex are becoming integrated into schools' institutionalized learning bit by bit. In the following, we will discuss two interrelated fields: the first is the sociocultural field, which considers the *mobile complex*; the second is the educational field, with its focus on learning as meaning-making and as appropriation of cultural artefacts.

TOWARDS A CULTURAL ECOLOGY OF M-LEARNING

In the introduction, we introduced a key notion within our conceptualization of the potential of mobile devices for learning, namely mobile devices and the artefacts accessed through and created with them as cultural resource. The concept of a resource is traditionally associated with the field of economics, where resources are assets and prerequisites for the production of goods and services in relation to the needs and desires of consumers and society. Such a conceptualization of resources does not sit easily with pedagogy, which looks for learning within the developmental processes of human beings rather than within consumption. In addition, pedagogy looks for learning in the context of identity formation of learners within a wider societal context. However, at the beginning of the twenty-first century, an economy-oriented service function of learning, driven by targets and international comparisons, has started to preoccupy education systems and schools within them. In part, this is the result of economic changes of the last two or three decades, away from production and the associated heavy industries, to creative and service industries. In this context, human resources, which are based on learning and competencies, are becoming essential for global market economies. The discourse of the knowledge economy, with its inherent logic of valuing learning as an economic resource and the results of learning as human capital, has dominated policy thinking for some decades now. Dunning (2000, pp. 9ff.) describes the lengthy transformation process from 'natural assets' (land, unskilled labour) to 'tangible assets' (machinery) to 'intangible created assets' such as 'knowledge and information of all kinds'. He reports OECD data for the period from 1975 to 1995 on expenditure for research and development (a threefold increase), and increases in patents (48 per cent in the USA in the 20-year period) and participation in further and higher education (according to World Bank data from 1997, an increase in the proportion of learners aged 15–24 from 35 per cent in 1980 to 56 per cent in 1993). Araya and Peters (2010, pp. xx) describe the development of the last 20 years in terms of phases: 'from the postindustrial economy to the information economy to the digital economy to the knowledge economy to the "creative economy"'. Economic development in the field of human and cultural resources, as well as the related structuration, has since become rather more subtle.

This brief foray into economic policy lays bare that the concept of cultural resources, in the form of mobile devices and associated services and competencies as cultural resource for learning, is economically rooted. As educators, we need to take a critical stance towards these developments and ask ourselves how to respond to them.

Inherent in the historical development of the concept of *resource* is also a critical approach. In particular, the concept of a *cultural ecology* is helpful here. *Cultural ecology* can refer to the debate about natural resources. For some decades now, there have been discussions about the exploitation of energy and nature as societal resources. In this tradition, we argue for a critical debate about the new cultural resources, namely mobile devices and their services. For us, the focus must not be on the 'exploitation' of mobile devices and services for learning, but instead on the assimilation of learning with mobiles in informal contexts of everyday life into formal education.

Consequently, a key notion for us is assimilation, which needs to be rooted in traditional learning scenarios of school-based education. At the same time, processes of assimilation have to respect the rationale of mobile-device use by learners (and teachers). One central aspect is how learners appropriate mobile devices. As schools are still largely mobile-device-free zones, and as they tend not yet to afford working with mobile phones notable status for learning, the appropriation of mobile phones in everyday life and its rationale need to be considered. A second key aspect for us, therefore, is the personalized way in which life is constructed in societies characterized by individualized risks (see Beck, 1986). Under these conditions, human beings use mobile devices to construct their lifeworlds within particular sociocultural milieus and associated lifestyles. From this assimilative perspective, m-learning is located within the use of mobile devices in everyday life, as a result of personal appropriation, to which the challenges of the school curriculum and traditional teaching and learning practices stand in juxtaposition. This is where the notion of an 'ecology' is helpful. We propose to take into consideration Gibson and Pick's (2000, pp. 14ff.) ecology of perception. An ecology comes into being if there exists a reciprocity between perceiver and environment. Translated to m-learning processes, this means that there is a reciprocity between the mobile devices in the activity context of everyday life and the formal learning context. Reciprocity manifests itself as assimilation of learning in informal contexts into the formal curricular learning of the school. Another aspect of reciprocity of mobile devices, everyday life and formal learning is the naïve expertise (of media use) in everyday life that students bring into educational situations. Assimilation means to recognize such naïve expertise.

Reciprocity as a basis for the assimilation of cultural mobile resources by formal eduction can be realized practically through a mobile investigation of schools as learning environments. In a workshop for 16–20-year-old at-risk learners, participants started with an investigation of the college buildings and site. The participants wandered around to discover the facilities of the college. They were invited to take photos with their mobiles, one of which would be selected for printing on a T-shirt. The T-shirt offered a very personal perspective on appropriation of the college context, in the sense of learners adopting a stance towards the college through self-representation. In the opening phase of the workshop, the mobile phone offered concrete reciprocity of the participants' perspectives with the new learning context. Figures 4.1a–4.1d show some examples: one T-shirt depicts the image of a bench under a tree; another T-shirt adorns a row of mannequins from the sewing workshop of the school. Furthermore, there is a toilet sign with an interesting design, as well as a picture of paint traces on the floor of the art room. Other participants used their mobile phones just as tools for opening up their Web 2.0 context. One participant brought his self-image as a dancer in the form of a photo from Facebook into the workshop. Another T-shirt featured a collection of photos of friends. The photos chosen for the T-shirts highlight different aspects of reciprocity. Some photos can be seen as still-life compositions, which refer to objects of study. Others depict design aspects of the college. A third group refers to learners' everyday lives, their peers and their hobbies. They open up opportunities for the facilitator to address participants from their chosen perspective – design, hobby, peers – and to link these interests to the learning objectives of the curriculum. The reference to design is not a difficult task in a media-centred study environment. To refer to hobbies and peers is possible if the context of the school is seen as open to the outside world.

The facilitator accompanied one student group during the investigation of the college and took photos of his own of their activities for a *mobile teacher portfolio*. A mobile facilitator portfolio is an explicit way of setting up reciprocity between the college and new students. The facilitator's portfolio shows, for example, how carefully the group arrange a still life with their shoes and feet in a school corridor. The participants present themselves as fashion and art designers and certainly not as beginners, but as experts. With a such a mobile portfolio, a facilitator can adjust his/her perception of the learning habitus of participants. Their intention is to learn about design, but their idea of design is not just oriented towards traditional learning outcomes. For participants, play is an important element. Play plus target orientation is what they expect. The mobile devices of everyday life fit perfectly into this expectation.

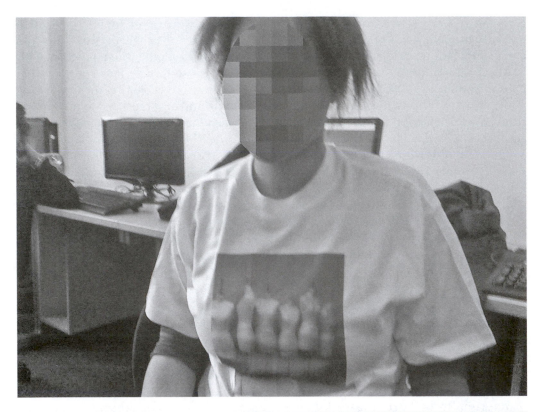

Figures 4.1a–d T-Shirts as Self-Representation (For Reasons of Personal Protection, the Faces Have Been Made Unrecognizable)

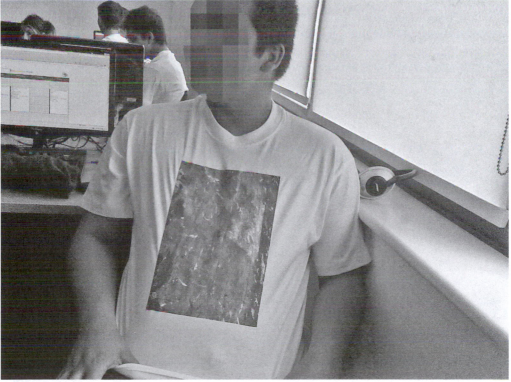

NEW DIGITAL RESOURCES WITHIN THE MOBILE COMPLEX OF STRUCTURES, AGENCY AND CULTURAL PRACTICES

Our engagement with m-learning does not focus on technological innovation as a stimulus for modernization of the education system, nor on school improvement in a paradigm that seeks maximum efficiency and attainment. Instead, as we have already noted, our focus is on mobile devices and the digital artefacts produced with, and accessed through, them as 'cultural resources'. These we deem to possess considerable affordances for learning. An important element of our theoretical perspective is the embeddedness of these resources in what we call the 'mobile complex', which is characterized by the disappearance of the world of discrete, bounded and clearly framed media, as well as a diverse set of modes of representation.

To capture the mobile complex, we propose a triangular model of structures, agency and cultural practices (see Pachler, Bachmair, & Cook, 2010, p. 25). This model widens the analytic perspective on the 'conditions governing the continuity or transmutation of structures, and therefore the reproduction of the social systems' ('structuration') offered by Giddens (1984, p. 25). Our model widens the dialectic, bilateral relation of structures and agency with the notion of cultural practices (see, among others, Lefebvre, 1961) because of the relevance of cultural practices to human beings, especially in terms of the differences in mobile-device use in everyday life and learning and teaching in formal education contexts.

In the following, we will discuss the three nodes briefly in turn.

Sociocultural Structures

Important contextual features of m-learning, for us, are the ongoing structural changes to mass communication, in particular user-generated content and individualized communication. These changes also affect the agency of the user and his/her relationship with media. Furthermore, we propose that users are routinely engaged in generating

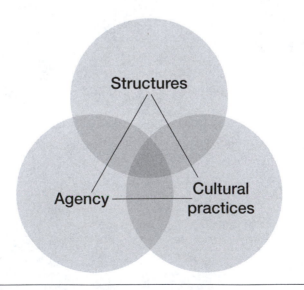

Figure 4.2 Key Components of a Sociocultural Ecological Approach to M-Learning

their own forms of individualized contexts for learning. Mobile devices enable new relationships of learners with space (the physical world) and place (space invested with meaning). They also enable and foster the broadening and breaking up of genres. We view the concept of 'learner-generated context' as an instantiation of a paradigm shift in which learning is viewed in categories of context and not content. And we view learning as a process of meaning-making that occurs through acts of communication, which take place within rapidly changing sociocultural, mass-communication and technological structures mediated, inter alia, by mobile devices. Mobile devices give users access to knowledge distributed across people, communities, locations, time, social contexts and sites of practice. Of particular relevance for us is how mobile devices mediate access to external representations of knowledge. Through mobile-device use, learners negotiate the world they live in, construct internal conceptualizations of knowledge and make social uses of knowledge.

Agency

Another important element of our theoretical perspective is the use of mobile devices for the formation of identity and subjectivity for finding a distinct way of being in the world. This element we call agency, which we see as the capacity to deal with, and to impact on, sociocultural structures and established cultural practices.

Agency includes the capacity to construct a personal lifeworld and to use media for meaning-making. It finds expresson in the learner's social and semiotic capacity, i.e. his/her ability to form technology-mediated relationships with others, make meaning in and of the world, and abstract representations of the world using a range of sign systems. This includes lifestyle and habitus, which frame people's life courses, organized into relatively stable sociocultural milieus and value orientations (see Schütz, 1932/1967).

In our example above, the introductory workshop for at-risk learners, habitus is important. Traditionally, the success of learning was thought to depend on the intellectual capacity and the attention of a student. The results of the Programme for International Student Assessment (PISA) show that there are significant social risks associated with failure in formal learning. Evidence from PISA suggests that the social risk of failure is correlated with variables such as being from a migrant background, coming from a poor family from a low social stratification, and being male. This is coupled with a de-traditionalization of the practices of learning, among other things, evident in the overall reduction in the proportion of learning undertaken in school as opposed to through lifelong learning. Linked to that is a significant increase in opportunities for learning in everyday life, for example, through television programmes. These programmes follow the traditional formats of formal learning fairly closely – for example, series such as *Who Wants to be a Millionaire*, which assume a particular habitus of learning based on knowledge acquisiton and reproduction, with the role of the teacher performed by a host; other elements are self-representation of contestants on screen and play through games. Target-oriented production of knowledge, as well as play and self-representation, we argue – on the basis of our development work with at-risk learners – should all be part of mobile-learning design and can be explained by the origin of mobile devices in the media ensemble of everyday life. This was self-evident for the student in the example above, who chose a photo of himself as an expert dancer for his T-shirt. Taken at face value, he did not follow the task brief. But, during his investigation of the college, he worked actively and with engagement on a *mis-en-scène*, a visual theme for still lifes, with his friends. For this, he used the mobile phone. However, for his self-representation on the T-shirt, he preferred to use an image from his Facebook page and he brought an already existing photo into the school context. For bringing together target- and result-oriented learning with play and self-representation, he utilized the affordances of media convergence and combined several contexts: the context of the college, the context of his hobby and the context of a social-network site.

Cultural Practices

By cultural practices, we mean routines in stable situations in relation to media use in everyday life, as well as in relation to the the pedagogical practices adopted by educational institutions.

For us, personal ownership is a defining characteristic of mobile devices, certainly as far as cultural practices are concerned, as it enables users to develop qualitatively and emotionally strong relationships with the devices and the services available through them. From an educational perspective, personal ownership means that it is the learner, rather than school, who develops the necesary skills to use the hardware and software effectively. Importantly, it also fosters processes of user-generated content, with users routinely capturing aspects of their everyday life, as well as user-generated contexts for learning through device use in the process, for example, of socializing and networking, communicating and the sharing of information and artefacts across time and place. Personal ownership also enables users to adopt personalized media and application preferences. Learners can make their own choices, rather than having to rely on those made by schools or teachers. Conversely, increasing choice brings with it some challenges, such as around the need to integrate a diverse range of devices, tools and applications and to ensure interoperability of devices and services. Cultural practices around media use in everyday life focus increasingly on so-called Web 2.0 practices, such as collaborating, exploring new literacies, pursuing enquiry and publishing to audiences (see Crook, 2012), and genres of participation such as hanging out, messing around and geeking out (see Ito et al., 2008). Crook's work (2012) identifies key differences in the 'operating characteristics' of out-of-school and in-school communication environments and how they apply to Web 2.0 practices.

Acceptable behaviour in the use of mobile devices links to social norms in the context of wider cultural practices surrounding the use of mobile phones, with traditional regulations of public and private spaces being renegotiated.

By capturing episodes from their everyday lives (and sharing them), mobile-device users create cultural artefacts, which we consider to have potential for learning. In this way, everyday events are afforded a certain status and permanence and can become the focus for later discussion, reflection and analysis. They also enable users to engage in processes of identity negotiation and renegotiation, as well as self-representation.

The multimodality of these technologies makes them more difficult to map onto traditional curricula and asserts pressure on established canons, i.e. definitions of what counts as valuable knowledge for teaching and learning. The communicative potential of mobile devices also opens up new possibilities in the relationships between teachers and learners, as well as learners and their peers, inside as well as outside the classroom. In our work, we focus in particular on the notion of what we call 'conversational bridges', by which we mean the need for school to adjust its cultural practices and become more open to the cultural practices of mobile-phone use in everyday life (see, e.g., Bachmair, Pachler and Cook, 2009).

THE APPROPRIATION OF NEW CULTURAL PRODUCTS AND A NEW HABITUS OF LEARNING

At the same time as mobile phones are becoming normalized in everyday life and the world of work, in particular business communication, worldwide, most schools are still banning mobile phones from their premises. One important reason is the fear that mobile devices represent a distraction for learners and from learning; another is the fear relating to e-safety, for example around bullying by means of the mobile phone. Underlying these fears is the strong connection between school instruction and the book, although, for reasons of financial exigency, e-books are starting to be considered as a viable alternative to the printed textbook in some districts. Furthermore, schools still tend to associate learning, first and foremost, with target-oriented instruction in which the teacher delivers knowledge and assesses the outcomes of learning. The ongoing de-traditionalization of learning in the context of the so-called *knowledge society* produces an increasing pressure on schools to engage positively with the societal trend towards individualized, mobile and convergent media, as well with the trend towards learning outside teacher-guided instruction, in informal contexts.

Appropriation

At this point, we want to turn to a well-established, key concept of education, namely appropriation. With the advent of industrialization at the end of the eighteenth and the beginning of the nineteenth century, a new self-perception of human beings as individuals emerged that entered as a new force of agency into the dynamic of society. The individual as a person could no longer be treated merely as a product constructed by institutions or social class. Educational theory of the time foregrounded the development of human beings. The idealistic approach embodied by Wilhelm von Humboldt (1792/2002) describes the development of humans as a dynamic of the appropriation of cultural products. Humans develop because they internalize the cultural products of the world and contribute to the world by externalizing what is in their inner world. In the context of de-traditionalization at the end of European feudalism, education hoped to guide child and human development, viewed from a perspective of appropriation, by offering the 'good, true and beautiful' (*das Gute, Wahre und Schöne*), embodied by the book, old languages and academic subjects and methods. Today, in a world dominated by people's everyday lifeworlds and economically driven global societies, the relevant cultural products have changed dramatically, and mobile phones, their services and the artefacts that can be accessed and produced with them are rapidly becoming cultural products relevant for education, not just as objects of literacy, but as a cultural resources for learning, understood as human development.

Furthermore, one of the results of the processes of individualization seemingly gaining relevance for teaching and learning is an emerging of a new habitus of learning. Differences in personality and personal activity patterns in society are becoming more evident in schools and in educational development (see, for example, recent policy initiatives in the UK around personalization). Teacher-guided instruction following target-oriented schemata are now increasingly less effective, particularly for some social groups. Creative and collaborative knowledge building is increasingly being deployed. On the basis of our work with m-learning, we argue that the following patterns are significant, interrelate and contribute to a new 'habitus of learning': target orientation, play and self-representation.

Learning as appropriation is one central element of our conceptual framework, in particular appropriation of cultural resources made available through, and created by, mobile devices and their services. In Pachler, Cook and Bachmair (2010), we define appropriation as the processes around the development of personal practices with mobile devices, and we consider these processes in the main to be interaction, assimilation and accommodation, as well as change. These are not the same as the development stages that are described in Piaget's (1955) theory of development. Following Vygotsky (1978/ 1930), we also consider 'responsive situations' – what, in the translation of Vygotsky's text from Russian, is called 'zones of proximal development' – to be essential in the context of child development, particularly in relation to the social negotiation of learning of children with cultural products. We deem it central for the cultural products that are to be appropriated to be grounded in child development. Artefacts produced with, and accessed through, mobile devices can be deemed to have such grounding.

We propose that developmental zones no longer be thought of mainly as temporal zones within a person's life course, but instead as situative contexts, which comprise user-generated contexts in the field of media as well as in the field of sociocultural milieus.

Our work is aligned with Piaget's (1955) description of learning and perception as a constant effort to adapt to the environment in terms of assimilation and accommodation. Therefore, assimilation in the context of learning means that a learner takes something unknown into his/her existing cognitive structures, whereas accommodation refers to the changing of cognitive structures to make sense of the environment. In addition, we see the context of appropriation as emergent and not predetermined by events. We place particular emphasis on practice, which can be viewed as a learner's engagement with particular settings, in which context becomes 'embodied interaction' (Dourish, 2004).

We view appropriation as operating within the triangular relationship between agency, practice and structures outlined above. This triangular relationship is evident in emerging cultural transformations, and appropriation provides an analytical perspective through which to engage with these changes. For example, media convergence, coupled with social milieus and their respective habitus of media use, leads to modes of appropriation that we interpret as individualized contexts for learning. In this way, everyday lifeworlds become contexts for learning, defined according to individual notions of relevance nested in cultural practices such as entertainment and school-based learning.

In our work, we are particularly interested in understanding the growing gap between the literacy practices developing outside school and those prevailing inside formal educational environments. By 'literacy practices', we mean the cultural techniques involved in reading and producing artefacts to make sense of, and shape, the sociocultural world around us. From our conceptual point of view, learners develop practices and meanings in and through the interactions embedded in their media use and attendant cultural artefacts. From a pedagogical perspective, a key challenge for us is to support learning between and across contexts outside and inside educational institutions. To achieve this, we argue that schools need to engage proactively with the emerging cultural transformations that mobile devices afford and bring about, as well as with the cultural products that result from, and are characteristic of, these transformations and that enable the individualized generation of content and contexts for learning.

In summary, appropriation for us is a generic term governing all processes concerning the internalization of, and externalization into, the pre-given world of cultural products across the breadth of learning, in educational institutions and in everyday life.

Appropriation and the pre-given world of cultural products work as context of development and are indispensible for the development of human beings. Today, every-day life works as a dominant context of development and is tied up with media use, notably the use of mobile devices, governed by structures of mass communication. Learning and media use, as modes of appropriation, are cultural practices that are determined inter alia by the agency of the user. Through appropriation, curricular practices, which take place in a context of social, economic, cultural and technological transformation, can be linked with child development, with children developing their inner capacities by internalizing cultural resources, including those artefacts made available by and through, and created with, mobile devices.

Habitus of Learning

Finally, for the purposes of this overview of key components of our sociocultural ecology of m-learning, we want to briefly discuss our perspective on learning, in which agency plays an important role. Rather than focusing on the acquisition of knowledge in relation to externally defined notions of relevance, increasingly, in a market-oriented system, an individual faces the challenge of shaping *his/her* knowledge out of *his/her* own sense of his/her world: 'Information is material which is selected by individuals to be transformed by them into knowledge to solve a problem in their life-world' (Böck, 2004). We consider the demands made of individuals in such contexts as a new habitus of learning, by which we mean 'constantly to see the life-world of the individual framed both as challenge and as an environment and a potential resource for learning' (Kress and Pachler, 2007, p. 22).

Two of the key characteristics of such a new habitus are an expectation of immediacy and ubiquity of access to the world of and in which meaning takes place. From the perspective of such a new habitus of learning, the world as learning resource becomes mobile, and learners are characterized by a constant expectancy, a state of *contingency*, of *incompletion*, of moving towards completion. Individuals with such a new habitus see the world as a 'curriculum' and expect always to be ready to be a learner (see Kress and Pachler, 2007, for a more detailed discussion).

REFERENCES

Araya, D., & Peters, M. A. (Eds.) (2010). *Education in the creative economy. Knowledge and kearning in the age of innovation.* New York, Bern, Berlin: Peter Lang

Bachmair, B., Pachler, N., & Cook, J. (2009). Mobile phones as cultural resources for learning: An analysis of educational structures, mobile expertise and emerging cultural practices. In *MedienPädagogik.* Retrieved from: www.medienpaed.com/2009/bachmair0903.pdf

Beck, U. (1986). *Risikogesellschaft. Auf dem Weg in eine andere Moderne.* Frankfurt, Germany: Suhrkamp.

Böck, M. (2004). Life worlds and information habitus. *Visual Communication, 3*(3), 281–293.

Crook, C. (2012). The 'digital native' in context: Tensions associated with importing Web 2.0 practices into the school setting. *Oxford Review of Education, 38*(1), 63–80.

Dourish, P. (2004). What we talk about when we talk about context. *Personal and Ubiquitous Computing, 8*(1), 19–30. Retrieved from: www.dourish.com/publications/2004/PUC2004-context.pdf

Dunning, J. H. (Ed.) (2000). *Regions, globalization, and the knowledge-based economy.* Oxford, UK: Oxford University Press.

Gibson, E. J., & Pick, A. D. (2000). *An ecological approach to perceptual learning and development.* Oxford, UK: Oxford University Press.

Giddens, A. (1984) *The constitution of society: Outline of the theory of structuration.* Berkeley, CA: University of California Press.

Humboldt, W. von (1792/2002). Ideen zu einem Versuch, die Gränzen der Wirksamkeit des Staates zu bestimmen. In A. Flitner und K. Giel (Eds.), *Wilhelm von Humboldt. Werke in fünf Bänden. Band I: Schriften zur Anthropologie und Geschichte* (4th ed., pp. 56–233). Stuttgart, Germany: Wissenschaftliche Buchgesellschaft.

Ito, M., Horst, H., Bittanti, M., Boyd, D., Herr-Stephenson, B., Lange, P., Pascoe, C., & Robinson, L. (2008). *Living and learning with new media: Summary of findings from the Digital Youth Project.* Chicago, IL: MacArthur Foundation. Retrieved from: http://digitalyouth.ischool.berkeley.edu/files/report/digitalyouth-WhitePaper.pdf

Kress, G., & Pachler, N. (2007). Thinking about the 'm' in m-learning. In N. Pachler (Ed.), *Mobile learning: Towards a research agenda* (pp. 7–32). London: WLE Centre. Retrieved from: www.wlecentre.ac.uk/cms/files/occasional papers/mobilelearning_pachler_2007.pdf

Lefebvre, H. (1961). *Critique de la vie quotidienne II, Fondements d'une sociologie de la quotidienneté.* Paris: L'Arche.

Pachler, N., Bachmair, B., & Cook, J. (2010). *Mobile learning: Structures, agency, practices.* New York: Springer.

Pachler, N., Cook, J., & Bachmair, B. (2010). Appropriation of mobile and cultural resources for learning. *International Journal of Mobile and Blended Learning, 2*(1): 1–21.

Piaget, J. (1955) *The construction of reality in the child.* London: Routledge and Kegan Paul.

Schütz, A. (1932/1967). *Der sinnhafte Aufbau der sozialen Welt. Eine Einleitung in die verstehende Soziologie.* Frankfurt, Wien: Julius Springer. English translation (1967). *The Phenomenology of the Social World.* Evanston, IL: Northwestern University Press.

Vygotsky, L. (1978/1930). *Mind in society. The development of higher psychological processes.* M. Cole et al. (Eds.). Cambridge, MA: Harvard University Press.

5

MOBILE LEARNING

New Approach, New Theory

Helen Crompton

The use of technologies is becoming ubiquitous throughout today's society. As philosophies and practice move toward learner-centered pedagogies, technology, in a parallel move, is now able to provide new affordances to the learner, such as learning that is personalized, contextualized, and unrestricted by temporal and spatial constraints. The unique attributes of mobile learning (m-learning) provide a new approach to learning, which requires a new theory.

This chapter begins by explicating the necessity for m-learning to have a theory of its own, describing exactly what makes m-learning unique from conventional, tethered electronic learning and traditional learning. This description includes the attributes afforded through the technological components, as well as the alternative approach to learning available through their use. Throughout this chapter, the suffix *learning*, as in m-learning, d-learning, and e-learning, refers to both the education and the learning that comes about from that particular form of education.

The next section summarizes the criteria, identified in the literature, of what should be included in an m-learning theory. Following this is an analysis of proposed theoretical models for m-learning, considering the existing theories used to underpin the new m-learning theory. Finally, I will unpack the themes emerging from the currently proposed theoretical models, namely *context*, *connectivity*, and *time*, which are nested within the concept of *personalization*, to make the argument that these attributes are the essence of m-learning.

DEFINITION AND DEVICES

In order to consider a theoretical approach to m-learning, it is imperative to establish what m-learning is and review how it is defined in the literature. M-learning is a relatively young field that is still rapidly evolving, and definitions have altered over time, depending on the technological attributes available and the new pedagogical opportunities provided by those technologies.

Definitions of m-learning in the past decade appear to have been constructed around four central constructs—learning pedagogies, technological devices, context, and social interactions—such as the definitions provided by Brown (2005), Sharples, Taylor, and Vavoula (2007), and Traxler (2009a). The definition selected for this chapter, provided by Crompton, Muilenburg, and Berge (Crompton, 2013), incorporates those four components to state that m-learning is "Learning across multiple contexts, through social and content interactions, using personal electronic devices" (Crompton, 2013, p. 4).

Determining which devices are included in m-learning has also been a topic of debate among scholars (Caudill, 2007; Traxler, 2009a). This can be highly problematic, because the m-learning field is so dynamic. For example, Traxler listed PDAs, palmtop, handhelds, and smartphones as mobile devices and questioned whether tablets deliver m-learning, owing to their lack of spontaneity, portability, and start-up time; one year later, tablets became commercially available, which addressed the earlier issues with mobility. So it is difficult, and ill advisable, to determine specifically which devices should be included in a definition of m-learning, as technologies are constantly being invented or redesigned. Therefore, one should consider m-learning as the utilization of electronic devices that are easily transported and used anytime and anywhere. Although the technological devices are an essential part of m-learning, the discussion in this chapter is mostly centered on the attributes provided by the devices, not just the devices themselves.

A NEED FOR A NEW THEORY

Although it is easy to see the differences between traditional learning and m-learning, it may not be so obvious to see how m-learning is different than electronic learning (e-learning). This section will make connections between the various learning approaches, while also revealing why an autonomous theory of m-learning is warranted. Tavangarian, Leypold, Nolting, and Voigt (2004) posited e-learning to be:

> *All forms of electronic supported learning and teaching,* which are procedural in character and aim to effect the construction of knowledge with reference to individual experience, practice and knowledge of the learning. Information and communication systems, whether networked or not, serve as specific media to implement the learning process.
>
> (Tavangarian et al., 2004, p. 274)

Thus, m-learning must be included in this definition, as the process of learning utilizes electronic technologies. This is similar to the relationship between distance learning (d-learning) and e-learning. The interconnected nature of d-learning, e-learning, and m-learning is portrayed in Figure 5.1.

The philosophy and approach of d-learning challenged the notion that learning is something that only happens face to face with the teacher, within the school environment. This changed as distance learners were given resources to study from home or from other off-campus locations. As the d-learning epoch began, students were provided with print materials; in time, this changed to multimedia materials on CD-ROM, and then multimedia materials via the World Wide Web (Keegan, 2002). This shift from print to electronic materials engendered the nomenclature transition from d-learning to e-learning. There are those who consider e-learning to be learning exclusively provided

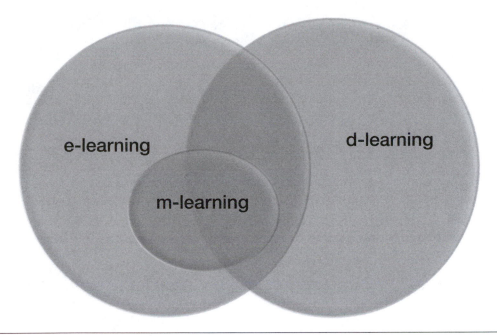

Figure 5.1 Interconnected Nature of D-Learning, E-Learning, and M-Learning. E-Learning in the Diagram is Referring to Tavangarian et al.'s (2004) Definition of E-Learning, Which Includes any Form of Learning That Utilizes Technology

through a network, such as the Internet, intranet/extranet, and satellite television (Ramshirish & Singh, 2007). However, as the definition provided by Tavangarian et al. (2004) states, e-learning does not have to be networked learning; therefore, e-learning activities could be used in the classroom setting, as they often are. This is identified in Figure 5.1, with e-learning overlapping d-learning, instead of nesting within it.

The attributes of m-learning can lead to a blurring of the boundaries between personal and academic life (Traxler, 2010), as the interactions with mobile technologies are woven into students' very existence. This is denoted in Figure 5.1, as m-learning is situated partially within d-learning to demarcate the learning taking place outside the typical academic setting, and m-learning is partly outside d-learning to recognize that some m-learning takes place within an educational setting. For example, m-learning can involve a person learning on a mobile device while traveling on a train, participating in a school field trip, or working in a classroom.

M-learning has always tacitly meant mobile e-learning (Traxler, 2009b); therefore, within Figure 5.1, m-learning is fully nested within e-learning. This could lead to the question of why m-learning needs a different theory beyond e-learning. Although all forms of e-learning utilize technologies, the attributes of mobile technologies provide a different learning experience to the one *conventional* e-learning technologies can offer. Conventional e-learning is tethered, in that students are anchored to one place while learning. Students typically have to designate a time to be situated at desktop computers, with their backs to the world; social and environmental contexts are generally incidental to learning. What sets m-learning apart from conventional e-learning is the very lack of those spatial and temporal constraints; learning has portability (Laurillard, 2007; Sharples, 2006), ubiquitous access (Melhuish & Falloon, 2010), and social connectivity (Koole, 2009).

Academics have determined a difference between conventional e-learning and m-learning through analyzing the nomenclature characterizing each field. Laouris and Eteokleous (2005) posited that dominant terms for m-learning should include spontaneous, intimate, situated, connected, informal, and personal, whereas conventional e-learning should include the terms computer, multimedia, interactive, hyperlinked, and media-rich environment. Traxler (2009c) conducted a similar activity, perusing m-learning conference proceedings to gather the words personal, spontaneous, opportunistic, informal, pervasive, situated, private, context-aware, bite-sized, and portable; and, from the literature, conventional e-learning searches contained words such as structured, media-rich, broadband, interactive, intelligent, and usable. Both Laouris and Eteokleous's and Traxler's lists appear to characterize the context for learning and the attributes of each field, with identical or synonymous terms found between the two lists for m-learning and for conventional e-learning. What could be described as a socially determined nomenclature reveals a clear, dualistic conceptualization of conventional e-learning and m-learning.

To provide further understanding of how the learning theories look differently at learning, Table 5.1 provides examples of how traditional learning, conventional e-learning, and m-learning compare when particular attributes are considered within pedagogical practice. The attributes were chosen from a consideration of Laouris and Eteokleous's and Traxler's lists, and from attributes highlighted in earlier descriptions of m-learning and conventional e-learning definitions from this chapter.

Table 5.1 Comparing Traditional Learning, E-Learning, and M-Learning with Various Learning Attributes

	Traditional learning	**Conventional tethered e-learning**	**M-learning**
Time	Often constrained by formal school hours	Constrained to time sat in front of a computer, but can occur at any time of the day	No time constraints. Learning can take place anywhere you can carry and use a mobile device at any time of the day
Personalized	Limited in all aspects of differentiation and concepts taught	Some personalization, with a choice of programs and concepts to be taught, but computers are typically shared and non-personalized	Personalization through applications, concepts, and often the ownership of devices modified for the user
Private learning	Not private	Typically private	Private
Context	Highly limited to a set location and framework	Various locations, although still tied to specific locations and milieu	Learning can take place in numerous environmental and social settings, where wireless access can be obtained
Formal/informal	Formal	Formal and informal	Informal and can also be formal
Socio-connectivity	Connections made to those in direct environment	Virtual connectivity to the networked world	Connections made to those in the direct environment and those networked
Spontaneity	Not spontaneous	Partially spontaneous	Highly spontaneous

Note: For particular attributes such as private learning and spontaneity, these describe opportunities available to that form of learning. It is not to propose that m-learning is always private and highly spontaneous, but that opportunities are available for it to be so.

Table 5.1 displays the pedagogical differences between traditional learning, conventional e-learning, and m-learning. Although there is a familiar continuation to each learning practice, what appears to have been limiting in each column is addressed by the evolving practice in the columns to the right. For example, socio-connectivity within traditional learning is limited to those in the immediate vicinity; conventional e-learning pushed the boundaries to also include virtual connections, and m-learning extended this to include both direct and virtual networked connections. This difference between the columns could be simply due to the technologies used for learning, or the way in which the technologies mediate and facilitate the learning experiences (Peters, 2009). It has also been suggested that the actual ubiquity and mobility make m-learning a discrete form of learning (Peng, Su, Chou, & Tsai, 2009).

This section has explicated the interconnected nature of various theories of learning, specifically studying the differences between m-learning and conventional e-learning. A strong argument has been provided, separating the two fields in terms of learner experiences and attributes provided through that field of learning, thus determining that there is a need for m-learning to have a theory of its own. The next section of this chapter explicates the criteria necessary for incorporation within a theory of m-learning.

CRITERIA FOR M-LEARNING

The first step in postulating a theory for m-learning is to determine what factors need to be considered. Sharples et al. (2007) specifically defined four criteria. The initial step is to acknowledge what distinguishes m-learning from other learning activities. This belief was also held by Traxler (2009c), who particularly wished to examine the differences between m-learning and conventional e-learning in regard to the underlying learning experience. A similar study was conducted in the previous section of this chapter.

The second consideration posited by Sharples et al. (2007) is that one must be cognizant of the substantial amount of learning taking place beyond the academic and workplace settings, such as in friends' houses, places of leisure, doctors' offices, cars, etc. (Vavoula, 2005). It is important to consider how the environment and activities create extemporaneous learning opportunities. Sharples, Sánchez, Milrad, and Vavoula (2009) split this second consideration into multiple parts to highlight the importance of the mobility of the conceptual space, physical space, and social space. In other words, the learning concept is often highly dynamic, with a learner's attention shifting through personal interest, curiosity, or commitment; the location may be relevant to the concept being taught and the social environment shifting to various social groups.

The third deliberation (Sharples et al., 2007) is that one must ensure learning is based on practices that have been deemed successful. The socio-constructivist approach is deemed to be a successful learning pedagogy (Sullivan Palincsar, 1998; Vygotsky, 1978), promoting higher-order thinking skills, reflection, and collaboration (Collison, Elbaum, Haavind, & Tinker, 2000; Ewing & Miller, 2002). Socio-constructivists view learning as an interdependent process between the social and the individual in the co-construction of knowledge (Vygotsky, 1978).

Sharples et al.'s (2007) final consideration was that heed must be paid to the ubiquitous use of personal and shared technology. This includes the various personal technologies commercially available, the functionality of the devices, and the personalized services available. Koole (2009) stressed the impact of m-learning devices on usability, suggesting that considerations of an m-learning theory should include the physical characteristics, input/output capabilities, and file storage and retrieval of the devices.

Laouris and Eteokleous (2005) listed a number of considerations similar to those described above, but they emphasized that, while the many parameters must be taken into account, one also has to be cognizant of the way in which they interact and influence each other. To this end, Laouris and Eteokleous proposed the mathematical formula mLearn = f\{t, s, LE, C, IT, MM, M\}, to draw attention to the point that m-learning is a function of each parameter; t = time, s = space, LE = environment, C = content, IT = technology, MM = learners' mental capabilities, and m = method of delivery and interaction with content.

This section of the chapter has identified criteria one must consider when constructing a theory for m-learning. The following section provides a summary of the m-learning theories presented in the literature thus far and explicates the approaches used to develop a new theory.

PROPOSED THEORIES

To propose a theory for m-learning is certainly not an easy task. The previous section named just a few of the criteria that a new theory must acknowledge, not to mention the confounding variables that cannot be controlled for. Nevertheless, there are those who have attempted such a task, such as Koole (2009), Laurillard (2007), Naismith, Lonsdale, Vavoula, and Sharples (2004), and Sharples et al. (2007), who all created frameworks to describe various aspects of m-learning. However, further understanding of the highly dynamic, emerging field is necessary before a final theory for m-learning can be determined (Ibid.).

Those who have constructed an early theory of m-learning appear to have directly connected m-learning to an existing theory or theories. Activity theory and conversational theory are popular choices for links to m-learning, but many other theories have also been used.

Activity Theory

Activity theory is a theoretical framework for analyzing people's practices as developmental processes, while considering individual and social influences as interlinked (Kuutti, 1996). Koole (2009), Uden (2007), and Zurita and Nussbaum (2007) all used activity theory to create conceptual frameworks for various aspects of m-learning. Koole designed the Framework for the Rational Analysis of Mobile Education (FRAME), based on activity theory as it pertains to Vygotsky's (1978) work on mediation and the zone of proximal development. Zurita and Nussbaum (2007) used activity theory to provide a framework for analyzing the tasks, needs, and outcomes for designing m-learning activities. Although they were interested in Vygotsky's (1978) philosophies, they chose to focus on Engeström's (1987) expanded activity theory, which was an extended version of Vygotsky's conceptualization of the mediated relationship between the learner and the object/mobile device.

Uden (2007) used activity theory as a framework for describing the parts of an activity system for designing applications for m-learning. Uden described how m-learning is fundamentally situated and socially mediated, which directly connects with the tenets of activity theory described by Engeström (1987). Sharples et al. (2007) also utilized

Engeström's 1987 expanded activity theory, although they dichotomized tool-mediated activity to highlight two layers: the semiotic layer, with learning as a semiotic system, in which the learner's object-oriented actions are mediated by cultural tools and signs; and the technological layer, in which technologies function as active agents in learning.

Sharples et al. (2007) also based the new theory of m-learning on the work of Pask's (1975) conversation theory. This theory was selected as Sharples et al. concurred with Pask's vision of communication as the sharing of understanding through a pervasive computational medium, rather than seeing communication as merely the exchange of messages through a transparent medium.

Conversation Theory

Conversation theory, developed by Pask in 1975, is a cybernetic and dialectic framework for how knowledge is constructed. Followers of conversation theory believe that knowledge is agreed upon through the exchange of knowledge through conversations. Laurillard (2007) used the conversation theory to create the conversational framework, in which new technologies could be assessed and utilized according to how the technology supports the learning process. Laurillard described that, although conversation is common to all forms of learning, m-learning activities can build in more opportunities for students to have ownership and control over what they are learning through digitally facilitated, location-specific activities. In another paper, Sharples et al. (2009) created a mobile theory based on Pask's conversational theory and the writings of Dewey (1916), proposing that students learn through conversation and exploration. In this theory, mobile devices act as a system in which knowledge can be created and shared.

It is interesting that, while activity and conversational theories are often utilized in the construction of a theory for m-learning, there are scholars who have made the point that connections can be made to multiple different theories.

Connecting to Multiple Theories

Both Naismith et al. (2004) and Keskin and Metcalf (2011) wrote articles that connected m-learning with multiple theories. Naismith et al. selected six categories of what they define as theory-based categories of activity: behaviorist, constructivist, situated, collaborative, informal and lifelong, and learning and teaching support. Within each of these theory-based categories are descriptions of the learning that would take place and how it connects with mobile technologies. Keskin and Metcalf named 15 different theories connected with m-learning: behaviorism, cognitivism, constructivism, situated learning, problem-based learning, context-awareness learning, sociocultural theory, collaborative learning, conversational learning, lifelong learning, informal learning, activity theory, and the more recent theories of connectivism, navigationalism, and location-based learning.

The argument has been made that m-learning is somewhat different from other technological learning approaches, and the emerging theories have been explicated. The next section reveals the themes that emerge from the proposed theories of m-learning.

EMERGING THEMES

Throughout this chapter, the meaning of m-learning has been unraveled to reveal various attributes. The socially determined nomenclature presented by Laouris and

Eteokleous (2005) and Traxler (2009c), as well as the connections made to preexisting theories, has created a pattern of themes: context, connectivity, and time, all nested within personalization. This section of the chapter will explicate how the four themes have emerged from the proposed lists and theories.

Figure 5.2 has both interconnected and nested attributes, providing a simplified overview of the complex field of m-learning. There are many attributes embedded within each theme that are discussed in this section. Some of those attributes overlap within each theme, although personalization is overarching in that it develops as a result of context, connectivity, and time.

Context

Within m-learning, different milieus are created with the changing sociocultural and technological structures (Cook, Pachler, & Bachmair, 2011). Sharples et al. (2009) described the interconnected nature of context with that of connectivity and time:

> Context is a central construct of mobile learning, not as a container through which we pass like a train in a tunnel, but as an artifact that is continually created by people in interaction with other people, with their surroundings and with everyday tools.
>
> (p. 4)

It is the accumulation of the multifarious nature of these components that describes m-learning.

Koole (2009) adduced that the devices themselves actively support learners in the comprehension and transfer of information by the nature in which m-learning allows access to content in multiple formats, emphasizing the contexts and uses of the

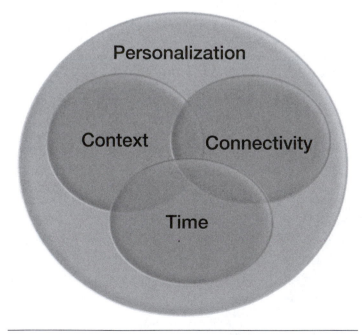

Figure 5.2 Overview of the Emerging Themes Surrounding M-Learning

information. Traxler (2011) described the role of context in m-learning as "context in the wider context" (p. 1), as the notion of context becomes progressively richer. This theme fits with Naismith et al.'s (2004) situated theory, which describes the m-learning activities promoting authentic context and culture.

Connectivity

Connectivity describes social interactions within the process of learning. Interactions can either be face to face or virtual, through the many networks provided; they can also be a combination of the two. The networks can connect learners to the vastness of the WWW, or to a learning partner via e-mail. Conversation theory (Pask, 1975), utilized by Laurillard (2007) and Sharples et al. (2009), provides testament to the strong connection of this theme to m-learning. Sharples et al. (2009), in particular, emphasized the importance of connectivity, stating: "It is not the learners, nor their technology, but the communicative interaction between these to advance knowing" (p. 4).

M-learning provides more opportunities for connectivity, as the networks reach far beyond what is available to those involved in traditional learning, and, unlike e-learning, the learner is not anchored to a set place. The connectivity theme also links to Vygotsky's (1978) sociocultural approach. Learning happens within various social groups and locations, providing a diverse range of connected learning experiences. Furthermore, connectivity is without temporal restraints, such as the schedules of educators.

Time

Sharples et al. (2009) described m-learning as "Learning dispersed in time" (p. 3). A significant difference between m-learning and other learning approaches is the erosion of formal learning times. Learners can now learn at a time they choose, and at times not traditionally used for learning. Banks (2006) described the additional learning time as a type of resource, giving it substance, such as a raw material or commodity.

The irrelevance of time is a significant shift in the learning paradigm. The shift emerged with the e-learning epoch, as students were able to learn at times beyond the typical work or school schedule, although they were still restricted to times of the day when the learner could sit in front of a computer. With the emergence of m-learning, learning happens whenever the student wishes to learn (Melhuish & Falloon, 2010).

Personalization

Context, connectivity, and time are all nested within personalization, as they afford learners the choice of what, where, when, and how they learn. Mobile devices also offer personalization, as they can be customized to the individual's unique learning pathway (Peters, 2009) through the plethora of available devices and applications. Earlier in this chapter, Laouris and Eteokleous (2005) and Traxler (2009c) provided lists of socially determined nomenclature describing m-learning. Many of the terms were directly connected with the themes context, connectivity, and time, such as context-aware, pervasive, portable, situated, connected, spontaneous, and opportunistic. Both these lists specifically included the word *personal*, as the affordances of the electronic devices offer the learner choice.

Consider these two examples of how different learning opportunities connect with the four themes. First, imagine a student who is trying to catch up with classwork while traveling home on a bus. Using a personal device, he or she listens to a podcast lecture and has personalized learning by choosing when and where learning takes place. Time, therefore, is inconsequential, as the student has chosen a time available, and further personalization happens, as the student can rewind or fast-forward the podcast to meet his or her unique learning needs. In this scenario, time and personalization are the main themes involved.

Second, consider a class homework project that requires students to take a trip to the local botanical gardens. The aim of the trip is to build a database of information about plant habitats. Context plays a significant role in this situation, as the students learn more information about the plants by scanning codes placed at the side of each plant. From the information gained, students connect with others by inputting data into a spreadsheet, which is shared by all the students. The time selected to accomplish the task is chosen by the student. Personalization takes place within context, connectivity, and time. Students can also choose how long they need to complete the task, or study an individual plant, and the level of difficulty can alter, as students of different abilities may choose to collect data on the more complex plant features or the simpler plants. In this final example, context, connectivity, time, and personalization are all involved in the learning process.

CONCLUSION

M-learning brings a number of unique attributes to learning, which provides a new approach to learning and requires a new theory. Although connections have been made to other learning approaches, the affordances of the technologies offer opportunities that have not been available to this extent before. Various early theories for m-learning have been created and studied, although, as the young field of m-learning continues to grow, the theory for m-learning will need to be constantly revised and revisited, probably changing beyond recognition of what we know as m-learning today. At this time, the theories and the nomenclature surrounding m-learning connect with the larger themes of context, connectivity, time, and personalization, to make the argument that these four themes are the essence of m-learning.

REFERENCES

Banks, K. (2006). L'ordre du temps: l'invention de la ponctualité au XVIe siècle. *French Studies, 1,* 97–98.

Brown, H. T. (2005). Towards a model for mlearning. *International Journal on E-Learning, 4*(3), 299–315.

Caudill, J. G. (2007). The growth of m-learning and the growth of mobile computing: Parallel developments. *International Review of Research in Open and Distance Learning, 8*(2), 1–13.

Collison, G., Elbaum, B., Haavind, S., & Tinker, R. (2000). *Facilitating online learning: Effective strategies for moderators.* Madison, WI: Atwood Publishing.

Cook, J., Pachler, N., & Bachmair, B. (2011). Ubiquitous mobility with mobile phones: A cultural ecology for mobile learning. *E-Learning and Digital Media, 8*(3), 181–195.

Crompton, H. (2013). A historical overview of mobile learning: Toward learner-centered education (pp. 3–14). In Z. Berge, & L. Muilenburg (Eds.), *Handbook of mobile learning.* New York: Routledge.

Dewey, J. (1916). *Democracy and education.* New York: Free Press.

Engeström, Y. (1987). *Learning by expanding: An activity-theoretical approach to development research.* Helsinki, Finland: Orienta-Konsultit.

Ewing, J., & Miller, D. (2002). A framework for evaluating computer supported collaborative learning. *Educational Technology & Society, 5*(1), 112–118.

Keegan, D. (2002). *The future of learning: From eLearning to mLearning.* Retrieved from: www.worldcat.org/title/future-of-learning-from-elearning-to-mlearning/oclc/77086825?referer=di&ht=edition

Keskin, N. O., & Metcalf, D. (2011). The current perspectives, theories, and practices of mobile learning. *The Turkish Online Journal of Educational Technology, 10*(2), 202–208.

Koole, M. L. (2009). A model for framing mobile learning. In M. Ally (Ed.), *Mobile learning: Transforming the delivery of education and training* (pp. 25–50). Edmonton, AB: Athabasca University Press.

Kuutti, K. (1996). Activity theory as a potential framework for human–computer interaction research. In B. A. Nardi (Ed.), *Context and consciousness: Activity theory and human–computer interaction* (pp. 17–44). Cambridge, MA: MIT.

Laouris, Y., & Eteokleous, N. (2005, October). *We need an educationally relevant definition of mobile learning.* Paper presented at the 4th World Conference on mLearning, Cape Town, South Africa.

Laurillard, D. (2007). Pedagogical forms for mobile learning: Framing research questions. In N. Pachler (Ed.), *Mobile learning: Towards a research agenda* (pp. 153–175). London: WLE Centre.

Melhuish, K., & Falloon, G. (2010). Looking to the future: M-learning with the iPad. *Computers in New Zealand Schools: Learning, Leading, Technology, 22*(3), 1–15.

Naismith, L., Lonsdale, P., Vavoula, G., & Sharples, M. (2004). Literature review in mobile technologies and learning. In *NESTA Futurelab Literature review series* (Report 11). Retrieved from: Futurelab http:/_/_archive.futurelab.org.uk/_resources/_publications-reports-articles/_literature-reviews/_Literature-Review203

Pask, G. (1975). Minds in media in education and entertainment: Some theoretical comments illustrated by the design and operation of a system for exteriorizing and manipulating individual theses. In R. Trappl & G. Pask (Eds.), *Progress in cybernetics and systems research* (pp. 38–50). London: Hemisphere Publishing Corporation.

Peng, H., Su, Y., Chou, C., & Tsai, C. (2009). Ubiquitous knowledge construction: Mobile learning re-defined and a conceptual framework. *Innovations in Education and Teaching International, 46*(2), 171–183.

Peters, K. (2009). M-learning: Positioning educators for a mobile connected future. In M. Ally (Ed.), *Mobile learning: Transforming the delivery of education and training* (pp. 113–134). Vancouver, BC: Athabasca University Press.

Ramshirish, M., & Singh, P. (2007, January). *e-Learning: tools and technology.* Paper presented at the DRTC Conference on ICT for the Digital Learning Environment, Bangalore, India.

Sharples, M. (Ed.) (2006). *Big issues in mobile learning* (Report of a workshop by the Kaleidoscope Network of Excellence Mobile Learning Initiative, pp. 14–19). Nottingham, UK: Learning Sciences Research Institute.

Sharples, M., Sánchez, I., A., Milrad., M., & Vavoula, G. (2009). Mobile learning: Small devices, big issues. In N. Blacheff., S. Ludvigsen., T. de Jong., A. Lazonder, & S. Barnes (Eds.), *Technology-enhanced learning: Principles and products* (pp. 223–251). Berlin: Springer-Verlag.

Sharples, M., Taylor, J., & Vavoula, G. (2007). A theory of learning for the mobile age. In R. Andrews & C. Haythornthwaite (Eds.), *The Sage handbook of e-learning research* (pp. 221–247). London: Sage.

Sullivan Palincsar, A. (1998). Social constructivist perspectives on teaching and learning. *Annual Review of Psychology, 49,* 345–375.

Tavangarian, D., Leypold, M. E., Nolting, K., & Voigt, D. (2004). Is e-learning the solution for individual learning? *Electronic Journal of E-learning, 2*(2), 273–280.

Traxler, J. (2009a). Learning in a mobile age. *International Journal of Mobile and Blended Learning, 1*(1), 1–12.

Traxler, J. (2009b). The evolution of mobile learning. In R. Guy (Ed.), *The evolution of mobile teaching and learning* (pp. 1–14). Santa Rosa, CA: Informing Science Press.

Traxler, J. (2009c). Current state of mobile learning. In M. Ally (Ed.), *Mobile learning: Transforming the delivery of education and training* (pp. 9–24). Edmonton, AB: Athabasca University Press.

Traxler, J. (2010). Will student devices deliver innovation, inclusion, and transformation? *Journal of the Research Center for Educational Technologies, 6*(1), 3–15.

Traxler, J. (2011). Context in a wider context. *Medienpädagogik, 19 Mobile Learning in Widening Contexts.* Retrieved from Medienpädagogik Zeitschrift für Theorie und Praxis der Medienbildung:_ www.medienpaed.com/_zs/_content/_blogcategory/_45/_82/_

Uden, L. (2007). Activity theory for designing mobile learning. *International Journal of Mobile Learning and Organization, 1*(1), 81–102.

Vavoula, G. (2005). A study of mobile learning practices, internal report. In *Deliverable 4.4 for the MOBIlearn project* (IST-2001-37440).

Vygotsky, L. S. (1978). *Mind in society: The development of higher psychological processes.* Cambridge, MA: Harvard University Press.

Zurita, G., & Nussbaum, M. (2007). A conceptual framework based on activity theory for mobile CSCL. *British Journal of Educational Technology, 38*(2), 211–235.

6

FRAMEWORK FOR MOBILE-LEARNING INTEGRATION INTO EDUCATIONAL CONTEXTS

Adelina Moura and Ana Amélia Carvalho

INTRODUCTION

For centuries, the hierarchical model of learning was accepted. Currently, new forms of learning are emerging, as there is unlimited access to information via the Internet, which can be accessed from mobile devices (smartphones, PDAs, pocket PCs, tablet PCs) too. This trend takes in the implementation of new educational models for teaching and learning, along with content distribution and management of school times and spaces.

M-learning is often understood as learning that takes place on a mobile device, but other meanings appeared during the last decade. The discussion about the best definition of m-learning is not fixed, and reflection will continue. According to Sharples (2005), there is a need to reconceptualize learning for the mobile age. In our study, we adopt the Crompton, Muilenburg and Berge definition of m-learning presented in chapter 1 (Crompton, 2013, p. 4), where learning across multiple contexts and using personal electronic devices is concerned.

Learning supported by mobile technologies can offer opportunities for both individuals and groups of students, but, as with any other approach to teaching, there are advantages, barriers and limitations (UNESCO, 2011). Nevertheless, some limitations of the past don't take place in the newer device models (screen size, battery life). As stated by Shuler (2009), m-learning may be the new frontier for students, from preschool to higher education. Some of the mobile devices are in the students' pockets, and they expect that academic content will also be made available through these handheld devices (Ally, 2009).

Understanding how individuals learn and how learning takes place is a key consideration for the design of learning strategies, particularly for the preparation of learning activities supported by mobile technologies. How can we effectively use mobile technology to improve teaching and learning? How can we motivate and engage students, both inside and outside the classroom? These questions are issues that have led us to develop the theoretical framework described here. This framework is based on constructivist approaches, Activity Theory (AT) and the Attention, Relevance, Confidence and

Satisfaction (ARCS) Model. It guides the design of learning experiences mediated by mobile technologies such as mobile phones, to promote educational success. Indeed, the devices that go into students' pockets are now part of the educational process, whereas in the past they were prohibited. To set a didactic model that can be applied to m-learning requires looking at the characteristics of specific devices and their capabilities to be integrated in educational contexts.

We carried out a study using students' mobile phones and different multimedia services and functionalities (video, audio, notes, podcasts, SMS) for learning a mother tongue and a foreign language, such as Portuguese and French. We used the framework proposed to describe the activities and to analyse data.

M-LEARNING-TECHNOLOGIES INTEGRATION IN THE LEARNING PROCESS: A FRAMEWORK

The framework for the mobile-technologies integration in education presented here is based on constructivist approaches (Fosnot, 1996), the Activity Theory (AT) principles (Engeström, 2001; Nardi, 1996) and on the ARCS Model (Keller, 1987; Shih & Mills, 2007), together with guidance provided by relevant research in the field of m-learning (Kukulska-Hulme & Traxler, 2005; Naismith, Lonsdale, Vavoula & Sharples, 2004; Shuler, 2009; Traxler, 2007; Vavoula, Pachler & Kukulska-Hulme, 2009).

When considering mobile technologies, we rely on the particularities of mobile devices for educational purposes, identified by Naismith et al. (2004, p. 9): *portability* (the learner can take the device to different places, due to its small size and weight), *social interaction* (data exchange and collaboration with others), *context awareness* (students gather and respond to real or simulated data anywhere, under any environmental conditions and at any time), *connectivity* (learners can create a shared network by connecting mobile data-collection devices or other devices to a common network), and *individuality* (difficult activities can be supported and customized for individual learners). As the authors mention, any of these features must be present in m-learning practices, but it is also relevant to take into account the objectives to be achieved.

AT has been used to explore educational innovations and innovative learning spaces (Trish & Du Toit, 2010; Waycott, 2004). This approach provides a useful lens to investigate the ways that students interact with innovative learning tools, such as mobile phones, in different educational contexts. In this framework, we highlight the elements of AT that are adapted to the learning environment. Subject, artefact, object and activity are the basic principles of AT (Leontiev, 1978) and should be considered as an integrated system (Nardi, 1996). In an activity system, subjects interact with objects to achieve common outcomes. Human interactions and human–object interactions are mediated through the use of tools, rules, community and division of labour (Engeström, 2001).

When applying AT to the mobile phone as a learning tool and describing the relationship of the subject with all elements of AT (Figure 6.1), the following situations arise: the subject is the owner of the mobile tool and can create a learning environment autonomously; he/she can determine his/her own learning needs and goals; he/she is responsible for managing learning material and content; and he/she can decide which group to join and can engage in collaboration. The subject also has control over the tool, the object, the rules, the community and the division of tasks. He/she can select and use the tool for learning according to his/her own needs; reuse and remix contents;

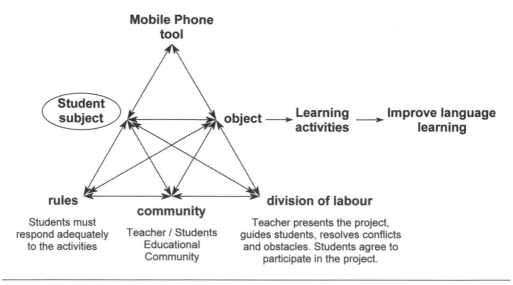

Figure 6.1 Articulation Between Subjects and Other AT Elements

manage and organize his/her own learning; configure the environment according to his/her own preferences; choose with whom to communicate; and self-monitor his/her own progress. Ownership and control are dimensions closely related to the notions of personal and personalized, two features of mobile devices that contributed to mobile-phone appropriation as a learning tool.

Constructivist approaches and AT provided support to analyse the dynamic context of learning, and to theorize learning as a constructive and social activity (Fosnot, 1996; Waycott, 2004). The motivational ARCS Model (Keller, 1987) was adapted to learning contexts based on teaching and learning that are supported by mobile devices. According to Keller's model, the learning cycle includes: Attention, Relevance, Confidence and Satisfaction (ARCS). Shih and Mills (2007) considered this model a new standard for m-learning. They proposed a new m-learning model, identified as the Shih Mobile Learning Model, based on Keller's ARCS Model. According to Shih and Mills (2007), Shih's model provides an innovation in instructional design that guides the use of enhancements for effective teaching and learning in today's virtual m-learning environments. By focusing on the use of mobile technologies in educational contexts, and on Shih's model, teachers can adapt to the different ways people learn and enrich their learning experiences. The learning cycle in Shih's model includes multimedia messages (attention), Web search (relevance), peer-to-peer discussion (relevance/confidence), digital story-telling (confidence) and simulated gaming (satisfaction). The authors acknowledged that this model is based on social-constructivism approaches through the use of collaborative discussion. Keller's model and the Shih Mobile Learning Model helped us to develop motivational strategies to integrate podcasts and SMS activities in the learning process (Moura & Carvalho, 2010). We think that when motivation increases, performance also increases. Motivation is the key to success in learning (Moura, 2010).

In this framework (Figure 6.2), m-learning is placed in the centre as a process of combination of the subject (the student) using a mobile artefact (mobile tool), which

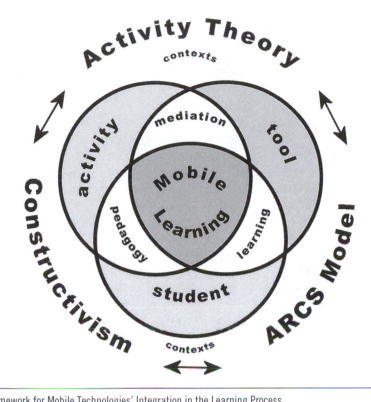

Figure 6.2 Framework for Mobile Technologies' Integration in the Learning Process

together mediate the learning action (activity) and go on to interactively change the object/motive (integration of mobile technologies in the learning process). The combination can facilitate the improvement of previous skills or the internalization of new knowledge (learning). Teaching strategies (pedagogy) conducted through mobile devices (mediation) facilitate the sharing of knowledge and engage students in their own learning and improve their academic achievement (learning).

Context is central in m-learning, both at pedagogical and technological levels. Context is not reduced to the education sector in which students are engaged, nor to the physical space in which learning takes place. Our analysis shows that there are other contexts of learning, such as on buses, while waiting for public transport or a meeting, in between classes, waiting in a queue or sitting comfortably at home.

Personal and portable mobile devices, such as mobile phones, make this technology a learning tool that can be appropriated by students to support their learning process (Moura, 2010). Some of the most accepted learning theories cannot explain the distinctive features of m-learning (Kukulska-Hulme & Traxler, 2005; Vavoula et al., 2009), because they are based on the idea that learning occurs in a classroom environment that is mediated by the teacher. However, when mobile devices are used, learning can occur across multiple contexts, because mobility is the key feature of mobile technologies. In our study, learning took place inside and outside classrooms, mediated by students' mobile devices.

These theoretical foundations underpin the integration of mobile technologies into different educational contexts and how they interact and influence each other. In the framework presented here, we highlight two important aspects of m-learning: pedagogy and technology. To better understand these two domains, we present a representation that helps to design suitable learning environments supported by mobile technologies, and we further explain our framework, presented above, centred in both technology (mediating tools) and educational activities (learning success).

Technological and Pedagogical Domains

Understanding the relationship between technological and pedagogical domains helps in the design of m-learning contexts. Both domains interact in the context of m-learning. Depending on the nature of m-learning experiences, those elements can be applied in separate steps. The conceptual framework presented by Parsons, Ryu and Cranshaw (2007) helped us to design our several m-learning experiences (podcasts, SMS, video, audio and notes).

Technological Domain

In the literature, m-learning is characterized by words such as personal, mobile, spontaneous, suitable, informal, pervasive, situated, private, context-sensitive, small size and portable (Traxler, 2007).

Users' role and profile determine their identities in the context of learning, and each user makes use of his/her mobile device in different ways. Young students used SMS and video capture more easily than adult students, as we saw in our study. *Mobility* is the most important feature in the mobile context and can be interpreted in varied perspectives. We focused on the mobility of students (home/school) and learning contexts, and we chose the most convenient time to send students SMS activities. It is crucial to pay attention to the *user–mobile interface*, because mobile devices present some restrictions, such as small screens and limited battery life. We opted for micro contents and privileged short podcasts, instead of long texts, encouraging micro learning. Users tend to employ a variety of rich *media* objects, and these different types of media should support educational contents appropriately. Taking advantage of the different multimedia services and functionalities of students' mobile phones, such as video, image, text and audio, diverse activities were proposed. Mobile devices allow a perpetual contact, and, therefore, this *communication support* could be used to develop the collaborative learning objectives in, for example, a field trip. SMS was the most adequate communication support between the students and the teacher, greatly appreciated by students during the study, because they could ask questions of the teacher, anytime and anywhere, and had quick responses to their doubts.

In what concerns m-learning contexts, there are some dimensions that we need to pay attention to, such as *identity*, required for the development of personalized learning experiences. When using SMS as a learning resource, as in our study, it is possible to personalize the contents to the students' needs, such as quizzes or text syntheses by SMS. The *learner* is also an important part of m-learning, because each user is different and has psychological features that interfere with his/her learning experience. M-learning is learner centred, and so we can focus on his/her learning profile or style and choose different media and different content formats. We used podcasts to improve pronunciation, micro stories by SMS to create reading habits, and images to explore creativity. *Activities* can be performed individually and also collaboratively, because mobile technologies enhance collective learning experiences. Although a mobile phone is a private device, it also enables students to engage in individual or collaborative learning activities, such as the creation of micro stories in pairs or responding to curricular quizzes. *Collaboration* can happen in many ways, inside or outside the classroom, with the teacher or mates. Students worked collaboratively (writing micro stories, creating a video and sending images to each other), in and outside the classroom, using their free SMS plans. *The spatial–temporal* dimension means learning anywhere and anytime and implies an awareness of time and location. The context of *facility* can have impact on the design of an m-learning interface as well, but, nowadays, more innovative technologies can enable a richer facility context. By using mobile devices, students can study anytime and anywhere and expand classroom boundaries (in our study, for example, students used their mobile phones as data repositories). Students received SMS activities and curricular information when in the bus or while waiting for transport to go to school or go home.

Pedagogical Domain

The combination of technological and innovative teaching strategies facilitates the emergence of opportunities for developing and enriching learning experiences appropriate to the learners' needs. With respect to learning experience and objectives, individual and collaborative learning need to be considered. To enhance the learning experience: we must carefully *organize contents*; we must present *goals and objectives* clearly, which helps the learner to engage—both can be adapted to the context (in this case, our students received lesson topics by SMS before class); we must use *outcomes and feedback* to measure learning goals and objectives and motivate learners (we sent students' activities results and exercise corrections by SMS); adequate and relevant *learning experiences* can be an important aspect in developing *new or improved skills* (our students appreciated podcasts because they helped them to study autonomously); *social interaction* means establishing some pertinent collective learning, for example group or peer experiences (tell a story with images or video). According to Parsons et al. (2007), providing learners with an individual or collective problem to solve is mostly a source of *conflict, completion, challenge* and *opposition*, but these opposing forces help the activity to advance, as supported by AT.

For a pedagogy appropriate to m-learning, there are three essential dimensions: learner, environment and mediating tool. In AT, the equivalent basic elements are: subject, object and artefact. These basic elements, associated with *context* – an important concept in m-learning – emerge as important contributions to the combination of technological and pedagogical perspectives. These elements help us understand how learning activities mediated by mobile technologies are developed. The use of the tool (mobile phone) by the learner and the recognition of its usefulness (immediate educational benefit) lead to its appropriation.

The ubiquitous and personal nature of mobile devices facilitates the synchronization between the individual development and the context, increasing the learner motivation, dialogue, interaction and communication.

MOBILE GENERATION PROJECT

We carried out a project that we entitled the 'Mobile Generation' project, about the appropriation of mobile phones as a learning tool. Table 6.1 summarizes the way both pedagogical and technological domains, described above, were integrated in our research to achieve educational objectives, and it helps to understand the Mobile Generation project. The project used relatively simple technologies, SMS, notes, digital pictures, videos and podcasts. In this project, different learning experiences were developed where students could explore their mobile phone as a learning tool and reflect about their own process of learning. The Mobile Generation project was developed to explore different

Table 6.1 Pedagogical and Technological Objectives

Technological domain (mobile phone) Learning contexts (learning inside and outside classrooms)		Pedagogical domain (learning success) Learning experiences	Educational objectives
Users' roles and profiles – Students discover new uses for their mobile phone as a learning tool – Adult students develop skills through the use of technology to support m-learning activities – Students participate in the work of peers – Teacher as facilitator and guide **Mobility** – Students use the mobile phone to receive curriculum content, answer questions, learn anywhere and anytime **Interface mobile** – Mobile-device limitations: memory, storage, and multimedia features (MP3) – Visualization, audition, and writing – Learning through small units, creation by SMS and *podcasts* **Media** – Multimedia functionalities (text, image, sound, and video) **Communication** – Voice, SMS, *e-mail,* and MSN	**Identity** – Young and adult learners **Learners** – High-school students (four multiple cases— day and night students) **Activities** – Access to different content in different formats (text, image, video, and audio), use of different senses (listen, read, text), answers to questions; student producer (*podcasts*) – Learning contents review and pronunciation training – Collaborative writing **Spatial–temporal** – Students access and receive information anytime and anywhere – SMS (during day and at night) **Facility** – Write text message without looking at the keyboard – Learning by micro contents (rapid and micro learning) is easier for retention (SMS) – Mobile phone at hand (always easy to access content) – "Always on" **Collaboration** – Collaboration writing (pairs)	**Contents organization** – Students organize contents (folders, write on computer, inbox) – Students create and organize **Goals and objectives** – Awareness of content relevant to students' learning – Discovering new ways to study – Enhance learning – New learning contents consolidation, their own podcasts **Outcomes and feedback** – Students use SMS to respond to teacher questions – Teacher feedback by SMS, e-mail, and MSN **Conflicts, competition, challenges** – Quizzes, games, tools limitation, adults' and students' limitation to send SMS **Social interaction** – Collaborative writing (micro story) – Teacher–student– student interaction (by SMS, e-mail, MSN)	**Individual learning (improve existing knowledge and make new learning)** – Exploration – Reflection – Communication – Consolidation **Collaborative learning (collaborative writing, group work)** – Collaboration – Discussion – Interaction

contexts using m-learning and mobile-phones use as an educational resource. The mobile phone is a technological device that students own, which is highly customizable and extensively used in informal contexts, but not in the classroom. Trying to reverse this situation, we proposed that our students explore different services and features available in most mobile phones to develop study and improve learning skills.

In Table 6.1, we present the activities and learning strategies designed for our research study. Our research questions were: How does mobile-phone appropriation as a learning tool occur? How are artefacts, such as mobile phones, used as a mediation tool in individual and collaborative learning?

Our study considers the application of educational objectives as they relate to pedagogical and technological domains. Although most of the proposed activities (Table 6.2) are individual in nature, there were activities that benefited from the collaborative nature, connectivity, mobility and portability of students' mobile phones.

We proposed that students explore, throughout a school year, different activities for language learning (Portuguese and French). Students used podcasts both to progress French pronunciation and to learn Portuguese content. They also received SMS for improving vocabulary, both in their mother tongue and in the foreign language.

From the individual learning perspective, the learning objectives are oriented towards exploration (learning activities supported by mobile phones, such as podcasts, sending answers by SMS), training (tests and quizzes, sharing findings), communication (contacting teacher and classmates by SMS or voice), consolidation (summaries, syntheses and taking class notes). From the collaborative learning perspective, the learning objectives are collaboration (writing micro stories in pairs, digital story, poetic calendar construction in a group, reading in different voices), discussion (group work, tweets, SMS discussion), interaction (sending and receiving SMS to and from the teacher and classmates).

Table 6.2 Activities Integrated in the Study

Mobile-phone applications	Class activities
Writing and reading	iDictionary
	Micro stories
	Haikais
	Notes
	Tweets
Record and audition	Teacher's and students' podcasts
Caption and visioning	Pictures
	Videos
SMS activities	Word of the day
	Curricular contents
	Thought
	Quizzes
	Play—*Who Wants to be a Millionaire?*
	Proverbs
	Riddles
	Daily reading—fables and stories
	Micro stories (distance and face to face)

Individual and collaborative activities are greatly appreciated by students, as they said in the interviews:

1. 'By SMS we can receive a lot of information, and be in touch with the teacher and classmates. I loved it.'
2. 'Having content in my mobile phone made me feel curious about reading more. I appreciated the content sent by our teacher.'
3. 'My mobile phone helps me very much to create a digital story with my classmates who are at a distance.'

As mobile phones are private tools, the organization of curricular content depends on the students. Some students organized content in folders, others left content in the SMS inbox or copied it to their computers. Students created and organized their own podcasts too. In what concerns content organization and device capabilities, students said:

1. 'I can study on my mobile phone and benefit from its storage capacity.'
2. 'It is easy to organize contents in my mobile phone, and check information anytime anywhere.'

Knowing goals and objectives is relevant to students' learning, as pointed out by a student:

1. 'I liked it when the teacher sent us the topics of the lesson before class and sent me activities to practice.'
2. 'My teacher sent SMS to stimulate me and sent me guidelines to achieve lessons' goals.'

By using mobile devices, students discovered new ways to study that enhance and consolidate learning.

Outcomes and feedback helped students to measure goals and objectives, because students used SMS to respond to the teacher's questions, and the teacher sent them performance-activities feedback by SMS, e-mail or in MSN conversation. The constant feedback to students about their work was very much appreciated by students: 'By using my mobile phone as a learning tool I'm always in contact with my classmates and my teacher. I can ask questions to the teacher any time and anywhere.'

To challenge students, we proposed playing *Who Wants to be a Millionaire?* over ten days. To develop this game, we sent one question by SMS every day and asked for responses. Most of the students liked receiving quizzes and games; even adults students did.

To help students develop social interaction, we proposed some collaborative activities, such as writing micro stories in pairs, reading a poem in different voices and creating a group digital story with a mobile-phone video camera. The teacher also promoted students' one-to-one interaction by SMS, e-mail or MSN discussion.

From the technological perspective, we were interested in studying the mobile phone as a learning tool in different contexts of learning (inside and outside the classroom). The study carried out was qualitative (Bogdan & Biklen, 1992), with multiple case studies (four), but with one unit of analysis only (Yin, 1994), the 'mobile phone as a learning tool'.

Table 6.3 Participants' Gender

Groups	A (n = 27)		B (n = 18)		C (n = 18)		D (n = 5)	
Gender	f	%	f	%	f	%	f	%
Female	0	0	18	100	10	56	3	60
Male	27	100	0	0	8	44	2	40

This study took place during the 2008–2009 academic year and had the participation of four Groups (Table 6.3). The participants were aged 15–20 years in Groups A, B and C, and 22–56 years in Group D. This study analysed a total of 68 participants, 46 per cent female and 54 per cent male. Participants from Group B studied in a vocational school, and the other groups were in a state high school. Participants from Group A were only male, and Group B was formed only of females, and both attended Portuguese language classes (mother tongue). Groups C and D were mixed gender and attended French classes (foreign language). Participants from Group D were adult students who had left school and returned to continue their studies in evening classes.

Participants were questioned about whether they considered their mobile phone a learning tool before they participated in this study. The majority of the respondents (71 per cent) did not recognize the usefulness or benefits of mobile phones to support school study. At the end of our research, we noticed a positive change of opinion about the potential of mobile phones in an m-learning context, apart from five students who responded negatively. The degree of agreement with the statement 'a mobile phone is a learning tool' was more than 84 per cent in all groups, which shows that students recognize mobile phones' new role (private tool), as a tool to support learning. A participant in the interview declared: 'Before I started using it, I never thought that a mobile phone could actually be useful to learn a subject. But nowadays, after the experiences made at school, I recognise that it is a great learning tool.'

Another participant said:

> I consider my mobile phone as a learning tool and I used it several times to support my study during the school year, to memorise vocabulary and to look up for some words in the dictionary. I also used my MP4 player to listen podcasts to improve my pronunciation in French language.

According to students' opinions, the mobile phone has great potential as a learning tool, owing to its convenience, usefulness and added value to the learning process. We believe that mobile devices, such as the mobile phone, can be integrated into different learning activities and can be a way to motivate students. The results revealed a high acceptance and appropriation of this tool for learning purposes. Most participants said they wished that other teachers would also use the mobile phone to develop learning.

CONCLUSION

The framework proposed helped us to design the research and analyse data. In this study, students accepted the use of their own mobile phone to support their study because they included them in their school learning practices on a daily basis. When students used a mobile phone in classroom activities, they felt it added some school benefits (convenience, utility, facility, motivation), and so they recognized this device as a learning tool. The majority of students felt that teachers and students need to change the current practice of forbidding mobile phones at school and instead look at them as a tool that supports learning tasks. The basic principles of AT (subject, artefact and object) helped us to describe how the use of new tools is shaped by cultural factors, and how, when the new tool is appropriate, it mediates the activities it supports.

The material sent by SMS and podcasts served as supplements to the learning and teaching processes inside or outside the classroom and provided the opportunity for the teacher to differentiate the students' learning profiles. An interesting outcome in our research was that participants who had more recent mobile-phone models incorporated these devices more successfully in school activities and became emotionally dependent on the artefact, in comparison with those who had basic models. Another finding was that students are strongly predisposed to use their personal devices, such as mobile phones, and learn with them at school.

Our findings are in line with those reported by Parsons and Ryu (2006), who state that there is positive evidence that m-learning can be a quality learning strategy, even in technically limited situations, as was the case with the mobile phones used in this study. We agree with the ideas of these authors when they indicate that technological sophistication is not necessarily a utility measure, as even the simplest technologies, such as SMS and basic mobile phones, prove stimulating, rich social practices around basic systems. The most important and complex are the teaching strategies and methods created with and for the technology.

The results also reveal that students can take advantage of a tool they are intimately familiar with and carry around at all times. The mobile phone offers increased opportunities, especially for language learning. Dealing with the challenges of using a mobile phone as a learning tool may seem intimidating, but students considered it added value to their learning time.

The data collected show evidence of the value of mobile-phone integration at school and its pedagogical exploitation as a complementary learning tool, but also the necessary integration of activities that require learner cognitive engagement. We suggest a deep reflection on the integration of mobile technologies in learning practices, emphasizing what really creates the quality of learning, rather than giving too much importance to technology.

REFERENCES

Ally, M. (2009). *Mobile learning: Transforming the delivery of education and training*. Athabasca, AB: Athabasca University Press.

Bogdan, R., & Biklen, S. (1992). *Qualitative research for education*. Boston, MA: Allyn and Bacon.

Crompton, H. (2013). A historical overview of mobile learning: Toward learner-centered education (pp. 3–14). In Z. Berge, & L. Muilenburg (Eds.), *Handbook of mobile learning*. New York: Routledge.

Engeström, Y. (2001). Expansive learning at work: Towards an activity theory reconceptualisation. *Journal of Education and Work, 14*, 133–156.

Fosnot, C. T. (1996). *Constructivism: Theory, perspectives, and practice*. New York: Teachers College Press.

Kukulska-Hulme, A., & Traxler, J. (Eds) (2005). *Mobile learning: A handbook for educators and trainers*. London: Routledge.

Keller, J. M. (1987). Strategies for stimulating the motivation to learn. *Performance & Instruction, 26*(8), 1–7.

Leontiev A. N. (1978). *Activity consciousness and personality*. Retrieved from: http://marxists.org/archive/leontev/works/1978/index.htm

Moura, A. (2010). *Apropriação do Telemóvel como Ferramenta de Mediação em Mobile Learning: Estudos de Caso em Contexto Educativo*. Retrieved from: http://repositorium.sdum.uminho.pt/handle/1822/13183

Moura, A., & Carvalho, A. (2010). Mobile learning: Using SMS in educational contexts. In N. Reynolds & M. Turcsányi-Szabó (Eds), *Key Competencies in the Knowledge Society*. IFIP TC 3 International Conference, KCKS 2010. Brisbane, Australia, 281–291.

Naismith, L., Lonsdale, P., Vavoula, G. & Sharples, M. (2004). *Literature review in mobile technologies and learning* (FutureLab Report 11). Retrieved from: www.google.com/url?sa=t&rct=j&q=literature%20review%20in%20mobile%20technologies%20and%20learning&source=web&cd=1&ved=0CDUQFjAA&url=http%3A%2F%2Fciteseerx.ist.psu.edu%2Fviewdoc%2Fdownload%3Fdoi%3D10.1.1.136.2203%26rep%3Drep1%26type%3Dpdf&ei=Ci3jUMHnOsXv0QHeyoGYDg&usg=AFQjCNHzDotK3rZxD2S07BaTSbvftTkwpg&cad=rja

Nardi, B. (1996). *Context and consciousness: Activity theory and human-computer interaction*. Cambridge, MA: MIT Press.

Parsons, D., & Ryu, H. (2006). *A framework for assessing the quality of mobile learning* (Massey University website). Retrieved from: www.massey.ac.nz/~dpparson/Mobile%20Learning%20Quality.pdf

Parsons, D., Ryu, H., & Cranshaw, M. (2007). A design requirements framework for mobile learning environments. *Journal of Computers, 2*(4), 1–8.

Sharples, M. (2005). Learning as conversation: Transforming education in the mobile age. *Proceedings Seeing Understanding, Learning in the Mobile Age*. Budapest, Hungary, 147–152.

Shih, Y. E., & Mills, D. (2007). Setting the new standard with mobile computing in online learning. *The International Review of Research in Open and Distance Learning, 8*(2). Retrieved from: www.irrodl.org/index.php/irrodl/article/viewArticle/361/872/

Shuler, C. (2009). *Pockets of potential using mobile technologies to promote children's learning*. New York: The Joan Ganz Cooney Center at Sesame Workshop.

Traxler, J. (2007). Defining, discussing and evaluating mobile learning: the moving finger writes and having writ ... *The International Review of Research in Open and Distance Learning, 8*(2). Retrieved from: www.irrodl.org/index.php/irrodl/article/view/346/875

Trish, A., & Du Toit, L. (2010). *Utilising Activity Theory and illuminative evaluation as a theoretical framework for ACTS learning space*. Retrieved from: www.swinburne.edu.au/spl/learningspacesproject/outcomes/files/ACTS_Evaluation_Theoretical_Framework.pdf

UNESCO. (2011). *UNESCO mobile learning week report*. Paris: UNESCO HQ. Retrieved from: www.bunyad.org.pk/index_files/UNESCO_MLW_Report_2011.pdf

Vavoula, G., Pachler, N., & Kukulska-Hulme, A. (2009). *Researching mobile learning: Frameworks, tools and research designs*. Bern, Germany: Peter Lang.

Waycott, J. (2004). *The appropriation of PDAs as learning and workplace tools*. Retrieved from: http://kn.open.ac.uk/public/getfile.cfm?documentfileid=9608

Yin, R. K. (1994). *Case study research: Design and methods*. Thousand Oaks, CA: Sage Publishing.

7

LEARNING AND TEACHING AS COMMUNICATIVE ACTIONS

A Theory for Mobile Education

Scott J. Warren and Jenny S. Wakefield

As mobile devices and applications have increasingly been employed to support formal and informal learning, theories used to guide such implementations have come from traditional sources: information processing, social and radical constructivism, and even behaviorist traditions. However, what differentiates these mobile tools from other technologies used for learning is that they stem from the primary purpose of the devices: communication. This communication comes from multiple avenues, ranging from voice calls and text messaging to global positioning systems that situate learning in the local space by embedding metadata and learning activities. Because mobile devices often include a broad array of communicative features, it becomes important to develop theory that guides their use and that focuses on the communication affordances. This is especially important when viewed from the perspective of their ability to support learning discourses that situate learners in meaningful, real-world contexts. Further, such a guiding theory should value discourse as a means to support students as they argue toward shared, intersubjective understandings about the topic at hand. The question, then, is what theory can be used to support the communication that mobile devices allow as a means of fostering learning? To that end, learning and teaching as communicative actions (LTCA) theory offers one possible avenue (Wakefield, Warren, & Alsobrook, 2011).

THEORETICAL FRAMEWORK: LEARNING AND TEACHING AS COMMUNICATIVE ACTIONS

In establishing LTCA theory, we claimed that current learning-theory frameworks, from radical behaviorism to social constructivism in education, artificially splinter the holistic experiences of teaching and learning (Warren, Wakefield, & Mills, 2013), creating differentiations that lead to false and unproductive distinctions. Sfard (1998) stated that it is dangerous, and possibly destructive, to choose a single metaphor or perspective on learning. Doing so denies the necessity of both acquisition-type and constructivist knowledge models that foster learning and unnaturally narrows the view of what learning is and how it may take place. Taking only a single view of what knowledge is and whether it is constructed or acquired can lead educational stakeholders to become unproductive and, therefore, leads to tensions between practitioners, who are most commonly teachers, and theorists.

Further, thinking that there is only one form of knowledge or truth artificially separates theorists and researchers from the daily experiences of teachers and learners and implicitly claims that there is only one path to learning. Teachers, however, tend to hold worldviews that do not fall neatly into one or another epistemology (Schraw & Olafson, 2002), and thus their views conflict with the intact, singular theories found in academia. Instead, teachers tend to understand, experience, and design instruction; that is, the objective, subjective, and relative realms exist concurrently for them. These are all viewed as necessary within an instructional sequence, not as separate, chained, reinforced stimuli and response, or as social construction of solutions to ill-structured problems. The difference between how we *theorize* about learning and teaching versus how learning and teaching are *experienced* thus becomes problematic when we employ only that single lens on either: behaviorist, cognitivist, constructivist, or some other (Cobb, 2002). In our field, however, it is common to view learning models as valid only if they are internally and externally consistent within a single epistemic and ontological frame, blinding us to the necessity of understanding the world in all its complexity (Walker & Evers, 1988).

COMMUNICATIVE ACTIONS

Education is not only an exclusively behavioral, cognitive, or social process; instead, it is all of these at once, expressed as the goals we have for student learning. In order to address the fragmenting of worldviews into objectivist, subjectivist, and relativist positions (Bernstein, 1983), as noted in the introduction, we begin by providing a theoretical overview of Jürgen Habermas (2003). This sociologist, pragmatist, and theorist provided a different lens that may allow us to better understand the complexities of learning, without privileging one form of knowledge over others. Instead, valid understanding is proposed to come from human communication toward goals—individual and shared—all geared toward getting what one wants or needs.

Criticism of Communication and Theory

Habermas's critique of ideology was meant to enable individuals to become aware of *distortions in knowledge* that emerge as a result of the very nature of human communication and that depend on the fundamentally imperfect understandings of both speaker and hearer (Habermas, 1981/1984). Empirical and interpretive social scientists use their senses to describe the world around them (Hollis, 1994). In contrast, critical theorists seek to understand *why* the world is as it is and leverage a critique of the social, political, and economic systems that create injustice. Rather than upholding a pessimistic worldview, as theorists such as Foucault (1981) have been accused of doing, critical theory is instead a view that the world can always be a better place (Bernstein, 1983; Slattery, 2006). Kincheloe and McLaren (2011, p. 288) stated that:

[a] critical social theory is concerned in particular with issues of power and justice and the ways that the economy; matters of race, class, and gender; ideologies; discourses; education; religion and other social institutions; and cultural dynamics interact to construct a social system.

Although Habermas (1981/1987) criticized systemic distortion of knowledge through the coercive and normative power inherent in social and political systems, he accepted that human communication is necessarily deformed because humans will always have an imperfect understanding of one another, because our communication tools are imperfect. Speech acts cannot fully convey our internal understandings, but we must, as Wittgenstein and Anscombe (1968) stated, assume that both speaker and hearer are making sincere expressions regarding their experiences and mental states. Within this context and set of assumptions, Habermas sought to comprehend mutual understanding, given this recognized limitation.

Communication to Reach Goals

As such, Habermas has worked to frame discourses geared toward understanding by focusing, not on the individual utterances made by people, but instead on how those utterances allow humans to reach particular goals and reach agreement through discourse and arguments regarding claims to truth made by interlocutors. Habermas's theory of communicative actions (TCA) focuses on how human speakers, by the act of communication and seeking understanding, i.e., shared meaning and mutual understanding, allow for "transmission of culturally stored knowledge," but also means to "coordinat[e] action ('fulfillment of norms') and socializ[e] actors ('formation of personality structures')" (Habermas, 1981/1987, p. 63). Communicative actions are "oriented to achieving, sustaining, and reviewing consensus" (Habermas, 1981/1984, p. 17). They include personal goals such as (1) getting what one wants, (2) being understood by another, (3) being seen to tell the truth, (4) making a personal subjective claim to truth, or (5) making completely relative claims to personal truth and identity. The exchange of validity claims requires an end agreement among discussants resulting from discourse and the rejection or modifications of claims based upon the strength of the stronger argument or reason (Habermas, 1993). Within particular utterances, speakers contact the objective, social, and their own subjective worlds concurrently. This creates *intersubjectivity* (position taking), in which speaker and hearer regard knowledge as objective, subjective, *and* relative. It is this idea that forms the following theory of learning and teaching, guiding how mobile devices support education.

LEARNING AND TEACHING AS COMMUNICATIVE ACTIONS

In order to understand the role of Habermas's (1998) work in the context of educational settings, the theory of LTCA has been proposed (Warren, 2011). It seeks to contextualize teaching and learning in two ways. First, the theory claims that activities have inherent claims to truth that require critique in order to generate knowledge. Second, knowledge constructed through participatory discourses must be intersubjectively agreed upon by all participants in order to be viewed as valid by those participants.

We have proposed that such acts emerge from the designed instructional activities, as well as the social discourse that accompanies them (Warren & Wakefield, 2012).

Therefore, communicative goals from the teacher in instructional settings should include conveying structural content information (e.g., Detroit is the county seat of Wayne County, Michigan), and the teacher should follow by drawing out student responses that confirm understanding. In other goals, the instructor seeks to suggest and then negotiate normative rules within the class (e.g., you *should* provide both positive and negative feedback when critiquing your peers' work).

Learning goals that teachers have for their students can come from, for example, the state curriculum or from personal goals established for individual students in response to diagnostic testing or evaluation; however, each is communicated either directly, through such actions as writing them down and sharing them, or through the implicit goals of the specific activities and linkages to assessment. It is, thus, communicative actions that inform the design of learning activities, and each must be included to spur learning discourses within a classroom. These speech acts, as identified by Habermas (1998), include *normative* actions related to the validity of claims of truth about group, institution, and societal rules, *strategic* actions geared toward learners determining the validity of objective knowledge and truth claims made directing hearers to act, *constative* actions geared toward allowing students to interactively make and challenge claims to the validity of objective knowledge, and, finally, *dramaturgical* actions that allow for both individual and subjective expressions of truth through artistic forms of communication, as mentioned by Habermas (1998).

COMMUNICATIVE ACTIONS TO SUPPORT LEARNING AND TEACHING

In LTCA theory, each communicative action, as mentioned above, serves as a foundation for how teaching and learning can be designed. Further, within an instructional sequence, each type governs how the transmission, reception, critique, and construction of communicated knowledge takes place (Warren, Bohannon, & Alajmi, 2010). The following serve as examples for how each action functions in learning settings, with special attention paid to the use of mobile technologies.

Normative communicative actions generally frame how participants take part in learning activities. With mobile technologies, these are often rules for appropriate use given by the instructor. Generally, they have to do with what students are *allowed* to use the communication affordances for in a learning setting. For example, with learning activities that require the use of a mobile global positioning system, the instructor would tell students they *should* turn the device to airplane mode, so that the device cannot be used for phone calls or texting with friends during instruction. Such norms stem from societal expectations of fairness and legal rules. Normative communicative actions are regularly expressed as what students *should* do rather than as commands.

Normative actions may be negotiated at the outset of a learning activity or unit, along with possible consequences for violating the rules established through social discourse among class participants. For instance, a rubric can be developed in collaboration between teacher and learners. The teacher should be prepared to enforce these norms in accordance with what has been intersubjectively agreed upon among learners, rather than imposing his/her will on students. Doing so gives students buy-in to the process and helps learners reinforce the rules among themselves. These norms are often revisited throughout a semester and may be changed in response to discourse about them by stakeholders.

Another example would include learners using smart phones in class to complete assignments. When responding to instructor elicitations through a mobile application for a learning management system, they may discover that working on a problem in small groups with peers, using text messaging, would increase their ability to solve problems and answer questions. As such, a student begins a renegotiation of the rule that stated all phones should be turned to airplane mode, so that students may communicate through text messages, thus improving learning. The entire class participates in discourse toward a goal of mutual, intersubjective understanding that may lead to changing the rules for participation.

In today's schools, *strategic communicative actions* commonly follow the establishment of these norms. These speech acts are commonly expressed as imperatives, e.g., that learners complete a particular assignment, use particular applications, or engage in particular discourses (Warren, 2011; Warren & Stein, 2008). These acts are the most frequently used learning actions in today's educational settings and provide only dualistic options. These are (1) accept or (2) reject the presented direction.

In an educational setting, an example of such direction may require a learner to use the Twitter micro-blogging tool, with multiple mobile support applications. Recently, an instructor ordered students in a class to download the Tweetdeck application or any of the other mobile applications that facilitate access to Twitter over a student's phone. Through the communications and within the discourse that emerged, the applications allowed students to receive directions, clarified assignments, and challenged them to argue in response to the expressed truth claims. These claims were often unsupported and demanded critique, as the instructor engaged in what is commonly called playing the "devil's advocate." However, the central truth claim the instructor holds is that the knowledge communicated through an assignment that students complete using an LMS application is *useful*. If they do not agree, they reject the inherent truth of the claim, refusing to act, i.e. reject using such an app. If accepted, it is implied that a student views the claim as valid, and the knowledge gained from the related act is then further leveraged through constative communicative actions.

Constative communicative actions are discourses or arguments in which one participant makes a claim to truth. Learning in this context results from disagreements or truth claims shared between interlocutors about what is true knowledge, generally focused on complex topics that may have no one correct answer. Such discourses may lead to rejection, negotiation, and/or exchange of counter-claims among learners. Warren and Stein (2008) stated that constative speech acts allow for development of "critique [of] the theoretical understandings of speaker and hearer" (p. 276) toward intersubjective agreement and shared knowledge among learners. When engaged in constative acts, learners and instructor will challenge the validity of truth claims; failing to do so results in another form of communicative act, devoid of argumentation. We hear people engage in constative communicative acts daily as they are speaking or texting on their mobile phones, and we see them in e-mails. Once disagreement about the truth of an individual claim occurs, constative communicative acts follow.

Disputing truth claims generally comes through presentation of evidence and critique of the speaker's evidence or examples. This discourse generates new truth claims that are counter to the original claim. Such negotiation leads to the social construction of new knowledge or the acceptance of a different set of truth claims than those originally made. In some instances, the instructor's claims were intended to incite constative discourse, without the speaker intending to make a real claim to truth. Such claims can be leveraged to present, engage, or model critique. Students have used Twitter, Adobe Connect, or Skype, either synchronously or asynchronously, to engage in the construction of their own understandings and to generate their own accepted truths, which have sometimes been counter to accepted theory or knowledge.

Truth-claim critique is often supported by research findings or from student "*Lifeworld*" (italics added) experiences. Habermas (1981/1984) stated that these take place outside of institutional systems of communication. Within the educational setting, these are usually within a student's own lived experiences. As new consensus about truth is constructed through communications that students post, using, for instance, mobile blog apps or Twitter messages, this fosters additional communication and new arguments towards learning through supported, intersubjective agreement. Through these, the instructor further asks learners to express their thoughts within their individual blog reflections, through digital stories, or through visual design in dramaturgical actions.

In *dramaturgical communicative actions*, we adopt views from the perspective of "two worlds" (Habermas, 1981/1984, p. 93). The first is the subjective, interior view of the speaker. It is in this orientation that he or she articulates their personal identity and internal understandings about a topic. We see this commonly through a student's reflective video blogs posted to video-sharing sites (e.g., YouTube) that can be accessed anywhere, artwork uploaded to sharing sites (e.g., DeviantArt), and in discourses with peers using mobile apps that support voice-over-IP such as Skype or text messaging. The second world is the external, objective one, often expressed through participants' utterances of their individual understandings (Habermas, 1981/1984). Dramaturgical actions present our internal lifeworld and internal identity, through external expression, to the outside world. Dramaturgical acts are often individual, artistic creations such as poems, thoughtful blog reflections, paintings, graphic design, construction of digital avatars, or other expressions.

Another important feature of dramaturgical acts is that they are not constructed entirely relative to the individual speaker. They are mediated and can be improved through critique. For example, when a student posts a dance enactment to YouTube, it contains his/her individual or lifeworld understanding. However, the performance is open to examination by peers, experts, teacher, and others, toward a goal of improving the learner's expression in the future, making it more clearly understood by both speaker and hearer.

USING LTCA THEORY TO DESIGN INSTRUCTION FOR MOBILE LEARNING

In the spring of 2011, LTCA theory was combined with the use of mobile tools in order to support two blended courses. One was at the Masters level, and the other at the doctoral level. The design of these courses followed LTCA instructional design principles first framed by Wakefield et al. (2011) and presented in Table 7.1.

From these courses, and the use of mobile tools to support learners in the interstitial periods *between* class meetings, several lessons emerged that came from the theory and that apply directly to the use of mobile devices for learning and teaching.

Table 7.1 LTCA Instructional Design Principles and Directions

Communicative action	Instructional design principle	Design directive
Normative	Allow students an opportunity to negotiate norms and classroom rules that support their learning experiences. Students and instructor should construct norms that will guide effective communication in which all members of the classroom may fairly and respectfully critique claims to truth and knowledge	When preparing learning experiences, include and model initial rules for behavior and discourse, but allow for whole-class negotiation and modification of these norms early and regularly in response to expressed need. The instructor may start with the rule that no one may speak without raising their hand and being recognized by the teacher. However, through negotiation, students may instead establish conditions under which they may speak without the instructor's permission
Strategic	Instructor provides knowledge of, or access to, shared, socially validated facts that can be communicated by an instructor or technological tool, including textbooks, websites, and other repositories of reified knowledge	When designing instruction, include activities that communicate basic, socially validated knowledge to give students a framework for understanding, discourse, social and relative knowledge construction, and other future learning experiences. That knowledge which comes to schools from the state has been subjected to numerous challenges to claims to truth prior to inclusion in state standards. Although some may be faulty, it provides a starting point for shared understanding and a place to begin critique of validity
Constative	Give opportunities for students to engage in critical discourse centered on understanding truth claims and knowledge put forth by peers, instructor, textbooks, etc. Further, they have their own claims to truth and knowledge, critiqued and challenged toward a larger goal of constructing or acquiring valid knowledge toward making future change	Include specific opportunities for students to critique existing claims to knowledge and truth from texts, instructor, peers, and other sources of reified knowledge. Allow students to construct their own claims to truth and knowledge and allow them to be tested for validity by peers, instructor, and, if applicable, experts. As put forth in social constructivist views, communication among and between students is an effective means of constructing knowledge. However, any knowledge emerging from this discursive process must also be open to the crucible of critique in order to test its validity
Dramaturgical	Make available chances for students to safely express their personal identities, passions, and other internal, relative, or subjective truths and knowledge, which are open to respectful critique through discourse with peers, instructor, and others	Design instruction that allows students opportunities for safe personal expressions of identity—expressive understanding of the subject—while allowing for minor critique. Although a student's song is an expression of personal identity and truth, it remains subject to validity critique through discourse in social settings, as when critics review a Broadway musical

From Wakefield, Warren, and Alsobrook (2011)

MOBILE TOOLS FOR LTCA LEARNING

As the instructor designed each course, it was with the idea that students would come to campus six or seven times throughout the semester. As such, the two courses employed several mobile applications, allowing students access to course materials, discussion forums, and reading materials using smart phones and other mobile devices. These tools included online applications that facilitated access through either phone apps or Web browsers:

1. LMS with mobile support (e.g., Blackboard, Schoology);
2. social media including micro-blogs (e.g., Facebook, Twitter);
3. synchronous meeting tools (e.g., Adobe Connect, Wimba);
4. synchronous voice-over-IP tools (e.g., Skype);
5. smart-phone voice and text messaging.

Table 7.2 presents possible learning affordances of each tool and how they may be used to support learning.

Although some mobile tools duplicated the media or learning affordances of another, the instructor sought to have the class decide which worked best for the communication purposes established for them, to improve student buy-in.

THEORY INTO PRACTICE: STARTING WITH *SHOULD*

To holistically visualize how the LTCA theory can be utilized to guide in the m-learning environment, the following model is provided. As class begins, students should be engaged in the collaborative establishment of rules for *normative communications*

Table 7.2 M-Learning Tools in a Post-Secondary Course

Cognitive tool	Course enactment
Social support tools	Inform on available online discourse or sharing tools (e.g., Twitter) and synchronous class meeting apps (e.g., Adobe Connect) that allow access to learning-management systems
Information resources	A mobile learning-management system (LMS) can be used with connections to Internet resources; also, instructions to use search engines can be included to have students locate their own resources
Static and dynamic models	Provide models through links that students and the public provide through mobile tools such as Twitter and blogs
Mobile conversation and collaboration tools	Allow for numerous digital communication tools, to include e-mail, Skype, Twitter, Facebook, text messaging
Scaffolding	Embed specific supports and mild directives in the distributed learning activities (e.g., LMS itself, entries, interactions with peers and instructor)
Coaching	Provide coaching through each mobile app without requiring that students be physically present. Also provide cognitive challenge where needed and scaffolding as necessary
Assessment	Assess learning through instructor, peer, and public critique of student knowledge constructions (both group and individual) when posted on Twitter, blogs, and other social media tools accessed through mobile devices

regarding appropriate argumentation and truth-claim critique, as well as proper online interaction and mobile-application use. This is what the class and instructor believe that students *should* do in terms of use of the tool. For example, on many mobile devices, the Twitter app and text messages will either make a noise or vibrate the phone, or light up a tablet, to inform the receiver of an incoming communication. At 2 a.m., this can be disruptive to the privacy and family life of an instructor and may create tension among learners and instructor, who often work at different times of day and night. As such, instructor and students should develop social mores for when students may communicate or which type of application is most appropriate at what hour (e.g., blog at night, text during the day).

In face-to-face classes, the instructor should also establish norms for discursive critique through modeling. Such modeling is expected to transfer to students and include appropriate use of mobile social media for learning purposes. By doing so, students should more readily engage in respectful discussion about peer ideas. Additionally, these norms generally include consequences for inappropriate tool use. These are not substantially different from the types of punitive act they may experience in a face-to-face course with no mobile component, such as loss of points for non-participation.

Lifeworld Sharing

Beyond classroom discourse, students can also be encouraged, within reason, to share lifeworld experiences as part of establishing rapport among peers and with the instructor. These communicative acts can help participants to develop empathy and understanding for one another in the context of their daily lives and struggles, engendering the expression of what Nel Noddings (2003) called "care statements"—*affective communicative acts*. These statements help encourage cohesion among members of the class, which may be more difficult because of the distant nature of many mobile communications. By establishing relationships that emerge from such communications, students may develop appropriate social understandings about how and why they should use mobile devices and applications, both in class and later in the public sphere. They may also facilitate the sense of a social learning community and help participants get to know each other in a way different from that offered in classroom settings, where some learners may be intimidated about speaking up (Wakefield et al., 2011).

Strategic Acts

Following this establishment of basic guidelines for what students *should* do, the instructor is expected to then provide *strategic communications*, both at the outset of the use of the mobile tools for learning, as well as throughout the semester. These communications come in the form of directions to use the technologies. In following weeks, the instructor may post additional directions using mobile applications, in which he/she requires students to reply to a particular message, read a particular article, or other learning directives. Students will either use the mobile device and an associated application or they will not. Failure to use as directed implies the learner's rejection of the inherent validity of the instructor's claim and is often viewed as an act of transgression by the teacher.

In the post-secondary-course examples, the instructor required students to create a Twitter account and then follow and post messages in response to instructor prompts and peer responses. Many students followed this directive, although some did not.

Although there were class consequences to refusing to participate (loss of points), learning that should have come through the argumentative discourses had passed them by. Further, they also incurred a loss of resources provided by peers and instructor as they used the mobile devices outside of the classroom to help intersubjectively construct new meanings and knowledge.

Argumentative Communications: Learning Through Discord

Through *constative communications*, students engage in a give and take of truth claims: argumentation. Rather than use discussion boards alone, students employ mobile tools such as Twitter, blog reflections with comments, etc., to engage in communication. This ability to engage from anywhere at any time, as students have ideas, affords students the ability to receive feedback immediately. Further, students may engage in the disputation of peer and instructor truth claims through the provision of evidence and logical critique, which can be further supported by linking to online materials such as articles, images, and other relevant information. It is through this discursive process that the class seeks intersubjective agreement among members and to engage in knowledge construction.

Individual Expressions of Truth and Identity

Finally, learners should be encouraged, if not required, to provide *dramaturgical communications* tied to their individual understandings of a concept that also emerges or reveals their personal identity. These acts are a synthesis of a student's ideas that emerge from his/her social discussions with peers in constative communications, combined with other sources, such as reified information or knowledge embedded in texts. In some instances, this can simply be a research paper; in others, students may choose to engage in an artistic work. These may include such acts as photograph enhancing or modifying through a mobile app, before uploading to a site such as Flickr for sharing. It also may involve students developing data visualizations using mind maps or similar tools that tie mobile apps to online tools for later analysis and presentation. Or it can be capturing video using a smart phone that they then edit and share with the public through an application allowing for instant upload to a video-sharing site, such as YouTube. Although personal, these actions remain open to respectful critique by instructor, peers, and experts, toward a goal of improving student understanding and improving future performance. That is to say, they do not stand alone, purely relative to each learner.

To include communicative actions, learning activities should require learners to examine questionable truth claims made by the instructor or peers, or in theoretical and research articles. These activities can not only be distributed across the Internet, but also require students to use multiple mobile tools to communicate within the class and outside of class, with peers and with public figures who also use these apps to share information and engage in critique of ideas and research. By leveraging all that these mobile devices can do to support communication, learning can be improved by ignoring the chronological lines drawn by the system that restrict participant discourse to a limited number of hours a week.

CONCLUSION

As mobile devices continue to take hold in educational settings, it is important that there be a framework for why they can and should support learning. Given that their primary affordance is one of communication, it then makes sense to suggest a theory that acknowledges communication as central to learning and teaching and sees the importance of discourse in the educational setting. As such, this chapter offered one possible model for understanding how learning is supported through the use of mobile devices and applications. LTCA theory claims that the role of mobile tools is to connect instructor and students. This is expected to take place, not only in class, but also in the spaces between formal meetings. As a consequence, these devices provide learners with a valuable connection that allows them to receive instructor or peer support faster. In addition, it is possible they will receive feedback and/or critique of their ideas more quickly than they might have otherwise, and this can help provide students with up-to-the-moment, meaningful comments that allow for improved understanding. From our own experiences with mobile devices and applications, they can be powerful tools for supporting learning and improving instructor responsiveness to student ideas in ways that have not been available until now. Beyond the practical use, LTCA theory also provides a means of guiding m-learning tools philosophically, by situating the learning activities they support in the context of what they do best: improving communication, which leads to learning.

REFERENCES

Bernstein, R. J. (1983). *Beyond objectivism and relativism: Science, hermeneutics, and praxis*. Philadelphia, PA: University of Pennsylvania Press.

Cobb, P. (2002). Epistemological world views, subject matter context, and the institutional setting teaching. *Issues in Education, 8*(2), 149–158.

Foucault, M. (1981). *Power/knowledge: Selected interviews and other writings 1972–1977*. New York: Random House.

Habermas, J. (1984). *The theory of communicative action. Volume 1. Reason and the rationalization of society* (T. McCarthy, Trans.). Boston, MA: Beacon Press. (Original work published 1981, Frankfurt am Main, Germany: Suhrkamp Verlag.)

Habermas, J. (1987). *The theory of communicative action: Lifeworld and system* (T. McCarthy, Trans.). Boston, MA: Beacon Press. (Original work published 1981, Frankfurt am Main, Germany: Suhrkamp Verlag.)

Habermas, J. (1993). *Justification and application: Remarks on discourse ethics* (C. P. Cronin, Trans.). Cambridge, MA: MIT Press.

Habermas, J. (1998). *On the pragmatics of communication* (M. Cooke, Trans.). Cambridge, MA: The MIT Press.

Habermas, J. (2003). *The future of human nature*. Cambridge, UK: Polity.

Hollis, M. (1994). *The philosophy of social science: An introduction*. Cambridge, UK: Cambridge University Press.

Kincheloe, J. L., & McLaren, P. (2011). Rethinking critical theory and qualitative research. In K. Hayes, S. R. Steinberg, & K. Tobin (Eds.), *Bold visions in educational research: 32 key works in critical pedagogy* (pp. 285–326). Springer. DOI:10.1007/978-94-6091-397-6

Noddings, N. (2003). *Caring: A feminine approach to ethics and moral education*. Berkeley, CA: University of California Press.

Schraw, G., & Olafson, L. (2002). Teachers' epistemological worldviews and educational practices. *Issues in Education, 8*(2), 99–139.

Sfard, A. (1998). On two metaphors for learning and the dangers of choosing just one. *Educational Researcher, 27*(2), 4–13.

Slattery, P. (2006). *Curriculum development in the postmodern era* (2nd ed.). New York: Routledge.

Wakefield, J. S., Warren, S. J., & Alsobrook, M. (2011). Learning and teaching as communicative actions: A mixed-methods Twitter study. *Knowledge Management & E-Learning. An International Journal, 3*(4), 563–584.

Walker, J. C., & Evers, C. W. (1988). The epistemological unity of educational research. In J. P. Keeves (Ed.), *Educational research, methodology, and measurement: An international handbook* (pp. 28–36). Oxford, UK: Pergamon Press.

Warren, S. J. (2011). Learning and teaching as a communicative action. Retrieved from: www.ltca.us/LTCA_Theory.html

Warren, S. J., Bohannon, R., & Alajmi, M. (2010, April). *Learning and teaching as communicative actions: An experimental course design.* Paper presented at the annual meeting of The American Educational Research Association, Denver, Colorado.

Warren, S. J., & Stein, R. (2008). Simulating teaching experience with role-play. In D. Gibson & Y. Baek (Eds.), *Digital simulations for improving education: Learning through artificial teaching environments* (pp. 273–288). Hershey, PA: IGI Global.

Warren, S. J., & Wakefield, J. S. (2012). Learning and teaching as communicative actions: Social media as educational tool. In K. Seo (Ed.), *Using social media effectively in the classroom: Blogs, wikis, Twitter, and more* (pp. 98–113). London: Routledge.

Warren, S. J., Wakefield, J. S., & Mills, L. A. (2013). Learning and teaching as communicative actions: Transmedia storytelling. In L. Wankel & P. Blessinger (Eds.), *Increasing student engagement and retention using multimedia technologies: Video annotation, multimedia applications, videoconferencing and transmedia storytelling. Cutting-edge technologies in higher education* (pp. 67–95). Bingley, UK: Emerald Group Publishing Limited.

Wittgenstein, L., & Anscombe, G. E. M. (1968). *Philosophical investigations* (2nd ed.). Oxford, UK: Blackwell.

8

A FUTURE FOR M-LEARNING

Clark N. Quinn

To talk about the future of m-learning, several things are required: we must establish the "now," look at the trajectory, and then make inferences about the future. There are some interesting opportunities on the table, including what was mentioned as ubiquitous learning in Chapter 1, but also more. When we have ubiquitous information, what will learning interventions look like?

The path to be taken begins by examining the nature of mobile devices, including the breadth and depth of offerings, and their relative growth rates in usage. This will drive a different spin on a definition of m-learning, looking at patterns and categories of use. Together, the device and usage trends will enable a discussion of where we are at now and allow us to project forward. Short-term trends will be examined, and then longer-term possibilities. We'll also look at what is missing, and what the opportunities are. From these foundations, a vision of what future m-learning could look like will be derived.

DESCRIBING DEVICES

The nature of mobile devices has strong potential for determining the nature of m-learning. The definition of m-learning offered in Chapter 1, "learning across multiple contexts, through social and content interactions, using personal electronic devices" (Crompton, 2013, p. 4), leaves the nature of such devices largely open to interpretation. Although deliberate, that phrasing leaves open the possibility for some unfortunate inferences. For instance, a desktop is a personal electronic device, and yet it is definitely not a mobile device.

Indicative of the nature of a new and still-dynamic field, the definition of mobile devices has been the bane of many discussions to define m-learning. Clearly, smartphones and PDAs such as the iPod Touch are the prototypical device. Do laptops count? How about tablets?

The eLearning Guild's *Research 360° Report on Mobile Learning* (Wexler et al., 2007) defined a mobile device as "a compact digital portable device that the individual carries on a regular basis, has reliable connectivity, and fits in a pocket or purse." Ostensibly, this would preclude a laptop, though, if a laptop is doing more than merely serving as a portable desktop and is doing something unique or, as the report had it, "If an individual is out and about and is a 'learning target'", then a laptop could qualify.

As part of an effort to define successful characteristics of mobile applications, PalmSource (2003) documented the different uses of laptops and PDAs as many short, quick accesses of a PDA during a day, whereas laptop usages would be fewer and of longer duration. Since that time, tablets have emerged, with the Pew Internet & American Life Project (Rainte, 2012) documenting that US tablet ownership "nearly doubled from 10% to 19%" during the holiday period. This is a dramatic uptake, suggesting that tablets are making inroads into mainstream experience.

Here, it is proposed that the nature of the tablet experience is different than that of a laptop or a smartphone (Garg, 2011). It has previously been proposed (Quinn, 2011b) that two dimensions capture the differences between devices, intimacy and immediacy. Intimacy captures the relationship with the device, considering elements such as whether the device is used at arms length or close up, and as something you use for utilitarian needs compared with something you meet personal needs with. Immediacy is the speed with which the device is accessed and expected to be available, at any time. The proposal is that laptops are neither immediate nor intimate, tablets are intimate but not immediate, and smartphones and PDAs are both intimate and immediate (see Figure 8.1). The category of "immediate but not intimate" is open for debate, but a proposed example would be a kiosk used for quick information access, such as at a tourist destination or for check-in for travel. The likelihood, however, is that these are not categories but continua, and, as such, there will be devices that blur the boundaries.

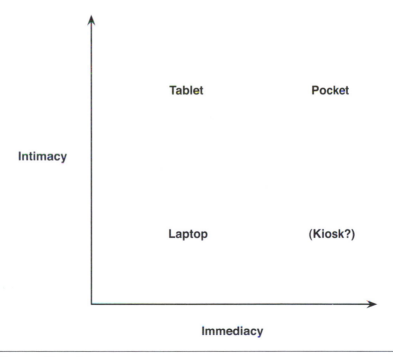

Figure 8.1 Intimacy and Immediacy

This distinction lumps smartphones and PDAs in one category, with some overlap from tablets, and then puts laptops as a separate category, again with some overlap with tablets. From there, more is common than dissimilar. Here, we will term the pocketable handheld, either a smartphone or PDA, as a "pod," a tablet as a "pad," and leave laptops out of consideration. When they're contextually relevant, they will be equivalent to a pad. We will also largely be considering the pod as the base-use case.

The devices themselves are refining into ones with connectivity, a screen, and audio capabilities, which run software under a variety of operating systems. More importantly, the additional hardware included is converging, with most devices having a large subset of: a camera, a second camera, a microphone, a speaker, a GPS, an accelerometer, and a compass. Most can communicate via Wi-Fi and Bluetooth wireless-networking standards. Some can use telecommunications standards (e.g., cellphone carrier signals) as well. This, then, characterizes the space of mobile devices and gives us a handle to examine the rest of the definition of m-learning.

DEFINING M-LEARNING

From the opening definition, it is also worth unpacking just what "learning" means. Although the definition is undoubtedly deliberately open, it is worthwhile to examine different scenarios. Looking at the patterns of usage, even with a tablet, it is improbable to think that the nature of m-learning is consumption of courses, certainly not on the pod in most instances. To the extent that m-learning is consumption of a course, there is no unique contribution of mobile, and it merely constitutes e-learning. Rather, the inference is that m-learning will really be about something different.

The unfortunate reality is that the use of the term *m-learning* likely implies courses on a phone, but, except for relatively unique instances, the most plausible scenario is to distribute the learning over a period of time and device accesses (Quinn, 2012). Spaced learning is not unusual in formal education settings, but, in organizational ones, and those contexts are not precluded in this discussion, the traditional learning model is the "event": people access learning in monolithic chunks, whether face to face as instructor-led training (ILT) or online via webinars or virtual classrooms, and asynchronous e-learning. The educational effectiveness of these is questionable at best, but the pragmatic constraints mitigate against change.

In the organizational setting, asynchronous courses may be delivered on pads as they are on desktops, with the caveat of adaptation to touchscreen interfaces. In educational institutions, the LMS-mediated distance of an online-learning environment may be delivered on a pad, but it is still likely to be spaced out over time. This is not an undesirable situation, as spacing is a necessary component of any suitably complex learning (Thalheimer, 2006). However, this is largely context-independent learning, and there is another opportunity.

A framework that informs the picture of particular forms of learning is that of performance support. Popularized by Gery (1995), the notion is of bringing information into the performance context that improves the ability of the individual to perform the task. Although this clearly is not learning in the traditional sense, it is possible that the learner can use that contextualized information to make connections and learn individually. Moreover, as Gery postulated, additional information could be provided to turn the performance instance into a learning moment (although, to date, that opportunity has been missed).

The point is to recognize that support for immediate performance is one form of mobile assistance, and learning is another. However, ideally, they are linked. There will be learning separate from performance, and vice versa, but, if there is performance, there is an opportunity for learning as well.

To unpack the forms of learning that will likely be found within the definition, and the basis for looking forward, we need to consider how the device situates in an overall context. There will be situations where the mobile device is merely a conduit for accessing learning, but more active roles are possible. To consider these, however, we need to invoke another framework.

The Four Cs

Referring again to the definition "learning across multiple contexts, through social and content interactions, using personal electronic devices," we see a specific mention of content and social interactions. The fundamental affordances of mobile have been proposed as the Four Cs (Quinn, 2011a): the consumption of *content*, interaction with *compute* capabilities, the ability to *communicate* with others, and the *capture* of our context (via video and/or audio, orientation, location, time, and increasingly more data; see Figure 8.2). An implicit fifth C is *combinations* of the above. In contrast to the definition in Chapter 1, here it is argued that it is important to separate pure consumption from interaction as distinct capabilities, as consumption at an appropriate time, in context, can be valuable without interaction.

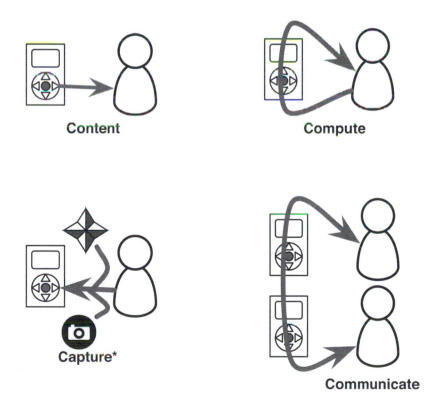

Figure 8.2 Four Cs of Mobile

Also necessarily separated, at this point, are performance support and formal learning. Despite the fact that there is, or can be, a continuum, we do different things to support each. Content for learning, by and large, is different for formal learning versus performance support. Organizations, at least, need to consider both. However, going forward, we should be mindful of what can and should be "in the head" and what can be in the world (via a device).

Augmenting

The common theme here is *augmentation*. In all cases, we're augmenting the learner/performer with resources, and augmenting the context for the learner or performance. To put it another way, m-learning is not about courses on a mobile device, but instead about augmenting several things. First, m-learning is about mobile performance support, ensuring a good outcome occurs, when necessary, whether the performer is really fully skilled or not. This can be also turned into a learning experience.

M-learning is also about augmenting a formal learning experience, or augmenting a performance experience to be a learning experience. We can extend the learning experience over time, which is a powerful support for ensuring that learning is retained, by reactivating that knowledge and reapplying it. We can also reactivate and contextualize by showing where and how that information plays out in the world.

The requirements for augmentation are severalfold. The goal is to provide the right resources, at the right time, to the right place and the right person. In many ways, this is related to work in the intelligent-tutoring-systems or artificial-intelligence and education field, where models of the domain, the learner, and the pedagogy were needed (c.f. Ohlsson, 1986). To adapt learning to the context, we need models of context. To adapt learning to the learner, we need models of the learner. To adapt the experience, we need to have a model of the resources at hand. And we may well need a model of the learner's tasks or goals in the context. Then, we will require a mechanism to adapt, making the pedagogy explicit (see Figure 8.3).

The definition of these models will include rules of pedagogy, we will stipulate, but ultimately may be derived from empirical results derived from analytics. To work at scale, such systems will also need to refer to individuals and content by description, requiring semantic tagging and taxonomies. These are the building blocks with which solutions can be assembled.

We will build on this broader definition of m-learning, but, to do so, we need to visit the current trends.

STATE OF PLAY

To look to the future, we must establish the present and the trajectory. In short, we are seeing convergence in devices, growth in penetration, and increase in capabilities.

As mentioned, the devices are getting more powerful and converging, and, in software, there is similar convergence. Most devices cannot succeed if they do not have the basic personal-information-management suite of apps—contacts or addresses, notebook or memos, calendar or events, and tasks or to-dos—that characterized the first successful mass-market mobile device, the Palm Pilot.

Devices typically have a browser and then the ability to run a suite of applications from a library of same. Even the so-called "feature phone" (the ordinary cellphone, as

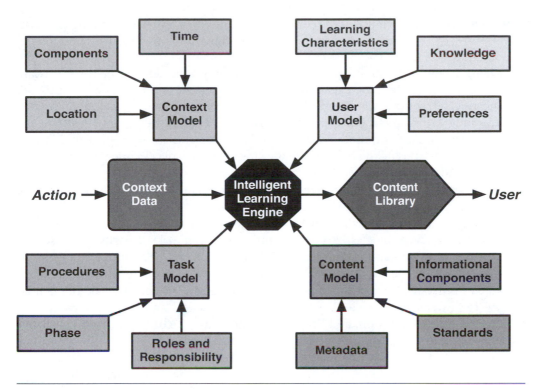

Figure 8.3 Adaptive Models

opposed to the smartphone, which really is an app-phone) now has a camera, screen, and a Web browser (over 85 percent of new handsets in 2011 will be able to access the mobile Web; in Europe and the US, 90 percent already possess such a phone; mobiThinking, 2012). Of course, the phone capability is independent of whether or not the user has access to, or has purchased, a data plan.

The penetration of these devices is growing. Globally, mobile subscriptions are at 86.7 percent; in developed nations, that's 117.8 percent (more subscriptions than eligible subscribers!), and even in developing nations, the penetration rate is 78.8 percent (International Telecommunications Union, 2011). Additionally, the developing world and global numbers have more than doubled over the past 5 years.

Use of mobile data is growing, too. There are now 1.2 billion mobile Web users (17 percent penetration, to date), with a 45 percent annual growth rate. Further, mobile Web subscriptions outpace fixed broadband at a 2:1 ratio (mobiThinking, 2012). The interest in digital data is increasing.

Beyond the devices, the market for software is also growing. Although apps can be developed for non-smartphones, the markets for smartphone and PDA apps are substantial: 300,000 apps have been developed in just over three years, and downloads, already at 10.9 billion in 2010, are expected to rise to 76.9 billion by 2014 (IDC, 2010).

Trends

What to make of all these statistics? Simply, that mobile is not going away. Further, we are seeing societal changes around mobile devices. Putting a phone on a table and turning it off signifies the importance of the conversation. Shopping patterns are being changed. The uptake of phones, smartphones, and apps signals a growing awareness of the opportunities on tap.

Other developments more specific to m-learning are the development of software platforms enabling the new capabilities. Although the developments are continual, significant changes are afoot. The performance problems with Adobe's Flash on mobile devices, long the Web standard for cross-platform advanced development, led to the abandonment of Flash on mobile devices, and HTML5 (the latest HyperText Markup Language standard) is taking off. Despite the cross-platform development barriers, tools are multiplying to support just these issues.

Related developments are important contributors. Semantics and analytics are taking off. WICHE Cooperative for Educational Technologies has received a grant to do advanced analytics from the Bill and Melinda Gates Foundation (WICHE Cooperative for Educational Technologies, 2011). Semantics has been at least partly addressed by work on learning standards (e.g., Quinn, 2000), and other work continues: tagging is possible within the Department of Defense's interoperable learning content standard, Standard Courseware Object Reference Model (SCORM); systems such as Augmented Reality for Interactive Storytelling (ARIS, 2012) provide frameworks for describing context-specific information; and Project Tin Can (Rustici, 2012) is providing a richer picture of defining a learning path, in a simple framework.

One other relevant factor is the rise in data collection. Anything done via a service, and services form the backbone of many mobile apps as the devices are still somewhat limited in capability, means that the actions of a mobile user are tracked. Although concerns for privacy are appropriate, there are certainly ways in which these data can be useful. Records of learner actions can be a rich source of data for reflection (Schauble, Raghavan, & Glaser, 1993).

The New Normal

The capabilities described are already leading to new visions of m-learning possibilities. Two major examples are the rise of the two "a" realities: augmented reality and alternate reality. These two developments bring new meaning to the notion of augmenting.

Augmented reality is where information is layered on top of the world, typically via a digital device. A common example is where the camera transmits a picture onto the screen, but the computer adds requested information on top of the image and adjusts the information relative to where the camera is pointing. So, for example, a user could ask for information about restaurants and pan the camera to see what restaurants were in which direction. The system uses the location of the device via the GPS and the direction being faced via compass, together with the information desired, and then can combine that information on top of the image from the camera. The educational applications include layering on context-sensitive information on top of the particular context.

Alternate reality is a notion of a separate universe. For mobile, this plays out as alternate reality games, whereby a fictitious reality is proposed in a way that intrudes upon the regular world. Typically, a story is created that then must be pursued by following clues and making decisions about actions. With the appearance of real events, by virtue of the game mechanics leaving real-world traces, such as Web pages, phone calls, e-mail, text messages, and more, the trail of the virtual world can be discovered and followed.

Although generally pursued for entertainment purposes, such stories can also be designed, as can other games (Quinn, 2005), for educational purposes.

These capabilities serve as the final piece to start looking at what can, will, and should happen in the future of m-learning.

GOING FORWARD

The task from here is to infer from the devices, trends, and emergent capabilities where mobile can be going. The task is to dive deeper, from a learning perspective, into those "seamless services, adaptive services, and context-aware services" (Yang, Zhang, & Chen, 2007) cited in Chapter 1. To do so, it is useful to examine what could be missing from the aforementioned elements.

What's Missing

Although content, computing, communication, and capture are valuable components, it is the important combinations that move the components from information to a learning experience. We need to explore the missing elements to consider how a learning experience could be construed, and then consider the mobile possibilities. Although augmenting formal learning is possible, an alternative is beginning to move formal learning away from the classroom, and also what would be distributed.

Abstracting the traditional classroom models of textbook, quizzes, exams, and instructor, a revised approach is to consider that the learning roles are information resources, formative and summative assessment, and mentor role (see Figure 8.4). The mentor role moves from lecturer to learning facilitator, as we advance our pedagogical model upon this model, and we shift from textbooks to rich media resources, formative assessment to meaningful practice, and summative assessment to a rich picture of learner performance. These are not unique to mobile, until we rethink the mechanisms for meaningful practice. We can decouple all of these from arbitrary locations and start connecting them to contextual locations.

Making Thinking Visible

Looking at models for learning, one of the top components is focusing on thinking skills, not just knowledge. What is key to success is making thinking, and learning, visible (Collins, Brown, & Holum, 1991). Learners need to be given meaningful tasks, attempt them alone or together, and watch others performing as well. Modeled examples, reciprocal practice, and scaffolded performance are critical. Contextualizing this performance, both in terms of what really happens in the world, and where, is a powerful learning opportunity (Quinn, 2004).

Learning traces can be not just semantic, but episodic (Rumelhart & Norman, 1988). Most of the information typically layered on via augmented reality is just semantic information, information "about." Layering on episodic information, traces of others' problem-solving made visible in the world, would be the mobile equivalent of Palincsar and Brown's reciprocal teaching (1984), and Schoenfeld's (1992) modeling of examples. You could see expert performances or novices.

Similarly, the underlying thinking behind things as disparate as advertisements, sports, architecture, and more could be made visible. Strategic decisions could be annotated. Similarly to the way first down lines are layered on television images of football, the

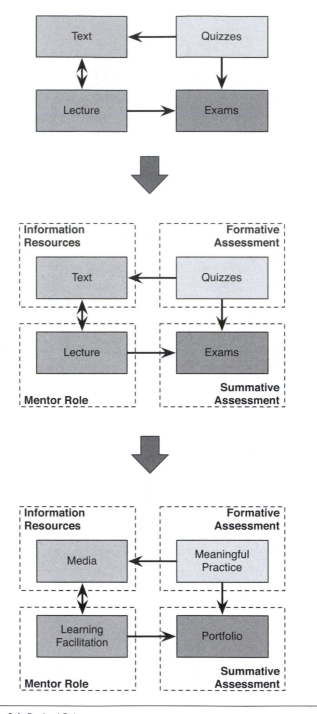

Figure 8.4 Revised Roles

placement of a billboard, the batter information, or the sightlines of a building could be displayed.

The point is to go beyond just putting semantic information in the world, and start exposing the underlying thinking that drives choices, to make that information available for inspection and learning. Just as reading someone's blog posts and following their tweets can allow you to follow their thinking, having them serve as "stealth mentors," so too can having the thoughts laid out on a site or event provide learnable insight. Both experts' and learners' paths could be made available.

This information can provide both performance support, showing invisible features or issues, and also learning, when the associated thinking is attached. Connecting both of these is an even richer experience. Moreover, individuals who so desire can choose to follow just what they are interested in. So, if someone is only interested in the outcome, just as a GPS shows you how to get somewhere, they can choose only to have support. If they want to learn, and currently GPS devices do not do this, they could also or only access geographic, demographic, or other geographical information systems (GIS) data to help understand the locale. The notion is that the individual can choose to perform, learn, or both.

Meta-Learning

Going beyond performance support and formal learning, there's also an opportunity for meta-learning, talking about relationships, systematicity, and more (e.g., Flavell, 1976). Ultimately, the ability to layer learning and meta-learning on top of performance support and around the events in one's life constitutes a version of m-learning very different from the notion of context-independent learning happening in free moments of time at convenient locations (see Figure 8.5). We can then provide information for any combination of performance support, learning, and meta-learning.

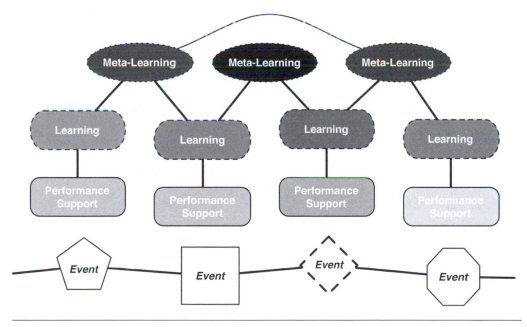

Figure 8.5 Layers of Learning

We can use the model of exposing information to start making comparisons. We can expose the learner's path to an expert's or other learners' paths for reflection, or just annotate those paths.

So, for example, we might have media files, such as podcasts or vidcasts, and documents including text and graphics, available on or through a mobile device. Connected to formal learning assessment in class or otherwise, these elements can constitute components of a learning experience and are valuable. In context, these can be great support for turning a contextual setting or event into a learning experience as well, by presenting relevant explanatory models, for example. For performance support, we might provide job aids, or troubleshooting videos, or voice-over task guides. For meta-learning, we can have concepts about good searches, videos on systematicity, or audio stories of instances of learning to learn (see Figure 8.6).

Assessment is required for formal learning and requires learner action. This goes beyond content consumption and, instead, is characterized as computation on the part of the device. The learner interacts with the system, expressing choices and decisions, and receives feedback. For performance support, the tools available are task-focused, whether to read and process data, or manage decision trees. For learning to learn, they might provide optimized help support tools, or allow learners to request their own or others' search processes.

Reaching out to someone at a point of need could be for expert support in the case of performance support, peer collaboration for either performance support or formal learning, or mentor support in formal learning or meta-learning.

Finally, contextual support can be in the form of capturing context to share for assistance, or providing specific help. Formal learning capture can be for learners to capture the local context for reflection or sharing, for creating media representations, as well as to layer on context-specific learning content. And for meta-learning, context-sensitive information could be to capture learner explorations.

	Performance Support	Formal Learning	Meta-Learning
Content	job aids, demonstrations	introductions, concepts, examples	learning guides, path capture
Compute	checklists, decision trees, calculators	practice: simulations, quizzes	interactive learning guides
Communicate	experts, peers	mentors, peers	learning mentors, approach collaborators
Capture	context capture	performance capture, representations	learner paths, processes

Figure 8.6 Models of Mobile

There would be filters to support under which conditions you might receive this information, on which devices, and for what subjects. The notion, however, is to augment the world in ways that support the development of us in the ways we wish to be developed.

In addition, the goal is to view the learning in the context of an "experience." We can make this learning work in the form of game, tuning the experience until it achieves the status of "hard fun." Pine and Gilmore (1999) have argued that we are currently in an "experience" economy and suggest that the next economy will be one that delivers a transformative experience. Here, we have that opportunity.

Learning Experience

Pulling together the notions of augmenting performance and learning, of supporting contextual learning, of making thinking visible, and making learning engaging, what might the experience look like?

Speculatively, the experience would ideally recognize the activity of the learner, both by location (GPS) and intended activity (calendar) and, then, by looking at the learner's learning path and current status, provide some engaging preparatory material designed to engage the learner's interest and set a goal a bit beyond his/her reach. A video might come in that sets the stage for a way to make this event more fun and meaningful, and guise the information in the form of a briefing or some other game element. The world might be annotated with information relevant to the decision-making, connecting to frameworks that either have been introduced or presented in the briefing, and then the learner can check with the device or make choices. Afterward, the learner could be connected with a mentor for both a learning and meta-learning review, with the learner's actions made visible as well.

This could play out in many ways, of course, depending on context, available resources, learner preferences, domain, and more. It could be a social activity, experts could be available, it could be not necessarily a game, if the learner were motivated enough, but just the information, and more. Even false events could be created as games to create learning opportunities, when insufficient such events are naturally occurring in the learner's current context.

CONCLUSION

This model has several benefits. The first is that the learner's experience is customized to the learner's goals. It may be that some collision detection and resolution are necessary, if several learner goals are relevant to the current moment, or a mechanism for integration. Yet, overall, the learning is layered across the learner's trajectory, not interrupting the learner for learning.

The second is that the learning can occur at the learner's own rate. Rather than try to force too much into a particular event, as with a face-to-face or online course, or have the learning experience stretch out too long, the learning experience can be more closely tailored to the rate at which learners can accommodate information. This is not unique to the mobile environment, but is more easily accomplished by achieving learner interaction in finer granularity.

The point is that the ubiquitous information environment is moving the learner along trajectories of development across the learner's events, not coupled to a classroom.

The formal learning both becomes more tightly linked to, and extends through, the learner's life. Ultimately, the experience becomes a continual partnership for development between learner and device, an individual personal mentor on tap, everywhere and everywhen.

REFERENCES

ARIS. (2012). Augmented reality and interactive storytelling. Retrieved from: http://arisgames.org/

Collins, A., Brown, J. S., & Holum, A. (1991) Cognitive apprenticeship: Making thinking visible. *American Educator*, 6–11, 38–46.

Crompton, H. (2013). A historical overview of mobile learning: Toward learner-centered education (pp. 3–14). In Z. Berge, & L. Muilenburg (Eds.), *Handbook of mobile learning*. New York: Routledge.

Flavell, J. H. (1976). Metacognitive aspects of problem solving. In L. B. Resnick (Ed.), *The nature of intelligence* (pp. 231–236). Hillsdale, NJ: Erlbaum

Garg, A. (2011). Tablet learning—Neither mobile learning nor elearning. Upside Learning Blog. Retrieved from: www.upsidelearning.com/blog/index.php/2011/11/29/tablet-learning-neither-mobile-learning-nor-elearning/

Gery, G. (1995). *Electronic performance support systems: How and why to remake the workplace through the strategic application of technology*. Toland, MA: Gery Performance Press.

IDC. (2010). IDC forecasts worldwide mobile applications revenues to experience more than 60% compound annual growth through 2014. Retrieved from: www.idc.com/about/viewpressrelease.jsp?containerId=prUS22617910

International Telecommunications Union. (2011). Key global telecom indicators for the world telecommunication service sector. Retrieved from: www.itu.int/ITU-D/ict/statistics/at_glance/KeyTelecom.html

mobiThinking. (2012). Global mobile statistics 2012: All quality mobile marketing research, mobile Web stats, subscribers, ad revenue, usage, trends. Retrieved from http://mobithinking.com/mobile-marketing-tools/latest-mobile-stats

Ohlsson, S. (1986). Some principles of intelligent tutoring. *Instructional Science*, 14(3–4), 293–326.

PalmSource. (2003). The Zen of Palm. Retrieved from: www.accessdevnet.com/docs/zenofpalm/Enlightenment.html

Palincsar, A. S., & Brown, A. L. (1984). Reciprocal teaching of comprehension-fostering and monitoring activities. *Cognition and Instruction*, 1, 117–175.

Pine, B. J. & Gilmore, J. H. (1999). *The experience economy: Work is theatre and every business a stage*. Cambridge, MA: Harvard Business School Press.

Quinn, C. N. (2000). Learning objects and instruction components. *Educational Technology & Society*, 3(2), 13–20. Retrieved from: www.ifets.info/journals/3_2/discuss_summary_0200.pdf

Quinn, C. (2004). Learning at large: Situating learning in the bigger picture of action in the world. *Educational Technology Magazine*, 44(4), 45–49. Englewood Cliffs, NJ: Educational Technology Publications.

Quinn, C. (2005). *Engaging learning: Designing e-learning simulation games*. San Francisco, CA: Pfeiffer.

Quinn, C. (2011a). *Designing mLearning: Tapping into the mobile revolution for organizational performance*. San Francisco, CA: Pfeiffer.

Quinn, C. (2011b). Intimacy & immediacy. Learnlets. Retrieved from: http://blog.learnlets.com/?p=2253

Quinn, C. (2012). *The mobile academy: mLearning for higher education*. San Francisco, CA: Jossey-Bass.

Rainte, L. (2012). Tablet and e-book reader ownership nearly double over the holiday gift-giving period. Retrieved from: www.pewInternet.org/Reports/2012/E-readers-and-tablets.aspx?src=prc-headline

Rumelhart, D. E., & Norman, D. A. (1988). Representation in memory. In R. C. Atkinson, J. J. Herrnstein, G. Lindzey, & R. D. Luce (Eds.), *Handbook of experimental psychology*. New York: Wiley.

Rustici (2012). Project Tin Can. Retrieved from: http://scorm.com/tincan/

Schauble, L., Raghavan, K., & Glaser, R. (1993). The discovery and reflection notation: A graphical trace for supporting self-regulation in computer-based laboratories. In S. Lajoie & S. Derry (Eds.), *Computers as cognitive tools* (pp. 319–337). Hillsdale, NJ: Erlbaum.

Schoenfeld, A. H. (1992). Learning to think mathematically: Problem-solving, metacognition, and sense-making in mathematics. In D. Grouws, (Ed.), *Handbook for research on mathematics teaching and learning*. New York: MacMillan.

Thalheimer, W. (2006). *Spacing learning events over time: What the research says*. Boston, MA: Work-Learning Research.

Wexler, S., Schlenker, B., Brown, J., Metcalf, D., Quinn, C., Thor, E., van Barneveld, A., & Wagner, E. (2007). *Research 360° Report on Mobile Learning*. Santa Rosa, CA: The eLearning Guild.

WICHE Cooperative for Educational Technologies (2011). WCET receives grant for groundbreaking higher education analytic research. Retrieved from: http://wcet.wiche.edu/advance/par-framework

9

SEAMLESS LEARNING

An International Perspective on Next-Generation Technology-Enhanced Learning

Marcelo Milrad, Lung-Hsiang Wong, Mike Sharples, Gwo-Jen Hwang, Chee-Kit Looi, and Hiroaki Ogata

THE EVOLUTION OF TECHNOLOGY-ENHANCED LEARNING

Personalized learning has been a goal for education during the past 40 years: to provide access to learning resources and activities that adapt to the needs and abilities of the learner (Dodd, Sime, & Kay, 1968). Mobile technologies can now offer adaptivity to the physical and social settings, and their use and adoption in education have generated a new approach for technology-enhanced learning (TEL) called mobile learning, or *m-learning* (Sharples, Milrad, Arnedillo Sánchez, & Vavoula, 2009). The rapid development of these technologies, combined with access to content in a wide variety of settings, allows learners to experience new learning situations beyond the classroom. Cross-contextual learning can enable a continuous learning experience across different settings, such as home–school, or workplace–college. This new view on TEL, supported by wireless technologies and ubiquitous computing, is termed ubiquitous learning or *u-learning* (Rogers & Price, 2006; Syvänen, Beale, Sharples, Ahonen, & Lonsdale, 2005). Although context is an important aspect of m-learning, it is the core concept of u-learning, owing to two important affordances of the learning environment, namely *context awareness* and *adaptivity*. By *context awareness*, we mean that the system providing pedagogical flow and content to the learning environment should be *aware* of the learners' situations. By *context adaptivity*, we mean that different learning contents should be adaptable to the particular settings in which the learners are situated.

Mobile and ubiquitous TELs offer the potential for a new phase in the evolution of the field, marked by a continuity of the learning experience across different learning settings. Chan and colleagues (Chan et al., 2006) use the term *"seamless learning"* to describe these new situations. Seamless learning implies that students can learn whenever they are curious, in a variety of situations. They can easily and quickly switch from one scenario to another, using their personal mobile device as a mediator, and can maintain the continuity of their learning across technologies and settings. These scenarios include learning individually, with another student, a small group, or a large online community, with possible involvement of teachers, relatives, experts, and members of other supportive communities, face to face or in different modes of interaction and at a distance, in places such as classrooms, outdoors, parks, and museums, or in cyberspace, such as in virtual worlds and social-networking spaces. Recent studies on seamless learning have been extending from teacher-facilitated classroom or outdoor learning into nurturing autonomous learners. Indeed, the ultimate motivation for learning scientists to promote seamless learning is to foster the habits of mind and abilities that support 21st-century skills among students (Anastopoulou et al., 2012). The aim is to design and enact not just episodic activities but ongoing programs, to gradually transform learners into more self-directed individuals being able to carry out learning tasks, not just anytime and anywhere, but perpetually and across contexts, with and without external facilitations. Mediated by technology, a seamless learner should be able to explore, identify, and seize boundless latent opportunities that his/her daily living spaces may offer, rather than always being inhibited by externally defined learning goals and resources (Wong, Chen, & Jan, in press). More research is certainly needed to improve our knowledge, to better facilitate the nurturing of seamless learners, as well as its technological support. It is necessary to further investigate how students interact with learning contents, peers, teachers, and parents through a variety of technologies and contexts (Wong & Looi, 2011).

The authors of this chapter bring together expertise in learning sciences and human–computer interaction to present and discuss the results of research experiences and projects conducted in Japan, Singapore, Sweden, Taiwan, and the United Kingdom. The main purpose of our current common efforts is to achieve synergy and research efficiency, especially in exploring and identifying how mobile technologies are nowadays shaping and creating innovative ways to share and construct information and knowledge in both formal and informal learning settings.

Our main contributions to this chapter are based on reflections upon our recent developments and experiences in Europe and in Asia regarding novel educational-design patterns, technologies, and tools to enhance learning. Having these points in mind, we propose and recommend possible directions for the design of future learning activities and technological solutions that can support seamless learning. To that end, we will discuss how the notion of *seamless learning* could be used to tackle some of the challenges our educational systems are facing in connection with the introduction of mobile technologies into classrooms settings, innovative educational practices, and sustainability.

CHARACTERIZING SEAMLESS LEARNING

The notion of *seamless learning* (Chan et al., 2006; Wong & Looi, 2011), which attempts to capture the opportunities for supporting learning across a variety of contexts offered by technological advancements in mobile computing and wireless communication, has been used for inspiring the efforts that will be described in detail later. These include learning outside the traditional classroom and learning across formal and informal contexts. The exploration of new physical contexts mediated by technologies certainly requires specific considerations about technological affordances, but also about the social and pedagogical arrangements for the activities. There are two main, important features that characterize seamless learning, namely, *seamless adaptivity* and *seamless connectivity*. Seamless adaptivity implies that the *technology adapts* to the learner without the learner being aware; for example, providing learning content or services that are appropriate to the learner and settings (in the learner's language, at the right level of difficulty, providing appropriate help, etc.). Seamless connectivity enables continuity of the learning experience by maintaining the learning across devices and settings, enabling learners to carry on where they left off, and to easily re-establish a learning activity from a previous time, by providing means to search back in time for a learning content or activity and then recall its context and connection.

Despite many promising TEL developments, such as the introduction of interactive whiteboards and personal (1:1) computing in the classroom, there is still a need to improve our knowledge in this field in order to better support the design of activities inspired by the educational qualities that have been identified in previous research related to seamless learning. For example, it is necessary to further investigate how students interact with learning materials, peers, teachers, and parents, through a variety of technologies and contexts (Looi et al., 2010). Wong and Looi (2011) have recently suggested 10 different dimensions characterizing activities for mobile-assisted seamless learning (MSL), as described below:

(MSL1)   encompassing formal and informal learning;
(MSL2)   encompassing personalized and social learning;
(MSL3)   across time;
(MSL4)   across locations;
(MSL5)   ubiquitous access to learning resources (online data and information, teacher-created materials, student artifacts, student online interactions, etc.);
(MSL6)   encompassing physical and digital worlds;
(MSL7)   combined use of multiple device types (including "stable" technologies such as desktop computers, interactive whiteboards);
(MSL8)   seamless switching between multiple learning tasks (such as data collection, analysis, and communication);
(MSL9)   knowledge synthesis (a combination of prior and new knowledge, multiple levels of thinking skills, and multidisciplinary learning);
(MSL10) encompassing multiple pedagogical or learning activity models.
                    (Wong & Looi, 2011; MSL5 as revised by Wong, 2012)

These 10 dimensions align well with many of the educational objectives and values expressed in national documents for schools in Taiwan, Singapore, Japan, Sweden, and the United Kingdom. The projects and activities described later will show how we have included these dimensions in relation to the design of the learning activities. It is important to mention that design considerations should also take into account the technological affordances and their functionalities that depend on the pedagogical and social features of the learning activities, as well as the characteristics of the subject matter. Within the subject domains of science, mathematics, and language learning, technological and pedagogical design choices have to be considered, not only with respect to the qualities described in the dimensions of MSL, but also with respect to the learning objectives of specific subject matters and the corresponding recommended learning trajectories.

CHALLENGES IN PEDAGOGICAL AND TECHNOLOGICAL DESIGN ASSOCIATED WITH SEAMLESS LEARNING

The vision of transforming learning practices with new technologies has not yet been fully crystalized, especially with regard to enabling learning and collaboration across contexts. The effort of designing effective computer support along with appropriate pedagogy and social practices is more complex than imagined (Stahl, 2002). There is no easy solution to the development of systems and technological tools to mediate autonomous and social learning in seamless-learning environments. Such technological solutions must be able to support individual learners in bridging their ongoing learning processes across contexts, as well as connecting multiple learners within the same learning community, but separated by time and (physical or digital) space. An even greater challenge lies in how to shift the epistemological beliefs of individual learners (as well as teachers who are to facilitate seamless learning) from absolutism and transmissionism to constructivism and socio-constructivism. This is because genuine seamless learning is about treating all the learning spaces and resources that learners have access to as ingredients to facilitate their ongoing self- and co-construction of knowledge, rather than believing in knowledge as composed of universal facts that are best learned through didactic teaching. Inquiry learning, distributed collaborative learning, authentic learning, and participatory learning are some of the approaches that can be enacted to nurture the habit of seamless learning in learners' minds.

Indeed, it is crucial for researchers and practitioners to find effective ways to design, implement, and evaluate innovative learning environments and technologies in a wide variety of learning settings. Some of the current design challenges faced by seamless-learning researchers and practitioners can be listed as follows:

- How to design seamless-learning activities that support innovative learning practices?
- How to design seamless-learning activities that integrate learning across informal and formal settings, with the eventual aim of nurturing autonomous learners?
- How to design learning activities that reflect the cultural diversity of learners?
- How to assess seamless learning in these new educational contexts?

Another significant issue pertains to the integration of software components in distributed environments (e.g., device- versus cloud-based) and also across a variety of software with new hardware and peripherals (e.g., sensors), as well as the support for content delivery and learner artifact creation on diverse types of device used across different *learning* contexts.

EXEMPLARS OF SEAMLESS-LEARNING ACTIVITIES IN ASIA AND EUROPE

During the last 5 years, we have been conducting research activities that explore new design approaches and innovative uses of social media, wireless, and mobile technologies in a variety of collaborative and inquiry-based learning settings (Hwang, Shi, & Chu, 2011; Hwang, Tsai, & Yang, 2008; Kurti, Spikol, & Milrad, 2008; Looi et al., 2010; Milrad et al., 2011; Ogata et al., 2010; Sharples, Taylor, & Vavoula, 2007; Wong, Chin, Tan, & Liu, 2010). Our approaches are not simply characterized by the provision of novel uses of rich digital media combined with mobile and wireless computational systems and tools, but also by the exploration of new and varied learning activities that become available when innovative approaches are applied for designing new technological solutions and utilizing existing ones to support seamless learning. This section presents a number of exemplars related to seamless-learning projects that show how learning can be supported across a variety of contexts, how students can be helped to explore the physical environment, and how mobile and ubiquitous technologies can be used to facilitate conversations for learning.

Inquiry-Based Seamless Learning Project in Taiwan

To investigate the effects of m-learning and assessment strategies on students' in-field inquiry activities, a 4-year national project was initiated in Taiwan in 2008 (Hwang & Tsai, 2011). In each year, there were nearly 1,500 students participating in the learning activities of this project. Figure 9.1 shows the Chiku ecological conservation area located in southern Taiwan, in which the learning activities were conducted for observing black-faced spoonbills, fiddler crabs, and mangroves (Hung, Lin, & Hwang, 2010). The learning activities were designed as an extension of the formal curriculum of elementary-school natural-science courses, to seamlessly integrate the learning experiences across various dimensions, including formal and informal learning contexts, individual and social learning, and physical world and cyberspace indicated by Wong and Looi (2011).

A three-stage, seamless-learning scaffolding process was provided to guide students to conduct extensive self-learning in the field (Hung, Lin, & Hwang, 2010). In the first stage, the students were guided to obtain background knowledge of the learning targets

Figure 9.1 M-Learning Activities Conducted in Chiku Ecological Conservation Area

Source: From Hung, Lin, & Hwang, 2010

by answering a series of structured questions based on the observations and interactions with the physical-world contexts. In the second stage, a set of open-ended questions was provided to guide the students to further observe and compare learning targets in the field. Moreover, they were asked to articulate their findings and propose questions accordingly. In the third stage, the students were encouraged to perform self-initiated learning by carrying out extended scientific explorations outdoors. It took 4 months for the students to experience the three-stage field trips. In each stage, the students were guided to observe, explore, and collect data in the field, one day per week. After each field trip, the students went back to the classroom and wrote digital learning diaries based on the progress and reflections on what they had observed and learned in the field.

During the field trips, each student was equipped with a mobile device, a telescope, and a digital camera for accessing the supplementary materials, taking notes, observing the learning targets, and collecting data. Moreover, they were encouraged to raise questions and discuss with peers. The collected data were uploaded to a workstation for analysis of the ecology of the area. A scale was proposed to assess students' inquiry performance based on the amount, accuracy, and quality of the observation records and questions raised during the m-learning process. From the experimental results, the students were categorized into different mastery levels, as follows: the basic-level students who took few records with rough descriptions, the master-level students who took many records with average quality, and the advanced-level students who took many records with high quality and detailed descriptions. Based on the findings, some differentiated remedial instructions and learning activities were provided for individual students. It was found that the approach was more effective than traditional in-field learning activities in improving students' learning achievement, motivation, and attitudes (Hwang, Wu, & Ke, 2011).

The Personal-Inquiry Project in the United Kingdom

The Personal-Inquiry (PI) project, a collaboration between the Open University and the University of Nottingham, helped young people aged 11–14 to understand themselves and their world through a scientific process of active inquiry. It addressed the need for young people to understand scientific methods and discourses by acting as scientists, carrying out personally meaningful scientific investigations. A computer toolkit, named nQuire, was designed to enable "scripted-inquiry" learning, where scripts are dynamic software guides, implemented on personal devices such as netbooks and smartphones, that support a continuity of learning between formal and informal settings. In a typical investigation, young learners started in the classroom, investigating a topic online, developing shared inquiry questions, and proposing methods of investigation, supported by the teacher. They used the nQuire software to plan what types of data to collect, ranging from social surveys to data probes, and how to organize the results. Then, at home, in the playground, or outdoors, they collected the data individually or in small groups, with the software providing data checking and visualizations. Back in the classroom, they shared and compared results, producing group presentations that addressed the inquiry questions. Here, management of the learning passed from the software back to the teacher, who could view the individual and group results and assisted the pupils in interpreting the findings and reflecting on the inquiry process. This seamless transition between learning within and outside the classroom was assisted by a shared representation of the inquiry process (Figure 9.2).

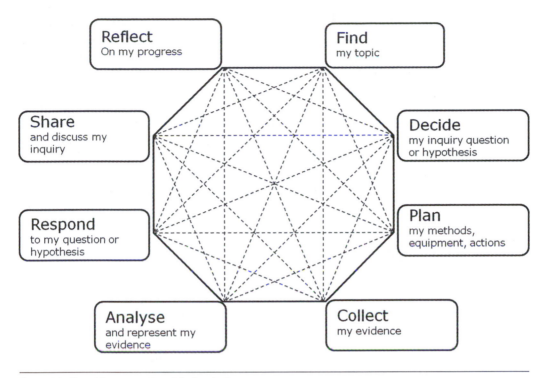

Figure 9.2 Shared Representation of the Inquiry Process

Source: From Anastopoulou et al., 2012

It functioned as a classroom aid (one teacher displayed a version as a large poster on the wall of the science classroom), a home page for the nQuire application, and a list of menu items on the main nQuire screen for selection of phases of the current inquiry. An authoring component of nQuire enabled a teacher or educational designer to select, author, and modify the scripts and to monitor and guide the student activity.

Six school-based trials were conducted to evaluate this combination of technology and pedagogy on topics of: urban heat islands (twice), heart rate and fitness, microclimates, healthy eating, sustainability, and effect of noise pollution on birds. Results that compared outcomes with those of a control class showed a positive effect on learning outcomes and a maintained enjoyment of science lessons. Interviews with participants across the trials provided evidence of increased understanding of the inquiry learning process, by children and teachers alike (Anastopoulou et al., 2012).

The Geometry Mobile Project in Sweden

Geometry Mobile (GEM) is an on-going m-learning project in the field of mathematics, trying to find alternative ways to support the learning of geometry using mobile and positioning technologies (Sollervall et al., 2011). The project brings together a group of researchers from Linnaeus University in the fields of media technology and mathematics education, working very closely with teachers and schools. The activities involved in this project are related to inquiry-based geometric learning tasks involving transitions between different contexts, including outdoors and classroom tasks. The focus is not only on the appropriation of technologies used within a specific learning context, but also on how the appropriated technologies support these transitions, and in particular how they enable effective communication of mathematical strategies. Our motivation has been to design learning activities that stimulated students' enactive modes of action by putting special focus on spatial orientation, while minimizing features related to spatial visualization.

Guided by design-based research and the notion of seamless learning, we have designed and implemented a series of learning activities in mathematics where mobile and Web technologies support transitions between outdoor and indoor learning contexts (Nilsson, Sollervall, & Spikol, 2010; Sollervall et al., 2011; Sollervall & Milrad, 2012). The students' initiatives during the self-regulated outdoor part of the activity are scaffolded by the use of mobile technologies and activity prompts, which provide means and demands for data collection, measurements, and on-the-spot oral and visual recordings of the groups' experiences and strategies. These efforts are carried out as a sequence of activities distributed across different contexts, according to the following:

- introduction and instrumentation;
- self-regulated outdoor activity;
- presentation and discussion of results in the classroom;
- problem-solving using interactive visualizations (Web visualizations and augmented reality).

These activities draw on the use of GPS technology, available in a mobile device. The research team has developed a set of mobile applications that allow students to measure distances between their own devices and mobile devices held by other students, as well as to collect data and record audio annotations. The data collected by these mobile applications are stored in a central repository for using later in the classroom. A Web-based geo-visualization tool and an augmented-reality application are used back in the classroom to visualize and reflect upon the activities conducted in the field.

Since 2010, we have been running these activities with five classes from four different elementary schools in our region. By participating in the activity, the students are offered opportunities to experience geometrical constructions in full-sized space. Specifically, they are stimulated to make use of their orientation ability, which differs cognitively from the visualization ability that is more commonly used to solve similar tasks in school. These kinds of learning activity offer the participating students enacted experiences of school geometry that are not commonly offered in school contexts (Sollervall, Otero, Milrad, Vogel, & Johansson, 2012).

The outdoor explorations, the use of mobile technologies, and the distribution of the activity across time and locations pose didactical as well as technological challenges that call for careful considerations regarding the design of the activity (Sollervall et al., 2012). The different learning tasks being distributed across time and locations means they fulfill 2 of the 10 dimensions (MSL3 and MSL4) characterizing MSL, as described earlier. We will discuss the dimensions of MSL in relation to these activities in further detail in the last section.

Sustainable Seamless Learning in a Singapore Primary School
Code-named "SEAMLESS Project," our longitudinal study of school-based research with a primary school in Singapore is now into its 5th year. In this project, we explore, apply, and refine the notion of seamless learning to design, as well as study, the integrated and

synergistic effects of learning in both formal and informal settings (Looi et al., 2010). Learning is distributed across different learning processes (emergent or planned), as well as across different spaces (in or out of class), as shown in Figure 9.3. Type I refers to planned learning in classrooms, and Type II means planned learning outside of school environments, such as field trips. Type III refers to emergent learning happening outside of school, mostly driven by learners' interests and initiatives. Finally, Type IV means emergent learning in class, such as unplanned teachable moments and serendipitous learning (Chen, Seow, So, Toh, & Looi, 2010). Mobile devices are used as mediating tools to facilitate the seamless integration of these different types of learning space.

We revised and *mobilized* 2 years' worth of the national curriculum for Primary 3 and 4 Science, which seeks to extend learning activities beyond the classroom from Type I to Types II, III, and IV (Zhang et al., 2010). To support the long-term learning activities, 34 students from the experimental class were each assigned a smartphone with 24/7 access, in order to mediate a variety of learning activities, such as in-class small-group activities, field trips, data collection and geo-tagging in the neighborhood, home-based experiments involving parents, online information search and peer discussions, and digital student artifact creation, among others. We carried out an ethnographic study of six students to explore the linkages of their learning and lived-in practices across these types of learning. Learning experiences are deepened when a virtuous cycle is created, where the students can establish continuity of experiences, connecting both the formal and informal learning spaces (Chen et al., 2010).

A separate thread of research, which stems from this seamless-learning research and which has grown into a distinct research program of its own, is the design of seamless learning for Chinese language learning. The "Move, Idioms!" (Wong et al., 2010) and the MyCLOUD (Wong, Chai, Chin, Hsieh, & Liu, 2012) projects seek to leverage mobile

	Planned	Emergent
Out of class	*Type II* **Planned learning out of class** E.g. Field trip to a heritage site which is part of the school curriculum	*Type III* **Emergent learning out of class** E.g. using mobile phones to capture pictures and video clips of animals and directed by self-interest
In class	*Type I* **Planned learning in class** E.g. Searching for answers in the classroom or using tools on the phone to create mind maps	*Type IV* **Emergent learning in class** E.g. Teachable moments not planned by the teacher

Figure 9.3 Matrix of Learning Spaces
Source: Adapted from So, Kim and Looi, 2008

technologies to mediate and support assimilation of language learning into the learners' daily life, followed by deep learning through personalized and social meaning making in the online-learning space.

Learning by Logging Project in Japan

Our current research focuses on how to capture learning experiences in our daily life, then share and reuse them for future learning. We have developed a ubiquitous learning log system called SCROLL (System for Capturing and Reminding of Learning Log) (Ogata et al., 2010). A ubiquitous learning log (ULL) is defined as a digital record of what the learner has learned in his/her daily life using ubiquitous technologies. It allows the logging of his or her learning experiences, with photos, audios, videos, location, quick-response (QR) code, RFID tags, and sensor data, and the sharing and reuse of the ULL with others. Using SCROLL, learners can receive personalized quizzes and answers for their specific questions. Also, they can navigate and be aware of their past ULLs, supported by an augmented-reality view. SCROLL supports learning in formal and informal contexts, both individual and collaborative, in the physical world and in cyberspace, using multiple devices such as desktop computers and Android tablets, PCs, and smartphones, and for multidisciplinary domains (Wong and Looi, 2011). Figure 9.4 illustrates the learning processes in the "learning by logging" model, called LORE (log–organize–recall–evaluate), and the system components, called the 4R model (record–regulate–remind–refine) (Ogata et al., 2011):

1. Log what the learner has learned: When the learner faces a problem in the daily life, s/he may learn some knowledge by him/herself, or ask others for help in terms of questions. The system records what s/he learned during this process as a ULL Object (ULLO).
2. Organize the ULL: When the learner tries to add a ULLO, the system compares it with other ULLOs, categorizes it, and shows if similar ULLOs exist. By matching similar objects, the knowledge structure can be regulated and organized.
3. Recall the ULL: The learner may forget what s/he has learned before. Rehearsal and practice can help the learner to recall past ULLOs and to shift them from short-term memory to the long-term one. Therefore, the system assigns some quizzes and reminds the learner of past ULLOs.

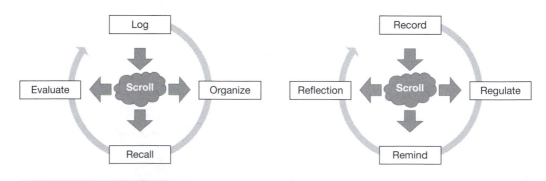

Figure 9.4 LORE (Left) and 4R Model (Right) for Learning by Logging

4. Evaluate: It is important to recognize what and how a learner has learned by analyzing the past ULL, so that the learner can improve what and how to learn in the future. Therefore, the system refines and adapts the organization of the ULLOs based on the learners' evaluation and reflection.

Based on the above models, Web and Android OS versions of the SCROLL system have been developed. An initial experiment has been conducted in an English course at university level in order to entwine vocabularies learned in class and out of class using the system.

DISCUSSION AND CONCLUSIONS

The five seamless-learning projects presented in this chapter exemplify diversified possibilities for designing for, facilitating, and practicing such a learning approach. The learning design applied in all five projects not only involves cross-time (MSL3), cross-locational (MSL4) activities, but also encompasses formal and informal learning settings (MSL1), personalized and social learning (MSL2), and physical and digital worlds (MSL6). However, if MSL1, MSL2, and MSL6 are conceptualized as three continua, then the five learning designs are in fact exhibiting varied emphases between the three respective pairs of poles. The different learning activities were designed for, and implemented in, formal and informal educational contexts, and we argue that they contain several features with strong impact for broadening students' learning experiences, both beyond the activities themselves and also beyond the learning context in which they take place. In a formal, school context, the flow of learning is controlled and supported by the teacher, whereas the learner him/herself becomes primarily responsible for his/her learning in informal contexts. As noted by Wong and Looi (2011), the "learners need to be engaged in an enculturation process to transform their existing epistemological beliefs, attitudes and methods of learning."

An analysis on the five reported learning designs with respect to the 10 MSL dimensions introduced earlier may result in the GEM and the SCROLL projects being placed at two different ends of a spectrum, while the other three projects are situated somewhere in the middle. The GEM project is more oriented to formal learning and social learning (MSL1 and MSL2), as the entire learning process is facilitated by the teacher and takes place at designated times and locations, with a group of learners learning together, face to face. The "learning by logging" activities in the SCROLL project are largely (individual) learner-driven and occur in formal and informal learning settings. In other words, the SCROLL system is intended to support highly personalized learning, while social learning is achieved in an indirect manner (e.g., reusing other learners' ULL). What is similar in both projects is the MSL6 dimension—both are employing augmented reality (certainly a technology that bridges the physical and digital worlds) in their technological solutions, which serve as the *enablers* of the respective learning activities (without the technology, such activities could not be carried out at all).

In between, the learning-process designs in the inquiry-based seamless-learning project in Taiwan, the PI project in the United Kingdom, and the SEAMLESS project in Singapore exhibit a similar learning flow pattern characterized by: (1) teacher-facilitated classroom activities, (2) out-of-class individual or small-group activities, (3) online or in-class data sharing or peer learning, and (4) in-class consolidation activities.

The three projects attempt to strike a balance between learning in formal and informal, and personalized and social, settings. The SEAMLESS project places a greater emphasis on leveraging 1:1, 24/7 access to the mobile devices for learner-initiated, personalized data collection in learners' own free time. The Taiwanese project focuses on teacher-facilitated field trips as the only means of data collection. The PI project ran a series of studies that connected classrooms with a range of formal and informal settings for data collection, including home, playground, fitness center, discovery center, and city street. In terms of MSL6, the three projects do encompass learning in physical and digital worlds. However, the digital technologies employed by these projects (with the affordances of data capturing and processing, student artifact creations, online discussions, etc.) serve as the *enhancers* of the learning activities, and the physical and digital-based learning aspects of the activities are not as tightly coupled as in GEM and SCROLL. That is, such seamless-learning processes could still be carried out without digital technologies. However, it is the technologies that vastly enhance the learners' learning experience and learning effectiveness across multiple spaces.

In essence, the similarities and variations across the five learning designs we have analyzed above are perhaps the result of the diversified research goals and the specific nature of the subject matters that have been addressed in these projects. However, the salient seamless-learning features, as encapsulated in the 10-dimensional model, are still exhibited by these learning designs. The formal education system all over the world has long been dominated by the instructionist and transmissionist views of learning, which carry the notion that knowledge can be decomposed into isolated basic elements and be transferred separately to the learners. Instead, the notion of seamless learning emphasizes "chain effects" across learning spaces that contribute to building learning progressively across contexts and time, using mobile technologies for augmenting human semantic and episodic memories by capturing and connecting previous learning activities and content, and to adapting the learning to the learner's current physical, social, and educational setting. Such a disposition is congruent with Sharples' (2009) assertion that, "it may not be possible to determine when the learning begins and ends" (p. 19).

Goodyear (2011) claims that we are facing two perceptible changes in the field of educational research. The first is a shift in our sense of the spaces and contexts in which education takes place, as different learning activities are becoming more commonly distributed across a variety of contexts. The second change is a wider understanding with regard to the conception of educational praxis, acknowledging the growing importance of design. Addressing these two challenges calls for new integrated-design approaches for technology-enhanced learning. One of the major challenges of today's education is no longer about finding the best ways for knowledge delivery, but, rather, designing, developing, and implementing interactive learning experiences and activities for learners to construct knowledge by engaging and inspiring them to learn. We believe that the notions and concrete examples presented in this chapter represent a step forward towards achieving such goals. Seamless-learning activities of the type illustrated in this chapter, which are highly self-regulated and involve collaboration and communication with peers, can contribute to preparing students for a future that requires them to take initiatives, be creative, and take informed decisions, and puts high demand on their social skills.

REFERENCES

Anastopoulou, A., Sharples, M., Ainsworth, S., Crook, C., O'Malley, C., & Wright, M. (2012). Creating personal meaning through technology-supported science learning across formal and informal settings. *International Journal of Science Education, 34*(2), 251–273.

Chan, T.-W., Milrad, M., et al. (2006). One-to-one technology-enhanced learning: An opportunity for global research collaboration. *Research and Practice in Technology Enhanced Learning Journal, 1*(1), 3–29.

Chen, W.-L., Seow, P., So, H.-J., Toh, Y., & Looi, C.-K. (2010). Connecting learning spaces using mobile technology, *Educational Technology, 50*(5), 45–50.

Dodd, B., Sime, M., and Kay, H. (1968). *Teaching machines and programmed instruction.* London: Penguin Books.

Goodyear, P. (2011). Emerging methodological challenges. In L. Markauskaite, P. Freebody, & J. Irwin (Eds.), *Methodological choice and design* (Vol. 9, Part 4, pp. 253–266). The Netherlands: Springer.

Hung, P.-H., Lin, Y.-F., & Hwang, G.-J. (2010). Formative assessment design for PDA integrated ecology observation. *Educational Technology & Society, 13*(3), 33–42.

Hwang, G. J., Shi, Y. R., & Chu, H. C. (2011). A concept map approach to developing collaborative Mindtools for context-aware ubiquitous learning. *British Journal of Educational Technology, 42*(5), 778–789.

Hwang, G. J., & Tsai, C. C. (2011). Research trends in mobile and ubiquitous learning: A review of publications in selected journals from 2001 to 2010. *British Journal of Educational Technology, 42*(4), E65–E70.

Hwang, G.-J., Tsai, C.-C., & Yang, S. J.-H. (2008). Criteria, strategies and research issues of context-aware ubiquitous learning. *Educational Technology & Society, 11*(2), 81–91.

Hwang, G.-J., Wu, P.-H., & Ke, H.-R. (2011). An interactive concept map approach to supporting mobile learning activities for natural science courses. *Computers & Education, 57*(4), 2272–2280.

Kurti, A., Spikol, D., & Milrad, M. (2008). Bridging outdoors and indoors educational activities in schools with the support of mobile and positioning technologies. *International Journal of Mobile Learning and Organization, 2*(2), 166–186.

Looi, C.-K., Seow, P., Zhang, B., So, H.-J., Chen, W., & Wong, L.-H. (2010). Leveraging mobile technology for sustainable seamless learning: A research agenda. *British Journal of Educational Technology, 41*(2), 154–169.

Milrad, M., Kohen-Vacs, D., Vogel, B., Ronen, M., & Kurti, A. (2011). An integrated approach for the enactment of collaborative pedagogical scripts using mobile technologies. *Proceedings of the International Conference on Computer Support for Collaborative Learning CSCL 2011.* Hong Kong, China.

Nilsson, P., Sollervall, H., & Spikol, D. (2010). Mathematical learning processes supported by augmented reality. *Proceedings of the 34th Conference of the International Group for the Psychology of Mathematics Education.* Belo Horizonte, Brazil.

Ogata, H., Li, M., Hou, B., Uosaki, N., El-Bishouty, M., & Yano, Y. (2010). Ubiquitous learning log: What if we can log our ubiquitous learning? *Proceedings of International Conference on Computers in Education 2010* (pp. 360–367). Putrajaya, Malaysia.

Ogata, H., Li, M., Hou, B., Uosaki, N., El-Bishouty, M., & Yano, Y. (2011). SCROLL: Supporting to share and reuse ubiquitous learning log in the context of language learning. *Research and Practice in Technology Enhanced Learning, 6*(2), 69–82.

Rogers, Y., & Price, S. (2006). Using ubiquitous computing to extend and enhance learning experiences. In M. van Hooftk & K. Swan (Eds.), *Ubiquitous computing in education: Invisible technology, visible impact* (pp. 329–347). Mahwah, NJ: Lawrence Erlbaum Associates.

Sharples, M. (2009). Methods for evaluating mobile learning. In G. N. Vavoula, N. Pachler, & A. Kukulska-Hulme (Eds.), *Researching mobile learning: Frameworks, tools and research designs* (pp. 17–39). Oxford, UK: Peter Lang Publishing Group.

Sharples, M., Taylor, J., & Vavoula, G. (2007). A theory of learning for the mobile age. In R. Andrews & C. Haythornthwaite (Eds.), *The Sage handbook of elearning research* (pp. 221–247). London: Sage.

Sharples, M., Milrad, M., Arnedillo Sánchez, I., & Vavoula, G. (2009). Mobile learning: Small devices, big issues. In N. Balacheff, S. Ludvigsen, T. de Jong, A. Lazonder, & S. Barnes (Eds.), *Technology enhanced learning: Principles and products* (pp. 233–240). Heidelberg, Germany: Springer.

So, H.-J., Kim, I.-S., & Looi, C.-K. (2008). Seamless mobile learning: Possibilities and challenges arising from the Singapore experience. *Educational Technology International, 9*(2), 97–121.

Sollervall, H., Gil de la Iglesia, D., Milrad, M., Peng, A., Pettersson, O., Salavati, S., & Yau, J. (2011). Trade-offs between didactical and technological design requirements affecting the robustness of a mobile learning activity. *Proceedings of the 19th International Conference on Computers in Education.* Chiang Mai, Thailand.

Sollervall, H., & Milrad, M. (2012). Theoretical and methodological considerations regarding the design of innovative mathematical learning activities with mobile technologies. *International Journal of Mobile Learning and Organisation, 6*(2), pp. 172–187.

Sollervall, H., Otero, N., Milrad, M., Vogel, B., & Johansson, D. (2012). Outdoor activities for the learning of mathematics: Designing with mobile technologies for transitions across learning contexts (pp. 33–34). *Proceedings of the 7th IEEE International Conference on Wireless, Mobile and Ubiquitous Technologies in Education*. Takamatsu, Japan.

Stahl, G. (2002). Contributions to a theoretical framework for CSCL. *Proceedings of CSCL 2002* (pp. 62–71). Hillsdale, NJ: Lawrence Erlbaum Associates.

Syvänen, A., Beale, R., Sharples, M., Ahonen, M., & Lonsdale, P. (2005). Supporting pervasive learning environments: Adaptability and context awareness in mobile learning. *Proceedings of the 3rd IEEE International Workshop on Wireless and Mobile Technologies in Education* (pp. 21–28). Tokushima, Japan.

Wong, L.-H. (2012). A learner-centric view of mobile seamless learning. *British Journal of Educational Technology*, *43*(1), E19–E23.

Wong, L.-H., Chen, W., & Jan, M. (2012). How artefacts mediate small group co-creation activities in a mobile-assisted language learning environment? *Journal of Computer Assisted Learning, 28*(5), 411–424.

Wong, L.-H., Chin, C.-K., Jan, M., & Chai, C.-S. (2011). The development of a seamless language learning framework mediated by mobile technology. *China Education Technology, 2011*(12), 1–7.

Wong, L.-H., Chai, C.-S., Chin, C.-K., Hsieh, Y.-F., & Liu, M. (2012). Towards a seamless language learning framework mediated by the ubiquitous technology. *International Journal of Mobile Learning and Organisation, 6*(2), 156–171.

Wong, L.-H., & Looi, C.-K. (2011). What seams do we remove in mobile-assisted seamless learning? A critical review of the literature. *Computers & Education, 57*(4), 2364–2381.

Zhang, B.-H, Looi, C.-K., Wong, L.-H., Seow, P., Chia, G., Chen, W.-L., So, H.-J., Soloway, E., & Norris, C. (2010). Deconstructing and reconstructing: Transforming primary science learning via a mobilized curriculum. *Computers & Education, 55*(4), 1504–1523.

10

SUBSTANTIVE EDUCATIONAL CHANGE IS IN THE PALM OF OUR CHILDREN'S HANDS

Cathleen A. Norris and Elliot M. Soloway

We have known for more years than we might care to admit (Bransford, Brown, & Cocking, 2000) what a classroom should look like in order for substantive learning to take place. However, instead of a learn-by-doing pedagogy (aka project-based learning, inquiry-based learning, active learning, etc.), didactic pedagogy/direct instruction still rules the land. Whether it is a teacher at the front of the room expounding, or a Khan video expounding, or an electronic whiteboard instead of a blackboard at the place of the expounding, or even if the students can immediately respond to the expounding with a clicker—that is still direct-instruction pedagogy, and we all know that direct-instruction pedagogy, although useful in places, ought not to be the overwhelmingly dominant pedagogy. So, why hasn't this pedagogy been replaced by the better, learn-by-doing pedagogy?

The truth is this: Enacting a learn-by-doing pedagogy (or project-based learning, inquiry-based learning, active learning) is really difficult to do; it requires considerable time on the teacher's part, as well as deep content knowledge, in order to tailor the learning experiences to the particular strengths and weaknesses of the student. Professors who devote their lives to what is, relatively speaking, a narrow area, and who teach one course per semester and have one to three doctoral students to help them, can enact a learn-by-doing pedagogy. Professional schools such as medicine or business schools, which need to provide a case-based learning environment, charge considerable sums and thus can bathe students in instructional support. Learn-by-doing pedagogy is challenging to enact and, without question, it is expensive, and it does not scale well at all.

However, if a K–12 student is lucky, he or she will experience a learn-by-doing pedagogy. Highly talented and motivated teachers—artisan teachers, as Tom Carroll (2011) calls them—can and do create classrooms with an active-learning pedagogy. Those teachers are the ones who are remembered by their students—remembered for having helped transform their lives in some significant way.

On the other hand, for the everyday teacher for whom teaching is a job not a calling, for whom working 16 hours a day—plus weekends—is not an option, enacting a learn-by-doing pedagogy with 20th-century technology (i.e., pencil and paper and textbooks) is simply too hard to do. Indeed, the textbook publishers—not known for innovation or leadership—produce materials that support direct instruction that teachers readily use on a daily basis. And, with state-mandated testing, No Child Left Behind, and merit-based pay breathing down their necks, what are teachers supposed to do? Tell the children what they need to know, tell them again louder, and get them through those horrible tests.

We hasten to say this: We are in no way blaming teachers for this situation—far from it. We sympathize and empathize with teachers whose class sizes are increasing, who are taking on more parental-style responsibilities as children from dysfunctional homes bring that baggage into the classroom, and who regularly read newspapers that heap scorn upon teachers and the teaching profession. At a recent political rally, one picketer had a sign that said: "You are glorified baby sitters who leave work at 3 p.m. You deserve minimum wage" (Gabriel, 2011). Under these conditions, again, what is a classroom teacher to do?

TECHNOLOGY = OPPORTUNITY

Although technology can be just a bunch of gadgets, *good* technology is really *good* opportunity—good technology enables people to do things they literally couldn't do before. For example: Dell Computer didn't use the computer *to keep track of its inventory* of millions of parts, like other PC manufacturers did. No, Dell used the computer and the Internet to *eliminate inventory*—and, in so doing, invented just-in-time PC manufacturing, scooping the industry and making big piles of money.

Company after company, industry after industry has leveraged those good gadgets—those good opportunities—and fundamentally changed the way they do business. Apple Computer is just Apple now, with half of its business coming from the iPhone; that transformation has happened in just 4 years. Oh, and Apple is the largest technology corporation in the world—all on the back of that miraculously thin slab of aluminum-encased glass called the iPhone.

Sadly, K–12 missed the desktop revolution, it missed the Internet revolution, and it missed the laptop revolution. Just having computers in your school doesn't mean your school leveraged the technology—leveraged the opportunity. For the most part, K–12 simply assimilated—integrated—desktops, the Internet, and laptops into the existing pedagogy; indeed, the electronic whiteboard and clickers just made direct-instruction pedagogy even easier. The clicker (response pad) took off in K–12 when it came with a test bank of questions that teachers could use to quickly and easily create tests. Playing *Jeopardy*, while certainly more fun than doing worksheets, is still, at its core, drill-and-practice; *Jeopardy* is an integral part of direct-instruction pedagogy.

However, K–12 is not going to miss the mobile-technologies revolution! K–12 will not be sitting out this opportunity—no way, no how!

THE AGE OF MOBILISM = OPPORTUNITY FOR K–12 TO FINALLY CHANGE

Steve Jobs proclaimed that we are in the Post-PC Era. That's a negative way of naming our times. Calling it the Age of Mobilism more accurately reflects what mobile technologies are enabling. Here are some observations from the pundits of mobile technologies:

Mobile is ramping up faster than any platform before it and will bring a staggering scale worldwide.

(Quotation by Mary Meeker in Fendelman, 2009)

There are 1.2 billion personal computers in use worldwide including desktops, laptops and tablet PCs like the iPad. There are 1.1 billion fixed landline phones. There are 1.0 billion automobiles registered and in use. There are 1.6 billion television sets, 1.7 billion credit card users, 2.0 billion Internet users, 2.2 billion people with a banking account, and 3.9 billion radio receivers in use worldwide. Mobile utterly dwarfs them all—with 5.2 billion currently active, i.e. fully paid mobile phone subscriptions.

(Ahonen, 2011)

The market dynamics are such that I think non-smart phones will disappear entirely from branded portfolios in 3 to 5 years.

(Dedieu, 2011)

And some interesting mobile facts:

- 15,000 new apps are published each week onto the smartphone marketplaces— 15,000—per week (Freierman, 2011)!
- More smartphones are now being purchased than PCs (Mckendrick, 2012);
- More time is spent using apps on a mobile device than is spent "surfing" the web (Gahran, 2012)!

Indeed, we are moving at bullet-train speed into the Age of Mobilism.

As we commented above, creating a learn-by-doing environment is the goal. However, learn-by-doing is a very challenging pedagogy—although the artisan teachers can pull it off, the everyday teachers typically find it overwhelming. Currently, the burden in a learn-by-doing classroom is primarily on the teacher; the teacher is the font of knowledge and help and resources; the teacher is, in some sense, a road block. The students need to go *through* the teacher to get to information, assistance, etc. No wonder learn-by-doing is not widely practiced in schools; it is very demanding on teachers.

However, mobile technologies are the opportunity that K–12 has been waiting for: just as a rising tide raises all boats, mobile technologies enable all teachers—not just the artisan teachers—to move to a learn-by-doing pedagogy. Why exactly do mobile technologies facilitate a learn-by-doing pedagogy?

The mobile technologies of the 21st century will "scaffold" learners and help learners take ownership and responsibility for their own learning. Mobile technologies enable students to go directly to all manner of information, people, places, data, events, and locations; the teacher (or the classroom textbook) no longer is the mediator. With a mobile device in each learner's palm, each learner can be active and engage in a learn-by-doing pedagogy.

Indeed, with the teacher freed from being the mediator, the teacher now can do exactly what the Father of learn-by-doing pedagogy, John Dewey, suggests: "They [teachers] give the pupils something to do, not something to learn; and the doing is of such a nature as to demand thinking, or the intentional noting of connections; learning naturally results" (Dewey, 1916).

As we describe in more detail below, mobile technologies can scaffold the thinking that is "demanded" by a learn-by-doing pedagogy. Unlike 20th-century paper-and-pencil technologies, mobile technologies can support students as they engage in "the doing," as they engage in the "noting of connections." Now, because students can more easily engage in a learn-by-doing pedagogy, that in turn enables teachers—*all* teachers—to more easily engage in a learn-by-doing pedagogy.

But, and this is a *huge* but, although mobile technologies are a necessary condition for classrooms moving to a learn-by-doing pedagogy, they are far, far from a sufficient condition. As we argue below, teachers must be provided with a curriculum—with that "something to do"—and with a great deal of professional development in order to support teachers making the biggest transformation of their professional career—a shift from an instructionalist pedagogy to a learn-by-doing pedagogy. First, however, let's address the way in which mobile technologies will scaffold students so they can engage in a learn-by-doing pedagogy.

SCAFFOLDING THE "DEMANDED THINKING"

Imagine the following: In a classroom of 30 fifth graders, each child has embedded in the palm of their hand an Internet-connected computing device (aka smartphone), accessible essentially 24/7, inside the classroom and outside the classroom. In a learn-by-doing pedagogy, here are the key types of activity that such an arrangement enables:

- *Learn in context:* Science is full of definitions and otherwise abstract ideas. However, in walking home from school, one young student notices an interesting root structure of an old, old tree. With the m-learning device in her hand, snapping a picture of that root system is easy. What has just happened is that student, in Dewey-talk, has engaged in "the intentional noting of connections"—she has linked a concrete image of a root system to an abstract idea discussed in the classroom. Moreover, the student has constructed an artifact, not just watched a video or listened to a lecture; the act of doing is the critically important element in learning.
- *Direct and immediate access to information, events, locations, data:* Following out this vignette, the student can use Google Goggles, an augmented-reality app, to identify the tree, immediately, and provide additional information about the tree from the vast Internet store of information. This student doesn't need to wait until he or she arrives home to look up the root system in a book, or even go online; with a device in his or her hand, access to information—events, people, places, and things—is immediate and direct. Still further, information is but one element becoming available over the Internet. There are mounds of databases containing archival data (e.g., weather data, population data, pricing data) available freely; and, increasingly, as sensors proliferate, there are real-time data available on the Internet. Also, events such as conferences, concerts, sales, etc., are also directly accessible, as are places all over the globe that have an Internet presence. The opportunity is this: If a student has an interest, no longer must their interest be mediated by a teacher or a textbook. Rather, the student can himself or herself immediately pursue, to virtually any depth, his or her interest in a topic, an event, a location, etc. This level of direct access is unprecedented; the real challenge is making access more accessible!

- *Discuss, collaborate, and work as a team*: Still further, the young student brings that photo of the root system back into the classroom to show his or her classmates, and then a conversation naturally ensues. "Wow, where did you get that picture? Look at the picture I took of a tree's root system. It looks different than your picture. Why?" Learning is in the conversation; learning occurs when there is discourse and discussion—in the context of information that can be immediately retrieved. What does a teacher do in this situation? Help the students learn; help the students understand what information to retrieve; work together, collaborate, to develop a deep, integrated understanding. In contrast to "I Teach," this is "We Learn."
- *All the time, everywhere learning*: In the past, we have seen the classroom as the major place where schooling—and learning—take place. However, in our 24/7 world, a child spends more time outside of school than in. Although some use "anytime, anywhere" learning, we feel that the term "all the time, everywhere learning" better represents what children (and adults) do in their everyday lives. An Internet-connected, m-learning device is truly a cognitive prosthesis and supports "all the time, everywhere learning."
- *Mobile devices are not just computers*: Although mobile devices can support computing activities such as text editing, spreadsheeting, etc., their functionality only *begins* there! These devices already come standard with a GPS, an accelerometer, a camera, a mic, an ambient light sensor, and a multi-touch screen. Tomorrow, these devices will come with all manner of sensors, e.g, galvanic skin response, temperature, EKG, etc. The functionality that these sensors unleashes is almost beyond imagining.

In sum, then, mobile technologies—devices, software, networks—provide learners with a broad range of tools with which they can truly take control and ownership of their own learning. Yes, students can do that with paper and pencil. It's just much harder to do so with those 19th-century technologies, and thus only the most competent, most assertive, most energetic students will likely take ownership of their own learning. Just as a rising tide raises all boats, mobile technologies enable all learners to be owners of their own learning.

ESSENTIAL USE VS SUPPLEMENTAL USE: WHEN COMPUTING DEVICES MOVE THE NEEDLE OF ACHIEVEMENT

In reviewing the empirical literature on the use of computing devices in the classroom—laptops on carts, desktops in a lab, even 1:1 laptop programs—we observed that, when computers are used as a supplement to learning, as an add-on to learning, student achievement is not positively impacted. When computers are used as glorified typewriters for an hour a week, or Google search engines in studying a science or social-studies unit, no discernible increase in student achievement is recorded (Norris, Hossain, & Soloway, 2012).

In contrast, when computing devices are used as essential tools, then increases in student achievement are observed. A necessary condition for "essential use" is 1:1—each child having his or her own computing device. (However, as we noted above and further analyzed in Norris et al. (2012), 1:1 is in no way a sufficient condition to ensure essential use.) Essential use is marked by the following:

- students use their devices for extended periods of time, inside the classroom and outside the classroom;
- students use their devices for a diverse set of learning activities;
- students use their devices to support collaborative learning activities.

In a truly learn-by-doing pedagogy, when the computing devices are used as essential tools, not supplemental tools, the learner can, in fact, take on the ownership of his or her learning. The teacher is a mentor, a guide, who shapes and directs, who encourages and presses. However, when the teacher walks away to work with another student, the m-learning device is still there, serving as an essential scaffold for a student's learning. If a learner is supposed to take ownership of his or her learning, it is only reasonable that the learner be provided with tools that can support that responsibility. Mobile technologies, finally, provide learners with the opportunity to take ownership of their learning and thereby enable all teachers to engage in a learn-by-doing pedagogy. Mobile technologies, as essential tools for learning, are the key to scaling up learn-by-doing.

BARRIERS TO CHANGE

While the opportunity is at hand, and while the need to change is great, there are still significant barriers that need to be overcome in order to take advantage of this exciting and important opportunity:

- *Lack of vision*: There are still the deniers: no, there is nothing wrong with the current system that a bit of tweaking won't correct; no, that technology-infused future is not needed in schools, since that's not the way our parents learned; etc. Stay the course! And there are pessimists: the educational system is immutable, unchangeable. Indeed, all three reviewers of this chapter echoed some form of: "I don't see how education is going to change."
- *"But we don't have the money"*: When a parent says "we don't have the money for that" to their child, it really means: "we don't value that." Ditto for schools; we have heard the lament "we don't have the money" so many times it can make one pessimistic! That said, although there may not be sufficient funds to go 1:1 across the whole district, or even across a school, every superintendent and every principal worth their salt has a pot of money stashed away for interesting ideas. It's time to dip into that stash and use it to fund a pilot to start learning about 1:1 learn-by-doing. It's time to start valuing mobile technologies.

A rejoinder that we hear is this: "We have spent a great deal of money on technology already and we have not seen any benefit, any increase in student achievement. So, why should we invest more money in technology? What is different this time?" That is indeed a fair question. First, the reason that schools have not seen any movement of the achievement needle as a function of technology spending is because schools have, by and large, used computers as supplements to their existing curriculum and pedagogy. As a supplement, there wasn't sufficient oomph to make a significant difference in learning. Still further, adding new technology (e.g., a cart of iPads) to an old curriculum/pedagogy (drill-and-practice, instructionalist pedagogy) will not move the needle either; doing drill incrementally or even substantially better is not going to result in significant increases in student achievement (Norris et al., 2012). What we have argued for here is using the new technology (mobile) with a new pedagogy (learn-by-doing), and using those devices as essential tools, not as supplemental tools for learning. Therein lies the difference.

As computing devices move from supporting enterprises to supporting individuals, the cost of those devices and the connection services has come way down. However, for the 55 million K–12 schoolchildren in the US—and the billions outside America—that cost is still too high—*much* too high. We estimate that an affordable price point for an Internet m-learning device for students—be they parent-supported or school-supported—is $10 per month per student, where that cost includes a m-learning device and an always-on, available-everywhere Internet connection plan. That sounds low, but the telecommunications companies will still be making a profit at that price point.

Bring-your-own-device (BYOD) will happen; schools will stop banning mobile devices and allow the students to "bring your own device." Although schools will no longer need to purchase the majority of devices, there are still costs involved in moving to 1:1, e.g., networking, software, professional development, etc. BYOD will help; but, as always, there is no free lunch.

Finally, the $100 computer envisioned by Nicholas Negroponte (Dybwad, 2005) has indeed arrived: it isn't the laptop he envisioned, but an m-learning device. Today, there are $100 Android-based tablets with WiFi (no cellular) that could make excellent learning devices in a classroom, when equipped with suitable software, and with curriculum and professional development for the teacher. And, over the next 2–3 years, that same $100 will be able to buy increasingly more powerful m-learning devices—with cellular connections!

The excuse, "We don't have the money," is more a statement of not valuing technology than a statement about purchasing power.

- *Curriculum, curriculum, curriculum*: Frankly, the biggest barrier is the lack of curriculum to support teachers as they transition outside their comfort zone. A well-articulated curriculum is needed by everyday teachers as they move from direct instruction to learn-by-doing. There is ample evidence that a thoroughly described curriculum helps teachers, especially the everyday teachers, to be more effective. Schools provide teachers with textbooks, guidebooks, professional development—for direct-instruction pedagogy.

However, we have seen school after school move to 1:1 and provide teachers with precious little *curricular* support. Thus, it is not surprising that the teachers simply assimilate the technology into their direct-instruction lesson plans: they do as they were instructed—they "integrate" the technology into their existing lesson plans. And what are the results? Correspondingly precious few gains in student achievement. We can't expect to transition to 1:1 computing using devices—be they laptops, netbooks, tablets, or smartphones—on the backs of the teachers; we can't expect teachers, who already have full-time jobs, to recreate a whole new curriculum for a whole new pedagogy to leverage the affordances of 1:1! What are we thinking?

Waiting for the textbook companies—which are petrified that their fundamental business model is in the process of being totally disrupted—to develop the needed curriculum is not a good idea. Rather, as we are seeing, districts are forming teams of teachers who, over the summer, are being paid to create new curriculum. (Why more districts don't band together is a mystery; the water cycle in Hoboken is the same water cycle in Newark, last we heard.) Now, district-based curriculum development is not a long-term, scalable solution, but textbook companies, as they see that districts want new curriculum to support learn-by-doing, will produce it—eventually.

- *Need for ongoing professional development*: The dirty little secret that no one wants to talk about is this: even when curriculum is provided to teachers, unless the teachers are supported with a significant level of professional development, the vast majority of the teachers simply will not come to use the mobile-device-enabled curriculum in an effective manner—for good reason. The evidence is that teachers teach the way they are taught; therefore, changing a teaching style—didactic, instructionalist— that is deeply ingrained in them is not going to be in any way easy. It is going to take time, it is going to take support, it is going to take motivation, it is going to take mentoring in order for most teachers to switch from their current mode of instruction to a learn-by-doing pedagogy.
- *Lack of leadership*: Change is not going to be without bumps and pains. When a teacher or class hits that inevitable bump, if the superintendent says, in response to a teacher's complaint, "this is optional," then it is "game over." Teachers will fall back into their comfort zone and not take on the challenge of moving to a learn-by-doing pedagogy. The superintendent or principal—and all those down the line—must uniformly say: change is *not* optional; "we are going to do this, and you will be provided with the necessary supports." Together, a school or a group of teachers can work through the bumps, but the administration must stand firm— and must come through on its promise of providing the necessary supports. Another form of leadership is this: local, state, and federal government must put pressure on the communications providers (e.g., the telecommunications companies, the cable companies) to give K–12 special pricing. The precedent is there: thanks to pressure from the public and government officials, the FCC just unveiled the "Connect to Compete" program (Miller, 2011) that provides poor families with the Internet for $9.95 per month. Although this fee is dramatically lower than the commercial fee, the cable providers say that this price is "roughly at-cost"—which means they are not losing money and, if anything, they are still making a profit! It's time for educators to step up and be proactive, not reactive— for a change—and demand special school pricing from the communications providers.
- *800 pound gorilla—assessment*: It's time to tell the emperor—you have no clothes! Statewide standardized testing drives instruction. Teachers teach to the test. They would be both impractical and unethical if they didn't: Tests are important, and the students need to be prepared. As long as the tests are fact-based, then instruction will focus on the facts—especially as teacher pay for student achievement becomes more prevalent. Although we have evidence that drill-and-practice is not necessarily the only pedagogy to prepare students for a fact-based exam (Looi et al., 2011), convincing schools of that claim is challenging—and risky for the schools.

Not only is valuable classroom time diverted so that teachers can better prepare their students to take the standardized, fact-based tests, we are seeing schools divert their precious funds toward buying computers and reclaiming valuable classroom space in order to reconstitute computer labs, so that online testing can be supported. Desktop-based computer labs? Schools are going backwards!

Perhaps the new crop of tests (Assessment & Teaching of 21st Century Skills Foundation, 2012) of 21st-century skills, such as collaborative learning, self-directed learning, etc., being developed by the Assessment & Teaching of 21st Century Skills Foundation, sponsored by three 21st-century corporations (Cisco, Microsoft, Intel), will be a beacon for the new generation of tests and will help to reset what is considered important to know and to be able to do. If we want a learn-by-doing pedagogy, then we need assessments that value what a learn-by-doing pedagogy enables—and we need learn-by-doing assessments!

CONCLUDING REMARKS

For the record, we predict that, by 2015, every child in every grade in every classroom in America will be using an m-learning device for curricular purposes, 24/7. You can take that to the bank! We feel that this prediction will hold true for the developed nations in general, and, as for the nations who are known as the Global South—those nations not considered to be in the developed category—they will not be far behind, as they have the greatest need to educate their people.

The only issue is this: how will those devices be used? Will the barriers stand, so that teachers will simply assimilate the m-learning devices into their existing curriculum—with little or no impact on learning, as the devices will be used as supplements, not as essential tools—or will schools overcome the barriers and move to a learn-by-doing pedagogy, where all the teachers are participating, and where students are being prepared for the knowledge–work, global marketplace? In the end, it is only a question of will: do we have it or not? Stay tuned!

ACKNOWLEDGMENT

An early version of this paper appeared in the *Educational Technology Magazine*, March 2011.

REFERENCES

Ahonen, T. (2011). All the numbers, all the facts on mobile the trillion-dollar industry. Why is Google saying: Put your best people on mobile? Retrieved from: http://communities-dominate.blogs.com/brands/2011/02/all-the-numbers-all-the-facts-on-mobile-the-trillion-dollar-industry-why-is-google-saying-put-your-b.html

Assessment & Teaching of 21st Century Skills Foundation. (2012). http://atc21s.org/

Bransford, J. D., Brown, A. L., & Cocking, R. R. (Eds.) (2000). *How people learn: Brain, mind, experience and school.* Washington, DC: National Academy Press.

Carroll, T. (2011). National Commison on Teaching and America's Future. Retrieved from: http://tinyurl.com/8xehoyq

Dedieu, H. (2011). Apple, RIM and HTC captured 75% of mobile phone operating profits in Q1. Retrieved from: www.asymco.com/2011/05/17/apple-rim-and-htc-captured-75-of-mobile-phone-operating-profits-in-q1/

Dewey, J. (1916). *Democracy and education.* New York: Macmillan.

Dybwad, B. (2005). Negroponte details specs on planned $100 laptop. Retrieved from: www.engadget.com/2005/09/28/negroponte-details-specs-on-planned-100-laptop/

Fendelman, A. (2009). Mobile Internet Report, quote from Mary Meeker. Retrieved from: http://cellphones. about.com/b/2009/12/16/mobile-internet-report-mobile-is-ramping-up-faster-than-any-platform-before-it.htm

Freierman, S. (2011). One million mobile apps, and counting at a fast pace. Retrieved from: www.nytimes.com/ 2011/12/12/technology/one-million-apps-and-counting.html

Gabriel, T. (2011). Teachers wonder, why the scorn? Retrieved from: www.nytimes.com/2011/03/03/education/ 03teacher.html?_r=1&scp=2&sq=teachers&st=nyt

Gahran, A. (2012) Phone, tablet users spend more time with apps than Web. Retrieved from: www.cnn.com/2012/ 01/20/tech/mobile/apps-web-gahran/index.html

Looi, C.-K., Zhang, B., Chen, W., Seow, P., Chia, G., Norris, C., & Soloway, E. (2011). 1:1 mobile inquiry learning experience for primary science students: A study of learning effectiveness. *Journal of Computer Assisted Learning, 27*(3), 269–287.

Mckendrick, J. (2012). Milestone: more smartphones than PCs sold in 2011. Retrieved from: www.smartplanet. com/blog/business-brains/milestone-more-smartphones-than-pcs-sold-in-2011/21828

Miller, P. (2011). FCC's Connect to Compete initiative offers low-income homes $9.95 broadband. Retrieved from: www.theverge.com/2011/11/9/2549626/fcc-connect-to-compete-low-income-homes-9-99-broadband

Norris, C., Hossain, A., & Soloway, E. (2012) Under what conditions does computer use positively impact student achievement? Supplemental vs. essential use. *Proceedings of the SITE 2012 Conference*, Society for Information Technology and Teacher Education, New Orleans, LA.

11

THE FUTURE OF MOBILE APPS FOR TEACHING AND LEARNING

Ferial Khaddage and Christoph Lattemann

A new definition of m-learning has been presented in the first chapter. It was modified from a definition presented by Sharples, Taylor, and Vavoula in 2007. In Chapter 1, Crompton, Muilenburg, and Berge defined m-learning as "learning across multiple contexts, through social and content interactions, using personal electronic devices" (Crompton, 2013, p. 4). This chapter departs from this definition and focuses on mobile applications (apps) and technologies in this context.

Mobile apps have come a long way in the past 2 years, especially in their applications for business, health, information, communication, and education. Most mobile devices are now capable of processing information in the same way as desktop computers. For example, many iPhone, iPads, and other similar smart devices are equipped with many functionalities and unique features that can be used for delivering learning content. However, mobile devices are considered as effective and efficient tools for teaching and learning, as mobile devices are being implemented as fusion devices that include some unique features and functionalities. Khaddage, Lanham, and Zhou (2009) listed some of these functionalities that are being implemented in one single mobile device, and they include the following (see Table 11.1).

Most of these features are already being used by students to help them during the learning process (Khaddage & Knezek, 2011). Currently, the rapid development of mobile apps for mobile devices is taking the educational world by storm.

The mobile-app sphere has grown tremendously in recent years and is showing no signs of stopping. The worldwide mobile-app market is expected to grow from US$6.8 billion in 2010 to US$25 billion by 2015 (Zedensk, 2011). A study by a mobile research

Table 11.1 Functionalities of Mobile Devices (Khaddage et al., 2009)

App technology	Video capturing and playback	Internet access	Interactive content
Text documents	Podcasting	Photo capturing	RSS feeds
Audio recording	Note-taking	Calendar/organizers	QR-code reader

specialist group confirmed that the mobile-apps market is moving rapidly, and this is affecting the world globally (Jahns, 2010). This fast penetration is due to open, easy, and direct access to app stores around the world, and it is due to the availability of tools and resources for developers to develop, manage, and maintain apps for any particular purpose. Currently, there are many stores worldwide, and mobile apps are spreading widely; there are apps for business, for health, and for music. However, there are only a few mobile apps in the area of higher education, especially at universities, and there is very little mobile support in the current online-course-delivery systems at most institutions (Seibu & Biju, 2008). With the advent of mobile technologies, such as smart phones, and the penetration of affordable flat-rate-based mobile connection, m-learning will become a major distributor of learning content to students at universities (Tatar, Roschelle, Vahey, & Penuel, 2003). It is a crucial fact that there is an urgent need to develop unique approaches that can form the base of new mobile apps for teaching and learning in higher education. This challenge could be made possible with the deployment of the emerging new, unique, cloud-based computing for teaching and learning via mobile apps. Cloud-based computing could form a foundation for a strong mobile-apps infrastructure; this is because there are few issues that still form a barrier for proper, effective mobile-device integration for education. These factors are listed in Table 11.2, along with the possible solutions to overcome the specific barriers.

Despite these rapid developments in mobile apps and devices, universities are yet to formally acknowledge and integrate apps for teaching and learning. The major issue claimed by universities is that there isn't yet one standardized mobile device to be used by all students. Therefore, all students have different mobile devices. This fact is an issue for universities to implement interoperable mobile apps, as different devices have different interfaces and use different technologies. Some universities have overcome this barrier by using only one set of devices with the same interfaces, such as the iPhone or the iPad, to

Table 11.2 Factors and Issues Related to Mobile Devices

Factors and issues	Possible solution
Cost and charges	(Wi-Fi) hotspot access/(Chrome access); no Internet connection
Privacy and security	Build access to apps via a secure private cloud
Battery life	Current devices are equipped with longer battery life (10 hours)
Screen display	Dynamic and interactive display
Data/text input	Touch screen for easy and direct interaction
Connectivity & communication options	Communication apps can connect and collaborate free, such as Viber, Skype, Facebook
Processing power	Advanced operating systems within smart phones are constantly improving; Android/iSO
Application tools	Building apps on the cloud will create a device-independent platform
Audio	Voice-recognition input/recording
Development and implementation	Use already existing apps
Storage capacity	Most smartphones already come equipped with 32GB and external storage (memory cards etc.)

provide access to learning content. A good example of such integration is Abilene Christian University in the United States. It integrated the iPhone for teaching and learning after a thorough investigation of students' and teachers' behaviors and demands and surveys on mobile technology and devices. The university was finally able to integrate the iPhone to promote m-learning from 2008 (Abilene Christian University, 2008).

As mobile devices and app technologies can provide an efficient delivery mechanism of learning content, universities should implement methods to integrate this technology. In the next section, mobile apps and technologies for teaching and learning are discussed, and cloud-based computing is described as an alternative and effective approach for successful mobile-app integration.

MOBILE-APP TECHNOLOGIES

Mobile apps, if integrated properly, can provide an efficient delivery mechanism for learning content. In this section, we investigate app integration, methods, and approaches that can be adapted to meet today's students' needs.

Oblinger (2003, 2004), Oblinger and Oblinger (2005), and McMahon and Pospisil (2005) describe today's learners as digitally literate, "always on," always connected and reachable. They want to stay connected and reachable, they also want to experiment and have community-oriented personalities and characteristics. They are collaborative and multitasking learners who like to study in a group-based environment (McMahon & Pospisil, 2005).

Khaddage, Lattemann, and Bray (2011) also stated that the methods of communication among students have changed over the years, and, these days, students stay connected with their peers via social media and Web 2.0 technologies, such as Facebook, Skype, Twitter, YouTube, blogs, wikis, etc. They belong to the new, digital mobile world. Universities and educators, on the other hand, are often still reluctant to use these technologies and, in particular, mobile apps for teaching and learning; they view these technologies as a distraction for students (Khaddage et al. 2011).

Mobile Apps for Teaching and Learning

There are many methods and approaches that can be adapted to integrate mobile apps, and this could make learning and teaching an easy task for students, as well as for teachers. Apps can be used for test preparation, study guides, and as new types of instructional material in the classroom environment. We believe that mobile apps can offer the following three "Ss" to the access of learning content in a university environment: "speed, security, simplicity." Figure 11.1 is an illustration of the three Ss:

- *Speed*: Apps are designed to be fast and efficient; they are very quick to load and start up remotely from any mobile device, regardless of how complex the query.
- *Security*: Apps are designed to keep users safe and more secure when using their mobile devices; they can be developed with built-in malware and phishing protection, and the auto-updates feature is an important feature to make sure that the app's functions are up to date with the latest security updates.
- *Simplicity*: Apps can be streamlined, clean and simple, efficient, and easy to use. Users can access and perform a search and navigate action via the same box and the same interface very easily.

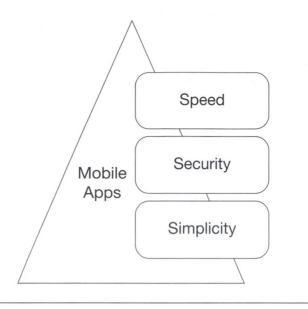

Figure 11.1 The Three Ss

There is also an important new feature of most of the Google apps that can be used for teaching and learning, such as Google Doc and Gmail. Since August 2011, Google has offered offline access to its web apps such as Gmail, Google Calender, and Google Docs (Geron, 2011). Google has provided this option to support the use of Google apps for business and education. Therefore, universities can take this challenge now and try to integrate app technologies to provide learning content to students. This feature can eliminate the costs and charges normally acquired by internet service providers (ISPs); this has been a major concern, in particular when accessing apps via a mobile phone using 3G networks. Hence, when the same access is offered free of charge and offline via Google Chrome technology, users will be encouraged to integrate this technology into their daily life and will use it to access learning content. With this offline access, users can interact with the mobile apps and their Gmail and communicate with their student peers or teachers.

Also, both the iOS and Android platforms provide development tools for making the app-development process easier and more coherent. This has helped in the development of a variety of apps that are freely available online for teachers and students to download, use, and adapt. It is also a crucial factor for developers to be knowledgeable about the platform-centric application programming interfaces and development tools provided by the platform being used by the particular institution, so that they can design and build apps according to their special requirements. Currently, Apple and Google are dominating the app market for business as well as for education; already some universities, such as Deakin University, are conducting an investigation into iPad (Apple) integration via apps for teaching and learning (O'Loughlin, 2011).

Research has suggested that the early 21st century is like the early 20th century, in that we are at the beginning of a new educational paradigm, and the engine of growth is communication and information (Daniels, 2009). As mobile technologies and tools are becoming more affordable, connectivity is becoming more ubiquitous, and ownership of mobile devices is constantly on the rise; hence, mobile apps will make their way into the mainstream of the educational environment. Currently, there are a growing number of m-learning apps that can be used for teaching and learning, and here are a few that we recommend:

- Mental Note (type, draw, add notes to pictures);
- iStudiez Pro (built-in planners for input and schedules, track workload);
- InClass (organize, share notes, save .doc files and Ace classes);
- Audio Note (write notes, set up recording, audio recording with time stamp);
- Kindle (reading, downloading books, etc.);
- PenUltimate (store information in a separate note; students can e-mail it and share it);
- Pages (word-processing program, sync docs. or create new ones);
- Some Google apps for educational use:
  - Gmail & Calender: communicating and sharing schedules;
  - Talk: synchronous (IM and video) communication;
  - Doc: real-time collaboration for Docs.
  - Group: form teams;
  - Sites: create their own sites.

Cloud Computing for Mobile-App Integration

Currently, with the development of cloud-based computing, developers of mobile apps are able to create cross-platform mobile applications using traditional Web technologies. Cloud-based computing is considered an innovative solution in relation to mobile-apps development. Recently, the development of cloud-based computing and its application and tools have become very popular for teaching and learning and are considered a step forward for educational institutions. Therefore, developing a shared, m-learning environment may now be possible through this advanced, emerging technology (Hamm, 2009).

Cloud-based computing consists of three layers, which form the three building blocks of cloud computing: the infrastructure as a service (IaaS), the platform as a service (PaaS), and the software as a service (SaaS). This gives the user flexibility in selecting the appropriate service of their choice (Creeger, 2009).

Khaddage and Knezek (2011) stated that the combination of the three layers allows users to run and access apps from anywhere and at anytime, and store information and content online. The three layers can be identified as follows:

- The IaaS is the major foundation layer, where everything is built; it is responsible for the cloud-hosting applications, and users can run any app of their choice, or any existing apps can be migrated to the cloud using the cloud hardware.
- The PaaS allows users to develop and implement their own apps using certain tool resources. A good example of this is Google App Engine: It allows users to develop their own app, tailored to their needs.
- The SaaS allows users to access and run existing online apps, such as Google apps. The advantages of these apps are their excellence for global collaborative work. Furthermore, they are free of charge (Khaddage & Knezek, 2011).

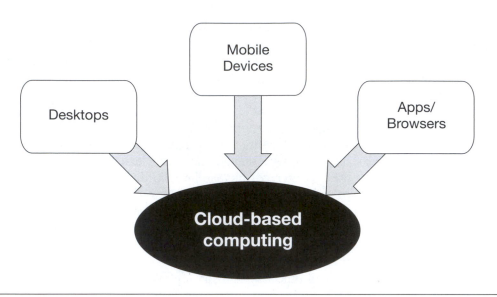

Figure 11.2 Building Blocks of Cloud-Based Computing

Cloud-based computing can enhance the process of developing cloud-based apps that work on multiple devices, such as mobile, desktops, browsers, and apps within the cloud-based environment (Khaddage & Knezek, 2011). Figure 11.2 is an illustration of this process.

The apps are stored in the cloud, and users can have fast, secure, remote or local access from just about any client device or operating system. The plug-and-play feature within the cloud-computing technology is responsible for publishing the apps onto the network or the Web. Tools such as cloud-based e-mail systems, calendars, chats, and forums, to improve messaging, as well as interaction capabilities and shared resources, data, and information, can all be integrated. The students can make multiple copies of the learning content, viewable on a variety of devices that can be synchronized, and, hence, all users within the same field can have access to share and use the information in their account. Cloud-computing applications should be designed for scalability to support large numbers of students and surges in demand. Universities can develop and remotely host custom-built educational applications within the cloud, and this can reduce costs and time spent, thus providing benefits to students as well as to the university. In order to create such apps, it is necessary to develop these applications on the underlying platform in order to cover different mobile devices, such as iPads, Blackberries, iPhones, Windows Mobiles, etc. There are many good examples of cloud-based mobile applications, such as Gmail's mobile provided by Google, Google Documents, etc., and they are all accessible via the mobile-app technology. These technologies may take universities toward a more open and global educational environment, and ensure greater future prospects for today's students, as they strive to reach out to an open-access, global learning environment via mobile apps.

The Future of Mobile Apps for Teaching and Learning

In the near future, we may see that Apple follows the Kindle model of cloud-synced books. Kindle and the iBooks app allow students to share their notes and bookmarks. Interoperability between applications and devices is given, and data can be synchronized.

Universities should implement an education strategy that can merge the tools and technologies, apps, and pedagogical factors. Therefore, we may see that educational institutions start to acknowledge and formally recognize informal learning (learning that happens outside a classroom environment), as mobile-app technologies and methods of communication are already enforcing this push into the curriculum, hence giving mobile apps capability to bring together informal and formal learning approaches (Knezek, Kwok-Wing, Khaddage, & Baker, 2011).

A framework to evaluate how this technology can improve learning should be implemented in the near future, as technology keeps evolving rapidly, and changes should occur along the way. It is also believed that iPads/iPhones/iPods and their apps will be real winners in the teaching and learning environment. Although making textbooks digital won't revolutionize education, it will improve the medium that can offer the three Ss mentioned earlier (speed, security, and simplicity), and, therefore, a change in teaching methods and a focus on social factors are what are needed to change education for the better. Today's society needs critical thinkers, inventors, creators, and not just ordinary students who acquire one-way, static education, and mobile apps could provide this dynamic, collaborative method of learning.

Mobile cloud computing holds great promise for delivering cloud-based mobile apps by enabling access from anywhere, but there may still be several barriers that need to be addressed to elevate its usefulness and capabilities. For mobile cloud computing to reach its full potential, the following three critical challenges need to be addressed, as stated in a recent article by Betts (2011):

- lowering network latency to meet application and code offload interactivity;
- increasing network bandwidth for faster data transfer between the cloud and devices;
- providing adaptive monitoring of network conditions to optimize network and device costs against the user's perceived performance of cloud applications.

None of these is easy to accomplish, but service and network providers, in cooperation with educational institutions, are already making important steps to improve the mobile-cloud experience.

In the following section, an analysis of student perceptions of mobile apps for teaching and learning is described to support the integration and the acknowledgment of this unique type of access and delivery of learning content.

ANALYSIS OF STUDENT PERCEPTIONS OF MOBILE APPS FOR TEACHING AND LEARNING

From a didactical, methodological, and technical perspective, mobile apps seem to be an efficient means for teaching and learning purposes. Mobile devices such as smartphones provide the technological platforms for access and transfer of information. The open-source idea of the Android operating system pushes the development of educational apps. The majority of mobile devices and smartphones are easy to use and are seen as efficient tools for collaboration and data sharing. Didactical concepts derived from a constructivism perspective show ways to manage dispersed and self-organized work or group-work processes.

The survey was conducted to explore and analyze students' perceptions of mobile apps for teaching and learning. Student perceptions of mobile apps may be influenced by specific individual variables, such as gender and attitude toward technology, environmental variables, such as access to the Internet and supply of applications, as well as social variables and network effect, which may be based on groups' cohesion (Kaasinen, 2005).

Methodology

In order to study the attitudes of students toward the effectiveness of m-learning, a questionnaire with 20 items was developed, designed to measure students' attitudes toward, and perceptions of, the effectiveness of mobile apps for teaching and learning. The study was conducted between August 2010 and September 2011. A convenient sample of about 240 students in Japan, 80 in Germany, and 40 in Australia was taken. The students come from different academic fields, have different cultural backgrounds, and come from different universities in Australia, Japan, and Germany.

Results and Discussion

Our findings show that 90 percent of the surveyed students in Germany, 95 percent of the Japanese, and 98 percent of the Australian students use smartphones (iPhone, Blackberry, Samsung Galaxy/Wave, etc.). The analysis indicates that, although computer use is still dominant, a large number of university students use their mobile phones to access content, communicate, and share information. For example, 41.2 percent of the Japanese students reported connecting to the Facebook app via smartphones. Only 15 percent of the German students use Skype or Viber on their smartphones. All smartphone users use mobile apps, but only 20 percent are willing to pay for them.

About 70 percent of all surveyed German students perceive smartphones and mobile apps as useful for distance learning. This ratio was even higher among Australian students (85 percent). The following fields—where mobile phones can contribute to learning—were mentioned: collaboration and communication among students (perceived as useful by 50 percent of the students); communication with the teacher (perceived as useful by 30 percent of the students); quizzes (perceived as useful by 21 percent of the students); and up- and downloading of content (perceived as useful by 30 percent of the students). Gender-specific differences are not significant.

The most commonly used apps on a mobile device are language programs (such as the Chinese App or Spanish for Dummies) and apps for quizzes and tests (e.g., SAT test). The surveyed students complained that they do use mobile apps in an informal way and outside their learning context and their university, as this type of learning is still unrecognized and not formally acknowledged, and, thus, teachers and administrators are yet to formally integrate and implement these apps to help their students learn. Hence, it is not surprising that the adoption rate of this technology for teaching and learning in higher education is still low.

For now, the general sense gained from this preliminary analysis is that, in Japan, as well as in Australia and in Germany, the convenience of being able to connect to the Internet via apps, using mobile devices, is very appealing to students, but not so much to teachers yet. As mobile-computing technologies are currently being led by hi-tech mobile devices such as the iPad, iPhone, Samsung Galaxy/Wave, and Blackberry, and operating systems such as Android and iOS, and an increasing number of apps, the movement toward the use of mobile devices in education is on the rise. Not only is this trend likely in educational settings, but also for different organizations (Jahns, 2010). Apps are being developed on a daily basis and are ready to be used, and this rapid development can simplify the process of apps integration for teaching and learning for nontechnical users from all different educational backgrounds, as they would only be required to integrate a particular app and use it, without worrying about the technological aspect behind its development and implementation.

CONCLUSION

Mobile apps will soon reshape the future of the current learning settings at universities. Smart mobile devices such as smartphones, iPads, tablets, and e-readers are now surpassing laptops and desktop computers. The time has come for universities to integrate this technology into the curriculum and use it effectively. Mobile apps, along with cloud-based computing for teaching and learning, will soon become the future of higher education. Decision-makers, developers, teachers, administrators, and researchers will soon see that these technologies and applications will increase productivity among students, reduce paperwork, and grant immediate access to content. This can be achieved in a unique way that other devices simply do not offer.

REFERENCES

Abilene Christian University. (2008). *Connected* [Online video produced by ACU student and staff to visualize a new kind of learning]. Retrieved from: www.acu.edu/technology/mobilelearning/video/connected.html

Betts B. (2011). Overcoming mobile cloud computing challenges with distributed apps online. Retrieved from: http://searchnetworking.techtarget.co.uk/news/2240037496/Overcoming-mobile-cloud-computing-challenges-with-distributed-apps

Creeger, M. (2009). CTO Roundtable: Cloud computing. *Communications of the ACM, 52*(8), 50–56.

Crompton, H. (2013). A historical overview of mobile learning: Toward learner-centered education (pp. 3–14). In Z. Berge, & L. Muilenburg (Eds.), *Handbook of mobile learning*. New York: Routledge.

Daniels, R. (2009). A cloud in every garage. *Forbes,* May 7. Retrieved from: www.forbes.com/2009/05/07/cloud-computing-enterprise-technology-cio-network-cloud-computing.html

Geron, T. (2011). Google takes Gmail, Calendar, Docs offline: A big plus for Chromebook. *Forbes.* Retrieved from: www.forbes.com/sites/tomiogeron/2011/08/31/google-takes-gmail-calendar-docs-offline-a-big-plus-for-chromebook/

Hamm, S. (2009). How cloud computing will change business. *Business Week,* June 4. Retrieved from: www.businessweek.com/magazine/content/09_24/b4135042942270.htm

Jahns, R. G. (2010). Smartphone application market to reach US$15.65 billion in 2013. Retrieved from: www.research2guidance.com/smartphone-application-market-to-reach-us15–65-billion-in-2013/

Kaasinen, E. (2005) User acceptance of mobile services—value, ease of use, trust and ease of adoption. PhD thesis. *VTT Publications, 566, Julkaisija,* Tampere University of Technology, Finland.

Khaddage, F., & Knezek, G. (2011). Device independent mobile applications for teaching and learning: Challenges, barriers and limitations. *Proceedings of Global Learn Asia Pacific 2011* (pp. 1–7).

Khaddage, F., Lanham, E., & Zhou, W. (2009). A proposed blended mobile learning model for application in higher education. *Proceedings of the 4th International Conference on Interactive Mobile and Computer Aided Learning—IMCL 2009* (p. 141).

Khaddage, F., Lattemann, C., & Bray, E. (2011). Mobile apps integration for teaching and learning. *Proceedings of Society for Information Technology & Teacher Education International Conference 2011* (pp. 2545–2552).

Knezek, G., Kwok-Wing, L., Khaddage F., & Baker R. (2011). *TWG 2: Student technology experiences in formal and informal learning*. Discussion paper for TWG 2 the EduSummIT 2011, International Summit on ICT in Education, UNESCO Headquarters, Paris, France.

McMahon, M., & Pospisil, R. (2005). Laptops for a digital lifestyle: Millennial students and wireless mobile technologies. *Proceedings of ASCILITE 2005.* Retrieved from: www.ascilite.org.au/conferences/brisbane05/blogs/proceedings/49_McMahon%20&%20Pospisil.pdf

Oblinger, D. G. (2003). Boomers, Gen-Xers, and Millennials: Understanding the new students. *EDUCAUSE Review*, *38*(4), 38–47.

Oblinger, D. G. (2004).The next generation of educational engagement. *Journal of Interactive Media in Education, Special Issue on the Educational Semantic Web*, (8), 1–18.

Oblinger, D. G., & Oblinger, J. L. (2005). *Educating the net generation*. Melbourne, Australia: EDUCAUSE.

O'Loughlin, A. (2011). The use of iPads for educational purposes: A study of lecturer engagement within mobile learning environments. In S. Barton et al. (Eds.), *Proceedings of Global Learn Asia Pacific 2011* (pp. 1196–1198), AACE.

Seibu, M. J., & Biju, I. (2008). Mobile technologies and its impact—An analysis in higher education context. *International Journal of Interactive Mobile Technologies*, *2*(1), 10–19.

Sharples, M., Taylor, J., & Vavoula, G. (2007). A theory of learning for the mobile age. In R. Andrews & C. Haythornthwaite (Eds.), *The Sage handbook of e-learning research* (pp. 221–247). London: Sage.

Tatar, D., Roschelle, J., Vahey, P., & Penuel, W. R. (2003). Handhelds go to school: Lessons learned. *IEEE Computer*, *36*(9), 30–37.

Zedensk (2011) Mobile in the Enterprise. Retrieved from: http://gigaom2.files.wordpress.com/2011/05/mobile-help-desk-in-enterprise.jpg

12

MOBILE LEARNING ACROSS DEVELOPING AND DEVELOPED WORLDS

Tackling Distance, Digital Divides, Disadvantage, Disenfranchisement

John M. Traxler

HISTORY AND THE CONTEXT

Mobile technologies can clearly support, deliver and enhance learning. In doing so, they can tackle the barriers of distance, digital divides, disadvantage and disenfranchisement, however these concepts are defined. This chapter will explore the complexity of this agenda. We can orient ourselves by looking at accounts of initiatives and programmes that range from large scale to small scale, from urban to rural, from young to old, from north to south, to choose only a handful of dimensions.

In Europe, in the earliest days of learning with mobile devices, the European Commission's Information Society Technologies programme's *m-learning* project (www.m-learning.org/archive/index2.shtml), running from 2001 to 2004 and costing €4.5 million, tackled literacy, numeracy and life skills for the young NEETs (in the official jargon of the time, 'not in education, employment or training', from 16 to 24 years of age). It involved three countries, Britain, Sweden and Italy, and had considerable success in building and deploying what were very innovative technologies for those early days. The devices used were early PDAs and smartphones. Much of the effort, time and resource in those early days was devoted to developing a serviceable infrastructure and designing, developing and integrating the various educational systems, which included stand-alone games, a personalised portal, an online soap opera, an intelligent tutoring system and an LMS. The project took place, however, against a backdrop of constant technical change and churn, and this often provoked restarting the technical development in order to stay abreast of current technologies. In spite of these technical difficulties, trials involving some 200 learners across 12 different schemes showed increased motivation and engagement.

The project was based on a few underlying predicates and delivered some counter-intuitive findings. One of these predicates was that some form of social-constructivist pedagogy was most desirable. Another predicate was that the idiosyncratic and often unreliable devices being used out of necessity were, in fact, only proxies for an eventual, generic, *converged* device. Finally, there was the notion that informal learning with familiar mobile devices would entice learners into learning within formal settings with computers, en route to re-engaging with the economy and the world of work. In fact, it was the fairly behaviouristic games that were well liked, whereas the most social-constructivist element, the discussions accessed through personalised portals, needed trained moderators and, thus, only succeeded with learners already in educational groups. The mythic generic *converged devices* never did emerge, and it has become apparent in recent years that sustainable generic m-learning would generally depend on learners' own highly *diverged* devices. Many of the learners did indeed want to make the transition to formal learning, while just as many wanted to continue with informal m-learning and saw no reason to make the transition.

There was, at the time, survey data suggesting that the one universal possession of the young dispossessed and disengaged was their mobile phone. This was a final predicate and suggested that mobile devices did not just reinforce or replicate existing digital divides, and could thus be used as the technology that would take education to *the bottom of the pyramid.*

Many projects, directly or indirectly, knowingly or unknowingly, have built on this early work, especially in those countries, agencies and organisations where there are resources and responsibilities enabling or compelling pro-active educational interventions to catalyse social change. In Austria, for example, a recent project, ComeIn, also EU-funded, works with exactly the same constituency, now called *marginalised young people.* These young people, aged 14–21 years, are still at risk of exclusion, as they stand on the margins of society. Their experiences of marginalisation result from different factors, including educational or economic barriers. They are still a highly vulnerable group, as they confront challenges such as strong competition in the labour market and difficult transitions between different life phases. Mobile devices will still be the first choice for enabling them to access a learning platform, as, again, the project's early empirical work shows universal ownership of a mobile phone (Unterfrauner, 2011).

MOBILES FOR EDUCATION FOR DEVELOPMENT

In parallel developments, there were early attempts to use mobiles in the global South, often in South Africa. Here, the drivers were geographical or infrastructural distance and separation, rather the social and economic distance and separation found in Europe. The emphasis was on the support and management of existing conventional education systems, often distance-learning systems, rather than on pedagogic innovation.

One of the earliest projects was in Kenya. The project was unusual in being large scale and one off; it was neither a pilot nor a trial, but was driven largely by a vision and by some limited UK experience from the University of Wolverhampton (Traxler & Riordan, 2003). As a prelude to the project, Digital Links International undertook a scoping study in the autumn of 2004, looking at aspects of ICT attitudes, access and usage among teachers in eight case-study areas. This showed that teachers were likely to be early adopters of SMS technologies as soon as they received network coverage and had an interest in, and acceptance of, using SMS in learning (but also that teachers would be understandably unhappy with SMS schemes that displaced messaging costs onto them).

The study also considered the professional, institutional, logistical, and cultural and equity issues of access to information and communications technologies. In particular, it examined the likely feasibility and effectiveness of using multiple media to deliver the in-service training programme. The conclusion was that this approach would be successful, but would need careful organisation at district level to take into account the challenges posed by constraints in equipment and infrastructure. The scoping study was itself a significant achievement in accessing the views of teachers and advisors in deeply rural areas, rather than just accepting those of ministry officials.

In practical terms, Digital Links believed it was feasible to use videotape as part of any programme for primary headteachers throughout the country, with secondary schools willing and able to provide the key points of delivery. However, in some areas where distances were great and communications poor, a back-up plan would be needed, and the teachers' colleges would have to offer help. The use of audiocassettes as part of any key resource teacher's (KRT) programme was also felt to be feasible throughout, provided there was a clear plan to cover the costs of batteries for the cassette players in schools without a source of electrical power. Between 60 and 96 per cent of rural schools were without any source of electrical power. At the same time, there was almost universal interest among teachers in becoming computer literate and having access to computers. This survey and its conclusions reveal most of the factors at work in any comparable situation and emphasise the potential of mobile technologies in blended distance-learning systems. The successes and the failures of the subsequent project can be seen as implicit in this initial study.

The project, called SEMA (Traxler 2005), started development and procurement work in early 2006. It was inaugurated in mid 2006 to exploit messaging technologies based on mobile phones to support nationwide, in-service teacher training and educational information management in schools in Kenya. The project consisted of an initial pilot phase across two districts, followed by a much larger pilot phase with another ten districts. At the end of this second phase, the technical and organisational achievements of the system were impressive. A total of 12 districts in eight provinces and the Ministry of Education itself were involved, and the total number of users was about 8,000. Most of these had received face-to-face training. About 85 per cent of the registered users were active on the system, and over 3,000 participants, or approximately 40 per cent, were female. The project had consumed over a quarter of a million SMS messages and had involved the development and deployment of several different SMS technologies. It was intended ultimately to support 200,000 primary teachers on the School Empowerment Programme (SEP) and to gather, process and present class-enrolment data nationally with dramatically improved speed, visibility and accuracy, as part of the Educational Management Information Systems (EMIS) programme. SEP and EMIS were, at the time, core components in national strategies to address inefficiency, overcrowding, under-training, maladministration and wider social problems in the Kenyan education system, and, ultimately, to enhance the delivery of universal primary education.

The m-learning component was twofold: first, a bespoke managed and targeted messaging using SMS and users' own phones, exploiting the highly systematic nature of Kenyan teachers' teacher numbers, effectively their employee ID, to create multiple discussion groups, based around role and regions, from school up to province as appropriate, mediated entirely by SMS. This component also facilitated delivery of the following:

- study-guide material, giving week-by-week support, maintaining momentum, contact, morale and continuity;
- content such as hints, tips, outlines, lists, summaries, revision;
- reminders for assessment, contact, broadcast, discussion, video, meeting;
- discussion in the form of feedback, seminar, query;
- pastoral work giving support, encouragement;
- urgent messages about errata, cancellations and changes.

Second, an EMIS, mediated again by SMS, allowing headteachers to construct one rather terse and opaque message every week, giving enrolments – the *register* in UK educational parlance – broken down by class and gender. The server then did various calculations, allowing officials with the appropriate URL and password to go to an urban cybercafé and see tabulated national and provincial data representing the current state of the entire school system. This was a dramatic improvement on the previous paper-based systems, which needed a host of motorcycle couriers and manual counters to produce data that were too old and cumbersome to ever be verified, but nevertheless determined orphan feeding, textbook allocation and teachers' salaries.

An early, informal evaluation of the traffic, however, showed relatively little educational content in the discussions and showed many messages in error, especially in the EMIS system. Therefore, although the system was infrastructurally robust and technically adequate, there were apparently problems for users in understanding its role and intended use. This suggested that revisions to the policy, training and documentation of the system were needed in order to encourage an increase in the intended use of the system, but perhaps also an exploration of why users found the system so attractive for so many other uses. These never took place, and the final, formal monitoring and evaluation exercise, conducted in early 2008, which could have been crucial to exploring the context and causes for these apparent problems in the project's pilot phases and to understanding, improving and sustaining the project, however, faced a variety of infrastructural and technical challenges, alongside cultural and organisational constraints, and limitations on resources, personnel and logistics (Lightfoot, 2012). It also coincided with the outbreak of nationwide violence and chaos that followed the contested presidential election of 2007–2008.

Other initiatives exploiting SMS, for example those at the University of Pretoria (Traxler & Viljoen, 2007), were less ambitious and, with hindsight, more robust and straightforward, while DEEP, a major, contemporary DFID-funded teacher development project based in Egypt and South Africa's Eastern Cape Province, provided an interesting counterpoint (Traxler & Leach, 2006), in that its priorities were improved teacher efficacy and professionalism, but predicated on government-supplied PDAs. The improvements were indeed impressive, but financially unsustainable.

In contemporary South Africa, the Dr Math project uses the Mxit platform (Butgereit, 2007; Butgereit & Botha, 2011). This is an incredibly popular messaging technology that provides teenagers with a host of services, not all of them entirely safe, and hosts 40–50 educational and social services. Dr Math is a maths club or maths help system. Using only text, no graphics, learners connect to a volunteer university-based tutor or mentor. The format is very versatile and robust and overcomes a variety of barriers associated with traditional maths clubs: these clubs are *uncool* – and *cool*, by the way, crops up in many of m-learning's foundational myths – and there is perhaps a stigma to having extra lessons. In addition, there is a lack of suitable tutors, who may already be employed full time and are not available in the afternoon, while learners may not be available to return to school in the evenings, and there may be other scheduling conflicts between learner and tutor. Therefore, a large-scale mobile project solves these problems by connecting a large pool of tutors to learners at acceptable times. Dr Math is unusual in having created a benign and sustainable business model – users are prepared to pay Mxit for the connectivity, and tutors receive academic credit for the time. The organisers are now preparing to build on this success, not by scaling up, but by replicating the service across other university towns.

Also in South Africa, the Shuttleworth Foundation has been among a range of NGOs supporting large-scale and potentially sustainable projects delivering basic education and targeting teenagers and young people. In 2009, the m4Lit (mobile phones for literacy, now called *Yoza*) project set out to explore the viability of using mobile phones to support reading and writing by teenagers in South Africa. Two *m-novels*, in English and Xhosa, part of a series, were published on a mobile-friendly website and on the mobile instant-messaging platform, Mxit. In the 7 months following the launch, the stories had been read over 34,000 times, users had submitted over 4,000 entries in writing competitions for the stories, and readers had left over 4,000 comments on chapters. *Yoza* is now a library of 35 m-novels, in response to demand by readers for more m-novels. These are 35 m-novels written in ways that appeal to youth, by local authors. For some teenagers, mobile phones are a viable platform for distributing longer-form content and enabling reader participation. One girl commented, 'Awsum :) Im realy nt much of a reader but reading of my phone jst seems alot easier . . . and co0ler! :).' The library continues to grow.

Most of these and similar projects are not funded as academic research, and this means that they are less likely to be formally evaluated and formally published and disseminated than corresponding research projects. In fact, evaluation is likely to be a problem for a variety of reasons, even for academic research projects, and the role of evidence in the formulation of institutional or national policies for m-learning continues to be problematic (Traxler & Kukulska-Hulme, 2006).

In the Indian subcontinent, there are several valuable and interesting projects working in a similar space. The MILLEE (Mobile and Immersive Learning for Literacy in Emerging Economies) project, having started in 2004, has fostered English literacy of children in developing parts of India where English-language skills are widely seen as key for socioeconomic success, a *world language* or *power language* that accesses national educational opportunities, with government, health and legal services, and the global knowledge economy. The project provides interactive English-language games and has a positive impact on English acquisition. One goal of the project has been to investigate how to make localized English-language learning resources more accessible to underprivileged children, at times and places that are more convenient than schools. Reconciling localised resources with economies of scale and/or sustainable business models will be a recurrent theme. The project has focused on developing scalable, localizable design principles and tools for language learning and confronting the challenges of integrating sound learning principles, providing concrete design patterns that integrate entertainment and learning, and accounting for cultural and learning differences in children in developing regions. The project has received major sponsorship from the MacArthur Foundation, Microsoft, National Science Foundation, Nokia,

Qualcomm and Verizon. It has been featured in the press in India (where previous pilots were based), a Canadian Broadcasting Corporation television documentary, and ABC News. With a donation of 450 mobile phones from Nokia, there is now a controlled experiment with 800 rural children in 40 villages in India. Meanwhile, collaborators in Africa and China are replicating the work with rural learners in their local communities. It continues to attraction global attention, along with a handful of other projects, some also mentioned here. As m-learning attracts more corporate and policy attention, this is understandable, but worrying. We are expecting significant decisions around funding and policy to be made on the basis of policymakers being exposed to a handful – the recurrent, same handful – of successful projects. Other projects share this emphasis on basic literacy, aspects of local culture such as story-telling and games, and participative design deployed to reach children in remote rural areas (Kam, 2009; Kam, Rudraraju, Tewari, & Canny, 2007; Viswanathan & Blom, 2010; Winters & Mor, 2008).

They illustrate many of the issues of working with disadvantaged communities in developing regions. The challenge is finding design strategies that reconcile new, powerful and probably unfamiliar technologies with local, maybe traditional and conservative, expectations about learning and pedagogy. Partly because of the failings of the local school systems, these projects often build informal learning activities as a way of reaching youngsters, and sometimes adults, who have dropped through the school system. Although these are worthwhile alternatives to corporate or global ideas about what to learn and how to learn it, much more work is needed to identify and consolidate the genuinely general or transferable parts of these approaches. In essence, disadvantaged and distant communities need the educational version of mass customisation as the antidote to educational mass production, in order to access appropriate and sustainable m-learning.

Janala, a project headed by the BBC World Service Trust in Bangladesh and launched in 2009, is, like Dr Math, another example of simplicity and scale. It is funded by the UK Department for International Development as part of English in Action, a major educational initiative launched in 2008 to raise the language skills of 27 million people by 2017. The majority of Bangladeshis consider English essential to securing a good job and educating their children, according to a BBC survey, and wanted their children to learn it. This simple proposition, however, fails to reveal the ethical complexity around different languages in disadvantaged communities and developing regions.

Learners access the Janala system with a short-code and get hundreds of English-language audio lessons and quizzes. The service is picked up by many of the poorest, those living on less than $3 a day, and the BBC is proud of the proportion of users that continually return to the service. Content is updated weekly and caters to all levels of experience, with *Essential English* for beginners, *Pronunciation* for intermediaries and *Vocabulary in the News* for the more advanced. They agreed to cut the cost of calls to the service by up to 75 percent. Each lesson lasts 3 minutes and costs less than the price of a cup of tea from a Dhaka stall. Janala works with all six of Bangladesh's mobile operators. One of the major achievements of the Janala project has been getting these national network operators to meet and agree various technical issues. In emerging markets, with cut-throat competition and little customer loyalty, this is a considerable achievement.

As we have seen, mobile technologies and mobile networks can reach deep into remote rural regions and deliver learning to isolated communities. They can consequently upset the delicate ecological balance around their language, culture and learning. This is complex and not necessarily always malign.

On the one hand, even some European languages are increasingly marginalised by the globalisation of which mobile technologies are only one small symptom (and, indeed, these even distort the use of Chinese away from traditional but elitist characters and towards the demotic *pinyin* Romanisation favoured by mobile-phone keyboards).

In Kenya, worldreader.org provides e-book readers to various communities across southern Africa and attempts to grapple with assorted technical problems. These readers are a cheap, robust mobile technology to take content into remote regions in developing countries. One example comes from Ntimigom Primary and Nursery schools in Kilgoris, a town in the Rift Valley Province, Kenya, where the mother tongues might be that of the Maasai, with their traditional semi-nomadic lifestyle, or perhaps the Gusii-speaking Kisii. The e-book readers, however, deliver Swahili. In many parts of Kenya, Swahili is a lingua franca that has evolved along the entire coast and hinterlands of East Africa. English, however, is much higher status and educationally desirable; either may threaten mother tongues, and the linguistic ecology of different East African states is a politically charged issue. We should also remember that national education has often been the instrument to *sedentarise* nomadic communities who ignore national borders and do not pay taxes. M-learning is now a component in the scenario.

These are various counter examples that show that the exposure of small language communities is not always detrimental. In fact, the Internet and mobile devices can both link dispersed communities together that would otherwise be fragmented and swamped in the wider world. One example is the Tuvan community, which now has an iStore app, a talking dictionary, devoted to preserving its language and passing it on. It was created by the Living Tongues Institute for Endangered Languages and BoCoSoft Inc. Tuva is located in southern Siberia, and the Tuvan people have a rich tradition of orally transmitted folklore, including many genres, ranging from very brief riddles and aphorisms to tongue-twisters, magical tales, hero tales, scary stories and epics that would take many hours to recite. Another small, simple example of this is the San, the so-called Bushmen of the Kalahari, the original inhabitants of much of southern Africa, but now very marginal to the economic and educational worlds around them. There are 11 different language groups among the San. Many of these click languages have only existed in written form for fewer than 20 years. Some have fewer than ten adult speakers. Currently, there are 27 linguistic projects underway among San communities in southern Africa. One of these aims to support San language with enhanced e-book readers in their own languages (www.kalaharipeoples.org/). These may illustrate the balance between the mass production of learning and its mass customisation.

MOBILES FOR EDUCATION FOR DISADVANTAGE

Throughout this time, researchers, agencies and public bodies have also been promoting the use of mobile technologies for learners disadvantaged by physiological or cognitive challenges. This approach might have started through enumeration of how different technical features could address particular challenges (Rainger, 2005) but became part of a more inclusive characterisation of education and educational design – *education for all* – at the same time as mobile devices became pervasive and ubiquitous. There are obviously still many bodies supporting their respective communities and constituencies, but they are now able to place their work in a more inclusive ideology. In the UK, the work of TechDis (www.techdis.ac.uk) has demonstrated this trajectory and supports students across the national university population, while, at the same time, commercial system developers have responded to the stimulus of disability-discrimination legislation.

Projects using mobiles to support greater access to education and address issues of social exclusion have followed this trajectory, too. In 2004, Sony supported a project at the University of Wolverhampton for non-traditional students, those with no history of university in their families or their neighbourhoods, by providing PDAs (effectively, smartphones without telephone connectivity) for a cohort of students, giving them the necessary information to adjust to a complex new academic environment (Traxler & Riordan, 2004). This scheme, like so many others at the time, was unsustainable, as it depended on the institutional provision of devices. Now, the Mobile Oxford project and other open-source spin-offs occupy a similar space, but assume that students have their own personal, web-enabled, location-aware devices. Through a simple and accessible interface, these mash up public information, such as bus timetables, and institutional information, such as university timetables and library catalogues, in order to provide answers to a range of problems of living and working in complex urban and academic environments.

The reference to Sony reminds us of a perennial aspect of the technological approach to social problems, namely the seductive prospect of support and resources from corporate social responsibility. This plays out differently in different cultures and different political and economic climates. In much of Europe, in the first decade of this century, the states and their institutions were willing and still able to recognise their responsibilities in easing the access to education of disadvantaged communities, and mobile devices were an emergent, appropriate and attractive technology. This accounted for much public funding of m-learning and for the private sector receiving less attention from indigent researchers.

The relationships between the private-sector custodians of *corporate social responsibility* funds and the public-sector beneficiaries were by no means straightforward. In approaching sources of private finance, corporate social responsibility support was usually more attractive to educators than straightforward business partnerships. Often, however, this support was short term and fixed term. This meant that set-up and start-up were rapid, often not giving the technology or the learners the time to settle, and making competent evaluation methodologically and practically very challenging. It often meant that there were no formal ethics procedures and little peer-reviewed publication. A more damaging aspect was, however, that projects supported in this way were far less likely to think in terms of sustainable business models or responsible exit strategies. In the second decade of the century, amidst global economic gloom, this is all the more significant.

To close the circle, the *m-learning* project eventually led to the MoLeNET initiative. Although this had an explicitly vocational agenda, it nevertheless illustrated that the earlier projects had a demonstrable impact on policymakers and government budget holders. The initiative invested about £14 million in a range of projects in England and Wales, and, although the funding was fixed term, established a broadly based network of practitioners and mentors. In fact, this network may have been its most valuable legacy.

OBSERVATIONS AND ISSUES

As readers will notice, and as UNESCO noticed too in its recent regional reviews, the history of m-learning for the majority of its first decade has been dominated by a relatively small number of individuals and a relatively small number of institutions, quite often based in either England or South Africa. Certainly, activity in the non-English-speaking worlds has been minimal, and the working language of m-learning in conferences, applications, learners and journals has always been English. These are factors that make learning from, transferring from, and generalising from, our experiences problematic.

There are other factors. We have explored the interventions of m-learning research and development into those communities characterised by disadvantage or distance in relation to existing educational provision. We have, however, ignored the overriding influence of funding on these endeavours. These interventions could only happen if, and for as long as, they were funded. Although there may have been an element of purely academic research or technical development, the majority of this funding support came for departments, donors and agencies with a social or educational agenda. Rightly or wrongly, these departments, donors and agencies provided funding opportunities, broadly or narrowly defined, for m-learning researchers to demonstrate that their work could make a social or educational impact. In any review of the capacity of mobile devices to address kinds of social or educational disadvantage, we cannot ignore the extent to which the visions, values, performance indicators and preferences of the funding departments, donors and agencies have skewed or coloured the outcomes and impact of the work so far and the lessons we learn. We might, however, have to make some generalisations about these agencies, donors and departments, in order to see, at least to a first order of magnitude, how this skewing and colouring might work, and also where it might have come from. In some countries, those characterised by what has been called *big government*, there is an expectation that the state take lifelong responsibility for its citizens, certainly in much of health, education and employment. These governments have often funded research to promote their social agenda, and the work and outputs of the m-learning community have been skewed accordingly. The relationship between evidence and policy is not linear; it is cyclic and inter-dependent.

Small government, by comparison, can be characterised as the ideology that government has only an elementary responsibility to defend the border and fight crime. Its educational responsibilities might be quite limited, probably only primary or elementary schooling, and, obviously, in the developing countries, this may be further compounded by lack of resources and lack of capacity. This begs big questions about the role of researchers and activists, and the purpose of projects and evidence. Can these influence business and government, and, if so, how? This takes us back to the role of corporate social responsibility on the one hand and the need for the m-learning community to produce cogent business arguments on the other.

Either way, we must recognise that educational interventions for social reasons, unlike interventions for research reasons, are far more likely to be attempting to meet an ongoing need or demand; some have argued that an unsustainable intervention might cause more harm, by diverting resources or raising expectations, than good and could be construed as unethical if there is no exit strategy.

We must also, however, take into account the historical dimension and recognise that perfect hindsight is now redundant. The work of the m-learning community started in an era when mobile devices were expensive, fragile, rare and difficult, and policymakers and funders might have easily deferred to researchers as the recognised experts. It ends in an era when mobile devices are cheap, robust, universal and easy, and policymakers and funders might quite easily have very comprehensive and confident views about what mobile devices can and cannot do. The empirical evidence coming from subsidised, small-scale, fixed-term pilots run by enthusiasts does not necessarily transfer to larger, sustained programmes embedded within bigger organisations and institutions. Furthermore, the evidence generated by these pilots might address the question of educational impact or value in relation to the resources invested in the project, but will not address the question of the relative educational impact of mobile technologies as opposed to, say, equivalent resources invested in school libraries or subsidised school meals. At worst, the work of the m-learning community may have demonstrated merely that increased resources in education improve learning.

Finally, there is a growing interest among educationalists in *resilience*, both education for cultural, social, personal and economic resilience in increasingly unstable and turbulent times, and resilient education services in the face of the varied disruptions that have faced both Gaza and Haiti, the disruptions of geology and of geopolitics. Mobile technologies and the work of the m-learning community can make valuable contributions to these disasters and dislocations.

In the context of the current chapter, the definition of m-learning as *learning across multiple contexts, through social and content interactions, using personal electronic devices* both reveals and conceals. As a tool for addressing educational exclusion and marginalisation, the key attribute and defining characteristic of m-learning has been the capacity of the technology to cross distance rather than context. Even this distinction is not, however, straightforward, as we argue that the nature of the distances that we describe are not only geographical or geometric, but also infrastructural, social, economic, physiological or cognitive, allowing educational interventions to reach across the separation between *most of us* and *the rest of us* in ways that were not previously possible. Talk of context can obscure these varied but simple possibilities. Increasingly, addressing educational exclusion and marginalisation rests, not on the capacity of the technology to cross distance or context, but on the nearly universal access, ownership, appropriation and use of the technology. This, however, does not make learning or m-learning merely sustainable or equitable but otherwise unchanged. In fact, it fundamentally changes the nature of learning. Learning is now increasingly nothing but mobile, and societies around the world are increasingly defined by their mobility and connectedness, transforming learning by altering the ways in which people and communities generate, acquire, share, discuss, emphasise, store, transmit and consume the ideas, information, images, identities and opinions that constitute the knowledge and epistemologies that underpin the conception of learning.

In this context, much work has been done using mobiles within the open- and distance-learning community, rather than the self-identifying m-learning community, and this fact suggests that too tight an adherence to definitions might have the effect of excluding valuable contributions from our discussions.

THE COMING DECADE

This chapter builds on 10 years of experience with m-learning and, standing back from the specifics of projects, initiatives and interventions, it attempts to explore the nature of these propositions about mobiles, learning and forms of disadvantage. In a global context, this exploration is timely. There has been a discernible increase and a discernible shift in interest in using mobiles to support and deliver learning in the developing countries among the wider world of agencies, corporates and ministries. In October 2010, for example, the UNESCO chair in e-learning in Barcelona sponsored an international seminar that focused on mobiles, learning and development. At about the same time, the GSMA Development Fund published its *mLearning: A platform for educational opportunities at the base of the pyramid* (GSMA 2010), intended to give the mobile-network operators a sense of the business case. In February 2011, the World Mobile Congress in Barcelona sponsored its first awards for learning and attracted an impressive field from organisations working in development. In August 2011, USAID convened the first m4Ed4Dev symposium in Washington, DC, as a prelude to launching the mEducation Alliance in February 2012. In November 2011, the WISE debate supported by the Qatar Foundation focused on mobiles, education and the hard-to-reach, and, in December 2011, UNESCO in Paris convened its first Mobile Learning Week, consisting of both closed sessions for experts and open sessions for the wider community. These sessions focused, regionally and globally, on policy issues and teacher development, the latter seen as a crucial place to break into the educational cycle and promote education for all. In March 2012, there was a further International Symposium in Washington, organised by UNESCO and drawing together major practitioners and stakeholders, and graced by the presence of Sir Bob Geldof. These are just events and publications that have crossed my personal horizon.

Because of the changes signified by recent events, there is a likelihood that m-learning for the disadvantaged and m-learning in development contexts may move from small-scale, fixed-term projects run by the enthusiasts from the m-learning community towards larger, sustained projects run by ministries and corporates.

Many of these events were focused on new audiences and, perhaps understandably, never unpacked a fundamental paradox in their own analyses and recommendations. This paradox is represented by the competing views of mobile technologies as instrumental in fundamental social changes that increasingly render formal education systems intrinsically less credible, authoritative and authentic – the phrase *Arab Spring* is frequently used in this context – and as a technology that formal education systems may co-opt and appropriate in order to regain their authority, credibility and authenticity. Currently, this tension remains tacit. A similar but more obvious tension occurs between scale, sustainability and appropriateness. Technology and infrastructure will scale, and their protagonists and stakeholders know how to assemble business models, but these may be inimical to local, indigenous and informal cultures and habits.

PERSONAL REFLECTIONS

My early work in m-learning was with the *m-learning* project, mentioned earlier, starting back in 2001, working with the literacy of young people, perhaps homeless or job-less, in the UK and other European countries. Then, later, I worked in Kenya, with

SEMA, to support in-service teacher training and educational information gathering using a bespoke SMS system. These were, at the time, easy to conceptualise as two separate, parallel strands, one domestic, in the *developed* North, the other, a long way away, geographically and culturally, in the *developing* South, at some opposite extreme.

Subsequent work in Cambodia and elsewhere in South Asia complicated the *developed/developing* dichotomy. It introduced an *East/West* component to my thinking alongside the *North/South* one; moving away from anglophone Africa and its legacy of European education systems and moving into societies with strong historical, local formal education institutions introduced another variable or dimension. This, along with ongoing work in southern Africa, highlighted and promoted the pedagogic aspects of m-learning, based within communities, their cultures and their epistemologies, and demoted the more obvious technical and infrastructural aspects.

Some experience in the US and South Africa, and in the UK, Scandinavia and Singapore, further complicated my thinking about the contexts of m-learning by introducing government as an additional dimension, specifically, as we have said, in the ideological contrast between *small* government and *big* government, and in the way these bound an uncertain space between research-based evidence in the process of *evidence-based policy formulation* – sometimes, understandably, derided as *policy-based evidence formulation* – and the role of sustainable business models involving corporate and community players.

This chapter was started as I returned from scoping visits for both the United Nations Relief and Works Agency and the British Council, looking at opportunities to use mobiles to support the education of nearly half a million Palestinian children and tens of thousands of their teachers, spread across camps in the West Bank, Gaza, Jordan, Syria and Lebanon. These are not only *challenging* environments, but ones that add further dimensions to the contexts within which we try to use mobile technologies: ones where educational organisation, infrastructure and capacity have existed, but have been destroyed or displaced, and where the educational role of mobile technologies can be caught between conflicting interpretations, seen sometimes as *progressive*, sometimes as *un-Islamic*, both *cargo cult* and *Trojan horse*.

This confused, fragmented and personal account taught me that m-learning, in attempting to address issues of access, inclusion and equity, is operating in an incredibly complex space. In the last 10 years, maybe more, we have seen technical progress and social change (Traxler, 2010). We have seen this across every sector and region of global education, but many factors militate against any process of abstraction, generalisation, prediction or even the most cautious reasoning about what is happening, beyond accounts of the lived experience of the participants.

This is true for populations in general and must be equally true when we explore our work with communities characterised as disengaged, disadvantaged, disenfranchised or distant. Of course, these characterisations may only be those from outside the communities in question, they may be the views of the *normal* or national mainstream. In some cases, the power of mobile devices to deliver education, the education of the *normal* mainstream, as expressed through ministries, curricula, schools, textbooks, qualifications and teachers, may be of questionable worth. Here, when we consider mobile technologies, we are attempting to balance two questions, namely *what is the nature of our duty to educate others?* with *what is the nature of our right to educate others?*

Many communities, from endangered-language communities in Africa, to Romany traveller communities in Europe, to the hearing-impaired in Britain, see knowledge, language and learning as vital components of their individual and collective identities. The affordances of mobile technologies and m-learning are different and much more potent than their static and sedentary equivalents. In ethical terms, there is an unresolved and unrecognised tension between *informed consent* and *blissful ignorance*. So, learning with mobile devices, across developing and developed worlds, can indeed tackle distance, can tackle digital divides, disadvantage and disenfranchisement, but the process and the prospects are complex and confused.

REFERENCES

Butgereit, L. (2007). Math on MXit: Using MXit as a medium for mathematics education. *Meraka INNOVATE Conference for Educators* (p. 13). CSIR, Pretoria, South Africa, 18–20 April.

Butgereit, L., & Botha, R. A. (2011). Stop words for 'Dr Math'. In P. Cunningham & M. Cunningham (Eds.), *Proceedings of IST-Africa*. IIMC International Information Management Corporation.

GSMA. (2010). *mLearning: A platform for educational opportunities at the base of the pyramid*. London: GSMA Development Fund. Retrieved from: www.gsmworld.com/documents/mLearning_Report_Final_Dec2010.pdf

Kam, M. (2009). *Designing digital games for rural children: A study of traditional village games in India*. Retrieved from: www.cs.cmu.edu/~anujk1/CHI2009.pdf

Kam, M., Rudraraju, V., Tewari, A., & Canny, J. (2007). Mobile gaming with children in rural India: Contextual factors in the use of game design patterns in situated play. *Proceedings of DiGRA 2007 Conference*.

Lightfoot, A. (2012). Signal poor on m-learning's impact. *The Guardian*, March 13. Retrieved from: www.guardian.co.uk/education/2012/mar/13/mobile-learning-research-language-teaching

Rainger, P. (2005). Accessibility and mobile learning. In A. Kukulska-Hulme & J. Traxler (Eds.), *Mobile learning: A handbook for educators and trainers* (pp. 58–59). London: Routledge.

Traxler, J. (2005). Using mobile technologies to support learning in Sub-Saharan Africa. In *Proceedings of MLEARN2005 Cape Town*, South Africa, 25–28 October.

Traxler, J. (2010). Sustaining mobile learning and its institutions. *International Journal of Mobile and Blended Learning, 2*(4), 58–65.

Traxler, J., & Kukulska-Hulme, A. (2006). The evaluation of next generation learning technologies: The case of mobile learning. In *Research Proceedings of ALT-C2006*. Oxford, UK: ALT.

Traxler, J., & Leach, J. (2006). Innovative and sustainable mobile learning in Africa. In *Proceedings of WMUTE* (IEEE), Athens, Greece, November.

Traxler, J., & Riordan, B. (2003). *Evaluating the effectiveness of retention strategies using SMS, WAP and WWW student support*. Galway, Ireland: ICS-LTSN.

Traxler, J., & Riordan, B. (2004, September). *Using PDAs to support computing students* [voted best paper]. Paper presented at LTSN Annual Conference. Belfast: ICS-LTSN.

Traxler, J., & Viljoen, J.-M. (2007). Mobile educational messaging—Scaling-up and sustaining. In *Proceedings of eLearning Africa*. Nairobi, Kenya, May.

Unterfrauner, E. (2011). Mobile learning based intervention—A case study among marginalised young people. *Eleed—E-Learning & Education*, (7). Retrieved from: http://eleed.campussource.de/archive/7

Viswanathan, D., & Blom, J. (2010). New metaphors from old practices—Mobile learning to revitalize education in developing regions of the world. *IEEE Transactions on Learning Technologies, 3*(1), 18–23.

Winters, N., and Mor, Y. (2008). IDR: A participatory methodology for interdisciplinary design in technology enhanced learning. *Computers & Education, 50*(2), 579–600 (see telearn.org).

Part II

Learning and Learner Support

13

MOBILE LEARNERS

Who Are They and Who Will They Become?

Agnes Kukulska-Hulme

More than a decade of research and practice testifies to the fact that mobile technologies offer many learning benefits that apply to a wide range of people (see Hwang & Tsai, 2011; Kim, Mims, & Holmes, 2006; Rochelle, 2003; Sharples, 2000). Nevertheless, we can notice that specific learner groups have been targeted by researchers, developers, practitioners, and others. The target groups have been variously determined by imperatives such as researchers' curiosity, funders' agendas, national education strategies, organizational priorities, and commercial interests. As m-learning becomes increasingly widespread—partly as a side effect of the mass adoption of mobile devices in personal and working lives—discrete mobile learner groups become less discernable in the population, and identification of any neglected groups becomes more challenging. Learners' particular needs may remain undiscovered, unless more effort is put into understanding the development of m-learning in terms of the learners involved and how their engagement is evolving.

We can observe that m-learning is rapidly becoming universal, in the sense that mobile technology is increasingly already in the hands of those who can make use of it for learning (International Telecommunications Union, 2012). This new universality is a potential that must be interpreted by those in charge of education systems, institutions, and classes, as well as by ordinary individuals who need to comprehend the personal-learning implications of the cell phones and other devices they carry around with them. Incorporating m-learning into e-learning or into traditional-learning settings takes time and effort, and, if we ask "Is it worth it?", part of the answer has to be provided through an understanding of how it will benefit learners. On a small scale, this might be reasonably obvious; for example, mobile technologies can significantly enhance the experience of a school trip or field trip by making it possible for learners to collect, share, and analyze data in situ and to integrate this seamlessly with preceding or subsequent learning (e.g., Vavoula, Sharples, Rudman, Meek, & Lonsdale, 2009). On a larger scale, such as mobile-activity design for work-based, community-based, distance, or lifelong learning, we have to understand the diverse learner populations in terms of common opportunities and challenges, such as distributed locations, ability to contribute global or geo-referenced data, patterns of available time, access to mobile apps and resources, and common disabilities and impairments. We can also envisage ways in which mobile technologies can respond to highly personal needs and preferences, normally requiring individualized tutorial support.

The chapter begins with an example illustrating how, through the use of mobile technologies, learners may become lifelong participants in episodes of formal and informal learning. For m-learning, this is a new kind of challenge, inasmuch as those who design for formal learning need to be more aware of how, thanks to lifelong and life-wide perspectives, the formal learning fits into a broader repertoire of ongoing, informal, and out-of-class activity that, at times, may also need to be pedagogically supported if it is to be effective and efficient. A person who has been targeted as a mobile learner for a specific activity in an educational establishment (e.g., a science lesson, a business simulation, a geography trip) may also be, or indeed become, a mobile learner in other settings. The chapter moves on to a characterization of mobile learners based on an analysis of published conference papers in the field of m-learning. The interest in knowing more about mobile learners was developed through several recent projects, in which the author and her colleagues have carried out surveys and interviews seeking learners' perspectives and eliciting detailed descriptions of their m-learning practices. The findings illustrate a close connection between personal life circumstances and the opportunity to use a mobile device to realize personal learning goals (Kukulska-Hulme et al., 2011; Kukulska-Hulme, Traxler, & Pettit, 2007). Language learners in particular are adopting mobile technologies to support independent and social learning (Kukulska-Hulme & de los Arcos, 2011). Although much of this research has been carried out from the perspective of adult, distance, and lifelong learning, students and other learners in all educational settings increasingly have similar needs and challenges in respect of time pressures, multitasking, and being able to have ready access to learning networks and digital learning resources. Furthermore, it is recognized that the prospect of lifelong learning in response to frequent job changes and long-term career development is the new reality for school, college, and university graduates.

PROBLEM STATEMENT

Imagine a target group or population of business-management students. Alongside any m-learning they engage in as part of their formal studies, members of the group will have additional reasons for using mobile technologies. Some students will be facing specific personal challenges such as dyslexia, which may be helped through the assistive aspects of mobile devices. All the students are likely to come into contact with learners from other countries who are using mobile devices to improve their proficiency in the target language necessary for their studies, for example by audio recording their tutors and peers. When the business students graduate, they themselves may be in the position of having to refresh or acquire knowledge of a foreign language, in order to function more effectively in an international work arena. We can predict for the group as a whole that many of the students are likely to continue learning during their working lives: they will become mobile professionals, lifelong learners and networkers. In their private lives, they will probably continue to learn in a mobile way, in small doses of available time, for practical reasons, for career advancement, and for pleasure.

As the above example illustrates, learner characterization with regard to m-learning cannot and should not be confined to a narrow focus. Mobile technologies will increasingly support lifelong professional and voluntary learning, as portable devices continue to facilitate connections and continuity between settings. In future, a learner progressing through life may not be referred to as a "mobile learner" but will still derive certain benefits from m-learning that may also be common to other learners finding themselves in analogous situations or having similar personal goals and needs.

Existing work on student profiling, which owes much to research in the field of distance education (e.g., Woodley & Ashby, 1994), suggests that this should take into account demographic information and previous learning, as well as a host of other study factors grouped around access to equipment, motivation, experiences that learners can draw on, and possible barriers to completion. Although all these aspects remain relevant in profiling for the design of m-learning, contemporary learning designs must cater for increasingly mobile learners, who are intent on efficiency, often wish to limit their spending, and yet have more opportunities to learn in increasingly diverse, technology-rich environments, which might include the multifunctional phone in one's pocket, free Wi-Fi on the train, interactive mobile experiences in the city, and access to networks of tutors, peer learners, or mentors on the move.

However, the matter is further complicated by the ambiguity of "mobile." One distinctive feature of mobile technologies is that, paradoxically, they support learners who are immobile, as well as those who are habitually or exceptionally mobile—people who are unable or unwilling to sit upright at a desktop computer, as well as people for whom it would make no sense at all to do so. The spotlight in m-learning is most frequently on physical mobility and movement between different locations or settings. In a broader perspective, it has been noted that mobile devices enable, not just greater mobility, but also emancipation from spatial, temporal, and contextual constraints (Kakihara & Sørensen, 2002). Nevertheless, practices that are largely hidden from view, such as those that take place in and around the home, may attract less attention and can be difficult to investigate.

The field of m-learning research has reached a point where it is necessary to generate an overview that will illuminate who has been targeted for specific experiences of m-learning and identify populations that have not yet had the opportunity to experience it or to have a high-quality experience of m-learning. In other words, it is important to characterize the groups or populations that could become mobile learners of the future. Increased appropriation of portable, content-rich media, such as podcasts, mobile apps, e-books, and mobile social networking in daily life and work, plays a salient role in accelerating the diffusion of both formal and informal varieties of m-learning (Kukulska-Hulme et al., 2011), and so this is a rapidly shifting landscape, but the important point is to become accustomed to questioning the direction of travel.

CHARACTERIZING MOBILE LEARNERS

Existing literature on learner characteristics provides a general foundation in terms of describing learner diversity and the breadth of learning approaches, strategies, and styles (see, e.g., Coffield, Moseley, Hall, & Ecclestone, 2004; Pollack, 2009; Richardson, 2000; Riddell, Tinklin & Wilson, 2005). Complementary literature on online learners emphasizes the particular characteristics and backgrounds of those who choose virtual study over face-to-face study (Palloff & Pratt, 2003), and how lifestyles may determine the mode of study. Pedagogical descriptors such as incidental learning (Song & Fox, 2008) and serendipitous learning (Calori, 2009) suggest that learners use new technologies to enrich their learning, in some cases profiting from chance encounters and opportunities that present themselves, whereas, in other cases, they display more deliberate autonomy and agency (Pachler, Bachmair, & Cook, 2010); it is worth emphasizing that both dispositions are well aligned with m-learning. Published accounts of adult learning indicate self-direction and self-determination as important traits (Hase & Kenyon, 2007; Knowles, 1980), which has relevance for mobile applications requiring learners to work actively yet remotely from their teacher, and to exercise a good deal of self-reliance. An interesting question that can be formulated on the basis of this literature is: Who is the most likely to benefit from m-learning, and what personal attributes, if any, should they have?

Researchers have already noted that overall effort to engage learners in the use of mobile devices is not necessarily distributed evenly or in the most appropriate ways. Frohberg, Göth, and Schwabe (2009) have argued that, whereas most m-learning projects support novices, the real potential is in supporting advanced learners. This is because m-learning "can best provide support for learning in context. There, learners are asked to apply knowledge and not just consume it. Novices are often not ready to do so" (Frohberg et al., 2009, p. 323). Other researchers have found further imbalances across the spectrum of m-learning initiatives and projects. Hwang and Tsai (2011) took six major technology-based-learning journals as the basis for an analysis of research trends in mobile and ubiquitous learning. They found that, in the period 2001–2010, most reported studies were in higher education, followed by elementary-school and high-school settings. Furthermore, they found that students from higher education (and, to a lesser extent, from elementary school) have consistently dominated mobile and ubiquitous learning research during this period. Teachers and working adults were rarely the focus of studies, and Hwang and Tsai (2011) have proposed that it is worth paying more attention to teachers' and working adults' mobile and ubiquitous learning in the future.

The focus on higher education may reflect a bias towards convenient samples, as researchers choose to work with learners who are within easy reach, or they wish to trial a new technology within their own classes. It may be the effect of local, institutional, or national funding and backing for certain types of study. It is also the case that some projects generate a large number of papers, occasionally appearing in issues of the same journal, and so a simple paper count may disguise the fact that several published studies in higher education refer to the same project or investigation. Furthermore, studies published in major journals do not reflect the full range of research and development work submitted for publication, or that appears in other outlets. Anecdotal evidence further suggests that numerous studies have never been written up or made available beyond an internal audience, partly reflecting the rapid pace of technological change. It is reasonable to assume that at least some contemporary m-learning research and practice are therefore not documented in a public way; this has already been noted by Kukulska-Hulme, Shield, and Hassan (2010), based on a small, open survey of mobile-device use in language teaching and learning. Conference papers and presentations give a more accurate indication of the breadth of actual research, development, and practice in m-learning. Conference content may, however, disproportionately represent major funded projects (that also provide funding for conference participation) and the specific interests and expertise of hosting institutions, often in higher education.

In general, information about specific learner groups that have been targeted or have been shown to benefit from m-learning can be found in disparate sources, as the field of m-learning has expanded into other specialisms (e.g., medical education), as well as continuing to grow in broad domains such as elementary-level education across the whole curriculum. Information about m-learning research and practice is thus dispersed across a wide variety of outlets, including dedicated sources (books and theses on m-learning; m-learning journals and conferences); ad hoc sources (journal special issues devoted to the theme of m-learning; publications based on events, project outcomes, case studies, and policy; blogs and other social media; commercial product information; publications showcasing the winning entries in awards and competitions in m-learning); as well as publications or presentations relating to particular fields of application, such as science education, medical education, language education, international-development studies, and disability studies. Finally, m-learning research is to be found in the broader or related fields of learning technology, online and distance learning, e-learning, information science, cognitive science, computer science, and human–computer interaction.

Observations about target learners, presented in the next section, are drawn from 10 years of published conference proceedings of the *mLearn: World Conference on Mobile and Contextual Learning*, which is overseen by the International Association for Mobile Learning (IAmLearn, www.iamlearn.org). It is the main international research conference dedicated to m-learning and has taken place every year since 2002; the body of papers analyzed here is, therefore, from the period 2002–2011. For each paper, the target learners were identified from information included in each paper, if the information was present.

TARGET LEARNERS IN M-LEARNING

In line with what has already been noted by Hwang and Tsai (2011), a large number of studies and projects reported at mLearn conferences are also concerned with students in schools and higher education, but the range and variety of learners involved in m-learning reach far beyond these formal-education settings.

Schoolchildren and Their Carers

Several papers concerned with school education address broader societal issues, such as whether the children come from poor homes or affluent homes equipped with computers, and how m-learning can advance social inclusion. Parents of schoolchildren are sometimes part of the m-learning initiative, and all stakeholders are increasingly consulted. Several reported projects have had a special focus on bringing culturally divided groups together to promote peace, dialogue, and multicultural interaction.

Higher-Education Students

Papers reporting research in higher education are mainly focused on the students, with occasional mention of lecturers, instructors, teachers, or tutors. First-year students are sometimes a special focus of attention for m-learning deployments. There are some efforts to bring m-learning to groups of young people from different social strata and from different regions and countries, and to cater for those whose careers will involve traveling or that already require combining work with study (e.g., maritime-studies students, military students, MBA students). Papers also report on the use of mobile devices to support foreign students in their learning of the local language, thereby extending the reach of education to those from abroad; other papers report on new ways for students to engage with learning English as a foreign language. Students' everyday use of mobile phones and other devices is sometimes the starting point for developing ideas for m-learning.

Young Adults Not in Education or Work

Beyond school and higher education, m-learning projects have frequently targeted young adults who are described as disaffected, disengaged, reluctant, marginalized, or disenfranchised. These young people are unwilling to take part in education, or they may have experienced educational failure; they may have no opportunity for face-to-face teacher contact, or lack access to computers for remote study; they may be unemployed, under-employed, homeless, or suffer from mental illness. As with higher-education students, the teenage or young-adult mobile-phone user is used as a means of generating new ideas and to understand how these users could relate to m-learning. Development of numeracy and literacy skills, survival skills, job hunting, and other socially valuable competences are highlighted as the most pressing need, and considered to be a good use of mobile technologies with these target groups of learners.

The Underserved in Development Contexts

International development contexts form the basis of another important collection of papers across the proceedings. The target learners are often described as "underserved" and may reside in rural settings; projects have also targeted refugees and immigrants, and intercultural competence has been identified as a worthwhile goal. M-learning for development is concerned with the digital divide, developing citizens, and may be located within broader initiatives to develop populations through open and distance learning, lifelong learning, and free access to content repositories. Postgraduate students working in development organizations, although not "underserved," are another group that has benefited from m-learning.

World of Work: Employees, Professionals, Apprentices

Vocational, professional, and employee learning/training constitute another substantial target area for m-learning. Included here are apprenticeships, students on internships and work placements, as well as school or college leaders and managers who need to be trained and form communities to share their practice. Teacher professional development and toolkits for education and training providers are not prominent, but they are represented, along with m-learning as part of initial teacher training. Travel for business, sport, or education is a recognized factor in the adoption of m-learning; another is learning while employed in a travel-related job, for example as a lorry driver or a taxi driver. Medical team support for emergency situations and disasters is also an important theme, and, therefore, emergency-service operators, emergency managers, ambulance companies, doctors, and other health care professionals are targeted in a number of projects. Papers also report on work with hard-to-reach learners in jobs such as caring and cleaning.

Communities, Friends and Families

Another large group of studies and projects concerns learning in communities, families, and informally as part of lifelong learning. Here we encounter the "mobile-society" type of initiative, where the general public and local communities may be involved as part of a drive to change how technology is used across a whole region or nation. We also see "citywide" learning, where the city becomes a learning environment, and all its diverse resources come into play for students, citizens, and immigrants, but may also highlight the digital divide and other divisions or exclusions within a society (e.g., issues with traveler families). M-learning for community interest in local history, for tourists, and for visitors to art galleries, museums, gardens, and other scenic places, is well represented in the mLearn conference proceedings. Geosocial games create new opportunities for groups and communities to interact and learn together, and informal language learning can be a binding element for a family or community. Parents and caregivers are involved in projects that support parents-to-be, young parents, and early-childhood learning. Informal, community, and family learning is also focused on personal medical information and care, including peer support (e.g., peer educators for sex-worker health care) and medication management (e.g., by adolescent diabetics).

Learners With Special Needs and Disabilities

There is one more group of learners targeted by m-learning projects, and these are learners with special needs, disabilities, or impairments. They include sign-language users, learners with severe disabilities, and those whose disabilities may be hidden or have not yet been addressed. For example, students may elect to use a games console as an assistive technology support for numeracy skills and hidden disabilities such as dyscalculia. M-learning projects not focused on disability support occasionally state that they aim to make accommodations for people with disabilities and impairments.

DISCUSSION

The analysis has enabled a high-level review of the types of learner who have participated in m-learning projects and studies, as reflected in the mLearn international conference series. It is worth mentioning that some of the identified target groups are also represented in specific dedicated publications and resources on m-learning. To give just a few examples, the MOTILL project's case studies and critical review database cover applications of mobile technologies, specifically in lifelong learning (Arrigo, Kukulska-Hulme, Arnedillo-Sánchez, & Kismihok, in press; see also www.motill.eu); work-based learners feature strongly in Pachler, Pimmer, and Seipold (2011); and research and practice in m-learning for visually impaired people has been published in Allegra et al. (2012). By bringing together case studies and other resources illustrating how m-learning applies to particular target groups, these publications are in a good position to influence policy and practice.

The conference papers reviewed for this chapter's analysis reveal seven target learner groupings, with a certain degree of overlap between them. Overlaps occur in common themes around mobility, access, and attitudes to education, but they are also detectable in attempts to address learners' personal vulnerabilities and to use m-learning as a way to bring people together and confront cultural difference in positive ways. Questions raised by the analysis include whether learners who have had positive experience of m-learning in one particular context go on to generate their own opportunities for m-learning in other settings and other areas of their lives. Learners are partly subject to decisions made by others, such as those concerning what materials, resources, and technologies will be made available to them, and partly self-determining, able to decide what they want to do on their mobile device and working out how this helps them reconcile work, life, and learning. It seems that the learner-centric ethos of distance education is being adopted more widely in higher education and in the growing domains of semi-formal and informal learning. Distance education has sometimes attracted those who otherwise would not wish to engage with learning, but, for the majority of enrolled students, it is simply a convenient and flexible mode of learning, and, in the same way, m-learning may be considered a preferred or more efficient way to train or study.

The analysis of who is mentioned as target learners within published papers in the mLearn conference proceedings also reveals that papers describing systems architectures, user interfaces, and interaction designs, as well as those that make contributions to research methodology and theory, generally refer to broad categories such as learners, users, students, course developers, and research participants. It is a challenge to find technical or theoretical papers that also provide details of specific learners or learner groups. This may be owing to length constraints or convention, but more discussions of system features and theoretical considerations in direct relation to specific target learners would be a welcome development.

M-learning has become commonplace in that mobile phones and other portable devices are widely available; however, it is not the case that every person who could be a mobile learner has the device they want, that they can afford to use freely, or that best suits their need. Furthermore, learners need excellent guidance and support in using these tools to best effect. The following target groups are largely missing in the conference papers examined:

- The older, retired population is potentially a target group for m-learning, but it is very much underrepresented in reported projects and studies.
- Engaged, enthusiastic, and talented (young) adults are also not featuring in this literature, other than partially through their roles as workers or employees.
- Mobile learners who may be getting their inspiration within tight communities and families appear to have been out of scope of research over the past 10 years.
- Support for disabilities is only rarely the subject of m-learning studies, despite the fact that undiagnosed vision problems are common, and many mobile-phone users complain about the difficulty of reading from their screen.
- Those who are underserved are narrowly defined as being located in developing countries, whereas all continents have learners who are underserved for reasons of relative poverty or inability to use the prevailing language.

CONCLUSION

This chapter has provided an overview of target learner groups in reported m-learning projects and studies over the past 10 years, as reflected in a series of conference proceedings. The evolution of multiple ways to characterize mobile learners will enable educational researchers, practitioners, managers, administrators, and policymakers to adopt a richer descriptive language and to elaborate more transparent and compatible visions of educational futures. It will also make it easier for instructors and researchers to design m-learning experiences for a range of target learners, informed by broader knowledge about which other groups the learners might also be considered to belong to, now or in future, and what other groups of mobile learners they may come into contact with. This is not the way m-learning is currently conceptualized, but it is how it needs to be thought of in a world where planning and designing for m-learning is becoming a more challenging activity than was the case previously, when the landscape of m-learning consisted largely of clearly delimited, self-contained, and time-bound projects.

REFERENCES

Allegra, M., Arrigo, M., Dal Grande, V., Denaro, P., La Guardia, D., Ottaviano, S., & Todaro, G. (Eds.) (2012). *Mobile learning for visually impaired people.* Palermo, Sicily: Consiglio Nazionale delle Ricerche, Istituto per le Tecnologie Didattiche.

Arrigo, M., Kukulska-Hulme, A., Arnedillo-Sánchez, I., & Kismihok, G. (in press). Meta-analyses from a collaborative project in mobile lifelong learning. *British Educational Research Journal.*

Calori, I. (2009). *Awareness for learning through serendipitous interaction in public intelligent environments.* Paper presented at the 5th International Conference on Intelligent Environments (IE'09). July 20–21, Technical University of Catalonia, Barcelona, Spain.

Coffield, F., Moseley, D., Hall, E., & Ecclestone, K. (2004). *Learning styles and pedagogy in post-16 learning: A systematic and critical review.* London: Learning & Skills Research Centre.

Frohberg, D., Göth, C., & Schwabe, G. (2009). Mobile learning projects—A critical analysis of the state of the art. *Journal of Computer Assisted Learning, 25*(4), 307–331.

Hase, S., & Kenyon, C. (2007). Heutagogy: A child of complexity theory. *Complicity: An International Journal of Complexity and Education, 4*(1), 111–118.

Hwang, G.-J., & Tsai, C.-C. (2011). Research trends in mobile and ubiquitous learning: A review of publications in selected journals from 2001 to 2010. *British Journal of Educational Technology, 42*(4), E65–E70.

International Telecommunications Union. (2012). Key 2000–2011 country data (released June 2012): Mobile-cellular subscriptions. Retrieved from: www.itu.int/ITU-D/ict/statistics/index.html

Kakihara, M., & Sørensen, C. (2002). Mobility: An extended perspective. In *Proceedings of the 35th Hawaii International Conference on System Sciences* (HICSS-35) (pp. 1756–1766). January 7–10. IEEE, Big Island, Hawaii.

Kim, S. H., Mims, C., & Holmes, K. P. (2006). An introduction to current trends and benefits of mobile wireless technology use in higher education. *AACE Journal, 14*(1), 77–100.

Knowles, M. (1980). *The modern practice of adult education: From pedagogy to andragogy.* Wilton, CT: Association Press.

Kukulska-Hulme, A., & de los Arcos, B. (2011). Triumphs and frustrations of self-motivated language learners using mobile devices. In *The CAL Conference 2011—Learning Futures: Education, Technology & Sustainability.* April 13–15, Manchester, UK.

Kukulska-Hulme, A., Pettit, J., Bradley, L., Carvalho, A. A., Herrington, A., Kennedy, D. M., & Walker, A. (2011). Mature students using mobile devices in life and learning. *International Journal of Mobile and Blended Learning, 3*(1), 18–52.

Kukulska-Hulme, A., Shield, L., & Hassan, X. (2010). Mobile technologies for language learning and teaching: An exploratory investigation. In A. Gimeno Sanz (Ed.), *New trends in computer-assisted language learning: Working together* (pp. 167–174). Gandia, Spain: Macmillan.

Kukulska-Hulme, A., Traxler, J., & Pettit, J. (2007). Designed and user-generated activity in the mobile age. *Journal of Learning Design, 2*(1), 52–65.

Pachler, N., Bachmair, B., & Cook, J. (2010). *Mobile learning: Structures, agency, practices.* New York: Springer.

Pachler, N., Pimmer, C., & Seipold, J. (Eds.) (2011). *Work-based mobile learning: Concepts and cases.* Oxford, UK: Peter Lang.

Palloff, R., & Pratt, K. (2003). *The virtual student: A profile and guide to working with online learners.* San Francisco, CA: Jossey-Bass.

Pollack, D. (Ed.) (2009). *Neurodiversity in higher education: Positive responses to specific learning differences.* Chichester, UK: Wiley-Blackwell.

Richardson, J. T. E. (2000). *Researching student learning: Approaches to studying in campus-based and distance education.* Philadelphia, PA: Society for Research into Higher Education & Open University Press.

Riddell, S., Tinklin, T., & Wilson, A. (2005). *Disabled students in higher education: Perspectives on widening access and changing policy.* London: Routledge.

Rochelle, J. (2003). Unlocking the learning value of wireless mobile devices. *Journal of Computer Assisted Learning, 19*(3), 260–272.

Sharples, M. (2000). The design of personal mobile technologies for lifelong learning. *Computers & Education, 34*(3–4), 177–193.

Song, Y., & Fox, R. (2008). Using PDA for undergraduate student incidental vocabulary testing. *ReCALL, 20*, 290–314.

Vavoula, G., Sharples, M., Rudman, P., Meek, J., & Lonsdale, P. (2009). Myartspace: Design and evaluation of support for learning with multimedia phones between classrooms and museums. *Computers & Education, 53*(2), 286–299.

Woodley, A., & Ashby, A. (1994). Target audience: Assembling a profile of your learners. In F. Lockwood (Ed.), *Materials production in open and distance learning* (pp. 18–26). London: Paul Chapman Publishing.

14

MINDTOOLS FOR SUPPORTING MOBILE-LEARNING ACTIVITIES

Gwo-Jen Hwang

In an m-learning activity, the students are situated to learn in real-world contexts with learning supports from the digital learning systems via mobile devices and wireless communications. The learning supports can be supplementary materials related to the learning context or some particular learning targets, hints for the learning tasks related to the contexts, feedback to the students based on their learning status or performance, or tools for helping the students organize what they have learned from the textbooks and what they have observed from the real-world learning environments (Chu, Hwang, Huang, & Wu, 2008; Hung, Lin, & Hwang, 2010; Hwang & Chang, 2011; Hwang, Chu, Shih, Huang, & Tsai, 2010; Hwang & Tsai, 2011; Hwang, Tsai, & Yang, 2008; Hwang, Yang, Tsai, & Yang, 2009). Without proper supports, such in-field or contextual m-learning scenarios might become too complex for most students.

Jonassen, Carr, and Yueh (1998, p. 1) have indicated that "technologies should not support learning by attempting to instruct the learners, but rather should be used as knowledge construction tools that students learn with, not from." Several educators have pointed out that computers can be a potential tool for supporting learning and instruction, such that the learners function as designers, and the computers function as Mindtools for interpreting and organizing their personal knowledge (Jonassen, 1994/1999; Jonassen et al., 1998; Kommers, Jonassen, & Mayes, 1992). Therefore, it has become an important and challenging issue to develop and employ Mindtools to assist learners to interpret and organize their personal knowledge in m-learning environments, in particular, for those in-field learning activities (Chu, Hwang, Tsai, & Tseng, 2010; Hwang, Chu, Lin, & Tsai, 2011; Hwang, Wu, & Ke, 2011). In this chapter, two types of Mindtool are presented. Moreover, the effectiveness of applying the Mindtools in several m-learning activities is reported.

LITERATURE REVIEW

Using mobile devices to provide learning supports for indoor or outdoor learning activities has been recognized as being an important instructional model nowadays

(Chiou, Tseng, Hwang, & Heller, 2010; Hwang et al., 2008); in particular, the necessity and importance of "authentic activities," in which students can work with problems from the real world, have been emphasized by educators for decades (Herrington & Oliver, 2000; Lave, 1991). On the other hand, researchers have also pointed out several critical tasks involved in instructional design for supporting students to learn while taking part in authentic activities (Hwang et al., 2008; Young, 1993), such as scaffoldings to assist novices in completing learning tasks within complex real-world contexts (Bruner, 1986; Hwang et al., 2009; Williams van Rooij, 2009; Vygotsky, 1978), the supports to enable teachers to interact knowledgeably and collaboratively with individual students or co-operating groups of students, and the facilities for designing and conducting situated-learning activities to assist students in improving their ability to utilize skills or knowledge (Collins, 1991; Leng, Dolmans, Jöbsis, Muijtjens, & Vleuten, 2009; Nussbaum et al., 2009; Ogata & Yano, 2004).

The advance and popularity of mobile and wireless communication technologies have enabled the implementation of such learning systems that situate and support students to learn in real-world contexts. In such a contextual learning environment, learners usually hold a mobile device to interact with real-world targets, with supports from the learning system via wireless communications. In the past decade, various studies have been conducted to demonstrate the benefits of employing mobile and wireless communication technologies in supporting contextual learning in the real world. For example, Hwang et al. (2009) developed a contextual learning system for training students in the use of the "single-crystal X-ray diffraction" procedure in a chemistry course; Chen, Hwang, Yang, Chen, and Huang (2009) developed a ubiquitous performance support system to assist teachers in classroom management and student consultation. Hwang et al. (2010) further employed a decision-tree approach for providing learning guidance and instant feedback to the students who were learning, in a butterfly museum, to identify different breeds of butterfly based on their physical characteristics. In those studies, m-learning systems mainly played the role of a personalized instructor or tutor who guided the students to learn and helped them resolve their learning difficulties in the real-world environment, by providing learning guidance, feedback, or supplementary materials following some learning-support mechanisms.

In addition to guiding the students to learn or solving their learning problems, researchers have tried to provide further support to help students construct and organize knowledge in m-learning activities. Mindtools are such learning support tools that have been adopted by researchers in several m-learning studies. A Mindtool is a computer-based tool or learning environment that serves as an extension of the mind. Jonassen (1994/1999, p. 9) described Mindtools as "a way of using a computer application program to engage learners in constructive, higher-order, critical thinking about the subjects they are studying."

Educators have identified several potential Mindtools, such as databases, spreadsheets, semantic networks (e.g., concept maps), computer conferencing, hypermedia construction, microworld environments (dynamic modeling tools, e.g., active-learning environments that simulate real-world phenomena), expert systems, and information and communication technologies (ICT, e.g., online discussion groups and search engines) (Jonassen et al., 1998; Valcke, Rots, Verbeke, & Braak, 2007). Many practical applications have demonstrated how Mindtools can benefit students in organizing their knowledge in m-learning activities. For example, Chu, Hwang and Tsai (2010) reported the effectiveness of using a knowledge-acquisition method as a Mindtool for assisting students in organizing their knowledge and learning experiences in an m-learning activity, and, hence, the learning achievements of the students were significantly improved. Their study also showed that the learning attitudes of the students were promoted as well. A recent study conducted by Hwang, Chu, et al. (2011) further showed that Mindtools could help students share as well as organize knowledge in contextual-learning environments. In the meantime, another study, conducted by Hwang, Shi and Chu (2011) showed that using Mindtools for collaborative m-learning could even improve the learning achievements and attitudes of students, more than individual learning.

MINDTOOLS FOR M-LEARNING

Concept Map-Oriented Mindtools for M-Learning

Concept maps have been recognized as being an effective tool for organizing and visualizing knowledge and learning experiences (Anderson-Inman & Ditson, 1999; Chiou, 2008; Fischer, Bruhn, Grasel, & Mandl, 2002; Reader & Hammond, 1994), as well as an assessment tool for evaluating the cognitive degree of a set of relevant concepts for individuals (Liu, Don, & Tsai, 2005; Peng, Su, Chou, & Tsai, 2009; Ruiz-Primo & Shavelson, 1996). Concept mapping was developed by researchers at Cornell University for representing conceptual-knowledge structures (Novak & Gowin, 1984; Novak & Musonda, 1991). In the past decades, many studies have shown that concept maps are helpful for the promotion of meaningful learning, and, hence, their positive effects can act upon students (Horton et al., 1993; Hwang, Wu, & Ke, 2011; Trent, Pernell, Mungai, & Chimedza, 1998). For example, the study by Kao, Lin and Sun (2008) showed that, with the help of concept maps, students' creativity could be promoted, and their self-awareness could be improved through reflective thinking. They also indicated that the visualization of concept maps provided not only a way for peers to share their knowledge, but also an effective facility for helping them integrate their concept maps into a more complete one.

In the following, a contextual-learning activity for butterfly ecology observations is presented to show how concept map-oriented Mindtools can be used to support m-learning activities, based on the learning case presented by Hwang, Shi and Chu (2011). The objective of the learning activity is to help the students understand the butterfly ecology by observing the butterflies and the related host plants in a butterfly ecology garden. Such learning activities are part of the regular natural-science curriculum of the target school and have been conducted for years.

Figure 14.1 shows the m-learning environment for conducting the learning activity. It consists of a computer classroom and the butterfly ecology garden, with wireless-communication networks. There are several ecology areas in which particular kinds of butterfly and the related host plants of the butterflies are raised. In each ecology area, a radio-frequency identification (RFID) tag is placed. Meanwhile, each student has a mobile device (i.e., PDA) with an RFID reader. With the help of such sensing technology, the learning system is able to detect the location of individual students, and, hence, proper learning instructions or supports can be provided to meet the real-world contexts.

In this case, the students are asked to develop their own concept maps based on what they have learned from the textbooks and the instructions of the teacher, before going

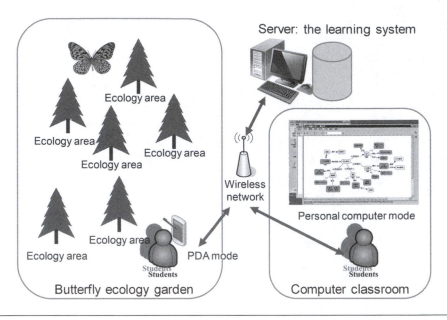

Figure 14.1 M-Learning Environment for Butterfly Ecology Observations

into the field for observations. While learning in the butterfly garden, each student inter-acts with the learning system and invokes the Mindtool to browse the concept maps they have developed via the mobile devices with the wireless-communication facility. The learning system detects the location of the students and guides them to find the learning targets for making observations, as shown in Figure 14.2a. When the students have arrived at the location of the learning targets, the learning system shows the students the learning tasks, as well as some supplementary materials, as shown in Figure 14.2b. The students then start to observe the learning targets and to compare what they find in the field with their original concept maps.

In the study of Hwang, Shi and Chu (2011), CmapTools, developed by the Institute for Human and Machine Cognition of the Florida University System (Novak & Cañas, 2006), is employed as the concept-map development system. CmapTools is a well-known tool that enables users to construct, navigate, and share knowledge models represented as concept maps. It allows users to construct concept maps on personal computers and share them on servers via the Internet (http://cmap.ihmc.us/conceptmap.html). The concepts can be described with multimedia (i.e., texts, hypertexts, photos, or videos).

As it could be difficult for the students to modify their concept maps in the field with mobile devices, while observing the butterfly ecology, Hwang, Shi and Chu (2011) suggest that different facilities should be supported for the students to develop and modify their concept maps at different learning stages; that is, the students can use both personal computers and mobile devices to develop and modify their concept maps. For example, a student might prefer using a personal computer to develop the first version of the concept map in the computer classroom, and then use a mobile device to browse and modify the concept map in the field. Figure 14.3 shows the interface for browsing the concept maps via the mobile device. Such a facility enables the students to compare the real-world butterfly ecology with the concepts they have learned from the text books.

Figure 14.2a Learning System Guides User to Learning Target

Figure 14.2b At Learning Target the Learning Task is Presented

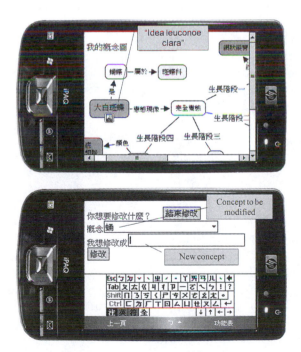

Figure 14.3 Interface for Browsing and Modifying the Concept Maps Via Mobile Devices

On the other hand, some students might want to modify the concept maps in the computer classroom after making the observations. In that case, they can take notes on the mobile devices first, and make the modifications via personal computers after going back to the computer classroom.

Expert System-Oriented Mindtools for M-Learning

An expert system is an artificial-intelligence program that simulates expert reasoning based on the knowledge base constructed by collecting knowledge from domain experts. Past experiences have shown that the most challenging task in developing expert systems is to acquire and organize knowledge from domain experts, which has been called *knowledge acquisition* by researchers (Chu & Hwang, 2008; Shaw, Turvey, & Mace, 1982). Jonassen (1994/1999) indicated that the process of collecting and organizing domain knowledge for constructing knowledge bases could engage students in critical thinking. Chu, Hwang, and Tsai (2010, p. 2) further indicated that "learners are likely to interpret and organize their personal knowledge while participating in the knowledge acquisition process." Consequently, the most effective way of employing expert systems as Mindtools is to engage students in collecting and organizing knowledge related to the course content they aim to learn, following a knowledge-acquisition approach.

Among various knowledge-acquisition approaches, the repertory grid method that originates from the Personal Construct Theory proposed by Kelly (1955) has been recognized as being an effective one (Boose & Gaines, 1989; Hwang, Chen, Hwang, & Chu, 2006). For example, Chu, Hwang, and Tsai (2010) developed a learning environ-ment in which students learned to identify and classify various plants on a school campus by observing the plants and organizing what they found in a repertory grid using mobile devices. A single repertory grid is represented as a matrix whose columns are element labels and whose rows are construct labels. Elements could be decisions to be made, objects to be identified, or concepts to be learned (Chu & Hwang, 2008). Constructs represent the features for describing the similarities or differences among the elements. A construct consists of a trait (e.g., "large") and the opposite of that trait (e.g., "small"). A 5-scale rating mechanism is usually used to represent the relationships between the elements and the constructs; i.e., each rating is an integer ranging from 1 to 5, where 1 represents that the element is very likely to have the trait; 2 represents that the element may have the trait; 3 represents "unknown" or "no relevance"; 4 represents that the element may have the opposite characteristic of the trait; and 5 represents that the element is very likely to have the opposite characteristic of the trait (Chu & Hwang, 2008).

Table 14.1 shows an illustrative example of a repertory grid for describing a set of plants on a school campus. In this case, the elements are Lalang grass, variegated-leaf croton, Cuphea, Indian almond, money tree, crown of thorns, and pink ixora, and the constructs are leaf shape, leaf point, leaf edge, and number of leaf-vein branches. For example, the value of the <Lalang grass, leaf shape> entry is 1, indicating that the leaf shape of Lalang grass is "long and thin." On the contrary, the value of the <Indian almond, leaf shape> entry is 4, implying that the leaf shape of Indian almond tends to be "flat and round."

There are several ways of using repertory grids as Mindtools to support m-learning activities, depending on the objective of the learning activities. In the study by Chu, Hwang, and Tsai (2010), the teacher was asked to develop an objective repertory grid

Table 14.1 Illustrative Example of a Repertory Grid

Trait	Lalang grass	Varie-gated-leaf croton	Cuphea	Indian almond	Money tree	Crown of thorns	Pink ixora	Opposite
The leaf shape is long and thin	1	2	2	4	2	2	2	The leaf shape is flat and round
The leaf has a tapering point	1	1	1	4	2	1	3	The leaf has a hollow point
Perfectly smooth leaf edge	1	1	4	1	1	5	1	The leaf edge has deep indents
The leaf vein has few branches	5	3	2	2	3	3	3	The leaf vein has many branches

(i.e., the repertory grid with correct ratings for each <element, construct> pair) before conducting the learning activity in the field. As the elements and constructs were provided by the teacher, the students only needed to fill in the rating for each <element, construct> entry, based on their observations in the field. Assuming that the example given in Table 14.1 is the objective repertory grid, Figure 14.4 shows the interface of an m-learning system that guides students to observe the leaf point of the target plant, Lalang grass. The five choices represent the 5-scale rating (i.e., 1–5) of the <Lalang grass, leaf point> entry of the repertory grid; that is, values 1–5 will be stored in the entry if the students choose "tapering to a long point", "arrowhead-shaped point", "stem attaches to tapering point", "round with a blunt tip," or "leaf with a hollow point", respectively.

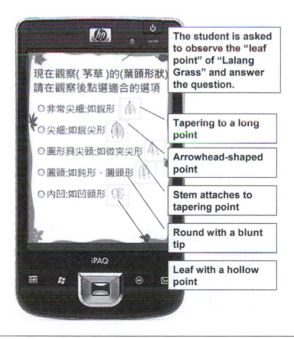

Figure 14.4 Interface for Browsing and Modifying the Concept Maps Via Mobile Devices

If the students fail to give the correct rating compared with that given by the teacher in the objective repertory grid, the learning system would guide them to observe another learning target with "incorrect main feature" and compare it with the learning target. For example, if a student observed the plant (learning target) Lalang grass and described its leaf point as "round with a blunt tip" (by giving rating 4), and the student's answer is compared with the rating given by the teacher (i.e., "tapering to a long point" with rating 2), it would be found that the student's answer was incorrect. From the objective repertory grid, the learning system would find that the leaf point of another plant, Indian almond was "round with a blunt tip," matching the incorrect answer given by the student. Therefore, the student would be guided to observe the Indian almond and compare its leaf point with that of Lalang grass, as shown in Figure 14.5. After making the comparison, the student would be asked to answer the question again.

Another way of using repertory grids as Mindtools was reported by Hwang, Chu, et al. (2011), who aimed to engage students in more challenging learning tasks. In their study, the teacher only assigned the target plants (i.e., elements of the repertory grid) to be observed; that is, the students needed to determine the constructs for identifying and differentiating the plants, as well as fill in the rating of each <element, construct> entry on their own. It can be seen that such an approach is more challenging, as the students not only need to observe and compare the appearance of the plants, but also need to determine which features (i.e., constructs) are significant for identification purposes.

EFFICACY OF MINDTOOLS IN SUPPORTING M-LEARNING

Several studies have reported the effectiveness of using Mindtools to support m-learning activities in terms of learning attitudes, learning motivations, and learning achievements.

Figure 14.5 Example of Guiding the Student to the Plant With the "Incorrect Feature"

For example, Chu, Hwang, and Tsai (2010) employed a repertory grid-oriented Mindtool in an m-learning activity "knowing campus plants" of an elementary-school natural-science course and found that students' learning motivation, as well as their learning achievements, was significantly improved. One year later, Wu, Hwang, Tsai, Chen, and Huang (2011) developed a repertory grid-oriented m-learning system for training nursing-school students to identify the status of the target patients. The experimental results showed that the approach is helpful to students in improving their learning achievements and mastery of their clinical skills. Furthermore, Hwang, Wu and Ke (2011) conducted a concept map-supported m-learning activity "knowing butterfly ecology" of an elementary-school natural-science course and found that the approach not only enhances learning attitudes, but also improves the learning achievements of the students.

In addition, researchers showed that engaging students in collaborative m-learning activities using Mindtools could further achieve better learning efficacy. For example, Hwang, Shi and Chu (2011) conducted a collaborative m-learning activity using concept maps. In comparing "mobile learning with concept maps" and "mobile learning without concept maps," they found that the students who learned collaboratively with concept maps showed significantly better learning performance in terms of learning attitudes toward science courses, self-efficacy of computer skills, and self-efficacy of group learning, as well as learning achievements. Moreover, they also found that such a sound complicated learning activity did not significantly increase the cognitive load of the students. Similar findings were reported by Hwang, Chu, et al. (2011), who developed a repertory grid-oriented Mindtool for supporting collaborative m-learning activities.

Furthermore, Hung, Hwang, Su, and Lin (2012) conducted an inquiry-based m-learning activity using concept maps for comparing the scientific-observation-competence progress of gifted and average students in an ecology park in southern Taiwan. The experimental results showed that, although the learning performance of the gifted students did not significantly differ from that of the average students during the learning activity, the learning retention of the two groups was quite different. It was found that the average students forgot some of the concepts or knowledge in the follow-up test, whereas the gifted students kept on internalizing what had been learned after the intervention. Such a finding has demonstrated the potential and importance of investigating the effects of carrying out m-learning activities with Mindtools on the learning performance of sudents with different knowledge levels, learning styles, genders, or preferences in the future.

REFERENCES

Anderson-Inman, L., & Ditson, L. (1999). Computer-based concept mapping: A tool for negotiating meaning. *Learning and Leading with Technology, 26*(8), 6–13.

Boose, J. H., & Gaines, B. R. (1989). Knowledge acquisition for knowledge-based systems: Notes on the state-of-the-art. *Machine Learning, 4*(4), 377–394.

Bruner, J. (1986). *Actual minds, possible worlds.* Cambridge, MA: Harvard University Press.

Chen, C. H., Hwang, G. J., Yang, T. C., Chen, S. H., & Huang, S. Y. (2009). Analysis of a ubiquitous performance support system for teachers. *Innovations in Education and Teaching International, 46*(4), 1–13.

Chiou, C. C. (2008). The effect of concept mapping on students' learning achievements and interests. *Innovations in Education & Teaching International, 45*(4), 375–387.

Chiou, C. K., Tseng, J. C. R., Hwang, G. J., & Heller, S. (2010). An adaptive navigation support system for conducting context-aware ubiquitous learning in museums. *Computers & Education, 55*(2), 834–845.

Chu, C. H., & Hwang, G. J. (2008). A Delphi-based approach to developing expert systems with the cooperation of multiple experts. *Expert Systems with Applications, 34*, 2826–2840.

Chu, H. C., Hwang, G. J., Huang, S. X., & Wu, T. T. (2008). A knowledge engineering approach to developing e-libraries for mobile learning. *The Electronic Library*, 26(3), 303–317.

Chu, H. C., Hwang, G. J., & Tsai, C. C. (2010). A knowledge engineering approach to developing Mindtools for context-aware ubiquitous learning. *Computers & Education*, 54(1), 289–297.

Chu, H. C., Hwang, G. J., Tsai, C. C., & Tseng, J. C. R. (2010). A two-tier test approach to developing location-aware mobile learning systems for natural science courses. *Computers & Education*, 55(4), 1618–1627.

Collins, A. (1991). The role of computer technology in restructuring schools. In K. Shingold & M. S. Tucker (Eds.), *Restructuring for learning with technology*. New York: National Center on Education and the Economy.

Fischer, F., Bruhn, J., Grasel, C., & Mandl, H. (2002). Fostering collaborative knowledge construction with visualization tools. *Learning and Instruction*, 12, 213–232.

Herrington, J., & Oliver, R. (2000). An instructional design framework for authentic learning environments. *Educational Technology Research & Development*, 48(3), 23–48.

Horton, P. B., McConney, A. A., Gallo, M., Woods, A. L., Senn, G. J., & Hamelin, D. (1993). An investigation of the effectiveness of concept mapping as an instructional tool. *Science Education*, 77, 95–111.

Hung, P. S., Hwang, G. J., Su, I. S., & Lin, I. H. (2012). A concept-map integrated dynamic assessment system for improving ecology observation competences in mobile learning activities. *Turkish Online Journal of Educational Technology*, 11(1), 10–19.

Hung, P. H., Lin, Y. F., & Hwang, G. J. (2010). Formative assessment design for PDA integrated ecology observation. *Educational Technology & Society*, 13(3), 33–42.

Hwang, G. J., & Chang, H. F. (2011). A formative assessment-based mobile learning approach to improving the learning attitudes and achievements of students. *Computers & Education*, 56(1), 1023–1031.

Hwang, G. H., Chen, J. M., Hwang, G. J., & Chu, H. C. (2006). A time scale-oriented approach for building medical expert systems. *Expert Systems with Applications*, 31(2), 299–308.

Hwang, G. J., Chu, H. C., Lin, Y. S., & Tsai, C. C. (2011). A knowledge acquisition approach to developing Mindtools for organizing and sharing differentiating knowledge in a ubiquitous learning environment. *Computers & Education*, 57(1), 1368–1377.

Hwang, G. J., Chu, H. C., Shih, J. L., Huang, S. H., & Tsai, C. C. (2010). A decision-tree-oriented guidance mechanism for conducting nature science observation activities in a context-aware ubiquitous learning environment. *Educational Technology & Society*, 13(2), 53–64.

Hwang, G. J., Shi, Y. R., & Chu, H. C. (2011). A concept map approach to developing collaborative Mindtools for context-aware ubiquitous learning. *British Journal of Educational Technology*, 42(5), 778–789.

Hwang, G. J., & Tsai, C. C. (2011). Research trends in mobile and ubiquitous learning: A review of publications in selected journals from 2001 to 2010. *British Journal of Educational Technology*, 42(4), E65–70.

Hwang, G. J., Tsai, C. C., & Yang, S. J. H. (2008). Criteria, strategies and research issues of context-aware ubiquitous learning. *Educational Technology & Society*, 11(2), 81–91.

Hwang, G. J., Wu, P. H., & Ke, H. R. (2011). An interactive concept map approach to supporting mobile learning activities for natural science courses. *Computers & Education*, 57(4), 2272–2280.

Hwang, G. J., Yang, T. C., Tsai, C. C., & Yang, S. J. H. (2009). A context-aware ubiquitous learning environment for conducting complex experimental procedures. *Computers & Education*, 53(2), 402–413.

Jonassen, D. H. (1994/1999). *Computers as Mindtools for schools, engaging critical thinking*. Englewood Cliffs, NJ: Prentice-Hall.

Jonassen, D. H., Carr, C., & Yueh, H. P. (1998). Computers as Mindtools for engaging learners in critical thinking. *TechTrends*, 43(2), 24–32.

Kao, G. Y. M., Lin, S. S. J., & Sun, C. T. (2008). Beyond sharing: Engaging students in cooperative and competitive active learning. *Educational Technology & Society*, 11(3), 82–96.

Kelly, G. A. (1955). *The psychology of personal constructs* (Vol. 1). New York: W.W Norton.

Kommers, P., Jonassen, D. H., & Mayes, T. (Eds.) (1992). *Cognitive tools for learning*. Heidelberg, Germany: Springer.

Lave, J. (1991). Situating learning in communities of practice. In L. B. Resnick., J. M. Levine., & S. D. Teasley (Eds.), *Perspectives on socially shared cognition* (pp. 63–82). Washington, DC: American Psychological Association.

Leng, B. A. de, Dolmans, D. H. J. M., Jöbsis, R., Muijtjens, A. M. M., & Vleuten, C. P. M. van der (2009). Exploration of an e-learning model to foster critical thinking on basic science concepts during work placements. *Computers & Education*, 53(1), 1–13.

Liu, C. C., Don, P. H., & Tsai, C. M. (2005). Assessment based on linkage patterns in concept maps. *Journal of Information Science and Engineering*, 21(5), 873–890.

Novak, J. D., & Cañas, A. J. (2006). The origins of the concept mapping tool and the continuing evolution of the tool. *Information Visualization*, 5, 175–184.

Novak, J. D., & Gowin, D. B. (1984). *Learning how to learn.* Cambridge, UK: Cambridge University Press.

Novak, J. D., & Musonda, D. (1991). A twelve-year longitudinal study of science concept learning. *American Education Research Journal, 28,* 117–153.

Nussbaum, M., Alvarez, C., McFarlane, A., Gomez, F., Claro, S., & Radovic, D. (2009). Technology as small group face-to-face collaborative scaffolding. *Computers & Education, 52*(1), 147–153.

Ogata, H., & Yano, Y. (2004, March). *Context-aware support for computer-supported ubiquitous learning.* Paper presented at the 2nd IEEE International Workshop on Wireless and Mobile Technologies in Education, JhongLi, Taiwan.

Peng, H. Y., Su, Y. J., Chou, C., & Tsai, C. C. (2009). Ubiquitous knowledge construction: Mobile learning re-defined and a conceptual framework. *Innovations in Education and Teaching International, 46*(2), 171–183.

Reader, W., & Hammond, N. (1994). Computer-based tools to support learning from hypertext: Concept mapping tools and beyond. *Computers & Education, 12,* 99–106.

Ruiz-Primo, M. A., & Shavelson, R. J. (1996). Problems and issues in the use of concept maps in science assessment. *Journal of Research in Science Teaching, 33,* 569–600.

Shaw, R., Turvey, M. T., & Mace, W. (1982). Ecological psychology: The consequence of a commitment to realism. In W. B. Weimer & D. S. Palermo (Eds.), *Cognition and the symbolic processes* (pp. 159–226). Hillsdale, NJ: Lawrence Erlbaum Associates.

Trent, S. C., Pernell, E. Jr., Mungai, A., & Chimedza, R. (1998). Using concept maps to measure conceptual change in preservice teachers enrolled in a multicultural education/special education course. *Remedial and Special Education, 19,* 16–30.

Valcke, M., Rots, I., Verbeke, M., & Braak, J. V. (2007). ICT teacher training: Evaluation of the curriculum and training approach in Flanders. *Teaching and Teacher Education, 23*(6), 795–808.

Vygotsky, L. (1978). *Mind in society: The development of higher psychological process.* Cambridge, MA: Harvard University Press.

Williams van Rooij, S. (2009). Scaffolding project-based learning with the project management body of knowledge (PMBOK®). *Computers & Education, 52*(1), 210–219.

Wu, P. H., Hwang, G. J., Tsai, C. C., Chen, Y. C., & Huang, Y. M. (2011). A pilot study on conducting mobile learning activities for clinical nursing courses based on the repertory grid approach. *Nurse Education Today, 31*(8), e8–e15.

Young, M. F. (1993). Instructional design for situated learning. *Educational Technology Research & Development, 43*(1), 43–58.

15

RETHINKING SCAFFOLDING IN MOBILE CONNECTIVIST LEARNING ENVIRONMENTS

Ozlem Ozan and Mehmet Kesim

As learning moves into an informal, networked, technology-enabled realm, the major theories of learning, which are behaviorism, cognitivism, and constructivism, do not fully describe learning. Downes (2006) adds a fourth approach to these theories: the view of knowledge as composed of connections and networked entities (Siemens, 2008). Siemens defines this fourth approach as "connectivism." In connectivism, learning (defined as actionable knowledge) can reside outside of ourselves (within an organization or a database). Learning is focused on connecting specialized information sets, and the connections that enable us to learn more are more important than our current state of knowing (Siemens, 2004). Mobile technology is one of the newest enablers of connectivist learning environments, because it promotes the combination of mobility, social media, and learning by providing basic infrastructure.

In this changing learning environment, which is triggered by new mobile information and communication technologies, we find a variety of new learner needs. Learners need to know how to learn in a networked environment, how to manage their networked learning process, how to exist in a networked society, and how to use the tools belonging to the network society. In this chapter, we will describe how Vygotsky's "scaffolding" concept, Berge's "learner support" strategies, and Siemens' "connectivism" approach can be used together to satisfy mobile learners' needs. Vygotsky's scaffolding concept tells us how we can provide just-for-me and just-enough help and guidance to learners in a social context. Berge's learner support strategies help us understand always-connected mobile learners' needs. Siemens' connectivism approach provides us the context of a new learning paradigm, and the connectivist mobile platforms allow us instant communication and enable just-in-time learner support.

VYGOTSKY'S SCAFFOLDING CONCEPT

Scaffolding is a metaphor to describe and explain the role of a more knowledgeable peer in guiding, learning, and development processes (Verenikina, 2003), and it is an umbrella term to describe the means of supplying learners with the tools they need in order to

166

learn, not only through teachers, but also through peers (Jacobs, 2001). The term "scaffolding" in this context comes from the works of Wood, Bruner, and Ross (1976). It was developed as a metaphor to describe the type of assistance offered by a teacher or peer to support learning (Lipscomb, Swanson, & West, 2001). The concept of scaffolding is grounded in the developmental theories of Vygotsky (1978).

Fundamental to Vygotsky's theory is the idea that higher mental functions, such as thinking, voluntary attention, and logical memory, and human consciousness in general, have their origins in human social life; the theory derives from internalized social relations (Vygotsky, 1981).

In order to gain an understanding of Vygotsky's theories on cognitive development, it is important to understand two of the main principles of his work: the more knowledgeable other (MKO) and the zone of proximal development (ZPD) (Lipscomb et al., 2001). According to Lipscomb et al., MKO refers to someone who has a better understanding or a higher ability level than the learner with respect to a particular task, process, or concept. It could be anyone, such as parent, teacher, caretaker, instructor, or peer. ZPD is the distance between the "actual developmental level as determined by independent problem solving and the level of potential development as determined through problem solving under adult guidance or in collaboration with more capable peers" (Vygotsky, 1978, p. 86). The MKO and ZPD together form the basis of the scaffolding component of the cognitive apprenticeship model of instruction (Berk, 2002; Daniels, 2001; Krause, Bochner, & Duchesne, 2003; Lipscomb et al., 2001; McDevitt & Ormrod, 2002; Verenikina, 2003; Wells, 1999). Vygotsky believed that, when a student is at the ZPD for a task or concept, providing the appropriate scaffolding will give the student enough of a "boost" to achieve the task (Galloway, 2001).

The goals of scaffolding are teaching specific knowledge and skills, building general intellectual habits, and fostering motivational and effective outcomes (Hogan, 1997). According to Lipscomb et al. (2001), in the process of scaffolding, the teacher helps the student master a task or concept that the student is initially unable to grasp independently. The teacher offers assistance with only those skills that are beyond the student's capability; of great importance is allowing the student to complete as much of the task as possible, unassisted. The teacher only attempts to help the student with tasks that are just beyond his current capability. When the student masters the task, the teacher begins the process of "fading," or the gradual removal of the scaffolding, which allows the student to work independently.

Instructional materials may also be used for scaffolding. Many different facilitative tools can be utilized in the scaffolding process, such as using "think aloud," or verbalizing thinking processes when completing a task; cooperative learning, which promotes teamwork and dialogue among peers; concrete prompts; questioning; coaching; cue cards or modeling; activation of background knowledge; giving tips, offering explanations, asking, implying, cues, and procedures; inviting students to contribute clues and students' participation; encouraging; verifying and clarifying students' understanding; modeling desired behaviors; and breaking the task into smaller or more manageable parts (Lipscomb et al., 2001; Roehler & Cantlon , 1997) .

Teachers have to be mindful of keeping the learner in pursuit of the task, while minimizing the learner's stress level; skills or tasks too far out of reach can lead a student to his/her frustration level, and tasks that are too simple can cause much the same effect (Lipscomb et al., 2001). According to Hogan (1997), to be successful, scaffolding requires a convivial atmosphere in which students can let their defenses down, and in which teachers make students feel at ease in taking intellectual risks. When these conditions are met, scaffolding helps to create thoughtful environments.

As the nature of scaffolding requires tracking the learner and one-to-one communication when needed, and as it is a kind of social process, which requires just-in-time, just-enough, just-for-me, and just-in-case help, it was only used in face-to-face education until recent years. It was not possible to apply this strategy effectively in open- and distance-learning environments prior to the usage of social networks. However, it can today be used effectively, as networked learning environments and mobile technologies (m-technologies) provide us with the appropriate infrastructure. Although scaffolding is a very useful strategy to facilitate learning, we should reinterpret it for use in networked learning environments. In this regard, Berge's learner support strategies can be used for analyzing always-connected learners' needs, and connectivism provides deeper understanding about the ways scaffolding can be used in today's networked learning environments.

BERGE'S LEARNER SUPPORT STRATEGIES

The term "learner support" is associated with distance-learning environments. Learner support is the nomenclature for a particular set of practices that have been developed within open and distance learning (Thorpe, 2003). It describes a holistic approach to the provision of support, which operates from the first inquiry to the completion of studies, for individual learners (Phillips, 2003). Learner support in open and distance learning refers to the meeting of needs that all learners have. As it is central to high-quality learning, learner support covers guidance about course choice, preparatory diagnosis, study skills, access to group learning in seminars and tutorials, and so on (Thorpe, 2003). Phillips (2003) gives examples of students' needs that arise in the scope of learner support in distance-learning environments, as follows:

- information and admission guidance prior to enrollment;
- "study at a distance" support for new students;
- guidance about course choices, study skills, and planning of education process;
- provision to learners of opportunities to monitor and review their progress;
- career guidance to enable students to link study plans to their career interests;
- guidance about available facilities for those with disabilities;
- guidance about the university's administration.

Berge (1995) proposes a widely used classification of supporting activities for online education under four categories:

- pedagogical
- social
- managerial and
- technical.

Pedagogical support is related to instructional and intellectual tasks, such as helping students to focus discussion on critical concepts, and stimulating learner participation and interaction. Social support concerns creating a friendly social environment in which learning occurs, by promoting human relationships, developing group cohesiveness, maintaining the group as a unit, and in other ways helping members to work together for a mutual cause. Managerial support helps students with organizational, procedural, and administrative processes, events, and activities. It involves providing objectives and setting timetables, procedural rules, and decision-making norms. Technical support is related to making learners comfortable with the system and the software. The aim of technical support is to make the technology transparent and to help students concentrate on the academic task rather than the technology.

Berge's (1995) categorization of student support summarizes the basic needs of online learners. The utilization of this approach in networked learning environments is actually applicable to identify ways to keep networked learners satisfied and productive. However, augmentation of this approach is necessary by considering social context and social learners who are able to communicate and interact instantly. In this regard, Vygotsky's scaffolding and Siemens' connectivism approaches are very helpful, as both of them are based on social interaction.

SIEMENS' CONNECTIVISM APPROACH

Connectivism is a learning theory for the digital age (Siemens, 2005). According to Siemens, connectivism is the integration of principles explored by chaos, network, and complexity and self-organization theories; learning is a process of connecting specialized nodes or information sources; and learners can exponentially improve their own learning by plugging into an existing network.

Some of the principles of connectivism given by Siemens (2006) are as follows:

- Learning may reside in nonhuman appliances. Learning can rest in a community, a network, or a database.
- The capacity to know more is more critical than what is currently known. Knowing where to find information is more important than knowing information.
- Connection-making provides far greater returns on effort than simply seeking to understand a single concept.
- Learning happens in many different ways through courses, e-mail, communities, conversations, Web searches, e-mail lists, reading blogs, etc. Courses are not the primary conduit for learning.
- Different approaches and personal skills are needed to learn effectively in today's society. For example, the ability to see connections between fields, ideas, and concepts is a core skill.
- Organizational and personal learning are integrated tasks. Personal knowledge is comprised of a network, which feeds into organizations and institutions, which in turn feed back into the network and continue to provide learning for the individual. Connectivism attempts to provide an understanding of how both learners and organizations learn.
- Currency (accurate, up-to-date knowledge) is the intent of all connectivist learning.
- Decision-making is itself a learning process. Choosing what to learn and the meaning of incoming information is seen through the lens of shifting reality. Although there is a right answer now, it may be wrong tomorrow, owing to alterations in the information climate impacting the decision.

Siemens (2006) states that, in a networked society, the concepts of *knowledge, learning,* and *culture* are changing: consequently, *structures, spaces,* and *tools* used for learning are evolving. Learning is a network-formation process of connecting specialized nodes or information sources. Social acts that bring out identities, awareness, relationships, connections, and interactions among and between learners are necessary for interactive learning (Tu, Blocher, & Roberts, 2008). The ability to see connections, recognize patterns, and make sense between fields, ideas, and concepts is the core skill for individuals today (Siemens, 2006).

Although connectivism explains new knowledge, learning, and changing structures, spaces, and tools, it does not provide deep information about micro-design issues, in other words, teaching and learning. It doesn't answer the questions, "how will we teach?" and "how will we support students?" deeply enough. To fill this gap, additional approaches, which can blend harmoniously with connectivism, are necessary, such as Vygotsky's and Berge's work.

MOBILE CONNECTIVIST LEARNING ENVIRONMENTS

A distinguishing feature of our society at the beginning of the 21st century is the rapid rate of technological and social change (Peters, 2009) and the need to be able to access information anytime and anywhere. Hence, m-technologies become more popular owing to their portability and facility for wireless connection. The communication and data-transfer possibilities created by m-technologies can significantly reduce dependence on fixed locations for work and study and, thus, have the potential to revolutionize the way we work and learn (Peters, 2009). M-technologies leverage the opportunities offered by e-learning and enable brand new opportunities. In this context, m-learning is considered a new channel for the individuals who are mobile. Today, m-technologies have become an integral part of learning activities.

Mobile ecosystems combine mobile telephony, removable memory chips, e-mail, the Web, social networking, basic word-processing and spreadsheets, data input, storage, and transfer. According to Jaokar and Gatti (2010), mobile ecosystems cover entertainment and games, Web browsing and search, voice-over-Internet protocol, voice, messaging, mobile TV, Internet protocol television, mobile video, social networking, and augmented-reality applications. It provides basic infrastructure to combine mobility, social media, and learning. The mobile connectivist learning environment (MCLE) is where mobile social-media tools come together for the purpose of learning in multiple contexts. MCLE covers mobile content and learning-management systems, blog-platform apps, social-bookmark apps, picture apps, social-video and audio apps, mobile versions of wikis, event and document apps, aggregation apps, location-based applications, professional networks, friend and community networks, short message service (SMS), voice and e-mail messaging through mobile technologies, and mobile augmented reality (see Figure 15.1).

SCAFFOLDING IN A MOBILE CONNECTIVIST LEARNING ENVIRONMENT

The rapid development of technology and exponential growth in the use of the Internet, along with Web 2.0 and mobile developments, make new and different educational

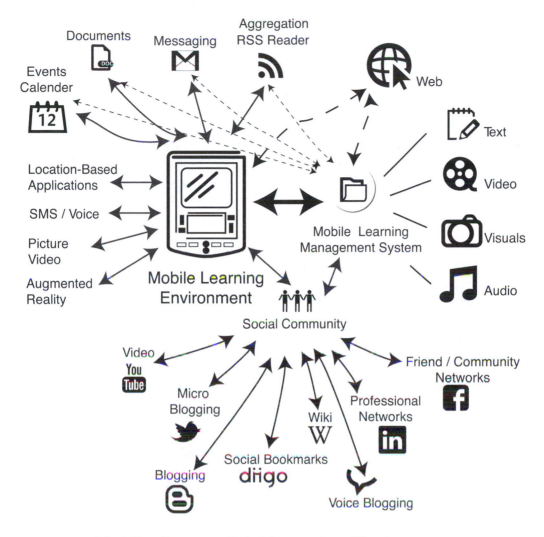

Mobile Connectivist Learning Environment

Figure 15.1 Mobile Connectivist Learning Environment (MCLE)

structures, organizations, and settings a possibility (Kop & Hill, 2008). As mentioned earlier, in a networked society, the concepts of *knowledge, learning,* and *culture* are changed; consequently, *structures, spaces,* and *tools* are evolving and becoming mobile. As stated above, Siemens (2006) has redefined learning as the network formation process of connecting specialized nodes or information sources. Siemens has also stated that knowledge rests in the networks, making the ability to see connections and recognize patterns and make sense between fields, ideas, and concepts the core skill for individuals today.

Learners are, henceforth, at the center of their own learning experiences, and the role of the teacher is evolving from instructor to guide/facilitator/mentor. As a consequence of this change, we came across the question, "How will we teach in a learner centered, mobile, and connected environment?" According to the authors of this chapter, to answer this question, it is important to understand emerging learner needs, and to review learning guidance and support. Today, individuals need to know how to learn in a networked environment and manage this educational process, how to exist in a networked society, and how to use the tools belonging to the networked society. On one hand, Berge's (1995) approach presents a visionary perspective at this point. It gives us ideas about how we can configure new strategies about this issue. On the other hand, mobile technologies provide an opportunity to provide just-in-time, just-enough, just-in-case, just-for-me help—in other words, scaffolding—to learners, without the constraints of tightly delimited physical location. Thus, we could provide learners instant:

- *instructional scaffolding* for learning in a network;
- *social scaffolding* for learners to interact in a network;
- *technical scaffolding* to assist learners in utilization of tools belonging to the networked society; and
- *managerial scaffolding* to allow learners to manage their educational process in the connectivist learning environment.

Considering the aforementioned four types of scaffolding, strategies and mobile tools to provide support to learners in a mobile connectivist learning environment are provided in Table 15.1.

Examples for the apps and tools that are provided in Table 15.1:

- Mobile collaboration apps: nozbe, CloudOn, Educreations Interactive Whiteboard, Whiteboard Lite, Collaborative Drawing, Sketchio, Skype for iPad, FaceTime, DropBox, Screen Chomp
- Productivity apps:
  – To-do lists: 2Do, Priority Matrix, Omnifocus, Todo, Taska
  – Calendars and reminders: Pocket Informant HD
  – Checklist and rubrics: rubrix, nozbe
  – Quiz: Quiz Creator
  – Portfolio: Behance Network, Minimal Folio
  – Office: CloudOn, Notes Plus, Pages, Keynote, iAnnotate PDF
- Social-media apps
  – Blogging: Blogsy, BlogPress, WordPress
  – Photo blogging: Tumblr, Posterous, Flickr
  – Video blogging: Flixwagon
  – Voice blogging: Bubbly, Bubble Motion
- Idea-mapping apps: SimpleMind+, Popplet, Popplet Lite, Screen Chomp, iBrainstorm, Inspiration Maps Lite, iThoughtsHD
- Bookmarking and social-tagging apps: RadBox, Skyloog, Symbaloo, Videolicious, pinterest
- RSS apps: Feedler RSS Reader, Reeder, NewsRack
- Social-networking apps: Facebook, Twitter, LinkedIn, Four Square, Discovr

Table 15.1 Scaffolding Strategies in Mobile Connectivist Learning Environment

Type of scaffolding	Strategy	Scaffolding providers and tools that can be used by provider		
		Instructor	Peer	Materials
Instructional scaffolding (Aim: To help students to learn in a network)	Just-in-time review & sharing	Bookmarking and social tagging apps, office and note-taking apps	Bookmarking and social-tagging apps, office and note-taking apps	—
	Brief information sharing	Blog apps, micro-blog apps	Blog apps, micro-blog apps	Glossary, how-tos, and FQAs
		Podcasts (instructor generated)	Podcasts (student generated)	—
	Multisensory learning	Photo blog apps, iBooks, video-blog apps, voice-blog apps	Photo-blog apps, iBooks, video-blog apps, voice-blog apps	Mobile course contents
	Aggregating information	Bookmarking apps	Bookmarking apps	—
	Improving access to resources	RSS		RSS
	Idea formation and sharing	M-forum, idea-mapping apps	M-forum, group-games apps, idea-mapping apps, office and note-taking apps	—
	Encouraging individual thought and reflective activities	Blog apps		—
	Collaborative writing	Wiki apps	Wiki apps	—
	Showing cases	Vodcasting (instructor-generated)	Vodcasting (student-generated)	Vodcasting
	Visualization of thinking process	Idea-mapping apps	Idea-mapping apps	—
	Students' participation	Collaboration apps	Collaboration apps	—
	Connection-making	Social-media and networking apps	Social-media and networking apps	—
	Peer evaluation		Portfolio apps, rubrics	—
Social scaffolding (Aim: To help students to promote human relationships and work together)	Guide and help others	Social-media apps, screencasting apps	Social-media apps, screencasting apps	—
	Cooperate with others		Office and note-taking apps	—
	Negotiate with others, to invite students to contribute clues	Social-media apps	Social-media apps	—
	Fostering sense of presence	Friend-network apps	Friend-network apps	—
	Supporting community building	Community-networks apps, SMS	Community-networks apps, SMS	—
	Enhancing collaboration	Social-networking apps, bookmarking and social-tagging apps, collaboration apps	Social-networking apps, bookmarking and social-tagging apps, collaboration apps	—
Managerial scaffolding (Aim: To help student to manage his/her own learning in connected environment)	Planning/organization	To-do list apps		Syllabus, calendars and reminders
	Monitoring him/herself			Checklist, rubrics
	Self-evaluation			Quizzes
Technical scaffolding (Aim: To ensure student's comfort and ease in using the system)	Brief information sharing	Blog apps, e-mail, m-chat	Blog apps, e-mail, m-chat	How-tos and FQAs
	Providing showcases	Video-blog apps, vodcasting	Video-blog apps, vodcasting	Vodcasting
	Encouraging asking questions and helping each other	Social-media apps	Social-media apps	Forum

- Podcasting apps: iPadio, Cinch, AudioBoo, Posterous
- Vodcasting apps: iMovie, Vimeo, Silent Film Director
- Screencasting apps: Show Me, Screen Chomp, Explain Everything, Educreations
- Course-content apps: iTunes, iBooks, Khan Academy, Wolfram Alpha, Muscle System Pro II, Britannica Kids, Molecules, Simple Physics, NASA, OnScreen DNA Model, Math Ref, Science Glossary
- Wiki apps: PikoWiki, Wikispaces Mobile
- Mobile group games: Hanging With Friends, Scrabble, Parallel Kingdom
- Mobile LMS: MLE-Moodle, MOMO (Mobile Moodle), Blackboard Mobile, Sakai Mobile.

CONCLUSION

Mobile information and communication technologies are an important part of the new social structure. They provide the opportunity to move between indoors and outdoors settings, across formal and informal settings, and between social and individual platforms. The usage of social media and mobile platforms are creating a major impact on the learning and teaching processes. Social media create an atmosphere in which individuals can learn from their peers about communication norms and cultures. For instance, in a study funded by the MacArthur Foundation, Ito et al. (2008) found that youth participate in social media within the contexts of two primary genres: friendship driven and interest driven. In friendship-driven genres, youth go about their day-to-day negotiations with friends and peers. Such friends can include peers from school, sports teammates, religious-group friends, and other activity peers. Interest-driven genres of participation focus on particular hobbies and interests or niche communities. In both of these types of genre, youth are a part of the peer-based learning process, as they "can both produce and evaluate knowledge and culture." In this context, while social learning facilitates collaborative learning, the contact with a tutor will become less prominent: students will come together, learn from each other, and occasionally assess each other. As a consequence of this change, new forms of scaffolding are emerging, which are necessary in the mobile connectivist world.

Currently, individuals and learners need to know how to learn in a networked environment and manage networked educational processes, how to exist in a networked society, and how to use the tools belonging to the networked society. It is our belief that combining the aforementioned approaches would be very useful to create new strategies in this area. Vygotsky's "scaffolding," Berge's "learner support," and Siemens' "connectivism" approaches can be utilized simultaneously; a combination of them can be used to satisfy emerging learner needs. The main characteristics of this scaffolding include three approaches; internalized social interaction, deep understanding of always-connected learners, and usage of significant scaffolding strategies—which belong to face-to-face education—on the mobile platforms. A variety of mobile applications can be utilized to provide this type of scaffolding, such as m-calendars, m-checklists, m-rubrics, m-quizzes, m-portfolios, m-blogging, mobile networks and collaboration tools, mobile mind maps, games, augmented-reality apps, podcasts, and video casts, to name but a few.

REFERENCES

Berge, Z. L. (1995). Facilitating computer conferencing: Recommendations from the Field. *Educational Technology*, *35*(1), 22–30.

Berk, L. (2002). *Child development* (5th ed.). Boston, MA: Allyn and Bacon.

Daniels, H. (2001). *Vygotsky and pedagogy*. New York: Routledge Falmer.

Downes, S. (2006). Learning networks and connective knowledge. Retrieved from: http://it.coe.uga.edu/itforum/paper92/paper92.html

Galloway, C. A. (2001). Vygotsky's learning theory. In M. Orey (Ed.), *Emerging perspectives on learning, teaching, and technology*. Retrieved from: http://projects.coe.uga.edu/epltt/index.php?title=Vygotsky%27s_constructivism

Hogan, K. (1997). Introduction. In K. Hogan & M. Pressley (Eds.), *Scaffolding student learning: Instructional approaches and issues* (pp. 1–5). Cambridge, MA: Brookline Books.

Ito, M., Bittanti, M., Horst, H. A., Doyd, D., Herr-Stephenson, B., Lange, P. G., Pascoe, C. J., & Robinson, L. (2008). *Living and learning with new media: Summary of findings from the Digital Youth Project*. Retrieved from Digital Youth Project: http://digitalyouth.ischool.berkeley.edu/report

Jacobs, G. (2001). Providing the scaffold: A model for early childhood/primary teacher preparation. *Early Childhood Education Journal*, *29*(2), 125–130.

Jaokar, A., & Gatti, A. (2010, 27 May). Open mobile-understanding the impact of open mobile: Implications for telecoms/devices, web, social networks, media and personal privacy. Retrieved from: http://openmobile.futuretext.com/

Kop, R., & Hill, A. (2008). Connectivism: Learning theory of the future or vestige of the past? *The International Review of Research in Open and Distance Learning*, *9*(3),1–13. Retrieved from: www.irrodl.org/index.php/irrodl/article/view/523/1137

Krause, K., Bochner, S., & Duchesne, S. (2003). *Educational psychology for learning and teaching*. Southbank, Australia: Thomson.

Lipscomb, L., Swanson, J., & West, A. (2001). Scaffolding. In M. Orey (Ed.), *Emerging perspectives on learning, teaching, and technology* [e-Book]. Retrieved from: http://projects.coe.uga.edu/epltt/

McDevitt, T. M., & Ormrod, J. E. (2002). *Child development and education*. Upper Saddle River, NJ: Merrill Prentice Hall.

Peters, K. (2009). M-learning: Positioning educators for a mobile, connected future. In M. Ally (Ed.), *Mobile learning transforming the delivery of education and training* (pp. 113–134). Edmonston, AB: AU Press.

Phillips, M. (2003). Delivering learner support on-line: Does the medium affect the message? In A. Tait & R. Mills (Eds.), *Rethinking learner support in distance education* (pp. 168–184). London: RoutledgeFalmer.

Roehler, L. R., & Cantlon, D. J. (1997). Scaffolding: A powerful tool in social constructivist classrooms. In K. Hogan & M. Pressley (Eds.), *Scaffolding student learning: Instructional approaches & issues* (pp. 6–42). Cambridge, MA: Brookline Books.

Siemens, G. (2004, December). *Connectivism: A learning theory for the digital age*. Retrieved from elearnspace: www.elearnspace.org/Articles/connectivism.htm

Siemens, G. (2005). Connectivism: A learning theory for the digital age. *Journal of Instructional Technology and Distance Learning*, *2*(1). Retrieved from: www.itdl.org/Journal/Jan_05/article01.htm

Siemens, G. (2006). *Knowing knowledge*. Lulu.com. Retrieved from: www.elearnspace.org/

Siemens, G. (2008). *Learning and knowing in networks: Changing roles for educators and designers*. AECT Instructional Technology Community. Presented to ITFORUM for discussion. Retrieved from: http://it.coe.uga.edu/itforum/Paper105/Siemens.pdf

Thorpe, M. (2003). Collaborative on-line learning: Transforming learner support and course design. In A. Tait & R. Mills (Eds.), *Rethinking learner support in distance education* (pp. 198–2011). London: RoutledgeFalmer.

Tu, C.-H., Blocher, M., & Roberts, G. (2008). Constructs for Web 2.0 learning environments: A theatrical metaphor. *Educational Media International*, *45*(4), 253–269.

Verenikina, I. (2003). Understanding scaffolding and the ZPD in educational research. *International Education Research Conference AARE—NZARE*. Auckland, New Zealand: Australian Association for Research in Education. Retrieved from: www.aare.edu.au/03pap/ver03682.pdf

Vygotsky, L. S. (1978). *Mind in society: The development of higher psychological processes* (M. Cole, V. John-Steiner, S. Scribner, & E. Souberman, Eds.). Cambridge, MA: Harvard University.

Vygotsky, L. S. (1981). The genesis of higher mental functions. In J. V. Wertsch (Ed.), *The concept of activity in soviet psychology*. New York: Sharpe.

Wells, G. (1999). *Dialogic inquiry: Towards a sociocultural practice and theory of education*. New York: Cambridge University Press.

Wood, D., Bruner, J., & Ross, G. (1976). The role of tutoring in problem solving. *Journal of Child Psychology and Psychiatry*, *17*, 89–100.

16

A MOBILE PEDAGOGY APPROACH FOR TRANSFORMING LEARNERS AND FACULTY

Scott Hamm, George Saltsman, Breana Jones, Stephen Baldridge, and Scott Perkins

Education is undergoing a retooling. The word "tablet" no longer conjures up images of the Big Chief notebook; rather, it represents a portable digital device situated in the social, vocational, and educational habits of our interconnected daily lives. Smartphones are increasingly becoming a normative and expected tool in a global culture where smartphone sales have outpaced PC sales (Canalys, 2012) and with over 6 billion mobile subscribers worldwide (International Telecommunications Union, 2012). The ways education might harness the power and ubiquity of these devices to access content, learn, and teach with these devices are profound. This opportunity has not gone unnoticed. President Obama singled out mobile connectivity for students in the 2011 State of the Union Address (Obama, 2011), and Department of Education Secretary Arne Duncan and Federal Communications Commission Chairman Julius Genachowski announced an aggressive 5-year goal for the adoption of digital textbooks on mobile devices across the United States (Genachowski, 2012). This chapter explores that promise of mobility in education by examining the theoretical background of m-learning, emerging themes of user practice, evaluation of one campus-wide program at Abilene Christian University (ACU), and a discussion of the reimagined classroom in a fully mobile setting.

THEORETICAL BACKGROUND OF M-LEARNING

Mobile technologies, by their very nature, are designed to be mobile—to be used in motion. The original patent for the wireless telephone (Stubblefield, 1908) states the primary use as "securing telephonic communication between moving vehicles and way stations" (p. 1). The embedded batteries and wireless radios of modern mobile devices are obviously designed to facilitate transportable use. However, current practice in formal, instructor-led education also includes the use of mobile devices in fixed education settings, where neither the student nor instructor is mobile or engaged in nontraditional pedagogy.

Attempting to situate existing pedagogical approaches to m-learning is inherently complex, given the breadth of m-learning's definition. Crompton, Muilenburg, and Berge provide the working definition of m-learning in the first chapter as "learning across multiple contexts, through social and content interactions, using personal electronic devices" (Crompton, 2013, p. 4). This definitional iteration includes devices such as laptops, smartphones, connected media players, and tablet devices. It includes inter-actions between persons and/or content in the context of learning. Ironically, m-learning does not necessarily imply mobility beyond the inherent mobility of the device, as the use of any of these mobile devices in a traditional setting qualifies. Review of current literature demonstrates that, indeed, many m-learning approaches do not invoke mobility, just the use of devices designed for mobility in the context of education.

This inherent dichotomy in the definition is challenging, especially when attempting to apply pedagogical approaches. In one case, m-learning is highly device-centric, for example encompassing the use of iPod Touches in a traditional classroom to expedite paper-based test taking. In other contexts, m-learning is highly context specific, for example describing informal learning by an independent person using a smartphone to access the history of a lighthouse seen from the side of a highway. In other instances, m-learning is often the traditional, industrial-era schooling model utilizing technological affordances to increase efficiency and convenience. Roschelle (2003) identified these complexities for education researchers, citing that existing "pedagogical applications are often led down the wrong road by complex views of technology and simplistic views of social practices" (Roschelle, 2003, p. 260). Laurillard (2007) agrees, noting "there is still work to be done in characterising the critical factors that make it distinctive" (p. 155).

The existing literature in distance education would provide applicable theory and researched-based pedagogical approaches, if only m-learning were consistently applied in distance-education settings. Likewise, frameworks from computer-based education practice would inform formal classroom settings, if these approaches were only consistent with its pedagogical application in fixed settings. The breadth of context in m-learning requires the application of a blended approach; however, the existing definitions for blended learning (or hybrid learning) are yet again too narrow for the extensiveness of m-learning.

Any attempt to define and categorize a pedagogical approach and tag a theory for m-learning will be eclectic in nature and problematic at best. A dose of Social Construction Theory here and a few others there for good measure might be a start, but perhaps a futile attempt at finding a suitable theoretical approach. M-learning also has a great deal of implied informal learning, such as the example of the individual using a smartphone to access the history of a lighthouse. As for pedagogical approaches on informal learning, there is a stark realization that scant depth of literature on this topic exists (Siemens, 2005). The theoretical misfit of mobility within existing theoretical bases encourages understanding it in broader learning theory. This reconceptualization allows for peda-gogical maturation in this rapidly developing field (Brown, 2004). Introducing theory into the m-learning discussion is an important step in merging theory and praxis. However, searching for a theory of m-learning may be missing the point. Instead, placing the affordances of mobility within Social Construction Theory offers theoretical insights into the methods by which mobility may enhance and shape learning.

Vygotsky (1978), Social Construction Theory's founder, examines the activity involving a person and an object using a tool to accomplish a task (Kuutti, 1996). Vygotsky describes an apprenticeship of learning in which a knowledgeable peer assists the learning peer in acquiring new skills and understanding. With this apprentice learning, mobility allows for an extended Zone of Proximal Development (ZPD) (Berger, 2011). Mobility moves beyond the physical requirements of the ZPD and extends its boundaries in ways and places at a pace faster than our ability to define them will allow. A mobile pedagogy operates in a situated ZPD, where the learner is intentionally engaged with peers and guided by a knowledgeable mentor. This theoretical affiliation recognizes that mobility augments "a society in which people on the move increasingly try to cram learning into the gaps of daily life" (Sharples, Taylor, & Vavoula, 2007, p. 223).

THEMES OF USER PRACTICE

Despite the challenges in defining m-learning, actual practice continues to emerge, as faculty and students utilize mobile devices to accomplish academic tasks in formal and informal settings. Four emergent themes can be observed arising from the emerging literature and praxis of m-learning: the ability of mobile devices and wireless infrastructure to provide ad hoc infrastructure for formal and informal learning, the potential for increased learner independence, the capacity for greater learner engagement, and increased communication between teachers, learners, and content.

Ad Hoc Infrastructure for Learning

During their inception, mobile technologies were seen as extensions to existing infrastructure (Stubblefield, 1908), and, in many ways, m-learning currently extends existing infrastructures. One frequent application is enlarging the formal institutional learning network with the global reach of cellular data networks. Blackboard Mobile Learn and iTunesU illustrate just two of many approaches educational institutions have taken to extend access to institutional learning materials via student-owned mobile devices. This approach has been an effective strategy, owing in large part to the preexisting habits of mobile-device users. Tanya Luhrmann, Stanford University, provides strong evidence that students not only carry their mobile devices, but they have furthermore become an extension of the mind (Carey, 2010). Existing pedagogical approaches for online and distance learning appear to be solidly applicable in these cases.

Today, however, mobile devices may also replace existing infrastructure, such as the one-third of U.S. families who now live without landline phones (Blumberg & Luke, 2011), or augment locations where previous infrastructure never existed, as has happened in many developing countries (Donner, 2008). Within education, teachers augment traditional classrooms by creating ad hoc, one-to-one computing environments that transform a room into a computer lab, without the expense or time required to construct a traditional lab. Classroom quantities of inexpensive mobile media players are effortlessly transported from room to room in a container no larger than a briefcase. The bring-your-own-device concept (Consortium for School Networking, 2012) seeks to further minimize cost by utilizing student-owned devices that they likely already have in class. In these instances, theory and practice from computer-based instruction pedagogy remain relevant.

Increased Learner Independence

The idea that students should grow more autonomous as they advance through their coursework is deeply embedded in educational culture. The literature of learner autonomy and, similarly, the focus of inquiry-based learning, discovery learning, and other constructivist-based learning approaches describe methods to develop self-sufficient learners. Holec (1981) proposed learner autonomy as both the means and end to instructional activity. Holec suggests the goal of education should be to produce learners who are autonomous and capable of sustaining lifelong learning, and the way to achieve these goals is the practice of autonomous learning within the formal educational structures. The connected nature of handheld digital devices provides scaffolding for the pedagogical applications of constructivist-based learning that lead to autonomous learning.

An example of developing autonomous learners can be served from the teaching practices at ACU, where all students have access to a mobile device. Faculty enthusiastically supported students' use of mobile devices, with 82 percent of faculty indicating they encouraged students to perform independent, in-class Internet searches, to research words or concepts, or to locate supporting information during formal class activities (Perkins & Saltsman, 2010). Students appear to equally embrace these habits, with 87 percent of respondents indicating their use of a mobile device provided increased control of the learning environment (Perkins & Saltsman, 2010). Powell's (2009) study of inquiry-based methods to support instruction in the chemistry laboratory demonstrated that the application of m-learning resulted in fewer clarifying interactions among students and teachers.

Increased Learner Engagement

In the mid 1980s, researchers established the "correlation between students' investment of time, effort and interest in a range of educationally orientated activities, and favourable outcomes such as increased performance, persistence and satisfaction" (Trowler & Trowler, 2010, p. 7). Now, three decades later, strategies to increase student engagement are still ardent topics of discussion in the literature. An early approach in researching the effectiveness of mobile devices to impact student academic performance was to measure the impact of student engagement.

Review of research related to the emerging practice of m-learning does conclude that the use of m-learning strategies can increase engagement within higher education in both graduate education (Goff, 2011) as well as undergraduate education (Abilene Christian University, 2012). These increases in engagement have further been observed inside and outside of traditional classroom settings (Abilene Christian University, 2012).

In the traditional classroom setting, Phillips (2011) and Baldridge (Baldridge, Moran, & Herrington, 2011) experimented with replacing existing classroom exercises with m-learning activities that generated positive results in student engagement (Abilene Christian University, 2012). Over a decade ago, Crouch and Mazur (2001) demonstrated that peer-instruction techniques increased performance in traditional courses. Similarly, Sutherlin and Powell (2011), applying these techniques with mobile devices, replicated the positive student engagement using peer-instruction techniques in traditional lectures.

Using m-learning approaches in place of formal lecture activities has likewise demonstrated improved student engagement. In multiple studies in both the United States (Powell, 2009) and United Kingdom (Evans, 2008), the practice of replacing traditional lectures with podcasts delivered on mobile devices verified increased levels of student engagement, as well as student-perceived improvement in academic performance. Statistical analysis of the data from those experiments revealed that students did engage more deeply and more frequently than with traditional lectures alone.

In a graduate-level therapy class, students reported increased participation, interest, and quality of the class experience as a result of the course being enhanced with m-learning teaching methods (Goff, 2011). In an undergraduate art course, students demonstrated greater learning efficiency using an iPhone to assess art layered with images from their iPhone, with ability to assess art using augmented reality (Jones, 2011). Shepherd and Reeves (2011) similarly reported greater student engagement outside traditional classroom times when comparing student access to an LMS using a personal computer and a mobile device.

Increased Communication

During the now legendary introduction of the iPhone in 2007, Steve Jobs stood on stage touting the new Apple device as three devices in one: a widescreen iPod, a phone, and an Internet communicator (Wong, 2007). That trio of capability now defines the category of mobile devices described as smartphones. Mobile media players and tablet devices have at least two of the three capabilities. Given that mobile devices are intrinsically designed to facilitate communication, it would be notable if usage did not increase communication between students, faculty, and educational content. As expected, research validates, in formal m-learning programs, that communication increases between teachers, learners, and content (Abilene Christian University, 2012).

Communication increases are being observed outside campus-wide m-learning programs as well. The 2011 ECAR National (US) Study of Undergraduates Students and Information Technology (EDUCAUSE) (Dahlstrom, de Boor, Grunwald, & Vockley, 2011) reports that 99 percent of students have access to e-mail, a core feature of mobile devices (p. 13). Of the 55 percent of students who own smartphones, two-thirds use e-mail on their device to communicate with professors (p. 8), 59 percent look up information outside class, and a majority use text, e-mail, or both, to communicate with peers over academic work (p. 15). This emerging trend illustrates how the growing ubiquity of mobile devices is leading to pedagogical approaches that build on the existing frameworks from online and blended education.

EXAMPLES OF PRACTICE: TOWARD AN M-LEARNING PEDAGOGY

An example of praxis and research, ACU launched a campus-wide m-learning program in the fall of 2008 by distributing mobile devices to incoming first-year students. Distribution continued in subsequent years, resulting in an undergraduate campus saturated with mobile devices by the fall of 2010.

ACU's program used three overarching strategies to guide planning and deployment: (a) program participation would be optional for faculty and students; (b) faculty early adopters would be encouraged and supported with incentives and resources; (c) numerous, regular opportunities would be provided for faculty to become involved at their own pace, allowing them to experiment and adopt based on their own capability and comfort; and (d) empirical evaluation of the impact of the program would be conducted by faculty researchers.

Goals for m-learning research were established to assist in evaluating the success of the program. Briefly summarized, these goals focused on assessing the following dimensions: (a) faculty participation, excitement, and utilization of devices both in and out of the classroom; (b) student excitement, device utilization patterns, and device preferences; (c) the effectiveness and impact of academic usage on student engagement and performance; and (d) formation of data-based recommendations for program modifications and targeted future investigations.

The conclusions of the first 3 years of data establish three findings evident from the research to date, namely: (a) both faculty and students at ACU are very positive about the program (See Appendix 16.B, Tables 16.2 and 16.3); (b) iPhones present a more attractive platform for learning over the iPod Touch (See Appendix 16.C, Table 16.4); and (c) learning activities can be successfully transitioned to mobile-device platforms. On the basis of these results, it can be concluded that, in order to be successful in educating 21st-century learners, educators will be increasingly challenged to understand the role mobility plays, because it is increasingly apparent students consider mobile-device implementation as not only desirable, but essential to their academic pursuits and success (Dahlstrom et al., 2011).

REIMAGINING A PEDAGOGY IN A MOBILE CONTEXT

As the capability of mobile devices increases, so does the opportunity to use them as an integral part of learning. National policy is encouraging movements toward the formal adoption of digital handheld devices in schools, and widespread consumer adoption is increasing familiarity with these devices outside education. It isn't just educators who are anxious to uses these devices in education. Since the advent of the podcast and text messaging, students have been eager to use these technologies as a vehicle for learning (Litchfield, Dyson, Lawrence, & Zmijewska, 2007). This emerging movement presents ways to realize a true m-learning pedagogy that uses the always-connected nature of mobile communications devices to rethink formal and informal education.

Rethinking Formal Learning in a Mobile Context

To reimagine the classroom, the most challenging hurdle may be the academy's hesitation to question the modality of learning and the traditional role of the teacher in the classroom. For most students, past and present, a majority of their education consisted of a teacher standing in the front of the room while the students sat in rows watching, listening, and recording information. Even with the popularity of online and hybrid learning, the teacher-centric methods of teaching and delivery still subsist.

One of the noted changes an actualized m-learning program presents to formal learning is a possible shift in authority within the classroom, or lack of a classroom altogether. When students are mobilized and involved in community-based learning, for example, the teacher is no longer the primary source of knowledge. The idea that one person (the instructor) has all the knowledge and power each learner needs is already somewhat unrealistic, and perhaps irresponsible. Consider an example of a social-sciences course learning about social justice and inequality. If this course were taught by someone lacking first-hand knowledge and experience, then s/he would be simply speaking in theory or concept only. However, if the class is mobilized, and the students are allowed to interact with the community, documenting and recording their own ideas and observations of injustice and equality, this methodology could greatly enhance the depth and breadth of learning. Instead of having just one person's perspective on injustice (the instructor's), there is now a wealth of concrete data gathered by students from different cultures, backgrounds, and ideals, who can all share what they view as unjust in the community. Students who have taken part in this type of learning at ACU report that they feel more involved in the course, and affording students the ability to take learning immediately from theory to reality provides exciting opportunities (Baldridge et al., 2011).

For students engaging in practice or internships, this mobile connectivity could also be particularly useful. Traditional field-education models may dictate that students acquire a certain number of hours within an agency or placement, then meet weekly to discuss their experiences. However, if connected by a common mobile site, students could interact with one another in real time throughout their experiences. If a student encounters an issue or has a question for a specific situation in an internship, they have the opportunity to present that issue to the class immediately for feedback, instead of waiting (possibly many days) to relay that information. Doing so allows for the immediate and real capture of emotion and inquiry, instead of forcing the student to hold the question until the next class meeting.

Although the distraction factor of these social-networking sites has been documented (Bugeja, 2006), and potential for students to over-disclose exists (Mazer, Murphy, & Simonds, 2007), the use of this method to connect learners grants the opportunity for students to interact on a more frequent basis than they might in a traditional classroom. Students who are uncomfortable talking in front of the group may be more inclined to interact regularly via social media. A student in a course at ACU utilizing this type of learning stated,

> I really like this type of classroom, because we can be where we are comfortable and I feel like I am more open to "talk" . . . I have some time to think more before posting or commenting and no one is interrupting. I feel more comfortable than in a classroom.
>
> (Anonymous student, assignment evaluation, 2011)

Rethinking Informal Learning in a Mobile Context

Aside from the marked shift in formal learning, m-learning has incredible potential to vastly alter (and even form) informal learning. The fact that students are already comfortable with social media and mobility (Wade, Jacobsen, & Forste, 2011) connects a cohort or class of students beyond their limited time in the classroom. If a course utilizes a Facebook group, and the students are in that group with their primary Facebook account, they have the ability to interact with the class 24 hours a day. Then, students' constant connection via social media extends to a class environment as well, furthering the possibility of community-based learning, even on an informal level, beyond the structured class time or content.

Incorporation of m-learning activities into a course, not just on a part-time basis, but as a continual tool may challenge the relevance of the formal classroom of years past. Limiting instruction to that which happens only in a classroom or in homework assignments outside of class hours forces students to compartmentalize learning. However, connecting students by using media they are already comfortable with and engaged with frequently nurtures a continual-learning environment, allowing students to interact anytime and all the time. This shift from tradition creates a new learning pedagogy, one that encourages constant interaction and feedback, one in which students are able to learn, not just from the book or the instructor, but from their environment, peers, and life, no matter when or where they are. This truly introduces the idea of learning that takes place everywhere, all of the time.

SUMMARY

The use of mobile technologies in education is increasing. Current policy regarding digital textbooks and digital learning materials will likely accelerate the use of mobile tools and m-learning strategies dramatically. Although these emerging forms of praxis don't fall nicely into existing definitions or established theories, that alone is unlikely to slow the use and adoption of m-learning. As evidenced at ACU, there exists great potential for m-learning to transform both formal and informal models for learning, even though it may threaten the established culture of instruction in the same way m-learning has challenged its own definition. This isn't necessarily a harmful occurrence, as many formal structures require reinvention upon the introduction of new technologies; however, it must be done with care and continued empirical assessment of the measurements of effectiveness.

APPENDIX 16.A

Table 16.1 Faculty Report of Personal and Academic Usage

	2009	2010	2011
Consider program a success	89	94	85
Have not used device in a class	20	19	12
Use regularly for class activities	46	83	84
Use regularly for non-class activities	89	88	89
Students positive about using for class	75	92	93
Always bring my device to class	39	76	89
Had students use in every class meeting	9	15	44

Note: Displays percentages of survey responses that were "agree" and "strongly agree."

APPENDIX 16.B

Table 16.2 Faculty Perceptions of Academic Impact on Students

	Year 1	Year 2	Year 3
Grades in class improved	18	25	38
Cooperation and collaboration increased	42	69	62
Were more productive	35	61	53
Increased participation	53	78	61
Increased involvement	55	80	65
Enhanced overall experience	61	78	74
Increased student–student contact about class activities and assignments	69	94	90
Comfortable using for required course activity	87	92	90

Note: Displays percentages of survey responses that were "agree" and "strongly agree."

Table 16.3 Student Perceptions and Utilization Patterns

	Overall agree, %	Agree + strongly agree, %
Use regularly	91.3	77.5
Carry to class daily	96.8	95.5
Improved the quality of my academic work	90.1	68.6
Increased communication with classmates	74.5	44.3
Increased contact with professors and TAs	82.9	64.3
Increased involvement in class	90.5	70.8
Increased interest in class	91.8	74.8
Improved organization	89.6	69.4
Improved quality of work	83.3	52.8
Helped me do things more quickly	88.9	69.8
Increased control of my learning environment	89.9	64.9
Helped me find out about campus events	92.4	74.5

Note: Displays survey responses from entering freshmen (n = 782) in the 2010 academic year.

APPENDIX 16.C

Table 16.4 Student Engagement Ratings by Device

Using my device in this class has . . .	iPhone (n = 570)	iPod Touch (n = 201)	t-value
Use regularly (all purposes)	5.15	4.87	2.81*
Carry to class daily	5.83	5.50	4.04**
Use for academic work	4.97	4.52	4.24**
Increased contact with professors and TAs	4.77	4.31	3.78**
Increased involvement in class	4.96	4.70	2.57*
Increased interest in class	5.09	4.71	3.79**
Improved organization	5.05	4.54	4.84**
Improved quality of work	4.61	4.20	3.61**
Helped me do things more quickly	5.05	4.41	5.95**
Increased control of my learning environment	4.93	4.39	5.21**

Note: Illustrates results of MANOVO on comparisons of iPhone and iPod Touch student response means exhibiting statistically significant differences.
* significant at p < .01; ** significant at p < .001.

REFERENCES

Abilene Christian University. (2012). *Mobile learning research*. Retrieved from: www.acu.edu/technology/mobile learning/research/index.html

Baldridge, S. N., Moran, A., & Herrington, W. (2011). Evaluation of the use of mobile technology in the social science classroom. *National Social Science Association National Technology and Social Science Conference Proceedings* (pp. 19–29).

Berger, S. B. (2011). *The developing person through the life span*. New York: Worth Publishers.

Blumberg, S. J., & Luke, J. V. (2011). Wireless substitution: Early release of estimates from the National Health Interview Survey, July–December 2009. National Center for Health Statistics. Retrieved from: www.cdc.gov/nchs/data/nhis/earlyrelease/wireless201112.pdf

Brown, T. H. (2004). The role of m-learning in the future of e-learning in Africa. In D. Murphy, R. Carr, J. Taylor, & Tat-meng, W. (Eds.), *Distance education and technology: Issues and practice* (pp. 197–216). Hong Kong: Open University of Hong Kong Press.

Bugeja, M. J. (2006). Facing the facebook. *The Chronicle of Higher Education, 52*(21), C1.

Canalys. (2012, February). Smart phones overtake client PCs in 2011. Retrieved from: www.canalys.com/newsroom/smart-phones-overtake-client-pcs-2011

Carey, P. (2010, March). Research proves it: Undergraduates crazy for device. *San Jose Mercury News*, p. 1C.

Consortium for School Networking. (2012). *Cost value of investment case studies/Student mobile learning/Summary.* Retrieved from: www.cosn.org/Initiatives/LeadershipforMobileLearning/tabid/8108/Default.aspx

Crompton, H. (2013). A historical overview of mobile learning: Toward learner-centered education (pp. 3–14). In Z. Berge, & L. Muilenburg (Eds.), *Handbook of mobile learning.* New York: Routledge.

Crouch, C. H., & Mazur, E. (2001). Peer instruction: Ten years of experience and results. *American Journal of Physics, 69,* 970–977.

Dahlstrom, E., de Boor, T., Grunwald, P., & Vockley, M. (2011). *The ECAR National Study of Undergraduate Students and Information Technology.* Boulder, CO: EDUCAUSE Center for Applied Research. Retrieved from: www.educause.edu/ecar

Donner, J. (2008). Research approaches to mobile use in the developing world: A review of the literature. *Information Society, 24*(3), 140–159.

Evans, C. (2008). The effectiveness of m-learning in the form of podcast revision lectures in higher education. *Computers & Education, 50*(2), 491–498.

Genachowski, F. C. (2012, Feburary). Transcript from digital learning day town hall. *Prepaired Remarks at Digital Learning Day Town Hall.* Washington, DC: Federal Communications Commission.

Goff, J. (2011). *The impact of mobile learning methods on graduate student engagement.* Retrieved from: www.acu.edu/technology/mobilelearning/documents/research/goff/full-report-goff.pdf

Holec, H. (1981). *Autonomy and foreign language learning.* Oxford, UK: Pergamon.

International Telecommunications Union. (2012, November). Key global telecom indicators for the world telecommunication service sector. Retrieved from: www.itu.int/ITU-D/ict/statistics/at_glance/KeyTelecom.html

Jones, K. (2011). Use of augmented reality interfaces to enhance art student learning: An experimental comparison of learning platforms. Retrieved from: www.acu.edu/technology/mobilelearning/documents/research/kenny-jones/jones-final-report-2011.pdf

Kuutti, K. (1996). Activity theory as a potential framework for human–computer interaction research. In B. A. Nardi (Ed.), *Context and consciousness: Activity theory and human–computer interaction* (pp. 17–44). Cambridge, MA: MIT Press.

Laurillard, D. (2007). Pedagogical forms for mobile learning: Framing research questions. In N. Pachler (Ed.), *Mobile learning: Towards a research agenda* (pp. 153–176). London: WLE Centre, Institute of Education.

Litchfield, A. J., Dyson, L. E., Lawrence, E., & Zmijewska, A. (2007). Directions for m-learning research to enhance active learning. *ICT: Providing choices for learners and learning: Proceedings ascilite Singapore 2007* (pp. 587–596).

Mazer, J. P., Murphy, R. E., & Simonds, C. J. (2007). I'll see you on "Facebook": The effects of computer-mediated teacher self-disclosure on student motivation, affective learning, and classroom climate. *Communication Education, 56*(1), 1–17.

Obama, B. (2011). *The State of the Union 2011.* Retrieved from White House website: www.whitehouse.gov/state-of-the-union-2011

Perkins, S., & Saltsman, G. (2010). Mobile learning at Abilene Christian University: Successes, challenges, and results from year one. *Journal of the Research Center for Educational Technology, 6*(1), 47–54.

Phillips, M. (2011). *Connected Learning Project Report.* Retrieved from: www.acu.edu/technology/mobilelearning/documents/research/phillips/phillips-final-report.pdf

Powell, C. (2009). Using iPhones to support student learning in inquiry based laboratory experiments. Retrieved from: www.acu.edu/technology/mobilelearning/documents/research/cynthia-powell/powell-using-iphone.pdf

Roschelle, J. (2003). Keynote paper: Unlocking the learning value of wireless mobile devices. *Journal of Computer Assisted Learning, 19*(3), 260–272.

Sharples, M., Taylor, J., & Vavoula, G. (2007). A theory of learning for the mobile age. In R. Anderews and C. Haythornthwaite (Eds.), *The Sage handbook of e-learning research* (pp. 222–223). London: SAGE.

Shepherd, I., & Reeves, B. (2011). iPad or iFad: The reality of a paperless classroom. Retrieved from: www.acu.edu/technology/mobilelearning/documents/research/ipad-or-ifad.pdf

Siemens, G. (2005, June). Theories for informal learning design? [Weblog message]. Retrieved from: www.connectivism.ca/?p=21

Sutherlin, A., & Powell, C. (2011). *Final project report for mobile learning fellows program 2010–2011 academic year.* Retrieved from: www.acu.edu/technology/mobilelearning/documents/research/cynthia-powell/powell-sutherlin-final-report-2010-11.pdf

Stubblefield, N. B. (1908). *U.S. Patent No.0887357.* Washington, DC: U.S. Patent and Trademark Office.

Trowler, V., & Trowler, P. (2010). *Student engagement evidence summary.* York, UK: The Higher Education Academy.

Vygotsky, L. S. (1978). *Mind in society: The development of higher psychological processes.* Cambridge, MA: Harvard University Press.

Wade, C., Jacobsen, B. S., & Forste, R. (2011). The wired generation: Academic and social outcomes of electronic media use among university students. *Cyberpsychology, Behavior, and Social Networking, 14,* 275–280.

Wong, K. (2007, January). *The introduction of the iPhone from an Apple first-timer's perspective.* Retrieved from: http://abcnews.go.com/Technology/Business/story?id=2783651&page=1

17

THE POWER OF THE PERSONAL

Discovering the M in M-Learning

Colleen Carmean, Jill L. Frankfort, and Kenneth N. Salim

As we've seen in the struggles of previous chapters, m-learning is difficult to define in a meaningful way. *Everything learning but with personal electronic devices* creates a framework for shared understanding, but tells us little about the transformation we've seen in informal, just-in-time, and personalized learning brought on by mobility of devices. The negative space in shared understanding of a just-in-time learning shift is the reason this book is necessary, and for those of us seeking to create meaningful learning experiences with mobile devices, the book has arrived none too soon.

Our goal is to capture practice in m-learning in terms of what these small-device technologies newly offer the education landscape. We've seen in previous chapters that the feature of mobility alone is not to be discounted, for it is, as this book's shared definition implies, at the heart of m-learning. But, if we rest there, we lose sight of discovering the deeper *affordance* (Carmean & McGee 2008; Gibson, 1977; Norman, 1988) of immediacy and connection natively built into use of small-device technologies. Understanding the potential for new learning experiences and supports built into *mobility + design* is the purpose of this chapter: understanding new learning and support possibilities when designing for mobile technology in new learning uses, designing with mobility, and designing to leverage mobility as a unique feature for the learning experience.

Donald Norman (1988) claims that *affordance* is built in human–computer interaction as the specific possibilities of the experience that are readily perceivable by an actor. Seen as a combinatory experience of multiple, distinct variables, one could make the case that any specific combination is the unique sum of a formula where affordance of technology = (device + software):

$$A = d + s$$

For Norman (1988), design for the unique interaction between the features of a device and the software, as perceived by the user (in our case, the learner), provides the affordance of experience for that object. If this is so, we are missing transformative possibilities of *designing* for m-learning by leveraging affordance as a sum value, rather than simply leveraging mobility as an innate feature of the hardware. Until now, m-learning has been assumed as a characteristic of the mobile device, and minimally leveraged but little explored in the history of these devices. Much richer possibility appears when the intersection of feature sets and user perception becomes a formula to be solved, where each of the variables adds to the experience and possibilities.

Approached in this way, it is easy to recognize that simply reading a homework assignment on a couch instead of at a desk does not change the learning experience. Our flat, self-contained content remains the same, whether accessed via a book, a printout, a computer, or an electronic mobile device. As related to the learning outcome, our learning experience of a PDF is unchanged by the medium. What then is the *affordance* of a mobile device? What are the unique *actionable properties* of affordance, referenced by Gibson (1977, 1979), that are perhaps latent, but uniquely available, and exist between mobile electronic devices and the learner?

For Gibson (1977, 1979), access to content on the go would be less a perceived design affordance and more a by-product of mobility. Affordance lies in the actor's use and the features of design for use. Mobile electronic devices have, before today, provided little that is unique within Gibson's notion of actionable properties and the user experience. Indeed, the actor perceives the unique ability of taking the content from the desk to the couch (or plane, train, waiting room), but learning remains unchanged between mobile and non-mobile experience. Our personal electronic devices have great *potential* regarding convenience and mobility, but when do the awareness and needs of Norman's actor and Gibson's properties by design become realized, not just in mobility, but in m-learning? Are there unique affordances to the learner in m-learning, and how do we leverage this in design that has not before been possible via books and paper, and even desktop computers?

EXPLORING THE AFFORDANCE OF MOBILE DEVICES

Let's put the learner on an airplane, far removed from the content he/she could reach out for in an office, with or without an Internet connection. If content is accessed via a laptop rather than a book, having access to a dictionary on the hard drive is certainly a new affordance of mobile technology. That affordance means ready integration of ancillary resources *as needed, wherever needed*. Certainly, many of us could have previously carried small pocket dictionaries with us in the past, but the constraints of air travel made it unlikely that we would carry one in our luggage bin or book bag when in flight.

$$A = m + (d + s)$$

Affordance = mobility + (device + software), where the device (a laptop carrying these valuable, as-needed resources) creates access to a dictionary, whenever and wherever the user needs it. The mobile device can also carry years of historical documents, reports, lists, tables—whatever the user has chosen to place on the hard drive, including software needed to interact with the content. Affordance lies at the intersection of the user's perceived capability of the device (mobile mass storage), plus the software (unique to the needs of the user), available wherever the user needs to be at any time.

Leveraging the Touch Screen

Move the content to a tablet, and the simple design of *integration* expands the user's experience. Now the user stops searching for software, stops searching for the right menu to accomplish a task, leaves behind the stop–go flow of interaction built into the multitasking but serial experience of accessing software on a laptop. A new affordance is due to touch-screen interactions built into the design of tablet + software. The user can reach a dictionary by simply touching the word not known. By design, the user is more likely to use the embedded dictionary to look up a word if he/she can touch the word with a finger and watch the definition pop up. With a touch screen, learning a definition does not take us out of the flow of the content or the experience. Integration of content with definitions becomes the affordance to be leveraged in experience design.

As Norman (1988) sees it, experience exists in the design of possible actions embedded in the device. When design is intentional, each variable changes the experience, and, as with any formula, the value of each variable changes the solution. The potential affordance of an experience when using a tablet device significantly changes over that of using another, non-touch-screen mobile device. Whether this affordance is realized in the design of the software, and whether it is done well enough to be perceived by the user, is a question of affordance realized.

Leveraging the Internet

Move the learner off the airplane to a train (or a bus or a waiting room somewhere), with cellular service now available on his/her device. The user experience expands to an open-ended, more individualized exploration of terms, ideas, or histories.

$$A = m + (d + s) + i$$

Affordance thus changes to a new set of possibilities for the user, when the feature set integrates Internet connectivity into the design for use. The learner now has access to just-in-time answers, solutions, shared knowledge, job aids, and help sites. More than ever, the presence of the Internet changes the experience and moves it closer to a learning environment. Design of the device for Internet-awareness, plus the software in use and design for mobility, shapes a unique affordance built into the combinatory formula of user experience.

Computers, including mobile laptops, were designed to conveniently store materials and dictionaries in the same place, always available within the same context. Touch-screen tablets were designed to allow for integration of these separate materials within the application. Cellular devices were designed to incorporate outside materials, at the user's discretion and according to a personalized decision path. Note that, in this experience, the user is not yet necessarily the *learner*, for we have not yet designed for the possibility characteristics of mobile *learning*. We have moved closer when adding Internet connectivity, as the combination of features available creates instant access to information, anytime and anywhere, embedded in the cellular feature of the devices.

Affordance expands exponentially as each variable brings richer possibilities to the equation. Embedded within each variable is an expansion of the complexity of the formula, creating new realizations of design for individualized use, value, and need.

Leveraging the Mobile App

One more feature variable, not to be ignored if we are moving to a state where we design for learning, is the mobile app: software designed for a small job or singular purpose, to be run on a mobile device. This includes simple menus that allow the user experience to be focused and clutter-free. Apps now run in the multiple hundreds of thousands, with fast, engaging, uncomplicated small device interfaces that are never as frustrating as the complex versions on laptops or desktop devices.

App design is intended to be so specific to the intention that the user never struggles with where in the menu to find an option, never wonders what the App was fully intended to do, never worries whether we are fully utilizing functionality. Users search and seek single-purpose apps for almost any product of function (often for free or at little cost), through the massive and collectively created app stores (iTunes, Apple Store, Google Play, Windows Marketplace, Blackberry App World) specific to their device platform.

With mobile apps, we begin to see design emerge as the stronger component of the experience, and the user able to now choose the app experience over the same content via the Web. In the simplest case of design for learning, we can look to the work of public libraries, where the user is able to check out library books via the Kindle app, a broader set of computer ePub and PDF apps for diverse mobile devices, or Web-based PDF readers for desktop/laptop machines. Few users would argue against the enhanced experience of using the Kindle app. Designed for the feature set of the Kindle (or Kindle-compatible touch tablet), this tiny app focuses on the experience of reading a text. Simply that.

Its features are designed for the best possible reading experience, individualized for the user: size of font with one click, color of the background, night lighting, touch-word definition. Library users now tell librarians that they would prefer to wait for the limited-supply Kindle copies of a book, rather than return to the paper experience. Unlike reading a PDF on a mobile device, the user experience of a mobile app often changes his/her reaction to the content. The app is designed *for* the content.

The affordance to be explored in m-learning can't ignore the new user experience now available within the attraction of small-function design, within software uniquely designed as a mobile application. Affordance expands to include mobility plus device and software, Internet connectivity, and the focused intention of mobile apps (MA).

$$A = m + (d + s(MA)) + i$$

With this new function, design for learning begins to emerge, creating a unique set of questions:

- What happens when we move understanding of the mobile experience to variables within the formula that allow for never-seen-before possibilities and expectations inherent in design for the mobile experience?
- What if m-learning can be more than what learning has been before, because of new functionality in personal electronic devices?
- What if the affordance of a combination of variables creates *m-learning as an experience built for the user, whenever, wherever, however*?

In other words, mobile, connected to the Internet and its web of individualized choices, built for access in small chunks, and customizable to individual's needs and experience—

does this not change m-learning from learning that is mobile, to something more and not yet experienced or understood?

For instance, in our first chapter, Crompton spoke of the use of QR codes to obtain further information about a painting in a museum. The affordance of QR codes is a unique quality of small function interaction between device camera, QR mobile application software, Internet, and desire of the actor (now learner) to explore the context around a specific painting more deeply, following chosen links in an online world of information.

We now begin to see m-learning as actionable possibility built on the learner's context, action, choices, and needs in the moment. This combination of features creates a learner-centered connection to the world and the individualization of knowledge yet to be understood in learning design.

The formula may continue to expand with each actionable possibility designed by an expanded technology or new use design intention. Going back to Norman's (1988) notion of possibilities of the experience, the equation may continue to grow in complexity if new technologies or new uses of technology continue to create new possibilities for how we learn or how we more successfully, more deeply approach learning.

Thus, an inherent part of the affordance equation in mobile value is the ability of the learner to incorporate the possibilities in his/her specific configuration of personal electronic device to link out to the wide world of information, history, images, and meaning that surround his/her contextual framework. Currently, our formula moves toward m-learning as distinct from mere use of mobile device in its realization of the combinatory value of a *whole greater than the sum of its parts*, and the unique possibility for design of a richer learner experience based on that understanding.

What then is m-learning that differentiates itself from reading a text in ways that remain the same experience, despite the use of mobile or fixed device, despite the location, despite the prescribed learning outcome? When is m-learning to be dismissed as merely *learning but on personal electronic devices*, and when does the experience of personal electronic devices change the nature and affordance of learning? Perhaps it is not the m of m-learning, but rather the nature and boundaries of learning the topic forces us to explore.

REIMAGINING A LEARNING FRAMEWORK

In higher education, the learner has changed. Academia is no longer a place for only the elite, prepared, and privileged. A global nation is now seeking higher education, and the diversity of the population demands a new diversity in understanding how we learn, and how best to support the individual needs of the learner. This wide umbrella of support for diversity in learning preferences, needs, and abilities is largely possible owing to technology.

In the best of conditions, technology opens options for more flexible and accessible learning. We now offer environments that are less place-bound, time-bound, or approach-bound. We offer a range of services to allow learners to enter the content in their own way, and we support the whole learner in his/her ability to make learning applied, context-rich, and meaningful. Good instructors have always known that the most meaningful learning comes when embracing and making the content and understanding one's own.

As we've seen with our affordance examples, personalization is the significant factor in exploring mobile electronic devices as learning tools. And, as personalization expands to a wider context of learning than the classroom, so does our understanding of affordance built into the possibility of mobile applications that support the whole learner.

The boundaries on the learning experience have expanded to include smart tools, interactive and just-in-time software, analytic performance trends available to learner and instructor, and real-time response systems. These all create more personal, responsive, and learner-centered possibilities for engaged learning. Whole-learner support tools also now play a larger role in learning, and the role of smart machines and real-deep pattern-matching allows for machines to provide individualized "nudges" to support learner self-awareness and success.

This chapter calls into question how individualized response and support software creates a new m-learning that changes the learner and the learner experience. New research suggests that the experience of learning changes when m + learning is individualized, responsive, and learner aware.

The health care and wellness sector offers an interesting example. There are now more than 40,000 mobile health apps and SMS solutions providing personalized and just-in-time support and education to individuals looking to stop smoking, exercise more, better control their alcohol usage, or manage chronic diseases (Cohn, 2012). For example, the MyQuit Coach app provides adults looking to quit smoking with motivational tips and photos that are customized based on their goals, progress, real-time cravings, and preferences. The RunKeeper app provides novice and experienced athletes with personalized training suggestions, as well as audio feedback on real-time pace and distance while the athletes are on the go. The apps with the largest numbers of users are those that make the mobile experience most relevant and specific to each user. At the same time, research shows that these mobile tools have great impact when they are designed for integration of progress tracking, goal attainment, and behavior change (Cole-Lewis & Kershaw, 2010; Weitzel, Bernhardt, Usdan, Mays, & Glanz., 2007).

M-LEARNING AND HIGHER EDUCATION

What does this m-learning shift look like for college students? Can m-learning engage and support students to increased persistence and success? Now is the time to apply lessons learned in motivational health and personalized awareness apps to learning. Too many students today fail to earn a college degree after beginning their studies. The Institute of Education Sciences reports that only 55 percent of full-time first-time students who begin a 4-year degree finish it in 6 years (Knapp, Kelly-Reid, & Ginder, 2012). Although financial barriers and lack of academic skills prevent some students from earning a degree, research has shown that many students struggle because they lack the academic behaviors and mind-sets associated with college success (Lotkowski, Robbins, & Noeth, 2004).

What does it look like then when m-learning includes personalized m-support, focused on helping students define their goals, deal with academic setbacks, successfully manage their time, and reach their short- and long-term goals—the very skills and attitudes associated with academic persistence (Kennett & Reed, 2009)? And what is the potential when these mobile interactions can be personalized, based on a specific university's academic requirements and expectations, student progress and performance, and student feedback in the moment?

Worth considering is how m-learning in the academy can use social networks to employ social accountability and peer pressure around positive academic behaviors. The idea of networks influencing behaviors is the cornerstone of the provocative hypothesis—*your friends' friends make you fat*—in Christakis and Fowler's book, *Connected* (2009). Years of research by other behavioral psychologists support the influence of social networks. Allcott (2009) described a large-scale pilot study run by an electric company, OPOWER. In the pilot, the company sent a group of residential utility consumers information about their household energy use, as well as the energy use of their neighbors. Residents in the treatment group reduced energy consumption after seeing how their energy usage compared with neighbors. Let's imagine then the power of m-learning in this regard: a student who publicly "checks in" to the library on his mobile app to study for a calculus exam would increase the likelihood that other connected peers would also go to the library and begin studying.

Theory Meets Practice

In early 2012, Persistence Plus and University of Washington–Tacoma (UWT) began a collaboration to pilot this very approach—personalized support and behavioral interventions delivered through mobile devices—to students enrolled in online introductory math courses. By leveraging the affordance created by mobile, connected, and personalized experiences, Persistence Plus and UWT sought to create a new experience of learning for the online student.

UWT is one of three urban campuses that compose the University of Washington system, and this urban campus serves a student population diverse in age, ethnicity, and experience. More than 80 percent of UWT students enroll after transferring from one of the area's community colleges or other universities, and 42 percent of students are first in their families to attend college. In 2012, UWT introduced online introductory math courses to provide its students with increased flexibility in their studies. Recognizing that online students and students in introductory math classes are at greater risk of not completing their courses successfully, UWT worked with Persistence Plus to provide students with a program of mobile support that would uniquely engage students and foster key academic behaviors. Persistence Plus, a social enterprise that was launched through the Kauffman Foundation's Education Ventures program in 2011, marries mobile technology and behavioral psychology to help colleges engage and motivate students to success and completion.

Over the course of the semester, students participating in the Persistence Plus mobile support pilot received personalized daily nudges, customized on the basis of course data, student grades, and student inputs, via text message or through a specially designed iPhone app. Grounded in behavioral research, these nudges served to foster the behaviors and mind-sets associated with increased engagement and achievement. For example, Persistence Plus prompted students to commit to studying at a specific time before a major test, because research shows that commitment to completing a task at a desig-nated time increases the likelihood of task completion. In another instance, Persistence Plus provided students with personalized support messages based on their current grades and their cumulative responses regarding how they were feeling about the course.

Persistence Plus also leveraged research that found powerful effects of exercises that enhance students' resiliency in the face of obstacles. Research has found that resiliency exercises and interventions that affirm students' values and beliefs can result in greater achievement, particularly among African–American and female students (Cohen, et al., 2009). In a more recent study, Walton and Cohen (2011) found that a social-belonging intervention improved achievement results and social well-being for African–American students in the treatment group. During the semester, Persistence Plus shared "resiliency stories" and advice from older students as a strategy for increasing the resiliency of participants.

The mobile platform design enabled Persistence Plus to collect the self-reported data on students' attitudes and behaviors, so that interventions could be designed based on the students' needs at the moment. This design was based on research showing that providing feedback based on individual data can positively impact student behavior and emotional state. In one study, Chiauzzi, Brevard, Thurn, Decembrele, & Lord (2008) found that students using interactive student stress-management software experienced lower levels of anxiety and engaged in greater physical activity.

Nudging Each Student to Success

Early results from this pilot were very promising. Student usage and engagement surpassed what was expected; students freely shared their progress, goals, and challenges via the mobile interface in response to interactive nudges. More than 85 percent of participating pilot students responded to a question nudge at least once, and students expressed unprompted enthusiasm—"Thanks again. Feels good to be supported"—for the feedback and interactive nudges.

Data collected from the mobile platform input also showed that Persistence Plus engaged a segment of the student population that did not seek out help from faculty or other campus resources. This finding was particularly exciting, because it supports the idea that some students feel comfortable sharing struggles through real-time mobile technology in a way that they simply don't through face-to-face interaction. Accordingly, this finding suggests that the non-public nature of mobile support is a key element of its power.

What about impact on student behavior and achievement? In both introductory pre-calculus and statistic courses, students participating in the pilot performed better academically than students who did not. Additionally, nudges were correlated with increased academic performance on specific assignments, as well as the uptake of positive behaviors, such as meeting with a study group. Student comments collected at the end verified these data: students interviewed after the pilot reported that the Persistence Plus mobile support program caused them to study earlier for tests and to be more conscientious in their study habits.

CONCLUSION

In physics, they say that the whole is greater than the sum of its parts. This is also true in learning theory, and in research related to the combinatory variables embedded in our m-learning affordance formula: $A = m + (d + s(MA)) + i$. M-learning creates a real-time, personalized connection between the learner, the content, and the digital world that extends what we now know about deeper learning, engagement, and supporting persistence.

Mobility, smart devices, a globally connected world, mobile apps, data analytics, and the real-time personalization of learning can now support new ways of learning and engaging behaviors that create stronger resilience and persistence. We are now at a stage where learning, especially in higher education, is no longer simply the experience of the classroom or the transference of subject matter. M-learning opens the door for delivery of constructed knowledge, new skills, and changed behavior. M-learning provides a unique affordance in a digital age of personalized finding, sharing, focusing, evaluating, and responding. The challenge is leveraging this affordance for increasingly digital and mobile learner populations and world.

REFERENCES

Allcott, H. (2009) *Social norms and energy conservation*. Cambridge, MA: Center for Energy and Environmental Policy Research, Massachusetts Institute of Technology.

Carmean, C., & McGee, P. (2008). A singular affordance model for emerging technologies. Retrieved from: https://sites.google.com/site/cmcarmean/samodel

Chiauzzi, E., Brevard, J., Thurn, C., Decembrele, S., & Lord, S. (2008). MyStudentBody-Stress: An online stress management intervention for college students. *Journal of Health Communication, 13*(6), 555–572.

Christakis, N. A., & Fowler, J. H. (2009). *Connected: The surprising power of our social networks and how they shape our lives*. New York: Little, Brown and Co.

Cohen, G. L., Garcia, J., Purdie-Vaugns, V., Apfel, N., & Brzustoski, P. (2009). Recursive processes in self-affirmation: Intervening to close the minority achievement gap. *Science, 324*, 400–403.

Cohn, M. (2012). Hopkins researchers aim to uncover which mobile health applications work. Retrieved from: http://articles.baltimoresun.com/2012-03-14/health/bs-hs-mobile-health-apps-20120314_1_health-apps-mhealth-mobile-health

Cole-Lewis, H., and Kershaw, T. (2010). Text messaging as a tool for behavior change in disease prevention and management. *Epidemiologic Reviews, 32*(1), 56–69.

Gibson, J. J. (1977). The theory of affordances. In R. E. Shaw and J. Bransford (Eds.), *Perceiving, acting, and knowing*. Hillsdale, NJ: Lawrence Erlbaum Associates.

Gibson, J. J. (1979). *The ecological approach to visual perception*. Boston, MA: Houghton Mifflin.

Kennett, D. J., & Reed, M. J. (2009). Factors influencing academic success and retention following a 1st-year postsecondary success course. *Educational Review and Evaluation, 15*(2): 153–188.

Knapp, L. G., Kelly-Reid, J. E., & Ginder, S. A. (2012). *Enrollment in postsecondary institutions, Fall 2010; financial statistics, fiscal year 2010; and graduation rates, selected cohorts, 2002–07 (NCES 2012–280)*. Washington, DC: National Center for Education Statistics, U.S. Department of Education. Retrieved from: http://nces.ed.gov/pubs2012/2012280.pdf

Lotkowski, V. A., Robbins, S. B., & Noeth, R. J. (2004). *The role of academic and non-academic factors in improving college retention*. ACT Policy Report. Retrieved from: www.act.org/research/policymakers/pdf/college_retention.pdf

Norman, D. (1988). *The design of everyday things*. New York: Doubleday.

Walton, G. M., & Cohen, G. L. (2011). A brief social-belonging intervention improves academic and health outcomes of minority students. *Science, 331*(6023), 1447–1451.

Weitzel, J. A., Bernhardt, J. M., Usdan, S., Mays, D., & Glanz, K. (2007). Using wireless handheld computers and tailored text messaging to reduce negative consequences of drinking alcohol. *Journal of Studies on Alcohol & Drugs, 68*(4), 534–537.

18

SOCIAL VERSUS INDIVIDUAL FLOW IN MOBILE LEARNING

Ah-reum Lee and Hokyoung Ryu

The ubiquity of mobile devices is having a profound effect on our lives. We increasingly expect to be able to work, learn, and play whenever and wherever we want to, and even this contemporary snapshot of mobile technology is only a step on the way to ever more opportunities that will continue to unfold. For example, a new m-learning application called Spy Listening E.I.A presents several game missions, such as eavesdropping on the native speakers' conversation as a spy. It is expected to convert boring English study to exciting, mobile game-based learning.

Although there are many definitions of m-learning, there is a common thread through these definitions that we somehow involve electronic mobile devices, such as handheld devices or iPads, in designing learning activities (e.g., Vahey & Roschelle, 2007). One important issue that m-learning researchers must therefore address is measuring the benefits when we utilize such devices for learning, which may then enable us to create new and better types of learning activity.

The benefits that have been asserted for different contexts of m-learning are many. Some studies regard the use of mobile devices as being primarily an issue of access and economy of delivery (Mayer, 2002). Small portable devices are cheaper and more easily used in the classroom than large desktop computer systems, so they bring the (assumed) benefits of e-learning to a wider constituency, and the delivery of the learning content can be made in a more economical way than the face-to-face classroom setting (Soloway et al., 2001).

The aim of this chapter is, thus, to identify some particular outcomes from m-learning that could be seen as addressing the contribution of mobile devices, when compared with both more traditional alternatives and immersive e-learning tools. The main focus of our analysis was to apply the concept of flow experience (Csikszentmihalyi, 1990) to the process of learning with mobile devices. In so doing, this chapter empirically tested three types of learning system through which learners could briefly explore a physical (or virtual) workspace, to be trained as security guards for a specific workplace as part of a simulated training program. The main theme of this chapter is to argue that m-learning activities can achieve the desired conditions for learners' optimal flow experience. Further, it claims that the flow-learning experience can be extended to when the learners are working together. From this perspective, we will be able to see how mobile technology can provide an effective learning experience and, thereby, influence a trajectory of m-learning curriculum development.

UNIQUE BENEFITS OF M-LEARNING

Learning has been characterized in a number of ways. For example, traditional *constructivism* emphasizes that learning is internal and personal, involving the generation of new understanding and knowledge and active changes in conceptual understanding. More recent views of learning (Gagne & Deci, 2005) have asserted that intellectual development is largely at the mercy of self-control, by which learners may find their own way to make a learning situation personalized and sensitized to them. Such *socio-cognitive perspectives* now place emphasis on learning as an active, social process, in which the learner is a central participant in his or her own learning process, and collaborative interactions are viewed as a key determinant of the content of learning activities (Lave & Wenger, 1991).

However, previous studies have mostly measured quantitative metrics such as "time on task," "task completion rate," and so forth. These might, in some circumstances, give a useful approximation of the benefits of m-learning activities, but it may be problematic to rely on such quantitative measures, e.g., time data or tests administered after learning activities, in order to draw inferences about m-learning outcomes, in that these are not amenable to justify a larger investment of m-learning initiatives.

Any educational or learning activity concerns itself with improving learning performance, and this should also be true of m-learning. However, m-learning needs to be seen as more than simply enhancing rote knowledge acquisition, as it is not easy to observe any significant instant benefits from m-learning when compared with traditional classroom pedagogy or distance learning. Instead, as many of its proponents claim, m-learning is largely at the mercy of self-determination or self-management (i.e., self-control) (Deci & Ryan, 1985), which requires learners to find their own way to make the learning situation work for them. If this is the case, a logical research question, which is central to this chapter, is how we can assess these new forms of m-learning experience.

A practical m-learning application may suggest a possible answer. In Japan, the Nintendo DS console has been widely used as a mobile multimedia-based English-learning tool, holding out the promise of fun and playful access to an otherwise frustrating learning activity (*Guardian Weekly*, August 8, 2008). In this nationwide project, the learning outcomes were simply measured by counting how many English words had been remembered by those using the Nintendo DS, as opposed to others who had not used it, and this was claimed as solid evidence of a preference for m-learning. In a similar vein, another Nintendo game called *Enchanted Learning 1000 Chinese Characters DS* is also helpful for Korean primary students to enjoyably learn Chinese characters. However, these facts alone did not answer the question of what made this happen, and, in particular, how self-determination or self-management with the m-learning may be important factors.

A possible explanation for this would be that the best learning moments usually occur when a learner is stretched to the limit in a voluntary effort to accomplish something difficult, challenging, and worthwhile (Presnky, 2003), consistently producing *flow experience* (Csikszentmihalyi, 1990) that sustains the learner's efforts to achieve something. To understand why some learning activities are more effective than others, and are able to sustain motivation, one should review the concept of flow experience as proposed by Csikszentmihalyi (1990). This theory, which to a large extent provides the theoretical foundation of this chapter, can help us to understand how learners might pursue whatever they are doing from internal motivation (Malone, 2005).

MEASURING LEARNING EXPERIENCES

Assessing m-learning from the perspective of user experience seems to have been a popular practice in the m-learning research community. However, while we are combining sophisticated mobile technologies for perceived benefits in user experiences, many m-learning projects do not explicitly address how we can present learners with appropriate learning experiences. By and large, empirical studies on positive attitudes or level of engagement have been undertaken, without addressing how we might systematically measure the learning experiences initiated by m-learning technologies.

In this regard, Csikszentmihalyi's flow experience (Csikszentmihalyi, 1990) sheds light on a way to incorporate learning experiences with the known benefits of m-learning. Though there are many different definitions of flow, it is generally said that flow is a holistically controlled feeling where one acts with total involvement or engagement with a particular activity, with a narrowing of focus of attention (Csikszentmihalyi, 1990). From an m-learning perspective, it implies that, in order for learners to experience flow, they must perceive a balance between their controls and the challenges of the activity, which should present them with playful interaction, exploratory behavior, and positive subjective experience (Hoffman & Novak, 1996).

Given that self-control is intrinsic to m-learning, the relative levels of challenge and skill may either facilitate or block the motivation to learn. That is, at a given moment, individuals are aware of a certain number of opportunities challenging them, while they assess how capable they are of coping with these challenges. If the challenges of an activity are beyond the individual's skill level, demanding more than the individual can handle, they may disengage from further learning; conversely, boredom may be the result, also leading to disengagement. This game-based m-learning may suggest why the Japanese and Korean students had such learning benefits (via engagement) from the Nintendo-based m-learning.

However, the role of flow experience in m-learning activities is not easy to see, mostly because it is a subjective experience. There have been many attempts, using tools such as focus groups and questionnaires, that have aimed to capture the behavioral metrics of m-learning and used them to measure aspects of flow experience. Most notably, Microsoft does extensive user-experience testing, mostly via measures of enjoyment, by interrupting the user's interaction every few minutes via a dialogue box asking them for their current level of engagement. However, collecting data with this interrupted mechanism in m-learning would be, to say the least, challenging (i.e., the *flow paradox*— it cannot be called a flow state as soon as it is interrupted by the mechanism). In effect, although flow experience is considered to be a useful measure for evaluating m-learning systems, little empirical work has yet been undertaken.

To apply flow experience in assessing learning outcomes, several human–computer interaction (HCI) practitioners (e.g., Katuk & Ryu, 2012; Park, Parsons, & Ryu, 2010) have demonstrated that the optimal flow state in learning activities can be characterized in four dimensions. These four dimensions of flow incorporate the extent to which (a) the learner perceives a sense of *control* over the learning activity, (b) the learner perceives that his or her *attention is focused* on the learning activity, (c) the learner's *curiosity* is kept aroused during the learning activity, and (d) the learner finds the learning activity *intrinsically interesting*. For more detail of these four dimensions of flow, refer to Ryu and Parsons (2012).

INDIVIDUAL VERSUS SOCIAL FLOW EXPERIENCE

Learning has been characterized in a number of ways. For example, traditional *constructivism* (Strommen & Lincoln, 1992) emphasizes that learning is internal meaning-making, involving the generation of new understanding and knowledge and active changes in conceptual understanding. In contrast, socio-cognitive perspectives on learning theory now place emphasis on learning as an active and social communication process (Lave & Wenger, 1991; Vavoula & Sharples, 2002), in which collaborative interactions are touted as a key construct of learning activities. In this way, learners are impelled to construct knowledge, not only for themselves but also for one another, to collectively elaborate shared meanings. Many m-learning projects thus owe much to interactive outdoor learning activities, where the context can extrinsically trigger the social cognition of learning and, at the same time, develop the learner's internal cognition.

In approaching to these two types of learning experience (i.e., individual vs. collaborative learning), however, learners would have a rather different flow, though they must perceive a balance between their skills and the challenges of the activity. The balance between skills and challenges is a sufficient condition for both learning experiences, but the ways that come to mind are not the same. For instance, the Savannah project (Facer et al., 2004) let students know animal behaviors by using a mobile game when they moved around on the school playing field. It also allowed a high level of individual self-control and group self-control over the learning content to construct a more pleasing cooperative learning experience in addressing the given collective challenges. Given that individual self-control of learning activities is intrinsic to all m-learning, however, the relative levels of group self-control may either facilitate or block the motivation to learn of each individual.

For any learning experience, Csikszentmihalyi's flow (depicted in Figure 18.1) can be applied, in that, if a learning activity is developing skills but not increasing the level of challenge (A_1–A_2), a learner will no longer be in the optimal flow channel, as his or her skills are higher than the level of difficulty of the learning activity. If the challenge increases without an associated level of skills development (A_1–A_3), there will be anxiety rather than optimal flow. Thus, to keep the learner in the optimal flow channel (A_1 or A_4), learning activities should be redesigned in such a way that the levels of knowledge and levels of difficulty are counterbalanced.

An important note on flow experience here is that human beings cannot constantly get pleasure from doing the same activity for long, and, therefore, changes to the optimal flow channel (e.g., A_1–A_4) are inevitable. In that case, the optimal flow experience can only be achieved when the challenges given by new learning activities are dynamically synchronized with the learners' skill sets, leading to the growth and discovery of new

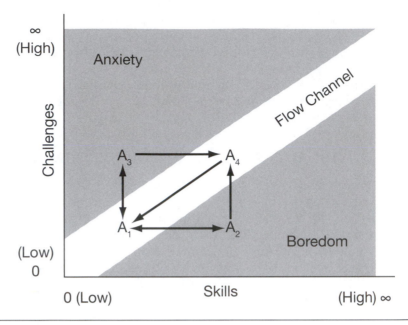

Figure 18.1 Csikszentmihalyi's Flow of Activities

Source: Extended from Csikszentmihalyi, 1990

knowledge or repeating less difficult activities by positive or negative feedback. This proposition is rather differently applied to collaborative-learning activities, where more opportunities for discovery of new knowledge are presented when "others" raise the level of challenge. If this is not the case, the collective-learning benefits presented by others or peers might be simply ignored to do a less challenging or more mundane activity.

This kind of collaborative-learning management, adjusting levels of joint challenges against the collective levels of skill, has been found to contribute to the development of group knowledge structure and acquisition (Kozlowski et al., 2001), although a likelihood of "*social flow*" experience has not been considered at its core. From an individual learner's perspective, at a given moment, each individual is aware of a certain number of opportunities challenging him or her, while, together, the group can assess how capable they are of coping with these challenges. If the challenges of an activity are beyond the learners' collective skill level, demanding more than they can handle, they together may disengage from further learning.

A simplistic way of extrapolating individual to social flow experience might be to say the social flow experience is equal to the total of individual flow experiences of all individuals. However, people do not necessarily associate their own interests with the group's interest, and vice versa. Therefore, the kind of social state required for this social flow experience has to be compartmented, particularly for collaborative-learning activities. The following section explains how this social flow can be triggered and maintained in collaborative-learning activities, and why this type of flow would have a separate effect from the learning outcomes for individuals.

RAISING CHALLENGE THROUGH COLLABORATION: SOCIAL FLOW

Playing or working together seems to appeal to some intrinsic aspects of human nature, that if we are playing (or learning) with others, then we may contribute to someone else's happiness, which historical social scientists and philosophers (e.g., Aristotle and Bentham) have claimed as a human aspiration. This implies being in the company of other people can make a great difference to the quality of our experience. Csikszentmihalyi (1990) maintained that the flow experiences in either "being alone" or "being with others" might differ. In some situations, of course, being alone can help us to accomplish learning goals that cannot be reached in the company of others (e.g., preparing for final exams). On the other hand, if solitude is seen as something to be avoided rather than a challenge, the person will resort to distractions that cannot lead to higher levels of engagement. Here, what we think of as critical to motivating collaboration is appropriate risk-taking by someone else in a group (as an external stimulation), helping the individual to update his or her own learning goals in conjunction with the group's goals.

Of course, collaborative learning is not a panacea. Its benefits can only be achieved at extra cost to the individual, such as requiring more effort and time to complete a collaborative activity within a group. In collaborative activities, "*social loafing*," which is the phenomenon of people making less effort to achieve a common goal when they work in a group than when they work alone, is not uncommon (Steven & Kipling, 1993). Because of the collective costs involved in collaboration, people may rationally choose "not to learn" together. When people begin to learn together, they must accept certain constraints that each person alone did not have. To some extent, they will have to respond similarly to the challenges they encounter, or the relationship may come apart. Hence, we must differentiate and integrate the two learning circumstances (Csikszentmihalyi, 1990). Differentiation means that each person is encouraged to develop his or her unique learning paths, maximize his or her skills, and set his or her own goals. Integration, in contrast, guarantees that what happens to one person will affect all the others. In particular, this integration in collaborative-learning activities would be legitimatized only by communication between learners (e.g., to make a shared meaning). In that case, it is simply a matter of keeping open channels of communication, where m-learning provides an intrinsic advantage. Otherwise, conflicts between individuals are not easily solvable, simply because each individual learner has his or her own goals that are, to a certain extent, divergent from those of all other learning partners. Through this negotiation process of collaborative-learning goals, they are able to find a new set of activities that will continue to keep them involved together.

An important note is needed here. In most cases, the obvious challenges that collaborative learners find together will be exhausted over time. The only way to restore flow to the integration relationship is by finding new challenges through *risk-taking*. In solitary learning activities, there is less impetus to replace the old challenge with a new one. The learner can, thus, simply choose not to learn at no cost, maintaining the status quo. By comparison, collaborative learning would have a greater chance of developing a new challenge, depending on the partners' level of skill, and, in turn, more complex challenges can be tackled. With this in mind, learning designers often try to implement "*sociability by design*," that is, to structure learning activities so that learners will have

Figure 18.2 Risk-taking Works as a Necessary Condition for Social Flow Beyond Individual Flow Experiences

numerous opportunities to simply "hang out" with each other and, thus, form interesting relationships to work together. This implies that one of the most important elements of the social experience might be shared social interaction, where people can go above and beyond their own normal range of ability.

The concept of social flow can account for why those participants who had found their tasks more challenging felt more flow experience than those who did not, in that people working together can voluntarily raise the levels of the challenge of a learning task while performing it. In particular, the instant communication channels of mobile devices could help them to promptly share challenges within activities to keep them working together. This triggering mechanism, as illustrated in Figure 18.2, would explain how collaboration could maintain their motivation, strengthening their social flow.

A CASE STUDY: LEARNING EXPERIENCE AND SOCIAL FLOW

To empirically show how social flow, discussed above, can be maintained and triggered in the collaborative-learning activity, we designed a learning program for trainee security guards to explore a physical space (or virtual space in the case of game-based learning) to become competent in securing specific premises. Three types of instructional design were made to see the differences in flow experience: traditional map-based instruction, a game-based system, and an m-learning system.

The first (map-based) condition was regarded as a control condition, and the game-based system was built upon the assumption that game-based learning activities would present a highly engaging and immersive learning experience. However, this game-based system did not provide the same physical mobility as the real world. This limitation was mitigated as much as possible by concealing all the possible landmarks in the building environment for both the map-based and m-learning. Further, for the virtual game, we provided a 3D map of the premises, as realistic as possible, that allowed the participants to see all the landmarks covered and perceive the depth or the relative volume of each room via the space-view option.

For this case study, a total of 53 trainee security guards voluntarily participated in the study, none of whom had physically explored the premises before. Twenty-five of them were females. All of them had a similar tertiary educational background and were aged 19–26. Nine of the fifty-three participants were assigned to the map-based learning system. There were differences in the size of each group (paper-based, mobile based, and game-based instruction), owing to the random way participants were assigned to conditions, and, to increase the power of the two experimental conditions (i.e., mobile-based and game-based learning) of interest, the number of participants in the control condition was intentionally minimized.

The traditional paper-based security training system contained a map of the five rooms to be visited, their security key codes, and their names on a sheet of paper. The game-based learning system was created using Active Worlds with the same information, but allowing the participants to navigate the experimental space virtually. A PDA with narrative information developed using Microsoft PowerPoint was used for m-learning.

As they completed their own learning session with the given learning system (the premises contains 23 rooms on the second floor, and the participants were guided by the system given to visit five of them, plus remembering other information related to security services), all of them were then asked to answer the 12 questions relating to flow experience in a five-point Likert scale (from 1 = strongly disagree to 5 = strongly agree). For the negative questions, their ratings were reversed to be equivalent to the positive questions. These questions were based on Webster, Trevino, and Ryan's categories (Webster et al., 1993):

- Control:
  (a) When using the mobile device (paper/game), I felt in control over everything.
  (b) I felt that I had no control over my learning process with the mobile device (paper/game).
  (c) The mobile device (paper/game) allowed me to control the whole learning process.
- Attention focus:
  (a) When using the mobile device (paper/game), I thought about other things.
  (b) When using the mobile device (paper/game), I was aware of distractions.
  (c) When using the mobile device (paper/game), I was totally absorbed in what I was doing.
- Curiosity:
  (a) Using the mobile device (paper/game) excited my curiosity.
  (b) Interacting with the mobile device (paper/game) made me curious.
  (c) Using the mobile device (paper/game) aroused my imagination.
- Intrinsic interests:
  (a) Using the mobile device (paper/game) bored me.
  (b) Using the mobile device (paper/game) was intrinsically interesting.
  (c) The mobile device (paper/game) was fun for me to use.

Table 18.1 gives the mean ratings for the three experimental settings of the flow experience. In particular, both cognitive curiosity and intrinsic interests seem to be critical motivators of the learning experience among our participants, which would motivate them to make the required effort to learn to use the sophisticated mobile-based or game-based instructional design.

For each factor, an ANOVA was applied, followed by a Tukey test (at $p \leq .05$). Taken together, the benefit of m-learning can be seen by the optimal flow experience aroused by "cognitive curiosity" and "intrinsic interests," compared with the other learning systems.

Table 18.1 Mean Ratings of the Flow Experience for Three Treatment Groups

System	Learning control	Attention focus	Cognitive curiosity	Intrinsic interest
Paper	3.56	3.78	3.44*	2.78*
Mobile	3.38	3.96	4.04	3.88
Game	3.60	2.90*	3.75	3.75

* = Statistically significant Tukey test at $p \leq .05$.

As seen in Table 18.1, the flow-experience effect can be seen as one potential analytical tool to explain the benefits of m-learning. It explicitly confirmed the significant advantages of the m-learning and game-based learning systems over the traditional pedagogy, in terms of both cognitive curiosity and intrinsic interest.

However, the flow experience observed in the learning program above is solely in the individual learner's sphere, and it is necessary to explore further whether collaboration via mobile devices could be associated with unique aspects of learning flow. To elaborate our case study, a simulated but realistically situated learning program was developed in the same domain of security-guard training. Three types of learning configuration— "*solitary mobile learning,*" "*instant collaborative mobile learning,*" and "*time-delayed collaborative learning*"—were deployed to assess the differences in both learning outcomes and flow experiences rated by the participants. All three learning settings allowed the "trainee guards" to participate in a security patrol mission using a mobile device, encouraging them to act both on their own and collaboratively, as well as sharing knowledge with other "trainee guards."

The same six locations were used throughout this study. Each subject in the two collaborative conditions only visited three areas personally, to deliberately emulate a collaborative-learning context. This learning program thus required each pair to learn about the six locations together. The participants in the solitary-learning condition were asked to complete the six patrol tasks alone, as a control condition.

Figure 18.3 The M-Learning System Guidance (Left) and Instructions for Learning Activities (Right)

Again, 45 security guards volunteered, none of whom had physically explored the premises in a security role before. They had a similar educational background and were aged between 20 and 28. Only five were assigned to the solitary-learning system.

Each participant was equipped with a mobile device (Nokia E71 or E66) installed with the Online Patrol Training System. The difference between the two collaborative configurations was that the instant mobile collaboration supported instant exchange of text and photo messages between the trainees. On the other hand, the time-delayed collaboration only allowed the uploading of photos to a server for later, face-to-face collaboration.

In the instant mobile collaboration, as soon as new text or photos were added, the partner was automatically notified. In contrast, the time-delayed collaboration did not allow this instant communication. We believe that comparing these forms of

Figure 18.4 Text/Picture Based Collaborative Communication

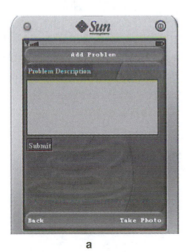

a   b

Figure 18.5 Working With Each Other. (a) Adding New Information; (b) As Soon as New Information is Added, the Partner is Automatically Sent a Notification

collaboration can reveal what is lacking in this time-delayed collaborative learning experience, in terms of social forms of flow and learning outcomes.

The six statements relating to flow experience were then rated on a five-point Likert scale, having been identified in the previous case study as key to see the optimal flow experience created by the two necessary conditions—"*cognitive curiosity*" and "*intrinsic interest.*" The additional seventh statement ("working with my partner allowed me to look into other issues other than the patrol instructions given") was inserted to see if working in a group had encouraged them to tackle more challenging tasks.

Table 18.2 gives the mean ratings for the three learning settings across the two contributors to the flow experience, and the "risk taking" measure relating to collaborative benefits. In all three measures, the instant mobile collaboration gains the higher ratings, which indicates that our participants had somewhat different flow experiences in the instant mobile collaboration. Clearly, with only the small sample size using the solitary mobile system, statistical comparisons are inappropriate. Nonetheless, at the very least, the values in Table 18.2 demonstrate that the instant mobile collaboration might be legitimatized for better forms of flow experience beyond individual flow experience (mean 3.80 vs. 2.52 for cognitive curiosity; 3.88 vs. 2.71 for intrinsic interest), and the higher risk-taking attitude inspired by the instant mobile collaboration (mean 3.95 vs. 3.25 vs. 1.35 for risk-taking) may be proposed as a factor to help explain the differences between the three learning systems.

The results suggest the distinctive nature of m-learning and, possibly, the implications of social forms of flow experience. "Cognitive curiosity" and the desire to attain competence with the learning application may motivate learners to develop more skills or further examine the learning space, and so higher ratings on these statements imply a willingness to exploit the learning activity further. "Intrinsic interest" can be deemed subjective experiences during interactions that are characterized by perceptions of pleasure and involvement. Higher ratings on these statements mean the learners are so intensively involved in the learning activity that putting additional time and cognitive effort into the learning activity is done willingly. Finally, "risk-taking" behavior is associated with these two contributors, in that it can generate a further motivation to learn. This is more likely to lead the group to find new sources of knowledge through collaboration, outweighing the possible costs of collaboration such as the additional time and cognitive effort required. Hence, it can be seen that higher risk-taking behavior by individuals may have benefited the group as a whole, because the group would reap the rewards of the higher risk-taker's discoveries.

Table 18.2 Mean Ratings of Flow Experience for Three Levels of Collaboration

System	Cognitive curiosity M (SD)	Intrinsic interest M (SD)	Risk-taking M (SD)
Mobile solitary	2.52 (0.83)	2.71 (0.92)	1.35 (0.77)
Instant mobile collaboration	3.80 (0.77)	3.88 (0.75)	3.95 (0.89)
Time-delayed collaboration	3.20 (0.95)	3.00 (1.08)	3.25 (0.79)

Note: Responses to all items except risk-taking were averaged to obtain the mean.

CONCLUSIONS AND DISCUSSION

The educational benefits of learning with others may be difficult to assess, but are nevertheless widely acknowledged. Many have claimed collaborative-learning activities enable exchanges of thoughts, emotions, and ideas among learners. In turn, this bonds them with others participating in the same learning activity.

In this chapter, in considering the impact collaboration has on an m-learning activity, the case study showed two preconditions of social flow: (1) potential learners should feel challenges given by others are manageable, and (2) they together or individually could see the challenges as positive self-improvement opportunities within the time pressure. This social form of learning experience deserves to be uniquely considered in collaborative-learning situations and implies that the development of knowledge in collaboration can be attributed to dynamic interaction with other learners. In this light, we suggested that the benefits of collaboration within a social-flow experience overcame any costs involved in the collaboration activity, and this might be a novel stance to account for the benefits of collaboration. That being said, designers might facilitate social-flow experience with mobile content design that can inspire a higher risk-taking attitude.

This chapter also raises several research themes of collaborative learning. Through conversing with Muilenburg and Berge (editors of this book), we found that studying how peers might co-develop a challenging task for their learning activity, and how they would work adaptively together on that task, would be an interesting question for validating the social-flow experience effect in collaboration (i.e., whether they are able to improve their collective skill set to meet the challenging task). This research on social forms of flow may reveal when groups can maximize their potential, and when they do not. That is, how m-learning can facilitate this social form of flow—as a relatively extrinsic motivation—is urgently needed to catalyze the adoption of m-learning in much learning-activity design.

ACKNOWLEDGMENT

This work was supported by the National Research Foundation of Korea (NRF) funded by the Ministry of Education, Science and Technology (MEST) (No. 20110028992) and Basic Science Research Program (No. 20110021398).

REFERENCES

Csikszentmihalyi, M. (1990). *Flow: The psychology of optimal experience*. New York: Harper Perennial.

Deci, E., & Ryan, R. (1985). *Intrinsic motivation and self-determination in human behavior*. New York: Plenum Press.

Facer, K., Stanton, D., Joiner, R., Reid, J., Hull, R., & Kirk, D. (2004). Savannah: Mobile gaming and learning? *Journal of Computer Assisted Learning, 21*(6), 204–216.

Gagne, M., & Deci, E. (2005). Self-determination theory and work motivation. *Journal of Organizational Behavior, 26*(4), 331–362.

Hoffman, D., & Novak, T. (1996). Marketing in hypermedia computer-mediated environments: Conceptual foundations. *Journal of Marketing, 3*(60), 50–68.

Katuk, N., & Ryu, H. (2012). Seeing is believing?: Rehearsing Mayer's multimedia effects in intelligent tutoring systems. *Computers and Education, 51*(2), 787–814.

Kozlowski, S., Gully, S., Brown, K., Salas, E., Smith, E., & Nason, E. (2001). Effects of training goals and goal orientation traits on multidimensional training outcomes and performance adaptability. *Behavior and Human Decision Processes, 85*(1), 1–31.

Lave, J., & Wenger, E. (1991). *Situated learning: Legitimate peripheral paraticipation.* Boston, MA: Cambridge University Press.

Malone, T. (2005). Toward a theory of intrinsically motivating instruction. *Cognitive Science, 5*(4), 333–369.

Mayer, R. (2002). Multimedia learning. *Psychology of Learning and Motivation, 41*, 85–139.

Park, J., Parsons, D., & Ryu, H. (2010). To flow and not to freeze: Applying flow experience to mobile learning. *IEEE Transactions on Learning Technologies, 3*(1), 56–67.

Presnky, M. (2003). Digital game-based learning. *ACM Computers in Entertainment, 1*(1), 1–4.

Ryu, H., & Parsons, D. (2012). Risky business or sharing the load? Social flow in collaborative mobile learning. *Computers & Education, 58*(2), 707–720. DOI:10.1016/j.compedu.2011.09.019

Soloway, E., Norris, C., Blumenfeld, P., Fishman, B., Krajcik, J., & Marx, T. (2001). Devices are ready-at-hand. *Communications of the ACM, 44*(6), 15–20.

Steven, K., & Kipling, W. (1993). Social loafing: A meta-analytic review an theoretical integration. *Journal of Personality and Social Psychology, 65*(4), 681–706.

Strommen, E., & Lincoln, B. (1992). Constructivism, technology, and the future of classroom learning. *Education and Urban Society, 24*(4), 466–476.

Vahey, P., & Roschelle, J. (2007). Using handheld technology to move between the private and public in the classroom. In M. van't Hooft & K. Swan (Eds.), *Ubiquitous computing in education: Invisible technology* (pp. 187–210). New York: Lawrence Erlbaum Associates.

Vavoula, G., & Sharples, M. (2002). *KLeOS: A personal, mobile, knowledge and learning organisation system.* Paper presented at the IEEE International Workshop on Mobile and Wireless Technologies in Education, Vaxjo, Sweden.

Webster, J., Trevino, L., & Ryan, L. (1993). The dimesionality and correlates of flow in human–computer interactions. *Computers in Human Behavior, 9*(4), 411–426.

19

THE "REFLECTIVE STUDENT"

The Use of Mobile Devices Through Seamless Educational Spaces and Authentic Learning Scenarios

Maria Cinque

The use of mobile devices—mobile phones, MP3 players, Tablet PCs, iPods, and iPads—has grown so much in recent years that their spread now exceeds that of personal computers in most modern professional and social contexts. However, it seems that these tools are used less in learning contexts, and some authors (for example, Herrington, Herrington, Mantei, Olney, & Ferry, 2009; Kukulska-Hulme, 2007) point out that there isn't a pedagogical theory for ubiquitous learning or m-learning. Although the so-called *early adopters* are willing to use new technologies for educational purposes, it is still unclear whether there are good theoretical reasons for using mobile devices for learning (Herrington et al., 2009). On the other hand, it must also be considered that the majority of m-learning activity continues to take place on devices that were not designed with educational applications in mind, and usability issues are often reported (Kukulska-Hulme, 2007). As a matter of fact, we must admit that the term "mobile" indicates tools with different features and functionalities, and there is no unifying theory for using them for learning, just an unending parade of tools that sometimes can be puzzling, even for a teacher well acquainted with technologies.

On the other hand, we must consider that m-learning challenges the wisdom, timing, and fixed spaces of established pedagogies and the usefulness of traditional tools and resources.

PEDAGOGICAL FOUNDATIONS

Bridging Technology and Learning

Many projects have already focused on metacognition and technology-enhanced learning (TEL), to develop and assess information technology-based learning environments that foster: student development of rich mental models through the scaffolding of meta-cognition; manipulation of multiple representations; the development and testing of conceptual models based on available evidence; exposure to authentic, complex, and ill-constrained problems; and understanding of complex, dynamic systems. Through some case studies based on projects carried out in different educational contexts (Cacace, Cinque, Crudele, Iannello, & Venditti, 2004; Cinque, 2008; Cinque, 2011; Cinque, Crudele, Gagliani Caputo, & Iannello, 2005; Cinque & Pensieri, 2009), this chapter will illustrate how m-learning can enhance metacognition, creative skills, and learning behaviors such as: problem-solving, reciprocal learning, experiential learning, progressive mastery, self-correction, critical reflection, and active seeking of meaning.

Our aim in these case studies was to test the different possibilities and opportunities of using mobile devices during the training of medicine and nursing university students. Some smaller projects were also carried out in a catering school, with younger students.

Seamless Spaces and Authentic Frameworks

Crompton, Muilenburg, and Berge, in Chapter 1 of this volume, state that m-learning is "learning across multiple contexts, through social and content interactions, using personal electronic devices" (Crompton, 2013, p. 4). The authors, based on Sharples, Taylor, and Vavoula (2007), explicitly refer to the main challenge of m-learning, which is to enable students to learn whenever and wherever they want and to seamlessly switch between different contexts, i.e., between formal and informal contexts and between individual and social learning, by extending the social spaces in which learners interact with each other. In this sense, the Crompton, Muilenburg, and Berge definition of m-learning implicitly includes that of Looi et al. (2010), who pointed out that, rather than trying to define m-learning in comparison with e-learning—as some authors have done—it would be better to think of "seamless learning spaces" and "continuity of the learning experience across different scenarios or contexts" (Looi et al. 2010, p. 154).

The adoption of the term "seamless" in the expression "seamless learning spaces," or in the synonymous expression "seamless educational environments," acknowledges an evolution of the technology and of the educational culture at the end of the 20th century. Based on a comprehensive review of the literature, Wong and Looi (2011) identify 10 dimensions of seamless learning: (1) encompassing formal and informal learning; (2) encompassing personalized and social learning; (3) across time; (4) across locations; (5) ubiquitous knowledge access (integrating context-aware learning, augmented reality learning, and ubiquitous Internet access); (6) encompassing physical and digital worlds; (7) combined use of multiple device types (including "stable" technologies, such as desktop computers, interactive whiteboards with mobile devices); (8) seamless switching between multiple learning tasks (such as data collection, analysis, presentation, and communication); (9) knowledge synthesis (integrating prior and new knowledge, abstract and concrete knowledge, and multidisciplinary learning); and (10) encompassing multiple pedagogical or learning-activity models.

The main theoretical and pedagogical framework of this chapter takes into account contemporary theories of learning, including situated learning (Lave & Wenger, 1991), activity theory (Engeström, 1993; Kofod-Petersen & Cassens, 2005), conversational theory (Pask, 1976), reflection-on-action model (Schön, 1983), and authentic learning (Herrington, 2006, 2010). These theories provide a consonant and coherent model of meaning making, offering a clearer understanding of the complexities of learning and conceiving "meaningful learning" as a willful, intentional, active, conscious, constructive, and socially mediated practice that includes reciprocal intention—action—reflection activities.

We studied all the structures of communication and organized the interaction between learners and technology, learners and teachers/tutors, and learners and their peers. We used the activity theory to map students' tasks during on-the-job training and to define what context aspects are related to the current user activity. We decided what kind of input could be given to stimulate student reflection and to offer them "authentic tasks."

In particular, we draw from literature the concept of "authentic learning environment" (Herrington, Reeves, & Oliver, 2010), which can be defined in terms of context, tasks, and roles of the participants. In an "authentic learning environment," problems are set within an authentic and realistic context; they are "ill-defined" (the solution of the problem does not have a clear path, requiring students to define the tasks and subtasks needed to complete the activity) and complex; they require a significant investment of time and intellectual resources, examination from multiple perspectives, and collaboration and reflection; they are integrated with assessment and supported by scaffolding.

RESEARCH

Context and Population Targeted

As a recipient of an HP 2003 Mobility Grant and an HP 2005 Technology for Teaching Grant, Campus Bio-Medico University of Rome carried out many projects to assess the use of wireless networks and portable devices (pocket and tablet PCs) for both classroom activities and on-the-job training. The projects, concerning the Faculties of Medicine (including Medicine, Nursing, Dietetics, and Science of Nutrition) and Engineering, involved more than 300 students in 4 years. At the beginning of 2007, we launched a new, wider program called We-Com (Wireless Educational Communities), destined to enhance the use of mobile technology at the university and to encourage teachers to adopt new pedagogical models that could benefit from the presence of wireless connections. This changed teachers' attitude toward technology. From the beginning of 2008, we started intensive use of mobile devices in classroom experiences, involving those teachers who were ready to redesign their courses.

Simultaneously, some smaller projects were undertaken. Mobile Wireless Education in a Catering School (MoWECS; 2004–2005) was aimed at investigating the best use of mobile wireless devices in a catering school to enhance teaching "on the job" (in the kitchen, in the laundry, in the rooms). Social Networking for Catering Schools (SoNECS; 2007–2008) expanded the educational opportunities through the creation of social networks among students of a catering school between 14 and 18 years old (Istituto Professionale Alberghiero, undergraduate school).

In total we carried out seven different projects, involving a total of 522 users (students, teachers, and health care professionals), some of whom participated in more than one project (see Figure 19.1).

In the majority of these projects, mobile devices were used for on-the-job training, that is, the teaching and learning that takes place in normal working situations, using the actual tools, equipment, documents, or materials that trainees will use when fully trained. However, after a first phase, characterized by the adoption during on-the-job training, the project outcomes went beyond our expectations, and there was a real "domino effect," with the spreading of new ideas and projects. As reported in the literature, the devices were used "in ways that never even occurred to their designers" (Keinonen, 2003, p. 2), and "the scope of use expanded to fulfill emergent needs" (Gilbert, Sangwan, & Han Mei lan, 2005, p. 207).

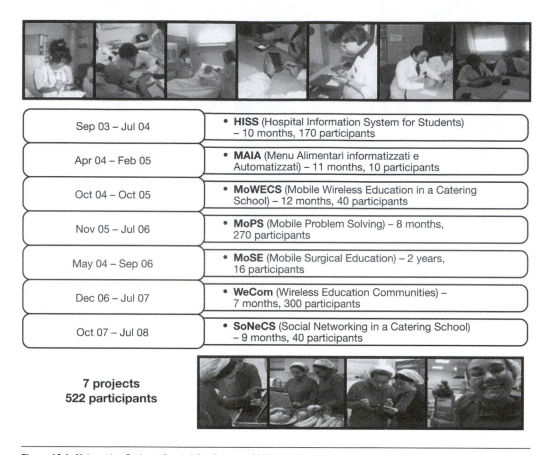

Sep 03 – Jul 04	• **HISS** (Hospital Information System for Students) – 10 months, 170 participants
Apr 04 – Feb 05	• **MAIA** (Menu Alimentari informatizzati e Automatizzati) – 11 months, 10 participants
Oct 04 – Oct 05	• **MoWECS** (Mobile Wireless Education in a Catering School) – 12 months, 40 participants
Nov 05 – Jul 06	• **MoPS** (Mobile Problem Solving) – 8 months, 270 participants
May 04 – Sep 06	• **MoSE** (Mobile Surgical Education) – 2 years, 16 participants
Dec 06 – Jul 07	• **WeCom** (Wireless Education Communities) – 7 months, 300 participants
Oct 07 – Jul 08	• **SoNeCS** (Social Networking in a Catering School) – 9 months, 40 participants

7 projects
522 participants

Figure 19.1 M-Learning Projects Carried Out Between 2003 and 2008

Desired Outcomes

The indicators used to evaluate the projects concerned both student learning and other factors, such as their greater involvement in learning activities, interaction, the climate of collaboration between students and tutors, and the ability of tutors to improve their teaching strategies and use technology as a support activity for tutoring and mentoring.

Activities designed for the projects were intended to make each student capable of the following learning behaviors: problem-solving, experiential learning, self-correction, progressive mastery, active seeking of meaning, critical reflection, and reciprocal learning. For a detailed description of these items, see Table 19.1.

PROJECT DEVELOPMENT

Wireless University

Learning on the job has always been considered a basic methodology for medical-related professions. The main aim of this process is to build a bridge between the "knowledge dimension" (what the student is learning at university) and the professional training. An important part of the teaching is accomplished in the wards, while visiting patients. The typical way of memorizing what is said or done by the teachers, nurses, or physicians

Table 19.1 Learning Behaviors

Behavior	Description
Problem-solving	Students are expected to engage with complex situations and decide what information and skills are needed in order to manage those situations effectively
Experiential learning	Students face real experiences from which they can draw the necessary stimuli as sources of learning and of motivation
Self-correction	Students will understand when and why they have made a mistake and can correct themselves without a direct, external request/indication
Progressive mastery	Students will gain increasing and progressive control of all topics/material, measuring themselves with increasingly difficult tasks
Active seeking of meaning	Students will give meaning to whatever they are doing in order to overcome difficulties that arise during study
Critical reflection	Students will be able to share reflection and awareness while learning
Reciprocal learning	Students are expected to learn by meeting up and working with their peers

is to take written notes in an exercise book. This leads to unstructured data and makes it difficult to rapidly access specific information. Postproduction is usually needed to reorganize the notes in a practical way for easy recovery of any part of them.

In 2003, we introduced wireless networks and portable devices at the Campus Bio-Medico University of Rome, starting a number of projects for assessing the use of this technology. In the Hospital Information System for Students (HISS) project, 170 students used wireless devices to collect data concerning more than 1,500 patients in the campus hospital.

An accurate analysis phase was necessary in order to create really useful modules: In some cases, the forms were created following the examples of existing paper forms, with appropriate modifications to make them suitable for a mobile device with a small screen; in other cases, it was necessary to create new modules for existing practices not otherwise documented, so as to make possible the recording and monitoring of activities previously not standardized. Consequently, the introduction of mobile devices facilitated the rationalization and structuring of contents to be transmitted, allowing much of the "tacit" knowledge in many departments to be made explicit. Furthermore, we designed activities to enhance students' reflection on their practice and on the connection between practice and theory. For this reason, it was necessary to put online resources (treatises on anatomy, pathophysiology, the composition of drugs) that students, on request, could download or access online to enhance their knowledge.

Students were also involved in the design of interfaces: Medical students gave suggestions to software developers for the creation of an electronic form to enter clinical information at the bedside; nursing students focused on modules concerning nursing diagnosis, and calculation of entrance and exit fluids; students of the dietetics curriculum addressed the construction of an order entry system for diets.

After the design of the interface, the main problem was content adaptation, depending on mobile devices' features and the frequent changes in the interface definition. The possibility to rapidly change the contents through an XML schema, without varying the code, allowed us to improve the application day by day.

The positive effects of the project went beyond our hopes. Two companion projects started, following the enthusiasm of some members of the staff: The first one, for the surgery-department physicians, has completely changed the method of rapid data entry at the bedside, which was previously done on a sheet placed on a wooden tablet. The second one, carried out in collaboration with the Campus Information System software developers, converted all dieticians' activities (such as bedside–kitchen communication) to an electronic version.

Two years later, we developed the Mobile Problem-Solving (MoPS) project for engineering students, which was funded under an HP Technology for Teaching Grant (2005). Problem-solving is a compulsory course for all students in the first year of the Masters course in bioengineering. The course includes both activities in the classroom and observation/intervention on the field. Mobile technology helped us achieve a fundamental goal of this course: immediate interaction for faster problem-solving. Students equipped with tablet PCs participated in periodic briefings held in the classroom, and then went to the hospital for observation, taking notes and images of the problems, and sending them to the tutors when needed.

Mobile School

A catering school normally offers a good part of its teaching in a training environment. It is difficult to access textual or multimedia resources while in a kitchen, or in an ironing room or a bedroom. Books can be too heavy to carry, whiteboards cannot be placed where they are most needed, digital projectors and screens are almost impossible to integrate in a kitchen and cannot be carried into all the bedrooms. Therefore, the introduction of wireless mobile devices helps in providing the necessary information in any location.

The MoWECS project was aimed at investigating the best use of mobile wireless devices in a catering school to enhance teaching "on the job" (in the kitchen, in the laundry, in the rooms). Within this scenario, we analyzed all the existing structures of communication and monitored the change in these structures during the phases of users' training to the new technologies and of development of mobile contents.

Students were able to access from anywhere multimedia resources, such as recipes with photos and a check-list of instructions; video instructions for the oven, for the vegetables and meat cuts; images of fruit scupltures; forms to calculate the cost of a meal and the total expenses of a day; forms to collect the number of guests in the different areas, to plan the menu of the day, to modify it for dietary needs, to record new recipes, to check the things to buy, and to assign tasks to the students. Besides the teaching material prepared specifically, students could also access resources on the Web.

The enthusiasm spread so much that the teachers of Italian literature, French, and English grammar at the culinary school changed their way of doing lessons and used pocket PCs. The teaching became more interactive; instead of books, students used handheld devices where they could read, hear the exact pronunciation of words, listen to music, see pictures of famous paintings, watch videos, and search for specific subjects.

Pocket PCs proved even more useful for new creative tasks, for which the device does not substitute some other medium (paper, desktop PC, etc.). First-year students used handheld devices to create vegetable sculptures from pictures scanned from books or found on the Internet. They looked at the models and the instructions on the mobile device and carved fruit and vegetables into creative shapes, such as flowers, animals, etc. Then they photographed their own products and sent them to the teachers.

The students in the second year were able to perform research on the traditional method of cooking in their region, Lazio. Equipped with pocket PCs, they were able to take, at the same time, written notes, photos, and audio recordings. They asked their grandmothers for recipes and for information on rites, anecdotes, and everything concerning food in the past. They went into traditional restaurants and interviewed the oldest people in the kitchen, taking pictures of preparation, tools, and the environment. They visited antiques markets to identify the objects used in traditional popular cooking. They also studied all the religious and familiar feasts in which food played an important role, and recorded the music played in those circumstances on the pocket PC.

A further project was SoNeCS, which was aimed at creating social networks among students of different catering schools. This goal has been achieved using different approaches.

Students and teachers were given the opportunity to publish their own content through an LMS or through blogging. Students used blogs as online portfolios, reflecting on what they were learning and sharing resources with other students. We enhanced the relationship between schools and families and among different, similar institutions by rebuilding the school website, in order to show all school activities, but also to make useful information easily available: job opportunities, historical archives, etc.

Using mobile devices, students could connect to the school website, looking for information or posting comments, could publish messages and photos on their blogs, and could share resources using a special networking website created for the schools participating in the project. Thus, mobile technologies were supporting new forms of distributed participation among different schools.

Evaluation Methodology

We used different tools to collect data about m-learning efficacy during on-the-job training: The evaluation methodology was based on user observations, user interviews, and questionnaires administered to students and to their tutors.

We developed specific indicators for the projects in order to investigate four main areas: education, communication, mobility, and user interface.

The indicators concerned:

- activities performed (time needed to accomplish a task, accuracy degree, the possibility of preventing mistakes);
- difficulties in using the device and time to learn;
- general improvements in training and learning;
- specific indicators concerning learning outcomes (see Table 19.1).

In addition to these areas, our research has also examined issues such as training in complex environments, including both formal and informal communication structures and the human–machine interface, that is, the "metaphors" more suitable for learning applications.

Our point of view was ethnographic more than technological. Starting from studies on collaboration and communication (Plowman, Rogers, & Ramage, 1995) and from the research on communities and technologies, we analyzed all the existing structures of communication in the university and in the school: the interaction between students and their tutors, the organization in the different areas, the different ways of communicating among them, and the contents of messages.

Furthermore, we tried to monitor the users' feedback using categories created by Everett Rogers, a theorist who spent over 30 years studying the diffusion of innovations, from QWERTY keyboards to new agricultural methods in developing countries. According to Rogers (1995), the characteristics of an innovation, as perceived by the members of a social system, determine its rate of adoption. Five attributes of innovations are: (1) relative advantage; (2) compatibility; (3) complexity; (4) trialability; and (5) observability.

PROJECT OUTCOMES

Students' Feedback on Wireless Training

Interesting results came from a questionnaire administered to all the students (medicine, nursing, and dietetics) involved in the project. They were asked to indicate the main advantages and drawbacks of using a pocket PC instead of a paper questionnaire. The majority of dietetics students indicated two main advantages: (a) speed in finding the answers and (b) time spared in the transcription of data from paper to PC. Usability was also indicated as one of the criteria of preference of a handheld: The pocket PC does not need a stand and it is not "uncomfortable" (not heavy to carry, in comparison with a normal PC). Furthermore, 80 percent of the interviewed students think that the presence of a keyboard would not help them in data entry. The three main requirements of innovation acceptance (advantage, compatibility, and acceptable complexity) were therefore fulfilled. The students we interviewed considered the other two indicators less important—trialability (the degree to which an innovation may be experimented with on a limited basis before making an adoption/rejection decision) and observability (the degree to which the results of an innovation are visible to others).

As to nursing students, great importance was given to the "relative advantage" factor. In the first phase, only 60 percent of them felt to be advantaged by the use of PDAs. As the attitude of some tutors toward the HISS project was negative, the students' feelings were biased. In this case, we had to work on the tutors to achieve good results with the students. Only when the tutors began to perceive the innovation as being better than the activity it superseded (writing on a piece of paper and then rewriting on a PC, or delivering it to the physicians), they motivated the students to use the new system.

A crucial indicator for PDA acceptance was "accuracy." We demonstrated that students using handheld devices for data entry in structured forms were more accurate than those writing on a blank piece of paper; they were able to observe and write down more things (having different questions to answer) and were more precise.

The most critical approach was by medicine students. The complexity of the tasks and the different approach for data entry (free text, multiple choices, drop-down lists, check lists, "frequently used" options, etc.) contributed to a very low degree of acceptance of the new technology. It is probable that medical students were so well acquainted and highly successful with the traditional academic practices they had been using, so that they perhaps were less motivated to try something new. Even the lack of motivation of their tutors was crucial for the acceptance of the new tools.

After a first phase that involved all the students in the different wards, we concentrated on a specific target. A pilot project started in the surgical ward: MoSE (Mobile Surgery Education). All the medical staff were involved, not only the students and their tutors. This phase showed that the presence of a leading figure is a key element for the acceptance of innovation: The fact that the director was keen on using the devices motivated all the staff.

Mobile Affordances and Efficacy of Learning: The Tutors' Perspective

The projects demonstrated that some affordances of mobile devices enhance meta-cognitive processes and promote communication among different actors (students–students; tutors–students; teachers–students):

1. Mobile technologies are *personal* and *portable*. They can be used at any time and in any place, enabling data collection, access to online resources and tutors, sharing of multimedia contents; students are given opportune *scaffolding* for reflection and personalization of learning.
2. Mobile devices, unlike a laptop, *can be used with a pen or with the fingers*. This makes them more appropriate to be carried and used in working environments, such hospitals or hotels.
3. Mobile technologies are *networked*. Wireless connectivity allows students to be in constant contact with their tutors and with their colleagues, facilitating collaboration, and promoting greater interest in, and wider exchange on, their training experiences.

Indicators of the efficacy of m-learning in these specific contexts can be grouped into the following categories:

- *Critical reasoning.* Students gain insight into the concepts and are able to better integrate the "practice" (what they learn during the training) with what is learned in the classroom. They also improve their analytical competences, communication, and problem-solving skills.
- *Involvement in the activities.* The collected data are more accurate, and the students attend the training more regularly and with more enthusiasm. Furthermore, students' perception of their capability to improve learning through training is enhanced and, consequently, their self-assessment and self-regulation skills are improved.
- *Collaboration and cooperation.* Students feel less "alone" cooperating and collaborating online with other students and with their tutor. At the same time, they develop their ability to work independently and feel "protected" (being able to ask for help at any time).
- *Immediate access to information.* Some tutors reported how convenient for the students it was to have immediate access at the bedside to reference information, such as drug interactions and lab values. In their opinion, m-learning can add to medical and nursing students' level of confidence in their practice.
- *Improved communications with tutors.* Our tutors commented on the difficulties that they experience staying in touch with their students on a regular basis once

these students are out on practice experiences. Mobile devices made it easier for tutors to contact students, and vice versa.

- *Tutor professional development.* Tutors learn to design educational activities in order to rationalize the stages of student learning during on-the-job training. Learning is not based on the imitation of activities, but on learning outcomes to be achieved at different times and in different ways, depending merely on the student. The personalization of the activities is a key consequence of the use of mobile technologies, which provide greater equity, allowing for everyone's active participation.

Teachers' Feedback on M-Learning

Teachers were interviewed collectively during focus groups. Their opinions on the advantages of m-learning were later clustered into six macro areas, as illustrated in Table 19.2.

Taking into account the expected outcomes, learning behaviors and skill development were monitored through teachers' observations (free and/or with observational grids). The skills were further grouped into three main macro areas, including not only the "expected" learning outcomes, but further—unexpected although "related"—issues:

- *complex thinking*: problem-solving, reciprocal learning, experiential learning;
- *social skills and participatory learning*: interaction with tutors and other learners, active participation in learning, interdependence;
- *personal shaping of knowledge*: progressive mastery, individual pacing, self-correction, critical reflection, active seeking of meaning, empowered self-direction, internal drive/motivation.

As reported in the literature (Wong & Looi, 2011), our projects demonstrated that m-learning can encompass different aspects of learning: formal and informal, personalized and social, "physical" and digital environments. It can enhance learning across time and locations, allowing ubiquitous access to tutors and information. Teachers

Table 19.2 Advantages of M-Learning: Teachers' Perspective

Advantages	Description
"Beyond the classroom"	Efficacy of systems that allow learning to be extended, even in places where a desktop PC can't be used
Rapid access to information and tutors	Systems that allow access to resources and online tutors and teachers at different moments of the day
Graphical and multimedia annotations	Both students and teachers can draw notes on their slides and include images, audio and video files, etc.
"Real-time" answers	The teachers can quickly test student understanding through feedback systems (polling) or collecting the annotated slides of their students
Collaboration	Mobile technologies can support the creation of new forms of interactive discussion, student–student or teacher–student, group projects, preparation of notes, collaborative review
Accessibility	Help people with disabilities

pointed out that m-learning must not be limited to tasks performed "on the move," but it must be seen as part of a *learning continuum*, which involves combined use of multiple device types (desktop and mobile, "traditional" and digital, etc.) and seamless switching between multiple learning tasks and multidisciplinary learning.

Measurement of Learning Outcomes

One important issue related to the projects was the measurement of learning outcomes. It is a complex question, as many dimensions and different approaches are involved. On the basis of a literature review (International Society for Technology in Education, 2010), it is possible to identify three domains with four factors:

- the cognitive domain (information management, knowledge construction, knowledge utilization, and problem-solving abilities);
- the affective domain (self-identity, self-value, self-directedness, and self-accountability);
- the sociocultural (social membership, social receptivity, socialization, and social fulfillment factors).

Specific learning indicators take into account three principal axes: (x) personal and environmental conditions (i.e., the *relational axis*), (y) decision-making/management factors (i.e., the *productivity/goal achievement axis*), and (z) creativity indicators (i.e., the *learning outcomes axis*). This framework—coming from educational programs to develop clinical reasoning skills (Terry & Higgs, 1993)—provides an overview of environmental conditions that promote creative learning, teaching decisions the educator and the learner need to make to engage successfully in learning and the characteristic behaviors of effective learning.

DISCUSSION

Reflection In and On Action

Practice-based learning and on-the-job traing are important elements in study programs educating professional practitioners, either in a university hospital or in a catering school. They are characterized by a focus on students' transition from university/school to professional working life. The students are exposed to real work challenges within the pedagogical scaffolding of the university/school program. An essential aspect of the learning process during on-the-job training is students' reflection on the relationship between school/university and real life, between theory and practice.

In order to foster students' reflection during the training, we created tools and forms that could *scaffold* student learning. Scaffolding means providing the support for the learner to gradually master what is needed to complete a task. Scaffolding is about processes, artifacts, and supporting technology. So, for example, as previously mentioned, students with a structured form on their PDA were able to observe more things, and they were more precise. In this way, they were able to *reflect in action* (Schön, 1983), i.e., during the training, on the tasks assigned to them.

Furthermore, we thought to involve students in the interface design: Students were invited to reflect on *what* was useful to read and/or to write during their training and *how* to build forms to gather information. They were forced *to reflect on action*

(Schön, 1983), i.e., upon their own learning during the training on the job. Understanding how learning happens in a given setting is never a straightforward task: It involves assumptions about the right type and the amount of support needed, based on the learning objectives of the course, initial knowledge and skills, the challenges of the learning setting, and many other different variables. This is why only tutors and older students could be involved in the interface design.

A further model of *reflection on action* was represented by the "companion" project carried out in the surgical ward (MoSE). All the staff were involved in data collection on mobile devices; all the information gathered was presented in a weekly meeting. Besides discussing the contents of the notes, we also compared the traditional way of taking them with the new system. We studied the data loss that occurred with paper forms, during the replacement of paper sheets. We analyzed the passage from a note to the next one. The circumstances of data loss; the percentage and quality of data loss, etc. In this case, the use of mobile technologies was a way to *rethink* the process of data gathering in the surgical ward, *reflecting on* the actions performed daily.

Deductive/Inductive Models of Reasoning

In the previous paragraph, we have argued that reflection is a key element during on-the-job training. Students in practice-based learning need to reflect to succeed with their work tasks and to achieve the learning goals set for their course.

In our experience, it was really amazing that, in a low-stakes social setting such as interviewing community members about cooking techniques, the mobiles were highly successful. However, in higher-stakes academic settings such as taking patient notes during medical training, they were less successful.

Many reasons can be found to explain these phenomena.

First, *mobile natives* are more likely to be found in a school than at university, where we can find the generation of *digital natives*, as Prensky (2001) calls them. Of course, these "labels" hide "generalizations," and sometimes the categorization by generation has been overrated. However, as a matter of fact, we can observe that, in our projects, catering-school students demostrated more acquaintance with mobile technologies and with the use of multimedia, whereas people in medical school, highly successful with the traditional academic practices, as noted before, were less motivated to try something new.

Futhermore, we must observe that the predominant model in university teaching in Italy is still based on *deductive reasoning* (from the more general to the more specific) and on a face-to-face transmissive model. This is why, at the beginning of their training, medical students find it difficult to change this framework and embrace a more *inductive* (i.e., moving from specific observations to broader generalizations and theories), or *abductive* (from a hypothesis to the observation and then back to a new hypothesis or theory) approach, which is fundamental for their profession. This is true for many other curricula that require students to work out a relationship between university and real life, between theory and practice, and we are convinced that m-learning could be very helpful for that.

In a catering school, the "theory" is not so important as to be intrusive during the practice, and very often the inductive model (from the practice to the theory) is used to stimulate students' motivation to learn.

Interactional Mobility and Communities of Practice

In practice-based learning, students relate to different communities. By participating in a community, the student takes part in the sense-making of that community. Students in the catering school are, as a matter of fact, a community of practice, characterized by key elements such as:

- *distributed co-ordination*: distributed nature of the tasks and activities;
- *plans and procedures*: organizational support for the work;
- *awareness of work*: students and their tutors need to keep themselves aware of others' work.

In medical/nursing training, students alternate between engaging in the practices of different communities, such as a university student or a novice practitioner, and collaborating with participants in other communities, e.g., a physician, a nurse, etc. Understanding the needs of different interacting communities is also important, even if the student is not her/himself a member. In negotiating or aligning the interests of different communities, it is thus vital to be able to take or appreciate the perspectives of the different communities. However, sometimes, the "shift" makes it diffcult to reflect on differences and similarities between communities, and to include both reflection in action and reflection on action (Schön, 1983). Students perceive themselves more as "outsiders" than as part of a community. This is why, perhaps, mobile technologies were not so successful, as it was not possible to identify the traits of a community of learners, where "each learner can contribute and build on other people's experience, combining different perspectives across classes, groups, organizations, and cultures" (Agostini et al., 2005, p. 5). Perhaps most of the health care students/professionals fail to acknowledge that knowledge is not an asset of the individuals or the groups, but rather of the community as a whole. This is why, probably, the mobile interaction was not as successful as we expected.

In the catering school, the success of the project went beyond our expectations and demonstrated that, "ubiquitous computing can be used to enrich the spaces in which the community lives with traces of other community members, of the past and envisioned future" (Agostini et al., 2005, p. 2). The SoNeCS project and the research on traditional cooking (intergenerational communication) demonstrated that mobile technologies can support new forms of distributed participation—across different communities—enlarging and enriching the community spaces.

CONCLUSIONS

Effects on Learning

The experiences confirmed the effectiveness of m-learning to develop metacognitive, creative, and critical skills, fostering self-regulation and stimulating "reflection on action" and "reflection in action" (Schön, 1983). As a matter of fact, learning on the job is learning in communities of practice, and mobile technology can support the interplay between learning and working. Furthermore, ubiquitous computing can be used to enrich the spaces in which the community lives with traces of other community members, of the past and envisioned future.

M-learning offers students the possibility of working in "authentic environments" and "continuity of the learning experience across different scenarios or contexts" (Looi et al., 2010, p. 154).

The project demonstrated that authentic learning is possible, not only for on-the-job training, but also in the classroom. M-learning offers opportunities and tools to improve creativity in the learning process, enhancing non-linear and non-standard thinking, and problem-solving in real cases/situations, shifting the focus from teaching to learning and stressing the participatory nature of knowledge creation.

As some teachers pointed out, it would be better to think of mobile as a part of a *learning continuum*, which involves combined use of multiple device types (desktop and mobile, "traditional" and digital, etc.) and seamless switching between multiple learning tasks and multidisciplinary learning.

In technology-enhanced learning discussion, there is a strong trend that promotes the change from LMS, course-centric, to personal learning environment (PLE), people-centric, and then to personal learning network (PLN). Mobile technologies can encourage forms of peer-to-peer learning, such as peer tutoring, and collaborative and cooperative learning, help students build their PLE and PLN, and enhance students' capability to reflect on what they are learning.

Sustainability, Teacher Training, and Other Barriers

One of the problems that often arises at the end of projects—particularly if these have been successful—is sustainability. The domino effect of the first projects, far from exhausting itself, created the base for the search for new grants or to modify some activities in order to include Web 2.0 tools and student smartphones.

Another critical aspect is the training of teachers, who often are not able to design learning activities to integrate new technologies. To solve this problem, we designed and implemented a course of e-teaching for both teachers and tutors who wanted to extend the range of their action to multimedia communication and social networking.

Some other barriers were represented by usability of the devices; the complex task of measuring learning outcomes; the teaching model that, in Italian universities, is predominantly based on vertical transmission and deductive reasoning.

These—together with other important issues such as the development of the broadband infrastructure, the readiness of the population to use broadband-based technologies—are some of the barriers that still limit the spreading of mobile technologies in Italian schools and universities and represent the reason why we can say that m-learning in Italy is still in its "infant" stage.

REFERENCES

Agostini, A., Colley, J., Divitini, M., Farooq, U., Kavanaugh, A., & Stone, A., (2005). Learning communities in the era of ubiquitous computing. *2nd International Conference on Communities and Technologies*, Milan, Italy, June 13–16.

Cacace, F., Cinque, M., Crudele, M., Iannello, G., & Venditti, M. (2004). The impact of innovation in medical and nursing training: A hospital information system for students accessible through mobile devices. *Proceedings of MLEARN 2004*, Bracciano, Italy, July 5–6.

Cinque, M. (2008). Mobile School e Wireless University: l'introduzione di tecnologie senza fili in ambienti complessi per aumentare produttività e creatività. In E. Marino (Ed.), *E-learning e multimedialità. Conoscenze senza frontiere* (pp. 477–489), Lecce: Pensa Editore.

Cinque, M. (2011). Lo "studente riflessivo": l'uso di dispositivi mobili tra formazione on-the job e PLN (Personal Learning Network). *Form@re. Open Journal per la formazione in rete, 73*. Retrieved from: http://formare.erickson.it/wordpress/it/2011/%C2%ABlo-studente-riflessivo%C2%BB-l%E2%80%99uso-di-dispositivi-mobili-tra-formazione-on-the-job-e-pln-personal-learning-network/

Cinque, M., Crudele, M., Gagliani Caputo, L., & Iannello, G. (2005*)*. PpMC (Pocket PC-mediated communication) in a catering school. In A. Agostini et al. (Eds.), *Learning communities in the era of ubiquitous computing. 2nd International Conference on Communities and Technologies* (pp. 33–37). Milan, Italy, June 13–16.

Cinque, M., & Pensieri, C. (2009). Campus We-Com. University students attitude towards didactical innovation. *Je-LKS (Journal of e-Learning and Knowledge Society), 1*, 57–65.

Crompton, H. (2013). A historical overview of mobile learning: Toward learner-centered education (pp. 3–14). In Z. Berge, & L. Muilenburg (Eds.), *Handbook of mobile learning.* New York: Routledge.

Engeström, Y. (1993). Developmental studies of work as a testbench of activity theory. In S. Chaiklin and J. Lave (Eds.), *Understanding practice: Perspectives on activity and context* (pp. 64–103), Cambridge, UK: Cambridge University Press.

Gilbert, A. L., Sangwan, S., & Han Mei lan, H. (2005). Beyond usability: the OoBE dynamics of mobile data services markets. *Personal and Ubiquitous Computing, 9*(4), 198–208.

Herrington, J. (2006), Authentic e-learning in higher education: Design principles for authentic learning environments and tasks. In T. Reeves & S. Yamashita (Eds.), *Proceedings of World Conference on E-Learning in Corporate, Government, Healthcare, and Higher Education* (pp. 3164–3173). Chesapeake, VA: AACE.

Herrington, J. (2010). Revisiting the link between teaching and learning research and practice: Authentic learning and design-based research. In: International Association for Scientific Knowledge (IASK). *International Conference Teaching and Learning*, November 29–December 1, Seville, Spain.

Herrington, J., Reeves, T. C., & Oliver, R. (2010). *A guide to authentic e-learning.* New York: Routledge.

Herrington, J., Herrington, A., Mantei, J., Olney, I., & Ferry, B. (2009). Using mobile technologies to develop new ways of teaching and learning. In J. Herrington et al., *New technologies, new pedagogies: Mobile learning in higher education.* Faculty of Education, University of Wollongong. Retrieved from: http://ro.uow.edu.au/cgi/viewcontent.cgi?article=1077&context=edupapers

International Society for Technology in Education. (2010). Developing an educational performance indicator for new millennium learners. *Journal of Research on Technology in Education, 43*(2), 157–170.

Keinonen, T. (2003). Introduction: Mobile distinctions. In C. Lindholm, T. Keinonen, & H. Kiljander (Eds.), *Mobile usability: How Nokia changed the face of the mobile phone.* New York: McGraw-Hill.

Kofod-Petersen, A., & Cassens, J. (2005). Using activity theory to model context awareness. In T. R. Roth-Berghofer, S. Schulz, & D. B. Leake (Eds.), *MRC 2005*, LNAI 3946, pp. 1–17.

Kukulska-Hulme, A. (2007). Mobile usability in educational contexts: What have we learnt? *The International Review of Research in Open and Distance Learning, 8*(2). Retrieved from: www.irrodl.org/index.php/irrodl/article/view/356/879

Lave, J., & Wenger, E. (1991). *Situated learning: Legitimate peripheral participation.* Cambridge, UK: Cambridge University Press.

Looi, C.-K., Seow, P., Zhang, B., So, H.-J., Chen, W., & Wong, L.-H. (2010). Leveraging mobile technology for sustainable seamless learning: A research agenda. *British Journal of Educational Technology, 41*(2), 154–169.

Pask, G. (1976). *Conversation theory: Applications in education and epistemology.* Amsterdam: Elsevier.

Plowman, L., Rogers, Y., & Ramage, M. (1995). What are workplace studies for? In *Proceedings of the Fourth European Conference on Computer Supported Cooperative Work* (pp. 309–324). Dordrecht, The Netherlands: Kluwer.

Prensky, M. (2001). Digital natives. Digital immigrants. *On the Horizon, 9*(5). Retrieved from: www.marcprensky.com/writing/Prensky%20-%20Digital%20Natives,%20Digital%20Immigrants%20-%20Part1.pdf

Rogers, E. M. (1995). *The diffusion of innovations* (4th ed.). New York: Free Press.

Schön, D. (1983). *The reflective practitioner: How professionals think in action.* New York: Basic Books.

Sharples, M., Taylor, J., & Vavoula, G. (2007). A theory of learning for the mobile age. In R. Andrews & C. Haythornthwaite (Eds.), *The Sage handbook of e-learning research* (pp. 221–247). London: Sage.

Terry, W., & Higgs, J. (1993). Educational programs to develop clinical reasoning skills. *Australian Journal Physiotherapy, 39*, 47–51.

Wong, L.-H., & Looi, C.-K. (2011). What seams do we remove in mobile assisted seamless learning? A critical review of the literature. *Computers & Education, 57*(4), 2364–2381.

20

MUSEUMS

Gateways to Mobile Learning

Denise M. Bressler

For over 60 years, mobile technology has been part of the museum-going experience (Proctor, 2011). Audio tours started in the late 1950s, with clunky technology that offered learners a linear audio commentary. As technology changed, the linear tour model changed too. More recent iterations allowed visitors to select their tracks, giving the learner more control and an improved learning experience.

Museums have always been great content providers, and, as technology changes, museums adapt and try to provide the most engaging learning experience that the technology can offer. Museum visits are voluntary, and so museums are always looking for ways to deepen the visitor's onsite learning experience. With the pace of change in today's world, engaging visitors can be challenging and complicated. Visitors "increasingly expect information and experiences on demand, whenever and wherever they are" (Proctor, 2011, p. 14). Fortunately, today's mobile technology uniquely affords the flexibility, interactivity, and personalization that today's learners demand.

In Chapter 1, Crompton, Muilenburg, and Berge state that m-learning is "learning across multiple contexts, through social and content interactions, using personal electronic devices" (Crompton, 2013, p. 4). Museums are well known for their content, and research shows that museum learning is intimately tied to social interactions (Falk & Dierking, 2000; Leinhardt, Crowley, & Knutson, 2002). Now that visitors are using their personal mobile devices in the museum context, it's appropriate to investigate m-learning within the framework of museum learning. Falk and Dierking's (2000) contextual model of learning summarizes the three factors that influence museum learning, including personal context, sociocultural context, and physical context. This chapter will present an exploration of mobile projects in the museum field, highlighting the elements of Falk and Dierking's model as it relates to each mobile initiative.

By taking advantage of all the affordances of today's mobile technology, museums are engaging learners in new ways with their copious content. More museums are launching mobile initiatives; according to Tallon (2012), 29 percent of the museums surveyed were currently offering a mobile experience, with an additional 27 percent planning to launch a mobile experience within 12 months. There has been momentum building over the past decade, with museums designing opportunities for learners to create content, share content, play with content, and even extend the museum content well beyond the physical walls. By detailing examples of these opportunities and related research findings, this chapter will build the case that museums are increasingly becoming the ideal gateway for m-learning.

CREATE CONTENT

Although now considered convenient hubs for social interaction, museums have long followed the model of spectator culture: the museum community provided a place for learners to come and view the content. Around 2005, mobile-phone and podcast tours began and followed a similar model of delivering museum-created content to learners' own phones (Nickerson, 2005; Samis & Pau, 2006). However, spectator culture was rapidly transitioning into participatory culture. So, it was not long before learners decided to create content themselves, with the first known account of guest-created podcasts coming from a group of students known as ArtMobs.

ArtMobs made its splash when it took the front page of the *New York Times* during spring of 2005 (Kennedy, 2005). Under the leadership of Professor David Gilbert, a class of Marymount Manhattan College students produced their own freely available podcasts—casual art critiques that were original, fun, and even irreverent—about artwork in the Museum of Modern Art. At a cursory glance, ArtMobs was a simple class project, but, from the museum community's standpoint, it changed everything. As stated by Samis (2008), "the news rippled like shock waves from an earth tremor in the museum world. For the first time . . . someone had publicly usurped the museum voice from an esteemed, authoritative institution" (p. 6). Since ArtMobs, museums have started to embrace participatory culture by finding ways to engage visitors by allowing them to create their own custom content. In this way, visitors are given the opportunity to make meaning for themselves and develop deeper, personal connections to their learning in the process.

Initial attempts were small and contained. One of the early cell-phone audio tours, Walker's *Art on Call*, gave visitors the chance to leave their own audio comments about the art through the program's TalkBack feature (Dowden & Sayre, 2007). The San Francisco Museum of Art, one of the first museums to experiment with podcasting, invited both experts and non-experts alike to contribute creative responses to the museums' collections (Samis & Pau, 2006). In both cases, the institutions had to approve the content before it was officially published to the general audience. Regardless, the conversation was started, and the shift from one-way spectator culture to two-way participatory culture had begun.

CONVERSING ABOUT CONTENT

Museums attract such a widely diverse audience, making it hard to create a one-size-fits-all learning experience, and yet almost every visitor has a mobile device. Early research from London's Tate Modern showed that visitors using handheld tours were having more extensive learning experiences, developing a deeper understanding of the content, and making more connections to their personal experiences (Proctor & Burton, 2004). As the next step toward embracing participatory culture, museums started to create ways for visitors to collect content and share their learning experiences from their mobile.

Although some early research indicated that mobile devices isolated visitors (Hsi, 2003), more recent evidence overturns that concern. The following research shows that, when visitors use their own mobiles, they make meaning out of the content through self-directed learning *and* social interaction.

Conversing Inside the Museum

Learning in a museum context means being with friends and family—the people who know you best. Museum-based research shows learning is profoundly impacted by the people with us (Falk and Dierking, 2000). The following examples show evidence of how mobile learners located in museums make meaning by engaging in social interactions.

The *Science Now, Science Everywhere* (SNSE) project, one of the first informal education mobile projects to receive funding from the National Science Foundation, yielded several indicators of mobile learners interacting socially while in the museum (Katz, Haley Goldman, & Foutz, 2011). Almost half of SNSE users shared audio content by physically passing the phone back and forth or by using speakerphone. Also, according to Katz et al. (2011), "visitors who texted the exhibition component or used their phone to save content they had created showed increased interaction, including more pointing at the component and more social interaction" (p. 358). Research results showed evidence that SNSE users had a deeper interactive experience than non-SNSE users and were more apt to report learning something new.

At the Exploratorium in San Francisco, research was conducted to compare two different types of mobile interface for interacting with a simulated-surgery exhibit (Lyons, 2009). In one case, visitors used the mobile as a simple remote control to steer items on a larger display. In another case, visitors used a more complex mobile interface, manipulating items on-screen and drawing circles to make incisions. Although the complex interface required more heads-down attention, "participants were more likely to make utterances that were *on-task* and focused on the *functional* aspects of the joint task" (Lyons, 2009, p. 382). Additionally, the complex interface afforded better task performance and better understanding of underlying science concepts.

Conversing Beyond the Museum

As a mobile device goes with the learner, researchers are building mobile platforms that can be used to connect the learning inside and away from the museum. These platforms often incorporate many factors within Falk and Dierking's (2000) contextual model of learning, including personal context, sociocultural context, and physical context. Students create a personal connection to the content by collecting data in the physical context, and then they discuss interpretations in a sociocultural context that extends beyond the museum.

One of the first of these platforms was *MyArtSpace*, developed in the United Kingdom. Piloted between 2006 and 2007 with over 4,000 students, it is now commercially available as *OOKL* (Rudman, Sharples, & Lonsdale, 2008). The software enables students to use phones during a museum visit to collect artifact information; they take photos, record audio, and write text comments, which are archived on a personal website. Upon collection, students find fellow classmates who also collected that artifact. Back at school, students review and reflect on their collections, often organizing the information into personal galleries.

Research findings were extensive. During onsite data collection, Rudman et al. (2008) found strong engagement and focused attention. They observed conversations among co-located learners, especially when finding classmates who selected the same artifact. Additionally, participants seemed to critically reflect on museum content during post-visit online activities. Overall, Rudman et al. (2008) found that the "software creates an environment in which students are able to collaboratively construct and share representations of their interpretations both within and outside school" (p. 159).

MyArtSpace was the pioneering project in this area, but others have followed in its steps and contributed additional support for this model of museum-based m-learning. At the Exhibit Museum of Natural History at the University of Michigan, researchers compared learners using a mobile platform called *Zydeco* with those using a worksheet. With the *Zydeco* system, students created tags before the museum visit to elicit prior knowledge. At the museum, tags were used to annotate data. Cahill et al. (2011) found that collecting the museum data and tagging them promoted deeper in-museum reflection, more discussion among students, and more deliberate data collection. Overall, researchers found that "the *Zydeco* system increased active sociocultural engagement" (p. 21), whereas the worksheet did not.

At the Astrup Fearnley Museum of Modern Art in Norway, students used mobile blogging as a means to develop and share interpretations of the art. While at the museum, students were observed both collaborating and working independently, blending both the personal context and social context of museum learning (Pierroux, Krange, & Sem, 2011). Blog conversations were started at the museum and continued post-visit. Researchers determined that the blog conversations illustrated critical thinking about art. This study also revealed that today's students are true natives of participatory culture who "viewed their blog entries about artworks at the museum as what genuinely 'counted' as meaning making for them" (p. 43).

PLAY WITH CONTENT

As Squire (2011) eloquently stated, games "have taken their place alongside books and television and media integrated into the fabric of our lives" (p. xi). More and more, people are playing games on their mobiles (Smith, 2010). A few museums are capitalizing on this by creating downloadable, stand-alone games. Two notable examples are *Launchball* and *MEanderthal* (Burton, 2011). The Science Museum of London produced *Launchball*, which challenges players to guide a ball through obstacles while utilizing basic principles of science. *MEanderthal*, from the Smithsonian's National Museum of Natural History, transforms facial photos into photos of early humans. Both of these are opportunities for learners to play and explore museum-related content anytime, anywhere, on their mobile.

M-learning games in museum settings present an exciting new area of m-learning research. Eric Klopfer (2008), who has been studying participatory handheld simulations for over a decade, suggested that m-learning games represent a largely untapped area of study. He argued that a well-designed mobile game that uses "the physical and social context of the player as integral components of the game" (Klopfer, 2008, p. ix) creates an effective playing and learning environment.

Museums offer plenty of physical and social contexts, making them desirable locales for such games. Some games take full advantage of the museum context, allowing players to play at the museum and deeply engage with the content in a fun yet meaningful way. Other games utilize the museum as part of a more comprehensive participatory experience, called an alternate reality game, or ARG.

Playing at the Museum

One of the earliest museum mobile games was a scavenger hunt at the Chicago Historical Society (Kwak, 2004). Software was developed on pocket PCs. The game included 10 questions, with multiple-choice answers. Children had to explore the galleries to find the answers. Kwak found that children were excited to use the device and liked playing the game with their friends.

Shortly thereafter came two mystery games, one set in a science center and the other in a historical cultural museum. These games were more robust and required players to solve problems collaboratively. In both cases, players received separate information that required them to cooperate in order to solve the mystery. At the Boston Museum of Science, Klopfer, Perry, Squire, Jan, and Steinkuehler (2005) found that *Mystery at the Museum* fostered feelings of connection between the visitors and the museum. Feedback from players confirmed that they were engaged, not only with individual exhibits, but also with the larger context of the museum and with their fellow players. At the Museum of Solomos in Greece, researchers created a mystery-themed mobile activity aiming to foster knowledge acquisition through collaboration. They found that the activity successfully promoted various forms of collaboration and proposed that different museums could adopt a similar gaming scenario (Cabrera et al., 2005).

Newer games are building on these concepts, and yet they allow players to use their own phones and they are seeking to discover more creative ways to engage the players with the content. *Prisoner Escape from the Tower* was one of the first location-aware mobile games set in a museum context (Reid et al., 2008). Players are challenged to free the prisoners without getting caught by the Beefeaters (Pearson, 2007). The software tracked players' positions using the GPS and radio-frequency transmitters so that players' locations would trigger certain parts of the story. Reid et al. (2008) found that triggered interactions with characters were a great way to engage people in gameplay. Overall, players found the game to be a fun way to learn about the Tower of London. According to Historic Royal Palaces (2010), visitors can now use their own iPhone to play an updated version of the game.

EGO-TRAP, one of the first games to utilize visitor-owned devices, was a gaming narrative tying together several individual exhibits within the Experimentarium in Denmark (Kahr-Højland, 2011). First, visitors received phone calls from a woman challenging them to use certain exhibits. In the next level, she challenged players to work together. Finally, players were encouraged to break into a secret room and reveal the woman's identity—and it's a rat! Kahr-Højland "designed [the game] with the aim of supporting pleasurable engagement as well as critical reflection in the exhibition" (p. 227). She found that players had pleasurable engagement with the game, spent longer in the exhibition, and interacted with exhibits again and again.

Playing Beyond the Museum

Simple mobile games, such as a scavenger hunt, can promote the act of looking closely and discovering new parts of the museum, which are key elements of informal learning (Burton, 2011). Robust collaborative games reinforce sociocultural learning and offer deeper engagement with the museum content. The newest museum gaming experience, Alternative Reality Games (ARGs), bring together both of these elements.

As explained by Jane McGonigal (2011), a preeminent game designer, "ARGs are games you play to get more out of your real life, as opposed to games you play to escape it" (p. 125). ARGs are part of the real world, and yet players experience the game through personal technologies and other virtual media. The collective intelligence of the players helps to process clues, allowing the game narrative to evolve. As summarized by John Maccabee, an ARG designer, this type of game is less about winning and more about playing (Hunter, 2008). It's an interesting new direction for museums, because, "an ARG places its content within the pedagogical context of participatory experience" (Kocher, Rusnak, & Eklund, 2010, p. 224). The experience may take place in the museum or away from the museum, but it revolves around the museum content and context.

Referred to by McGonigal (2011) as a groundbreaking project, *Ghosts of a Chance* was the first museum ARG. Played in 2008 at the Smithsonian American Art Museum, and created by City Mystery, the game challenged players to create exhibit artifacts and provide them to the museum (Bath, 2008). The reasoning for this was encapsulated in a storyline about two fictional curators who were haunted by ghosts. While on site at the museum, players received directions via text and remained engaged with their quests for up to 5 or 6 hours, were motivated to finish all the tasks within the game, and explored parts of a museum they had never seen before (Bath, 2008).

With museum ARGs being a recent development, there is limited research about the learning that occurs during game play. But Kocher et al. (2010) argued that, "ARGs exhibit pedagogically desirable qualities that are ideally suitable for learning purposes." In a pilot of an educational ARG called *ViolaQuest*, participants reported having to think laterally and outside of the box (Whitton, 2009). They also enjoyed the mobile elements of the game, such as walking around to solve puzzles. Basically, ARGs put players into a framework where they can acquire 21st-century skills. Klopfer (2008) expanded this idea by saying, "games that are situated in the real world indeed have a firm foundation in a number of powerful learning traditions and set the bar for new learning styles demanded in the twenty-first century" (p. 57).

EXTEND CONTENT

For museums to be of most benefit to mobile learners, they have to extend their content beyond the fixed location of a brick and mortar building. Over a decade ago, Falk and Dierking (2000) asserted that "museum professionals need to recognize that museum learning does not occur merely within the limited temporal and physical envelope of the museum" (p. xv). They were emphasizing that museum learning is part of lifelong learning that occurs within the larger context of society. The difference between then and now is that mobiles can help reinforce museum learning, regardless of time and space.

Let's walk through an example: A mobile learner visits Monterey Bay Aquarium and learns that some fish farming techniques are sustainable and environmentally friendly, while others are harmful. Inspired by this new knowledge, the learner downloads the museum's *Seafood Watch Guide* available at http://seafoodwatch.org. Now, when in an appropriate context such as a restaurant, the learner has the content necessary to put knowledge into action.

Content is best used in context. Museums offer great content, while larger society offers powerful contexts. According to Hulser and Bull (2011), we are at a point where "museums realize that their holdings ought to be seen inserted into their original contexts and cityscapes" (p. 205). The latest museum m-learning projects try to do just that, through augmented-reality (AR) and location-based, narrative experiences.

Layering the Environment

The newest m-learning trend to reach the museum field is AR, which has the potential to give new life to museum content well beyond the walls of the museum. Some museums are making their visual images accessible as overlays in a freely available AR application, such as Layar or Junaio, which run on most smartphones. Overlaid onto the cityscape, the learner can see buildings that are no longer there or artistic renderings of the future built environment. The Museum of London, the Powerhouse Museum in Sydney, and the City of Philadelphia all made their historical imagery available to city goers using AR (Boyer & Marcus, 2011). The Netherlands Architecture Institute (http://en.nai.nl/) helped create a three-dimensional architecture application in Layar called *Urban Augmented Reality*.

Imagery in context plants a seed for discovery-based learning and generates enthusiasm for a museum's collection, but the Exploratorium is pushing the envelope of using AR to truly extend its museum's learning experience. Using Layar, the Exploratorium has developed science inquiry-based activities at specific locations around San Franscisco (Rothfarb, 2011). One notable example is the *Fog Altimeter*: learners view the Golden Gate Bridge through their mobile devices and then use a measurement tool superimposed on the image to measure the height of the fog near the bridge.

Desiring to be the frontrunner for AR in museums, the Stedelijk Museum in Amsterdam has been experimenting with several pilot AR projects (Schavemaker, 2011). *ARtotheque* enabled users to design their surrounding urban context with their favorite artwork and explain their design rationale. In order to build *Me at the Museum Square*, the museum asked interactive-media students to propose AR artwork. One of the winning ideas built in AR was a springboard by a small pond entitled, *The most fun you will never have*. Although a lot of museum AR applications are starting out in the one-way spectator model, the Stedelijk Museum wants the public to use AR to interact with their design collection. After all, museum learning is social; as Schavemaker (2011) stated, "augmented reality applications become especially significant by way of extra communication tools . . . [they] elicit communication among the users" (p. 53).

Narrating the Environment

Although AR may be the next big thing for museums, according to Johnson, Adams, and Witchey (2011), it's possible for museums to extend their content with context-aware audio and images. The trick is to get users to envisage a cohesive experience inside an interactive, location-based narrative.

One of the first projects of this kind was a mobile sound installation called *Trace*, created in 1999 by Teri Rueb (2004). The project enabled hikers to automatically listen to poems, stories, and songs triggered by their geospatial location. More recently, Alyssa Wright (2007) at the MIT Media Lab created *Cherry Blossoms*, another GPS-activated mobile art installation. Participants would wear a backpack with a GPS unit. Bombing sites from Baghdad were correlated to real places around Boston. So, as participants walked around Boston, they would have chance encounters with "bomb sites," and the backpack would detonate, with confetti representing smoke and shrapnel.

Merging narrative content with location can promote powerful learning experiences. Boston and New York both have a lot of history that can be revealed with the right smartphone app. Available as an iPhone app or vodcast, *Murder at Beacon Hill* is a location-aware experience that takes participants through an interactive story about the 1849 disappearance of George Parkman, a wealthy businessman (Untravel Media, 2009). Content is adapted from a major documentary film, but the photo and video sources credit an amalgam of public libraries and museums. The 200-year-old New York Historical Society decided to give new life to their content by creating a walking tour (Hulser & Bull, 2011). At specific locations, relevant historical stories and images are available, along with suggested activities, such as going into a pharmacy where Underground Railroad activities took place. With over 10,000 downloads, these types of experience are clearly meeting the demands of the mobile-minded museum audience (Hulser & Bull, 2011).

CONCLUSION

In museums, learners have always been mobile—moving between exhibitions in a non-linear fashion, pausing briefly to look, listen, or otherwise engage with something that captures their attention. Now, museum learners are still mobile—they just may not be in the museum any more. As Samis (2008) articulated,

> The museum visit no longer begins when a person enters the building, nor need it end when she or he leaves. The museum's physical space is but one site—albeit a privileged one—in the continuum of the visitor's imaginative universe.
>
> (p. 3)

Museums will always have content to share, but, with mobile connectivity, they may no longer need walls to share it. Ultimately, in order to thrive in the Age of Mobilism, museums need to integrate mobile initiatives into the exhibition development process. In 2011, the Christina Ray gallery in New York City attempted this new model of development. In conjunction with *Mission:Edition*, limited-edition prints related to gallery artwork were hidden throughout the city (Wasserman, 2011). The gallery offered clues through FourSquare and Twitter, but citizens did not need to visit the gallery to encounter the prints. Prints procured by citizens directed them back to the gallery. The exhibition experience was developed around the mobility of the learner.

Another challenge museums face in the Age of Mobilism is to adapt and develop new learning models that work across multiple contexts. Some of the research in this chapter shows evidence of mobile technology effectively bridging contexts (Pierroux et al., 2011; Rudman et al., 2008). As learners move across multiple contexts, the mobile serves as a scaffold and supports continuity of learning. Timothy Zimmerman (2011) has started developing an approach called learning across contexts (LAC), which seeks to promote deeper student learning and provide researchers with a framework to understand the nature of learning across various contexts.

Overall, museums are in a liminal space; a state of transformation between museums past and museums future. In the past, museums were places people visited to experience the content. Museums of the future will offer context-aware content experiences to every mobile learner, regardless of time or space.

REFERENCES

Bath, G. (2008). *Ghosts of a chance alternate reality game (ARG): Smithsonian American Museum of Art.* Retrieved from: http://ghostsofachance.com/GhostsofaChance_Report2.pdf

Boyer, D., & Marcus, J. (2011, April). *Implementing mobile augmented reality applications for cultural institutions.* Paper presented at the meeting of Museums and the Web, Philadelphia, PA.

Burton, J. (2011). Playful apps. In N. Proctor (Ed.), *Mobile apps for museums: The AAM guide to planning and strategy* (pp. 71–75). Washington, DC: The AAM Press.

Cabrera, J. S., Frutos, H. M., Stoica, A. G., Avouris, N., Dimitriadis, Y., Fiotakis, G., & Liveri, K. D. (2005). *Mystery in the museum: Collaborative learning activities using handheld devices.* Paper presented at the 7th International Conference on Human–Computer Interaction with Mobile Devices, Salzburg, Austria.

Cahill, C., Kuhn, A., Schmoll, S., Lo, W.-T., McNally, B., & Quintana, C. (2011, June). Mobile learning in museums: How mobile supports for learning influence student behavior. In T. Moher, C. Quintana, & S. Price (Eds.), *Interaction design and children: Proceedings of the 10th International Conference on Interaction Design and Children* (pp. 21–28). Ann Arbor, MI. June 20–23. ACM.

Crompton, H. (2013). A historical overview of mobile learning: Toward learner-centered education (pp. 3–14). In Z. Berge, & L. Muilenburg (Eds.), *Handbook of mobile learning.* New York: Routledge.

Dowden, R., & Sayre, S. (2007). The whole wide world in their hands: The promise and peril of visitor-provided mobile devices. In H. Din & P. Hecht (Eds.), *The digital museum: A think guide* (pp. 35–44). Washington, DC: American Association of Museums.

Falk, J. H., & Dierking, L. D. (2000). *Learning from museums: Visitor experiences and the making of meaning.* Walnut Creek, CA: AltaMira Press.

Historic Royal Palaces. (2010, December). Escape from the tower: First ever Tower of London iPhone app [Video file]. Retrieved from: www.youtube.com/watch?v=ZJPI32mVApo

Hsi, S. (2003). A study of user experiences mediated by nomadic web content in a museum. *Journal of Computer Assisted Learning, 19*(3), 308–319.

Hulser, K., & Bull, S. (2011). Click history: Wherever, whenever. In J. Katz, W. LaBar, & E. Lynch (Eds.), *Creativity and technology: Social media, mobiles and museums* (pp. 204–225). Edinburgh: MuseumsEtc.

Hunter, M. (2008, August). The Smithsonian's got game. *ABC News.* Retrieved from http://abcnews.go.com/Technology/story?id=5490189&page=1#.TvnrfNRQ74t

Johnson, L., Adams, S., & Witchey, H. (2011). *The NMC horizon report: 2011 Museum Edition.* Austin, TX: The New Media Consortium.

Kahr-Højland, A. (2011). EGO-TRAP: The design and implementation of a digital narrative. In J. Katz, W. LaBar, & E. Lynch (Eds.), *Creativity and technology: Social media, mobiles and museums* (pp. 226–263). Edinburgh: MuseumsEtc.

Katz, J., Haley Goldman, K., & Foutz, S. (2011). Mobile phones for informal science center learning: A socio-technical analysis. In J. Katz, W. LaBar, & E. Lynch (Eds.), *Creativity and technology: Social media, mobiles and museums* (pp. 346–379). Edinburgh: MuseumsEtc.

Kennedy, R. (2005, May). With irreverence and an iPod, recreating the museum tour. *The New York Times.* Retrieved from: www.nytimes.com

Klopfer, E. (2008). *Augmented learning: Research and design of mobile educational games.* Cambridge, MA: The MIT Press.

Klopfer, E., Perry, J., Squire, K., Jan, M.-F., & Steinkuehler, C. (2005, May–June). Mystery at the museum: A collaborative game for museum education. In T. Koschmann, D. Suthers, & T. W. Chan (Eds.), *Proceedings of the 2005 Conference on Computer Support for Collaborative Learning: Learning 2005: The next 10 years!* (pp. 316–320). May 30–June 4. Taipei, Taiwan.

Kocher, M., Rusnak, P. J., & Eklund, K. (2010). Breaking boundaries: Learning by ARG within an academic conference presentation. In B. Kapralos, A. Hogue, S. Xu, & J. Rajnovich (Eds.), *Future Play: Proceedings of the International Academic Conference on the Future of Game Design and Technology* (pp. 223–226). May 6–7, Vancouver, BC, Canada.

Kwak, S. Y. (2004). *Designing a handheld interactive scavenger hunt game to enhance museum experience.* Unpublished Master's thesis, Michigan State University, Michigan, USA.

Leinhardt, G., Crowley, K., & Knutson, K. (2002). *Learning conversations in museums.* London: Erlbaum.

Lyons, L. (2009, June). Designing opportunistic user interfaces to support a collaborative museum exhibit. In C. O'Malley, D. Suthers, P. Reimann, & A. Dimitracopoulou (Eds.), *Computer supported collaborative learning practices: CSCL2009 Conference Proceedings* (pp. 375–384). International Society of the Learning Sciences (ISLS). June 8–13, Rhodes, Greece.

McGonigal, J. (2011). *Reality is broken: Why games make us better and how they can change the world.* New York: The Penguin Press.

Nickerson, M. (2005, April). *1–800-FOR-TOUR: Delivering automated audio information through patron's cell phones.* Paper presented at the Meeting of Museums and the Web, Vancouver, Canada.

Pearson, A. (2007, October). Escape Old London's most feared prison—Guided by GPS. *Wired.* Retrieved from: http://www.wired.com

Pierroux, P., Krange, I., & Sem, I. (2011). Bridging contexts and interpretations: Mobile blogging on art museum field trips. *MedieKultur. Journal of media and communication research, 27*(50), 30–47.

Proctor, N. (2011). Mobile business models in a 2.0 economy. In N. Proctor (Ed.), *Mobile apps for museums: The AAM guide to planning and strategy* (pp. 15–24). Washington, DC: The AAM Press.

Proctor, N., & Burton, J. (2004). Tate Modern multimedia tour pilots 2002–2003. In J. Attewell & C. Savill-Smith (Eds.), *Learning with mobile devices: Research and development* (pp. 127–130). London: Learning and Skills Development Agency.

Reid, J., Clayton, B., Melamed, T., Hull, R., Stenton, P., Peirce, A., et al. (2008). The design of prisoner escape from the tower: An interactive location aware historical game. *Tate 2008 Handheld Conference.* Retrieved from: http://tatehandheldconference.pbworks.com/f/DesigningPrisonersv3.doc

Rothfarb, R. (2011, April). *Mixing realities to connect people, places, and exhibits using mobile augmented-reality applications.* Paper presented at the Meeting of Museums and the Web, Philadelphia, PA.

Rudman, P., Sharples, M., & Lonsdale, P. (2008). Cross-context learning. In L. Tallon & K. Walker (Eds.), *Digital technologies and the museum experience: Handheld guides and other media* (pp. 147–166). Lanham, MD: AltaMira Press.

Rueb, T. (2004). *Trace* [Web page]. Retrieved from: www.terirueb.net/trace/

Samis, P. (2008). The exploded museum. In L. Tallon & K. Walker (Eds.), *Digital technologies and the museum experience: Handheld guides and other media* (pp. 3–17). Lanham, MD: AltaMira Press.

Samis, P., & Pau, S. (2006). "Artcasting" at SFMOMA: First-year lessons, future challenges for museum podcasters. In J. Trant & D. Bearman (Eds.), *Museums and the Web 2006: Selected papers from an international conference* (pp. 79–91). Toronto: Archives & Museum Informatics.

Schavemaker, M. (2011). Is augmented reality the ultimate museum app? Some strategic considerations. In N. Proctor (Ed.), *Mobile apps for museums: The AAM guide to planning and strategy* (pp. 46–55). Washington, DC: The AAM Press.

Smith, A. (2010). *Mobile access 2010.* Washington, DC: Pew Internet & American Life Project. Retrieved from: http://pewInternet.org/Reports/2010/Mobile-Access-2010.aspx

Squire, K. (2011). *Video games and learning: Teaching and participatory culture in the digital age.* New York: Teachers College Press.

Tallon, L. (2012). Museums & mobile in 2012: An analysis of the Museums & Mobile Survey 2012 Responses. Retrieved from: www.museums-mobile.org/survey

Untravel Media, Inc. (2009). The story [Web page]. Retrieved from: http://parkmanmurder.com/Parkman_Murder_History.html

Wasserman, S. (2011). Beyond information: Ritual, relationship, and re-encounter through mobile connectivity. *Curator, 54*(1), 11–24.

Whitton, N. (2009). *ARGOSI evaluation report.* Manchester, UK: Manchester Metropolitan University. Retrieved from: http://argosi.playthinklearn.net/evaluation.pdf

Wright, A. (2007). *Portfolio: Cherry blossoms* [Web page]. Retrieved from: http://alumni.media.mit.edu/~alyssa/

Zimmerman, T. (2011). Mobile devices for promoting museum learning. In J. Katz, W. LaBar, & E. Lynch (Eds.), *Creativity and technology: Social media, mobiles and museums* (pp. 264–291). Edinburgh: MuseumsEtc.

21

E-BOOK READERS AND PDAs FOR
WORK-BASED LEARNERS

Ming Nie, Terese Bird, and Palitha Edirisingha

Work-based learning plays an important role in the development of students' professional and social skills and, therefore, has a positive impact on increasing the employability of university graduates (Clamp & Warr, 2002; Hills, Robertson, Walker, Adey, & Nixon, 2003). Many higher-education (HE) institutions in the UK have already included work-based learners as a vital segment of their target audience in their teaching and learning agendas. The University of Leicester, for example, is a sector leader in postgraduate distance education. The university currently has over 7,000 students on 40 distance learning programs offered by 13 departments. Most of the students on these programs are part-time, work-based learners.

Work-based learning is defined by Seagraves et al. (1996) as learning that takes place at work, for work, or from work. A similar definition considers work-based learning as learning for work, at work, and through work (Gray, 2001). These definitions bring to the fore learning that is acquired through professional practice at the workplace and learning that arises from active participation in the day-to-day work life. Barr (2003) considers work-based learning more widely to include both learning that occurs at the workplace (work-located learning) and learning that occurs outside the workplace but with the aim of improving the work (work-related learning).

In this chapter, we discuss how two different groups of work-based learners used mobile devices for their formal learning activities. The first group included a cohort of distance learners studying a Masters program in applied linguistics and teaching English to speakers of other languages (TESOL) at the School of Education, University of Leicester, and a cohort of distance learners studying two Masters programs in occupational psychology (OP) at the School of Psychology, also at Leicester. Most of the students on the TESOL program were graduate teachers with at least 2 years of English-language teaching experience, who wanted to enhance their teaching and academic practice through this Masters program. The students on the OP programs were from a wider range of professional backgrounds, including human resources, marketing, consultancy, and management, who wanted to further their professional development through the Masters programs. For this particular group of distance learners, work-based learning occurred mostly as work-related learning. Our second group of learners who used mobile devices for their work-based learning were teaching assistants (TAs) who studied a foundation degree (FD) in educational studies at Leicester College. For them, the work-based learning occurred mostly at the workplace.

TAs fall under the general category of support staff within a local school. They are employed to carry out a variety of duties in support of teachers, varying from school to school. Some TAs support individual pupils with special needs, and others support the whole class or groups within the class in subject areas such as literacy and numeracy. In some instances, TAs also provide administrative or technical support, or pastoral care.

MOBILE DEVICES AND WORK-BASED LEARNING

Handheld devices such as PDAs were widely used to access learning material, take notes, capture reflections, and collect data and evidence at the workplace (Taylor, Sharples, O'Malley, Vavoula, & Waycott, 2006; Scanlon, Jones, & Waycott, 2005). These devices were found to be particularly useful for teachers' professional development (Aubusson, Schuck, & Burden, 2009; Power & Thomas, 2007). In one study of the use of PDAs with school teachers, the devices were found to be effective in enabling teacher reflections, capturing the spontaneity of learning moments, and promoting collaboration between teachers and students in the classroom (Aubusson et al., 2009). Similar results have been reported in other studies. For example, Power and Thomas (2007) reported that PDAs have been effectively used by teachers as tools for collecting data in the form of photos and voice-recordings. The word-processing, spreadsheet, and electronic planning functions of the PDA offered the teachers an "anytime, anyplace" learning tool for their professional learning and development (p. 379).

Medical and health care is another field in which mobile and handheld devices have been widely used to support work-based learning. Access to essential digital learning resources was identified as a challenge for students and professionals in health care in their workplace (Walton, Childs, & Blenkinsopp, 2005). For this reason, focus has been placed on the development of mobile resources, applications, and platforms to enable health professionals to access e-resources in clinical settings. Some initiatives in this area include the development of the ebrary Reader for medical texts (Ross-White, 2008); building a collection of electronic books for medical libraries (Heyd, 2010; White, 2011); the development of a variety of mobile resources, including smartphone applications, mobile websites, and e-books (Havelka, 2011); and the creation of an electronic reference shelf (Lomax & Setterlund, 2005).

Mobile and handheld devices have also been used to support other aspects of work-based learning in clinical settings. For example, Mini-DV video cameras were used to capture what happened in clinics. The videos were used to help students in placement to gain clinical skills (Edwards, Jones, & Murphy, 2007). Kindle e-readers were used with medical students in clinical settings, with portability and searchability reported as the major advantages, and slow connection speed, difficulty in navigation, and lack of color display identified as the major limitations (Shurtz & von Isenburg, 2011).

Our chapter examines the outcomes from two case studies at the University of Leicester, where two mobile devices, namely e-book readers and PDAs, were introduced into the teaching of three programs between 2008 and 2010.

An e-book reader is an electronic device designed primarily for reading digital files such as electronic books (e-books). The model used in the case study was the Sony PRS-505. The Amazon Kindle is another model of e-book reader.

In each case study, we describe the educational challenges faced by the students in the programs, and explain how the mobile devices were used to help overcome some of these challenges. We discuss the key findings in terms of the potential and limitations of each mobile device as a learning tool for work-based learners.

CASE STUDY 1: E-BOOK READERS FOR WORK-BASED DISTANCE LEARNERS

Context

In this case study, three programs were involved in using e-book readers to support distance work-based learners between 2009 and 2010.

The MA distance program in applied linguistics and TESOL has been delivered by the School of Education, the University of Leicester, since 1995. Two distance programs, the MSc in occupational psychology and the Diploma/MSc in the psychology of work, have been delivered by the School of Psychology at Leicester since 2000. All three programs attract part-time, work-based learners. The objective of these students was professional development through these distance-taught programs.

Most students on the three programs lead busy and demanding lives. They travel a lot, especially the English-language teachers in the TESOL program. Finding enough time to study is a major challenge for them. Students in these programs expressed a need for better, easier, and mobile access to reading material to make the most of their limited study time. With this group of students, the challenge was how to use the mobile devices to support their work-related learning outside the workplace.

Implementation

In order to address the above need, 28 Sony e-book readers were used in the three programs (17 given to TESOL and 11 given to OP students) between October 2009 and March 2010. The e-book readers were preloaded with learning materials (in ePub format) from modules produced by the TESOL and OP course teams. A sociolinguistics textbook was also made available on the e-book readers given to the 17 TESOL students.

Below is a description of the implementation involved in this case study, including material preparation and conversion, delivery of e-book readers, and student support.

- Preparation: The course teams updated and proofread all materials.
- Conversion: The materials were converted into ePub format by a learning technologist using Calibre (http://calibre-ebook.com), a free, cross-platform e-book reader management system.
- Preloading: The materials in ePub format were copied onto the e-book readers.
- Delivery: The e-book readers were posted to students.
- Update: Updated versions of the materials and new resources were uploaded to the university's Virtual Learning Environment (VLE) in ePub format for students to download onto their e-book readers.
- Guidance: Guidance and instruction were provided to guide students on how to add new materials onto their e-book readers.

Results

The initiative was evaluated using a questionnaire completed by 28 students and qualitative interviews with 12 students from both disciplines. Key benefits and limitations in association with the use of e-book readers for work-based distance learners were reported as follows:

Learning Time

The participating students from both disciplines highly valued the portability and flexibility that the e-book reader offers to their studying. The readability of the text on e-book readers under different conditions, the opportunity to access course materials from a single device, without an Internet connection, long battery life, capacity to accommodate many readings, and a user-friendly interface were all considered advantages that resulted in better access to essential readings and an enjoyable reading experience. For these reasons, students used their e-book readers in different locations, for example, homes, airports, parks, cafés, and on the move, including on trains, buses, or airplanes.

The portability of the e-book reader was found to be extremely convenient for students to take all course materials with them anywhere and read whenever they had a small chunk of time. Functionalities such as "bookmarking" and "continue reading" made the e-book reader easy for students to turn off and then pick up again from where they had left off. These functions of e-book readers increased the likelihood that students would study during their short breaks and while travelling.

This evidence showed that the device had a positive impact on students' learning time. It helped students to make better use of "dead time" and enabled them to fill gaps in a purposeful way.

Learning Cost

We looked into the cost for students associated with using learning materials. We found that using e-book readers helped them to reduce costs. Some students from both disciplines became less dependent on printed materials or more selective in what they printed out, as a result of having access to essential course materials on their e-book readers.

Learning Strategy

Using the e-book reader enabled some students from both disciplines to change their learning strategies, for instance, for keeping notes and approaching assignments.

For some students, the e-book reader was a welcome addition to the devices they had at their disposal for studies, so that they could choose appropriate devices for reading to suit their situations and needs. For example, one student reported that he used his laptop and textbooks when conducting research, because he felt that cross-referencing was faster and easier this way. He used printed materials when taking notes. He found it difficult to read from his e-book reader on public transport because the environment was noisy. Therefore, he preferred to use the e-book reader at home. He sometimes used his iPhone for a quick check of the materials when he was out or on the move. This finding showed that student reading habits became highly situational as a result of having access to different types of mobile device.

Copyright Issue

Copyright restrictions were major challenges encountered in our study. Despite extensive help from the university library, only a single education e-book on sociolinguistics was made available on the e-book readers after obtaining agreement with the publisher. The e-book reader could have been much more useful if all essential readings, including the core textbooks and journal articles, had been preloaded on them.

Technological Limitations

Limitations in functionality, such as lack of note-taking and delays in page-turning, which causes "flickering," constituted a hurdle for some students. Some students from both disciplines went back to the printed materials, where they could underline and make notes, especially during revision and preparation for assignments or the dissertation. Some considered e-book readers more useful and appropriate for reading for leisure than for study purposes. These limitations in functionality have been, to some extent, overcome in later models of e-book readers.

CASE STUDY 2: PDAs FOR WORK-BASED LEARNERS

Context

A key priority of the UK government and local Learning and Skills Council is to ensure that all TAs are professionally qualified to the undergraduate degree level. To achieve this, further-education (FE) colleges and universities offer FDs in educational studies for TAs who want to gain an HE qualification. Leicester College is one of the FE Colleges that offer this FD for TAs.

This FD course at Leicester College was delivered through a combination of lectures, tutorials, and reflective activities in the classroom settings where they worked as TAs. Students' learning was assessed through a combination of formative and summative methods, and based on evidence that the TAs collate as a portfolio.

The TAs' FD curriculum includes a variety of subjects, such as science, education in practice, literacy, and numeracy with ICT. In their workplaces (i.e., schools), they must fulfill several roles in different teaching settings. Sometimes they act as a teacher of the entire class, a one-to-one teacher, a participant tutor, or a facilitator. One of the challenges faced by TAs in FD courses is how to systematically record classroom activities in a complex working environment and to develop a portfolio of evidence for their degree program. For this group of TA students, the challenge was how to use mobile devices to support their learning in the workplace.

Implementation

In order to address the above challenge, Hewlett Packard Rw6815 PDAs were used to help the TAs record classroom observations and reflections, and access relevant learning resources. Twenty TAs in this FD course participated in the study during 2008–2009. The TAs were given PDAs from which they could access the college's VLE. They could download relevant tasks and content from the VLE onto their PDAs via their home computers. They could bring the PDAs to their workplaces, where they could record classroom evidence such as pictures, movies, and reflective notes to develop their portfolios. They could also use the PDAs to make reflective notes during their working time in the classroom. Returning home, students were required to upload the recorded evidence and reflective notes onto the college VLE for feedback and assessment.

The technology implementation involved in this case study included the following four areas:

- Preparation: Reviewing existing electronic course materials and, where necessary, redesigning for PDA use.
- Development of PDP (professional-development planning) portfolios: Development of the wiki and blog features within the VLE to facilitate TAs to incorporate reflections from their work-based experience in their PDP portfolios by uploading content from PDA onto the VLE.
- Multimedia enhancement: Use of multimedia (text, voice, and images) to enhance PDP portfolio development and learning content by using PowerPoint viewer (available in PDA) and support for audio files.
- Support: Development of training materials and guidance for use by tutors and TAs.

Results

Evidence on TAs' use of PDAs was gathered from 20 TAs studying the FD course at Leicester College. Data were collected through semi-structured one-to-one interviews, focus-group discussions with some TAs, studying the evidence captured by the TAs at their workplace using PDAs (photos, voice, and text), and portfolios developed by the TAs. Our analysis revealed a number of potentials and limitations with the use of PDAs for work-based learners.

Learning Support

All 20 TAs used their PDAs at their workplace to collect evidence for the development of their portfolios. The PDAs were found to be easy to use and effective as a tool to collect evidence for portfolios in various classroom settings. TAs were able to integrate the evidence they gathered from their classroom observations into the VLE.

Learning Design

Learning activities in which the PDA becomes the natural choice to carry out tasks increase the possibility that students use the device for learning. In our case study, we found that activities designed around assignments promoted the use of the PDA.

The tutor on the FD course used the text chat facility in the VLE (named "e-tutorial") to provide feedback on the reflective journals developed by the TAs. The TAs commented positively on this novel approach that linked their use of the VLE with the PDA. We found that the tutor's feedback promoted TAs' further reflection.

We also found that the PDAs were a useful tool in many teaching and learning settings for capturing evidence to build portfolios, including the traditional classroom settings, small groups, classrooms in a nursery or kindergarten learning environments, and outdoor settings.

Learner Support

The initial period of using PDAs was a learning curve for both the TAs and their tutor on the FD course. We found that the TAs' previous experience with technology was linked to their level of competence and confidence with the PDAs. The differences in competence and confidence dictated the level of support that they required from the college learning technologist. Learning with PDAs required a certain level of personalized support, mainly in the early stage of introduction of PDAs. Peers and family members were found to be effective sources of support for TAs for their learning with PDAs.

Ethical Issues

School policies and ethical considerations shaped the way in which TAs used PDAs. Taking photographs and video recordings of children in the classroom raised certain ethical issues that presented constraints on how PDAs could be used in schools.

Technological Limitations

The technological features of the PDAs affected TAs' use of them too. The quality of output from the PDA was questioned by our TAs. Some TAs had access to alternative technologies, such as cameras at school, which produced higher-quality output than the PDAs. This, therefore, limited TAs' use of PDAs.

DISCUSSION

Our findings from the two case studies revealed a variety of issues related to introducing and using two different types of mobile device to support work-based learners. Mobile technologies develop quickly, and, currently, there are far more superior devices than the ones we used in our case studies. In the following section, where necessary, we review some of the more recent developments of digital mobile devices, for example tablet computers, for their potential to support learners with similar learning needs to those in our case studies.

Learners' Mobility And Learning Time

In both case studies, the mobile devices used were found to be effective in supporting the work-based learner on the move. E-book readers were particularly effective in enabling student access to essential readings from various locations, such as at the workplace, in public places, and on public transport. The PDAs were useful for collecting evidence and capturing reflection by the TAs at their workplaces. By supporting learners' mobility, e-book readers enabled students to make better use of their limited study time.

These findings suggested that the mobile devices we used in our case studies, especially e-book readers, were effective in supporting work-based learners on the move and improving efficiency in their use of study time.

Learning Cost

E-book readers had a positive effect on the learning cost. Students reported cost savings as a result of using the device for reading instead of printing. This is in line with findings at the Oklahoma State University (2011) where the iPad was used as the e-reader. The study found that students were able to save money if they bought many e-books rather than paper books, and, in two semesters, the savings could cover the cost of the iPad.

The two case studies reported here raise an important question for scalability: How can educational providers reduce the transferring of the costs to the students where mobile devices are integral technology for teaching and learning?

Since we conducted the two case studies in 2008 and 2009, mobile devices have become more and more affordable. The Oxford Internet Survey revealed that almost one-third of British Internet users had an e-reader or a tablet computer in 2011 (Dutton & Blank, 2011). Research conducted by Google revealed that, in the UK, over 45 percent of the population own a smartphone (Shield, 2012). These technological developments have created a suitable context for institutions to implement mobile devices more widely.

Institutions can take two approaches when implementing m-learning widely: purchasing and giving out devices for students (similar to the approach in our case studies), and encouraging the use of student-owned devices. The University of Leeds in the UK, for example, provides iPhones to their fourth- and fifth-year medical students. The iPhones are preloaded with medical texts that a medical student can refer to in the clinical setting (Coughlan, 2010). The second approach, making use of students' own mobile devices, was not possible at the time we carried out our case studies. In this approach, the institution only needs to provide access to the Internet through Wi-Fi connections and a number of devices for those who do not have their own devices, rather than providing an institution-purchased device for each student. There are issues when using students' own devices, however. Traxler and Campus (2009) pointed out obstacles to widespread acceptance of using students' own devices, such as the perception of inequality and disadvantages created by the fact that some students have and others do not have.

Learner Support

In our case studies, users of the e-book reader needed minimal support, as the device was very easy to use for reading as well as transferring new reading materials onto the device. The TAs who used PDAs required considerable support, especially at the initial stage of the study. This raised issues regarding the technical competence of the learner and how to provide necessary support. This suggested that learning anywhere and at anytime required some technical support, at least in the early stages of introducing a new mobile device for learning. Our PDA study showed that building a support mechanism is needed for work-based learners, especially if their learning is likely to occur outside a formal institution.

Learning Design

In our e-book-reader study, we implemented a simple idea—to make essential reading materials available on the mobile device. More considerations were given to learning design for PDAs. We found that activities designed around assignments promoted engagement. The approach that links students' use of the VLE with the PDA was considered innovative. Feedback from the tutor on submitted portfolios promoted further reflection.

We also found that the environment in which the TAs worked strongly influenced how and why the PDAs were used. We found, for example, it was more effective to use the PDA in small-group teaching settings, compared with when the TAs were with a whole class of students. Classrooms full of pupils tend to be naturally noisy and busy, where the use of PDAs posed a challenge to the TAs.

These findings indicated the importance of learning design for different mobile devices in order to achieve different pedagogical purposes.

With the development of new devices, using apps has become a trend in learning design for mobile devices. For example, a leading LMS provider, Blackboard, offers apps to allow students to use mobile devices to participate in discussion boards, write blog posts, and post photos to journals. To support a work-based learning scenario, students studying an occupational-therapy program at the University of Northampton visit patients in their homes and bring along iPads loaded with the "Dr Goniometer" app. This app allows students to take photos of the patient's damaged limb or joint. The damage is then measured and evaluated by the app.

Technical Limitations

In both of our case studies, we identified technological limitations associated with the particular mobile device used. These technological limitations restricted, to some extent, how and for what students wanted to use the device. Mobile technology is a fast-growing field, and many of these limitations are being overcome, to some extent, in later models.

In HE, an increasing number of institutions have begun to explore the affordances of the iPad as a learning tool. Institutions were attracted to the promise of being able to pack all of the textbooks, now enhanced with multimedia, and other reading material and more functionality in one handy device, although at a higher price than an e-book reader. A couple of iPad initiatives have found mixed results. Students reported positively about the portability, light weight, and long battery life of the iPad (Wieder, 2011), very much in line with the findings from our e-book-reader study. However, studies also found that students used the iPad less as an e-reader than they originally thought they would (Angst & Malinowski, 2010; Handy, Suter, & Hooper, 2010). Students also felt negative about typing longer documents or using the iPad for their finals (Wieder, 2011).

The iPad seems to have lived up to its hype to some extent and succeeded in more areas than the Kindle and other e-readers (Eloff, 2011), but still does not fully remove the need for a laptop or desktop computer, for example for typing long documents, as some had hoped. It would, therefore, be of interest to further investigate its affordance to HE, especially with regard to work-based learning.

Challenges

Challenges were encountered in the two case studies. With the PDAs, a key challenge was mainly to do with ethical issues and what is considered to be proper use of PDAs with pupils in school settings. In maximizing the capacity and benefit of e-book readers, the major challenge was to overcome the copyright issues.

There have been some developments in overcoming copyright issues since we carried out our e-book-reader study in 2009. Using open textbooks is one of these developments. The idea is to develop open textbooks that can be used and adapted by teachers and students for free, instead of using textbooks provided by publishers. In one of these initiatives, the Utah State Office of Education, in the US, promoted the development and use of open textbooks in key curriculum areas, including secondary language arts, science, and mathematics (Peterson, 2012). Another example is the OpenED project led by the Open University in the UK, in which an open course in business was developed and implemented. Also, Apple's release of the free iBooks Author software in January 2012 has made it easy for any teacher to create his/her own multimedia-rich e-books for the iPad, encouraging teachers to avoid copyright issues by creating e-texts themselves.

Publishers have become more open towards e-textbooks since our pilot. More and more textbooks in e-book format have become available at an affordable price since 2009. For example, the Indiana University was able to negotiate a favorable pricing with the publisher for their students to use the eText version of textbooks instead of traditional textbooks (Dawson, 2012).

CONCLUSIONS

Our chapter addresses some pertinent issues in mobile and work-based learning scenarios, such as learners' mobility, learning time and cost, learner support, learning design, technical limitations, and challenges. Our study demonstrated that devices with the limited technological features of the 2008–2009 timeframe proved to be effective in meeting the needs of mobile and work-based learners. What is important today is designing for learning to take advantage of the new capabilities offered by new technologies.

The results from the e-book-reader study in particular have had an impact on the library at the University of Leicester. New service initiatives have now been developed to lend e-books to students. The outcomes from the two case studies have resulted in further developments in m-learning by other departments and disciplines within the university. For example, the Department of Criminology has launched a new Masters program in which iPads are shipped to distance students, along with instructions to download a free bespoke app containing all of the module's learning materials. The university's Museum Studies is piloting the use of tablet computers for use by their Masters students on field trips to places such as the British Museum.

It is necessary for institutions to have strategies for m-learning, particularly with regard to supporting work-based and distance learners. A Morgan Stanley report (Meeker, Devitt, & Wu, 2010) on Internet trends predicted that, by 2015, more people will be accessing the Internet from mobile devices than by fixed Internet connections. Work-based learners are increasingly and eagerly using mobile devices to keep on top of all their commitments in life, and this will only increase in years to come.

REFERENCES

Angst, C. M., & Malinowski, E. (2010, December). *Findings from eReader project, phase 1: Use of iPads in MGT40700, Project Management.* Mendoza College of Business, University of Notre Dame. Retrieved from: http://www.nd.edu/~cangst/NotreDame_iPad_Report_01–06–11.pdf

Aubusson, P., Schuck, S., & Burden, K. (2009). Mobile learning for teacher professional learning: Benefits, obstacles and issues. *ALT-J, 17*(3), 233–247.

Barr, H. (2003). Interprofessional issues and work based learning. In J. Burton & N. Jackson (Eds.), *Work based learning in primary care* (pp. 73–86). Abingdon, UK: Radcliffe Medical.

Clamp, E., & Warr, E. (2002). Addressing employability through implementation of work related learning. *Proceedings of the Third Annual Skills Conference: Skills Development in Higher Education: Forging Links.* July 10–11, University of Hertfordshire, UK.

Coughlan, S. (2010, September). University gives students text books on iPhones. *BBC News.* Retrieved from: www.bbc.co.uk/news/education-11427317

Dawson, K. (2012, January). Digital shift: e-books rising in popularity. *Indiana Daily Student.* Retrieved from: www.idsnews.com/news/story.aspx?id=85043&search=Digital%20shift&section=search

Dutton, W. H., & Blank, G. (2011). *Next generation users: The Internet in Britain.* Oxford Internet Institute, University of Oxford. Retrieved from: http://microsites.oii.ox.ac.uk/oxis/publications

Eloff, K. (2011). *Mobile devices in education: A report on five case studies involving the use of the Amazon Kindle DX ereader and the Apple iPad media reader for educational use* [PowerPoint slides]. Retrieved from slideshare: www.slideshare.net/kosieeloff/case-studies-of-mobile-device-usage

Edwards, M., Jones, S., & Murphy, F. (2007): Handheld video for clinical skills teaching. *Innovations in Education and Teaching International, 44*(4), 401–408.

Handy, B., Suter, T., & Hooper, B. K. (2010). *Executive summary: Oklahoma State University/Apple iPad pilot program*. Retrieved from: http://news.okstate.edu/images/documents/ipad_research_exec_summary.pdf

Havelka, S. (2011). Mobile resources for nursing students and nursing faculty. *Journal of Electronic Resources in Medical Libraries, 8*(2), 194–199.

Heyd, M. (2010). Three e-Book aggregators for medical libraries: NetLibrary, rittenhouse R2 digital library, and STAT!Ref. *Journal of Electronic Resources in Medical Libraries, 7*(1), 13–41.

Hills, J. M., Robertson, G., Walker, R., Adey, M., & Nixon, I. (2003). Bridging the gap between degree curricula and employability through implementation of work-related learning. *Teaching in Higher Education, 8*(2), 211–223.

Gray, D. (2001). *A briefing on work-based learning.* Learning and Teaching Support Network Generic Centre, Assessment Series No. 11. York: LTSN. Retrieved from: www.bioscience.heacademy.ac.uk/ftp/Resources/gc/assess11Workbased.pdf

Lomax, E., & Setterlund, S. K. (2005). A virtual reference shelf for nursing students and faculty. *Journal of Library Administration, 44*(1–2), 429–445.

Meeker, M., Devitt, S., & Wu, L. (2010). *Internet trends.* Morgan Stanley. Retrieved from: www.cionet.com/Data/files/groups/01006%20Internet_Trends.pdf

Oklahoma State University. (2011, May). *iPad study released by Oklahoma State University.* OSU News and Communications. Retrieved from: http://news.okstate.edu/press-releases/929-ipad-study-released-by-oklahoma-state-university

Peterson, M. (2012, January 25). *Utah State Office of Education to create open textbooks.* UtahPublicEducation.org. Retrieved from: http://utahpubliceducation.org/2012/01/25/utah-state-office-of-education-to-create-open-textbooks/

Power, T., & Thomas, R. (2007). The classroom in your pocket? *Curriculum Journal, 18*(3), 373–388.

Ross-White, A. (2008). ebrary reader and medical texts. *Journal of Electronic Resources in Medical Libraries, 4*(4), 67–71.

Seagraves, L., Osborne, M., Neal, P., Dockrell, R., Hartshorn, C., & Boyd, A. (1996). *Learning in smaller companies: Final report.* Project report. Educational Policy and Development, University of Stirling, UK. Retrieved from: http://eprints.gla.ac.uk/56297/

Scanlon, E., Jones, A., & Waycott, J. (2005). Mobile technologies: Prospects for their use in learning in informal science settings. *Journal of Interactive Media in Education, 25,* 1–17.

Shield, R. (2012, January). *UK smartphone ownership nears 50%.* newmediaage. Retrieved from: www.nma.co.uk/news/uk-smartphone-ownership-nears-50/3033601.article

Shurtz, S., & von Isenburg, M. (2011). Exploring e-readers to support clinical medical education: Two case studies. *Journal of the Medical Library Association, 99*(2), 110–117.

Taylor, J., Sharples, M., O'Malley, C., Vavoula, G., & Waycott, J. (2006). Towards a task model for mobile learning: A dialectical approach. *International Journal of Learning Technology, 2*(2/3),138–158.

Traxler, J., & Campus, P. (2009). Students and mobile devices: Choosing which dream. In H. Damis and L. Creanor (Ed.), *In dreams begins responsibility—Choice, evidence and change. The 16th Association for Learning Technology Conference* (pp. 70–81). September 8–10 , University of Manchester, UK.

Walton, G., Childs, S., & Blenkinsopp, E. (2005). Using mobile technologies to give health students access to learning resources in the UK community setting. *Health Information and Libraries Journal, 22,* 51–65.

White, M. (2011). Maximizing use and value of e-books in the medical library. *Journal of Electronic Resources in Medical Libraries, 8*(3), 280–285.

Wieder, B. (2011, March). iPads could hinder teaching, professors say. *The Chronicle of Higher Education.* Retrieved from: http://chronicle.com/article/iPads-for-College-Classrooms-/126681/

Part III
Teaching and Instructional Design

22

M-LEARNING AS A CATALYST FOR PEDAGOGICAL CHANGE

Thomas Cochrane

There have been many voices calling for new approaches and new pedagogies in higher education. According to Laurillard (2012), pedagogical change does not happen of itself—it is a design science. Reeves makes a plea for new approaches to technology adoption research in education, "Instead of more media comparison studies or studies investigating the effects of isolated media variables" (Reeves, 2009, p. 6). Herrington and Herrington (2007) note that the disruptive nature of the integration of new technologies in education often results in practitioners relying upon tried and proven pedagogical approaches, leading to "one step forward for technology and two steps back for pedagogy" (2007, p. 4).

Reeves (2005) calls for four major changes in educational-technology research and adoption that involve: collaborative research methodologies, new support strategies, new reward strategies, and new methods of disseminating research to practitioners. These strategies will minimize the reliance upon old pedagogies as we explore the potential of new technologies to enable new pedagogical paradigms. These four strategies are used to inform the following discussion on the potential pedagogical impact of m-learning research.

THE IMPACT OF M-LEARNING

Teaching and learning innovations are best implemented when informed by learning theory (Ally, 2008; Mishra, Koehler, & Zhao, 2007). A review of the literature (Cobcroft, 2006; Koszalka & Ntloedibe-Kuswani, 2010; Laine & Suhonen, 2008; Naismith, Lonsdale, Vavoula, & Sharples, 2004; Wingkvist & Ericsson, 2009) indicates that the field of m-learning educational research is relatively young, and theoretical-framework development has been hampered by the rapid changes in mobile technologies.

There exist as yet no comprehensive theoretical and conceptual frameworks to explain the complex interrelationship between the characteristics of rapid and sometimes groundbreaking technological developments, their potential for learning, as well as their embeddedness in the everyday lives of users (Pachler, Bachmair, & Cook, 2010, p. 3).

Theorists in the field of m-learning have been filling the void described by Pachler et al. (2010) by drawing upon established pedagogical theories and frameworks for application to m-learning. For example, Sharples, Taylor, and Vavoula (2007) utilized a combination of Activity Theory and a modified version of Laurillard's Conversational Framework. Wali, Winters, and Oliver (2008) appropriated Activity Theory, and Herrington, Herrington, Mantei, Olney, and Ferry (2009) used Authentic Learning (based upon situated learning and social constructivism) as a theoretical framework for their m-learning research projects.

The literature indicates that much of the early m-learning research and implementation focused upon the potential of m-learning to facilitate ubiquitous access to lecturer-created content, without a significant change in pedagogy from established instructivist pedagogies (Herrington & Herrington, 2007; Kukulska-Hulme & Traxler, 2005; Traxler, 2007).

Activity Theory has been used by many as a theoretical frame for m-learning, stemming largely from Sharples et al.'s (Sharples, Taylor, & Vavoula, 2005; Sharples et al., 2007) research, but, because of the operational complexity of Activity Theory (Pachler et al., 2010), this has led to impractical and convoluted implementation methodologies for the general practitioner.

Chen, Millard, and Wills (2008) evaluated the 40 research papers submitted to MLearn2007, categorizing the 17 m-learning scenarios described according to a four-category framework (learning objective, learning environment, learning activity, and learning tools) to establish how student-directed these projects were. Only two papers demonstrated alignment with being student-directed in all four categories (one of these was the author's paper (Cochrane, 2007a)). This selection of the m-learning research literature therefore indicates that the majority of current research has focused upon delivery of content to mobile devices (teacher generated and controlled), rather than student-generated content and contexts.

Another review of MLearn2007 and 2008 papers (Wingkvist & Ericsson, 2009) classified and critiqued the research methodologies reported in these papers. All 76 full papers were classified according to eight research methodologies (case study, field study, action research, experiment studies, survey research, basic research, applied research, and normative research) and four research purposes (describing, developing, understanding, and evaluating). The reviewers found that the representative m-learning research consisted predominantly of small-scale descriptive case studies, with little evaluation and reflection witnessed. An action-research methodology was used by only 5 percent of these papers. This indicates that there is a significant gap in the literature of m-learning research dealing with longitudinal action-research projects. With some notable exceptions (for example: MoLeNET), m-learning research has been predominantly characterized by short-term case studies focused upon the implementation of rapidly changing technologies with early adopters, but with little evaluation, reflection, or emphasis on mainstream tertiary-education integration.

Therefore, there is a need to focus on design frameworks that can be implemented by the general practitioner and provide sustained collaborative support, rather than introductory workshops or a reliance on high-intensity mobile application or multimedia development. A review of the literature led the author to draw on concepts from communities of practice (Lave & Wenger, 1991), a conversational framework (Laurillard, 2001), learner-generated content and learner-generated contexts (Luckin et al., 2008;

Luckin et al., 2010), and authentic learning (Herrington & Herrington, 2007; Herrington, 2006; Herrington & Oliver, 2000).

Reeves' (2005) call for design-based research can be applied to m-learning. Design-based research extends action research by making the development of implementation strategies and theory explicit. Thus, one of the goals of design-based research is informing practice beyond the specific context of the research itself.

Second, researchers need to move beyond a focus on information delivery via the institutional learning-management system (LMS) or replicating current pedagogies on new devices. Herrington, Reeves, and Oliver (2005) term this fascination with limiting technology appropriation in education within the official LMS as "digital Myopia." Utilizing freely available mobile Web 2.0 tools for social-constructivist learning provides a way of correcting digital myopia (Cochrane, 2011b; Cochrane & Bateman, 2010b) and provides a powerful toolset for enabling authentic learning that bridges formal and informal learning environments.

Significant pedagogical change is possible as a result of m-learning integration, when it is explicitly part of the design goal of technology integration innovation in teaching and learning.

TRANSFORMING PEDAGOGY VIA M-LEARNING

M-learning is a disruptive technology that can be utilized to empower social constructivism in education, thus acting as a catalyst for pedagogical change. An example framework for how this can be achieved is presented by the author at: http://prezi.com/jxupenofiwdj/

Sharples (2001) has long been an advocate of the "disruptive" nature of m-learning. This disruption can be a positive influence upon pedagogy, as it enables a refocus away from teacher-directed content to student-generated content and student-generated learning contexts. Kukulska-Hulme (2010) also emphasizes the positive catalytic nature of m-learning, and there is a growing body of examples; see, for example, Traxler (2011), who describes five ways m-learning can impact education, illustrated by a series of case studies.

Thus, m-learning presents rich opportunities for pedagogical change. In the rest of this section, we discuss an example methodology of how this can be achieved.

A NEW RESEARCH METHODOLOGY

Reeves (2005) calls for longitudinal collaborative research between educational researchers and practitioners. The author believes this can be achieved through modeling research partnerships around communities of practice (Lave & Wenger, 1991; Wenger, 1998; Wenger, White, & Smith, 2009). Forming a community of practice (COP) of the lecturers and researchers involved in an m-learning project creates a sustained collaborative partnership that can also draw in other interested lecturers from the periphery of the COP. The reified activities of these COPs can be used to broker m-learning best practice beyond the COP itself.

Pedagogical Frameworks

Heeding Reeves' (2005) call for a focus upon the unique affordances of new technologies, m-learning research projects should focus upon what can be achieved via the unique affordances of these tools, rather than replicating what can be done on more traditional computing platforms, such as desktop or laptop computers. Also, heeding Herrington et al. (Herrington & Herrington, 2007; Herrington et al., 2005), there should be a focus away from teacher-generated content delivery to these small-screened devices. Mobile devices (and, in particular, smartphones) by their design are ubiquitously connected, portable collaboration and communication tools and, therefore, can be used within social-learning environments in and beyond the classroom. A move from instructivist pedagogy can be achieved by choosing social-learning theory as a basis for m-learning implementation. Thus, choosing pedagogical frameworks that support the implementation of social constructivism will guide the design of m-learning projects.

Measuring Pedagogical Change

A measure of the impact of m-learning integration can be achieved by mapping the pedagogy–andragogy–heutagogy (PAH) continuum (Luckin et al., 2010) to the changes to pedagogy achieved via an m-learning project. That is, scaffolding pedagogical change from teacher-directed pedagogy, to student-centered andragogy, and then student-directed or student-negotiated heutagogy (Cochrane et al., 2011; Cochrane & Rhodes, 2011). Continuous reflection and refinement of the m-learning project outcomes and activities will allow for monitoring and evaluation of pedagogical change.

New Support Strategies

Supporting m-learning projects via sustained COPs made up of the project participants is one way to satisfy Reeves' call for sustained collaborative partnerships in educational-technology research (Cochrane, 2007b; Cochrane & Narayan, 2011; Garnett, Cochrane, Lowe, & Ecclesfield, 2011). The educational researcher can take the role of the technology steward (Wenger et al., 2009) within such COPs. The technology steward is a participant within the COP who has the expertise to guide the group in its choice of appropriate supporting technologies. Wenger et al. (2009) have identified this as a critical role in the interplay between technology and community building. This involves the development of trust and collaboration between the technology steward and the other COP members. We have found that basing COP meetings around social interaction, such as meeting at a local café, helps build this sense of relationship and trust.

New Research Dissemination Strategies

The reified activities of m-learning project COPs can include collaborative research outputs in the form of conference papers, workshops, presentations to colleagues, and journal papers. The partnership between an educational researcher and course lecturers can function as an apprenticeship into educational research for lecturers who are used to research within their disciplined-based research only (Cochrane & Bateman, 2010a; Cochrane & Flitta, 2009). Targeting respected open-access journals (such as the recent shift of *ALT-J* to open access) for these research outputs will also provide wider access for practitioners wishing to learn from others experiences in m-learning implementation.

EXAMPLES

Collaboration between researchers and practitioners removes the "gap" between educational research and practice, resulting in significant pedagogical change. This is illustrated by the following four example case studies: The first two are situated in New Zealand's largest institute of technology, and include the film and television course within the Bachelor of performing and screen arts at Unitec New Zealand (Cochrane, 2011a), and the Bachelor of architecture course at Unitec New Zealand (Cochrane & Rhodes, 2011). Both of these examples represent 3 years (2009–2011) of iterative collaborative m-learning research between an educational researcher (the author) and course lecturers, and their students. The second two examples are drawn from the author's experience of transferring this framework for m-learning integration into New Zealand's newest university. These two examples include the Bachelor of product design course at AUT University, and the Graduate Diploma of journalism at AUT University.

Performing and Screen Arts Students

The film and television elective course was the focus of the collaborative partnership of the researcher and the course lecturer that explored changes in pedagogy within the course enabled by m-learning integration. The initial 2009 m-learning project focused upon guided student exploration (andragogy) of the unique affordances of smartphones for film distribution. The 2010 m-learning project focused upon guided student exploration of mobile film creation using smartphones. Having built the course lecturer's confidence in the previous two projects, the 2011 m-learning project extended this by taking a heutagogical approach to facilitating team-based, student-generated mobisodes, or short mobile films, filmed, edited, and shared using smartphones (in this case, utilizing the iPhone 3G/S for recording and iPad1 for editing). The course was re-envisioned from a series of lectures to a semester-long COP comprising the students, the course lecturer, the researcher, and three external international mobile film experts. An example mobisode titled *Hardcore Parkour* by the "iSquad" team can be found at: www.youtube.com/watch?v=GgnbWiMd2C0. An example of PASA student feedback on m-learning integration 2011 can be found at www.youtube.com/watch?v=uq6YUt9UAJU

Architecture Students in the iArchitecture 2010 Project

An initial partnership between the researcher and architecture course lecturers grew out of a first-semester 2009 lecturer COP established to explore the potential of m-learning to enhance architecture education. Following this COP, all students and lecturers in the second-year Bachelor of architecture course were supplied with netbooks and smartphones to explore the integration of e-portfolios for the course. However, the project failed to get unanimous support from all course lecturers and floundered as an optional extra for the course. A rethink between the researcher and several committed architecture lecturers led to a smaller m-learning project in 2010. The 2010 m-learning project was implemented within a third-year elective course that was previously focused on teaching students how to use Flash to create a portfolio of their work. The course was rewritten by the researcher and participating lecturers as an exploration of mobile Web 2.0 and took an explicitly heutagogical approach to building student capability to create team-based m-learning projects using the unique affordances of smartphones (for example: geotagging and augmented reality) within the context of architecture situated around the city—beyond the confines of the classroom. The elective-course students, lecturers, and the researcher formed a COP that met weekly to explore the potential architectural affordances of smartphones, followed by the formation of student-negotiated projects. Assessment criteria and processes for the student m-learning projects were negotiated between the students and the participating lecturers. An example of a 2010 student-generated project is the ArchiFail augmented-reality project. This student team created a Wikitude layer titled "Archifail" that documented examples of "failed" architecture throughout the city. As part of the project, they produced a project presentation using Prezi (http://prezi.com/byy1rnidvw-i/archifail/) and used a Wordpress blog as a team hub. Students even produced tutorials for their student peers on how to use these tools (http://dave16288.blogspot.com/2010/11/wikitude-tutorial.html). Non-solicited example student feedback from 2010 can be found at http://dave16288.blogspot.com/p/gadgets.html. Building on the success of the 2010 project, the 2011 student teams within the elective course took this approach further, establishing partnerships with local councils to create Wikitude augmented-reality layers promoting local events and attractions, with one team entering into a commercial agreement with Auckland City Council based upon their project. Example 2011 student feedback on the project can be found at http://megkoolaid.wordpress.com/course-feedback/

During late 2011, the researcher moved institutions from Unitec New Zealand to AUT University in Auckland, New Zealand. The following two m-learning scenarios were developed in partnership with lecturers at AUT University in 2011 and 2012.

Augmenting the Design Thinking Studio

A partnership between the researcher and the head of the product-design department at AUT University lead to the establishment of a lecturer COP exploring the potential of mobile social media to enhance the physical design studio. The product-design course was established in 2007 at AUT University with a focus upon developing a traditional physical collaborative studio space for interacting with relatively small student classes ($N = 20$). Although the course is heavily computer-aided, using high-end 3D and CAD software for model development and rapid prototyping, there was little integration of online course interaction, and, consequently, student projects for real external clients were limited to presentations within the physical studio space. Brainstorms with the researcher and the lecturers explored the potential of mobile and social media to augment (rather than replace) the fantastic physical studio experience of the course. This included a focus upon student-owned smartphones for enabling student-generated content within authentic situated-learning experinces beyond the studio. Thus, students could interview clients and consumers, gather data on real-world experiences, collaborate in teams, and experience a more flexible and interactive exchange within the studio space as well.

The project initially established a COP of product-design lecturers to provide the lecturers with a personal experince of mobile social-media tools, such as iPhones and iPads, and wireless sharing of mobile media via Apple TV connected to projectors in the design studios. A survey of student mobile-device ownership revealed the ubiquity of student ownership of these devices. The use of several basic productivity social-media tools was established, such as Dropbox and Google drive storage (with students as well), followed by two exploratory projects with students using social media such as Posterous for team blogs of their projects (see, for example, http://autdesignjournal.posterous.com). Student engagement, research output, and client interactivity were all markedly higher than previous, similar traditionally paper-based projects (Withell, Cochrane, Reay, Gaziulusoy, & Inder, 2012). Over the first 6 months of the mobile social-media project within the product-design course, the following outcomes have been achieved:

- A reflective collaborative research paper has been written for the Ascilite 2012 Conference.
- A program blog has been established (http://autproductdesign.wordpress.com).
- The design thinking toolbox has been redone from a Flash interface to an iOS-friendly format.
- A Vodafone NZ application for project funding for 2013 has been made.

Images of the development of the lecturer COP have been collated using Picasaweb as a way of reifying the activity of the lecturer COP (https://picasaweb.google.com/104071444159890894025/ProductDesign2012). The success of the impact of the mobile social-media project on the product-design course has been described by the lecturers as "transformative." The goals for Semester 2 2012 now include the following:

- the continuation of the lecturer COP;
- the studios will be set up for wireless iPad teaching;
- all studio groups will use personal blogs in Semester 2 2012;
- there will be a major focus on the design thinking project during Year 1, taught via the iPad;
- the course now makes significant use of student mobile social media;
- a research paper is planned for presentation at Design Ed Asia.

Planning for next year is well underway, with the redesign of new studios to make the most of the integration of mobile and social media to augment the physical space.

Journalism 2.0

The Journalism 2.0 project at AUT university aims to influence the development of the journalism curriculum by encouraging lecturers to integrate the use of mobile social media using student-owned devices (smartphones, laptops, tablets). Previously, the approach taken by journalism lecturers was to present case studies on the impact of social media on journalism as photocopied excerpts of newspapers distributed to the class, with the students instructed to turn off their cellphones during class to minimize the disruption of their use during class. The establishment of a COP between the researcher and journalism lecturers exploring the impact of mobile social media on teaching rapidly changed this approach, convincing the lecturers that the rapid growth of social media and their use by journalists and their sources must be reflected in the courses they teach and in their own teaching practice. Lecturers were encouraged to model the professional use of mobile social media within the classroom, rather than see it as a disruption to the classroom dynamic. Further, by incorporating real experiences of social media and the modeling of its use within courses, the project aims to engage and empower students. Therefore, the project afforded opportunities to use social media to communicate inside and outside the classroom and reworked several traditional assessments (Cochrane, Sissons, & Mulrennan, 2012).

In the second semester of 2011, Twitter was introduced into the live classroom environment as a way to encourage further discussion, during and after class. In 2012, this was extended to reinvent the academic essay. Thus, in Semester 1 of 2012, for the first time, an essay assignment was introduced in one postgraduate class that, instead of being written in a traditional format, could be compiled using actual source media via

Storify.com. Storify allows the writer to curate, critique, and embed into their work a variety of social media sources, such as photos, tweets, and blog posts that have been posted on social-media sites. In order to create a story, the website asks for a title and a description, after which it directs the writer to the search tool where he/she can search for information relating to the topic on the Internet. Once the appropriate information is found, it is dragged and dropped into the story. The user can then write his/her thoughts and link to the content found online. We asked that the students mix academic sources, referenced as usual, with at least three social-media sources.

Students were allowed to choose whether to utilize Storify, although they were encouraged to have a go with the application before making their decision. Of 24 students in the class, only 3 did not use Storify: one because he had problems with an Internet connection during the time set aside to write the essay, and another because the software failed him.

The question the students had to answer was: "How if at all have social media altered the way journalists and public relations practitioners interact? Use real examples from at least three social media platforms as well as academic sources to back up your arguments."

Two journalism lecturers marked the essays and very quickly realized that, although a Storify essay can take longer to mark, a well-crafted one is far more engaging, being multimedia, than a traditional essay. The marks students received were spread from C to A+, which is the spread we would expect in a traditional essay. Several students lost marks because they failed to address the question and because their examples lacked relevance. Other students failed to make the most of the new format and wrote their essays as they would a regular essay, and used the minimum of social-media examples.

The best essays, however, made the most of the platform and the freedom to include multimedia examples. These students also altered their style and the way they wrote into the examples to make their essays fit the medium. Further, by using a mixture of books, journal articles, and discussions on social media, these students were able to explore the question far more deeply than most of those who stuck to the more traditional format.

Initial feedback from students suggests they enjoyed the opportunity to explore social media in a way other than for social purposes. Most also realize the need to be confident using social media for their future role as professional communicators. In conclusion, we believe the use of Storify to create an authentic, rich-media essay was a success, and the integration of mobile social media within the course has revolutionized the teaching of journalism at AUT University.

DISCUSSION

Facilitating pedagogical change in HE is often a difficult and slow process, and the educational-technology research literature is littered with examples resulting in no significant pedagogical difference in comparison with the traditional model. However, the introduction of m-learning into a course can act as a catalyst for pedagogical change by disrupting existing power relationships within the teaching and learning environment, creating a foundation for facilitating student-generated content and student-generated contexts. Thus, an ontological PAH shift can be facilitated, that is, a move from pedagogy (lecturer-directed and lecturer-generated content) to andragogy (student-centered and student-generated content) and, finally, heutagogy (student-directed or student-negotiated and student-generated contexts). This has been illustrated by four examples from critical reflection upon the author's experience of 5 years of action research on mobile Web 2.0 implementation, with an evaluation of 35 m-learning projects between 2006 and 2011 (Cochrane, 2012). These m-learning projects have evidenced different levels of pedagogical change. One of the keys to achieving significant pedagogical change has been the establishment of sustained collaboration between the researcher as an educational-technology steward and course lecturers. Supporting these projects via a COP of the participants creates the foundation for change, as called for by Reeves (2005, 2009) and Herrington et al. (2009). Taking an informed, design-based-research approach to m-learning integration forms the basis for facilitating ontological shifts (or a reconceptualization), creating the foundation for lecturers to reconceptualize pedagogy, and for learners to reconceptualize their role as learners, becoming co-creators of content and situated-learning contexts enabled by the integration of m-learning. Our example scenarios illustrate a radical conceptual shift in the understanding of the affordances of mobile social media to augment traditional physical learning spaces and interaction. In these cases, mobile social media were reassigned from the category of purely social tools for informal use into powerful tools for enabling student-generated content and collaboration within student-generated learning contexts. Previously, the extent of course online activity within these courses had been the administrative use of the institution's LMS and institutionally hosted student e-portfolios. In comparison with the level of

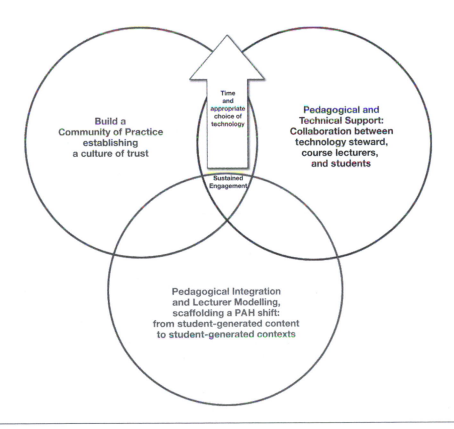

Figure 22.1 Facilitating Ontological Shifts in Education

student engagement and student empowerment evidenced by the previous student use of the LMS and e-portfolios, the level of student engagement and critical thinking, as well as teamwork building, evidenced via their use of mobile social media was revolutionary for these courses.

Key to this has been the sustained engagement of a supporting COP comprised of a collaboration between the course students, the course lecturers, and a technology steward, focusing upon scaffolding the pedagogical integration of mobile Web 2.0, creating the foundation for an ontological PAH shift among the participants (Garnett et al., 2011). This approach can be illustrated by Figure 22.1.

These ontological shifts provide the foundation for the redesign of learning activities and assessment procedures to focus upon student-generated content and contexts, rather than teacher-directed content delivery.

CONCLUSION

Reeves (2005, 2009, 2011) argues that the failure of educational-technology research to demonstrate any significant difference from that of traditional face-to-face classroom pedagogies is due to poor research methodologies that do not explicitly support pedagogical change. This chapter argues that m-learning can indeed be a powerful catalyst for pedagogical change when implemented within a sustained collaborative action-research methodology that includes the specific goal of designing for change. Four examples are provided across four different course contexts and two HE institutions, illustrating a support framework based upon developing and sustaining collaborative communities of practice.

REFERENCES

Ally, M. (2008). Foundations of educational theory for online learning. In T. Anderson (Ed.), *Theory and practice of online learning* (2nd ed., pp. 15–44). Edmonton, AB: AU Press, Athabasca University.

Chen, W. P., Millard, D. E., & Wills, G. B. (2008). Mobile VLE vs. mobile PLE: How informal is mobile learning? In J. Traxler, B. Riordan, & C. Dennett (Eds.), *Proceedings of MLearn08: The bridge from text to context* (pp. 82–88). Ironbridge Gorge, Shropshire, UK: School of Computing and IT, University of Wolverhampton.

Cobcroft, R. S. (2006). Literature review into mobile learning in the university context (p. 138). Retrieved from: http://eprints.qut.edu.au/4805/

Cochrane, T. (2007a). Mobile blogging: A guide for educators. In C. Oliver (Ed.), *Proceedings of MLearn 2007—Making the Connections 6th International Conference on Mobile Learning* (pp. 26–34). Melbourne Exhibition Centre, Melbourne: MLearn 2007.

Cochrane, T. (2007b, October). *Moving mobile mainstream: Using communities of practice to develop educational technology literacy in tertiary academics.* Paper presented at the MLearn 2007—Making the Connections 6th International Conference on Mobile Learning, Melbourne Exhibition Centre, Melbourne, Australia.

Cochrane, T. (2011a). mLearning: Why? What? Where? How? In G. Williams, P. Statham, N. Brown, & B. Cleland (Eds.), *Proceedings of the 28th ASCILITE Conference, ASCILITE 2011: Changing demands, changing directions* (pp. 250–262). Hobart, Tasmania, Australia: The University of Tasmania.

Cochrane, T. (2011b). Mobile cloud services as catalysts for pedagogical change. In L. Chao (Ed.), *Cloud computing for teaching and learning* (pp. 164–184). Hershey, PA: IGI Global.

Cochrane, T. (2012). An mlearning journey: Mobile Web 2.0 critical success factors. *International Journal of Handheld Computing Research, 3*(2), 44–57.

Cochrane, T., & Bateman, R. (2010a). *A mobile learning journey: Or "A tale of two academics pedagogical partnership."* Paper presented at the 6th International Conference on Technology, Knowledge and Society 2010. Retrieved from: http://t10.cgpublisher.com/proposals/89/index_html

Cochrane, T., & Bateman, R. (2010b). Smartphones give you wings: Pedagogical affordances of mobile Web 2.0. *Australasian Journal of Educational Technology, 26*(1), 1–14.

Cochrane, T., Bateman, R., Buchem, I., Camacho, M., Gordon, A., Keegan, H., et al. (2011). Mlearning 2.0: Fostering international collaboration. In I. Candel Torres, L. Gomez Chova, & A. Lopez Martinez (Eds.), *ICERI2011: 4th International Conference of Education, Research and Innovations* (pp. 42–51). Madrid, Spain: IATED.

Cochrane, T., & Flitta, I. (2009, November). *An MLearning journey: Critical incidents in transforming pedagogy.* Paper presented at the International Conference of Education, Research and Innovation (ICERI2009), Madrid, Spain.

Cochrane, T., & Narayan, V. (2011). Defrosting professional development: Reconceptualising teaching using social learning technologies. In D. Hawkridge, K. Ng, & S. Verjans (Eds.), *Proceedings of ALT-C 2011—Thriving in a colder and more challenging climate: The 18th international conference of the Association for Learning Technology* (pp. 158–169). University of Leeds, UK: ALT Association for Learning Technology.

Cochrane, T., & Rhodes, D. (2011). iArchi[tech]ture: Heutagogical approaches to education facilitated by mlearning integration. In K. Fernstrom & C. Tsolakidis (Eds.), *Proceedings of the International Conference on Information and Communication Technologies in Education ICICTE 2011* (pp. 112–121). Rodos Palace Hotel, Rhodes, Greece: University of the Fraser Valley and the University of the Aegean.

Cochrane, T., Sissons, H., & Mulrennan, D. (2012). Journalism 2.0: Exploring the impact of mobile and social media on journalism education. In I. A. Sánchez & P. Isaias (Eds.), *Proceedings of the IADIS International Conference on Mobile Learning 2012* (pp. 165–172). Berlin, Germany: IADIS International Association for Development of the Information Society.

Garnett, F., Cochrane, T., Lowe, P., & Ecclesfield, N. (2011). *Heutagogy and technology stewardship; Theory, practice and mobile social media.* Paper presented at the ECE 2011: Education In a Changing Environment, 6th International Conference Creativity & Engagement In Higher Education. Retrieved from: www.ece.salford. ac.uk/programmes-2011/papers/paper_135.pdf

Herrington, A., & Herrington, J. (2007). *Authentic mobile learning in higher education.* Paper presented at the AARE 2007 International Educational Research Conference. Retrieved from: www.aare.edu.au/07pap/abs07.htm

Herrington, J. (2006). Authentic e-learning in higher education: Design principles for authentic learning environments and tasks. In T. C. Reeves & S. Yamashita (Eds.), *Proceedings of World Conference on E-Learning in Corporate, Government, Healthcare, and Higher Education 2006* (pp. 3164–3173). Chesapeake, VA: AACE.

Herrington, J., Herrington, A., Mantei, J., Olney, I., & Ferry, B. (Eds.) (2009). *New technologies, new pedagogies: Mobile learning in higher education.* Wollongong, Australia: Faculty of Education, University of Wollongong.

Herrington, J., & Oliver, R. (2000). An instructional design framework for authentic learning environments. *Educational Technology Research and Development, 48*(3), 23–48.

Herrington, J., Reeves, T., & Oliver, R. (2005). Online learning as information delivery: Digital myopia. *Journal of Interactive Learning Research, 16*(4), 353–367.

Koszalka, T. A., & Ntloedibe-Kuswani, G. S. (2010). Literature on the safe and disruptive learning potential of mobile technologies. *Distance Education, 31*(2), 139–157.

Kukulska-Hulme, A. (2010). Mobile learning as a catalyst for change. *Open Learning: The Journal of Open and Distance Learning, 25*(3), 181–185.

Kukulsa-Hulme, A., & Traxler, J. (2005). Mobile teaching and learning. In A. Kukulsa-Hulme & J. Traxler (Eds.), *Mobile learning* (pp. 25–44). Oxford, UK: Routledge.

Laine, T. H., & Suhonen, J. (2008). Establishing a mobile blog system in a distance education environment. *International Journal of Mobile Learning and Organisation, 2*(2), 149–165.

Laurillard, D. (2001). *Rethinking university teaching: A framework for the effective use of educational technology* (2nd ed.). London: Routledge.

Laurillard, D. (2012). *Teaching as a design science: Building pedagogical patterns for learning and technology.* New York: Routledge.

Lave, J., & Wenger, E. (1991). *Situated learning: Legitimate peripheral participation.* Cambridge, UK: Cambridge University Press.

Luckin, R., Clark, W., Garnett, F., Whitworth, A., Akass, J., Cook, J., et al. (2008). *Learner generated contexts: A framework to support the effective use of technology to support learning.* Retrieved from: http://knowledgeillusion. files.wordpress.com/2012/03/bookchapterluckin2009learnergeneratedcontexts.pdf

Luckin, R., Clark, W., Garnett, F., Whitworth, A., Akass, J., Cook, J., et al. (2010). Learner-generated contexts: A framework to support the effective use of technology for learning. In M. Lee & C. McLoughlin (Eds.), *Web 2.0-based e-learning: Applying social informatics for tertiary teaching* (pp. 70–84). Hershey, PA: IGI Global.

Mishra, P., Koehler, M. J., & Zhao, Y. (Eds.) (2007). *Faculty development by design: Integrating technology in higher education.* Charlotte, NC: Information Age Publishing.

Naismith, L., Lonsdale, P., Vavoula, G., & Sharples, M. (2004). *Literature review in mobile technologies and learning* (No. 11). Birmingham, UK: University of Birmingham.

Pachler, N., Bachmair, B., & Cook, J. (2010). *Mobile learning: Structures, agency, practices.* London: Springer.

Reeves, T. (2005). No significant differences revisited: A historical perspective on the research informing contemporary online learning. In G. Kearsley (Ed.), *Online learning: Personal reflections on the transformation of education* (pp. 299–308). Englewood Cliffs, NJ: Educational Technology Publications.

Reeves, T. (2009). *The application of "design research" to e-learning.* Paper presented at the the First International Conference for e-Learning and Distance Learning. Retrieved from: www.eli.elc.edu.sa/2009/content/Reeves [research].pdf

Reeves, T. (2011, July). Authentic tasks and collaborative group work: Key factors for effective e-learning. *Effective elearning in practice.* Retrieved from: http://unitube.otago.ac.nz/view?m=9WOR29G9iGC

Sharples, M. (2001). Disruptive devices: Mobile technology for conversational learning. *International Journal of Continuing Education and Lifelong Learning, 12*(5/6), 504–520.

Sharples, M., Taylor, J., & Vavoula, G. (2005, October). *Towards a theory of mobile learning.* Paper presented at mLearn 2005, Cape Town, South Africa.

Sharples, M., Taylor, J., & Vavoula, G. (2007). A theory of learning for the mobile age. In K. Littleton & P. Light (Eds.), *The Sage handbook of e-learning research* (pp. 221–247). London: Sage.

Traxler, J. (2007). Defining, discussing, and evaluating mobile learning: The moving finger writes and having writ . . . . *International Review of Research in Open and Distance Learning, 8*(2), 12.

Traxler, J. (2011). Introduction. In J. Traxler & J. Wishart (Eds.), *Making mobile learning work: Case studies of practice* (pp. 4–12). Bristol, UK: ESCalate, University of Bristol, Graduate School of Education.

Wali, E., Winters, N., & Oliver, M. (2008). Maintaining, changing and crossing contexts: An activity theoretic reinterpretation of mobile learning. *ALT-J, Research in Learning Technologies, 16*(1), 41–57.

Wenger, E. (1998). *Communities of practice: Learning, meaning, and identity.* Cambridge, UK: Cambridge University Press.

Wenger, E., White, N., & Smith, J. (2009). *Digital habitats: Stewarding technology for communities.* Portland, OR: CPsquare.

Wingkvist, A., & Ericsson, M. (2009). Current practice in mobile learning: A survey of research method and purpose. In D. Metcalf, A. Hamilton, & C. Graffeo (Eds.), *MLearn 2009: 8th World Conference on Mobile and Contextual Learning* (pp. 103–111). Orlando, FL: The University of Central Florida.

Withell, A., Cochrane, T., Reay, S., Gaziulusoy, I., & Inder, S. (2012). Augmenting the design thinking studio. In M. Brown (Ed.), *ascilite 2012: Future challenges, sustainable futures* (pp. in review). Wellington, New Zealand: ascilite.

23

FLIPPED CLASSROOM MEETS MOBILE LEARNING

Aaron J. Sams

The concept of the flipped classroom has recently garnered the attention of educators, lawmakers, the media, and the public. This is largely owing to the increased attention given to numerous educators who have adopted the model (Green, 2012; Toppo, 2011). The flipped-classroom concept also overlaps greatly with other educational frameworks, such as blended learning and m–learning. Essentially, a flipped classroom leverages technology and utilizes a time shift in which elements traditionally used in class are moved outside of class to meet the needs of students in their unique educational setting (Bennett et al., 2011). In its crudest form, a flipped classroom is aptly named because what has traditionally been done in class (direct instruction) is now done outside of the class, and what was traditionally done outside of class (homework assignments) is now done in class (Schaffhauser, 2009). In more complex forms, teachers direct students to instructional video content when needed, during various stages in complex learning cycles (Musallam, 2011). Most commonly, the flip occurs in the form of shifting the time at which direct instruction is given. Many teachers who flip their class remove the direct instruction from the class time and, instead, they record the instructional content and deliver it outside the class (Bergmann & Sams, 2011/2012). This is where m-learning and the flipped classroom merge. By leveraging this time shift, students gain control over the time and location where they will receive instruction, and the teacher recuperates valuable class time, in which deeper and more personalized learning can take place. The time shift is a commonality in all flipped classrooms, but an even more powerful flip occurs when the flipped-classroom model is adopted: the attention in the class is shifted away from the teacher and "flips" toward the students, creating a student-centered learning environment (Bennett et al., 2011).

The popularity of the flipped-classroom concept has not come without its detractors. The three most common criticisms of the flipped-classroom approach are: (1) the flipped-class model simply perpetuates bad teaching (lecturing) through new technology; (2) not all students have equitable access to technology, and the model therefore widens the divide between the privileged and the poor; and (3) many students do not have a stable life at home, nor do they necessarily have time at home to work on school assignments, and, therefore, homework should not be given, and a flipped classroom necessarily requires that some work be done outside of the classroom (Nielsen, 2011b; Socol, 2012). These concerns are largely a result of the media-created term "flipped classroom" (Pink, 2010). No teachers who flip their classes operate under the flipped-classroom moniker with the exclusive intent to change the time in which homework and classwork are given, but they do so to create a more student-centered classroom (Bennett et al., 2011; Bergmann & Sams, 2012). The three stated objections could be addressed and answered sufficiently by a right understanding of a good flipped classroom, viewed through the lens of the benefits of m-learning.

APPROACHING A FLIPPED CLASSROOM

The questions that all educators who are interested in m-learning and are considering a flipped classroom must consider are: (1) What can be removed from class time that can be better placed outside the classroom by leveraging technology, and, subsequently, what will be done with the recovered class time that will enhance the face-to-face interactions with students? (2) How can the focus and attention of the classroom be turned away from the teacher and toward the students, giving the students more control over their learning? (3) How can the legitimate concerns of those skeptical of a flipped-classroom approach with respect to lecturing, equitable access, and respect for the time of the students outside of the scheduled school day be addressed?

TARGET POPULATION

This article will address a flipped classroom as viewed in light of m-learning in a middle-school or high-school environment. Although many who teach using a flipped-classroom model do so in elementary and college settings, those settings fall outside the expertise of this author.

FLIPPED-CLASSROOM MODELS

Although not essential, one of the typical components of a flipped classroom is the utilization of video as an instructional tool (Bennett et al., 2011). The video is utilized as the primary means of delivering direct instruction to the students in a class, thereby leveraging a time shift in which the direct instruction is delivered outside the parameters of the class period. Students are directed to view the lesson outside of class, be that at home, before or after school, in the library, or during a study-hall period (Bergmann & Sams, 2011/2012). Class time is then free from the restraints of whole-class direct instruction, and the class time freed by the time shift is capitalized on by the teacher for increased student interaction and learning activities that focus on building the cognitive frameworks and understanding of the students (Musallam, 2010; Musallam, 2011).

Pre-Training Model

The video can be utilized throughout various places in the learning cycle. One model is the pre-training model, in which the video is used to provide background and to front-load the students with information about an upcoming lesson (Musallam, 2010). In using the pre-training method, the teacher is able to provide a cognitive framework for the student in the video—thereby reducing cognitive load to the student—on which they later further their understanding in class.

Inquiry Model

Another place within a learning cycle where the video can be used is in the middle of an inquiry cycle. The explore–flip–apply model, as proposed by Dr. Ramsey Musallam (2011), a science teacher in San Francisco, allows students to explore a topic in class and begin to construct their own knowledge about the topic. The video is then used to enhance the student understanding and, in doing so, helps fill any gaps and clear up any misconceptions. Finally, the students are asked to apply their learning to a new situation.

Flipped-Mastery Model

Yet another approach is the flipped-mastery model, as proposed by pioneers in the flipped-classroom model Jonathan Bergmann and Aaron Sams (Schaffhauser, 20009; Toppo, 2011), in which the videos are utilized by the student as needed during asynchronous learning. Here, the videos provide direct instruction to the students at the point in time when it is immediately relevant. As students progress through learning objectives, there often comes a point at which the student needs to learn about a particular topic, or how to perform a specific skill. By accessing the video at the point in time at which it is most appropriate, the student can move through a course of study at his/her own pace and progress once mastery of the topic is attained.

Project-Based Model

On the more experimental front is the hybridization of project-based learning (PBL) with a flipped-classroom approach. Under this model, students work on relevant projects that have been devised by each student or group of students, and the instructional videos are used as needed to study a topic necessary for completion of the project. For example, if a student is working in a chemistry course on a project relevant to chemistry, the student will inevitably need to know how to balance a chemical equation. Ideally, the student will determine that certain skills are necessary, or perhaps the teacher would recognize this deficiency in the student's understanding and direct the student toward the appropriate instructional video. Either way, the video is available as a resource to be used when appropriate to enhance student understanding and progression through this project.

IMPLEMENTING, SUSTAINING, AND DEFENDING A FLIPPED CLASSROOM

As proposed in the introduction, the flipped-classroom model can be effectively implemented through an m-learning approach by answering these three questions: (1) What can be removed from class that will enhance face-to-face time? (2) How can the focus of the classroom be turned away from the teacher and toward the students? (3) How can the concerns of skeptics be addressed?

The Big Question

What can be removed from class time that can be better placed outside the classroom by leveraging technology, and, subsequently, what will be done with the recovered class time that will enhance the face-to-face interactions with students? Teachers who implement the flipped-classroom approach usually answer this question by removing direct instruction and replacing the time with individualized attention to more students (Bergmann & Sams, 2011/2012, 2012). From the perspective of a practicing teacher, this time shift allows the teacher to spend more time doing what they likely got in to the teaching profession to do: help students. However, from an m-learning perspective, this time shift also hands over "the when and the where" the direct instruction will take place. The students have the power to view the instructional videos on their own time, in as many sittings as they deem necessary, and as many times as they want. Additionally, they have control of the pause and rewind buttons that allow them to access the instruction at their own pace. This component of a flipped classroom falls directly in line with the essence of m-learning.

The Role of the Video

How can the focus and attention of the classroom be turned away from the teacher and toward the students, giving the students more control over their learning? In addition to giving control of the when and where of learning to the student, a flipped classroom also gives control of the context of the learning to the student. In a traditional classroom, all students are doing the same activities at the same time, on the same day. This is done, in part, because of pacing calendars, teacher-created schedules, exam schedules, and material management. However, in a flipped classroom utilizing either the mastery model or a PBL model, the students are all working on different topics and projects at a flexible pace (Bergmann & Sams, 2012; Schaffhauser, 2009). Within these two scenarios, a student accesses instructional videos when ready to learn a particular topic. The videos are archived, tagged, and searchable for easy access, and the teacher also points the student to appropriate videos when needed. The video instruction can come in two possible forms: teacher-created videos or videos from the Internet at large. Both forms have advantages and disadvantages.

Teacher-Created Videos

Videos created by teachers are customized to the learning needs of their own students. The students hear their teacher's own voice, see their teacher's own (digital) handwriting, and see their teacher's own face. The students have a connection to the teacher during class that is extended to outside the class through the video. Although not every teacher will feel comfortable creating videos and distributing them online, it is preferable to create original content for a specific set of students (Bergmann & Sams, 2012).

Videos From the Internet at Large

If a teacher chooses not to create videos, other options exist. There are an increasing number of quality instructional videos online that can meet specific learning needs (Overmyer, 2010; Toppo, 2011). The role of the teacher in this situation moves away from video creator to video curator. In this situation, teachers are not responsible for producing videos, but they use their professional skills to find quality instructional videos for their students that meet individual learning needs. They do not simply direct students to YouTube; instead, they direct them to a few YouTube channels of specific teachers that they have vetted as quality video instructors. Not all instructional videos are created equal. Students who access instructional videos from the Internet may find a teacher with whom they resonate, but feedback from students indicates that videos created by their own teacher are preferable.

Dealing With Skeptics

How can the legitimate concerns of those skeptical of a flipped-classroom approach with respect to lecturing, equitable access, and respect for the time of the students outside of the scheduled school day be addressed? Three common objections to a flipped classroom can be addressed and answered sufficiently when viewed through the lens of the benefits of m-learning.

The Flipped-Class Model Simply Perpetuates Bad Teaching (Lecturing) Through New Technology

This objection is less of a critique of the flipped-classroom model than it is of lecturing in general. If the instructional videos are simply videos of lectures, then this concern is valid. However, the power of video as an instructional tool goes far beyond lecture captures. In addition to lectures, flipped-classroom videos can include demonstrations (Bergmann & Sams, 2012), video-story problems (Rimes, 2011), writing prompts, how-to instructions, summaries of project requirements, short tutorials, or anything else that would have traditionally been given to a whole class by the teacher in a face-to-face setting (Bennett et al., 2011). By creating videos to deliver any of the above scenarios, the teacher effectively primes the class for learning, so that class time can be used for individualized learning opportunities instead of content delivery, whole-class instruction, or large-group demonstrations.

Not All Students Have Equitable Access to Technology, and the Model Therefore Widens the Divide Between the Privileged and the Poor

Although equity is a very valid concern, the digital divide between the poor and the rich, the haves and the have-nots, the Luddite and the technophile is not insurmountable. If a teacher requires students to view instructional videos outside of class, equitable access to the videos by each student must be ensured. Many students will access the videos on an Internet-connected computer, a computer connected to a digital medium such as a data DVD or flash drive, mobile device connected to Wi-Fi or mobile network, or video DVD played on a home television (Bergmann & Sams, 2011/2012, 2012). Any student who cannot access the videos in one of these ways will need an individualized solution created by the teacher, parent, and student. Possible alternatives to relying on student-owned technology are writing grants to fund the acquisition of iPods to be checked out to students, giving a donated computer to the student with parent permission, or securing time in the school or public library for student computer use. Additionally, many schools are exploring one-to-one programs in which each student has his own computer to use during the course of the school year. Although none of these solutions will be applicable in every situation, most situations can be accommodated through one of these solutions, or a combination of a few of them.

Homework Should Never Be Given

Some educational commentators argue that homework should never be given under any circumstances, because of the inequity students face at home (Nielsen, 2011b; Socol, 2012). Although some students have a safe home to go to, not all students have this luxury. Many students go home to watch younger siblings while parents work, other students work themselves, and others do not leave school for a home but for a shelter instead. Homework-free-schooling advocates argue that asking students in these situations to do homework creates an inequitable educational setting and is inappropriate and should be avoided. Although the validity of homework is controversial, the concern is not universal. Teachers and schools in settings that do not accept homework need not be excluded from a flipped-classroom environment, nor from m-learning.

If a teacher is interested in adopting a flipped-classroom model and teaches in a community where homework is not acceptable, the class will necessarily need to be structured in such a way that all students have time to complete the work and have access to appropriate technology within the parameters of the class period. Again, this may be difficult, but it is not an insurmountable task. Many of the solutions addressed in the previous objection (one-to-one computing, donations, grants, etc.) can be applied to this objection as well, but, in this situation, the acquired technology is put into the classroom for student use instead of in the home for student use.

If a school is interested in adopting a flipped-classroom model and is in a community where homework is not acceptable, a school culture and climate must be created that are conducive to students completing all their work for school during the school day. Time must be provided for students to work independently and freely in an environment that has adequate technology that is equitably available to all students. If homework is not part of a school culture, the school must create an environment that gives all students ample time and opportunity to complete all required work. In an environment such as this, the "mobile" portion of m-learning becomes mobility within the confines of the school day. If students have completed all their work in one class, they must be allowed the mobility to move to an environment in which they can effectively complete their work for another.

Whose Technology?

Although many of the objections to homework stem from equity issues, other schools have adopted a no-homework policy for another reason, such as respect for family time together at home (Kohn, 2007). In cases where equity is not an issue, but respect for family time is, an option may be a solution that has come to be known as BYOD: bring your own device. In a school environment where students have access to their own personal-computing devices, they can be encouraged to bring them to school to reduce the resource strain put on the school by adopting a technology-intensive model of instruction, such as the flipped classroom. BYOD is controversial and is not universally accepted, but some classes and schools that have adopted BYOD report an increase in access to technology and Internet resources by students who do not have their own devices, because the burden of ownership is spread between the school and the families in the school, thus leaving more school-owned computing devices available for students who do not have their own device (Nielsen, 2011a). A school considering this model can move away from funding the perpetual purchasing of new PCs and focus that money on infrastructure and support that will allow students (and teachers, for that matter) to bring their own computers to school. Schools who have not yet wrestled with this issue need to consider the possibility that the students who have their own devices likely have a device that is more up to date, faster, and more powerful than the antiquated and aging computers sitting down in the computer lab. Tapping into this resource not only relieves the funding strain on the school and gives students the ability to work on a better machine, it also taps into the mobility of devices that having a fixed lab location does not. Students may not have access to a 24/7 learning environment, but they do have control over the when and where of learning within the school day. One imperative placed on a school with a BYOD policy is ensuring that students who do not have their own device are provided with one. Although this could seem daunting, the school will only be outfitting classrooms with a limited number of computers, instead of providing a computer for each student. Schools who require students to wear uniforms face a similar challenge that can equally be overcome. Students who cannot afford the uniform must be provided one by the school. This has not dissuaded schools from adopting a uniform policy, if they believe the uniform will create a more effective learning environment. In the same manner, schools that desire a BYOD policy need not reject it because some cannot bring their own tech; they must evaluate whether or not the cost of providing the appropriate tools for those who cannot afford it is worth the systemic change caused by the BYOD policy.

UNIQUE QUALITIES

Teachers who implement a flipped classroom will quickly find that their classes operate differently. Students become self-directed learners, and management of the classroom is no longer one teacher attempting to have 30 students do the same thing at the same time, in an orderly manner (Bergmann & Sams, 2012). The class becomes more student-centered and less teacher-focused. Although the typical understanding of a flipped classroom is a time shift of content delivery, the more powerful shift seen in a flipped class is the shift in power and control over learning from the teacher to the students. This shift could come as a surprise to an administrator or teaching coach who expects uniformity and teacher control in the classroom, but, hopefully, the administrator will notice the engaged students learning, and the active teacher mentoring and guiding the students as needed.

RESPONSES TO A FLIPPED CLASSROOM

Student, Parent, School, Community, and Worldwide Response
Several personal anecdotes based on responses I have received from my own students, parents, community members, and the global community demonstrate the success and growth of the flipped-classroom model.

Student Response
After 6 years of experimenting with a flipped-classroom model of instruction, I am happy to report that most students like it, and only a few dislike it. The students who appreciate the model the most are those who have struggled to "play school," and those who dislike the model are those who traditionally "play school" well (Bergmann & Sams, 2012). The appreciative students have thanked me for the flipped class because I gave control of the learning to the students. Those who are less appreciative resent the fact that they have spent the majority of their lives learning the rules of the "game of school," and I changed the rules on them. Other schools using the flipped-classroom concept report

a decrease in failure rates and increased student engagement (Green, 2012). Some students are still motivated only by grades and not by an intrinsic desire to learn. A flipped classroom helps transition students from this mindset, some more reluctantly than others. The students who like the model the most are the very busy students who appreciate the flexibility it gives to them (Bergmann & Sams, 2012). They decide when and where they learn; they can pause and rewind their instructors; they can choose to work ahead, or take a break and catch up later, with minimal consequence.

Parent Response

Most parents I have spoken with do not understand the flipped-class concept at first. It is much different than any instructional model they have been exposed to or have experienced during their time in school. Once parents do understand, they love the fact that the model is so student-centered. Occasionally, I encounter the skeptical parent who claims that their student cannot learn from a video, but, when I explain that the videos are optional and we determine what is best for that student, the concern is usually dropped.

Community Response

Unfortunately, I get little feedback from my community about the instructional model. Occasionally, I do meet a community member at a youth soccer game or swimming lesson who has seen an article in the local paper (McMillin, 2010) or a clip on local news about the work I have done in my school. Generally, the ensuing conversations have been positive, and the individual is interested in talking more about the flipped-classroom concept, thanks me for what I have done, and often punctuates the conversation with a quip about how they wish they had experienced a class like this when they were in school.

Worldwide Response

The response around the world continues to grow. In 2011, I spoke at an education conference in Norway, and in 2012 I gave a presentation at a university in Germany. I also have helped coordinate a worldwide flipped-class open house, in which teachers across the globe volunteered to open up the doors to their classes and invited anyone to come observe a flipped classroom in action. The event brought educators into flipped classrooms in 30 cities, in 20 states and three countries. I have also had the opportunity to train educators from across the globe in the flipped-class model at my own conference that I host every summer.

CONCLUSION

M-learning has the potential to give more control to students as they take ownership of their learning. Educators in traditional brick-and-mortar schools can tap in to the flexibility of m-learning and hand over the reins of education to students by implementing a flipped classroom. Flipping a classroom can be done equitably and in a way that meets the individual learning needs of students.

REFERENCES

Bennett, B. E., Spencer, D., Bergmann, J., Cockrum, T., Musallam, R., Sams, A., Fisch, K., & Overmyer, J. (2011). The flipped class manifest. *The Daily Riff*. Retrieved from: www.thedailyriff.com/articles/the-flipped-class-manifest-823.php

Bergmann, J., & Sams, A. (2011/2012). Remixing chemistry class. *Learning & Leading With Technology, 36*(4), 24–29.

Bergmann, J., & Sams, A. (2012). *Flip your classroom: Reach every student in every class every day*. Washington, DC: ISTE.

Green, G. (2012, January). *My view: Flipped classrooms give every student a chance to succeed* [Web log]. Retrieved from: http://schoolsofthought.blogs.cnn.com/2012/01/18/my-view-flipped-classrooms-give-every-student-a-chance-to-succeed/

Kohn, A. (2007, January/February). Rethinking homework. *Principal*. Retrieved from: http://www.alfiekohn.org/teaching/rethinkinghomework.htm

McMillin, S. (2010). Woodland Park science teacher wins presidential award. *The Gazette: Colorado Springs*. Retrieved from: http://www.gazette.com/articles/teacher-100182-science-park.html

Musallam, R. (2010). *The effects of using screencasting as a multimedia pretraining tool to manage the intrinsic cognitive load of chemical equilibrium instruction for advanced high school chemistry students*. Unpublished doctoral dissertation, The University of San Francisco, San Francisco, CA. Retrieved from: http://flipteaching.com/resources/Dissertation_Musallam.pdf

Musallam, R. (2011). Should you flip your classroom? *Edutopia*. Retrieved from: http://www.edutopia.org/blog/flipped-classroom-ramseymusallam

Nielsen, L. (2011a). 7 myths about BYOD debunked. *T.H.E. Journal*. Retrieved from: http://thejournal.com/articles/2011/11/09/7-byod-myths.aspx

Nielsen, L. (2011b). *Five reasons I'm not flipping over the flipped classroom* [Web log]. Retrieved from: http://the innovativeeducator.blogspot.com/2011/10/five-reasons-im-not-flipping-over.html

Overmyer, G. R. (2010). *History and effectiveness of mastery learning in mathematics: From B.F. Skinner to the Internet* [Unpublished article]. Colorado State University, Fort Collins, CO. Retrieved from: http://api.ning.com/files/qfafTtfmGD4DQQVPavHjslHPF4IZdOM0Nro8rJxdaHIiCnLaFUR97yX-qfRAuprYzSuidtLCOtlYPNfK2dwhNK1nc77qOAv9/HistoryofMasteryLearning.pdf

Pink, D. (2010). Think tank: Flip-thinking—the new buzz word sweeping the US. *The Telegraph*. Retrieved from: www.telegraph.co.uk/finance/businessclub/7996379/Daniel-Pinks-Think-Tank-Flip-thinking-the-new-buzz-word-sweeping-the-US.html

Rimes, B. (2011). *Come join the video story problems channel* [Web log]. Retrieved from: www.techsavvyed.net/archives/1931

Schaffhauser, D. (2009). The vod couple. *T.H.E. Journal*. Retrieved from: http://thejournal.com/articles/2009/08/09/vodcasting.aspx?sc_lang=en

Socol, I. D. (2012). Changing gears 2012: Rejecting the "flip" [Web log]. Retrieved from: http://speedchange.blogspot.com/2012/01/changing-gears-2012-rejecting-flip.html

Toppo, G. (2011). "Flipped" classrooms take advantage of technology. *USA TODAY*. Retrieved from: www.usatoday.com/news/education/story/2011–10–06/flipped-classrooms-virtual-teaching/50681482/1

24

TEAM AND COMMUNITY BUILDING USING MOBILE DEVICES

Jackie Gerstein

People in the 21st century are using their own mobile devices—iPads, netbooks, laptops, and smartphones—to be consumers and producers of digital content, and to be active participants in online communities. They are connecting with one another through mobile technologies in unprecedented ways. Computers, Wi-Fi networks, and smartphones allow young people 24/7 access to technology and to one another. They are familiar and comfortable with social networking and using a variety of apps via their devices. Nielson (2010), in a survey of teen mobile-device use, reported that 94 percent of teen users identified themselves as advanced data users, turning to their mobile devices for messaging, Internet, multimedia, gaming, and other activities such as downloads.

When educators leverage these types of informal learning by giving agency to the students to use their mobile technologies and by providing the structure and skills for their use within more formal educational settings, motivation and learning are increased. Using mobile devices in educational settings as learning and community-building tools can promote interpersonal communication, encourage young people to positively express their individuality, and build their student-to-student, and student-to-educator relationships. The strategic and intentional use of cell phones, social-networking sites, laptops, blogs, and digital cameras can build diversity and cultural sensitivity, teamwork and problem-solving, self-reflection and self-exploration, and communication and self-expression.

This chapter introduces the use of mobile devices as a means to build community and teamwork within a variety of classroom settings: face-to-face, blended, and virtually. This discussion has four components: research that supports the use of student-owned mobile devices for building community in the classroom, evidence to support the importance of promoting community in the classroom, team-building activities using mobile devices, and the results of a end-of-course student survey about using mobile devices for community building.

BUILDING COMMUNITY IN THE CLASSROOM

Most classes, beginning around middle school and continuing through college, begin with reviewing the content to be covered, expectations regarding grades, and other academic information provided by the teacher or instructor. The human or social element is often disregarded. Most students enter the classroom wondering who is in their class. They want to know about the teacher and the people in the class, not what material is to be covered. This is supported by brain research that indicates that brain/mind is social, that learning is social (Caine & Caine, n.d.). Learning should begin with a social connection—between the educator and the learners, and between the learners themselves.

In this section, four separate but interconnected 21st-century trends are presented to support the importance of building a learning community and developing team-building skills as part of one's educational experience.

Benefits of Community Building in the Classroom

The importance of building a sense of community in the classroom cannot be understated or overlooked. Schaps (2003) in her *Educational Leadership* article, "Creating Caring Schools," discussed some of the benefits, based on research, of building a sense of community in the classroom:

> A growing body of research confirms the benefits of building a sense of community in school. Students in schools with a strong sense of community are more likely to be academically motivated . . . to act ethically and altruistically . . . to develop social and emotional competencies . . . and to avoid a number of problem behaviors, including drug use and violence.
>
> (Schaps, 2003, p. 31)

When a sense of community is promoted in the classroom setting, learning and achievement are enhanced. Vesely, Bloom, and Sherlock (2007) noted in their literature review that research has clearly shown that functioning in a community can enhance the learning that occurs among the learners. Woods and Ebersole (2003) assert that optimal learning outcomes are "directly tied to the establishment of social networks among participants engaged in a collaborative learning enterprise" (para. 1). In other words, desirable learning outcomes have a greater chance of being actualized when students feel they are engaged in a common purpose, when they feel they are part of a larger community of learners.

In their report, *Schools as Caring, Learning Communities. A Center Practice Brief,* California University researchers (2006) also give credence to the value of community building in the classroom. There appears to be significant relationships between classroom climate, student engagement, behavior, self-efficacy, achievement, and social and emotional development. Research also suggested that these effects of a positive classroom climate may be greater on students from low-income homes and groups that often are discriminated against (California University, 2006).

These benefits are not only applicable to face-to-face classroom environments, but are also relevant to virtual learning. The advances in technology in recent years have enabled learning communities to transcend physical space. The ubiquitous nature of today's technologies provides unique opportunities for individuals from all over the world to participate in online-learning communities, anytime and anywhere.

The sense of community in online settings does not come naturally. Online-course designers and educators need to be proactive in building a connected learning community, but the results can be similar to those found in face-to-face classrooms. Brown (2001) believes that, when distance learners feel a sense of community within the virtual learning environment, this emotional connectedness provides the support needed for them to successfully complete a class or a program. LaRose and Whitten (2000) found a significant relationship between students' perceived sense of community and the achievement of learning outcomes in online courses.

In essence, building community and facilitating a sense of affiliation within any learning environment, face-to-face or virtual, increase the potential of student success. Research suggests that a sense of community can be encouraged through: (1) actively cultivating respectful, supportive relationships among students and teachers; (2) emphasizing common purposes and ideals; (3) providing regular opportunities for cooperation and collaboration; and (4) providing developmentally appropriate opportunities for autonomy and influence regarding the classroom operations (Schap, 2003).

Community building should be emphasized, not just for the sense of togetherness it provides students, but because it also helps keep the students in the class, promotes full engagement in the class activities, facilitates effective collaborative learning, and encourages continued communication after the course or program is complete (Brown, 2001). The development of community should be an intentional goal when designing class activities—both in online and face-to-face learning environments.

Characteristics of the Millennials and iGeneration

An underlying foundation of this chapter is the importance of bringing the devices, methods, and strategies that learners are using in their personal lives for informal community building and learning into the more formal educational setting. According to a report disseminated by the Austrian Institute for Applied Telecommunications (2010), young people are emotionally attached to their mobile devices. Mobile devices act as a means of personal communication, of maintaining networks and friendships, and of expressing thoughts and feelings.

The use of mobile devices has created a means for informal learning and a desire on the part of young people to learn in social settings. Research supports that today's students, mostly Millennials (born between the early 1980s and 2000) and the iGeneration (2000 to the present) prefer to learn in groups. Based on this research, some of the recommendations for teaching millennial students include the following:

1. Millennials like to work collaboratively with their peers to enhance their own learning. As working with others can strengthen the learning experience for all students, educational activities should be designed that teach and facilitate cooperative and community-based learning.
2. Millennials prefer hands-on, active learning. Active learning strategies such as discussions, group projects, and cooperative problem-solving can deepen students' understanding of the content areas and their ability to apply new ideas. As Millennials have a group orientation, they should enjoy and benefit from active, cooperative-based learning opportunities (Wilson, 2004).

The tendency for collaborative interactions within social-networking sites and informal learning environments has grown even more for the iGeneration. As Rosen (2009) notes, this generation is primed for cooperative learning, owing to their types of electronic communication:

> Educational models must consider social networks as a valuable source for enhancing student interest and participation in the classroom. The kids are there in droves. The trick is to leverage their love of social networks to create educational tools built around them.
>
> (Rosen, 2009, p. 49)

Collaboration as a 21st-Century Skill

Young people are using their mobile devices to communicate and develop social skills, skills that have been identified as important for 21st-century living, learning, and working. Communication and collaboration form one set of learning and innovation skills identified by the Partnership for 21st Century Skills. The Partnership for 21st Century Skills is a national organization that advocates for 21st-century readiness for every student. One category of skills is the learning and innovation skills. These are skills that assist students in being prepared for increasingly complex life and work environments in the 21st century. Among these are communication and collaboration skills. The specific skills in this category that are directly related to the skills acquired through community-building activities within the learning environment include:

1. *Communicate clearly* (Partnership for 21st Century Skills, n.d., para. 1):
   - Listen effectively to decipher meaning, including knowledge, values, attitudes, and intentions.
   - Use communication for a range of purposes (e.g., to inform, instruct, motivate, and persuade).
   - Utilize multiple media and technologies, and know how to judge their effectiveness a priori as well as assess their impact.
   - Communicate effectively in diverse environments.
2. *Collaborate with others* (Partnership for 21st Century Skills, n.d., para. 2):
   - Demonstrate the ability to work effectively and respectfully with diverse teams.
   - Exercise flexibility and willingness to be helpful in making necessary compromises to accomplish a common goal.
   - Assume shared responsibility for collaborative work, and value the individual contributions made by each team member.

Future Work Skills

In addition to promoting 21st-century learning skills, another reason for promoting community building in the classroom is that it assists students in developing skills that have been identified as important for functioning in the future workforce. The Institute for the Future, an independent, nonprofit research group, released a report, *Future Work Skills 2020*. The report identified the key skills that will be needed in the workplace over the next 10 years (Davies, Fidler, & Gorbis, 2011).

Two of the 10 identified future skills in the report have a direct connection to the skills related to learning in a community, especially when mobile devices are used to do so.

1. *Social intelligence*: Social intelligence is the ability to connect to others in a deep and direct way, to sense and stimulate reactions and desired interactions. "This has always been a key skill for workers who need to collaborate and build relationships of trust, but it is even more important as we are called on to collaborate with larger groups of people in different settings" (Davies et al., 2011, p. 8).
2. *Virtual collaboration*: Virtual collaboration is the ability to work productively, drive engagement, and demonstrate presence as a member of a virtual team. "Online streams created by micro blogging and social networking sites can serve as virtual water coolers, providing a sense of camaraderie and enabling employees to demonstrate presence" (Davies et al., 2011, p. 12).

The report concludes with some implications and recommendations for educational institutions to prepare elementary-through-graduate-school students for the future workforce. One of the recommendations is to include in the classroom "experiential learning that gives prominence to soft skills—such as the ability to collaborate, work in groups, read social cues, and respond adaptively" (Davies et al., 2011, p. 13).

MOBILE-DEVICE-USE PATTERNS SUPPORT COMMUNITY BUILDING

People of all ages, almost from all parts of the world, are using their mobile devices to communicate, connect, and share personal experiences. They are building their own informal learning and social communities via their mobile devices and social-networking sites. This section discusses the research about mobile-device-use patterns. It becomes the foundation, not only for providing a rationale for the use of mobile devices in the classroom, but also serving as a guide for the types of technology and activity that are best suited for mobile-driven community-building activities.

Mobile-Phone Ownership and Use Patterns Among U.S. Teens

A Pew Research report entitled, *Teens and Mobile Phones*, released April 2010, noted that, as of September 2009, 75 percent of American teens aged 12–17 own a cell phone. This number has steadily increased from 45 percent of teens in November 2004. Cell phones have become ubiquitous in the lives of teens today, with ownership cutting across demographic groups and geographical locations.

As expected, texting was the top activity of cell-phone-using teens, with taking and sharing pictures, playing music, and recording and exchanging videos also being popular uses (see Figure 24.1).

Worldwide Use of Cell Phones

Mobile-device use has become a worldwide phenomenon, allowing informal learning and social networking to cross over geographical divides. Pew Research (2011) released a report entitled *Texting, Social Networking Popular Worldwide*. The three key findings from this report that support mobile-driven community-building activities are:

1. Cell phones are owned and used throughout the world.
2. Cell phones are being used for texting, taking photos, and using the Internet. Cell phones are owned by large majorities of people in most major countries around

The % of teen cell phone owners who have used the following functions on their cell phones

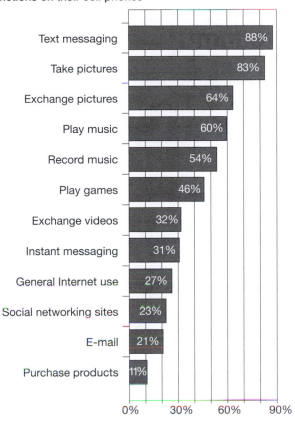

Figure 24.1 Cell-Phone-Use Patterns of Teens

Source: Pew Research Center's Internet and American Life Project, Teens and Mobile Phone Survey conducted from June 6 to September 24, 2009. n=625 teen cell phone owners ages 12–17 and the margin of error is ±5%

On your cell phone, do you regularly ...*

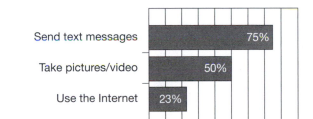

*Asked only of those who say they own a cell phone.
Based on median % across the 21 nations where 2011 data is available.

Figure 24.2 Texting Around the Globe

Source: Pew Research Center Q70b–d

Table 24.1 Cell-Phone Usage

	% Saying They Own a Cell Phone	On your cell phone, do you regularly . . .*			
		Make Phone Calls? %	Send Text Messages? %	Take Pictures or Video? %	Use the Internet? %
US	85	96	67	57	43
Spain	96	98	70	59	21
Britain	89	87	79	54	38
Germany	88	82	56	27	18
France	85	95	77	51	28
Lithuania	91	99	79	47	24
Russia	86	99	75	50	27
Ukraine	84	100	72	48	19
Poland	78	99	85	56	30
Turkey	84	97	64	44	22
Jordan	95	94	63	44	22
Israel	95	99	73	57	47
Lebanon	79	100	87	33	19
Egypt	71	98	72	58	15
China	93	99	80	54	37
Japan	86	98	81	72	47
Indonesia	55	96	96	38	22
India	53	98	49	26	10
Pakistan	48	97	44	9	6
Mexico	57	89	82	61	18
Kenya	74	100	89	31	29
Median	85	98	75	50	23

*Asked only of those who say they own a cell phone.
Source: Pew Research Center, Q68 & Q70a–d, Pew Research, 2011.

the world. They are used for much more than just phone calls. In particular, text messaging is a global phenomenon—across the 21 countries surveyed, a median of 75 percent of cell-phone owners say they text.

3. Young people worldwide are likely to use their cell phones for social networking (Pew Research, 2011).

The usage is similar to that seen with U.S. teens. Text messaging is prevalent in 19 of 21 countries, with a majority of cell-phone owners regularly sending text messages. Many also use their cell-phones to take pictures and record video (Pew Research, 2011).

Mobile-device use crosses socioeconomic boundaries and geographic locations. People are using them for texting, photo sharing, and other forms of social networking. In other words, people are already using mobile devices to build their own informal learning and sharing communities, and so it becomes a natural progression and extension to bring this type of learning into the educational environment.

TEAM-BUILDING ACTIVITIES USING MOBILE DEVICES

As has been the theme throughout this chapter, in order for mobile-driven team-building activities to be effective, it is best to leverage the ways people are using their cell phones in their own lives. In this way, the focus can be on the community-building activities, as opposed to teaching the technologies driving the activities. As was discussed in previous sections of this chapter, texting, photo taking and sharing, and social networking are the primary and most common mobile-device-use functions. These are the major types of technology used for the team-building activities described below. This section discusses some of the challenges and recommendations associated with mobile-device-driven community-building activities, guidelines for implementation, and sample mobile-driven activities that can be used for community-building.

Challenges and Recommendations for Using Mobile Devices

Using mobile devices for community-building presents some unique challenges. Suggestions and recommendations when designing and choosing the technology-driven team building activities include the following:

The learning activities need to be designed with the students' devices in mind. Students' technologies need to be able to do what is needed to complete the learning activities. Slow connections, dropped calls, and inadequate equipment can lead to frustration and anger and override the goals of the activities (Abrams, Scannell, & Mulvihill, 2011).

Devices need to possess the functions to complete the activity. The participants need to own devices that have the capabilities to access the technologies needed to complete the activities. The ability to download and use apps is specific to some, not all, mobile devices/smartphones. This is currently being discussed as the App Gap. See Edutopia's *Should We Be Concerned About an "App Gap"?* (www.edutopia.org/blog/app-gap-digital-divide-audrey-watters). It is best to design activities that use more universal cell-phone functions such as texting, photo taking, e-mailing, and video, so all participants can complete the activities with the devices they own.

Activity selection should be based on participant skills. Learners need to possess necessary skills and be comfortable using the different types of technology for the mobile-driven team-building activities (Abrams et al., 2011). Training might have to be provided on how to use the different technologies, but the learning of the technologies should not become the focus of the activities. Basic technologies and skills, however, can be the foundation for introducing other related technologies. For example, most students know how to text. It then becomes easy to introduce text-based games and services.

Proven technologies should be used. Mobile device functions, apps, and Web 2.0 tools should be selected that have been around for a while and have a good track record. Trying out and testing the newest, just-released app or service for the first time during the team-building activity may lead to unforeseen problems.

Any technologies selected for the activities need to be easy to use/easy to learn. If possible and plausible, students could be given a list of mobile-device functions and any apps or Web 2.0 tools that are going to be used, prior to or during the first meeting. Students could be encouraged to learn and practice using the technologies (Abrams et al., 2011).

The technologies and activities need to be appropriate for the group. It's important to choose team-building tools that match the way class members naturally prefer to communicate. Some members may like communicating by phone, face time or Skype, whereas others prefer e-mail, texting, or instant messaging. They also may have preferred mobile devices. They may own portable laptops and netbooks and prefer to use those. A survey of members can be taken of member preferences, and activities can be adapted to match these preferences.

Privacy and security need to be considered. Because of laws related to privacy in educational settings (see the Children's Online Protection Act for more details), the educator needs to be aware of the terms of service for any technology used, as well as to follow the acceptable-use policies for that organization where the activities are being implemented. For more information, see the Consortium for School Networking article, *Acceptable Use Policies in the Web 2.0 and Mobile Era* (www.cosn.org/Default.aspx?TabId= 8139), which provides some good information about these policies.

Guidelines for Implementation in Face-to-Face and Blended Settings

Face-to-face settings have some unique challenges that should be flushed out prior to the implementation of mobile-driven team-building activities. Many of the face-to-face community-building activities ask for class members to get into smaller groups. Strategies can be based on the following:

1. Some classes (especially those with students who have grown up with cell phones and who access them throughout the day) may need to have a device-down policy. This is because they can easily become distracted with their devices in hand— checking for text messages or Facebook status. The educator may have to implement a policy of asking students to put devices down during instructional time where the devices aren't needed or required.
2. The educator should stress to the class members that patience and perseverance come with the use of technology. The educator needs to learn to troubleshoot and problem-solve with members when the technologies do not worked as desired, and have back-up plans if all else fails.
3. If photos of class members are to be taken and used on social websites, e.g., Flickr or Facebook, photo releases need to be obtained. This applies for all age groups, but, with minors, parent permission is required. It should be emphasized that the right to privacy is just that—a right, and that the rights of any member who does not want his or her photo posted will be respected.
4. Some of the activities ask for the formation of smaller groups. Grouping strategies can be based on the following:
   (a) It may help to group participants by the devices that they own. Having at least one smartphone in the group can be beneficial if the facilitator wants to use some apps in the team-building activities. Some smartphones also have better photo and video taking and uploading capabilities.
   (b) If possible, each group should contain one or more members who are comfortable with and have expertise in mobile technologies. They can assist other members when they run into problems using the technologies. This process reinforces that the group is a learning community.

Example Team- and Community-Building Activities

What follows are some example community-building activities. They rely mostly on texting, e-mailing, and photo- and video-taking activities. Free, group-sharing Internet sites are also used that require access to the Internet via a smartphone or computer. Sites such as Flickr Photo Sharing, Facebook, Google Docs, and Web 2.0 tools supplement some of the activities.

Activity 1: Cell Sharing

- Goal: To connect with other members through sharing of personal artifacts. It is a good introductory activity.
- Procedures:
  1. Ask participants to locate a photo, song, or video from their mobile device that best represents them.
  2. Each person then shares with the group his or her media selection and the reason it was selected.
  3. For photo or video sharing: Ask students to pass the device around so all students can view the image, or use a webcam to project the image onto a larger computer screen or whiteboard.
  4. For sharing of music: Attach portable speakers to assist with the sharing of songs so others can hear them.
- Adaptation for virtual classes and teams:
  - Set up a Wiki or a group Facebook page and ask members to join. Request that members post a favorite picture, YouTube video, and/or a link to piece of meaningful music. (Note: This adaptation requires the use of a smart mobile device or a computer.)
- Student reflection:

I thought it was awesome that you wanted everyone to show the class a picture or type of music that had meaning to us. By doing this we got to see and learn a little bit more of our peers.

(20-year-old undergraduate on an interpersonal-relationships course)

Figure 24.3 Examples of Student Cell Sharing

Activity Two: Texting Interviews

- Goal: To get to know another group member and to report to the rest of the group what was learned.
- Procedures:
  1. Designed for virtual or face-to-face students to use at the beginning of the class or program.
  2. Randomly pair students (can be either face to face or virtually).
  3. Ask them to exchange contact information (e-mail or phone numbers).
  4. Explain that their task is to interview each other by developing questions that they would ask to help them get to know someone better, and texting or e-mailing their questions and answers back and forth.
  5. Interviewers summarize what they found out about their partners by posting the partner's name, the question asked, and the response received on a sticky-note board such as Wallwisher. This way all the members can learn about one another.
- Follow-up: Encourage the paired members to use one another for support during the class or program.
- Student reflection:

I enjoyed the texting exercise. It's pretty cool when your teacher lets you use your phone for the activities especially since I got to learn more about my partner.

(17-year-old undergraduate on an interpersonal-relationships course)

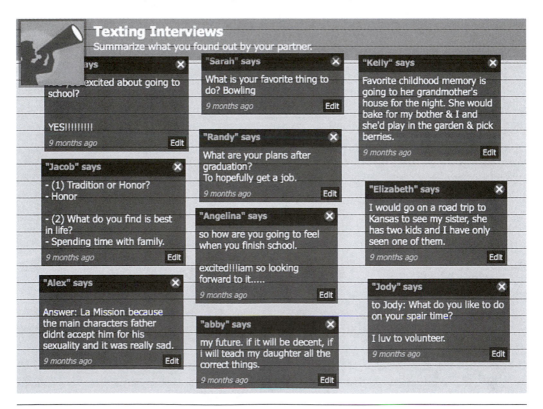

Figure 24.4 Wallwisher of Student Responses from Texting Interviews

Activity 3: Values Photos

- Goal: To learn about one another's values.
- Procedures:
  1. Can be used with either virtual or face-to-face students.
  2. Ask participants to choose their three top values. They can be provided with a list of values such as the list found at www.stevepavlina.com/articles/list-of-values.htm
  3. Give participants the task to locate objects in their environment that symbolize these values and take a photo using their mobile devices.
  4. Instruct students to e-mail their photos to a Flickr account set up for this purpose. Students do not need to have an account on Flickr to do so. The steps to set this up are as follows:
     (a) Set up an account on Flickr (www.flickr.com/)
     (b) Photos can then be e-mailed directly to this Flickr account. "You can upload photos to Flickr from your camera using your unique e-mail upload address. When you upload photos via e-mail, the subject line is used as the title of your photo, and the body of the e-mail is used as the description" (www.flickr.com/help/mobile/).
  5. Provide students with the e-mail address to send their photos to Flickr along with the instructions to put the name of their value in the subject line and why they selected that value in the description.

Teamwork
Click here to add a description

ⓒ ☐ Anyone can see this photo (edit)
Uploaded on Apr 12, 2012 | Delete
2 views / 0 comments

Electricity
Without this my laptop would die.

ⓒ ☐ Anyone can see this photo (edit)
Uploaded on Apr 12, 2012 | Delete
3 views / 0 comments

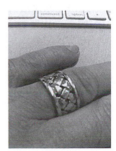

Making a difference
Rescuing dogs from the euthanasia list and urging others to adopt and not shop makes a difference!

ⓒ ☐ Anyone can see this photo (edit)
Uploaded on Apr 12, 2012 | Delete
2 views / 0 comments

No Calendar Worship
People Are More Important Than Deadlines.
Don't worship your planner / deadlines.

ⓒ ☐ Anyone can see this photo (edit)

FAMILY
Tap here to add sub caption.

Motivational Poster

Devotion / Love

Figure 24.5 Flickr Page of Values Photos With Captions

6. As all the group's images will be sent to this single Flickr account, members can view each others' via an account link provided to them, if a virtual class-room, or through the website projected on a screen if in a face-to-face setting.

Activity 4: What Do We Have in Common

- Goal: To assist members in discovering the commonalities among them.
- Procedures:
  1. Pair group members and ask them to exchange phone numbers.
  2. Request that they pass texts back and forth until they come up with four commonalities
  3. Two pairs are then formed, and they need to communicate with one another to discover four commonalities among the four of them.
  4. Ask each group to text their final four to the facilitator, who posts these.

Activity 5: Build a Bridge

- Goal: To explore teamwork, communication, and creative problem-solving.
- Procedures:
  1. This activity is designed for face-to-face environments.
  2. Spilt the group into two to four and give each group the same exact building supplies. Tinker Toys work well for this. Take the groups to separate locations so they have no visual or direct verbal access to one another.
  3. Ask the group to assign a communicator, someone who communicates with the other groups using his or her mobile device.
  4. Give them the instruction that they are to create three structures that look exactly alike and, to do so, they need to communicate with the other groups via their mobile devices. This can be done either through voice or texting, but no images can be sent. The communicator can only convey instructions and cannot be involved in the actual hands-on building of the structure
  5. Once the groups believe that they have completed the task, tell them that they can send pictures of their structure to the other groups for a final confirmation (see Figure 24.6).
  6. Bring the groups back together to have them compare their structures.
- Student reflection:

The most significant learning would be the "building the bridge" because that was fun to be able to know who would take charge and everything you said over the phone about what your team was building with the blocks would affect how their bridge would look. I had to be very precise and accurate, nearly perfect in order to get them to build it the same. Something I am going to improve on is the clarity of how I talk.

(19-year-old undergraduate on an interpersonal-relationships course)

Activity 6: Peer Feedback

- Goal: To provide a forum to allow participants to give feedback to one another.
- Option 1—texting or Facebooking feedback: This activity is designed for small working groups within the larger class or group to provide quick feedback.

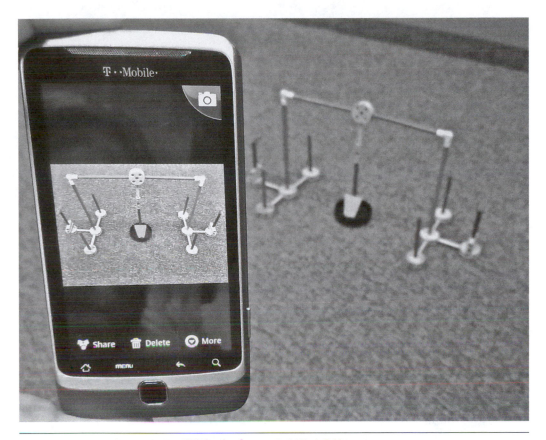

Figure 24.6 Students Communicating With Another Group to Build Their Bridges

- Procedures:
  1. If this hasn't already occurred, ask members of a smaller working group to exchange phone numbers and/or to friend one another on Facebook (this is determined by individual needs and preferences).
  2. After a small-group activity, instruct members to text or post on "friends'" Facebook page three adjectives that describes each other's performance during the group activity.
- Option 2—peer feedback through a group texting service: This activity is designed to provide real-time feedback via a texting service about a member's performance of a skill. It is designed for face-to-face learning environments.
  1. Ask members to join a group texting service such as Celly or Wiffitti.
  2. Request that they jot down notes about a student's performance during some skill-based activity—giving a speech, interviewing, performing a mechanical operation.
  3. Following the performance, ask members to text feedback about the performance to the texting service selected. Instruct them to use the first name only of the student getting the feedback, along with the feedback.
  4. These results can be projected onto a whiteboard for the entire group to see and discuss.

Figure 24.7 Interview Feedback Texted Through Celly

These, as well as other activities, can be viewed at http://community-building. weebly.com/

Some Evidence: End-of-Course Survey

The use of mobile devices to build community is new territory. To start preliminary discussion and research, this author examined how mobile devices facilitate community building by giving an end-of-course survey to students on an interpersonal-relationships undergraduate course that integrated mobile devices for team building. The two sections of the interpersonal-relationships course were offered during fall 2011 and early winter 2012. There were 20 students in the sections—8 were male, 12 female; 16 of the students were 17–20 years old, 1 was a 25-year-old male, another a 40-year-old female, and 2 of the students were females in their 50s. All of them owned some type of mobile device. No two of the owned devices were of the same make or model. At the end of the course, they were asked to answer a series of open-ended questions, using Survey Monkey to keep responses anonymous.

When they were asked if they felt that using students' mobile phones during class time was a good idea, there was an overwhelmingly positive response to mobile-device use in the class. A few problems were noted, but no students reported a purely negative response to their use. The reasons stated for positive feelings about mobile-device use seemed to revolve around three themes:

1. Technology is part of today's world.
2. It made the activities more engaging and interesting.
3. It provided the means for learning to be more personal.

When asked to describe the greatest advantage of using students' mobile phones to get to know one another and build a sense of community in the class, the student responses centered around the social nature of mobile devices adding to their feelings of getting to know one another. Several students mentioned that it provided them with a forum to open up with other students.

Based on student testimonials through both the survey and their end-of-course reflection paper, the following two themes emerged: students appreciated the use of mobile devices and believed they helped to increase their engagement, and students appreciated and learned best through the use of experiential and hands-on activities.

CONCLUSION

Using students' own personal devices in the classroom for community building makes good sense for several reasons: (1) they provide access for students across socioeconomic levels and geographical locations, making it viable for implementation, and (2) they lend themselves to being a natural and powerful team-building tool owing to the personalization and connection that people have to their own mobile devices. The recommendation is for educators to use the information and activities provided in this chapter as a rationale and as examples as to how they can incorporate their own mobile-driven community-building into their own learning environments. Educators are encouraged to take their own learning activities and adapt them to fit their own areas of interest and populations served.

REFERENCES

Abrams, Mi., Scannell, M., & Mulvihill, M. (2011). *Big book of virtual teambuilding games: Quick, effective activities to build communication, trust and collaboration from anywhere!* New York: McGraw-Hill.

Austrian Institute for Applied Telecommunications. (2010). *The mobile phone in school: Handling opportunities and risks appropriately.* Retrieved from: http://handywissen.at/downloads/

Brown, R. E. (2001). The process of community-building in distance learning classes. *Journal of Asynchronous Learning Networks, 5*(2), 18–35.

Caine, R., & Caine, G. (n.d.). *The brain/mind principles of natural learning.* Retrieved from: www.cainelearning.com/RESEARCHFOUNDATIONS/Brain-Mind-Principles.html

California University. (2006). *Schools as caring, learning communities: A center practice brief.* Center For Mental Health In Schools At UCLA.

Davies, A., Fidler, D., & Gorbis, M. (2011). *Future skills 2020.* Institute for the Future for University of Phoenix Research Institute. Retrieved from: www.iftf.org/futureworkskills2020

LaRose, R., & Whitten, P. (2000). Re-thinking instructional immediacy for web courses: A social cognitive exploration. *Communication Education, 49*, 320–338.

Nielson (2010). *U.S. teen mobile report: Calling yesterday, texting today, using apps tomorrow*. Retrieved from: http://blog.nielsen.com/nielsenwire/online_mobile/u-s-teen-mobile-report-calling-yesterday-texting-today-using-apps-tomorrow/

Partnership for 21st Century Skills. (n.d.). *Communication and collaboration*. Retrieved from: www.p21.org/overview/skills-framework/261-communication-and-collaboration

Pew Research (2010). *Pew Internet & American life project*. Retrieved from: http://pewInternet.org/Reports/2010/Teens-and-Mobile-Phones.aspx

Pew Research. (2011). Global digital communications: Texting, social networking popular worldwide. *Pew Research*. Retrieved from: www.pewglobal.org/2011/12/20/global-digital-communication-texting-social-networking-popular-worldwide/1/

Rosen, L. D. (2009). *Rewired: Understanding the iGeneration and the way they learn*. New York: Palgrave Macmillan.

Schaps, E. (2003) Creating caring schools. *Educational Leadership, 60*(6), 31–33.

Vesely, P., Bloom, L., & Sherlock, J. (2007). Key elements of building online community: Comparing faculty and student perceptions. *Journal of Online Learning and Teaching, 3* (3). Retrieved from: http://jolt.merlot.org/vol3no3/vesely.htm

Wilson, M. E. (2004). "Teaching, learning, and millennial students." In M. D. Coomes and R. DeBard (Eds.), *Serving the millennial generation*. New Directions for Student Services, no. 106. San Francisco, CA: Jossey-Bass.

Woods, R., & Ebersole, S. (2003). Social networking in the online classroom: Foundations of effective online learning. *E-Journal, 12/13*(1). Retrieved from: www.ucalgary.ca/ejournal/archive/v12-13/v12-13n1Woods-print.html

25

MOBILE TEACHING AND LEARNING IN THE CLASSROOM AND ONLINE

Case Studies in K–12

Michael M. Grant and Michael K. Barbour

There has been a push to introduce technology into K–12 classrooms since the 1980s. This has included the implementation of online learning and, most recently, the potential of teaching and learning with mobile computing devices. Mobile devices are becoming increasingly ubiquitous in society, particularly with youth. Recent survey research indicates that, overall, 75 percent of American teens own cell phones, with 58 percent of 12-year-olds owing cell phones to 83 percent of 17-year-olds owning cell phones (Lenhart, Ling, Campbell, & Purcell, 2010). Around the world, the numbers are just as remarkable (see, e.g., GSM Association & the Mobile Society Research Institute, 2010).

In addition to this market penetration, "cell phones are not just about calling or texting—with expanding functionality, phones have become multimedia recording devices and pocket-sized Internet connected computers" (Lenhart, 2010, p. 5). Yet that same research indicated, "most schools treat the phone as a disruptive force that must be managed and often excluded from the school and the classroom" (Lenhart, 2010, p. 4).

Even in its infancy, m-learning projects have begun to proliferate in educational environments. For example, publisher Houghton Mifflin Harcourt has created interactive curriculum apps for algebra and geometry, and K–12 online-learning programs such as the Florida Virtual School (FLVS) and K12, Inc. have created mobile apps to accompany their virtual-school offerings. Similar mobile campaigns have also occurred on college campuses.

In this chapter, we will briefly describe a series of projects designed to integrate mobile teaching and learning into K–12 schooling. In the first section, we outline the perceived rationale for increased use of mobile devices with today's K–12 students, and we will describe a professional development project to deploy iPads to classroom teachers in the science department at a suburban high school. Next, we will discuss the growth of K–12 online learning in the United States, and we describe a second project where the course content for students enrolled in an online advanced placement (AP) European history course was delivered through an m-learning content management system (mLCMS). This is followed by a discussion of some of the lessons learned from these limited pilot projects and some of the promise and challenges of mobile teaching and learning.

M-LEARNING IN K–12

The notion that today's students are different than previous generations has become a common one, both in the popular media and in more academic literature. Labels such as the "net generation" (Tapscott, 1998), "digital natives" (Prensky, 2001), and "millennials" (Rainer & Rainer, 2011) suggest that today's youth have grown up surrounded by digital technology since birth, and that has influenced how they live, work, play, and learn. Over the past two to three decades, these perceptions, along with a general belief in the power of technology to improve learning, have driven the purchase of technology to be placed in K–12 schools at a phenomenal rate. It is this belief that today's students are digitally savvy, as well as digitally immersive, that has prompted some schools to consider integrating mobile computing devices through school implementations or bring-your-own-device (BYOD) programs.

Until now, the adoption of m-learning and mobile devices in K–12 schools has been slow. One of the reasons for this lack of adoption is the fact that mobile devices are banned in many schools (Katz, 2005; Lenhart, 2010). As a potentially disruptive, non-educational device, many school and district administrators see the potential problems that cell phones and smart phones can cause in a classroom, and these potential problems have overshadowed their views on the promise these devices may have as educational tools. Further, there are reasonable concerns over the cost associated with many of these devices (and their associated data plans), along with the coverage provided by cellular companies (particularly in rural jurisdictions). Moreover, some school districts are admittedly reticent about implementing BYOD programs, owing to regulations associated with the Internet and the protection of children (see Nair, 2006), because smart phones and cell phones may use a cellular network bypassing the school's network altogether.

Project 1: Science Teacher iPad Deployment

The first project, entitled "Professional Development for Mobile Technology Integration," was funded by a small grant from the Michigan Association for Computer Users in Learning. The goal of this project was to provide professional development and ongoing support to four secondary-school science teachers on using the iPad as a tool for technology integration. Research has shown that there is an increase in teacher learning from professional development when teachers take ownership of that professional development (Loucks-Horsley, Love, Stiles, Mundry, & Hewson, 2009). As such, the focus of the professional development was based upon the teachers' specific interests related to using the iPad. In addition, research has shown there is a higher level of transfer in professional-development initiatives when ongoing support is provided to the teacher following the initial training (Desimone, Porter, Garet, Yoon, & Birman, 2002; DuFour, Eaker, & DuFour, 2005; Heck, Banilower, Weiss, & Rosenberg, 2008). As such, the provision of support after each professional development was planned to increase the level of effective use of the iPad as a tool for technology integration by the teachers in this project.

The initial professional-development session was designed to introduce the teachers to using the iPad, setting up their devices and iTunes accounts, and providing an initial orientation to some science-related applications (apps) that had been preloaded on their devices (e.g., 3D CellStain, Molecules, Rocks, WTunnel Lite, Video Physics, Science@VL, several periodic-table apps, etc.). The subsequent professional-development sessions would begin with each of the teachers describing how they had used the iPad over the past month, and then doing a show-and-tell of any new apps that they may have found. This was followed by an illustration from the researcher of how the iPad, or mobile devices in general, could be used in the classroom, as well as an orientation to any new science-related apps the researcher had discovered.

Most of the teachers used the iPads primarily as a personal learning tool. This meant that the professional-development sessions were largely focused on the potential of the devices and not necessarily on how these teachers were actually using them (or planned to use them during the life of the project). Beyond using them for their own learning, several teachers also used them as a teacher resource or supplemental tool for explaining concepts to students in the classroom. For example, a couple of teachers made regular use of one of the periodic-table apps (e.g., Memorex, AMC, EMD, etc.) as a reference when students had specific questions beyond the information contained on their paper copies of the table. The teachers felt each of these apps offered something a little different for the students.

Interestingly, although all of the teachers felt that the iPad was a potentially powerful pedagogical tool, only one of the four teachers felt confident enough with the device to attempt using it with his students. In this single instance, the teacher pooled together approximately a dozen iPads from colleagues in the school and also encouraged students to bring in their own devices. He began the lesson by having the students complete a quiz on their mobile device using the mLCMS *Mobl21*. This was followed by the teacher demonstrating a particular chemistry concept using a 99-cent app from his own iPad (i.e., QR Reference) and a document camera to project his screen to the class. After the demonstration, the students completed a set of activities using two free apps that had been preloaded on the iPads or that the students had been asked to download to their own devices (i.e., 3D Cell and VCell). The lesson concluded with the students completing a second quiz using *Mobl21*. Both the teachers and the students felt that this single mobile-integration activity was quite successful, as the students were engaged, and the teacher was able to integrate several different m-learning activities into that single lesson.

Among the teachers, including the one who attempted the mobile technology integration lesson, they felt the potential use of the iPad as a classroom device was limited at present. Teachers expressed concern about the student care with the devices. They felt that students would see and treat the iPad more as mobile devices to be handled with less care, as opposed to laptops or netbooks that were generally respected as a "computer." Teachers were also concerned about the cost of the iPad. As a single device, it was approximately the same cost as the purchase of two netbooks. Granted, the teachers did not consider other tablet devices that were cheaper in price than the iPads used in this pilot. However, the largest concern about the potential use of these devices was ensuring a one-to-one student-to-device ratio. All of the teachers felt that, without this student-to-device ratio, the potential of the device in the classroom was severely limited.

M-LEARNING WITH K–12 ONLINE LEARNING

One example of technology in education that has grown substantially over the past two decades, and somewhat successfully, is the use of K–12 online learning (also called virtual schooling or cyber schooling). To date, few K–12 online-learning programs have ventured into m-learning. For example, the FLVS was the first to introduce m-learning apps to its suite of tools with the creation of the *Revu4U* app. *Revu4U* was designed to assist students with test preparations by providing multiple-choice questions in algebra readiness, AP microeconomics, AP psychology, AP language, and AP literature. Since then, it has teamed with developer *GWhiz* to create a series of *meStudying* apps. These apps, which include Algebra 1, Reading for College Success, AP Language, AP Art History, and AP Psychology, generally provide students with a minimal amount of text, and visual and audio instructional content, and then provide students with significant amounts of test preparation. Finally, FLVS has been working with Emantras and Pearson Education to begin the process of converting some of its existing online courses to a truly mobile format.

Similarly, K12, Inc. has created a number of m-learning applications that can be used as a part of its online learning, although the K12, Inc. apps are more focused on the elementary- and middle-school population. For example, *Counting Coins* and *Counting Bills & Coins* are two apps designed to teach elementary students mathematics skills using money. Similarly, K12, Inc. has also released two *What's Sid Thinking* apps for middle-school students, which are memory games designed to help students memorize the 50 U.S. states and facts about the presidents, various land animals, and objects in the solar system. K12, Inc. also has an app that focuses upon Algebra I, and, like the FLVS, it provides minimal review and significant test preparation. K12, Inc.'s collection of apps—for both Apple iOS and Google's Android environments—is the most extensive of any K–12 online-learning program.

There are other K–12 online-learning programs that have created their own m-learning apps (e.g., the Virtual Community School of Ohio has created an app that allows parents/guardians to monitor their child's grades and attendance), and many others that use m-learning apps as a part of their instructional model. There are many more K–12 online-learning programs that leverage the m-learning apps created by various LMS companies to deliver their content to mobile devices. For example, a teacher in Tennessee collaborated with the Hamilton County Virtual School to produce course content inside *Mobl21* (see Meehan, 2010). However, beyond these individual efforts described above, there has been little success by K–12 online-learning programs to pursue m-learning in systematic ways.

M-learning has the potential to change K–12 online learning in significant and rapid ways, as applications are specifically developed to deliver content to mobile devices. At present, the majority of apps available for m-learning are those developed by Blackboard, Desire2Learn, and other course- or learning-management systems—and many of these apps simply convert Web-based or online content to be viewable on a mobile device.

Project 2: Virtual Schooling and mLCMS

The purpose of the study was to explore the use of m-learning in a virtual-school environment, specifically to gauge student perceptions and usage of the *Mobl21* app and m-learning in general. Students in an AP European History course, offered by statewide, supplemental K–12 online learning in the American Midwest, completed 2 of their 26 content units (i.e., approximately 4 weeks) using the *Mobl21* app. The remainder of the course was delivered using Desire2Learn. The 11 students enrolled in this course were in Grades 10–12 and lived primarily in rural areas. As with most supplemental online-learning experiences, the students were provided with a slot in their daily school schedule for their online course and a space in their school with computer access to engage in their online course.

Although the students were generally favorable towards the concept of m-learning, they indicated their experience with this particular project was somewhat negative. The content delivered through the *Mobl21* app represented less than 10 percent of their overall course and occurred at the beginning of the second semester. The students had already become comfortable with the other tools inside Desire2Learn's course management system. It was also interesting to note that, of the 11 students who participated in this project, only one of the students actually used the *Mobl21* app from a mobile device. The remaining 10 students used the desktop client on their school computer. When asked why they did not use their mobile devices, they stated that either their mobile device was not a smart phone (i.e., their phone did not support apps), the cost of data plans was so high they chose to limit their data usage, or they simply did not have a data plan on their mobile device.

In addition, the case here followed a more direct instruction model, which admittedly was reinforced by the *Mobl21* application. So, there were not opportunities for students to create artifacts or representations of their knowledge (see, e.g., Grant, 2011; Grant & Branch, 2005), nor were there opportunities to leverage other social media that might have encouraged informal learning.

LESSONS LEARNED FROM BOTH PROJECTS

Computing in the 21st century is becoming more powerful, and it continues to become available in more portable devices. Although both of the projects described in this chapter were limited pilot studies, with very small samples, there are some general lessons that can be taken from these projects, as well as trends that should be explored in the future.

Tablets, such as the iPad, are the first series of devices that provide the processing potential (and screen size) of a netbook, but the portability of a mobile device. Since the launch of the iPad, a number of other tablet computers have been deployed with Google's Android operating system, including Amazon's Kindle Fire and Samsung's Galaxy. Data from the iPad deployment with the science teachers indicated that the teachers believed the device could have many potential classroom uses. However, these teachers also felt extremely limited in their ability to use the device in the classroom by only having one iPad per teacher, as opposed to one device per student. Further, although the teachers used their iPads extensively as a personal and professional development tool, in a very pragmatic way they also believed the expense of providing tablets for every student was a luxury that schools simply couldn't afford. The teachers' alternative perspectives tempered enthusiasm for what was possible, with what was practical for these students.

A number of schools across the US are piloting tablet computers and e-readers as viable alternatives to print textbooks (see, e.g., Ferlander, 2012; Gleason, 2012; Hu, 2011).

In addition, most recently, the Partnership for the Assessment of Readiness for College and Careers (PARCC assessment), accompanying the Common Core State Standards for Math and Language Arts, announced that it would be compatible with iPads and Android devices (see www.parcconline.org/technology). So schools have added incentive to consider these devices.

At present, there has been little focus by K–12 online learning on developing m-learning as a part of what is already a technologically innovative course-delivery model. In fact, the only systematic efforts to develop substantial m-learning initiatives have been by FLVS and K12, Inc. However, the apps developed by these programs have been limited to knowledge and comprehensive review activities and test preparation. However, the process of turning these learning opportunities into smaller, more modularized segments that are suitable for mobile devices could assist in the process of providing a personalized learning experience. This personalized learning, particularly if it is based on a repository of learning objects that can be drawn upon based on individual student needs, could allow for K–12 education to truly be anytime, anyplace, any pace.

Given the proliferation of mobile devices among today's youth, data-driven information focused on how students perceive learning through these devices is important. However, there are still many geographic locations in North America where mobile access is limited, or data plans are simply too expensive for m-learning to be both possible and cost efficient. It is worth noting that many students engaged in K–12 online learning—particularly those engaged in supplemental K–12 online learning (such as the students included in the mLCMS project)—are located in rural areas where cellular networks are unavailable or limited, and the cost is prohibitive for these students. Additionally, many of the mLCMS apps that are currently available do not provide all of the same features or ease of use as the Web-based LMS programs. This makes students less inclined to use the mobile versions after becoming comfortable with the Web-based environment. This period of development provides both researchers and practitioners the opportunity to experiment on a small scale with this form of learning, to provide lessons that can be applied when mobile access becomes more complete.

Finally, students may need to overcome the stereotype of "a time for learning" to take full advantage of m-learning and mobile computing devices. For example, in the case of the online-learning students, only one of the students actually used a mobile device to complete the unit. Although some students reported they did not have a smart phone or data plan to take advantage of the unit, it is also probable that, when we dedicate specific time and place to learning, such as the case here, it may be more desirable for students to choose to use a larger screen and not be mobile. We have found similar reports from graduate students in other research. This certainly runs counter to more opportunistic definitions of m-learning (e.g., Quinn, 2000; Crompton, 2013, p. 4).

CONCLUSIONS AND RECOMMENDATIONS

Because of the increased availability of mobile computing devices, we are now seeing schools encouraging students to bring in their personal mobile computing devices (e.g., BYOD), as well as use school-owned devices in both K–12 and higher education. The increased availability of mobile computing devices "enables a transition from the occasional, supplemental use of classroom computers and school computer labs to the frequent, integral use of portable computational devices" (Swan, van't Hooft, Kratcoski,

& Unger, 2005, p. 100). However, we caution those who assume or believe that these devices have become ubiquitous. As we saw with the K–12 online learners, there are many youth who do not have access to these devices, or who choose not to use their devices to the fullest extent because of barriers such as cellular coverage or data-plan rates.

Mobile devices do not guarantee their potential or use. Liu, Han, and Li (2010) are explicit in their reminders that adoption or ownership of mobile devices will not assure that devices meet their potential for formal and informal learning. In our present cases, K–12 students chose to access curricular content designed for mobile computing devices on computers, and students may possibly dedicate time to studies, preferring a larger screen and dedicated computer.

Finally, adoption of mobile computing devices does not guarantee m-learning. For example, some K–12 schools are experimenting with classroom sets of mobile devices, where the teacher determines when the devices will be used, and the students are unable to take the devices home or use them with autonomy (e.g., Grant et al., forthcoming). Similar challenges existed in one of the K–12 projects described above, with the inability of teachers to envision ways to use the mobile devices without having a one-to-one environment, but at the same time questioning the expenditure necessary to provide one mobile device per student. Although we are not critiquing the value of using the mobile devices, we are highlighting that this use does not reflect the Crompton, Muilenburg, and Berge definition of m-learning presented in Chapter 1 (Crompton, 2013, p. 4), where learning occurs across multiple contexts. Indeed, m-learning may not work in all contexts, for all contents, or with all learners.

REFERENCES

Crompton, H. (2013). A historical overview of mobile learning: Toward learner-centered education (pp. 3–14). In Z. Berge, & L. Muilenburg (Eds.), *Handbook of mobile learning*. New York: Routledge.

Desimone, L. M., Porter, A. C., Garet, M. S., Yoon, K. S., & Birman, B. F. (2002). Effects of professional development on teachers' instruction: Results from a three-year longitudinal study. *Educational Evaluation and Policy Analysis, 24*, 81–112.

DuFour, R., Eaker, R., & DuFour, R. (Eds.) (2005). *On common ground: The power of professional learning communities*. Bloomington, IN: Solution Tree.

Ferlander, K. (2012, May). 21st-century technology in the classroom: Ten elementary schools doing it right. OnlineSchools.com. Retrieved from: www.onlineschools.com/blog/21st-century-technology-in-the-classroom-ten-elementary-schools-doing-it-right

Gleason, B. J. (2012, March). *The unlimited textbook—Schools in the age of the e-book*. Paper presented at the International Conference on Technology and Business Management. Retrieved from: www.ictbm.org/ictbm12/ICTBM12CD/pdf/D2018-done.pdf

Grant, M. M. (2011). Learning, beliefs, and products: Students' perspectives with project-based learning. *Interdisciplinary Journal of Problem-based Learning, 5*(2), 37–69.

Grant, M. M., & Branch, R. M. (2005). Project-based learning in a middle school: Tracing abilities through the artifacts of learning. *Journal of Research on Technology in Education, 38*(1), 65–98.

Grant, M. M., Tamim, S. R., Brown, D. B., Ferguson, F. K., Jones, L. B., & Sweeney, J. P. (forthcoming). *How are schools doing mobile?* Paper to be presented at the Association for Educational Communications & Technology meeting.

GSM Association & the Mobile Society Research Institute. (2010). *Children's use of mobile phones: An international comparison 2011*. Retrieved from: www.gsma.com/publicpolicy/childrens-use-of-mobile-phones-an-international-comparison-executive-summary-arabic-november-2011-japan-india-paraguay-and-egypt/

Heck, D. J., Banilower, E. R., Weiss, I. R., & Rosenberg, S. L. (2008). Studying the effects of professional development: The case of the NSF's local systemic change through teacher enhancement initiative. *Journal for Research in Mathematics Education, 39*(2), 113–152.

Hu, W. (2011, January). Math that moves: Schools embrace the iPad. *New York Times.* Retrieved from: www.pearson school.com/drm/2010/ipadpilot/NY_Times_iPad_story_1-4-11.pdf

Katz, J. E. (2005). Mobile phones in educational settings. In K. Nyiri (Ed.), *A sense of place: The global and the local in mobile communication* (pp. 305–317). Vienna: Passagen Verlag.

Lenhart, A. (2010). *Teens, cell phones and texting: Text messaging becomes centerpiece communication.* Washington, DC: Pew Internet & American Life Project. Retrieved from: http://pewresearch.org/pubs/1572/teens-cell-phones-text-messages

Lenhart, A., Ling, R., Campbell, S., & Purcell, K. (2010). *Teens and mobile phones.* Washington, DC: Pew Internet & American Life Project. Retrieved from: http://pewInternet.org/Reports/2010/Teens-and-Mobile-Phones.aspx

Loucks-Horsley, S., Love, N., Stiles, K. E., Mundry, S., & Hewson, P. W. (2009). *Designing professional development for teachers of science and mathematics* (3rd ed.). Thousand Oaks, CA: Corwin Press.

Liu, Y., Han, S., & Li, H. (2010). Understanding the factors driving m-learning adoption: A literature review. *Campus-Wide Information Systems, 27*(4), 210–226.

Meehan, T. (2010). Can social media help school phobia? *Elearn magazine.* Retrieved from: http://elearnmag.acm.org/archive.cfm?aid=1852159

Nair, A. (2006). Mobile phones and the Internet: Legal issues in the protection of children. *International Review of Law, Computers & Technology, 20*(1–2), 177–185.

Prensky, M. (2001). Digital natives, digital immigrants–Part II: Do they really think differently? *On the Horizon, 9*(6). Retrieved from: www.marcprensky.com/writing/Prensky%20-%20Digital%20Natives,%20Digital%20Immigrants%20-%20Part2.pdf

Quinn, C. (2000). mLearning: Mobile, wireless, in-your-pocket learning. *Linezine.* Retrieved from: www.linezine.com/2.1/features/cqmmwiyp.htm

Rainer, T., & Rainer, J. (2011). *The mellinnials.* Nashville, TN: B&H Books.

Swan, K., van't Hooft, M., Kratcoski, A., & Unger, D. (2005). Uses and effects of mobile computing devices in K-8 classrooms: A preliminary study. *Journal of Research on Technology and Education, 38*(1), 99–112.

Tapscott, D. (1998). *Growing up digital: The rise of the net generation.* New York: McGraw Hill.

26

USING MOBILE TECHNOLOGY TO ENHANCE TEACHING

Andrew M. O'Loughlin, Siew Mee Barton,
and Leanne Ngo

This chapter has been developed from a longitudinal study conducted over 12 months—from December 2010 to June 2012. The purpose of the research was to investigate how lecturers use mobile technology within a classroom setting. The technological basis for this study is the Apple iPad tablet, five of which were given to academics at an Australian university, with no instruction or guidelines for their use. This chapter examines the practical outcomes from the study, and the learning that has taken place, in order to arrive at some insights into managing mobile technology in the classroom. This chapter also develops a personal-development strategy for academics in the digital age.

BACKGROUND TO THE STUDY

Considerable research has been conducted into how students use mobile technology to enhance their learning (Hwang & Chang, 2011; Looi, Seow, Zhang, Chen, & Wong, 2010; Shih, Chuang, & Hwang 2010; Wang, Shen, Novak, & Pan, 2009). Similarly, there have been a large number of studies that look at how students engage with academics with regard to specific courses (Meurant, 2010). What is missing from the current array of research has been an investigation into how academics use technology as part of their teaching practice in general and, more specifically, mobile technology within their teaching practice.

The advent of cloud computing represents both an opportunity and a challenge to academics. First, there has been a noticeable tendency for universities to build new infrastructure in order to cater for changes in technology use. This, in itself, is somewhat perplexing and also paradoxical, as cloud computing has evolved to free the users from the traditional physical constraints that university campuses often bring (Round, 2011). It also challenges Australian universities' obsession with real estate and their adopted mantra (as well as that of many other universities globally) of "build it and the students will come." With this change, academics have been required to adopt new techniques with regard to mobile "*teaching*" (here we interpose the word "teaching" as opposed to learning, as this represents a new style for the delivery of information, rather than the traditional mechanisms associated with student learning). Traditional classroom activities associated with "chalk and talk," or "log in and lecture," are now under siege, as teaching moves to a more open frame of delivery, where students engage with the materials before many classes begin, and lecturers are required to add value, by making a significant contribution to students' understanding. It is the conundrum of balancing the need for value-added teaching and understanding that is challenging many of the existing teaching paradigms. Academics are feeling exposed, as Generation Y now demands greater digital interactivity, as well as facing "burnout" through 24/7 access to materials and support. Bonk and Graham (2006) discuss the widespread adoption and availability of digital-learning technologies, which have led to increased levels of integration of computer-mediated instructional elements into the traditional face-to-face learning experience. Further, these authors argue that blended learning is now a standard part of education and training, helping to link people across countries and the globe. In addition, it can help reduce travel time for employees undertaking management training, or be used to distribute corporate-developed material and resources to instructors all over the globe.

The problem for many academics is that teaching no longer begins and ends at the classroom door, but is now a constant process where students expect to be able to engage (when they want it), throughout their time at university. The advent of the computer tablet has meant that academics have had to come to terms with the "anytime, anyplace, anywhere" mentality that is increasingly pervading the university-education system. Considerable research has been undertaken that looks at how students both cope with and manage the digital university system (Bennett & Maton, 2010; Bullen, Morgan, & Qayyum, 2011; Morgan & Bullen 2011). However, there are limited studies investigating the strategies that lecturers have developed and are still developing in order to cope with these changes.

THE PARTICIPANTS

The current study involves five academics who teach business communications at one of Australia's mid-size universities. The unit teaches in excess of 4,000 undergraduate students per annum, requiring the academics to develop a variety of teaching and learning strategies (both digital and face to face) in order to teach the unit as well as manage a large administrative load. The five academics were each given an iPad and, adopting a naturalistic inquiry approach, were asked to use these iPads where they felt would be appropriate with regard to teaching the unit. No other training or instruction was given or offered, but was however, available on request. It is because the realities for each lecturer are multiple, and the cause-and-effect relationship are indistinguishable, that the study had adopted a naturalistic inquiry (Lincoln & Guba, 1985). This was a deliberate ploy in order to understand how academics would approach the problem of new technology being introduced into their "world" and, second, to allow them free reign regarding how they might use the technology, without imposing any immediate constraints. The iPads were both Wi-Fi and network enabled, but no SIM card was provided. It was down to each recipient as to whether they wished to avail themselves of the iPad's telephone network capability. In addition, an iTunes card to the value of

A$30 was provided in order to allow the academics to purchase any software apps that they might need, in order to carry out their teaching roles.

The remaining sections of this chapter set out what has been learned and provide a checklist for introducing technology into teaching.

THEORETICAL FRAMEWORK

As the basis for this study, the authors used an adaption of Revans' (1980) action-learning framework (see Figure 26.1).

Revans (1980) uses the following formula in order to explain the model's dynamics:

$$L = P + Q$$

L is the individual learning that takes places, which comprises programmed knowledge (P) (knowledge acquired from experts or through training courses) and questioning (Q). The argument presented is that programmed knowledge on its own is not sufficient to encourage learning, and that the questioning process (for example, closed, objective, relative, and open questions) allows us to reorganize our knowledge, so as to generate insights from a collective approach to learning and then put these into practice.

Marquardt (2009) extended Revans' (1980) formula to include reflection, which overcomes a gap in Revans' (1980) original framework involving the necessary aspects of "action":

$$L = P + Q + R$$

The current framework still presents a problem, and, although learning is the acquisition of "new" knowledge, it was apparent that different people treat knowledge

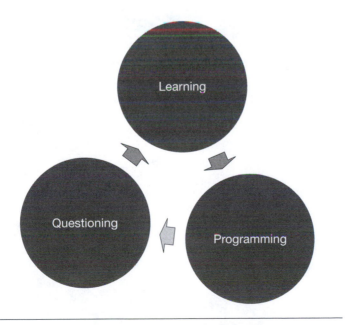

Figure 26.1 Revans' (1980) Original Action-Learning Framework

accumulation differently, and process it in very different ways. Importantly, without reflection taking place, little knowledge is acquired, but, if participants spend too much time reflecting, then the process slows significantly. In order to overcome this problem and understand how the participants engage with the mobile technology, we have added "*feedback*":

$$L = P + Q + R + F$$

The feedback loop is extremely important, as it allows for the monitoring and subsequent management of the possible effects caused by inertia and action without reflection. It is also very apparent that people process information in many different ways, and this study is no different in that respect. We were looking for academics to feed back to the head of the unit, for example, that they *might* need training, or that further enhancements would be required to enable them to fully utilize the technology in the classroom environment. Action learning was originally conceived of as an educational process where people learn together. The theoretical proposition that underpins action learning is that "learners" acquire knowledge through action, rather than instruction, and will in fact overcome various inhibitions when working in small groups. Therefore, an additional interest for the researchers was whether the iPad might

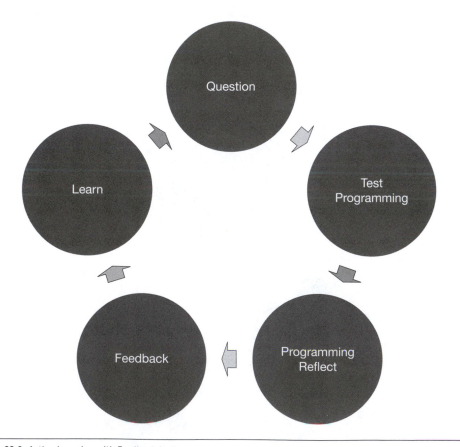

Figure 26.2 Action Learning with Feedback Loop

act as a catalyst to draw the unit team together (tablets are often advertised as a socially unifying tool), or, because of different competency levels, possibly push them apart.

LEARNING TO USE MOBILE TECHNOLOGY

Perhaps one of the most controversial findings from this study is that, although all of the academics had requested the use of an iPad for teaching and had cited improvements in their classroom delivery as the main reason, as well as ensuring familiarity with a communication technology that many students were now using, the study concluded that three out of five academics had never used Apple computers or phones prior to the study and had had little or no exposure to mobile technology.

Why is this important? There is a widely held belief (particularly in universities) that, when an employee requests access to a particular technology, her or she does have some comprehension of its operating features, and how it might enhance the productivity. This assumption appears to be incorrect, as evidence suggests that the majority (in this study at least) have no immediate sense of how the technology might add value, or indeed how it might be used to enhance their own in-class experience.

The use of iPads has been found to possibly enhance students' learning experience (Brand, Kinash, Mathew, & Kordyban, 2011; Fontelo, Faustorilla, Gavino, & Marcelo, 2012; Perez, Gonzalez, Pitcher, & Golding, 2011), but not necessarily to lead to better learning outcomes (Perez et al., 2011). Academic staff appear most likely to use the iPad primarily for administrative purposes, using applications such as e-mail, calendar, and meeting notes (Linsey, 2011), or for access to course resources and libraries, using applications such as e-books, as a means of communication with students using blogs, wiki, social media, and e-mail (Yeung & Chung, 2011), or as a projection device (Fontelo et al., 2012; Yeung & Chung, 2011) using various presentation applications. Only a small number of staff reported using iPads in their teaching activities in class.

The situation also arose where one of the academics gave his iPad to his son, on the grounds that he saw little or no value in its use, either for teaching or administration, and that there was no reason to undertake any form of training with regard to its operation, believing it would not enhance current practices. The academic in this case took no interest in the technology, not even asking for it back from his son when interviewed at the end of the 12-month research cycle.

Now, although this might appear unusual and perhaps a little extreme, the solution used here is not that uncommon. In another example, Academic 3 initially allowed her son to use the iPad and sat with him while he "played" with it. The learning that took place was action-based, but grounded in family experiences and expression. In this case, the academic recovered the iPad and went on to become a heavy user of the tablet.

M-learning is part of an ever-changing digital world in which "knowledge, power, and productive capability will be more dispersed than at any time in our history—a world where value creation will be fast, fluid, and persistently disruptive, a world where only the connected will survive" (Dorman, 2007, p. 6). In addition, in education, and in business, those who fail to grasp this reality will find themselves "ever more isolated, cut off from the networks that are sharing, adapting, and updating knowledge to create value" (Dorman, 2007, p. 6). This connected world is not constrained by physical space or time (Ng, Nicholas, Loke, & Torabi, 2010). The iPad-style tablet has very quickly become popular in higher education and has been adopted by the younger generation (Nielsen, 2010).

Questioning

What is perhaps most telling is that almost no questions were asked of the unit chair concerning iPad use (or of other colleagues), and indeed whether any training was available. Neither did the unit chair receive suggestions from the team that, where possible, the learning be captured and shared. As already noted, the strategy employed here was naturalistic inquiry, where the aim is to understand how people create meaning from, and interpret events in, their world (Lincoln & Guba, 1985). Initiation of discussions by the unit chair was deliberately withheld, so as not to bias the findings in any way.

Academics 4 and 5 were experienced Apple-technology users and found the transition seamless. They immediately took up the technology and started using it for both teaching and administration. Interestingly, neither chose to share their experiences with the other members of the team, and they had assumed that their colleagues had a reasonable level of familiarity with mobile technologies, or at the very least would ask. They did, however, talk together about what they had been doing with the iPad and shared various apps.

Academic 1 made one e-mail inquiry of the unit chair concerning why the telephone-network SIM card was not provided. Other than this she remained silent on how the iPad was used. In searching the university records, Academic 1 did make a request to the university IT department concerning training, but never attended the workshop, and did not follow up with further inquiries.

Academic 2, who relinquished use of the iPad to his son, was asked at one of the regular team meetings what he had been doing with it, and he openly admitted that he was not using it and felt that it was a more appropriate tool for "the younger generation . . . and that he could not see how to use it." Academic 2 made no attempt to discover how other academics were using the iPad and seemed oblivious to the fact that it was a requested tool for work.

Testing: iPad Use

Of the five academics, three used the iPad to various degrees, in their classroom and also for administrative work; one relinquished its use, and another used it sparingly:

- *Academic 1*: used the iPad to read and answer e-mails, only at work. Academic 1 refused to use the iPad for lecturing, or in the classroom, and explained that it was a distraction. Academic 1 deliberately did not take the iPad home, regarding its 24/7 functionality as an invasion of home life. Neither did Academic 1 take the iPad to meetings on other campuses. Its sole use was either as an additional office e-mail facility, or to take notes at local meetings. No apps were downloaded, and no SIM card was purchased.
- *Academic 2*: As already noted, he relinquished his iPad to a son. Prior to doing so, he did use it very briefly, but found that it was not intuitive and could see no way to use it in the classroom. Academic 2 did not download any apps or purchase a SIM card.
- *Academic 3*: After a relatively slow start, and with some guidance from her young son, she fully engaged with the technology, using it for lecturing, classroom teaching, and administration and, much later on, research. Academic 3 also used it socially at home and found that it significantly enhanced her teaching and classroom mobility. She did download a variety of productivity and social apps and, later on, purchased a SIM card.

- *Academic 4*: Already had her own personal iPad, and so was an experienced user. She had a high level of familiarity with Apple products and immediately uploaded a large number of apps. The iPad was used for lecturing, classroom teaching, administration, research, and full social engagement, both at work and at home. Academic 4 was using the full mobility provided by the iPad and purchased a SIM card upon receiving the iPad.
- *Academic 5*: Is an experienced Apple user and was very familiar with the technology, as he had been using an iPhone. Academic 5 immediately uploaded a variety of apps, most of which related to productivity, and a small number for social engagement. The iPad was used immediately for lecturing, in classroom teaching, research, meetings, administration, and limited social use. Academic 5 immediately purchased a SIM card on receiving the iPad, so as to exploit the technology's full mobility capability.

The variability of use is perhaps unsurprising. However, the extreme range was unexpected. Lower levels of technological engagement were both anticipated and expected, but completely relinquishing the technology was something that the researchers had not predicted.

Also evident was the fact that the technology was not proving to be the unifier that was expected. In fact, much of the testing and experimentation took place individually, and almost no cross-fertilization of ideas or discussion was entered into by the team.

Reflecting

Although the process of reflection was also variable, it is the range that was most notable. For example, Academic 2 only spent time using the technology to decide whether the iPad offered immediate value, but did not explore or reflect on what it might offer over the longer term. We have classified this Academic as a "*non-adopter*" (Hu, Poston, & Kettinger, 2011). Similarly, Academic 1 only spent time on immediate needs and not on what the technology might potentially offer. Some very limited reflection was undertaken, but not to any degree or depth, and there was an inherent refusal to explore beyond the technology's immediate functionality. The level of adoption here was classified as "*contained limited adopter*" (Venkatesh, Morris, Davis & Davis, 2003), in that she would use the technology, but only within existing limits, and sought no further capability or use.

Academic 3 was effectively a "*slow adopter*" (Venktash et al., 2003) of the technology and initially only spent time reflecting on the iPad's capability with family members at home. It took her approximately 6 months to become fully conversant with the technology and also to realize that it had potential benefits within a classroom setting. Once fully engaged with the iPad, Academic 3 integrated the advantages that mobile technology offered into her entire work and productivity cycle. It was apparent that Academic 3 needed both to be "shown" how to engage with the technology on different levels, as well as to be allowed to experiment with it in order to establish its purpose.

Academics 4 and 5 reflected in different ways and were seeking enhancements from the technology, rather than simple application. Although these two might be classified as "*early adopters*" (Wenger, White, & Smith 2009), their approaches were actually very different. Academic 4 saw greater versatility in the technology for social-interaction purposes, whereas Academic 5 focused much more on mobile productivity and the enhancements for teaching. Both reflected regularly on the various apps that were available and were prepared to purchase and try new products on the iPad beyond the A$30 allowance. Academics 4 and 5 were committed to using the portability functions of the technology in order to improve, not only their learning experience, but also those of the students.

The point to be noted here is that the provision of technology does not automatically encourage reflection to take place. There is a degree of scalability with regard to the reflective process, in that the user clearly needs to understand the technology's immediate value, in terms of being able to enhance the immediate experience . Indeed, in the case of Academic 3, experiential learning was a crucial part of the embedding of the technology into her daily use. For Academics 4 and 5, the importance of experience was also part of the reflection process, and, although both occasionally shared information on app use, they already had a good comprehension of the value that might be attributed to mobile technology.

Feedback

As mentioned earlier, the research ran for 12 months, and, during this period, only Academics 4 and 5 fed back what they had learned to the unit chair without needing to be prompted. Academics 1, 2, and 3 remained largely silent on their use of mobile technologies and only engaged in feeding back when they were interviewed for the research. What is perhaps most telling is that the researchers had assumed that feedback would be automatic and regular via meeting contact points, but there were clearly inherent problems preventing that process from taking place. In summary terms, Academics 1 and 2 did not think that it was their responsibility to provide feedback or seek support and help, nor to give guidance or advice. They argued that the technology had been given to them without instruction, and that it was the unit chair's (interestingly, not the university's) duty to organize some level of training for them, and find out *their* needs. Both disagreed with questions relating to their own accountability, particularly when they realized they had not been using the technology to anywhere near its full potential, and still insisted that it was the unit chair's obligation to train and provide them with support.

Why is it important to employ a feedback strategy? There was a significant delay in requesting feedback (12 months). The other problem with feedback is whether it should be based on *push* or *pull* strategies. Conceptually, the idea was not to burden any of the academics or influence their choice with regard to technology use. The study was predicated on the belief that each of the participants would, as action learning suggests, find learning easier in a small group where prescriptive techniques concerning technology use were eliminated, and that the technology would act as a catalyst for cohesion (Marquardt, 2009).

What happened, however, is that clear divisions evolved around competency and capability. Academics 1 and 2 saw little or no value in the mobile technology, but did not feed this back until the end of the research cycle. Academic 3 took time to understand how productivity could be enhanced through portability, but sought feedback from outside the team. Academics 4 and 5 spent time reinforcing their own knowledge and did not engage the other members because they were unaware that Academic 1 had disengaged, Academic 2 was a very limited adopter, and Academic 3 was a slow but competent adopter.

Earlier feedback might have encouraged greater sharing and improved the learning experience of Academics 1 and 2. Similarly, although the learning style involves seeking external support, Academic 3 might have recognized the value that mobile technology adds much earlier. It is unclear what value Academics 4 and 5 would have received from a comprehensive feedback process. However, it is suggested that learning throughout the entire unit might have improved, and a stronger and more cohesive team could have been established.

USING MOBILE TECHNOLOGY IN THE CLASSROOM

This study set out to discover how academics use mobile technology in the classroom. What is immediately apparent is that two of the five participants did not, and would not, use mobile technology to engage with students. However, the results from our study show that Academics 3, 4, and 5 use iPads extensively in their teaching:

(a) *Lecturing to students*: The iPad offers a lecturing capability, and Academics 4 and 5 used it instead of the fixed desktop computers. This allowed greater flexibility in terms of having the lecture already loaded, but the primary constraint was that a projector is still required for large audiences.

(b) *Instant information assistance*: It was also possible to use the iPad to gain immediate access to information contained within personal files, as well as on the Internet.

(c) *Personalized teaching and learning*: If the main computer and projector were being used, it was possible for the lecturer to move around the class with the iPad and call files up, or use the Internet to personalize the teaching for the students.

(d) *Loan of iPad*: On a number of occasions, equipment unpredictability in the classroom meant that students needed to borrow an iPad, in order to complete certain aspects of the assignment. Having an iPad available as an extra resource proved to be invaluable and freed the lecturer up to concentrate on other students, without having them drift off to other computer laboratories.

(e) *Problem resolution*: Students often had administrative problems that could be sorted on the iPad before or after class (and occasionally during class), without the need to use a public computer, or having to return to the office in order to complete the task.

The benefits that accrue from using mobile technology in the classroom are clearly evident, and they relate to a mixture of content management and technological flexibility. The problem of static class-based teaching paradigms is something that possibly hinders its wider application (as Academics 1 and 2 are testament to). In spite of this, mobile technologies do allow for a diverse range of possibilities and broaden the scope for a different level of teaching engagement. The main constraints are individual vision concerning the application of technology in the classroom and the current mechanisms of preferred delivery (fixed location and face to face).

WHAT WAS LEARNED FROM THE STUDY?

So what precisely was learned? There are a number of important findings from this study, which have beneficial practical application for the adoption of mobile technology by academics for teaching in a classroom setting, and also improving productivity. The iPad was mainly used for administrative and professional development (PD) (e-mail, conducting business during meetings, reading e-books, etc.), and only one-third used the iPad in actual teaching delivery (Linsey, 2011). Here, the lessons learned are applied to a higher-education establishment, but are of relevance to other organizations considering adopting mobile technology:

1. The iPad is merely one of a number of mobile platforms that are available, and all do much the same thing, although to varying degrees. The assumption that people are immediately familiar with the technology, no matter how widespread and pervasive it is, must be questioned. It is, therefore, extremely important that organizations that regularly use mobile technologies need to both have and continually develop a high level of training and input, to maximize employee performance and avoid the range and scalability issues described in this study.

2. Mobile technologies for educational purposes, along with cloud learning, are all pervasive and form part of the norming process that organizations undergo with regard to changes in their business environment. There is good evidence to suggest that use of mobile technologies in the classroom should now form part of an academic lecturer's PD. We suggest this on the basis that, for certain businesses, there is a high expectation that their staff will be automatically familiar with a range of mobile technologies. The evidence, however, suggests otherwise. Many employees have at best a mediocre understanding of technological use and the advantages that it offers, and, at worst, and as shown here, occasionally none at all. This variation is a worrying finding, given the importance that many universities are placing on the provision of m-learning as a platform for competitive advantage.

3. It is clearly necessary that appropriate PD processes, such as regular feedback reviews, be undertaken concerning mobile-technology use. This may include both formal and informal feedback, or team-based meetings to discuss how the technology can be leveraged for greater performance. What is apparent from this study is that employees cannot simply be left to their own devices, and that regular feedback sessions might identify productivity problems at a much earlier stage than the 12-month research cycle used here.

4. Developing a community of practice (CoP) provides an avenue for feedback, discussing practices, and sharing learning opportunities to enhance and expand practice (Lave and Wenger, 1991). CoP also allows for feedback, concerns, resolutions, and identification of PD opportunities. A CoP should be broader than the basic teaching unit and look to capture lessons learned from other academics in different disciplines. Academics 4 and 5 have been engaged in regular communication and sharing what they have learned, as well as leveraging off other professional communities that are also passionate about educational technologies. Both commented that they found these exchanges of ideas useful in their adoption and use of the iPad. It is also possible that a CoP support approach might have assisted Academics 1 and 2, who could have discussed and shared practices of iPad use with a community of practitioners. Academic 3 would certainly have benefitted from engaging with a CoP, given that Academic 3's preferred style was "external" experiential learning.

5. There also needs to be clear recognition at the outset concerning individual roles and responsibilities with regard to technological learning. For example, Academics 1 and 2 held the unit chair solely accountable for their failure to adopt the technology and their lack of engagement with the iPad, in spite of the fact that it was specifically purchased by the university for them to use as a teaching tool.

6. There is also an identified broader problem that, although universities are using mobile technology more than ever before, what seems to be evolving is a sort of *hybrid* approach to education. The demands of classroom attendance still take up much of an academic's time, and mobile-technology platforms are used largely to enhance, rather than supplant, this engagement. So the mantra of "log on and lecture" remains the dominant paradigm. Mobile technology in a classroom setting undoubtedly provides greater flexibility, which is a significant benefit, but it is questionable whether it offers any other substantial teaching or learning advantages, particularly while the current classroom model of teaching engagement continues to dominate the education process. The important point to make here is that mobile (able to engage anytime, anyplace, anywhere) does not equate to portable (same basic product that can be moved), and universities need to decide whether they are working toward/within a portable or mobile teaching framework, as this both influences and affects the way that lecturers deliver the content, as well as the student learning experience.

7. Our final learning point relates to the issue of human and social capital. Investment in technology is a significant draw card for employees, and being at the cutting edge of m-learning is becoming increasingly important for academics. While investing in technology, the universities clearly also need to invest in their staff. As evidenced here, two of the five academics have limited or no understanding of the technology provided to them. If this is reflective of the wider academic community (and we have no reason to doubt that it is not), there is both a productivity and human-capital problem simply waiting to happen. At our own university, discussion ranges about the value of giving all of the academics iPads. Although, in theory, this appears to be a reasonable suggestion, our study shows that, in practice, it is not without both human and social problems and concerns. Technology is changing how universities do business, but the teaching paradigms remain largely fixed in 20th-century delivery modes. This is partly attributable to an underinvestment in carefully *targeted* staff training and development and, in spite of the rhetoric, the inherent aversion to breaking with the historical legacy of "chalk-and-talk" (or the modern version of "log-on-and-lecture") teaching paradigms.

In this study, the use of iPads was embedded into the pedagogical design of an undergraduate subject. The results indicate that the use of Internet-connected technologies in the classroom was found to be useful only for *some* of the participants. Yeung and Chung (2011) reported initial findings from the first phase of their exploratory study to investigate the potential pedagogical use of iPads in higher education. Overall, iPads were found to be useful to provide instant access to the course resources and library databases, and as efficient means of communication with the students. However, the study raised a concern that the technology has yet to fully evolve for greater practical use in the classroom, particularly where there was a lack of university policy regarding technology support.

In using the action-learning framework developed earlier in the chapter in order to summarize the key learning outcomes, although all of the participants have learned from generating insights into their experience, as Revans (1998, p. 83) argues, "there can be no learning without action, and no action without learning." The lessons learned from this study can be summarized as *seven principles* for introducing and using mobile technology in the classroom. These are:

1. Never assume prior technical knowledge and *always* provide instructions concerning how the technology might and should be used.
2. Build academic staff capacity through PD to develop mobile-technology educational literacy.
3. Develop and *regularly* use both informal and formal feedback mechanisms to monitor and manage technology adoption.
4. Encourage and develop a CoP across the university.
5. Clearly define individual roles and responsibilities.
6. Challenge existing education paradigms in order to enhance the teaching and learning experience.
7. Along with technological investment, there is an urgent need to invest in human and social capital.

It is immediately evident that, although mobile technology provides a platform that allows for good practice to develop, it also highlights various levels of intransigence among users and problems associated with the existing teaching paradigms. There is a pressing need for a more focused pedagogical design of curricula, which is designed for mobile technology, as well as various applications for an innovative blended learning environment. Although there are clearly positive benefits to doing this, at the present time, reconciling these last two issues is proving to be both challenging (for example, cultural change) and enormously time consuming (such as, which mobile platform is best suited to teaching, and is this the same for learning?).

SUMMARY AND CONCLUSION

The study has focused on academic use of mobile technology within a classroom environment through a longitudinal study that was conducted over 12 months, an adapted action-learning framework, originally proposed by Revans (1980), modified by Marquardt (2009) to include "reflection," and in our study further adapted to include "feedback" in order to provide the theoretical framework for the study. It is apparent that the additional component of feedback provides a strong foundation for developing a practical framework for sharing and developing better teaching practices.

Although the seven key principles for introducing and using mobile technology in the classroom might seem obvious, it is evident that, when introducing mobile technology into educational environments, there clearly needs to be a substantive support mechanism already in place for academics to engage with. These principles have been used to good effect in a second study that has recently concluded, and the results are promising. In following the guidance from the key principles highlighted here, our preliminary results from a different cohort of six academics using mobile technology strongly suggest clear engagement with the iPad and have mostly reported greater satisfaction with the process and, in places, even potential stretching of the teaching paradigm.

Murphy (2011) compiled and analyzed secondary data from various sources, such as press commentaries, reports, and blogs on universities using or piloting iPads in their institutions, and concluded that iPads are used "*in a limited, content delivery capacity*" (p. 30), to predominantly deliver course materials, and many universities are "*still unsure of the best way to incorporate it into their existing programs and curriculums*" (p. 30). Murphy (2011) found that iPads were largely being used for course delivery, and not for teaching. Universities are almost exclusively focused on ubiquitous access to course and subject materials—typology 1 (Murphy, 2011, p. 21), followed by content generation and collaboration, but only 13 percent used iPads for administration, professional development, and research.

To conclude, the study has shown that there are some inherent benefits and weaknesses in how mobile technology is introduced to academics for use in a classroom setting, different levels of technology adoption and expectations of users, as well as what can be achieved. The key to successful implementation remains the careful management of people, product, and then process.

REFERENCES

Bennett, S., & Maton, K. (2010). Beyond the "digital natives" debate: Towards a more nuanced understanding of students' technology experiences. *Journal of Computer Assisted Learning, 26*(5), 321–331.

Bonk, C. J., & Graham, C. R. (2006). *Handbook of blended learning: Global perspectives, local designs.* San Francisco, CA: Pfeiffer.

Brand, J., Kinash, S., Mathew, T., & Kordyban, R. (2011). iWant does not equal iWill: Correlates of mobile learning with iPads, e-textbooks, BlackBoard Mobile Learn and a blended learning experience. *Proceedings ascilite 2011*, Hobart, Tasmania.

Bullen, B., Morgan, T., & Qayyum, A. (2011). Digital learners in higher education: Generation is not the issue. *Canadian Journal of Learning and Technology, 37*(1), 1–24.

Dorman, J. (2007). Engaging digital natives: Examining 21st century literacies and their implications for teaching in the digital age. Retrieved from: www.slideshare.net/cliotech/engaging-digital-natives

Fontelo, P., Faustorilla, J., Gavino, A., & Marcelo, A. (2012). Digital pathology—Implementation challenges in low-resource countries. *Analytical Cellular Pathology, 35*(1), 31–36. DOI:10.3233/ACP-2011-0024

Hu, T., Poston, R. S., & Kettinger, W. J. (2011). Nonadopters of online social network services: Is it easy to have fun yet? *Communications of the Association for Information Systems* (Article 25), 25. Retrieved from: http://aisel.aisnet.org/cais/vol29/iss1/25

Hwang, G. J., & Chang, H. F. (2011). A formative assessment-based mobile learning approach to improving the learning attitudes and achievements of students. *Computers & Education, 56*(1), 1023–1031.

Lave, J., & Wenger, E. (1991). *Situated learning: Legitimate peripheral participation.* Cambridge, UK: University of Cambridge Press.

Lincoln, Y., & Guba, E. (1985). *Naturalistic enquiry.* Newbury Park, CA: Sage.

Linsey, J. L. (2011). Leading change: going green with iPads. *International Journal of Business, Humanities & Technology, 1*(2), 10–16.

Looi, C., Seow P., Zhang, B., So, H., Chen, W., & Wong, L. (2010). Leveraging mobile technology for sustainable seamless learning. *British Journal of Educational Technology, 41*, 154–169.

Marquardt, M. (2009). *Action learning for higher education institutions.* Kuala Lumpur: AKEPT Press.

Meurant, R. C. (2010). Providing every student with an iPad as a means of helping develop Korean EFL digital literacy. In *Proceedings of the 6th International Conference on Networked Computing and Advanced Information Management* (pp. 242–247).

Morgan, T., & Bullen, M. (2011). Digital learners in higher education: A research project update. *Journal of Distance Education, 25*(1). (in FYI section).

Murphy, G. D. (2011). Post-PC devices: A summary of early iPad technology adoption in tertiary environments. *E-Journal of Business Education & Scholarship of Teaching* (Australian Business Education Research Association), 5(1), 18–32.

Ng, W., Nicholas, H., Loke, S., & Torabi, T. (2010). Designing effective pedagogical systems for teaching and learning with mobile and ubiquitous devices. In T. T. Goh (Ed.), *Multiplatform e-learning systems and technologies: Mobile devices for ubiquitous ICT-based education* (pp. 42–56). Hershey, PA: ICI Global Publishing.

Nielsen. (2010). *The connected devices age: iPads, Kindle, smartphones and the connected consumer.* Retrieved from: http://blog.nielsen.com/nielsenwire/consumer/the-connected-devices-age-ipads-kindles-smartphones-and-the-connected-consumer/

Perez, O. A., Gonzalez, V., Pitcher, M. T., & Golding, P. (2011). *Work in progress: Analysis of mobile technology impact on STEM based courses—Specifically, introduction to Engineering in the era of the iPad.* 118th ASEE Annual Conference and Exposition, Vancouver, BC.

Revans, R. (1980). *Action learning: New techniques for management.* London: Blond & Briggs, Ltd.

Revans, R. W. (1998) *ABC of action learning.* London: Lemos and Crane.

Round, K. (2011). E-learning 2.0: Cloud computing and the online learner. *Journal of Applied Learning Technology, 1*(4), 24–27.

Shih, J., Chuang, C., & Hwang, G. (2010). An inquiry-based mobile learning approach to enhancing social science learning effectiveness. *Educational Technology & Society, 13*(4), 50–62.

Venkatesh, V., Morris, M. G., Davis, G. B., & Davis, F. D. (2003). User acceptance of information technology: Toward a unified view. *MIS Quarterly, 27*(3), 425–478.

Wang, M., Shen, R., Novak, D., & Pan, X. (2009). The impact of mobile learning on students' learning behaviours and performance: Report from a large blended classroom. *British Journal of Educational Technology, 40*(4), 673–695.

Wenger, E., White, N., & Smith, J. D. (2009). *Digital habitats: Stewarding technology for communities.* Portland OR: CPsquare.

Yeung, M., & Chung, H. (2011). iPEP talk: Pedagogical conversations from the iPad exploration project. *Proceedings of Society for Information Technology & Teacher Education International.*

27

TEACHERS' TOOLS

Designing Customizable Applications for M-Learning Activities

Sara Price, Paul Davies, and William Farr

The functionality of mobile technologies makes them potentially important tools in the current and future landscape of teaching and learning. Although research has established learning opportunities that mobile technologies may provide for students (e.g., Klopfer & Squire, 2007; Kanjo et al., 2008; Rogers & Price, 2008; Franckel, Bonsignore, & Druin, 2010), successful integration into educational contexts requires a focus on teachers' use of technology. Although mobile tools to support classroom teaching for various purposes exist (e.g., Ratto, Shapiro, Truong, & Griswold, 2003), uptake in educational contexts remains limited. Previous work highlights a number of reasons for this, including concerns that technology does not reflect pedagogic approaches (Major, 1995), teachers' lack of training or familiarity with computers, and the time involved in learning a new tool (Mueller, Wood, Willoughby, Ross, & Specht, 2008). More importantly, teachers' beliefs about what and how they teach are instrumental in shaping their teaching practices (Luft, 2009).

With a continued shift in K–12 education toward mobile and 1:1 computing, growth in online learning, and increased bandwidth (Brown & Green, 2008), it is essential to consider new ways to engage teachers with technologies and new approaches for teaching with them. Traxler (2011) suggests five ways that m-learning offers new learning opportunities: contingent learning, situated learning, authentic learning, context-aware learning, and personalized learning, which may apply equally to teachers and learners. Furthermore, increased accessibility of GIS, such as Google Earth, together with GPS and Web 2.0 technologies, broadens the potential to support innovative ways of enhancing teaching (e.g., Anand et al., 2010), and provides opportunities to leverage change in pedagogical approaches to teaching science. Modern smartphone interfaces lend themselves to developing customizable applications, supporting teachers' creativity through modification and tailoring of activities to student age, ability, and subject.

This chapter explores the role of engaging in the design process (of developing a customizable smartphone application to foster a new approach to teaching science) in changing teacher beliefs about the value of technology for teaching and learning, and how it mediates new approaches to science teaching. The chapter draws on the GeoSciTeach project, which designed and developed a customizable smartphone application to support a geospatial approach to science teaching. It aimed to enable teachers to customize a mobile application, by selecting and organizing various tools for data collection, information sharing, and information visualization, to tailor the learning experience to support different science questions, age groups, and abilities. A participatory design approach involving pre-service science teachers (PSTs) was taken. These are science graduates training to teach science at 11–16 years, but with a specialist subject to post-16 years (i.e., chemistry, physics, or biology). The design process is described, with illustration of its approach to fostering teachers' belief development. Finally, the chapter outlines issues arising around the research process itself and challenges for implementing customizable tools such as these in teaching practice, and it indicates research directions.

OVERALL DESIGN CONSIDERATIONS AND APPROACH

A design process that aims to change beliefs held by teachers requires an involved and intensive timescale in the region of months and years (Trautmann & MaKinster, 2010). During pre-service training, however, beliefs are challenged during a pressured 9-month period. However, exposure to new procedural outcomes for PSTs, such as geospatial integration in educational settings, can have lasting effects on teacher knowledge, continuing professional development, and student progress (Hagevik, 2011). This section outlines the overall design approach and rationale behind the development of the GeoSciTeach application in this context of PST training.

Providing opportunities for teachers to take an active role in their learning, as well as fostering a collaborative learning process, with a focus on content knowledge, is central to successful teacher development (Constible, McWilliams, Soldo, Perry, & Lee, 2007). Taking a participatory design approach, the GeoSciTeach project worked with PSTs throughout the design and development process, involving them from the conceptualization of the application through to the final workable prototype. This approach has been shown to be effective in human–computer interaction (HCI), particularly when introducing new tools into current practices (e.g., Muller, 2002). In the context of teacher professional development, this is important in fostering new approaches to teaching familiar subject domains, developing clear links to the educational curriculum, engendering a sense of ownership with the technology, and enabling a deeper engagement with the motivation of the application. In so doing, this approach aimed to facilitate changes in "beliefs" about technology and geospatial ideas in science.

In addition, it is equally important that teachers are given the opportunity to reflect on their beliefs and abilities (Hagevik, 2011). Supporting this through using a contextualized approach has been shown to be effective (Penuel, Fishman, Yamaguchi, & Gallagher, 2007). The design of the GeoSciTeach application centered around a real-life example from the Royal Botanical Gardens, Kew, providing an authentic context for thinking about the design of the application interface and the tools needed to support appropriate learning activities. It also directly supported part of the training program, which required PSTs to undertake a field trip at Kew Gardens with groups of 11–12-

year-old students. The application was, therefore, used in an authentic teaching activity to promote in situ engagement with geospatial concepts and representations in science.

The value of effective subject-specific professional development in supporting both teachers' subject knowledge and pedagogical subject knowledge is well documented (Desimone, Porter, Garet, Yoon, & Birman, 2002). As the project specifically embraced geospatially related concepts to support the development of geospatial skills and awareness, the need to explore and support the development of PSTs' understanding of what "geospatial" means and its relationship to science was taken into consideration. Geospatial and spatial skills are used to understand and make sense of properties of space. This could be how we represent real things on maps, images, and diagrams, including how we visualize and think about things in two- and three-dimensional representations. Understanding science often requires students to use geospatial and spatial skills, for example, in ecological studies considering succession and habitat changes through time. Digital technologies such as GIS and GPS, together with sensing equipment (e.g., temperature, carbon monoxide), allow students to collect data and manipulate them in new ways. For example, students take pictures of plants in specific habitats and environmental measurements and tag them according to their location in the world. Pictures and information are automatically uploaded to Google Maps, where students can then examine the different plant and environment characteristics to reason about biological and ecological processes. Again, the use of an exemplary concrete activity enabled discussion with PSTs around these aspects.

Developing customizable applications also requires particular design considerations. Previous work has developed authoring tools to be usable by teachers without programming skills (Ainsworth & Fleming, 2006), and to empower them to be designers of learning environments (Major, 1995). However, they lack clear evidence of effectiveness and require time-intensive effort in initial learning and preparation of new activities (Ainsworth & Flemming, 2006). They also focus on content manipulation and foster a proliferation of activities such as quizzes (Hutchful, Mathur, Joshi, & Cutrell, 2010). Despite an "easy-to-use" design, these environments are not innovative in terms of the pedagogical approaches they encourage, nor the learning activities created (Mueller et al., 2008). In contrast, mobile applications foster more active learning experiences, empower student engagement, and offer portability, instant communication, and flexible and timely access to learning resources (JISC, 2005). For teachers, these tools, therefore, need to support customizable *orchestration*, as well as customizable content. Again, basing the design on a concrete example of student learning activity aims to ensure that the application "works" and enables PSTs to think about the technology—where and why it might be functionally useful—while also linking this with geospatial concepts. Once the application functionality has been created for the exemplary activity, then the customizable aspect can be developed. In this way, development ensures the end product is useable by teachers, alongside giving them better insight into the application functionality before having to think about different activities to customize. PSTs were fully involved in the whole design, that is, the customizable form and the functionality of the application.

Effective teacher development, conceptualized by Clarke and Hollingsworth (2002), provides a useful way to consider how teacher development is most productive. They conceptualize teacher progression (or growth) occurring through the dynamic interaction between domains, namely external sources of support—for example, involvement in the project described here; teacher beliefs; professional experimentation; and teacher values (described by them as "salient outcomes"). When professional development is most effective, "change sequences" are observed between one, or more, of these "domains," which leads to "growth development." Of particular significance is the observation that, for change to be long term, teacher beliefs are central, but that teachers need time and extended opportunities to refine their practices if change is to be permanent, something echoed in Trautmann and MaKinster (2010). The involvement in the GeoSciTeach project required long-term commitment from the PSTs (across and beyond their training program), as well as giving them opportunities to reflect on their practice, through exploring the use of new tools (smartphones) and new approaches to the thinking about science learning (geospatial). The approach to the design taken here is thus a good example of the Clarke and Hollingsworth professional development model for long-term growth and change.

The project provides an exemplary context within which to explore and discuss the process and outcomes of a customizable mobile-phone interface. In so doing, we aimed to also draw out key issues for future research to explicitly support teachers in their use and application of mobile technologies as an integral part of their teaching.

DESIGN PROCESS: IMPLEMENTATION

This section details the implementation of the design approach, illustrating how this approach sought to foster changes in teachers' beliefs, highlighting both practical and conceptual issues that arose during the process.

PSTs were introduced to the GeoSciTeach project and were recruited to participate on a volunteer basis, 6 months into their 10-month teacher-training course. This involvement aimed to ensure end-user input into the design and technical requirements of the application, and contribution to the pedagogical design of the learning activities. A series of four, 2-hour-long workshop sessions over a 5-month period were conducted to steer the development of the application and give participants the opportunity to feed back to designers over the progress of the application. A project blog was set up to encourage participants to generate ideas about science learning activities, discuss geospatial notions, and comment on the development of the application throughout the project.

During the first session, a fuller explanation of the project was given, together with an outline of expected participation in the planned program of work, and consent forms were completed. Participants began by describing the kinds of science practice and activity their students would currently engage in "in the field." An introduction to mobile smartphones was given, together with some example scenarios (plant response to climate change, electrical noise) for their use generated by a science-education lecturer. These were also available on the website for participants to look at and think about in preparation for the next workshop.

In the second session, participants were divided into small groups according to specific subject specialization (biology, chemistry, and physics) to brainstorm ideas about possible scientific activities, collaboratively with tutors, computer scientists, and HCI researchers. Eight Android phones were distributed across groups of five or six participants to facilitate this process. Most PSTs in the physics and chemistry subject groups found it difficult to link the capabilities of the phone to learning in science, while biology-based discussion centered around the use of data-logging sensors, which would require add-ons to phones. Biology graduates typically have experience using technology to support ecological investigations, and their focus on this use of technology in their discussions emphasized the importance that prior learning and experience play in teachers' thinking about pedagogical approaches (Luft, 2009; Trautmann & MaKinster, 2010). The combined expertise of the team and participants highlighted the need for PSTs to think more specifically about what they would want their students to do in a particular learning scenario or activity: for example, the kind of data they would need, what they would do with these data, and what they need to learn during the process. In so doing, they could help map smartphone potential and geospatial ideas more directly to teaching goals. This approach is essential if the teacher wants to go beyond thinking about the technology as simply an additional "add-on" to learning and actually use it to improve learning, both in terms of geospatial skills and specific subject content (McClurg and Buss, 2007). PSTs' lack of familiarity with, and understanding of, geospatial concepts emerged from this session. In the context of science, taking a geospatial perspective is fairly progressive and, as such, not explicitly written into the curriculum. Supporting the mapping of geospatial ideas to science teaching and the curriculum thus became a central part of the development process.

The next session focused on geospatial skills: an online survey of geospatial skills and current technology usage was circulated to participants, and the basic concept of layering of information was explained—a concept fundamental to geospatial thinking. It was found over the three sessions that PSTs struggled to comprehend science activities within the context of m-learning, with the use of a smartphone and geospatial ideas. Building on Haklay and Skarlatidou's (2010) three levels of geospatial reasoning (descriptive, analytic, inferential), a framework was developed to help PSTs map geospatial theory to science. It offers a description for each level, identifies ways in which the GeoSciteach application supports these, and maps them to related geospatial skills. This also indicates how curriculum development and geospatial skills move from the ability to identify and capture data, to making patterns and routes, and finally to understanding relationships and interconnected processes.

Development of the smartphone-application activity took place in parallel with these workshops. Similar to Trautmann and MaKinster (2010), our approach involved the introduction of geospatial tools and smartphone technologies through application to a specific exemplary activity to be employed in an authentic teaching context (Kew Gardens). An online Web application, Mockingbird, was used to produce mock-up designs for the application. These prototypes were made available to the PSTs for comment on the blog, as they were remotely situated in teaching placements. Opportunities for communicating and discussing ideas increase participant involvement in the design, improving the likelihood of long-term change (Trautmann & MaKinster, 2010).

A smartphone prototype was developed based on mock-ups, discussion among project team members, and feedback from PSTs. A number of data-collection tools considered necessary to support science fieldwork activity were made available as part of the application, including a camera, video camera, and data-logging of abiotic factors (e.g., temperature, humidity). Students were also given the facility to record taxonomic information about plants' characteristics (e.g., through a series of leaf silhouettes for matching entities in the environment), human uses, and plant significance within a

Table 27.1 Relating Geospatial Theory to GeoSciTeach and Geospatial Skills

Geospatial theory	Description	Sub-description	Procedural steps with GeoSciTeach	Geospatial functionality (of app)	Geospatial skill
Descriptive	Location: Where entity is	Identification of absolute place	GoogleMap, e.g., Kew (where you are now)	Representation of point locations within the model	Understand and identify own location, and collected data location
	Environment measure	e.g., soil, humidity, temperature	Record ambient data and link to location (country)	Associate meta-data & multimedia resources with specific points or areas	Identify and label Capturing, preserving, conveying appearances
	Feature	Shape, color, size, texture	Take photo: Upload to Google Earth	Render data with specific location into viewable image	
Analytic Understand structure of objects and phenomena	Comparison Relationship Patterns	Spatial, features Behavior relations	Photo tagging: relationship of one place compared to another	Ability to render model projections from different points of view	Reasoning about data Calculate and define distance and route Seeing patterns in data
Inferential Functional Evolutionary The "why?"	Integration with complex data Calculate relationships, e.g., time or distance		Leaf overlay/ silhouette	Ability to: Calculate relationships between areas, features, and points Calculate properties of specific areas	Understanding structure of objects Space in 2/3D Giving answer to evolution and functions of objects Cartographic configuration showing relationships between places

certain ecosystem. This gives the opportunity to gather information that is then mapped onto broader science learning ideas, for example, the importance of structure and function in biological thinking. The place of origin of a plant could also be tagged and layered onto Google Earth. These potential layers enable students to see patterns of plant distribution and adaptation throughout the world.

A fourth session with PSTs presented a working prototype as described above, and they were initially guided through the application in mock-up, before trialing it in pairs in an inner-city park. Participants provided feedback on aspects of the design they found useful, which ones needed additional modification, and what was lacking. The prospective Kew field trial was used as a concrete instance to work toward, providing a contextualized approach (Penuel et al., 2007). The application was made freely downloadable from the Android marketplace, with automatic update. Participants were each provided with Android phones, so that all iterations of development could be trialed. This was important, as PSTs on teaching placements could trial the application at any time. In so doing, PSTs were "given time to practice using new tools and data sources while also considering how they could apply these resources within their curriculum and with what pedagogical approaches" (Trautmann & MaKinster, 2010, p. 365).

One week prior to the field trip with 11–12-year-old students, the PSTs had an introductory meeting and planning day at Kew Gardens. During that time, logistics of teaching and planning activities were undertaken. Project participants were given time to explore the possibilities of using GeoSciTeach in their teaching with the pre-service tutor involved with GeoSciTeach. They were not obliged to use the smartphone application, but could do so if, and when, they thought it would support the learning activity. However, all project participants involved in teaching chose to use the application as part of the learning experience. PSTs devised questions that they felt could best be supported by GeoSciTeach, ranging from "How do plants maximize photosynthesis?" to "How do humans use plants?" These questions enabled exploration of how geospatial aspects of science learning might be foregrounded, through enabling students to harvest data and compare, contrast, and interact with that data locally and globally. The content of these questions suggests that the PSTs were beginning to change their understanding about geospatial thinking and develop a deeper appreciation of pedagogical content knowledge. This change implies that the participants' beliefs about the use of geospatial thinking in their practice was developing, and that they were starting to identify different "salient outcomes," as described by Clarke and Hollingsworth (2002). PSTs had 1 week to plan all activities for the student field trip, including their preparation of QR code links and selected video links.

During the exemplary activity day at Kew, children worked in groups of 16–18 and came around to each activity in turn. Where groups included project participants as teachers, the smartphone application became one aspect of the learning activity. Although teachers not directly involved in the project showed little interest in how the application worked, those who used the application reaped the rewards, as their students focused more on the specifics of geospatial relationships. For example, the prompt to upload photographs to Google Maps guided students to think about plant location in the world and its related habitat features.

In terms of beliefs and practice, different teaching approaches manifested differing use of the application. For example, while explaining how to use the application to each group of students, one teacher made clear reference to how the app can be used for both science (specifically in relation to the question they were asking) and for accessing geospatial concepts (focusing on where things are in the world). Analysis of this PST's interaction and use of the tool demonstrates developed competence in applying the technology to support a geospatial approach to science teaching. Another example (where one PST adopted a didactic teaching approach, while the other took a facilitative approach) illustrated how the application supported the facilitative approach to greater extent than the instructional approach. This suggests a design coherence with constructivist approaches, which are important in modifying underlying "traditional" beliefs of many science teachers about teaching science (Mansour, 2009).

Interviews with teachers and students about how well they thought the application worked revealed that both groups found it easy to use in context (teachers (novices to the app) took about 15 minutes, and students took 5), and that they themselves perceived that the application helped them to think geospatially about science. In terms of application design, one element that arose from discussion was that the application needed to have the option of being more structured or guided. PSTs were also concerned that collected data and planned activities on the application would have to be gathered, stored, and able to be distributed to students.

This was addressed during the development of the parallel mobile application enabling teachers to change the learning activity and the tools provided to guide or support the activity. The customizable part of the application begins by allowing teachers to choose the starting location for the learning activity—for example, Kew Gardens or the school grounds. In this way, the activity starts with the map (location) foregrounding geospatial notions. Teachers then type in the question they want their students to explore and select from a tick-box link which data-collection tools they would like to be made available to students. Teachers can modify supporting information and related information sites (e.g., in the form of YouTube video clips, text, or through QR readers), allowing them to tailor the experience to specific learning topics in fieldwork settings. However, during this phase of development, PSTs had finished formal training, and further attempts to arrange meetings and phone interviews with participants led to poor uptake. Instead, through contact from the Kew field trial, teachers from a school science department enrolled to trial the customizable application through a series of in-service training (known as INSET) sessions after school. However, owing to teacher time constraints and management pressures, this became increasingly difficult to implement. Real challenges to engaging in participant design are exemplified here. As in many training and workplace contexts, time pressures, management approaches, and the opportunity for consistent, long-term commitment are problematic.

However, eight PSTs from a different cohort of PSTs did volunteer to trial the application and its customizable interface. A workshop session provided the opportunity for trial and comment on the exemplary-activity application, as well as the customizable part of the application. The PSTs took around 10 minutes to find their way around the different tools for the exemplary activity and discussed how they thought it could be used to help students explore the question, "How do plants maximize photosynthesis?" Several suggestions for modifications or additions to future iterations were given, including a place for a guidance note on the question page (similar to a breadcrumb trail that guides the students through the task) and a timeline or a percent guide that showed how much of the activity is completed or how much time is left. One group wanted haptic feedback (hotter, colder, with the phone vibrating when you were near something of interest (Rogers & Price, 2008)). Others observed that there were a lot of tools/choices to make. However, the customizable nature of the application is precisely designed to allow teachers to choose as few or as many tools as they think appropriate for their question and students.

To trial the customizable interface, PSTs were asked to choose one of a set of science questions and, in pairs, to create a learning activity for their students using GeoSciTeach. This involved deciding what activities the students would need to undertake, for example, running, and what tools they would need to collect, record, and store data, such as measurement sensors, camera, Google Maps. Instead of using a "set" question, each pair formulated its own science-activity question. This is interesting, as it indicates that the exemplary activity provided an effective grounding for them to extend the application to new science contexts. For example, one pair designed an activity around the question "How fit are you?" For this, students would go on a run; use GPS tracking to see where they went, how far, and how long it took; and take recordings of pulse and breathing rate (and, in future iterations, carbon dioxide measurements to explore metabolic rate).

EMERGING ISSUES AND FUTURE RESEARCH DIRECTIONS

This section draws on findings from the project to highlight emerging issues from the design and development process, and its role in fostering change in teacher beliefs. Finally, key directions for future research are outlined that will engage with both the emerging opportunities for m-learning in teaching contexts and the principle challenges for research and situated application.

Engaging pre-service teachers in the design, development, and evaluation process proved fruitful in: (a) developing a prototype application that subsequent pre-service teachers were able to quickly grasp and use, to begin to develop their own new ideas of how to use the application in their science teaching; (b) developing ways to support the integration of new teaching approaches (in this case, geospatial skills) with the use of new technologies; and (c) indicating ways in which pre-service teachers' views of mobile technologies and the associated geospatial concepts could be useful in their science teaching. PSTs experienced each of the new learning opportunities afforded by m-learning (Traxler, 2011) at varying levels. Contingent learning occurred during the process of understanding the role of the smartphone application and the relationship between geospatial concepts and science. Engaging centrally in the design process highlighted PSTs' response to their changing experiences, enabling dialogue around, for example, what geospatial concepts in science mean. Situated learning took place during trials in the urban park and Kew Gardens, consolidating their competence in context. The project fostered an authentic learning approach, by engaging PSTs to think about and generate real science questions related to the curriculum. In terms of personalized learning, the application's customizable feature offers PSTs opportunity to think about how to tailor learning for different age groups and abilities.

Trautmann and MaKinster (2010) suggest that involvement in implementing new tools can mediate belief changes in teachers. However, their study comprised intensive technical and pedagogic support for teachers to implement geospatial approaches in their practice over the period of 1 year. In contrast, our study focused on the development of a tool that could be used in school, but primarily explored PSTs' development of geospatial awareness and competence with technology—an antecedent to full classroom implementation. This was considered an important part in the process of belief change, through the design process (technologically and pedagogically), and their developing understanding of the geospatial–science relationship. The design process offered access to a deeper-level understanding of the pedagogical and technological foundations of the tool. Nevertheless, across both studies, long-term commitment from participants was a central issue.

However, Mansour (2009) identifies a number of important barriers that impede teachers from putting their beliefs into practice. Time availability is problematic for teachers, and the pressure of working in a busy school environment often means they cannot commit sufficient time to both thinking about, and developing, novel resources. However, of greater importance to the project reported here is that some of the teachers felt that external pressures, for example, from school policies, would hinder their use of new technology in their practice. For example, during the interview, one project participant noted how the school he was now working in was not keen on the use of mobile phones and even stipulated the type of mobile phone allowable on school grounds. These types of problem are hard to overcome and, in part, rely on a case being built to support the benefits of using new technology. This move to want to change practice echoes the "salient outcomes" described by Clarke and Hollingsworth (2002): although they were discussing this in the context of individual development, this can be applied to the other levels of school organization, such as departmental or senior management. Being customizable, GeoSciTeach lends itself to teachers having autonomy over the "tool," allowing them to design activities that are specific to their learning context, and this may go some way in helping teachers to convince others of the benefits and applications of this technology.

Although future research continues to face challenges of long-term commitment from end users, this project illustrates how the development of an application such as GeoSciTeach, in the context of pre-service teachers, offers the opportunity for continued use and evaluation across subsequent cohorts. One fruitful avenue for research is to examine ways in which these kinds of technology or application can be embedded into teacher-training programs and so be usefully employed in the support and development of new approaches to science teaching.

REFERENCES

Ainsworth, S., & Flemming, P. (2006). Evaluating authoring tools for teachers as instructional designers. *Computers in Human Behavior, 22,* 131–148.

Anand, S., Batty, M., Crooks, A., Hudson-Smith, A., Jackson, M., Milton, R., et al. (2010). *Data mash-ups and the future of mapping.* Bristol, UK: JISC.

Brown, A., & Green, T. (2008). Issues and trends in instructional technology: Making the most of mobility and ubiquity. In M. Orey, V. J. McClendon, & R. M. Branch (Eds), *Educational Media and Technology Yearbook, 33,* 4–16.

Clarke, D., & Hollingsworth, H. (2002). Elaborating a model of teacher professional growth. *Teaching and Teacher Education, 18,* 947–967.

Constible, J. M., McWilliams, R. G., Soldo, E. G., Perry, B. E., & Lee, R. E. (2007). An immersion professional development program in environmental science for inservice elementary school teachers. *Journal of Geoscience Education, 55*(1), 72–79.

Desimone, L., Porter, A. C., Garet, M. S., Yoon, K. S., & Birman, B. F. (2002). Effects of professional development on teachers' instruction: Results from a three-year longitudinal study. *Educational Evaluation and Policy Analysis, 24*(2), 81–112.

Franckel, S., Bonsignore, E., & Druin, A. (2010). Designing for children's mobile storytelling. *International Journal of Mobile Human Computer Interaction, 2*(2), 19–36.

Hagevik, R. A. (2011). Five steps to success: Implementing geospatial technologies in the science classroom. *Journal of Curriculum and Instruction, 5*(1), 34–53.

Haklay, M., & Skarlatidou, A. (2010). Human–computer interaction and geospatial technologies in context. In M. Haklay (Ed.), *Interacting with geospatial technologies.* Chichester, UK: Wiley-Blackwell.

Hutchful, D., Mathur, A., Joshi, A., & Cutrell, E. (2010). *Cloze: An authoring tool for teachers with low computer proficiency.* Conference on Information and Communication Technologies and International Development, London, UK.

JISC. (2005). *Innovative practice with e-Learning: A good practice guide to embedding mobile and wireless technologies into everyday practice.* Retrieved from: www.jisc.ac.uk/whatwedo/programmes/elearninginnovation/practice.aspx

Kanjo, E., Benford, S., Paxton, M., Chamberlain, A., Stanton Fraser, D., Woodgate, D., et al. (2008). MobGeoSen: Facilitating personal geosensor data collection and visualization using mobile phones. *Personal and Ubiquitous Computing, 12*(8), 599–607. DOI:10.1007/s00779-007-0180-1

Klopfer, E., & Squire, K. (2007). Case study analysis of augmented reality simulations on handheld computers. *Journal of the Learning Sciences, 16*(3), 371–413.

Luft, J. (2009). Beginning secondary science teachers in different induction programmes: The first year of teaching. *International Journal of Science Education, 13*(17), 2355–2384.

Major, N. (1995). Modelling teaching strategies. *Journal of Artificial Intelligence in Education, 6*(2), 117–152.

Mansour, N. (2009). Science teachers' beliefs and practices: Issues, implications and research agenda. *International Journal of Environmental and Science Education, 4*(1), 25–48.

McClurg, P. A., & Buss, A. (2007). Professional development: Teachers' use of GIS to enhance student learning. *The Journal of Geography, 106*(2), 79–87.

Mueller, J., Wood, E., Willoughby, T., Ross, C., & Specht, J. (2008). Identifying discriminating variables between teachers who fully integrate computers and teachers with limited integration. *Computers and Education, 51,* 1523–1537.

Muller, M. (2002). Participatory design: The third space in HCI. In *The human–computer interaction handbook: Fundamentals, evolving technologies and emerging applications.* Mahwah, NJ: Lawrence Erlbaum Associates.

Penuel, W. R., Fishman, B. J., Yamaguchi, R., & Gallagher, L. P. (2007). What makes professional development effective? Strategies that foster curriculum implementation. *American Educational Research Journal, 44*(4), 921–958.

Ratto, M., Shapiro, R., Truong, T. M., & Griswold, W. (2003). The ActiveClass project: Experiments in encouraging classroom participation. In B. Wasson, S. Ludvigsen, & U. Hoppe (Eds.), *International Conference on Computer Supported Collaborative Learning* (pp. 477–486). Kluwer.

Rogers, Y., & Price, S. (2008). The role of mobile devices in faciliating collaborative inquiry in situ. *Research and Practice in Technology Enhanced Learning, 3*(3), 209–229.

Trautmann, N., & MaKinster, J. (2010). Flexibly adaptive professional development in support of teaching science with geospatial technology. *Journal of Science Teacher Education, 21,* 351–370.

Traxler, J. (2011). Introduction. In J. Traxler & J. Wishart (Eds.), *Making mobile learning work: Case studies of practice* (pp. 4–12). Bristol, UK: ESCalate Education Subject Centre: Advanced Learning and Teaching in Education.

28

iPAD HUMAN INTERFACE GUIDELINES
FOR M-LEARNING

Sabrina Huber and Martin Ebner

One of the most significant recent technologies is the tablet computer, such as Apple's iPad or its competitor tablets operating with Android. An increasing number of schools, such as the Kaiserin Augusta Schule, a high school in Germany (Digital Classroom Cologne, 2012), are making use of iPads in schools already.

This chapter will discuss whether and to what extent the development of iPad/iPhone apps for learning and teaching following the Human Interface Guidelines (HIG) helps to improve individual learning and teaching efforts.

The guidelines provide developers with a set of recommendations that should help to improve the user's experience in a certain environment, such as an application or a tool. There are guidelines for several platforms, and, in this chapter, we will focus on the iPad HIG (iPad Human Interface Guidelines, 2011), as well as the iOS Human Interface Guidelines (2012). Both concentrate on toolbar and visual design rules that should provide the user with reliable and intuitive interfaces. Designers should follow those guidelines when creating new apps to take full advantage of iPad features.

Owing to the fact that these are general guidelines for any app independent from the target group, we will examine whether the HCI guidelines are appropriate for apps designed for educational purposes and determine if there are further aspects that must be considered by developers and practitioners of learning apps.

As the guidance for iPad and iPhone is very much alike, this chapter will mainly focus on iPad apps.

iPAD HUMAN INTERFACE GUIDELINES: A SHORT INTRODUCTION

The iPad HIG are chosen according to their relevance mainly for the user, and not only the designer. Further, those guidelines contain four chapters, where the first provides an overview of the device, showing differences from the iPhone, such as its large screen and its highly interactive interface. In the second chapter, strategies for changing iPhone apps to iPad apps are described, where familiarity with the iPhone OS makes changing code relatively easy while developing the user interface, and experience is more of a challenge. This chapter now focuses on the third chapter, the iPad User Experience Guidelines, which help the designer and programmer to deliver a great user experience. The fourth chapter, the iPad User Inferface Element Guidelines, states how the user interface (UI) elements in iPad applications are an extension of chapter 3. Owing to the similarities of those chapters, they will be covered in one.

In the iPad, HIG interactivity and content come to the fore. The best apps promote those features by:

1. Downplaying application UI so that the focus is on the content that people want.
2. Presenting the content in beautiful, often realistic ways.
3. Taking full advantage of device capabilities to enable enhanced interaction with the content.

(iPad Human Interface Guidelines, 2011, p. 17)

The following guidelines and principles were selected and investigated in more detail (see examination of guidelines a little later):

- Aim to support all orientations—meaningfulness of rotating the device.
- Flatten your information hierarchy—the importance of auxiliary views, e.g., bars.
- Add physicality and heightened realism—real-life graphics to make users comfortable.
- Multi-touch gestures—performance of certain actions.
- File-handling—differences to other operating systems.
- Keyboard—hidden functions.

The following are human-interface principles:

- aesthetic integrity—measurement of the incorporation of an application's appearance with its functions;
- consistency—transferability of the user's experience and skills between different apps;
- direct manipulation—direct control through multi-touch gestures;
- feedback—immediate feedback after operations;
- metaphors—relation of virtual objects to real-world objects;
- user control—the user's responsibility for actions.

RESEARCH METHOD

During the winter term 2010, three applications were selected and tested in real-life school settings, among children between the ages of 8 and 10, on their iPads. In summer term 2011, a similar study was carried out with some improved scenarios.

In order to find out whether and to what extent the application of the iPad HIG was leading to the predicted user satisfaction, thinking-aloud tests, as well as user observations, were conducted in the field test. Finally, interviews helped to clarify user experiences and impressions.

In this chapter, we concentrate on the user observations done and the outcome lessons learned for interaction design. Finally, we provide a preliminary set of guidelines for how to use tablets for classroom instruction. From a didactical, technical, and also developmental viewpoint, the essential criteria to establish m-learning in the classroom will be shown.

EXAMINATION OF GUIDELINES

Aim to Support All Orientations

As the title suggests, the iPad is able to rotate to support multiple screen orientations. Once students found out that rotation was possible, they assumed that it would work for all applications and mostly wanted to turn the device to landscape mode because they could zoom in more. When apps did not support the landscape mode, students asked if something was wrong with their device and were distracted from their tasks.

On the other hand, at times, it can be better if the rotation mode is locked, because students were irritated by the screen rotating during activities that involved moving the iPad, e.g., interactive games where they had to move objects through shaking the device.

Some students were not aware of the advantages and disadvantages the alignment provides for certain exercises. Many apps have been designed to take advantages of the two orientation modes or have restrictions, e.g., when they used Mail, the default mail app on the iPad, they had a list of mails and accounts on the left pane in landscape mode but not in portrait mode. The majority of students who used portrait mode were confused and asked for a solution. Therefore, designers should always keep in mind the need to find a way to make users aware of auxiliary information that gets lost in portrait mode.

Another point: The iPad HIG focus on regarding rotating screens as reformatting. Students often lost their sentences when rotating their iPad from landscape to portrait mode. The younger ones repeatedly asked for help when that occurred. They should be told from the beginning that they should stay in one mode all the time when writing.

Also, if the device was in portrait mode and an application was starting in landscape mode, students sometimes got confused. They expected such apps to change into portrait mode, but they were not designed for that particular mode.

Flatten Your Information Hierarchy

Very likely, students forget where in their applications they currently are, and so most apps have additional tools on one screen so the user does not have to click through various places. Students should be familiar with auxiliary views right from the start. First, there are navigation bars, mostly on the left pane, that compresses the information hierarchy by one level; for example, in Dropbox, a Web-based file-hosting service that synchronizes files, when students open a folder, they can easily get back to the previous layer by clicking the button in the top left corner (see Figure 28.1).

Second, pop-up windows are often used so the user does not have to go to another screen to get additional information. The example in Figure 28.2 shows the bookmarks in Safari, Apple's Web browser, which appear as a pop-up window without leaving the page.

Third, segmented control in a toolbar enables the display of different categories, and the user does not have to leave the site. In iTunes, for instance, only the main content changes, while the buttons remain in the same place.

Last, very similar to those toolbars, tab bars are often used to display various categories without the need to move to another site or deeper into a hierarchy (see Figure 28.3). The buttons remain, but the main screen changes.

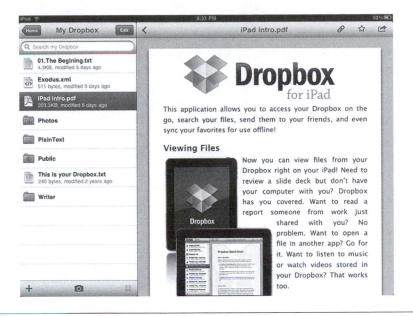

Figure 28.1 Navigation Bar in Dropbox

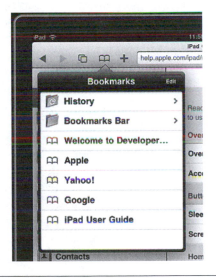

Figure 28.2 An Example of a Pop-Up Window in the Safari Web Browser

Figure 28.3 Tab Bar in iTunes Showing Segmented Controls

At the top edge of the iPad screen there is a status bar that displays the time, the battery charge, and the network connection. As it is important not only for teachers to control and keep track of the time, but also for students, no matter where they sit, the status bar should not be hidden. Also, the user should monitor the battery charge. Sometimes, students were worried when they had a low level of charge, e.g., 20 percent. However, the iPad's battery is quite powerful, and students should be told about it from the beginning, otherwise the same question will come up over and over again.

Add Physicality and Heightened Realism

Numerous apps provide the user with realistic dimensions so that it is easy to understand how they work, e.g., the address book, where students needed little explanation. Additionally, the iPad HIG suggest delighting the user with spectacular graphics so that they are drawn into an application. As long as those graphics and animations are not simply a distraction for the students, there is no problem. However, the 10-year-olds especially were easily diverted, particularly with e-books that contained a considerable number of animations and sounds. For a while, they forgot about reading and just played around.

Multi-Touch Gestures

The iPad user interface is based on multi-touch gestures to perform several actions, which students should know. With one finger, for instance, objects can be tapped to be selected. The one-finger swipe is used to move objects between two positions. Also, this gesture is known as the scroll gesture, because the user can scroll lists. Another gesture is the pinch, which usually implies using the thumb and a finger to zoom in or out of a position, e.g., a picture. Additionally, a page or an image can be rotated when the thumb remains in one position and the second finger rotates around it. Very little explanation was needed here, as students knew most essential gestures from TV or their smartphones, or immediately found them out themselves or together with their colleagues.

File-Handling

Those students who already worked with devices with operating systems that had a file browser soon got used to not thinking about those. They should be encouraged to view their documents as objects in various apps, such as Pages. Another difference from other systems is that the users do not have to save their work unless they cancel or delete, as iPad apps such as Pages or Keyword are responsible for saving.

Keyboard

The iPad keyboard is very briefly mentioned in the guidelines, but its usability and features are of great importance. For students, especially young learners, it was a big challenge to type their first sentences. They did not know about the touch-typing system, and it took them a very long time to figure out certain special characters, because they could only be found through pressing two keys, e.g., you need to press ".?123" and "#+=" to get to the percentage sign. If teachers do not encourage their students to search on their own before they ask for every detail, they will have nearly all the students putting their hands up at the same time.

In addition, there are numerous relatively hidden keyboard features that students randomly came across. When you write at least one word and double-click the space bar, you get a dot and a space. Or, when you hold down the comma, you get an apostrophe, and when you do the same with the dot key, you get a quotation mark, which saves a lot of time in longer texts. Try out various letters to get other versions, such as umlauts or letters with accent marks. Another new feature is the split keyboard, which one student found out about. When you click the show/hide button at the bottom on the right, you can undock or split the keyboard, which can be very handy. Undocking allows the keyboard to be moved to another position. The keyboard can also be split when you hold one finger on each side of it and just swipe them outwards. In reverse order, you can merge it again.

Depending on which language is selected, adapting the keyboard settings can be very useful too. For instance, our students had German settings, and, when they wrote their texts in English, autocorrection was turned on and distracted them. Under Setting > General > Keyboard, autocorrection can be turned off. Further, autocapitalization and caps lock can be turned on and off.

HUMAN-INTERFACE PRINCIPLES

A great user interface follows human interface design principles that are based on the way people—users—think and work, not on the capabilities of the device. A user interface that is unattractive, convoluted, or illogical can make even a great application seem like a chore to use. But a beautiful, intuitive, compelling user interface enhances an application's functionality and inspires a positive emotional attachment in users.
(iOS Human Interface Guidelines, 2012)

Aesthetic Integrity

Aesthetic integrity does not indicate the beauty of an app but measures how well the look of an application ties in with its function. Apps such as Pages and Keynote, which allow productive tasks, focus on simple design and not on spangly elements that could distract the user. Those two apps use straightforward buttons and provide the user with a clear understanding of their purpose. Also, students who were new to word-processing and presentation programs figured out the purpose of various buttons quite fast. Nevertheless, many had problems highlighting and copying words. They were not used to double-clicking words or tapping on words so that additional options would be available in a pop-up box, which is similar to a right click on a computer. Some stated they would prefer a mouse in the first lessons. However, after more practice, the majority felt comfortable with the apps.

Further, aesthetic integrity does not mean that all apps have to have reduced decorative elements. On the contrary, if an app promotes widespread tasks, e.g., a game, users do not want to get bored and they expect a pleasant appearance that guarantees a good time and promises greater discovery.

Consistency

Consistency in the interface is of great importance, as users can transfer their experience and skills between different apps. Students first learned how to work with Pages and then familiarized themselves with Keynote. Most symbols remained the same, and all the gestures, such as double-clicking for cutting and pasting, were not new for them anymore. The aforementioned apps were clearly developed according to standards the user is familiar and comfortable with from other leading productivity programs. Further, they are very intuitive for new users and follow the principle of consistency, which means they are consistent with iOS standards. The icons always have the same meaning, and the user can predict what they will do when they are in a different place.

Direct Manipulation

With the iPad, the user can directly manipulate objects, such as pictures, on-screen and does not have to use commands like buttons for that manipulation. Students soon understood how to control pictures, e.g., how to zoom in or make them bigger or smaller. They enjoyed the multi-touch interface straight away and started experimenting and passing on their knowledge; e.g., when one student found out how to rotate images, another way of experiencing direct manipulation, he immediately showed his colleagues. Students had immediate results that they could see from the beginning.

Feedback

Another essential principle is the immediate feedback the user wants and gets after operating a control. For example, when a word is highlighted in Pages, it turns blue. If the user tabs the info button, it glows for a second to indicate a successful operation. Such feedback is of great value for users, as they know whether something has worked or not and save time. Apart from visual feedback, audible feedback can also help the user to clarify results of actions. Students mainly got to know visible feedback because they had to turn off the sound most of the time to avoid a high noise level.

Metaphors

A principle that avoided many student questions that would certainly have come otherwise is the use of metaphors. As iOS offers numerous metaphors through graphics and gestures, the user can physically interact with realistic on-screen objects. Students quickly related virtual objects such as icons to real-world objects if they had a similar appearance, e.g., of folders. Mostly, those metaphors have fewer limits than the real-world object. Folders on the iPad can be filled with considerably more files than real ones. The user knows that the main purpose of folders is filing. If they also had to organize files into a registry, the usability of virtual folders would be diminished, which means that metaphors should not be expanded too far.

Metaphors in iOS include:
- Tapping Music playback controls
- Dragging, flicking, or swiping objects in a game
- Sliding On/Off switches
- Flicking through pages of photos
- Spinning picker wheels to make choices.

(iOS Human Interface Guidelines, 2012)

User Control

The last human-interface principle suggests that it should mainly be the user who starts and is in charge of the actions. It is considered a mistake if apps make decisions for the user on their own, unless they help to avoid risky results. Our students often used English apps, although they just started to learn the language. Additional messages and controlling actions would likely have led to distraction and more questions. Therefore, it is enough to have straightforward actions they could understand without difficulty, although they knew little about the language. Here, the aforementioned metaphors were of great help, as they were often symbols or icons without text.

SUMMARY OF OUTCOMES

Taking the aforementioned guidelines and principles into account, their thorough use definitely improves the development process, as well as the interface design, and leads to a better reception for learning apps. However, children, in our case young learners aged 8–10, still need further explanations from their teachers. Although the apps we used were mainly self-explanatory, many students needed additional help, as they often were afraid to do something wrong or were not motivated to explore on their own. After some encouragement and support, they first tried themselves and then asked their colleagues.

Importance of the Guidelines

Although students would sooner or later be well versed with the functions of the devices because they experimented or helped each other, it is of great importance that their teacher knows about gestures, bars, and orientations to provide all relevant information. Regarding the iPad HIG they should be aware of the following points:

- Not all applications allow rotation, and it should be pointed out when and why landscape or portrait mode is more appropriate, and which restrictions the two orientations imply.
- Students should know about the hierarchy, position, and function of auxiliary views such as bars, so that they do not get lost (e.g., in Dropbox).
- Students should be familiar with multi-touch gestures from the start to know how to perform various actions.
- File-handling on the iPad differs from other operating systems, and students should know how to find their files and why it is not necessary to save them in apps such as Pages.
- The keyboard offers numerous functions, but many of them are hidden. However, using them saves a lot of time when writing a longer text. Students should know how to find them.
- The appearance of an application does not necessarily say something about its content. Before students use it, teachers have to make sure they tried it out themselves to see whether the app delivers what its appearance promises. Often, the animations and graphics are better than the content and learning effect.

Criteria to Establish M-Learning in the Classroom
Visual Aid

In a class with more than 20 students who all have their own device, one teacher can hardly cope with all the questions that constantly emerge. From our experience, mentioning how certain apps work is not enough. Teachers need a projector or smart board to give explanations while all students are watching. Otherwise, the same instruction has to be given over and over again.

Organization

We suggest making folders to keep track of your apps, e.g., one folder for every subject or for all productivity apps, such as Pages and Keynote. Further, all files should be stored in a Dropbox account that is shared with all students. For instance, English students shared all their Keynote presentations, MP3 files, and worksheets.

Material

Currently, no digital schoolbooks for the iPad are available in Austria. Can teachers move forward with subject matters without them? Yes, they can, but with additional preparation time for the teachers. We split up a class (one half worked with iPads, the other half without) for a month and tried to complement the books with worksheets, online exercises, and apps and could practice listening, writing, speaking, and reading skills. There was no measurable difference between the two groups, and we managed to work on exactly the same subject matters. There are plenty of online exercises of all kinds available. However, teachers always have to be careful with copyright issues.

Choice of Applications

Teachers should try out apps before they show them to, or start them together with, their students. Sometimes, apps are more difficult than their title or description suggests. Further, teachers have to take into account that young learners of a new language might not even understand the error messages or buttons (if they have text on them). They should choose apps that offer great metaphors for children and are very intuitive. Moreover, some apps are really just fillers for 5 minutes because they do not have much content, or are too easy or too difficult for learners. It is the same with worksheets—teachers should look through them first, not only to be prepared for questions, but also to check whether they really fit the desired outcome or purpose.

Writing

As we did not want students' handwriting to be undervalued, we used apps such as neu.Annotate, which allows handwritten annotations for several worksheets. Additionally, they wrote some texts in Pages, which is useful for all subjects where students have to make notes too. As mentioned in the section about human-interface principles, the buttons are quite self-explanatory, but students had problems with deleting words or pictures. There is no metaphor for those actions, but when they were told via the aid of the projector, hardly anyone asked the same question again.

Managing Classes and Grades

Teachers can easily get themselves organized with apps such as TeacherPal, which offers a section to enter grades, students' cooperation, attendance, and behavior. A seating plan with pictures and additional information about students, such as names and e-mail addresses can be added too. In addition, there are numerous free apps to monitor tests and homework for students if they are allowed to take their devices home.

Connectivity

As the school network very likely cannot cope with 20 or more devices, an additional router is recommended to guarantee a stable Internet connection.

Internet Research

No matter which subject they currently have, students will need the Internet, e.g., for downloading worksheets, watching short clips, and most of all doing research. Therefore, it is of great importance to make them aware of copyright issues, proper methods for citations and references, and which websites are suitable for their research purpose.

Battery Life

Teachers/students should monitor battery life every day. Depending on how many hours the devices are used, the iPads should be charged. It can be very annoying if students do not have a device.

Read Full Books for Free

Shakespeare, Twain, or the *Three Little Pigs* by Halliwell-Phillipps—they can all be read for free. The iBook store offers numerous books for all age groups, which is great for all language teachers, but also technical, scientific, and health-related books can be found easily enough.

Group Projects

Students get instant access to information for their projects, can share it, split tasks, and make presentations. Once they are done, they can present projects in front of the whole class and upload them to their Dropbox. A great app for doing research is Wikipanion, where students can find out about nearly anything, can save a search history, add bookmarks, and save images. In addition, the World Atlas HD and GeoMaster Plus HD, where students learn interesting facts about countries and can test their knowledge, are very helpful.

Movies

Students can not only watch movies but also create their own, e.g., with iMovie, which costs about €4. They can record their own theatre plays or short dialogues, edit them, and add sounds and text. They can monitor themselves, e.g., their pronunciation and their colleagues', give better feedback, and understand the feedback they have been given better. Movies are not only a good idea in language subjects but also in science subjects such as physics or chemistry, where students carry out experiments from time to time and, later on, can add text for better understanding.

Finally, a checklist (see Figure 28.4) is presented for additional issues concerning an m-learning scenario with tablets in the classroom.

CONCLUSION

Active participation by students, which means more interaction between students and technology, in this case, the iPad, can lead to greater learning experience. Therefore, the development of appropriate learning apps can be promising for the future of teaching. Taking into account HIG improves the usage within real-life learning and teaching settings. Further, a beautiful, intuitive, and convincing graphical user interface adds to positive feelings in users. There is a strong relationship between good interface design and the ease of use of learning apps. However, the look of an app should also tie in with its function. Developers should always consider the needs of the target group carefully

Technical Issues	☑
Visual aid (beamer…)	☐
Battery life	☐
Connectivity	☐
Didactical Issues	☐
Choice of applications (to be checked beforehand)	☐
Administrative Issues	☐
Organization (folders…)	☐
Tool to manage classes and grades	☐
File-sharing (Dropbox…)	☐

Figure 28.4 Checklist for Teachers Who Want to Promote M-Learning

before they start designing and testing their apps, e.g., an app for young learners is not appropriate if it contains difficult buttons or too much text.

Learning objects of the future can be small apps, but we have to bear in mind that they will be designed for a special target group—the learner.

REFERENCES

Digital Classroom Cologne. (2012, January). iPad at Kaiserin Augusta Schule, Cologne. Retrieved from: http://digital classcologne.wordpress.com

iOS Human Interface Guidelines. (2012). Retrieved from: http://developer.apple.com/library/ios/#documentation/UserExperience/Conceptual/MobileHIG/Introduction/Introduction.html

iPad Human Interface Guidelines. (2011). Retrieved from: www.scribd.com/doc/61285332/iPad-Human-Interface-Guideline

29

THREE-DIMENSION DESIGN FOR MOBILE LEARNING

Pedagogical, Design, and Technological Considerations and Implications

Xun Ge, Dingchung Huang, Huimin Zhang, and Beverly B. Bowers

We live in a fast-paced digital world that places increased demands and challenges on working professionals across various disciplines. In order to remain current with emerging knowledge, we need to keep updated with advances in knowledge and technology. It is a daunting task for individuals with limited time to do so. We also realize that this digital world affords us untold benefits, including access to more powerful and advanced technologies that assist us to do our jobs more effectively and efficiently. Mobile technology is an example of a rapidly developing technology that shows promise as a solution to help learners meet accelerating needs for knowledge advancement within their own unique settings and time schedules.

Mobile technology is advancing at an amazing rate and has gained increasing popularity in recent years. Mobile devices include personal digital assistants (PDAs), laptop computers, smartphones, and other customized hardware (Liu & Hwang, 2010). According to the report of the International Telecommunication Union at Telecom World (2009), mobile-phone subscriptions reached 4.6 billion worldwide in 2009. Owing to its widespread use and unique capabilities and features, mobile technology has demonstrated remarkable potential for education and can be considered as a useful tool for learning and instruction (DiGiano et al., 2003).

Mobile devices offer a solution for accessing new knowledge and skills anytime and anywhere (Ally, 2009; Koole & Ally, 2006; Shih, Chuang, & Hwang, 2010). Mobile technology encourages self-paced and self-directed learning through use of the applications (apps) installed on them. Learners can receive individualized feedback and guidance instantly (Shih et al., 2010). Additionally, mobile technology has been recognized as an effective communication technology to promote collaborative learning and teamwork among students. Therefore, integrating mobile technology in education offers endless possibilities to provide alternative, high-quality educational experiences that are more inclusive, efficient, and effective (Elias, 2011). Mobile technology offers flexible learning capabilities that can be used to engage learners in a variety of strategies, including ubiquitous learning, active learning, interactive learning, situated learning, adaptive learning, and collaborative learning (Bomsdorf, 2005; Bradley, Haynes, Cook, Boyle, & Smith, 2009; Chen, Kao, & Sheu, 2003).

PURPOSE

As a new form of learning technology, mobile technology challenges educators to understand the affordances of the technology, learners' needs, societal needs, and contexts of instruction from new perspectives (Koszalka & Ntloedibe-Kuswani, 2010). Educators and researchers are compelled to examine research questions such as how mobile technology can be designed and integrated most effectively for learning and instruction. Research in m-learning has just begun, and there is a lot more to be explored and investigated. Although there is a myriad of literature discussing various aspects of m-learning, including design, implementation, delivery, and evaluation (Elias, 2011; Grasso & Roselli, 2005), there is rarely literature aimed at providing a theoretical framework for instructional designers to guide the design of m-learning. Therefore, in this chapter, we intend to discuss a three-dimension instructional design framework for m-learning: the dimension of pedagogy, the dimension of design, and the dimension of technology.

A computer-based simulation called *Putting It All Together* (Huang, Zhang, Higgins, Ge, & Bowers, 2011), which was developed to support the professional development of nurse learners, will be used to illustrate the instructional design framework. The pedagogical dimension, which is grounded in the theoretical assumptions for learning and involves situated cognition (Brown, Collins, & Duguid, 1989) and cognitive apprenticeship (Collins, Brown, & Holum, 1991), will be described. In addition, we will address the design dimension, which includes the underlying instructional design and multimedia learning principles to consider when designing an interactive, simulation-based learning environment. The technological features and issues for designing m-learning technology, including the advantages and features afforded by mobile technology, are discussed as the third important dimension. Additionally, instructional design guidelines specific to m-learning, based on both the literature and our own design experience, will be presented.

CONTEXT

There was an identified need for an instructional program to inform nurses and nursing students about immunizations across the lifespan and their roles in the immunization process. However, the topic of immunization was not covered sufficiently in the current nursing curriculum or in available nursing textbooks. To address the need, the University of Oklahoma (OU) College of Nursing (CON) received a large grant from the American Recovery and Reinvestment Act to create an online nursing immunization curriculum called the Nursing Initiative Promoting Immunization Training (NIP-IT). The Web-based NIP-IT curriculum, consisting of six modules of relevant topics, was designed to educate both current and future nurses about immunization. Course faculty hoped to create modules that were more interactive and clinically relevant to promote knowledge transfer to a real-world setting. Therefore, the CON faculty and the OU's instructional psychology and technology student instructional design team worked together to enhance the interactivity, authenticity, and complexity of the modules in order to promote learners' critical thinking and problem-solving.

One of the learning modules was designed to educate nurse learners about four important nursing roles related to immunizations: educator, communicator, care coordinator, and advocate (see Table 29.1). The educator role is one of the most important nursing roles, as nurses assess their patient's knowledge about immunizations and provide accurate information about vaccines. As educators, nurses need a strong background related to learning styles, how people learn, and how to effectively use techniques such as the "teach-back" to evaluate if learning has occurred. Nurses in the communicator role must have a good understanding of how to communicate effectively with patients in a variety of situations using an array of communication strategies. Immunizations can be an emotionally charged topic for many parents. If a parent gets upset about immunizations, the nurse needs to understand how to diffuse anger and to counteract misperceptions. Nurses also need to recognize verbal and non-verbal communication cues. As the care coordinator, the nurse has an important role in bringing together the many processes involved in immunizations. Nurses must be able to identify patients who are in need of vaccines, promote safe storage and handling of vaccines, assure adequate supplies are on hand, administer vaccines, monitor patients for potential adverse effects, and report reactions to the appropriate agency. The role of nurse advocate involves supporting and promoting the patient's individual health-care rights related to immunization, as well those of the community, through support of ethics

Table 29.1 Nursing Roles, Actions, and Exemplars

Nurse Roles	Nurse Actions	*Putting It All Together* Exemplar
Educator	Teach Knowledgeable about education theory; teaches patient and family about their condition and self-care; promotes health-care literacy	Provided information about vaccines Adjusted teaching to fit adult's or child's level of understanding Used teach-back
Communicator	Distribute and clarify information. Uses effective verbal, non-verbal, and written communications during patient interactions; recognizes verbal and non-verbal cues; communicates in culturally appropriate manner	Asked questions to confirm understanding Clarified misunderstandings Reflection Non-threatening manner
Advocate	Know about and distribute information about recent vaccination updates. Supports and promotes the patient's individual rights; supports policy initiatives that focus on the availability, safety, and quality of care	Discussed current recommendation for a new vaccine with the parent of child Respected parent's right to make decision not to vaccinate child
Care coordinator	Assess a patient's immunization status, recommend vaccination updates, and store/use vaccines properly. Facilitates and coordinates care with other disciplines to assure seamless, quality care; promotes effective follow-up care	Examined patient's chart to determine vaccine history Set up appointment for child to receive vaccines

and policy initiatives that focus on the availability, safety, and quality of care related to immunizations. For example, if a patient or a child's parent refuses a vaccine, the nurse accepts their decision and their right to make their own choices. These nursing roles are distinct but may overlap; more than one role can be assumed during any nurse–patient interaction.

The existing instructional materials did not provide learners with an opportunity to practice the four nursing roles. According to our needs analysis, most of the learners understood the concepts of the four roles; yet they lacked the experience of practicing these roles. Hence, we planned instruction starting from this point and moving forward, with the goal that learners would experience the four roles of a nursing professional through their engagement in interactive, simulated learning activities to promote deeper learning.

In order to bridge the gap between the current materials and the desired materials, we chose to use a real-world case study as the main storyline to create an interactive, Web-based, multimedia simulation. We hoped that the instructional activity would allow learners to discern and experience the distinctive characteristics of each nurse's role in a simulated clinical setting.

Considering the context and learners' prior knowledge and background, we first approached the design by following the general instructional design process—analysis, design, development, implementation, and evaluation (ADDIE). Then, we iteratively revisited and revised the design, which was summarized and conceptualized as three critical dimensions: pedagogical, design, and technological. We would like to offer this design framework to other instructional designers or those who are interested in designing technology for m-learning.

THREE-DIMENSION DESIGN FRAMEWORK

The three dimensions of the design framework discussed in this chapter are conceptualized as follows: The pedagogical dimension is defined by instructional approaches, specific to designing for a Web-based learning environment, which are grounded in learning theories and based on the outcomes of the needs analysis (including learner, task, and context analyses). The design dimension refers to the specific instructional strategies and activities that operationalize the identified instructional approaches, including instructional events, learning activities, sequencing and branching techniques, and screen and message design. The technological dimension involves examination of the features of a technological system, including the pros and cons of designing for a given learning environment, and addresses issues such as interface design and platform implementation. Each dimension will be discussed in further detail.

The Pedagogical Dimension

Similarly to designing for any learning environment, the pedagogical dimension should be the most essential consideration in designing for m-learning. The design of *Putting It All Together* was framed from the perspective of constructivist learning. According to constructivism, people construct their own knowledge based on their life experiences and prior knowledge (Jonassen, 1999). The ultimate learning goal in *Putting It All Together* was for learners to be able to perform the four nursing roles through their interactions with patients. To facilitate knowledge transfer, we purposely designed a simulation that placed learners in an authentic learning environment that mirrored real-life clinical scenarios. Instead of being presented with information, learners were guided through *Putting It All Together* as they solved a series of problems such as those they might actually encounter in their future workplace settings. As the problems encountered by nurses in real-world settings are ill-structured and dynamically changing according to many factors, including the nurse–patient relationship, we followed Jonassen's (1999) constructivist-learning environment to guide our design. A constructivist-learning environment is assumed to engage learners in meaning-making and knowledge construction process and provides learners with modeling, coaching, and scaffolding (Jonassen, 1999).

Simulation

One of the learning objectives in the design of *Putting It All Together* was to help learners understand, not only "what," but also "why" and "how" in their simulated problem-solving process. To this end, we applied simulation as a macro-strategy for our design. Simulation can be used as an effective tool to fulfill the requirement for complex, ill-structured problem-solving (Smith & Ragan, 2005). Learning with simulations has several advantages as compared with other formats of learning (Alessi & Trollip, 2001). First, a simulation can be complex, yet safe and easy to control at the same time; learners do not have pressure owing to fear of making mistakes. Second, simulations simplify reality, so they can be more conducive to learning; learners can concentrate on specific concepts or skills without distractions. Third, simulations enhance learners' motivation by being engaging, relevant, and challenging. Fourth, simulations can help with knowledge transfer, as they are designed to simulate real-world scenarios. The variety and complexity of situations in simulations can be adjusted to facilitate either near transfer or far transfer of knowledge.

The simulation begins with navigation instructions, including how to access help, how to exit at any time, how to return to where the learner might leave off, and reassurance that answers are neither right nor wrong. The conversation between the learner and the characters is guided throughout the simulation as the learner clicks on the "You" button to converse with the characters.

The learner enters the simulation and begins by meeting Rose, the nursing supervisor, outside of the hospital, as they enter the hospital. This is the first place the learner is asked about the four nursing roles. If the learner indicates they are comfortable with the four nursing roles, then they move to the next scenario. If they indicate they do not remember the four nursing roles, then the supervisor reminds the learner of the roles and reminds them to review the nursing roles in the NIP-IT module before they move to the next scenario.

In the next scene, the learner meets Jenny, a nurse colleague, in the hospital hallway. Jenny makes the learner feel welcomed and discusses the four nursing roles, giving the learner the opportunity to decide which role she has described. If the learner selects the correct role, a positive response is elicited from Jenny. If the learner selects an incorrect response, then Jenny provides the correct answer with rationale. Rose, the supervisor, re-enters at the end of this scenario and makes the assignment for the learner and Jenny to see the patient, Brett, who is at the clinic to get pre-kindergarten immunizations. He is accompanied by his mother, Mrs. Jonassen.

The learner meets and interacts with Mrs. Jonassen and Brett in the examination room. After the initial introduction and determination of the reason for the appointment, the learner has a choice to focus attention on, and interact with, Brett, who is upset about having to get a shot, or with Mrs. Jonassen, who is questioning why her child needs so many shots. Depending upon the learner's choice of who to interact with first, the scenario will branch off into either the educator role (interaction with Brett) or the communicator role (interaction with Mrs. Jonassen). Jenny, the experienced nurse, is a part of each scenario, offering expert guidance for the learner as needed.

In the educator role, the learner provides information about vaccines to Brett, adjusting teaching techniques to his developmental level. The learner assesses what Brett knows about causes of illness and how vaccines can protect him. The teach-back technique is used, as the learner asks Brett to repeat back what he just learned. At the end of the scenario, the learner gains Brett's agreement to take the vaccines. After completing the selected interaction, the learner is guided to a screen to reflect upon and select the role that they believe they played in the scenario. The learner also has the opportunity to reflect on how they thought they did during the scenario. After reflection, the learner is directed back to the scenario and is presented with two prompts that lead to a different scenario, which demonstrates a different role. For example, after completion of the scenario with Brett, the learner can choose to interact with Mrs. Jonassen and is directed to the communicator role.

In the communicator role, the learner interacts with Mrs. Jonassen, who seems reluctant to have her son immunized. In this role, the learner will clarify Mrs. Jonassen's understanding of how vaccine boosters work. The learner uses effective communication techniques such as reflection to indicate to the mother that her concerns are heard. After reflection on the communicator role, the learner is directed to a minor conflict situation with Mrs. Jonassen.

In the minor conflict situation, Mrs. Jonassen is upset and questions why her son needs so many vaccines, especially a flu vaccine. She voices a common misconception that, if he takes the flu shot, then he will get the flu. This is another example of the communicator role, as the learner clarifies misconceptions about vaccines, and then Mrs. Jonassen wants to know about a new vaccine to prevent human papilloma virus (HPV), a sexually transmitted disease. This leads into another branching scenario where the learner can choose to move into either the advocate role or the care-coordinator role. In the advocate role, the learner suggests that Mrs. Jonassen's teenaged daughter would be a good candidate for the new HPV vaccine and respects her decision to wait and think about it. In the care-coordinator role, the learner schedules an appointment for Mrs. Jonassen's daughter and prepares to administer the required immunizations to Brett.

This process of entering a scenario, interacting with the patient and his mother in one of the four nursing roles, and reflection continues until the learner has navigated through all four roles and has had the opportunity to reflect on each role. After completing the final role, the learner is guided back to meet with the supervisor, who reviews what was learned and provides feedback on what the learner did well in the scenario. Finally, the learner has the opportunity to reflect on the entire learning experience. Through actively engaging in the simulation, the learner has the chance to apply each role and has the opportunity to reflect upon each role, as well as upon the entire experience.

Underlying Theories

In designing the simulation, *Putting It All Together*, we followed the instructional model of goal-based scenarios (GBSs) (Schank, Berman, & Macperson, 1999). A GBS is a "learning-by-doing" simulation in which learners pursue their learning goals by practicing target skills and applying relevant content knowledge to help them achieve their goal. During the simulation, learners are provided with just-in-time coaching to help them apply knowledge to make a decision or solve a problem. Experts providing feedback and learner reflections of lessons learned are major characteristics of GBSs. The GBS approach is inherently motivating to learners.

In *Putting It All Together*, the main learning goal is for the learner to play the four nursing roles appropriately and effectively when he/she communicates with patients. We set up several scenarios for the learner (identified as "you" in the scenario) to interact with four characters in the simulation: the learner's supervisor (Rose), a colleague (Jenny), the patient (Brett), and the patient's mother (Mrs. Jonassen). During interactions with Mrs. Jonassen and Brett, the learner goes through each of the four nursing roles (i.e., educator, communicator, care coordinator, and advocate), which are specifically explained in Table 29.1.

Situated-learning theory indicates that learners learn better when they are placed in real-world contexts (Greeno, Smith, & Moore, 1993). These contexts are complex, with a social aspect (Anderson, Reder, & Simon, 1996). In *Putting It All Together*, we assign the nursing-intern role to a learner in a hospital, because it is important for the learner to assume the professional identity. However, as an intern, the learner does not perform the tasks by herself/himself, throughout the simulation. The learner acts in the four nursing roles with the guidance of a colleague, as in real situations. Learners enter the simulation and go through the four-stage problem-solving processes (i.e., problem presentation, information exploration, discovery, and reflection on solution) (Wang & Hannafin, 2005) as they play each of the four nursing roles. For instance, the patient will ask "you" questions at the beginning of each episode, and "you" have to analyze the problem based on the patient's responses, recall their prior knowledge, and come up with solutions to the problems. At the end of each episode, the learner will reflect on the problem-solving process and evaluate his/her own performance. By doing so, learners will develop problem-solving skills related to the four nursing roles and be able to transfer their experience to real-world jobs more effectively. Additionally, learners will reflect on their opinions and feelings toward the four roles in order to overcome attitudinal obstacles that could be interfere with their performance.

In addition, we incorporated cognitive-apprenticeship theory in our design to scaffold learners to learn expert thinking skills. An apprenticeship involves placing learners into a real-life learning activity, such as learning how to be a nurse by following and learning from an expert. By doing so, the apprentice learns the intellectual and psychomotor information necessary to do the nurse's job. Cognitive apprenticeship is similar, but the focus is on showing learners how experts think by verbalizing experts' thoughts (Collins, Brown, & Holum, 1991). In our design, an expert nurse will be the learner's mentor and will provide cognitive apprenticeship throughout the activity, using strategies such as question prompts, coaching, scaffolding, and self-reflection. The expert nurse asks questions, observes the learners, provides guidance in complex situations, and helps the learners reflect on the learning processes. According to Ge, Planas, and Er (2010), question prompts, scaffolding, and self-reflection are all useful mechanics to provide guidance.

The Design Dimension

In the design dimension, we further contextualize the pedagogical considerations in the specific design context of the project, which are translated into (a) design of strategies and activities, (b) activity sequencing and branching, and (c) screen design.

Design of Strategies and Activities

Figure 29.1 demonstrates the four critical problem-solving activities supported by *Putting It All Together*: problem representation, making decisions, self-reflection, and feedback from a subject-matter expert (SME).

Problem Representation

In the problem-representation stage, the learner has the opportunity to identify the problem based on the questions the patient or parent asks regarding vaccines. For

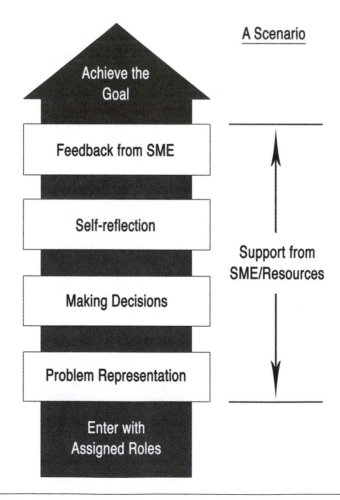

Figure 29.1 A Visual Representation of Major Learning Activites in *Putting It All Together*

example, Mrs. Jonassen asks the learner ("you") about the vaccine requirements for her son who is going to kindergarten, and if her son needs to have all the vaccines given during that appointment (see Figure 29.2). The learner, now in the role of the nurse communicator, is required to examine the parent's questions and analyze what her concerns are. The learner can then come up with a conclusion that the parent needs more information about different types of vaccine booster and the recommended vaccine schedule, which would then be taught as part of the nurse educator role.

Making Decisions

From the previous stage, learners should have identified a problem that they believed needed to be resolved for the patient. In this stage, learners are provided with different responses that they can make to react to the patient's or the parent's questions. There is no right or wrong response in the simulation. Different responses will lead to different nursing roles that learners will demonstrate. The decision-making activity is operationalized throughout the design with the simulation program branching to different paths (see Figure 29.3). Decision-making is guided so that eventually learners move through all four nursing roles and make decisions in each role, although the order in which they proceed through the simulation may differ.

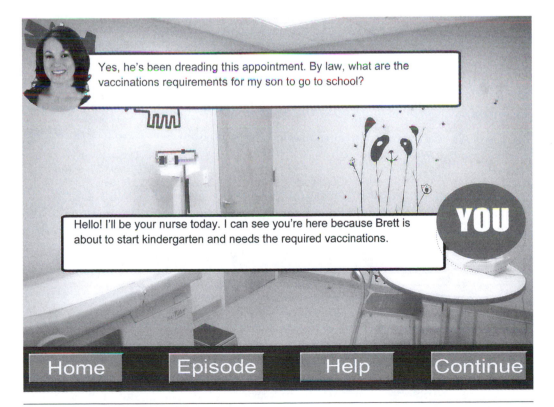

Figure 29.2 Conversation Between "You" and the Patient's Mom, Mrs. Jonassen. Mrs. Jonassen is Asking "You" About the Vaccine Requirements for Her Son, and "You" are Listening

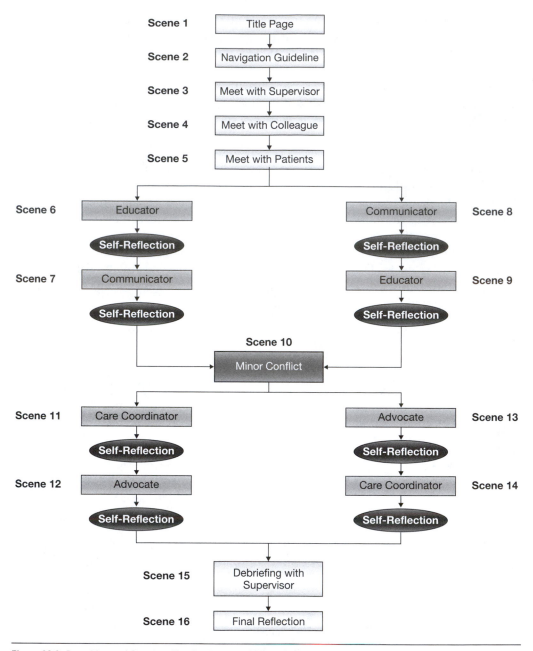

Figure 29.3 Branching and Structure Map for Putting It All Together

Self-Reflection

After making decisions, learners receive question prompts from the simulation program. The learner is asked to identify the role that he or she played (refer to Figure 29.4). The "reflection-prompts" function allows learners to reorganize the knowledge and principle they just applied and reflect on the role they demonstrated during their patient interaction.

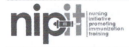

nipit
nursing initiative promoting immunization training
Think about your interaction with the patient...
What role do you think you were demonstrating? (Click all that apply.)
Communicator
Care Coordinator
Educator
Advocate

Figure 29.4 The Screen Shot Showing the Reflection Prompt

Feedback

In the last stage, learners have an opportunity to debrief with Rose, their supervisor in the story. Through the developing conversation, the supervisor debriefs the learners and helps them summarize what they have learned and practiced in the program. Questions from the supervisor also help learners perform a self-evaluation at the end of the program. For example, the supervisor reviews the performance of the learners in each role and asks questions to help them clarify activities of each role. These questions were designed to help learners recall and reflect upon their performance. The supervisor also helps the learners reflect on specific situations they encountered while they were performing a specific role. For example, the supervisor advises the learner to do a teach-back while in the educator role. This is a technique to enhance the patients' understanding of information by asking them to repeat back, in their own words, what the nurse has taught them.

Sequencing

Professional nurses play multiple roles when working with individual patients. When interacting with any patient, the nurse will transition back and forth through the different roles, based upon the patient's needs and care requirements. Therefore, instead of creating four separate cases to illustrate each role, which might seem artificial, a complete storyline was developed with an underlying structure consisting of four navigation

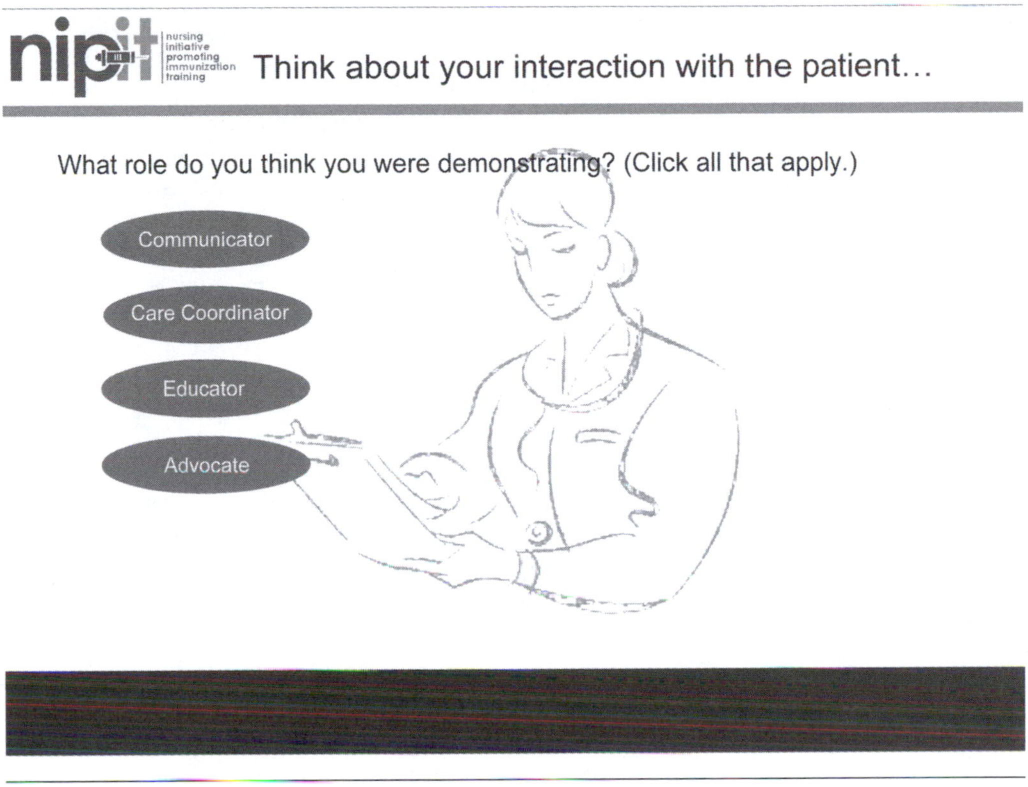

branches and paths (see Figure 29.4). Throughout the storyline, learners encounter different situations with the patient and his mother, which trigger one of the nursing roles. Learners interact with the same patient from the perspective of each nursing role. Afterwards, learners have the opportunity to identify which role they played in each situation. This design feature allows learners to experience and practice all the four roles through any branch or path they choose, in a random but natural sequence and in a realistically complex situation, without being interrupted in the flow of the story-line (see Figure 29.4). The design is intentional so that no matter which role learners begin with, they will eventually rotate through all four roles. This kind of design is intended to help learners understand and experience the four roles in a more realistic context.

Screen Design

The project *Putting It All Together* applied several multimedia principles proposed by Mayer (2005a, 2005b, 2005c, 2009) to avoid split-attention effect, redundancy, and other extraneous information that might be distracting and increase cognitive load. Three main principles were considered in designing and developing this project, including the segmenting principle, the spatial contiguity principle, and the personalization principle (Mayer, 2005a, 2005b, 2005c).

According to Mayer (2005a), people learn better when a multimedia lesson is presented in learner-paced segments, rather than in longer, continuous segments. In this regard, we broke down the scenarios into several episodes and the scripts into numerous segments. The "Episode" menu page and "Continue" button were designed to allow self-paced learning. The "Episode" menu screen allows learners to choose a specific section they would like to engage in, based on their own learning progress. The "Continue" button allows learners to move forward as they interact or "converse" with the characters (also called *avatars* in this chapter) in each episode. Learners can manage their own progress and re-access their performance at anytime if needed. Additionally, they can easily return to the previous screen or location and resume learning later, if they have to pause for any reason.

The spatial contiguity principle, that people learn better when words and pictures are closer together rather than farther apart on the screen, was considered another important design principle (Mayer, 2005b, 2009). The display of the simulation was designed as two dialogue panels on the same screen, to simulate the exchange of the conversation between avatar patient or parent and the learner ("You"). The color of the avatar or "You" indicates who is actively speaking. For example, an avatar who is speaking shows up on the screen in color and then turns gray when it is supposed to be listening (see Figures 29.5 and 29.6). On the screen, the graphics of the avatars were snapped with the dialogue frame to indicate to whom they were talking.

Putting It All Together is characterized by conversations (see Figures 29.2, 29.3, 29.5, and 29.6), which run through the entire simulation environment. Conversations were designed, not only to simulate a real clinical setting, but also to be congruent with the personalization principle, which states that people learn more deeply when a conversational style rather than a formal style is used (Mayer, 2005c).

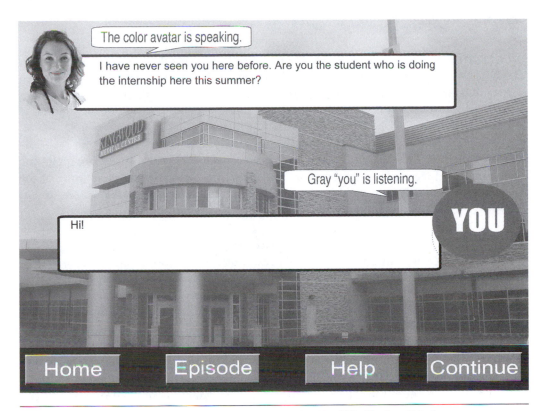

Figure 29.5 A Dialogue Between Avatar Jenny and "You." Jenny is Speaking While "You" are Listening

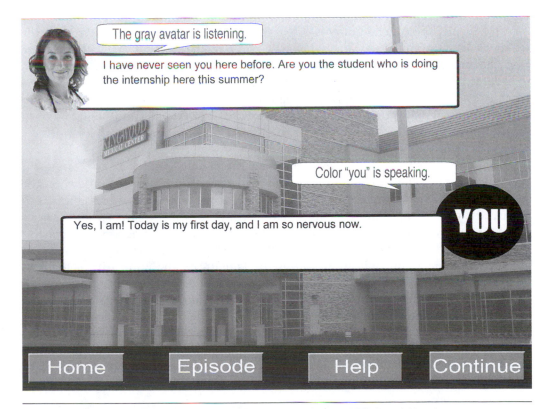

Figure 29.6 A Dialogue Between Avatar Jenny and "You." "You" are Speaking While Jenny is Listening

Overall, the techniques we used for the design of *Putting It All Together* were consistent with the design guidelines for mobile devices proposed by Grasso and Roselli (2005) in terms of content design (e.g., personalization, interactions, and multimedia design principles).

The Technological Dimension

There are many issues to consider in regard to the technological dimension, including user-interface design, platform selection, and implementation. To address some of the technological issues, the multimedia principles proposed by Mayer (2005a, 2005b, 2005c, 2009) provide valuable guidance for designing for m-learning.

User-Interface Design

A simple, intuitive user interface is particularly important for mobile devices (Elias, 2011). A usable interface can help to reduce the learning curve needed by learners so that they can use the application easily and focus on the domain content itself. *Putting It All Together* was designed to be used for both the online and mobile platforms. Therefore, four buttons of moderate size for the menu were designed to assist learners to intuitively use and navigate on mobile devices. All the screens presented are consistent in terms of layout, background, and color scheme. Owing to the restriction of mobile-device screen size, the text on each display has a limited size to avoid the need for frequent scrolling of the page. In addition, the "Help" function provides essential information learners can refer to if needed.

We chose the colors for dialogue boxes based on a critical analysis of the color schemes for the background pictures. No more than two dialogue boxes appear on the screen at once. The learner controls how fast the characters "talk" by clicking on the "Next" button. These techniques provide learners with autonomy and they can decide if they want to reread the dialogue before moving to the next screen, without being overwhelmed by the text appearing on the screen. We purposely did not include audios in order to reduce redundancy and to keep the mobile application simple and easy. The techniques we used for the interface design of *Putting It All Together* were consistent with the design guidelines for mobile devices proposed by Grasso and Roselli (2005) in terms of interface (e.g., menus, links, navigation, help, and feedback function).

Platform Consideration

In order to make the instruction accessible for both Web and mobile devices, the selection of technology platforms, based on the consideration of accessibility and popularity, was an important issue to be addressed. *Putting It All Together* was a Flash-based interactive application. Adobe Flash software, which allows creation of interactive media content for the Web, was chosen as the main tool for developing the *Putting It All Together* simulation application, because of its maturity and popularity at the time in 2010. In the past decade, with its flexibility and capability to create interactions, Flash has played a significant role in creating and making interactive media widespread, accessible, and popular. Currently, Flash is one of the few development tools that is popular with, and familiar to, many multimedia developers, instructors, and instructional designers. The learning object created by Flash technology can be easily loaded on Android-based mobile devices. These were the compelling and feasible reasons that Flash was selected as the development tool for designing our project.

However, the downside of the Flash technology is that it does not support Apple devices. Fortunately, there are quite a few apps developed by third-party developers for Apple iOS platforms, which provide alternative solutions to load Flash-based apps on Apple mobiles. In addition, Adobe, the company that owns Flash technology, has committed to converting all Flash-based applications into the latest HTML5 format, which can be run on Apple devices. Therefore, the most recent technology has made it possible and feasible to load most Flash-based multimedia projects onto Apple mobile devices.

DISCUSSION AND IMPLICATIONS

Mobile technology has opened up endless possibilities for learning, including simulation in the form of mobile apps. However, to achieve effective learning outcomes, instructional design requires alignment (a) between learning theories and their underlying assumptions for learning and instruction, (b) between pedagogical implications and instructional design, and (c) between multimedia design principles and technology affordances.

In our design experience, instructional design for m-learning has been guided by the philosophical perspective of constructivist learning, which aligns with learning goals and instructional needs based on our learner, task, and context analyses. The underlying assumption is that learners must have opportunities to experience real-world problem-solving (situated learning), which enables them to apply knowledge and skills and develop problem-solving skills, and facilitates knowledge transfer. With the affordances of mobile devices, real-world scenarios are not only embedded in the mobile apps, but are also situated within the context of everyday job settings. The ubiquitous feature of mobile technology allows learners to make connections between the problem scenarios in mobile apps and the real issues in their job settings and creates a seamless integration between formal learning in the classroom setting and informal learning in the real-world setting. With mobile technology, learners can have the benefit of a virtual mentor who helps them make connections (cognitive apprenticeship). The affordances of mobile technology have been advantageous to create instruction that is pedagogically sound and grounded in learning theories.

Learning theories and pedagogical approaches are essential foundations of instructional design. Once the learning and design goals are determined, it is important to lay out a blueprint to develop the learning environment, with special considerations to the design of instructional strategies and activities, sequencing of activities, branching of the program, and multimedia design principles. In *Putting It All Together*, our goal was to design a simulated learning environment that had a high fidelity to reality, which would offer an enabling context for learners to apply knowledge and skills and sharpen their problem-solving skills, with a focus on knowledge transfer. At the same time, we also ensured that multimedia design principles were followed, as we attempted to augment the advantageous features and overcome the constraints and limitations of the mobile technology. To further operationalize our design concepts and achieve the instructional goals, we developed a storyline with characters, activities, strategies, and learning episodes or events by following the GBS approach. Such a design was intended to help learners practice all of the identified concepts, skills, and complex problem-solving deemed essential to achieve the desirable learning outcomes.

As we moved deeper into the design, the design project became increasingly complex and intricate. Therefore, sequencing and branching became an important process within the design dimension. We arranged it so that whichever branch the learners chose to take, they would invariably have the same opportunities to practice the same sets of concepts and skills for each nursing role, and to solve the same sets of problems, although at different points in time. Clearly, all the design activities in the design dimension were further built on the pedagogical dimension, which was grounded in learning theories and philosophical perspectives.

Owing to the unique features of mobile devices, the screen design must follow the conventional method for games and simulations that is popularly used in the mobile-app industry. For example, it has to include a simple and clear interface design, conversational style, conversation bubbles, avatars, and navigation buttons. Our design for *Putting It All Together* reflects the features of a typical mobile app for simulations and games. Efforts were made to ensure that the design was consistent with the essential multimedia design principles generated from psychological theories about how people process information and transfer knowledge. Therefore, in the design dimension, designing the storyline, strategies, and activities, program sequencing and branching, and multimedia design principles should be considered.

Regarding the technological dimension, we have learned from our experience that it is important to examine and understand the advantages and limitations of a piece of emerging technology in order to fully take advantage of the technology affordances. At the same time, it is important to find means to address the constraints of technologies that will be used for learning technologies. In the design of *Putting It All Together*, we had to develop the screen design according to the characteristics of the mobile technology regarding screen size, color, navigation, message design (e.g., clarity and number of words), and the presentation format of the information and dialogues. We made the user interface simple, intuitive, and easy to navigate for a simulated-learning activity. All of these technology issues emphasize the important impact the technological dimension has on the design dimension.

Although a rich body of literature has provided much valuable insight into the design of m-learning (Elias, 2011; Grasso & Roselli, 2005), we argue that previous works have not tied the guiding principles together in a systematic and coherent manner by integrating literature from different research areas, such as learning theories, instructional design principles, multimedia principles, and interface design principles. Therefore, this chapter is an effort to conceptualize relevant instructional design concepts and principles into a sound conceptual design framework, consisting of the pedagogical, design, and technological dimensions, which is based on learning theories, pedagogical implications, and pragmatic considerations of technology affordances. In conclusion, we hope that the three-dimension design framework presented by this chapter will serve as a useful design tool for the instructional design community and offer valuable guidelines for other instructional designers who have an interest in designing m-learning technology.

REFERENCES

Alessi, S. M., & Trollip, S. R. (2001). *Multimedia for learning: Methods and development* (3rd ed.). Boston, MA: Allyn & Bacon.

Ally, M. (2009). *Mobile learning: Transforming the delivery of education and training.* Edmonton, AB: AU Press/ Athabasca University Press.

Anderson, J. R., Reder, L. M., & Simon, H. A. (1996). Situated learning and education. *Educational Researcher*, *25*(4), 5–11.

Bomsdorf, B. (2005). *Adaptation of learning spaces: supporting ubiquitous learning in higher distance education.* Paper presented at the meeting of Mobile Computing and Ambient Intelligence: The Challenge of Multimedia, *Dagstuhl Seminar Proceedings 05181*, Schloss Dagstuhl, Germany.

Bradley, C., Haynes, R., Cook, J., Boyle, T., & Smith, C. (2009). Design and development of multimedia learning objects for mobile phones. In M. Ally (Ed.), *Mobile learning: Transforming the delivery of education and training* (pp. 157–182). Edmonton, AB: Athabasca University Press.

Brown, J. S., Collins, A., & Duguid, P. (1989). Situated cognition and the culture of learning. *Educational Researcher*, *18*(1), 32–42.

Chen, Y. S., Kao, T. C., & Sheu, J. P. (2003). A mobile learning system for scaffolding bird watching learning. *Journal of Computer Assisted Learning*, *19*(3), 347–359.

Collins, A., Brown, J. S., & Holum, A. (1991). Cognitive apprenticeship: Making thinking visible. *American Educator*, *15*(3), 6–11, 38–46.

DiGiano, C., Yarnall, L., Patton, C., Roschelle, J., Tatar, D., & Manley, M. (2003). Conceptual tools for planning for the wireless classroom. *Journal of Computer Assisted Learning*, *19*(3), 284–297.

Elias, T. (2011). Universal instructional design principles for mobile learning. *International Review of Research in Open and Distance Learning*, *12*(2), 143–156.

Ge, X., Planas, L. G., & Er, N. (2010). A cognitive support system to scaffold learners' problem-based learning in a web-based learning environment. *Interdisciplinary Journal of Problem-based Learning*, *4*(1), 30–56.

Grasso, A., & Roselli, T. (2005). *Guidelines for designing and developing contents for mobile learning.* Paper presented at the IEEE International Workshop on Wireless and Mobile Technologies in Education, Washington, DC.

Greeno, J., Smith, D. R., & Moore, J. L. (1993). Transfer of situated learning. In D. K. Detterman & R. J. Sternberg (Eds.), *Transfer on trial: Intelligence, cognition, and instruction* (pp. 99–167). Norwood, NJ: Ablex.

Huang, D., Zhang, H., Higgins, E., Ge, X., & Bowers, B. (2011). "Putting It All Together"—The development of a simulation-based instruction to enhance nursing learners' experience of four professional roles. Presentation at the annual meeting of the International Convention of Association for Educational Communications and Technology, Jacksonville, FL, November 8–12.

Jonassen, D. (1999). Designing constructivist learning environments. In C. M. Reigeluth (Ed.), *Instructional-design theories and models: A new paradigm of instructional theory* (Vol. 2, pp. 215–240). Mahwah, NJ: Lawrence Erlbaum Associates.

Koole, M. L., & Ally, M. (2006). The framework for the rational analysis of mobile education (frame) model: Revising the ABCs of education practices. Paper presented at the Networking, International Conference on Systems and International Conference on Mobile Communications and Learning Technologies.

Koszalka, T., & Ntloedibe-Kuswani, G. S. (2010). Literature on the safe and disruptive learning potential of mobile technologies. *Distance Education*, *31*(2), 139–157.

Liu, G. Z., & Hwang, G. J. (2010). A key step to understanding paradigm shifts in e-learning: Towards context-aware ubiquitous learning. *British Journal of Educational Technology*, *41*(2), E1–E9.

Mayer, R. E. (2005a). Principles for managing essential processing in multimedia learning: Segmenting, pretraining, and modality principles. In R. E. Mayer (Ed.), *The Cambridge handbook of multimedia learning* (pp. 169–182). New York: Cambridge University Press.

Mayer, R. E. (2005b). Principles for reducing extraneous processing in multimedia learning: Coherence, signaling, redundancy, spatial contiguity, and temporal contiguity principles. In R. E. Mayer (Ed.), *The Cambridge handbook of multimedia learning* (pp. 183–200). New York: Cambridge University Press.

Mayer, R. E. (2005c). Principles of multimedia learning based on social cues: Personalization, voice, and image principles. In R. E. Mayer (Ed.), *The Cambridge handbook of multimedia learning* (pp. 201–228). New York: Cambridge University Press.

Mayer, R. E. (2009). *Multimedia learning* (2nd ed.). New York: Cambridge University Press.

Schank, R. C., Berman, T. R., & Macperson, K. A. (1999). Learning by doing. In C. M. Reigeluth (Ed.), *Instructional design theories and models: A new paradigm of instructional theory* (pp. 161–181). Mahwah, NJ: Lawrence Erlbaum Associates.

Shih, J. L., Chuang, C. W., & Hwang, G. J. (2010). An inquiry-based mobile learning approach to enhancing social science learning effectiveness. *Educational Technology & Society*, *13*(4), 50–62.

Smith, P., & Ragan, T. (2005). *Instructional design* (3rd ed.). New York: Wiley.

Telecom World. (2009). *The world in 2009: ICT facts and figures.* Geneva: International Telecommunication Union.

Wang, F., & Hannafin, M. J. (2005). Design-based research and technology-enhanced learning environments. *Educational Technology Research and Development*, *53*(4), 5–23.

30

MOBILE ASSESSMENT

State of the Art

Stavros A. Nikou and Anastasios A. Economides

MOBILE ASSESSMENT

New developments in assessment utilizing mobile devices contribute to an ongoing evolution in the context of m-learning. This chapter begins with a brief overview of the computerized assessment procedures that led to mobile assessment. It then defines mobile assessment and its pedagogy and explains relevant design issues and the implementing technologies. Then it describes the main mobile assessment practices used today, as well as their affordances and constraints. This chapter may serve as a useful reference for developers, teachers, trainers, educational administrators, researchers, and others with an interest in mobile assessment.

ASSESSMENT AND COMPUTING

Assessment is considered a fundamental part of the learning process, because teachers can evaluate and classify learners, encouraging and supporting the learning procedure (Ellis, 2001). The commonest distinction among assessment types in the literature is that made between formative assessment and summative assessment. A summative assessment certifies learning and reports about students' progress at the end of a unit or a course. It is usually referred to as assessment *of* learning. A formative assessment can be defined as activities undertaken by teachers and/or their students that provide information to be used as feedback, to modify the teaching and learning activities in which they are engaged (Black & William, 1998). It is usually refer to as assessment *for* learning.

Beyond paper- and pencil-based assessment, it can be computer assisted also. Computer-assisted assessment/computer-aided assessment (CAA) or computer-based testing (CBT) makes use of computer technology, enabling instructors to deliver, mark, and analyze assignments or exams (Sim, Holifield, & Brown, 2004). Advantages of CAA over paper-based assessment include accuracy, time savings, immediate feedback, enhanced validity, and improved security (Segall, Doolen, & Porter, 2005). The form of CAA that adapts to the examinee's ability level is called computer-adaptive testing (CAT). The basis for CAT systems is the Item Response Theory (IRT), which defines the relationship between examinees and items through mathematical models. The difficulty of each item is matched to the learner's knowledge level with adaptive item sequencing. The main advantage of computerized adaptive tests is that each examinee usually receives different questions than other examinees, with the total number of questions in a CAT usually smaller than the number of questions needed in a classic test. The majority of current CAT systems give priority to security, reliability, and maintainability, while they almost ignore issues related to presentation, functionality, and feedback (Economides & Roupas, 2007). Seventeen criteria for the evaluation of an adaptation engine (Economides, 2007) and twenty-one adaptive-feedback attributes (Economides, 2006a) could be considered in order for the designers and developers of CAT systems to produce effective feedback adapted to the learner or the educational context. The introduction of mobile devices to assessment practices has led to the development of a new form of assessment, the mobile assessment.

DEFINING MOBILE ASSESSMENT

Mobile device-based assessment is called mobile assessment (m-assessment). A range of mobile devices, such as laptops, netbooks, tablet PCs, and handhelds (PDAs, palmtops, mobile phones, and smartphones) facilitate exams across contexts, "anytime and anywhere." Taking into consideration the corresponding m-learning characteristics (Sharples, Taylor, & Vavoula, 2005; Traxler, 2005), m-assessment can also be characterized as: personalized, informal, learner-centered, collaborative, ubiquitous, bite-sized, lightweight, on demand, typically blended, situated, and context-aware.

M-ASSESSMENT PRACTICES

Different assessment practices can be conducted using mobile devices: classroom response systems, self-assessment, peer assessment, collaborative assessment, computerized adaptive testing on mobile devices, dynamic assessment, context-aware and location-aware assessment, as well as mobile game-based learning (mGBL) assessment.

Classroom Response Systems

Electronic classroom response systems (CRSs), audience response systems (ARSs), or synchronous e-voting systems (usually called "clickers") are small, wireless, specialized keypads, mobile phones, or handhelds used by students as an alternative method of "showing your hands" to answer questions posed by instructors. The responses (anonymous or not) can be aggregated and presented for class discussion. Individualized feedback to students is also possible. Examples of CRSs are Votapedia (Maier, 2009), TXT-2-LRN (Scornavacca, Huff, & Marshall, 2007), and Classroom Presenter (Anderson et al., 2004; Koile & Singer, 2006). When coupled with appropriate pedagogical methodologies, these systems can promote learning (Fies & Marshall, 2006), because they increase student engagement (through anonymity of data submission to the group), participation and attentiveness (all students can potentially answer all questions), interaction (the lecturer has immediate access to students' answers), and satisfaction

(Davis, 2003). They also provide an effective formative-assessment mechanism, where course material largely depends on student feedback, and students can work out misconceptions via peer or classroom discussion (Kay & Lesage, 2009). Although success with synchronous surveys in class is very well documented, asynchronous electronic surveys, usually conducted to gather feedback before or after teaching sessions, need to be evaluated (Tong, 2011).

Self- and Peer Assessment

Self- and peer assessment helps students monitor their own learning. Not much research about how to use mobile technology for self- and peer assessment has been reported. In m-assessment systems for self- and peer classroom assessment, students showed increased motivation, improved achievements, and positive acceptance, with the assessment procedure found to be flexible, convenient, and time-saving (Chen, 2010; de-Marcos et al., 2010).

Collaborative Assessment

Collaborative learning is a new educational approach where students work together in groups to improve their understanding of a subject. Computer-supported collaborative learning (CSCL) uses computer technology to support knowledge construction and sharing among participants (Stahl, Koschmann, & Suthers, 2006). The introduction of mobile devices in CSCL, as well as intelligent support tools in assessment, has great potential to contribute to the development of innovative forms of collaborative assessment (Gay, Stefanone, Grace-Martin, & Hembroke, 2001; Strijbos, 2011). Handhelds can facilitate the complex task of assessing group work (Yarnall et al., 2003). Furthermore, even examinations can be designed collaboratively (Swan, Shen, & Hiltz, 2006). Collaborative learning, including assessing students' knowledge, can also be conducted outdoors, in places with no pre-installed infrastructure, such as wilderness, national parks, and archaeological sites (Vasiliou & Economides, 2007a).

Computerized Adaptive Tests on Mobile Devices

The main components of a computerized-adaptive-tests-on-mobile-devices (CAT-MD) system are the item pool, the item selection procedure, the ability estimation, and the stopping rule (Triantafillou, Georgiadou, & Economides, 2008a). According to the general framework for adaptive m-learning by Economides (2006b), an adaptation engine acquires the context of the mobile learner as input data and accordingly personalizes the educational activity and/or the infrastructure. The adaptation procedure can produce a personalized exam adapted to the examinee's ability level, or even a dynamic-assessment module, and, furthermore (when the context relates to a ubiquitous environment), a context-aware assessment.

Dynamic Assessment

The dynamic-assessment (DA) strategy integrates assessment with instruction, providing teaching assistance during assessment, and thus supporting the idea of "assessment as teaching and learning strategy." It can have the "sandwich format" (pre-test, teach, and post-test) or the "cake format," where assessment is interwoven with teaching (Sternberg & Grigorenko, 2001). A DA approach can effectively support student learning in the field, by providing instant feedback when students need it, according to their performance evaluated by the DA (Chen, Chen, & Lin, 2009). GPS-embedded mobile devices, wireless networks, and radio-frequency identification (RFID) technology are potential enablers for the implementation of DA in any authentic situation. A Web-based DA system enables learners with low-level prior knowledge to experience more effective learning (Wang, 2010), and a decision-tree approach for such a DA had a positive effect on student motivation (Huang, Wu, Chu, & Hwang, 2008).

Context-Aware Assessment

A system is context aware if it can extract, interpret, and use context information and adapt its functionality to the current context of use (Byun & Cheverst, 2004). The context consists of the learner state, the educational-activity state, the infrastructure state, and the environment state (Economides, 2008, 2009). In order to facilitate the development of context-aware systems, relevant principles and models were described (Baldauf, Dustdar, & Rosenberg, 2007), and frameworks were analyzed (Martin et al., 2011). Twelve models for assessing the learning performance of the students, based on their real-world and online behaviors, are proposed in Hwang and Tsai (2011). In a context-aware u-learning environment, RFID-sensor technologies (Curtin, Kauffman, & Riggins, 2007), embedded in mobile devices, along with wireless networks, detect the environment and interact with students, guiding and assessing them as they are engaged in the learning activity (Liu & Hwang, 2010). Experimental results from real-world learning contexts indicate improved student-learning achievement, promoting the learning attitude (Chu, Hwang, Tsai, & Tseng, 2010; Hwang & Chang, 2011).

Location-Aware Assessment

Location-aware systems constitute a subfield of context-aware computing. These systems can sense the current location of a user and change behavior based on this location, using Wi-Fi or mobile-phone triangulation, GPS, or RFID. Evaluation of "assessment in situ (e.g., location)," using geo-located questions with GPS-enabled mobile devices, shows increased student motivation, reflection, and personal observation (Santos, Pérez-sanagustín, Hernández-leo, & Blat, 2011). The integration of location-aware services and Web 2.0 may offer great innovations in the delivery of education in the future (Cochrane & Bateman, 2010).

mGBL Assessment

Players use mobile phones as well as RFID and near-field communication (NFC) technologies to interact with a game scenario in any location (pervasive games). The assessment may have the form of explicit questions to be answered, or it may be based on the level of performance that the player reaches while playing. mGBL is mapped with existing learning theories (Zaibon & Shiratuddin, 2009). Examples from the literature (Garrido, Miraz, Ruiz, & Gómez-Nieto, 2011; Wang, Øfsdahl, & Mørch-Storstein, 2008) indicated that mGBL contributes to increased learning and motivation.

Several pedagogical principles and learning theories are combined in each m-assessment practice. Table 30.1 presents the relationship between learning theories and m-assessment practices (Naismith, Lonsdale, Vavoula, & Sharples, 2004; Orr, 2010; Ryu & Parsons, 2009).

Table 30.1 Learning Theories Along With Mobile Assessment Practices

Learning theory practice	Main feature	Example of m-assessment
Behaviorism	Immediate feedback provides the opportunity to adjust the learning behavior	CRS, CAT-MD, dynamic, context aware
Constructivism	Students construct their own knowledge based on interactions with the environment	Context and location aware, mGBL, collaborative
Situated learning	Learning takes place in authentic learning environments	
Collaborative learning	Learning is based on social interactions	Self- and peer assessment, collaborative

DESIGN AND IMPLEMENTATION TECHNOLOGIES

Design

The most popular standards available for m-learning and m-assessment are the Shareable Content Object Reference Model (SCORM) and the IMS Question and Test Interoperability Model. The first model enhances content's interoperability and reusability among learning objects. The second one defines a specification for representing questions and the reporting of results, allowing the exchange of data (item, test, and results) between multiple IT systems (Álvarez-gonzález, Araya, Nuñez, & Cárdenas, 2011; Zhang, Wills, & Gilbert, 2010).

Implementation

M-assessment systems can be delivered through short message service (SMS), client-server and/or mobile ad hoc networks (MANETs) implementations.

SMS

This is a text-messaging service between mobile-phone devices. It can be used as a quiz tool (fill in blanks, true/false, multiple-choice questions), with usually automated feedback. SMS technology fits to m-learning because it has low cost and is available on all mobile phones, and students are already familiar with it (Tretiakov & Kinshuk, 2005). Successful implementations of SMS assessment systems provide an additional channel of communication between teacher and students, making class more interactive and interesting; improve student examination performance (Morris, 2010); enhance formative assessment and feedback (Nagowah, Meghoo, & Gaonjur, 2010); and enrich the learning experience in general (Yengin, Karahoca, Karahoca, & Uzunboylu, 2011). SMS-based assessment systems could also be integrated with learning and exam-management systems (Riad & El-Ghareeb, 2008).

Client-Server

Another implementation of mobile exam systems links mobile application interfaces (clients) to XML database-management systems (servers) via a wireless communication system. The typical flow in such an m-assessment system includes the following steps: the teacher uploads questions to the server; the student downloads the m-assessment application to his/her phone and responds to the questions; the server tabulates scores and presents them to the teacher and/or the student. Such implementations (Cavus & Al-momani, 2011; Kim et al., 2010; Lu, Sundaram, Zhaozong, Arumugam, & Gehao, 2011; Madeira, Pires, Dias, & Martins, 2010; Otair, Tawfiq, Al-Zoubi, & Alkouz, 2008) have the following key advantages: location and device independence of application logic, centralized software maintenance and data management, fast data storage and retrieval to support a large number of concurrent users, multimedia support, and different privilege levels (instructor and learner).

MANET

In a MANET, there is no need for pre-installed infrastructure. Each mobile device is free to move independently, changing its links to other devices acting as server, receiver, and router. Mobile classrooms based on the instructional device of the teacher and the learning devices of the students can be "dynamically constructed" in both indoor and outdoor environments (Chang, Sheu, & Chan, 2003). Multicast MANETs, with their flexible and adaptive architecture, provide reliable and efficient communication, facilitating collaboration among teachers and students in places without communication infrastructure (Mamoukaris & Economides, 2003; Vasiliou & Economides, 2008).

AFFORDANCES AND CONSTRAINTS

The additional channel of assessment using small portable devices that facilitate "testing on demand" has both affordances and constraints resulting from the special character-istics of these new assessment media.

Affordances

The main affordances of m-assessment are described below:

- *Context awareness*: M-assessment can be conducted "anywhere and at anytime," in the classroom or in the field, in a ubiquitous fashion (Economides, 2009; Soloway, Norris, Blumenfeld, Fishman, & Marx, 2001), "providing access to tools and information within the context of learning activities" (Luchini, Quintana, & Soloway, 2004, p. 135).
- *Adaptability*: Development and evaluation of computerized adaptive testing on mobile devices (Triantafillou, Georgiadou, & Economides, 2008b) proved to be an effective, efficient, accurate, exact, and reliable formative-assessment tool.
- *Personalization*: Adaptability and differentiated instruction lead to a more personalized learning experience (Looi et al., 2009). Wireless communication devices equipped with sensors detect users and environment information in order to provide personalized services (Economides, 2009).
- *Feedback*: Mobile devices facilitate formative-assessment practices giving the opportunity for many assessment sessions during instruction. Immediate instructor feedback supports students as independent, self-motivated, and self-regulated learners (Al-smadi & Guetl, 2011), a primary goal for 21st-century education. Also, student feedback enables instructors to adjust course material in real time, avoiding any misconceptions (Koile, & Singer, 2006).
- *Collaboration*: Mobile devices can enhance online collaborative-learning activities and assessment strategies (group work, outdoor learning), supporting an active-learning environment (Vasiliou & Economides, 2007b).

- *Multiple uses*: PDAs as multimedia access tools, communication tools, capture tools, representational tools, or analytical tools (Churchill & Churchill, 2008) offer new potentials in m-assessment such as richer assessment items and feedback and, hence, more realistic testing environments.
- *Efficiency*: The efficiency (time it took students to complete a quiz) was found to be superior for the PDA-based assessment compared with the paper and pencil quiz, whereas no differences in effectiveness (students' test scores) were found between the two quiz types (Segall, Doolen, & Porter, 2005). Treadwell (2006) indicates that students express a high level of satisfaction with a PDA-based assessment system.
- *Anonymity*: Anonymous answer submission increases learners' self-confidence to be engaged in discussions (Attewell, 2005).
- *Cost*: Mobile devices are usually less expensive than desktops or laptops (Allan, Carbonaro, & Buck, 2006; Traxler, 2004).

Constraints

The main constraints of m-assessment are basically the physical attributes of the mobile devices:

- Small screen size with limited input capabilities has a negative effect in the usability of the mobile devices (Maniar, 2007).
- Other usability constraints include limited battery life, limited storage capacity and computational power, interface limitations, and inconvenient input (Chen, Chang, & Wang, 2008).
- Platform inconsistency among mobile devices and connectivity issues may be also a barrier (Churchill & Hedberg, 2008).
- Security issues should also be considered, such as device lost or theft, data vulnerability, and privacy.

CONCLUSIONS

M-assessment has been implemented so far in different disciplines and subject contexts such as K–12 and higher education, environmental and engineering education, outdoors, inquiry science learning, virtual experiments, museum visits, workplaces, and health care. Despite the difficulties and constraints, the general outcome is that it can enhance the assessment procedure and complement both e-assessment and traditional assessment and, hence, boost the learning experience. This is mainly because it enables more frequent formative assessment and it can be conducted in any authentic learning environment, providing personal learning support and improving instruction. However, problems such as access, pedagogical support, administrative encouragement, and perceived reliability often stand as barriers to its greater adoption (Penuel, Tatar, & Roschelle, 2004) and, thus, must be overcome. Developers and instructors should cooperate in order to produce quality m-assessment practices, while educational administrators and policymakers would encourage its adoption.

REFERENCES

Allan, C., Carbonaro M., & Buck G. (2006). A survey of Personal Digital Assistants (PDAs) use in a middle school environment: Perceptions of teachers, parents and students. *Meridian Middle School Computer Technologies Journal*, 2(9).

Al-smadi, M., & Guetl, C. (2011). Supporting self-regulated learners with formative assessments using automatically created QTI-questions. *Global Engineering Education Conference (EDUCON)*, 2011 IEEE, 288–294.

Álvarez-gonzález, L. A., Araya, E., Nuñez, R., & Cárdenas, F. (2011). Blue-QTI: A mobile learning system using bluetooth and IMS QTI specification. *eL&mL 2011 : The Third International Conference on Mobile, Hybrid, and On-line Learning*, Gosier, Guadeloupe, France.

Anderson, R., Anderson, R., Simon, B., Wolfman, S. A., VanDeGrift, T., & Yasuhara, K. (2004). Experiences with a tablet PC based lecture presentation system in computer science courses. *ACM SIGCSE Bulletin*, 36(1), 56.

Attewell, J. (2005). *From research and development to mobile learning: Tools for education and training providers and their learners*. Paper presented at mLearn 2005, 4th World Conference on Mobile Learning, Cape Town, South Africa.

Baldauf, M., Dustdar, S., & Rosenberg, F. (2007). A survey on context-aware systems. *International Journal of Ad Hoc and Ubiquitous Computing*, 2(4), 263–277.

Black, P., & William, D. (1998). Assessment and classroom learning. *Assessment in Education. Principles, Policy & Practice*, 5(1), 7–74.

Byun, H. E., & Cheverst, K. (2004). Utilizing context history to provide dynamic adaptations. *Applied Artificial Intelligence*, 18(6), 533–548.

Cavus, N., & Al-momani, M. M. (2011). Mobile system for flexible education. *Procedia Computer Science*, 3, 1475–1479.

Chang, C. Y., Sheu J. P., & Chan, T. W. (2003). Concept and design of ad hoc and mobile classrooms. *Journal of Computer Assisted Learning*, 19, 336–346.

Chen, C. H. (2010). The implementation and evaluation of a mobile self- and peer-assessment system. *Computers & Education*, 55(1), 229–236.

Chen, G. D., Chang, C. K., & Wang, C. Y. (2008). Ubiquitous learning website: Scaffold learners by mobile devices with information-aware techniques. *Computers and Education*, 50, 77–90.

Chen, C., Chen, C., & Lin, T. (2009). Dynamic assessment of fieldwork. *Development*, 1–8.

Chu, H. C., Hwang, G. J., Tsai, C. C., & Tseng, J. C. R. (2010). A two-tier test approach to developing location-aware mobile learning systems for natural science courses. *Computers & Education*, 55(4), 1618–1627.

Churchill, D., & Churchill, N. (2008). Educational affordances of PDAs: A study of a teacher's exploration of this technology. *Computers & Education*, 50(4), 1439–1450.

Churchill, D., & Hedberg, J. (2008). Learning object design considerations for small-screen handheld devices. *Computers & Education*, 50(3), 881–893.

Cochrane T., & Bateman, R. (2010). Smart phones give you wings: Pedagogical affordances of mobile Web 2.0. *Australasian Journal of Educational Technology*, 26(1), 1–14.

Curtin, J., Kauffman, R. J., & Riggins, F. J. (2007). Making the "MOST" out of RFID technology: A research agenda for the study of the adoption, usage and impact of RFID. *Information Technology and Management*, 8(2), 87–110.

Davis, S. (2003). Observations in classrooms using a network of handheld devices. *Journal of Computer Assisted Learning*, 19(3), 298–307.

de-Marcos, L., Hilera, J. R., Barchino, R., Jiménez, L., Martínez, J. J., Gutiérrez, et al. (2010). An experiment for improving student's performance in secondary and tertiary education by means of m-learning auto-assessment. *Computers & Education*, 55, 1069–1079.

Ellis, A., (2001). *Teaching, learning, and assessment together: The reflective classroom*. Larchmont, NY: Eye on Education.

Economides, A. A. (2006a). Adaptive feedback characteristics in CAT (Computer Adaptive Testing). *International Journal of Instructional Technology & Distance Learning*, 3(8), 15–26.

Economides, A. A. (2006b, November). *Adaptive mobile learning*. Fourth IEEE International Workshop on Wireless Mobile and Ubiquitous Technology in Education WMTE06, Athens, 26–28.

Economides, A. A. (2007). On evaluation of adaptation engines. In V. Uskov (Ed.), *10th International Conference on Computers and Advanced Technology in Education (CATE 2007)*, October 8–10. Beijing, China.

Economides, A. A. (2008). Context-aware mobile learning. *The Open Knowledge Society, A Computer Science and Information Systems Manifesto, First World Summit, WSKS 2008*, Athens, Greece, September 24–26. Proceedings. SPRINGER Communications in Computer and Information Science (CCIS), 19, 213–220.

Economides, A. A. (2009). Adaptive context-aware pervasive and ubiquitous learning. *International Journal of Technology Enhanced Learning*, 1(3), 169–192.

Economides, A. A., & Roupas, C. (2007). Evaluation of computer adaptive testing systems. *International Journal of Web Web-Based Learning and Teaching Technologies, 2*(1), 70–8.

Fies, C., & Marshall, J. (2006). Classroom Response Systems: A review of the literature. *Journal of Science Education and Technology, 15*(1), 101–109.

Garrido, P. C., Miraz, G. M., Ruiz, I. L., & Gómez-Nieto, M. A. (2011). Use of NFC-based pervasive games for encouraging learning and student motivation. *Third International Workshop on Near Field Communication*, Hagenberg, Austria, 32–37.

Gay, G., Stefanone, M., Grace-Martin, M., & Hembrooke, H. (2001). The effects of wireless computing in collaborative learning environments. *International Journal of Human-Computer Interaction, 13*(2), 257–276.

Huang, S. H., Wu, T. T., Chu, H. C., & Hwang, G. J. (2008). A decision tree approach to conducting dynamic assessment in a context-aware ubiquitous learning environment. *Fifth IEEE International Conference on Wireless, Mobile and Ubiquitous Technology in Education*, 89–94.

Hwang, G. J., & Chang, H. F. (2011). A formative assessment-based mobile learning approach to improving the learning attitudes and achievements of students. *Computers & Education, 56*(4), 1023–1031.

Hwang, G. J., & Tsai, C. C. (2011). Research trends in mobile and ubiquitous learning: A review of publications in selected journals from 2001 to 2010. *British Journal of Educational Technology, 42*(4), 65–70.

Kay, R. H., & Lesage, A. (2009). A strategic assessment of audience response systems used in higher education. *Australasian Journal of Educational Technology, 25*(2), 235–249.

Kim, S., Schap, T., Bosch, M., Maciejewski, R., Delp, E. J., Ebert, D. S., et al. (2010). Development of a mobile user interface for image-based dietary assessment. *Health San Francisco*, 0–6.

Koile, K., & Singer, D. (2006). Improving learning in CS1 via tablet-PC-based in-class assessment. *Proceedings of the 2006 International Workshop on Computing Education Research ICER 06*, 119.

Liu, G. Z., & Hwang, G. J. (2010). A key step to understanding paradigm shifts in e-learning: Towards context-aware ubiquitous learning. *British Journal of Educational Technology, 41*(2), 1–9.

Looi, C. K., Wong, L. H., So, H. J., Seow, P., Toh, Y., Chen, W., et al. (2009). Anatomy of a mobilized lesson: Learning my way. *Computers & Education, 53*(4), 1120–1132.

Luchini, K., Quintana, C., & Soloway, E. (2004). Design guidelines for learner-centered handheld tools. *Proceedings of the 2004 Conference on Human Factors in Computing Systems CHI 04, 6*(1), 135–142

Lu, J., Sundaram, A., Zhaozong, M., Arumugam, V., & Gehao, L. (2011, June). Mobile exam system—MES: Architecture for database management. *The International Conference on Education & Learning in Mobile Age—CELMA*, June 1–2, Lake District, UK.

Madeira, R. N., Pires, V.F., Dias, O.P., & Martins, J.F. (2010). Development of a mobile learning framework for an analog electronics course. *Engineering Education*, 561–567.

Maier, H. R. (2009). Student participation in lectures using mobile phones. *Engineering Education*, 43–48.

Mamoukaris, K. V., & Economides, A. A. (2003). Wireless technology in educational system. *11th International PEG Conference*, Russia, 28/6–1/7

Maniar, N. (2007). M-learning to teach university students. In C. Montgomerie & J. Seale (Eds.), *Proceedings of World Conference on Educational Multimedia, Hypermedia and Telecommunications 2007* (pp. 881–887).

Martin, S., Diaz, G., Plaza, I., Ruiz, E., Castro, M., & Peire, J. (2011). State of the art of frameworks and middleware for facilitating mobile and ubiquitous learning development. *The Journal of Systems & Software, 84*(11), 1883–1891.

Morris, N. P. (2010). Podcasts and mobile assessment enhance student learning experience and academic performance. *Bioscience Education, 16* (1).

Nagowah, S., Meghoo, L., & Gaonjur, K. (2010). A mobile framework for formative assessment for first year students. *3rd IEEE International Conference on Computer Science and Information Technology (ICCSIT), 4*, 492–499.

Naismith, L., Lonsdale, P., Vavoula, G., & Sharples, M. (2004). Literature review in mobile technologies and learning. *FutureLab Report, 11*.

Orr, G. (2010). A review of literature in mobile learning: Affordances and constraints. *6th IEEE International Conference on Wireless Mobile and Ubiquitous Technologies in Education*, 107–111.

Otair, M., Tawfiq, A., Al-Zoubi, A. Y., & Alkouz, A. (2008, April). A mobile quiz system for assessment of the learning process. *3rd International Conference on Mobile and Computer Aided Learning, IMCL*, April 16–18, Jordan.

Penuel, W. R., Tatar, D. G., & Roschelle, J. (2004). The role of research on contexts of teaching practice in informing the design of handheld learning technologies. *Journal Educational Computing Research, 30*(4), 353–370.

Riad, A., & El-Ghareeb, H. (2008). A service oriented architecture to integrate mobile assessment in learning management systems. *Turkish Online Journal of Distance Education-TOJDE, 9*(2), 200–219.

Ryu, H., & Parsons, D. (2009). Designing learning activities with mobile technologies. *Innovative Mobile Learning Techniques and Technologies, 64*(0), 1–20.

Santos, P., Pérez-sanagustín, M., Hernández-leo, D., & Blat, J. (2011). QuesTInSitu: From tests to routes for assessment in situ activities. *Computers & Education, 57*(4), 2517–2534.

Scornavacca, E., Huff, S., & Marshall, S. (2007). Developing a SMS-based classroom interaction system. In D. Parson & H. Ryu (Eds.), *Proceedings of the Conference on Mobile Learning Technologies and Applications MoLTA*, 47–54.

Segall, N., Doolen, T., & Porter, J. (2005). A usability comparison of PDA-based quizzes and paper-and-pencil quizzes. *Computers & Education, 45*(4), 417–432.

Sharples, M., Taylor, J., & Vavoula, G. (2005). Towards a theory of mobile learning. *Mind, 1*(1), 1–9.

Sim, G., Holifield, P., & Brown, M. (2004). Implementation of computer assisted assessment: Lessons from the literature. *AltJ, 12*(3), 215–229.

Soloway, E., Norris, C., Blumenfeld, P., Fishman, B. J., & Marx, R. (2001). Devices are ready-at-hand. *Communications of the ACM, 44*(6), 15–20.

Stahl, G., Koschmann, T., & Suthers, D. (2006). Computer-supported collaborative learning: An historical perspective. In R. K. Sawyer (Ed.), *Cambridge handbook of the learning sciences* (pp. 409–426).

Sternberg, R. J., & Grigorenko, E. L. (2001). All testing is dynamic testing. *Issues in Education, 7*, 137–170.

Strijbos, J. W. (2011). Assessment of (computer-supported) collaborative learning. *IEEE Transactions on Learning Technologies, 4*(1), 59–73.

Swan, K., Shen, J., & Hiltz, S. R. (2006). Assessment and collaboration in online learning. *Journal of Asynchronous Learning*, 45–62.

Tong, V. C. H. (2011). Using asynchronous electronic surveys to help in-class revision: A case study. *British Journal of Educational Technology*, DOI:10.1111/j.1467–8535.2011.01207.x

Traxler, J. (2004). Mobile learning—Evaluating the effectiveness and the cost. In J. Attewell & C. Savil-Smith (Eds.), *Learning with mobile devices* (pp. 183–188), London: Learning and Skills Development Agency.

Traxler, J. (2005). Defining mobile learning. *Learning, 40*, 261–266.

Treadwell, I. (2006). The usability of personal digital assistants (PDAs) for assessment of practical performance. *Medical Education, 40*, 855–861.

Tretiakov, A., & Kinshuk, K. (2005). Creating a pervasive testing environment by using SMS messaging. *IEEE International Workshop on Wireless and Mobile Technologies in Education WMTE05, 1*, 62–66.

Triantafillou, E., Georgiadou, E., & Economides, A. A. (2008a). CAT-MD: Computerized adaptive testing on mobile devices. *International Journal of Web-Based Learning and Teaching Technologies* (extended versions of the best papers presented at m-ICTE2006 Conference), *3*(1), 13–20.

Triantafillou, E., Georgiadou, E., & Economides, A. A. (2008b). The design and evaluation of a computerized adaptive test on mobile devices. *Computers & Education, 50*, 1319–1330.

Vasiliou, A., & Economides, A. A. (2007a). Mobile collaborative learning using multicast MANETs. *Information Journal of Mobile Communications, 5*(4), 423–444.

Vasiliou, A., & Economides, A. A. (2007b). Game-based learning using MANETs. In N. Mastorakis & Ph. Dondon (Eds.), *Proceedings of the 4th WSEAS/ASME International Conference on Engineering Education (EE'07)* (pp. 154–159). Agios Nikolaos, Crete, Greece.

Vasiliou, A., & Economides, A. A. (2008, April). MANET-based outdoor collaborative learning. In M. E. Auer & A. Y. Al-Zoubi (Eds.), *3rd International Conference on Interactive Mobile and Computer Aided Learning (IMCL),* Amman, Jordan, April 16–18, International Association of Online Engineering.

Wang, A. I., Øfsdahl, T., & Mørch-Storstein, O. K. (2008). An evaluation of a mobile game concept for lecturers. *IEEE 21st Conference on Software Engineering Education and Training*, 197–204.

Wang, T. H. (2010).Web-based dynamic assessment: Taking assessment as teaching and learning strategy for improving students' e-Learning effectiveness. *Computers & Education, 54*, 1157–1166.

Yarnall, L., Penuel, W., Ravitz, J., Murray, G., Means, B., & Broom, M. (2003). Portable assessment authoring: Using handheld technology to access collaborative inquiry. *Education, Communication & Information, 3*(1).

Yengin, I., Karahoca, A., Karahoca, D., & Uzunboylu, H. (2011). Is SMS still alive for education: Analysis of educational potentials of SMS technology? *Procedia Computer Science, 3*, 1439–1445.

Zaibon, S. B., & Shiratuddin, N. (2009). Towards developing mobile game-based learning engineering model. *Methods*, 649–653.

Zhang, P., Wills, G., & Gilbert, L. (2010). IMS QTIEngine on Android to support mobile learning and assessment. *Design*, 1–8.

31

mMOOC DESIGN

Ubiquitous, Open Learning in the Cloud

Inge de Waard

Mobile learning has had a long history running up toward its current, contemporary possibilities. When looking at cellular phones, up until 1973, they were limited to devices installed in cars and other mobile vehicles. However, from April 3, 1973 onward, the first analog mobile-phone calls became a reality when Martin Cooper from Motorola called Joel S. Engel of Bell Labs (Wikipedia, The Free Encyclopedia, 2012). In the next three decades, m-learning was embraced in a lot of places, including developing regions. The adoption rate and the types of device used are, however, still very imbalanced and depend on the socioeconomic background of the mobile user group.

The societal changes brought along with the Internet, social-media development, and the rise to ubiquity of a number of technologies (Wi-Fi, mobiles, etc.) have changed human society as a whole. Within only a decade, people from all continents started to use the same tools to connect with others and, most of all, to improve their lives or livelihoods. Looking at the m-learning boom of today, we can see that m-learning is now slowly coming of age, and, as such, a new era dawns in which mobile access becomes a growing, global reality. However, these changes are not limited to technology. As a result of the rise in social media, ubiquitous cloud computing, and new technologies, new educational formats emerge.

In this chapter, we look closely at the mobile Massive Open Online Course (mMOOC) design, which combines both MOOC and m-learning, because a MOOC complements all the educational changes, and m-learning offers the devices and characteristics to realize contemporary educational changes (de Waard, Abajian, et al., 2011). In order to do this, the chapter first looks at the parallels between the MOOC format and m-learning. After this, the educational challenges of this Knowledge Age are described, and, more specifically, how the mMOOC design addresses these challenges by producing a learning environment that answers these needs. The mMOOC design resulted from Mobile MOOC (MobiMOOC2011), the first MOOC that was designed to be accessible for mobiles and focused on m-learning as a topic.

SHORT LOOK AT MOOC AND M-LEARNING

Defining M-Learning

It is only in the last few years that the full capacity of m-learning has started to take shape, and ubiquity has become a reality. This evolution in learning with mobile devices has resulted in different definitions of m-learning that evolved over time, taking into account its most recent developments and understandings. M-learning is defined here as "learning across multiple contexts, through social and content interactions, using personal electronic devices," as stated by Crompton, Muilenburg, and Berge and presented in Chapter 1 of this book (Crompton, 2013, p. 4). The emphasis on interactions is of great importance here, as the mMOOC design focuses on human interactions, dialogues, and discussions as the main dynamic to enhance knowledge creation and formation. Another interesting point in this definition is "using personal electronic devices": this allows us to think wider than the mobile device itself, for m-learning in this day and age is not so much using mobile devices, but the fact that, as a learner, you are mobile and you use a wide variety of (personal) devices to stay in touch with the content and network of your choice.

Closer Look at MOOCs

A MOOC is best described by a short definition of the acronym. A MOOC is called massive as it draws in voluntary learners from around the world (e.g., 100,000 registered participants in the Artificial Intelligence MOOC of Stanford University). A MOOC is also a free course. If you—as a learner—are interested in a MOOC, you simply register for the course: there is no payment and very limited administration. A MOOC is not situated inside a learning-management system (LMS); it is, rather, a constellation of readily available social-media tools used by all the participants in the course to communicate/share/learn about a topic of mutual interest. As such, MOOCs are called open, because anyone can join and start a discussion. Not only that—the content shared and created in a MOOC is also open. Everyone is free to create content related to the course. This makes a MOOC ideal for creating open online resources (OER), as the content can be viewed by anyone interested. A MOOC is situated online. It is Web-based or in the cloud, allowing people to access the course from where ever they are and at any given time.

The fact that the participants of a MOOC are free to add, share, and remix content is of great importance to the course itself. A MOOC does not result in a classical course dynamic of provided content, teacher-driven information, group discussion, and personal or group assignments. A MOOC allows adult learners with or without experience in a particular field to exchange knowledge, build upon each other's ideas, and shape the course itself. This is a major difference with classical, linear course design. Participants are free in choosing how they will participate in the course, and they are free in where they add content they write or share. The course dynamics in a MOOC are multiple, varied, and complex. An example of a course dynamic is provided at the end of the mMOOC design section, allowing you to grasp all the different mMOOC parts.

The term MOOC was first mentioned by two separate individuals: Bryan Alexander and Dave Cormier, as mentioned by Siemens (2012). The concepts behind, and the actual realization of, MOOCs were first introduced by Stephen Downes and George Siemens as they were building a course format to fit with the theory of connectivism; this course came to be known as *Connectivism and Connective Knowledge* (CCK), which first ran in 2008. "In connectivism, the starting point for learning occurs when knowledge is actuated through the process of a learner connecting to and feeding information into a learning community" (Kop & Hill, 2008, p. 2).

Example of a MobiMOOC Dynamic

Only by engaging in a MOOC do the dynamics become apparent. It is hard to imagine all the dialogues and learner actions that take place without living it.

There follows a real-life example of a MobiMOOC dynamic to give an idea of what happens in a MOOC. In the course wiki a new topic is announced: collaborative-tool experiences. One of the MOOC participants has waited for this topic to launch because s/he has had difficulty finding the right mobile authoring tool. S/he shares this question regarding an authoring tool via the course discussion group. The reason this participant is searching for an authoring tool is because s/he wants to set up an m-learning project outline by the end of MobiMOOC. In response to the request, other MobiMOOC participants start sharing their experience with authoring tools. Some of them simply answer via the discussion group; others share a movie via YouTube in which an authoring tool is reviewed/shown; others launch a twitter "help-me" thread, in which the twitter-verse is asked (taking the learning experience outside of MobiMOOC). People outside MobiMOOC tweet their reply, and those tweets are redirected to #MobiMOOC (# is a hashtag that enables Twitterers to follow a certain topic). Others launch the question via Facebook.

The question is picked up by one of the guides on the side. S/he reads up on the answers and discussions that were happening on the subject after it had been posted by the initial MOOC participant. Having read all, and based upon his/her experience, this guide on the side will answer the question during a synchronous conference, showing a tool with the shared-application option (a way to share a computer screen in real time with others) in the synchronous-conferencing tool. These synchronous sessions are then recorded and prepared for mobile access via the course YouTube channel. All of this makes up a complex, yet resourceful and adequate, solution to the question stated by the MOOC participant at the beginning.

After just a couple of days, the initial question has been answered in a variety of ways (and has given rise to a multitude of strategies and dialogues). Each action is pushed based on:

- personal preference of the participant that is taking the action (social-media preference, personal-learning preference (visual, textual . . .));
- personal experience of the question at hand;
- personal will to engage in dialogue.

Personal motivation is close to intrinsic motivation, which is why the MOOC approach, combined with accessibility via (personal) mobile devices, fits human-learning nature (both informal and formal).

Combining M-Learning and MOOC

The format of a MOOC is a worthwhile pedagogical approach to combine with m-learning precisely because it explores new learning hypotheses (i.e., connectivism) that promote a higher quality of learning than traditional formats, especially in light of the affordances of these new mobile technologies (e.g., across location and time), as mentioned by de Waard, Koutropoulos, et al. (2011). MOOCs allow learning to happen across space and time owing to their mainly asynchronous and online architecture.

M-learning and MOOCs also allow learners to connect. Traxler (2010) mentioned that the "learners' experiences of knowing and learning . . . are changing with the experience of greater mobility and connectedness" (p. 13). Winters (2007) also listed three interesting aspects of m-learning: it enables knowledge building by learners in different contexts, it enables learners to construct understandings, and the context of m-learning is about more than time and space. Indeed, the same can be said about learning through a MOOC. A MOOC surpasses time and space, as all the resources are centralized in the cloud, and it enables personalized knowledge construction.

It is also the first time in history that learning content can be accessed via mobile devices and social media, which both fit into a MOOC. "This expands knowledge acquisition beyond the traditional classrooms and libraries, hence redefining those spaces and adding to knowledge spaces overall" (de Waard, Abajian et al., 2011, p. 108).

M-learning and the MOOC format fit contemporary learning and, as such, they lend themselves to be merged in a mMOOC design.

EIGHT CONTEMPORARY LEARNING NEEDS OF THE KNOWLEDGE AGE

As mentioned in the introduction, contemporary education and training need to be remodeled to fit the challenges of the Knowledge Age. Before elaborating on the practical part of the mMOOC design, it is of interest to look at the challenges that current educational designs need to embed:

- *Networked learning, connecting to people*: Networking among peers is essential for learning to appear. A mMOOC can be thought of as a "short-term" community of practice. All the participants are brought together to share community, domain knowledge, and practice for a short period of time, hence strengthening their knowledge through a network of specialized peers. A MOOC is all about connecting to others to strengthen learning and knowledge creation/exchange, as indicated by Siemens (2005). Mobile devices, on the other hand, have always been used to connect with others.
- *Becoming active, critical content consumers*: In a world where information is exploding exponentially, it is increasingly important that any learner finds his/her way to the most relevant information as the basis for knowledge construction. McElvaney and Berge (2010) came to the conclusion that, "when learners adopt personal web technologies, it enables and requires them to discard their roles as passive consumers of information, learners must become editors who critically question content and sources."
- *Emerging collaborative peer learning*: Networking in itself is not enough; in this increasingly connected world, collaboration becomes ever more important, not only to obtain relevant knowledge, but also to constructively scaffold on each other's expertise. Garrison (2000) mentioned that, "this adaptability in designing the educational transaction based upon sustained communication and collaborative

experiences reflects the essence of the postindustrial era of distance education" (p. 13).

- *Setting up communicative dialogues*: Conversations between people in learning communities are at the center of those online communities. This exchange of ideas that goes back and forth between members of a community is essential, because, "more than any other way, people learn not from courses or Web sites but from each other . . . through dialogue" (Rosenberg, 2006, p. 158).
- *Optimizing informal learning*: Informal learning happens depending on the context the learner is in and the learning needs s/he consciously or unconsciously perceives. As we move through life, we transfer our insights and beliefs from one experience to another, abiding by the flux of life and knowledge itself. By providing and disseminating information in such a way that a mobile device can log on to it whenever the need arises, informal learning is optimized.
- *Strengthening lifelong learning*: Allowing learners to acquire information and so construct knowledge using their personal learning device(s) will increase their lifelong learning capacity, as the learning facility is kept close to the learner her/himself. This acquired learning skill will also last a lifetime.
- *Supporting authentic learning*: As professions and subsequent education toward these professions diversify, authentic learning that fits the learner's needs is becoming crucial to allow tailored and relevant knowledge to be constructed. Naismith, Lonsdale, Vavoula, and Sharples (2004) mentioned that, "mobile devices can provide more direct ways for learners to interact with materials in an authentic learning context" (p. 13).
- *Enable self-regulated learning*: Pintrich (2000) indicated that most models of self-regulated learning include strategies to shape, control, or structure the learning environment as important strategies for self-regulation. A MOOC is built on a learner-centered approach. This means that each of the participants is responsible for his/her own learning.

mMOOC DESIGN

The mMOOC design is a step forward in realizing an m-learning format that fits the contemporary and future needs of education in this knowledge era. The mMOOC design is a design that can be used for setting up ubiquitous learning environments.

Background of the mMOOC Design

The first mMOOC design grew out of the demands and expectations of MobiMOOC.

Description of MobiMOOC

From April 2 to May 14, 2011, MobiMOOC took place—a 6-week MOOC format course on m-learning, organized by Inge de Waard, who also remained present throughout the course as one of the facilitators and the overall coordinator. MobiMOOC offered six m-learning topics, each covering one week: a session introducing m-learning, m-learning planning, m-learning for development (M4D), leading-edge innovations in m-learning, interaction between m-learning and a mobile connected society, and m-learning in K–12 environments. All the facilitators (Judy Brown, Niall Winters, David Metcalf, John Traxler, Andy Black, and the organizer) were *guides on the side*, sharing their expertise, but also actively participating as peers in the course.

Up until 2011, most MOOCs were mainly Web-based. They used software and spaces that were mainly accessible with desktop computers (Moodle, discussion without mobile options, wikis). In order to walk the talk, MobiMOOC was using resources that were accessible with a variety of mobile devices as much as possible. In the first version of MobiMOOC, that was not always easy, but lessons were learned that added to the mMOOC design. The design is explained in the mMOOC architecture section. There is still room for improvement to get mMOOC fully mobile, as indicated at the end of this mMOOC design section.

Data on Mobile Use by MobiMOOC Participants

During MobiMOOC, two surveys were provided and taken by the participants; the mobile-use statistics were described by de Waard, Koutropoulos, et al. (2011). In total, 319 of a total of 556 MobiMOOC participants took the surveys, of whom 270 filled in the first one at the beginning of MobiMOOC, and 49 answered the second survey after MobiMOOC had ended.

Mobile devices were used during MobiMOOC. Although participants did not always have to access materials via mobiles, many of them did use them to interact with course materials. Seventy-seven percent of course users indicated that they had used a mobile device to access MobiMOOC. Unfortunately, at that time, there were no learner analytics available to clearly indicate how much of the content was added or viewed via mobile devices.

In the final survey of MobiMOOC, participants indicated the reasons they preferred to use their mobile devices to access the course materials. The predominant factor for using a mobile device to access course materials was the location independence afforded by mobile devices (61 percent). Closely tied to the location independence is the temporal independence (57 percent). Another reason as to why participants used mobile technologies to access the course was simply because they were just there, they were something that was available (30 percent).

There were, however, restrictions to using a mobile device, the chief reason centering on mobile-device usability and user interface. The major reasons were the screen size of mobile devices (72.5 percent), the lack of a physical keyboard (65 percent), and the perceived device functionality (57.5 percent); a device, for example, may lend itself much more to read-only functionality than read–write functionality. Other factors that were important to participants when deciding when to use a mobile device were the cost of mobile data plans (25 percent), their speed when compared with traditional Internet connections (32.5 percent), and, as is usually the case, habit (30 percent).

This is why it is not enough to provide only mobile accessible resources. In order to give the learner an optimal learning environment, all the resources must be accessible both to static and mobile devices. Through provision of an open device design, the learner can use the type of device that suits their learning intent (e.g., catching up on discussions, writing reflections, etc.). The mMOOC design incorporates this as much as contemporary technological innovations allow.

mMOOC Architecture

The mMOOC design aligns with the very nature of human communication and reflection, bringing learning closer to the human mind, as Cafolla (2008) wrote when critiquing the old educational system: The nonlinear characteristics of the human mind and human social interaction render the Industrial Age paradigm of teaching ineffective and deeply flawed.

In order to allow nonlinear communication and reflection, mMOOC consists of seven building blocks (see Figure 31.1). The design itself resides in the cloud, which means all the course parts make up the complete design: There is a central agora for discussions, an adaptable online syllabus or course anchor, the (un)known learners who are guiding the tools used, a mobile-accessible social-media toolkit that is tailored to the affordances of the course, multimedia that are delivered in a mobile-friendly manner, and links to feeds and/or content harvesters in order for learners to self-regulate their learning.

MOOC Versus mMOOC

MOOCs started out as Web-based courses that were mainly accessed through a desktop computer. At the beginning, the central course location was an LMS, which made it difficult to access with mobile devices. The resources were online, but mobile access was not important in the early stages of MOOCs.

The shift to mMOOC gave rise to adaptations from the original MOOC format. However, the author does underline that, in a contemporary ubiquitous environment,

Figure 31.1 The Seven Building Blocks of mMOOC Design

it would be possible that certain bits of content are not built for mobile access (complex graphics/stats), while other bits are not made to be accessed through a desktop (on-location, augmented-reality-driven content). Only when mobile devices are equipped with a beamer (projector) as standard will more complex visuals be accessible via personal mobile devices. On the other hand, desktops will become more lightweight and mobile as technology evolves. To allow the reader of this chapter to get an idea of the mobile additions to MOOCs, each following mMOOC design section will feature a paragraph on *mobile additions*.

mMOOC in the Cloud

The mMOOC design resides in the cloud in order to create a design that is open to a variety of learners. A MOOC has a unique social edge that relates to a more open and connected way of thinking and conversing. This coincides with Downes (2007), who shared that learning activities are similar to how we connect to our friends, colleagues, and members of society overall. We connect with them and enter into dialogue while exchanging ideas, content, etc. Downes also underlined the importance of enabling an open, connected, and interactive learning environment, and the cloud is the ideal space where these characteristics are met, and, as such, it is at the center of mMOOC.

Mobile Addition

Moving the mMOOC completely into the cloud allowed learners to access content as directly as possible, avoiding the need to sign into an LMS.

Adaptable Course Overview/Syllabus

Courses tend to have a central starting point to provide an ongoing, online syllabus that can be adapted easily by participants and facilitators in order to keep all the participants up to date and in sync with the course as it rolls out.

Such a syllabus can be built using a wiki. The wiki functions as the course anchor. All the learners can come to the wiki to get oriented in the course, or to access repositories that are provided by the course organizers, facilitators, or even by the learners themselves, if the course is constructed as an un-course (a course that has no pre-fixed facilitators or teachers, but where the participants choose from whom they want to learn).

During the MobiMOOC, the online syllabus was on wikispaces (this offers educational benefits and easy pdf creation of all pages; http://mobimooc.wikispaces.com/).

Mobile Addition

Although most wikis are currently accessible with mobile devices, they are not ideal for mobile adaptation or viewing. There is, however, a mobile wiki: picowiki (www.picowiki.com). A solution that was used during MobiMOOC are updated pdf versions of the course wiki, allowing non-desktop users to keep on top of the course timeline, including when they are offline.

The Central Agora

Dialogue is at the center of constructing knowledge, for "dialogue is the primary mechanism for maintaining connections and developing knowledge through them" (Ravenscroft, 2011). Where a MOOC is an ideal place for dialogue to take place and, therefore, for knowledge to be constructed or appear, the same is said to be true for m-learning, as, "the learning environment is enhanced and ability to share knowledge through online discussion is strengthened through social media. The sharing of experiences in a network facilitates the transformation of learning outcomes into permanent and valuable knowledge assets" (de Waard & Kiyan, 2010, p. 5).

For dialogue to happen, one must have a central meeting place. The central meeting place, or agora, is a key ingredient of the mMOOC architecture and, therefore, it has to be fluently mobile accessible and demands a minimum of digital and/or mobile literacy from the learner. This element needs to be the most intuitive tool used to share ideas with. In early versions of MOOCs, an LMS was used.

Mobile Addition

One of the easiest, low-threshold online tools available for dialogue is the listserv. It is simple and chronologically organized and is accessible with simple WAP-enabled phones, smartphones, netbooks, and desktops. Furthermore, even with the slowest Internet connections, the text messages from listservs will come through. Another good option is a discussion forum. However, one must choose a discussion forum wisely when it is to be part of an mMOOC: Choose one that is accessible to mobile devices (the wider the range of supported mobile operating systems, the better); ideally, there should be an option for social-media embedding; and e-mail postings should be allowed (easy mobile e-mailing).

(Un)known Learner Audience

Target audience and learner characteristics are at the center of instructional design for online learning, as Reeves et al. (2002) mentioned: "a thorough description of the intended audience and their learner characteristics . . . will enable the expert to judge the appropriateness of the user interface" (p. 2). However, because a MOOC is open to all, an optimal design for the target audience is difficult, as this audience is unknown until the actual course takes off.

Mobile Additions

It is important to keep the mobile and digital literacy demands to a minimum, or provide resources that will increase those skills, and make sure the core spaces have low technological thresholds. However, if you know your target audience, you can use those mobile social-media tools and Internet options that you know your learners are already using. A pre-course survey on which mobile tools your target audiences are using can benefit the mMOOC design and user-friendliness.

Supporting Self-Regulated Learning

M-learning and MOOCs are only just starting to get into mainstream learning and training. As such, the chaos that comes along with an open course and the variety of content that is created by all the participants can be overwhelming to newcomers.

There are two simple ways to enable a more structured approach to the resulting information overload:

- Provide links to feeds from all the resources.
- Provide information on coping with information abundance or support self-regulated learning.

Social media, discussion forums, listservs, and wikis all offer RSS, OPML, or Atom feeds to be shared. Through the provision of feeds, the learner can stay on top of what has been written and shared, which enables comment and discussion. Apart from the feeds, it is also possible to use a content harvester, a curating program that gathers all the latest postings/comments—for example, Twitter-based harvesters such as paper.li or summify.com, or a great open-source harvester that is completely customizable: the gRSShopper tool built and provided for free by Stephen Downes (http://grsshopper. downes.ca/).

Apart from the feeds, the learners must be made aware of how to cope with all the information. During the 2011 MobiMOOC, the more experienced participants put their heads together and came up with some guidelines on how to regulate the information overload of a MOOC. This list was then added to the online wiki syllabus.

Mobile Additions

RSS feeds are not known to all mobile users. During the introduction week, an example of a mobile RSS-feed application is given, including how to search and install new mobile apps.

Mobile Multimedia

Multimedia are increasingly used for learning purposes and especially in MOOCs, but some mobile screens limit the way in which media can be delivered. WAP-enabled cell phones support only a limited array of multimedia (most of them only multimedia messaging services), and some e-book readers do not have multimedia capability. For that reason, this section on mobile multimedia considers smartphones, tablets, and other devices that have multimedia options.

Mobile Additions

Cross-platform mobile multimedia delivery has many implications:

- The financial benefit of using Wi-Fi is underlined at the beginning of MobiMOOC.
- Mobile-multimedia guidelines are given at the start of the course.
- Recordings of the synchronous sessions are converted for mobile delivery: The complete session is cut into smaller parts (to enable downloading), and converted into a mobile-friendly format (e.g., mp4).
- Pictures and graphs are adapted (if necessary) to allow increased readability (different pictures as zoom options).
- Audio files are delivered in MP3 format.
- Mobile apps that allow access to common file types such as PDF, Word doc, and Excel are shared with all the participants collaboratively.

Choosing From the Mobile-Enabled Social-Media Toolkit

Embedding social media in the mMOOC design increases the possibility of authentic learning and collaboration and addresses specific learning affordances. An overview of mobile-enabled social-media tools is given in Table 31.1. McElvaney and Berge (2010) listed a wide variety of social-media tools and linked them to their educational potential. They mentioned that, "mobile versions of personal web technologies give learners more options on where and when to learn" (p. 8).

Table 31.1 List of Mobile-Enabled Social-Media Tools

Mobile-enabled social-media tool	Why use it	Knowledge Age challenge addressed
Blogs (examples: Wordpress, Blogger, Posterous)	To reflect on what is learned, or what the learner thinks is of importance Keeping a learning archive Reflecting on the learning itself Commenting on content	Self-regulated learning Lifelong learning Becoming active, critical content producer
Discussion enabler: listserv or discussion forum (examples: Google groups, Yahoo groups)	Listservs use e-mail to keep everyone informed. With many of the listservs, you can choose how you want your mails to be delivered (e-mail digest: e.g., immediate, once a day, once a week), which adds to self-regulated learning Mobile-friendly discussion forums allow topics to be organized easily Generating and maintaining discussions Getting a group feeling going via dialogue	Enabling dialogue Collaboration Self-regulated learning Informal learning
Social networking (examples: Facebook, Google+, LinkedIn)	Building a network of people who can add to the knowledge creation of the learner	Enables networking Collaboration Enabling dialogue Informal learning Becoming active, critical content producer
Multimedia sharing: –Video (e.g., YouTube, Qik) –Audio (e.g., Skype) –Pictures (e.g., Flickr)	Sharing visuals, audio, and/or movies to give others an in-depth view of what is happening Ideal: for getting the learner to really share their own real-life experiences. Sharing videos, pictures, and/or audio also allows people to construct learning snippets and share those with others Extra: geotagging, sharing the location of the object of the video, audio, or picture that is shared. These metadata can later be used for additional learning tracks	Collaboration Lifelong learning Informal learning Authentic learning Becoming active, critical content producer
Virtual meetings (examples: Blackboard Collaborate, Big Blue Button)	Most of the social-media tools are asynchronous, but the virtual-meeting tools allow synchronous communication to take place Ideal: for putting one person/topic expert in the picture and exchanging ideas with her/him Planning where to go next with a course or course topic Synchronizing thoughts and possible problems between all learners	Embraces networking Enabling dialogues Lifelong learning Informal learning Authentic learning (when streamed from a location) Becoming active, critical content producer
Idea and content sharing Microblogging (example: Twitter, Yammer)	Twitter allows the learner group to share short messages with one another. This can be of great use to share, not only ideas, but also relevant content from other sources Keeping track of specific topics Exchanging ideas Generating Q/A chats	Embraces networking Enabling dialogues Informal learning
Social bookmarking (examples: Diigo, delicious)	Social bookmarking allows the learner group to find bookmarked items related to the topic at hand gathered in one place Ideal for organizing online resources that would otherwise be scattered across the Web	Collaboration Lifelong learning Informal learning Self-regulated learning Practice critical filtering of content

Table 31.1 continued

Mobile-enabled social-media tool	Why use it	Knowledge Age challenge addressed
Collaborative content creation spaces Google docs Wikis (Picowiki = mobile)	Wikis and collaborative documents offer an easy way to build substantial collaborative content, and an easy way to read and edit space Building a course syllabus Creating collaborative papers Creating story boards	Collaboration Enabling (written) dialogues and discussion Authentic learning Becoming active, critical content producer
Sharing presentations (examples: Slideshare, Prezi)	Sharing presentations offers an immediate way of enhancing knowledge on a certain subject Presentations can be part of the information resources that are shared during the course They can also be used to synthesize other presentations and thus organize the major key points of a course in one point	Lifelong learning Informal learning Becoming active, critical content producer
Collaborative reference managers (examples: Zotero, Mendeley)	For those learners interested in research or formal accreditation, reference managers offer a great way to easily pick up references and insert citations Easily accessing citations, building reference lists, creating literature reviews	Collaboration Lifelong learning Self-regulated learning Becoming active, critical content producer
Collaborative mindmapping (example: Mindmeister)	Planning or structuring thoughts, future steps, content	Collaboration. Lifelong learning Becoming active, critical content producer
Augmented-reality additions (examples: Wikitude, Hoppala augmentation, Junaio)	Great for adding authentic information to geo-located spaces Allows learners to produce and/or get more relevant information standing in a particular space	Authentic learning Lifelong learning Becoming active, critical content producer

Mobile Additions

The use of mobile-enabled social-media tools is central to the mMOOC design, as it allows the critical aspects of connectivity, openness, communication, and interaction to take place. The social-media toolkit is, however, constantly increasing and changing.

Assessment and survey options are not addressed in this toolkit.

Room for mMOOC Improvement

As indicated earlier, mMOOC still needs to be optimized to arrive at a fully mobile format. A few sidesteps were made to work around existing design obstacles that stand in the way of a fully functional mMOOC, including the provision of PDFs as exports from the wiki, converted multimedia files, and mobile tech support. As technology evolves, m-learning will most probably become a term that will no longer be used, as all learning will become just-in-time and incorporated into one personal device or even embedded in the body. Until that time, increased mobile access is enabling global learning.

CONCLUSION

The mMOOC design combines the characteristics and strengths of both m-learning and the MOOC format. By using emerging technologies and pedagogies, the course design allows learning to take place in the cloud and be directed by the learners. The mMOOC design fits the challenges of the current Knowledge Age, as it embraces networking and collaboration; it enables dialogue, lifelong learning, informal learning, authentic learning, and self-regulated learning; and it allows course participants to become active, critical content producers.

REFERENCES

Cafolla, R. (2008). Industrial age paradigm vs. information age (chaos) paradigm. Retrieved from: www.coe.fau. edu/faculty/cafolla/courses/eme6051/chaos/Applications.htm

Crompton, H. (2013). A historical overview of mobile learning: Toward learner-centered education (pp. 3–14). In Z. Berge, & L. Muilenburg (Eds.), *Handbook of mobile learning*. New York: Routledge.

de Waard, I., & Kiyan, C. (2010, October). Mobile learning for HIV health care workers' training in resource limited settings. *Proceedings from mLearn 2010*, Malta.

de Waard, I., Abajian, S., Gallagher, M., Hogue, R., Özdamar Keskin, N., Koutropoulos, A., & Rodriguez, O. (2011). Using m-learning and MOOCs to understand chaos, emergence, and complexity in education. *The International Review Of Research In Open And Distance Learning, 12*(7), 94–115.

de Waard, I., Koutropoulos, A., Özdamar Keskin, N., Abajian, S. C., Hogue, R., Rodriguez, C. O., & Gallagher, M. S. (2011, October). Exploring the MOOC format as a pedagogical approach for m-learning. *Proceedings from mLearn 2011*, Beijing, China.

Downes, S. (2007). What connectivism is. *Stephen's Web*. Retrieved from: www.downes.ca/post/38653

Garrison, D. (2000). Theoretical challenges for distance education in the 21st century: A shift from structural to transactional issues. *The International Review Of Research In Open And Distance Learning, 1*(1), 1–17.

Kop, R., & Hill, A. (2008). Connectivism: Learning theory of the future or vestige of the past? *The International Review Of Research In Open And Distance Learning, 9*(3), 1–13.

McElvaney, J., & Berge, Z. (2010). Weaving a personal Web: Using online technologies to create customized, connected, and dynamic learning environments. *Canadian Journal of Learning and Technology/La revue canadienne de l'apprentissage et de la technologie, 35*(2). Retrieved from: www.cjlt.ca/index.php/cjlt/article/view/524

Naismith, L., Lonsdale, P., Vavoula, G., & Sharples, M. (2004). *Literature review in mobile technologies and learning*. FutureLab Report, 11.

Pintrich, P.R. (2000). The role of goal orientation in self-regulated learning. In M. Boekaerts, P. R. Pintrich, & M. Zeidner (Eds.), *Handbook of self-regulation* (pp. 452–502). New York: Academic Press.

Ravenscroft, A. (2011). Dialogue and connectivism: A new approach to understanding and promoting dialogue-rich networked learning. *International Review of Research in Open and Distance Learning, 12*(3). Retrieved from: www.irrodl.org/index.php/irrodl/article/view/934

Reeves, T. C., Benson, L., Elliott, D., Grant, M., Holschuh, D., Kim, B., et al. (2002). Usability and instructional design heuristics for e-learning evaluation. *World Conference on Educational Multimedia, Hypermedia and Telecommunications* (pp. 1615–1621).

Rosenberg, M. J. (2006). *Beyond e-learning*. San Francisco, CA: Pfeiffer.

Siemens, G. (2005). Connectivism: A learning theory for the digital age. *International Journal of Instructional Technology and Distance Learning, 2*(1). Retrieved from: www.itdl.org/Journal/Jan_05/article01.htm

Siemens, G. (2012). *The future of higher education and other imponderables* [Web log]. Retrieved from: www.elearnspace.org/blog/2012/06/16/the-future-of-higher-education-and-other-imponderables/

Traxler, J. (2010). *The learner experience of mobiles, mobility and connectedness*. Paper published by ELESIG Evaluation of Learners' Experiences of e-Learning Special Interest Group. Retrieved from: www.helen whitehead.com/elesig/ELESIG%20Mobilities%20ReviewPDF.pdf

Wikipedia, The Free Encyclopedia. (2012). Mobile phone. Retrieved from: http://en.wikipedia.org/w/index.php?title=Mobile_phone&oldid=507448708

Winters, N. (2007). What is mobile learning? In M. Sharples (Ed.), *Big issues in mobile learning* (pp. 7–11). Nottingham, UK: LSRI University of Nottingham.

Part IV

Policies, Administration, and Management

32

BECOMING A MOBILE INSTITUTION

George Baroudi and Nancy Marksbury

The mobile platform is one of the fastest growing witnessed in the last 10 years. Media pundits point to compelling statistics: Half of all Internet searches originate from a mobile device (Kessler, 2011), and worldwide ownership of mobile devices is believed to now exceed ownership of toothbrushes (Garg, 2010). One in three smartphone users shopped on their device in September 2011, making their purchase while located in the physical retail location (Radwanick, 2011), and Morgan Stanley predicts mobile computing will outdistance desktop computing as the preferred method of access to the Internet in a few years (Meeker et al., 2009). These benchmarks refer chiefly to smartphone adoption; mobile media usage statistics will be driven even higher by tablets and e-readers with 3G and 4G compatibility. Factor in unlimited data plans and consider the extent to which mobile communication permeates our lives, our classrooms, and workplaces.

With adoption of mobile technology becoming ubiquitous, education at all levels is impacted. Students accommodate to 24/7 access to information and each other, and walk into the classroom with an unintentional expectation of the same. This points to an important transition for learning and teaching, particularly in higher education. With a device-development trajectory heading toward smaller, more affordable, and more portable, students are building a proficiency that can be leveraged in the classroom. They bring into the classroom a device with functionality that is nearly equal to desktops and laptops. Device ownership is the social norm. Their ease with tapping, pinching, and swiping across the Internet is a skill in a realm most campuses are not yet prepared to cohabit. Mobile devices assimilate easily into students' social lives, granting instant access to information, and anytime–anywhere communication, and yet institutional components have deterred a matching evolutionary process in higher education.

THE ACCIDENTAL MOBILE INSTITUTION

To some extent, every college campus is embracing, or oblivious to, the undercurrent of a mobile initiative. A laptop or tablet program is not required to impact a campus or university; its stakeholders bring their own devices, making every institution a mobile one, in absentia. With each new semester, hundreds of newly purchased devices enter our classrooms and networks. Demand on IT services for wireless (or Wi-Fi) access, to both Internet and academic resources, increases. Students text and search by tap faster on a non-QWERTY keypad than some faculty can find a website. Integrating a student preference for mobile communication impacts multiple aspects of the institution, its faculty, and support services.

This chapter describes how one institution implemented a strategic initiative among its students, faculty, and administrators by rolling out an enterprise deployment of 12,000 tablet devices. We begin by placing into context the driving economic forces, inspiration, and challenges of preparing a strategy and plan for deployment. We discuss outcomes attained in the cultural context of a multi-campus university during a 2-year initiative to drive enrollment. After describing plans for deployment and outcomes achieved, we conclude with suggestions for other institutions as they become accidentally mobile.

PREPARING FOR THE ALREADY THERE

In the aftermath of the one of the toughest recessionary periods since the Great Depression, universities are plagued by low enrollment, rising instructional costs, and, oftentimes, a lack of futuristic vision. As a privately funded, tuition-driven institution, we felt the sting of inflation, our national deficit, and unemployment. Looking internally, we also saw a great deal of slowed resources in the areas of admissions and in registration. The student lifecycle requires a great deal of administrative commerce: documentation for registration, payment-plan adherence, vaccination compliance, FAFSA filings, etc. Fulfilling these requirements complicates the higher-education landscape, often creating roadblocks and bureaucratic mazes students find frustrating. Internal and external factors set a challenging context.

With a focus on business-process improvement, attention turned to how to mobilize student fascination with mobile technology and break out of the mold of desktop computing. In a cost-cutting climate, most institutions of higher education are forced to cut spending on technology, at a time of device profusion. Administrative leadership calls for easy and efficient solutions. IT staff strive to systemize both people and process, while technology users persist in wanting customized solutions. Faculty technology adoption ranges wildly from categories of those who refuse to e-mail to boundary-pushing astrophysicists and programmers. There are still others who struggle with uploading content to their course-management system. Some may question the value of technology in their curricula, full stop. Meanwhile, nearly every student is already "there," with a smartphone and Facebook account. He's in constant contact with others, developing a social network; she's playing an asynchronous game, geocoding locations with friends. Students entering post-secondary education today are ready for an experience that is relevant in a world where individuals may interact across space and time.

Charged with the task of attracting new students and increasing retention of our existing enrollment, we clearly required an investment in technology, and the choice had to be something tangible to the students. Informal focus sessions with students suggested that individual devices would likely provide a means for drawing positive attention. We considered netbooks and laptops. Even though powered with additional RAM, everything appeared as late chapters out of the same old computing book. The iPad, together with its symbiotic relationship to cloud computing, was appealing from a number of standpoints. With the increasing and oftentimes crippling costs associated with academic software and computer maintenance, we had already been exploring cloud-based application sharing as a replacement for computing labs. With this planning, we viewed academic computing with new eyes and were thus ready to embrace a post-desktop model, one compatible with the lifestyle of a millennial student.

We argued that to maintain institutional competitiveness, institutional evolution requires moving beyond static computing assets and capabilities. Students require a learning environment that is relevant to their social lives. Capitalizing on the coincidence of the release of Apple's swipe technology on a larger display, the iPad, the strategy was presented to decision-makers.

Socializing a Good Idea

One of Bill Gates' smartest ideas in the late 1980s was the inclusion of games such as Solitaire, Minesweeper, and FreeCell into the Windows operating system. These fun and low-stakes activities taught everyone, incognito, eye-to-hand coordination with a mouse. Providing an enjoyable means for play helped generations of computer users learn to use the mouse and computer-keyboard commands, thereby growing their digital literacy. Convincing institutional decision-makers to agree to a multi-million-dollar investment in what was, at the time, a somewhat faddish speculation required a similar strategy for consensus. Articulating the benefits of mobile computing, through the experience of the new iPad device, to digital immigrants required arguing a variety of business-case perspectives.

To the chief financial officer, whose main concern is a return on investment, the case was made that hand-helds can reduce expenses. With essentially no moving mechanical parts, maintenance is minimal; staff and software costs are reduced by leveraging the manufacturer's service commitment. Distribution that is based on cleared bills and compliance requirements fulfilled provides an incentive to students to manage payment and documentation prerequisites. Arguing iPads are essentially self-maintaining, individually owned, and protected through a third-party warranty policy, it became clear the risk of exposure was mitigated. The device may even be found when lost. By transferring ownership from the institution to the student, recipients of the devices benefit from a sense of ownership that does not require a great deal of IT support. Essentially, these devices free their owners from having to rely on the geeks, while opening venues to information, communication, and entertainment.

To the chief marketing officer, a case was made to position the university as a technologically savvy institution, not so much so as rivaling our peers, but more so in the minds of potential students. Those peer institutions thought we were foolish to invest in the somewhat expensive device on such a grand scale. Many have since followed our lead. However, when viewed in light of the large amounts of financial aid and tuition assistance students now incur, spending $500 per potential student was easier to digest. If the offer of a device might attract an additional 100 students, retaining those students brings millions of tuition dollars to the institution. Marketing our institution with direct association to an exciting new device type added social prestige to individuals in the early majority of innovation adopters (Rogers, 2003), garnered media attention, and stimulated a marketing focus for incentivized enrollment. Institutional positioning may be positively affected by the reinforcement of university branding when associated with an exciting new technology.

For the chief academic officer, a case was made to connect the technology to learning and teaching. Tying mobile computing to an already-established institutional direction toward blended and online learning was a simple argument to make. The breadth and depth of educationally related apps available are astounding. The more difficult argument was emphasizing how the mobile device contributes to a progressive learning environment. After all, the device appears as the typical "black box," with no moving parts and a mysterious Wi-Fi-enabled way for transferring content and communication. How might content be created and collaboration encouraged, rather than merely extending isolated Web surfing? Although laptop initiatives provide obvious functionality, it is the almighty app on a device with swipe technology that makes a significant difference.

For individual decision-makers, idiosyncratic solutions were employed to introduce each to this new tablet. For some, we purchased devices with keyboards for replicating the desktop experience. For others, iPads were pre-installed with educationally related apps. To endorse the kind of risky investment the initiative presented, each decision-maker needed a sound business rationale and a positive hands-on experience. Making the case for institutional adoption was in effect driven by personal adoption. To forge connections in understanding, each individual had to experience how the device would inspire and excite.

From the CIO perspective, an approaching end to traditional lab-based computing environments was recognized. Student labs, although still necessary, are a barely sustainable resource. Steadily increasing software costs, hardware updates, and antivirus protocols and procedures dominate IT spending. A 1:1 device-to-student initiative was logical; providing students with unfettered access and device ownership was a no-brainer. Tablets such as the iPad are a fractional expense when compared with laptops at almost double the price. A key consideration for those who would endorse the investment was recognizing the tablet was not yet meant to fully replace a desktop or laptop, but rather accentuate it by providing mobile access to Web- and cloud-based institutional resources. Understanding the cloud concept and looking at the broad landscape of mobility and technology development was a required vantage from which to make the business case.

The Long Island University iPad Initiative

Long Island is a fish-shaped mass of land extending eastward from New York City. Its namesake university, LIU, is composed of two major campuses, one urban and one suburban, plus four regional locations throughout the greater New York area. With a combined enrollment of nearly 30,000 full-time and part-time undergraduate and graduate students and a low endowment, it was hard hit by the 2008 bank failures and subprime-lending crises. As a tuition-dependent institution, LIU suffered when parents were laid off or could no longer secure a second mortgage or home-equity loan. In the confluence of these economic conditions and faced with rising costs of maintaining the traditional computer laboratory model, LIU began its mobile journey.

As an enrollment incentive for the 2010–2011 academic year, newly enrolled freshmen, once their eligibility criteria were satisfied, received a free iPad. Criteria for eligibility required newly registered, full-time undergraduates to have made satisfactory payment arrangements and to have their vaccination records and admissions documentation all squared away. With the media launch announcing LIU's iPad initiative, continuing students galvanized and submitted to their respective provosts letters of petition; the administration relented and offered continuing full-time students in good academic standing the device at a half-price cost of $250, which was leveraged into the institution's billing cycle. This method of payment provided the means to students to include this cost within their tuition repayment plans. More than 6,000 devices were distributed over the course of the first academic year.

The following year, 2011–2012, the initiative was expanded to include newly enrolled graduate students and full-time as well as part-time undergraduate students. Both cohorts were offered the device at the reduced rate of $250, so long as the basic criteria for eligibility could be met. As with the previous year, students paying the reduced rate were able to add this cost into their tuition repayment plan. Student technology fees were increased to accommodate some of the additional budgeting resources.

Strategizing Deployment

From an institutional perspective, we knew from the start our departments responsible for student support and technology could be overwhelmed with questions about eligibility. We also knew our distribution channels could easily be swamped with long lines and ensuing chaos—at the moment of distribution and over time—in technical support. And a third challenge presented with Apple's mandate of serial-number registration with the iTunes store. If we followed this protocol and supported each student with each device set up, our deployment channels would have been essentially paralyzed. Instead, we leveraged our student-services system, MyLIU. Professional staff trained in early iOS development (Apple's proprietary operating system) created a software and procedural framework for installing a configuration utility and capturing the profile data, working within the iTunes application. We detail its description and functionality next.

The MyLIU App

At the outset of the initial communications, students were invited to log into a student information portal to access a checklist for tracking and passing the eligibility criteria. With each checklist item completed, students were able to measure their progress (see Figure 32.1). Once the checklist was satisfactorily completed, students then accessed an online scheduling system directing them to available appointments, based on their campus location. Students then selected their own appointment time, which was based on six deployments per half hour, during regular business hours, for the fall semesters.

At the appointed time of device distribution and upon the student presenting his/her campus ID, staff members rechecked each student's eligibility checklist, installed the MyLIU app, and configured the student's LIU e-mail account on the device. Students then were asked to sign a digital agreement indicating their understanding that the device was now their own property, for which the warranty agreement exists between Apple and the student recipient (see Figure 32.2.). The agreement also addressed the concern for students' awareness that any iTunes charges incurred by using the device were their sole responsibility.

To address institutional concerns about handling the tidal wave of questions regarding eligibility, avoiding the frustration of waiting in long lines, and to be able to account to our internal auditors as to whom these devices were distributed, the MyLIU app was created. While enabling the deployment directives as detailed above, it also includes a device interface linking to current events, weather, time, and the course-management

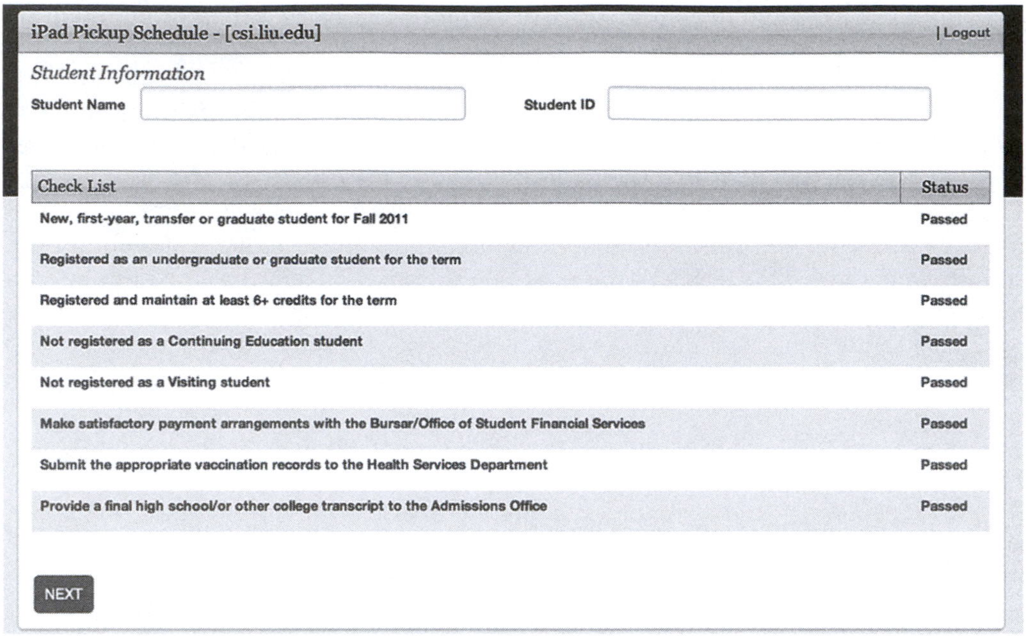

iPad Pickup Schedule - [csi.liu.edu]		Logout

Student Information

Student Name [   ]   Student ID [   ]

Check List	Status
New, first-year, transfer or graduate student for Fall 2011	Passed
Registered as an undergraduate or graduate student for the term	Passed
Registered and maintain at least 6+ credits for the term	Passed
Not registered as a Continuing Education student	Passed
Not registered as a Visiting student	Passed
Make satisfactory payment arrangements with the Bursar/Office of Student Financial Services	Passed
Submit the appropriate vaccination records to the Health Services Department	Passed
Provide a final high school/or other college transcript to the Admissions Office	Passed

[NEXT]

Figure 32.1 The Eligibility Checklist. When All Items Were Completed, Students Were Then Able to Access an Online Scheduling System

system and other academic-related resources. The app enables students to register for classes online and check their bursar balances and class schedules. Important to the deployment process, the app includes a configuration utility that automatically extracts the serial number and device MAC address for audit control. The repository of serial numbers, MAC addresses, names, dates, and times of deployment became invaluable for resolving a number of complaints and challenges that surfaced and satisfied auditor expectations for accountability. These data will also allow us to analyze retention patterns in the coming years and to consider trends in enrollment, student life participation, and other correlates to technology adoption.

LAUNCHING A DEPLOYMENT

A successful deployment is multifaceted. How does an institution prepare for thousands of additional devices going online? Are helpdesks structured to react and respond to user feedback in a timely fashion? Who handles requests for students whose eligibility is not as clear cut as the system requires? Considerations such as these, left unresolved, can make or break a deployment.

Preparing the infrastructure is an ongoing activity for any enterprise, and a requirement for a bricks-and-mortar institution. For ours, the previous decade of capital wireless investments helped to mitigate the requirement of a large lump sum expense in fortifying a wireless network. With the annual infusion of capital, our expansion of wireless access points continued. In preparing to manage the expected two or three times the number of mobile devices on the network, authentication management for Wi-Fi access was unified. Previously, it had been decentralized. Density of the wireless-network

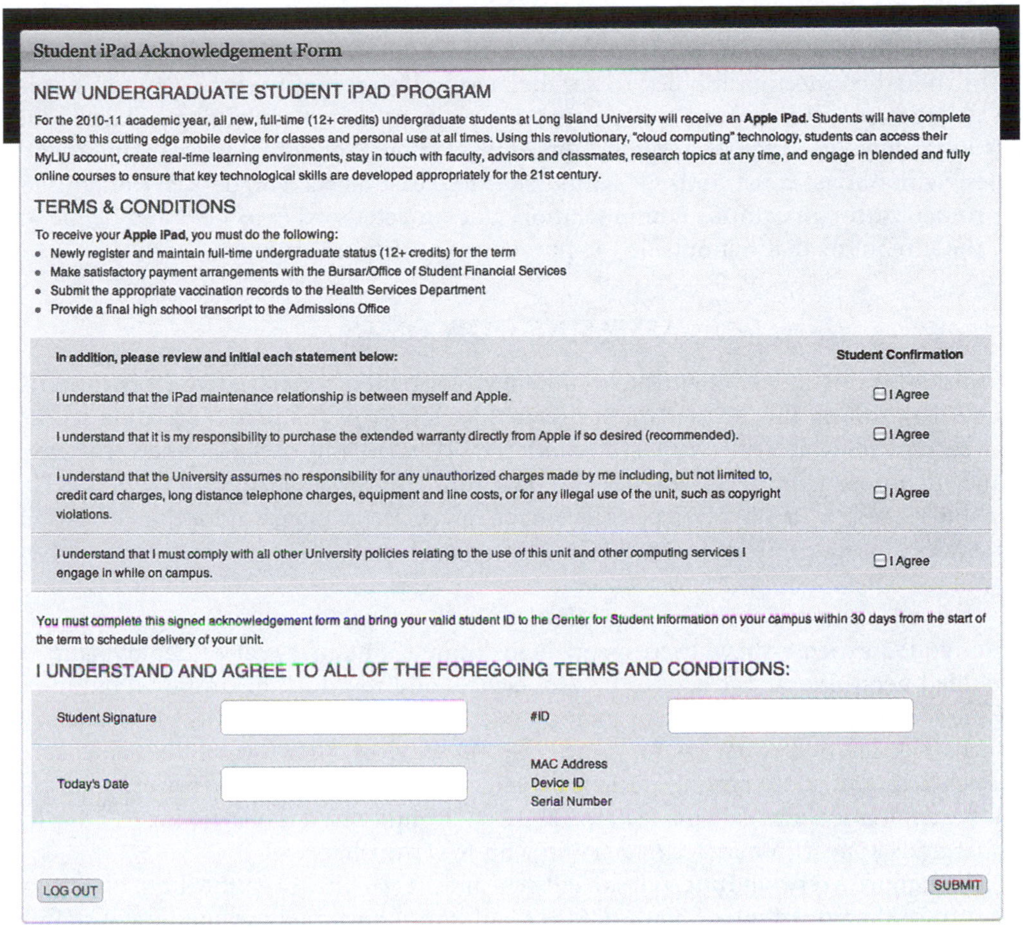

Student iPad Acknowledgement Form

NEW UNDERGRADUATE STUDENT iPAD PROGRAM

For the 2010-11 academic year, all new, full-time (12+ credits) undergraduate students at Long Island University will receive an **Apple iPad**. Students will have complete access to this cutting edge mobile device for classes and personal use at all times. Using this revolutionary, "cloud computing" technology, students can access their MyLIU account, create real-time learning environments, stay in touch with faculty, advisors and classmates, research topics at any time, and engage in blended and fully online courses to ensure that key technological skills are developed appropriately for the 21st century.

TERMS & CONDITIONS

To receive your **Apple iPad**, you must do the following:
• Newly register and maintain full-time undergraduate status (12+ credits) for the term
• Make satisfactory payment arrangements with the Bursar/Office of Student Financial Services
• Submit the appropriate vaccination records to the Health Services Department
• Provide a final high school transcript to the Admissions Office

In addition, please review and initial each statement below:	Student Confirmation
I understand that the iPad maintenance relationship is between myself and Apple.	☐ I Agree
I understand that it is my responsibility to purchase the extended warranty directly from Apple if so desired (recommended).	☐ I Agree
I understand that the University assumes no responsibility for any unauthorized charges made by me including, but not limited to, credit card charges, long distance telephone charges, equipment and line costs, or for any illegal use of the unit, such as copyright violations.	☐ I Agree
I understand that I must comply with all other University policies relating to the use of this unit and other computing services I engage in while on campus.	☐ I Agree

You must complete this signed acknowledgement form and bring your valid student ID to the Center for Student Information on your campus within 30 days from the start of the term to schedule delivery of your unit.

I UNDERSTAND AND AGREE TO ALL OF THE FOREGOING TERMS AND CONDITIONS:

| Student Signature | | #ID | |
| Today's Date | | MAC Address Device ID Serial Number | |

LOG OUT   SUBMIT

Figure 32.2 The Online Agreement. Students Provided Their e-Signature in Agreement With Accepting Full Ownership of the Device, Which Transferred a Support Relationship to the Student and to the Manufacturer

grid had to be increased, with the prioritization of classroom and instructional spaces over faculty offices and common areas. Internet protocol (IP) address assignments were limited to two per account, but the time limit per lease was an illusive matter to pin down.

Aspects of a centralized IT structure aided the process. Working closely with the IT helpdesk team once the deployment process started, IP address lease limits were monitored and adjusted accordingly. Ultimately, we opted for shorter lease periods and continue to maintain a healthy balance of access to all end users. The scaled deployment of devices, with appointments staggered to introduce a limited number of new devices per campus, per day, also aided in balancing the upward increase in demand on the wireless infrastructure.

The Me Toos

Through the months leading up to deployment and to the present, IT has been inundated with requests from all manner of individuals advocating their own eligibility criteria.

Staff assumed IT was selling half-priced tablets, non-qualifying students and their parents sought to convince theirs was an exceptional case, and everyone else with a shred of institutional connection lobbied to get theirs as well. Any entity embarking on a give-away initiative will encounter the somewhat unpleasant task of explaining and defending eligibility guidelines; it is the responsibility of the deployment system to maintain staunch rules. With budget constraints, it is impossible to please all stakeholders. We established a protocol through campus administration, unconnected to IT, to field and deliberate on these requests that fell outside the purview of qualifying criteria.

ASSESSING OUTCOMES

Within weeks of the deployment, technology blogs cited the initiative (Jordan, 2010; Lai, 2010), noting LIU as the largest private distributor of the iPad, exceeding schools and enterprises worldwide. Almost 2 years later, LIU is still one of the largest distributors, standing on par with larger colleges and for-profit enterprises (Lai & Siegl, 2011). This can be viewed as a staggering achievement, given the sluggish adoption of mobile strategies among companies today (Greengard, 2011; Lai, 2011) in a static economy.

Hidden Costs

Unintended expenses have been surprisingly limited. The first year of deployment, we included neoprene zipper bags to protect devices and to attach institutional branding. By the second year of deployment, snap-on Lucite cases were provided as a less expensive alternative. Despite concerns for protecting the devices, there was little evidence of carelessness and abuse among student ownership. Even reports of theft were minimal. Unlike device deployments made in the K–12 environments, it is heartening to note that undergrads appear to manage ownership with fewer mishaps.

Much more overwhelming, but not entirely unexpected, has been the drain on staffing resources. Even distributing 30 devices per half hour consumed the energies of staff, as each device was prepared, configured, and labeled prior to the student's appointment. Although the deployment pace is controlled in a manageable fashion, by limiting the number of appointments per day and by opening appointments no earlier than one week in advance, staff resources are consumed by preparations and questions from those who hope to qualify and argue their case when they do not.

Another hidden cost has risen from faculty. Those quick to innovate with the devices in the classroom learned with the first generation of devices that the ability to project a presentation or simulation was severely limited. This limitation is lesser with the iPad2, but does require the purchase of a projection adapter.

LIU intentionally distributed devices, first to students, and then to faculty. We knew students would have little adjustment in using the iPad for communication and information access. By seeding the devices among students, faculty adoption was invigorated by device envy. Rogers' innovation-adoption categories (2003) were clearly defined among LIU faculty, and the next section provides evidence of such delineation.

The Range of Faculty Technology Adoption

As new freshmen and transfer-student deployment progressed, faculty were invited to participate in our learning community. Academic leadership created a request for project proposals and circulated the opportunity to all full-time faculty early in the first semester.

Selection criteria included identification of courses, as well as academic experiences and student populations with whom faculty would work on specified projects. Particular emphasis was placed on pedagogical purposes and strategies, expected student-learning outcomes, and a proposed assessment plan. Faculty development initiatives included campus-based events for informal networking, user-group meetings, and presentations at the university's technology conference.

One challenge facing faculty was incorporating this new technology in a classroom where some students had and some did not. Because the eligibility criteria limited distribution to select categories of students, namely new students, and because distribution was scaled, distribution among all class members was not the reality. Still, successes were achieved. For example, one math professor reported success with using the iPad to demonstrate complex visual representations of formulae and as a course administration tool, bringing into a static classroom instant access to grades, attendance, etc., but less useful as a calculating tool as one would have presumed (A. Borde, personal communication, November 29, 2010). Art faculty found the device threatening at first, but in time, engagement-inducing by providing quick references to terms and theories in the classroom. User-group meetings with participating students, faculty, and staff, were formed to bring commonality. The user group aided the institution in reaching a critical mass by providing an opportunity for sharing of knowledge and interesting experiences and community building.

How did our faculty adjust to the pedagogical shifts in learning? Grassroot movements by both faculty and students interested in stepping further into app creation and problem-solving surfaced. One student single-handedly moved the student newspaper to a Flipbook format, and other inspired instructors worked collaboratively with their students to adapt coursework to the device and to create applications. Perhaps the most notable project incorporating the device was a Wi-Fi-mapping project for a graduate environmental-science course. Students involved in the project measured campus wireless signals. Their measurements and signal-strength analyses were synthesized into a signal visualization map (see http://gis.liu.edu) in a class project.

As may be predicted, not all faculty were enthusiastic about the idea of Web-enabled devices in their classrooms. Students clearly saw the benefits mobility added to their academic life, citing affordances in studying, note-taking, and productivity. However, some faculty refused to allow the devices in their classroom, complaining this merely distracted students while providing them with limitless game play (DeSalvo, 2011).

What might the near future hold for the mobile institution? The e-text is the killer app to come. Our students carry significant poundage in books on their backs. Complaints about cost are tired and worn out. The evolution of mobile devices into the educational landscape is transforming the world of academic publishing. Publishing companies today are scrambling to catch up with technology, reinventing themselves from content distributor to content provider and aggregator. They struggle against each other in their aim to adapt and stay afloat in shifting tides. Some seek to attach claim to portions of institutional technology fees, while others position themselves in the role of device support to faculty and students in the form of bookstore with technological support services. Yet others pursue novel ways to integrate content into proprietary learning-management systems. While this industry remains adrift in an environment where only a fraction of texts are converted to an electronic format, we await the maturation of technology providers, publishers, and educators. When more content becomes available, and students develop their preference for reading and studying within the e-text format, that will be the tipping point. Until then, faculty will remain in the role of information gatherer, and students as shoppers for the best value from the best source of information.

DIY DEPLOYMENT

Relating the reader's potential do-it-yourself deployment to this case study, one may find similar parallels. Ours is a tuition-dependent institution impacted by the economic challenges of the present day. Our students have launched their own mobile initiative with ubiquitous access and mobile devices. We hoped to attract larger numbers of students and leverage cloud computing to move away from traditional computing labs. Through the lens of business-process improvement, we identified a gap between students' expectation of computing resources on campus, declining enrollment, and the ever-increasing complication of governmental compliance.

LIU's mobile initiative was a move to provide the connectivity and mobility today's learners expect to find in higher education. We were amazed to find the power of a $500 device to motivate students to square away payment arrangements on a $10,000 bill. However, manufacturer requirements can cripple a deployment, and teaching philosophies distrustful of technological change may be antithetical to success. The tablet that includes swipe technology appeals to millennials and mouse-inhibited users alike. However, the focus of being a mobile institution should not be device-dependent or brand-oriented. The journey is really about capitalizing on the natural evolution of the Internet, and about bringing ownership and mobile access to those who may not have been able to afford the original cost of a device. Today's institutions must be agile, nimble, and evolving similarly to students' technological maturation.

The impact of a mobile initiative is likely to result in a blurring of traditional boundaries between the academic setting and the rest of the world. Factors that facilitate learning are less about the tools and more about interaction and relevance. Every teacher has a different method for teaching, for discerning ways to connect students' understanding to knowledge, for encouraging engagement and curiosity. From chalkboard to green boards to whiteboards to the iPad, the tools will continue to evolve, while the process of teaching remains the same. The offer of the device lent to students the promise of access to rich information from scholarly sources, educational applications, and communications on the go.

For the institution, the initiative reported on in this chapter began as a recruitment tool. To sustain a forward-thinking direction, we must use the momentum gained and direct our strategy to retention through faculty development and student support. The communication evolution that the Internet created and mobility enables is unstoppable. As was witnessed during recent events of the Arab Spring, the Occupy movements, and Russian and Egyptian election demonstrations, mobility is pervasive, because it provides the individual with access to the world stage. Our students are already there, and it is now time for institutions to prepare for that which they can no longer ignore.

ACKNOWLEDGMENTS

The authors acknowledge the fiduciary relationship between Apple and Long Island University and establish that Apple provided no financial discounts to the University based on quantity purchases, except by packaging in lots of ten devices. No other remuneration has been exchanged.

REFERENCES

DeSalvo, J. (2011). How's your iPad doing? *Post Pioneer*. Retrieved from: http://liupostpioneer.com/2011/03/23/how%E2%80%99s-your-ipad-doing/

Garg, A. (2010). Interesting mobile statistics by Tomi Ahonen: mLearnCon. Retrieved from: www.upsidelearning.com/blog/index.php/2010/07/07/interesting-mobile-statistics-by-tomi-ahonen-mlearncon/

Greengard, S. (2011). Can IT manage mobility? *Baseline, Jan/Feb*, 5.

Jordan, P. (2010). iPad in education: Long Island University deploys 6,000 iPads. Retrieved from: http://ipadinsight.com/ipad-in-education-2/ipad-in-education-long-island-university-deploys-6000-ipads

Kessler, S. (2011). Mobile by the numbers. Retrieved from: http://mashable.com/2011/03/23/mobile-by-the-numbers-infogrpahic/

Lai, E. (2010). (Updated) 20 largest iPad rollouts by enterprises or schools. Retrieved from: www.forbes.com/sites/sap/2010/11/10/20-largest-ipad-rollouts-by-enterprises-or-schools-as-of-nov-10/

Lai, E. (2011). In enterprise mobility, dreamers outnumber rookies (but laggards dwarf them all). *ZDNet*. Retrieved from: www.zdnet.com/blog/sap/in-enterprise-mobility-dreamers-outnumber-rookies-but-laggards-dwarf-them-all/2221

Lai, E., & Siegl, J. (2011). iPad and iPad 2 deployments. Retrieved from: http://ipadpilots.k12cloudlearning.com/

Meeker, M., Huberty, K., Gelblum, E., Nema, N., Dawson, J., Standaert, P., et al. (2009). *The mobile Internet report*. Morgan Stanley & Co. Incorporated.

Radwanick, S. (2011). 1 in 3 smartphone buyers made purchase on their phone while in a store. comScore, Inc. Retrieved from: www.comscoredatamine.com/2011/12/1-in-3-smartphone-buyers-made-purchase-on-their-phone-while-in-a-store/

Rogers, E. M. (2003). *Diffusion of innovations* (5th ed.). New York: Simon & Schuster.

33

A FRAMEWORK FOR IMPLEMENTING
MOBILE TECHNOLOGY[1]

Ryan M. Seilhamer, Baiyun Chen, and Amy B. Sugar

In this chapter, we outline the systematic approach to successfully implement a mobile technology at the University of Central Florida (UCF). The developed mobile implementation framework provides scalable solutions to plan, test, and implement a mobile technology on a campus, considering the student and instructor perspective, impact on infrastructure, and technical support across the university. Following a brief background of mobile initiatives in higher education, we discuss the mobile implementation framework, share lessons learned during each phase, and discuss the results of our pilot study. Finally, we summarize our findings and call for future research on this mobile implementation framework at the institutional level.

MOBILE INITIATIVES IN HIGHER EDUCATION

Research has shown that m-learning, when designed properly, can be used to engage college students and to teach cognitive, affective, and psychomotor concepts and skills (Dearnley et al., 2009; El-Bishouty, Ogata, Rahman, & Yano, 2010; Pursell, 2009; Sauder et al., 2009). The exponential growth of mobile devices has infiltrated the educational arena and shifted our thinking about how these devices can be used in education (comScore, Inc, 2011). Since 2008, universities have adopted mobile initiatives to embrace this technology shift by making their online content compatible on mobile devices, through creating mobile-optimized versions of their websites, or building stand-alone applications that can be downloaded from the iPhone, Android, and Blackberry app stores (Abilene Christian University, 2011; Rellinger, 2011; Schaffhauser, 2011). Universities provide mobile access to online courses for students and instructors via either a mobile application for their course-management system (CMS) or iTunes University. Most successes come from small-scale and private universities, such as Stanford, Yale, and Duke, owing to costs and availability of resources (Abilene Christian University, 2011; Perkins & Saltsman, 2010; Wasserman, 2010).

The number of educational applications available for mobile devices, such as smartphones and tablets, is growing at a rapid rate (Abilene Christian University, 2011;

Rellinger, 2011). There are many questions regarding, not only which applications to use, but also how to integrate them into a CMS and implement these applications campus-wide. The successful implementation of mobile technology is important to its adoption and sustainability on a college campus (Churchill, 2011; Hall, 2010; Herrington, Mantei, Olney, & Ferry, 2009; Huang & Sung, 2010). Little research has been conducted on the implementation of mobile technologies as an institutional strategy. In the 2010 EDUCAUSE Learning Initiative Online Spring Focus Session on m-learning, among 79 participating institutions, only five of them reported to have a mobile strategy for their institution (Wasserman, 2010). Implementing m-learning as an institutional strategy is more difficult for large-scale universities such as UCF, with over 59,000 students and nearly 2,000 teaching faculty and adjuncts. In the Fall 2011 semester, over 27,000 UCF students enrolled in at least one Web- or video-based course, and over 6,200 UCF students took only online classes (Center for Distributed Learning, 2011). Having more than 60,000 students and instructors access university information and course content via mobile devices involves issues of adequate bandwidth and available support.

MOBILE INITIATIVE AT UCF

UCF adopted a mobile initiative in 2010 that included the following goals: expose students and instructors to m-learning tools to implement new learning strategies, expand the accessibility of campus information, and enable students to access needed information effectively and efficiently. In order to accomplish these goals, we formed a mobile-initiative team to help streamline the integration of m-learning at our institution. The mobile-initiative team consists of four instructional designers from UCF's Center for Distributed Learning (CDL). CDL serves as the central agent for online learning at UCF, providing distance-learning strategies and policies, online course design and development support for instructors, and technical support for instructors and students.

Our first initiative started in 2011, when the university launched the UCFMobile application, a set of smartphone applications that provide access to UCF information, including news, events, course listings, athletics, images, video, and social media. Later iterations of the UCFMobile application integrated the Blackboard Mobile Learn application. This application allows students and instructors access to their online courses from their mobile devices to complete certain tasks, such as reading course content, posting to discussions and blogs, and checking grades, assignments, and assessments. As of Fall 2011, 15.5 million courses have been viewed in Blackboard Mobile Learn, which has over 1 million users worldwide (Blackboard, 2011). Our mobile-initiative team was responsible for the successful integration of this application into UCFMobile and launch of the stand-alone application provided by Blackboard.

MOBILE IMPLEMENTATION FRAMEWORK

A scalable, systematic, and sustainable method was needed to integrate the Blackboard Mobile Learn application with our CMS. In order to successfully implement this application on our campus, the mobile-initiative team designed the mobile implementation framework (Figure 33.1).

This framework consists of four phases: plan, test, pilot, and release. Evaluation occurs during each phase and is a key component of this framework. The first two phases

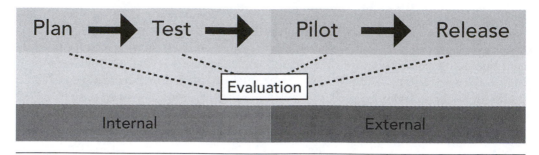

Figure 33.1 Mobile Implementation Framework

of this framework are internal, and the last two are external, involving instructors and students. Each phase of this mobile implementation framework is discussed below.

Plan

The purpose of the planning phase was to identify the stakeholders, project goals, available resources, and project timeline based on the institution's mobile initiative.

Stakeholders

We identified several internal stakeholders for our project, including the mobile-initiative team, the chief information officer of our university, the vice president of our department, our CMS administration team, and representatives from UCF's computer services and telecommunications (CS&T). The external stakeholders included instructors and students.

Project Goals

The next step in the planning phase was to meet with the internal stakeholders to select the mobile technology/application to be implemented and identify the desired outcomes and goals. After identifying Blackboard Mobile Learn as the application to be implemented, our internal stakeholders identified the following goals for this project:

- Evaluate Blackboard's Mobile Learn.
- Collaborate with instructors and students to test Mobile Learn.
- Create a marketing and support structure.
- Survey to evaluate Mobile Learn experience.

In order to meet these project goals, the internal stakeholders decided to conduct a small-scale pilot of the Mobile Learn application, prior to rolling it out to the entire university. This pilot provided several benefits, including the ability to collect feedback from instructors and students regarding the application, optimize the application for our university's needs, monitor the application for server load to determine how it fits into our current infrastructure, test support materials, and report call volume.

Resources

During the planning phase, we evaluated existing resources available, including technology/mobile devices, funding, and personnel to assist in the planning and implementation of the remaining phases of the framework. We also identified additional resources that might be needed and internal/external funding sources available to acquire them.

When we began this project, we had no mobile devices on the mobile-initiative team. The team determined the need for a wide variety of mobile devices and operating systems in order to thoroughly test the application. We acquired internal departmental funds to purchase two mobile devices and explored grant opportunities to purchase an additional four devices for the test and pilot phases (i.e., two iPod Touches and two iPads). During the test and pilot phases, Sprint loaned us a Blackberry and Android phone. This gave us a variety of mobile devices and operating systems to test the application during these phases.

In addition to determining technology and funding resources, we identified available personnel to assist with the various phases of this framework. Our mobile-initiative team established 13 internal testers within our department, consisting of full-time employees and part-time students. We also identified key personnel from the CMS administration team, CS&T, and the instructional design team to assist us with testing, support, and infrastructure issues.

Project Timeline

After identifying the overall project goals, the mobile-initiative team determined the desired outcomes for each phase of this framework. This helped us determine the length of time needed for each phase and establish a project timeline. Milestones and tasks were delegated to the members of the mobile-initiative team, to be completed before each remaining phase of the framework. We used Basecamp, a project-management system, to assign milestones and tasks, create a project calendar, and organize files relevant to this project.

We discovered that some phases would take longer to complete than others, depending on the goals and outcomes for each phase. In our project timeline (see Appendix 33.A), the planning and implementation phases each spanned two semesters, and the pilot and testing phases each spanned one semester. In addition to identifying the key goals and tasks for each phase, we learned the importance of concurrently planning for the next phase. For example, the planning phase should include tasks related to this phase and also include tasks to prepare for the testing phase. Similarly, the testing phase should include tasks to prepare for the pilot phase, and the pilot phase should include tasks to prepare for the implementation phase. This ensured the subsequent phases were not delayed owing to a lack of planning and helped us meet milestones identified in our project timeline.

Evaluation of the planning phase was formative. We collected feedback from informal interviews with the internal stakeholders throughout this phase.

Test

The testing phase provided internal stakeholders the opportunity to become familiar with the mobile application, report technical and usability issues, and determine how this application fitted into the current infrastructure. This phase also provided the opportunity to determine how to optimize the mobile application to meet institutional needs (e.g., customize tools, interface, branding). Testing is a critical step before conducting a pilot for a mobile technology, as major issues are identified, and a support structure is established during this phase. In addition to testing, preparation for the pilot phase occurred during this phase.

Testing Plan

Developing a testing plan identifies the most critical tools in the application to be used with the testing group and determines how these tools will be tested. An easy, yet sufficient, testing plan focused on the critical tools and activities allowed us to collect valuable information about the mobile application without confusing the user or focusing on less commonly used tools or activities.

When creating our Mobile Learn testing plan, we identified 11 critical tools in the Mobile Learn application for students and 10 critical tools for instructors, including Learning Modules, Course Content, Assignment, Assessments, Discussions, Blogs, Journals, Announcements, Roster, Media Library, and My Grades. We identified these tools as critical based on their frequency of use in online courses at our university.

We devised a testing plan that consisted of access instructions and four sections (see Appendix 33.B). The first two sections identified the tool being tested, then provided the steps to replicate when testing the tool. One example is: "Read through the Learning Modules. Can you access modules 1–5?" The remaining two sections focused on the testing results and specific comments related to each tool. We received feedback from internal testers that the testing directions were clear and concise, which facilitated testing for those who were not familiar with the mobile application, device, or operating system.

In conjunction with creating a testing plan, we identified the testing group. Specific applications may require personalized roles or access to sensitive information that may dictate who can participate in the testing. Attributes to consider include technology and educational level, role (student/instructor), and personal bias toward the technology/application. We identified a testing group consisting of five instructors, seven students, and one CMS administrator, representing a variety of the aforementioned attributes. Three of the five instructors in our testing group were part of the mobile-initiative team and very familiar with the Mobile Learn application, whereas the remaining two had little or no knowledge of this application. None of the student testers had experience using the Mobile Learn application.

Testing the Application

After creating the testing plan and selecting the testing group, we identified the time frame for the testing to occur. We conducted the testing over a 4-week period in order to allow enough time for everyone in the group to complete testing and provide feedback. The average time to complete each test was 30 minutes. We discovered the importance of being flexible and allowing sufficient time for the testing group to complete testing, owing to their limited time and availability and the fact that compensation was not an option. The extended testing period also allowed us to retest the application once our CMS administration team resolved minor technical issues.

In order to test the application across multiple devices and operating systems, we asked our testing group to test the application multiple times on different devices. We encouraged them to check out the mobile devices we acquired to aid in testing the application on different devices and operating systems (e.g., iOS, Android, Blackberry). As we did not have enough mobile devices to provide to the entire testing group, several testers conducted the testing on their personal devices. Five of the ten instructor tests were completed on a device and/or operating system of which the user had little or no experience. Four of the eight student tests were completed on a device and/or operating system of which the user had little or no experience. This provided us with a diverse pool that helped us consider the technology barriers this application might present to potential users.

Testing Results

The results of the testing phase identified the technical and usability issues of the application before the pilot release. We placed more emphasis on technical issues reported during testing rather than usability issues, as we chose to adopt an application from a software vendor and did not have the ability to change the structure of the application. Our main concern was how the application integrated with the current hardware and software infrastructure being used at our university. We categorized the issues reported during testing by priority, with the most critical to be addressed first. Critical issues were defined as anything that would prevent users from completing basic tasks in the software (e.g., posting to a discussion board). Some issues were determined to be less critical as they didn't prevent the user from using the basic functions of the application (e.g., formatting issues and supplemental media elements not functioning properly across multiple platforms).

The student side of our internal testing identified 27 issues within the application over five devices, of which 10 were critical. The instructor side identified 10 issues over five devices, of which 5 were critical. All issues were reported to our CMS administrator, with the most critical given priority. Once the issues were fixed, a small internal team performed focused testing on only these issues, to make sure they were resolved before the pilot. In addition to the testing plans, we evaluated the testing phase by collecting informal feedback from the CMS administration team and the mobile initiative team.

Preparing for the Pilot

To expedite pilot testing, we concurrently created a pilot plan during the testing phase that identified the timeline of the pilot. Based on feedback and results from the testing phase, we developed training documentation for the pilot participants. We customized the training documentation provided by Blackboard and created a resource page on UCF's Teaching and Learning Online websites. This resource provided an overview of the Mobile Learn application and identified the available tools in the application, directions on how to access and use the application, and who to contact for help.

We developed a communication plan to determine how to communicate with pilot participants and identified a main point of contact from our mobile-initiative team. We created several templates to use when communicating with pilot participants, including a letter to the pilot instructors outlining the details of the pilot and the resources available, and an announcement inviting students to participate in the pilot that we posted in each pilot course. We also created an HTML resource page that we uploaded and linked on each pilot-course home page to provide student and instructor support.

We invited 23 instructors, with a variety of technology skills and course disciplines, to participate in the pilot. Out of this pool, 12 instructors agreed to participate. We benefited from starting this recruitment process early, as this provided us with sufficient time to correspond with them regarding the pilot and finalize our pilot group. As a result, we were able to quickly launch our pilot, and pilot instructors were able to incorporate the mobile application into their curriculum if they chose to do so.

Finally, a survey utilizing the technology-acceptance model (Davis, 1986; Siegel, 2008) was drafted to measure student and instructor satisfaction when using this application during the pilot. This survey asked students and instructors how they used the application, what features they liked and disliked, and general mobile-user information.

Pilot

The purpose of the pilot phase was to roll out the new mobile technology on a smaller scale, to ensure the technical-support structure was in place, develop training materials for instructors and students, train support staff, and anticipate possible issues. We conducted this pilot study of Blackboard Mobile Learn involving 20 fully online and mixed-mode classes with 12 instructors in summer 2011. Two instructors checked out a mobile device for the pilot, and the remaining used their personal devices. At the end of the pilot, we invited all student and instructor participants to complete a voluntary survey to provide feedback regarding the application.

System Analytics and Support-Call Volume

A total of 20 classes participated from a variety of disciplines: anthropology, history, French, psychology, health informatics, hospitality, and journalism. Three were graduate-level classes, sixteen were undergraduate and one was special topic. Thirteen were fully online classes, and seven were blended. There were five different course terms (A, B, C, D, and Special topics) in the summer semester (see Table 33.1). Table 33.1 presents a detailed breakdown of the class duration and support-request numbers on Mobile Learn for each course term. The system analytics indicate that Mobile Learn was used more extensively in the Summer A and Summer B terms.

A total of 136 users accessed the application during the summer semester. Table 33.2 illustrates the number of page requests (i.e., times a user accessed any component of Mobile Learn during the summer semester). The majority of the page requests (103 out of 126) were below 100. All instructor page requests were below 60.

Table 33.1 Participating Class Duration

Summer term	Start date	End date	No. of classes	No. of requests (not unique)
A	May 13	June 24	5	413
B	June 24	August 5	7	543
C	May 13	August 5	6	263
D	May 13	July 15	1	33
Special topic	May 13	August 5	1	45
Total			20	1,297

Table 33.2 Mobile Learn Usage—Summer Semester

Role	No.	Page requests Min.	Page requests max.	Page requests median
Student	126	3	1,992	34.5
Faculty	10	3	56	22.5
Total	136	3	1,992	33

During the pilot, our online technical-support team received a total of four phone calls from students seeking help to access the UCF Mobile Learn application. Instructors also received student questions regarding initial access. Once Mobile Learn was set up on the phone and connected to the UCF CMS, it appears that students did not request additional assistance.

Survey Demographics

The survey investigated users' attitudes towards the use of Mobile Learn, their actual use of the technology, and participants' demographic information. A total of 69 respondents participated in the survey: 49 were female, and 20 were male. The majority of the participants were students, Caucasian, under the age of 25. Among all participants, five were instructors and 64 were students. Participants reported a variety of devices used to access Mobile Learn. Figure 33.2 shows detailed breakdowns of the reported devices. The majority of users reported using either an iPhone or Android device.

Self-Reported Mobile Learn Usage

The most frequently used features reported in the survey include: assignments, course content, announcements, discussions, grades, and assessments. More than 60 percent of participants reported that they used these features. Some of the less frequently used activities include: post discussions, access media files, access class roster, post comments on blog/journal, and create announcements. These features were not used as widely by participants as the other features in the CMS. The results indicate that users tend to read, not compose messages for teaching and learning purposes on their mobile devices.

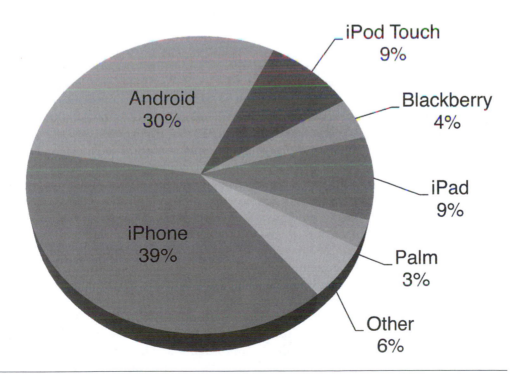

Figure 33.2 Devices Used by Participants to Access Mobile Learn (Self-reported N = 67)

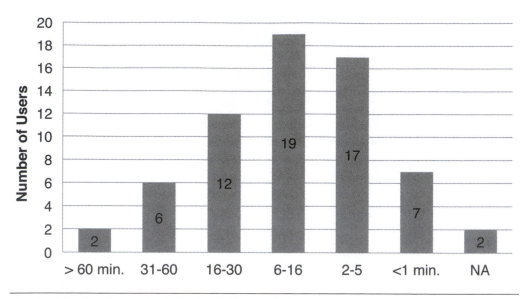

Figure 33.3 How Long the Participants Spent on Mobile Learn Each Time They Logged-in (Self-reported N=65)

We also asked our participants about their Mobile Learn usage. The results show that most users used their mobile devices to access the CMS several times a week. Only one in five of our participants used Mobile Learn once a day or more frequently. In terms of time duration, the majority of our participants reported that they spent between 5 and 30 minutes each time they logged into Mobile Learn. Figure 33.3 shows these details.

Student and Instructor Perception of M-Learning

Based on the technology-acceptance model, the survey investigated different aspects of user perceptions of Mobile Learn: perceived organizational support, perceived usefulness, perceived ease of use, intention to use, and satisfaction towards the application. For each aspect, respondents were asked to rate their level of agreement with proposed statements on a 5-point Likert scale. The survey results indicated that participants agreed that they had directions to access the application and support services for technical assistance. They agreed that using Mobile Learn made it easier for them to access the CMS, but were neutral on the statements regarding efficiency and work-quality improvement. For all measures, participants agreed that it was easy to download and access the application, to do what they wanted, and to become skillful. The overall satisfaction level was high. Our respondents agreed that it was beneficial and fun to use the application. The overall experience was good, and use of Mobile Learn improved their online-learning experience. The intention was rated the highest among all measures. High intention indicated that our participants showed a strong interest in using m-learning in the future and demanded more features, as well as more mobile applications for their use.

The results indicated that students found the application more useful than instructors did. Instructors were neutral on the usefulness of the application, but highly rated the other aspects, such as ease of use, attitude, and intention. The findings enabled us to measure student and instructor satisfaction, while guiding our feedback for future improvements to the application.

Release

The purpose of the release phase was to notify external stakeholders of the new mobile application and implement the support structure for this application. In order to accomplish this, we created a marketing plan and a support plan.

Marketing Plan

Being a larger university, the release phase of the Mobile Learn application had the potential to reach 3,328 course sections, which made a marketing plan a necessity for us.

We created a marketing plan that outlined a campus-wide communication strategy among the internal stakeholders and various departments on campus involved in this project. We leveraged existing tools within our enterprise resource planning (ERP) system and CMS to market the application, including a portal pagelet within our ERP promoting Mobile Learn and the institutional messaging feature inside our CMS to notify students of the new application once they logged into their course the first time. Blackboard also provided us with the Mobile Learn Adoption Kit to help explain and promote the application through ready-made materials such as fliers, guides, and FAQs.

In order to send a consistent message across our campus regarding Mobile Learn, we created a centralized website, UCFMobile, which serves as the authoritative source for information about the application. This site includes an overview of the application, directions on how to access it, upcoming features, and support materials. Having a centralized website helps to avoid mixed information and confusion when releasing the application and provides the campus community one source for the most up-to-date information.

We also identified channels available through our university's marketing department that could be used to promote Mobile Learn, including exposure on high-traffic websites, print campaigns, and social-networking sites. In addition to giving Mobile Learn high visibility on the UCFMobile website, it was featured in campus newsletters and promoted on official Twitter and Facebook accounts.

Support Plan

Our support plan identified how the application will be supported campus-wide and how the user will find support information. The implementation of this application went beyond the scope of CDL's online technical course support. For the first time, we had to think about how to support the installation of an application on a mobile device. The service desk, a different department on campus, supports the application's authentication method, and so we worked closely with them to determine when a user would contact CDL or the service desk. We determined that the service desk would handle login issues, while CDL would be in charge of issues with content inside the application. A decision was made for the user to contact the phone or software manufacturer when having issues installing the application on their device.

In addition to the UCFMobile website, we integrated additional support into our existing Teaching and Learning Online websites. This allowed us to provide role-specific information for instructors and students on these sites—for example, how to use the application to complete a course versus how to teach a course using the application. We also added a link to these Mobile Learn resources in the standard online course template provided to instructors.

We evaluated the release phase by identifying the percentage of total users who accessed the application. Our goal was to have 10 percent usage in the first semester, with the number increasing thereafter. We also analyzed the number of support requests related to the application from CDL and the service desk.

CONCLUSION

The mobile implementation framework introduced in this chapter provided us with scalable solutions to plan, test, pilot, and implement a mobile technology on our campus, while considering the student and instructor perspective, impact on infrastructure, and technical support across the university. Using this systematic approach, we identified the key objectives, tasks, and milestones for the overall project and each phase of the project. As a result, we completed key tasks for each phase before moving to the next, and stayed on track to meet our overall project goals. The evaluation process built into each phase of this framework provided internal stakeholders the opportunity to share feedback, which helped us identify and resolve issues before moving forward in the project.

We learned the importance of maintaining flexibility throughout this implementation framework, as we had to make minor adjustments to the project timeline owing to unforeseen issues, such as procedural, budgetary, or technical. Concurrent planning and evaluation across phases allowed us to make these changes to the timeline while still meeting crucial project deadlines. As a result, subsequent phases were not delayed owing to a lack of planning.

In addition, we learned that the support and involvement of the internal stakeholders was key to the successful implementation of an enterprise-level application in a large university such as ours. The systematic approach of this framework enabled us to work and communicate efficiently with the various departments and stakeholders across our campus, which ensured they were informed and prepared for the campus-wide launch of this mobile application.

The information obtained from our pilot research helped us facilitate the marketing, training, and support systems for the implementation of this mobile technology on a large scale. As indicated in our survey results, instructors and students showed consistent satisfaction regarding the use of Mobile Learn at UCF. They also expressed strong interest in using m-learning in future classes and demanded more features, as well as more mobile applications for their use. There is still a need for more research to be conducted on this mobile implementation framework at the institutional level, and, as we continue to scale this initiative, we hope to continue to add to the body of research on effectively using mobile technologies in education.

APPENDIX 33.A

Project Timeline
Semesters 1 and 2: Planning Phase

- Form mobile team/committee to implement the various phases.
- Acquire funds to purchase devices—internal and external.
- Identify initial task for mobile team.
- Identify internal testers.
- Plan for testing phase.

Semester 3: Testing Phase

- Research mobile technologies.
- Conduct internal testing of the application.
- Develop training documentation for students and instructors.
- Plan for pilot phase:
  –Create a pilot plan.
  –Create a survey for pilot.
  –Recruit instructors to participate in the pilot.
  –Create a pilot communication plan (how to communicate with instructors and students).

Semester 4: Pilot Phase

- Launch the pilot of mobile application.
- Conduct student and instructor survey.
- Analyze survey data.
- Create a campus-wide implementation plan.
- Plan for implementation phase.

Semesters 5 and 6: Implementation Phase

- Develop plan to roll out mobile application to entire campus.
- Schedule training and information sessions for instructors.
- Identify advertising and marketing plan.
- Revise training documentation based on instructor/student feedback.

APPENDIX 33.B

Test Plan for Bb Mobile Learn—Instructor/Designer Functionality Testing
Course Title: Mobile Learn—Instructor Testing—ENC6217
Name:
Date:
Device Hardware & Operating System:
Instructions: Follow the Steps to test the Bb Mobile Learn tools in the instructor/designer role; indicate in the Results field whether the tools load properly; and write further comments in the Comments Field.

Table 33.3 Example Test Plan for Bb Mobile Learn

Tool	Steps to replicate	Results	Comments
Learning modules	Read through the learning modules Can you access modules 1–5?		
Course content	Read through course content Did you receive any errors?		

NOTE

1 The authors thank Dr. Aimee deNoyelles, Dr. Patsy Moskal, Dr. William Phillips, and Luisa Cintron for their helpful comments, suggestions, and contributions regarding this manuscript.

REFERENCES

Abilene Christian University. (2011). *2009–10 mobile learning report.* Abilene, TX: Abilene Christian University. Retrieved from: www.acu.edu/technology/mobilelearning/Research/presentations.html

Blackboard. (2011). *Blackboard mobile apps reach nearly three million downloads.* Retrieved from: www.blackboard.com/About-Bb/Media-Center/Press-Releases.aspx?releaseid=1618480

Center for Distributed Learning. (2011). *University of Central Florida distance learning Fall 2011 semester report.* Orlando, FL: University of Central Florida.

Churchill, D. (2011). Conceptual model learning objects and design recommendations for small screens. *Subscription Prices and Ordering Information, 203.*

comScore, Inc. (2011). *The 2010 mobile year in review.* Retrieved from: www.comscore.com/Press_Events/Presentations_Whitepapers/2011/2010_Mobile_Year_in_Review

Davis, F. (1986). *A technology acceptance model for empirically testing new end-user information systems: Theory and results.* Sloan School of Management, Massachusetts Institute of Technology.

Dearnley, C., Taylor, J., Hennessy, S., Parks, M., Coates, C., Haigh, J., et al. (2009). Using mobile technologies for assessment and learning in practice settings: Outcomes of five case studies. *International Journal on E-Learning, 8*(2), 193–207.

El-Bishouty, M. M., Ogata, H., Rahman, S., & Yano, Y. (2010). Social knowledge awareness map for computer supported ubiquitous learning environment. *Subscription Prices and Ordering Information, 27.*

Hall, G. (2010). Technology's Achilles heel: Achieving high-quality implementation. *Journal of Research on Technology in Education, 42*(3), 231–253.

Herrington, A., Mantei, J., Olney, I., & Ferry, B. (2009). *New technologies, new pedagogies: Mobile learning in higher education.* Wollongong, Australia: University of Wollongong. Retrieved from: http://ro.uow.edu.au/edu papers/91

Huang, S., & Sung, Y. (2010). Empowering teaching through instruction-adapted technology: Case studies on mobile learning. *Society for Information Technology & Teacher Education International Conference 2010, 2010*(1), 3265–3272.

Perkins, S., & Saltsman, G. (2010). Mobile learning at Abilene Christian University: Successes, challenges, and results from year one. *Journal of the Research Center for Educational Technology, 6*(1).

Pursell, D. (2009). Adapting to student learning styles: Engaging students with cell phone technology in organic chemistry instruction. *Journal of Chemical Education, 86*(10), 1219.

Rellinger, B. (2011). *Impact of mobile devices on universities.* Retrieved from: http://docs.google.com/viewer?a=v&pid=sites&srcid=ZGVmYXVsdGRvbWFpbnxicmlhbmFyZWxsaW5nZXJ8Z3g6NmY5MmQ2M2FmN2Q1YzY2Yw&pli=1

Sauder, D., Timpte, C., Pennington, R., Tsoi, M. Y., Paredes, J., & Pursell, D. (2009). Adapting to student learning styles: Using cell phone technology in undergraduate science instruction. *Proceedings of World Conference on Educational Multimedia, Hypermedia and Telecommunications,* Chesapeake (pp. 3066–3071).

Schaffhauser, D. (2011). A mobile education: Student-created apps. *Campus Technology, 24*(5), 28–32. Retrieved from: http://campustechnology.com/articles/2011/01/01/a-mobile-education-student-created-apps.aspx

Siegel, D. (2008). *Accepting technology and overcoming resistance to change using the motivation and acceptance model.* Doctoral dissertation, University of Central Florida, Orlando.

Wasserman, A. (2010). *Your campus on a smartphone, and the future of mobile education.* Paper presented at the ELI Meetings, EDUCAUSE. Retrieved from: www.educause.edu/Resources/YourCampusonaSmartphoneand theF/200400

34

SO WE HAD THIS IDEA

Bring Your Own Technology at Brebeuf Jesuit

Jennifer LaMaster and J. D. Ferries-Rowe

Traditionally, school decision-making is based on control of tools and resources. Student A uses school resources, in the school building, during school hours, monitored by school personnel, and so on. Today, however, our students are blogging, videoconferencing, file sharing, collaborating—creating day and night, at home, at school, in the car (hopefully not when driving!). Teachers communicate and collaborate with students in asynchronous channels such as e-mail or learning management systems. Those of us in IT departments are on call 24/7.

In this new world, those of us in school administration must shift how we make decisions related to access, retrieval, and use. The type of device, the acceptable online tool, should no longer be the focus of teaching and learning—or even administrative decision-making. The paradigm shifts from enforcing centralized control to engaging student choice.

THE PROBLEM: DEMAND FOR TECHNOLOGY INCREASES WHILE FUNDING STAYS THE SAME

Over the last 20 years, educational technology has differentiated instruction, simplified routine tasks (e.g., electronic grade books), and expanded the curriculum. With each year, a new gadget or website or classroom management system makes its way onto instructors' collective radar. One challenge for technology integration in education is that purchasing decisions focus on a certain price point (cutting edge, last year's model, wow-they-still-make-that?). As programs and interactive websites take advantage of newer and faster processors, technology must be upgraded to keep pace with the demand for the resources being accessed by students and teachers.

Compounding the problem, unlike other industries, advances in educational technology do not automatically lead to a reduction in workforce or other significant expense, so there is no significant cost savings or notable increase in productivity. The dubious merits of robo-graders and factory-style online courses notwithstanding, under the dominant model of education used today, a certain number of teachers are required to obtain a certain level of quality instruction. Additionally, a specific investment in technology is required to offer a certain level of integrated learning.

When the demand is for more access (e.g., increased bandwidth, newer wireless technology) and higher-quality end-user technology, such as more stability or faster technology, then the only solution in traditional models is to spend significantly more money—or slow the pace of technology integration. Neither of these solutions was acceptable to our parents, students, and teachers.

THE PROCESS

Setting the Context

Brebeuf Jesuit Preparatory School (Brebeuf Jesuit) is a Jesuit Catholic high school of 800 students, located in Indianapolis, Indiana. A 2002 facilities upgrade created classrooms with ceiling-mounted projectors tied to computers, mobile pen-based tablet PCs for all faculty members, in-room DVD players, and a smattering of interactive whiteboards. In 2010, Brebeuf Jesuit enjoyed a 2:1 student–computer ratio, yet still faced times in the day when every lab was in use, and demand still exceeded supply. Mobile carts, instituted as a solution to access in 2005, were locked away from student access during student "free" periods. Teachers complained about their inability to communicate electronically with students during and after the school day. One teacher remarked, "I hate that when I ask [a student] if she read the notes online, her response is 'I couldn't get to a computer. The library was full.'" Frustration abounded about the lack of access to technology. Despite these frustrations, however, there was a lot of integrating taking place in the school.

Integrating Mission, Education, and Technology

A priority of any integration initiative must be to align the technology objectives with the educational objectives of the organization. Brebeuf Jesuit Preparatory School is driven by a centuries-old learning paradigm developed out of the Spiritual Exercises of St. Ignatius Loyola. Revised in the 1980s, the "Ignatian Pedagogical Paradigm" informs our teaching and learning. That five-stage learning process—Context, Experience, Reflection, Action, Evaluation) aided in the discernment of bring your own technology (BYOT) as the best option for our students (LaMaster, 2012a).

First, we had to start with the context of our current technology integration in the classroom. Framing the context within the National Educational Technology Standards for Students and the Jesuit Secondary Education Association, "What Makes a Jesuit School Jesuit," proved invaluable (International Society for Technology in Education, 2011; Jesuit Secondary Education Association, 2005). One of the first assignments in the PBS Teacherline/ISTE Certificate program is to create "My NETS Organizer." This chart asks the responder to take the National Educational Technology Standards for Teachers by indicator and reflect on current practices with the indicator in the current teaching environment, specific examples of the indicator in practice, additional ideas for implementing the indicator, tools one could use, and resource links relevant to the indicator. Using this chart to align mission-driven technology integration grounded our decision-making.

The next year was spent in cycles of experience, trying out new tools, tricks, and methods. This was followed by periods of intentional reflection, answering the question "how did it go?" The authors found ambitious faculty members to run pilot programs with educational gaming (Redistricting Game), social media (Edmodo and Twitter), collaborative presentation (Prezi, Google Docs), and open student device use (phones and tablets). Teachers and students were asked by the authors to reflect on their experiences in focus groups, one-on-one conversations, and surveys. The process helped determine our future direction, create enthusiasm for new tools, and re-energize teaching and learning.

Finally, we decided to expand integration across the entire school population. A great deal of momentum for the decision occurred by word of mouth—it is amazing how one teacher's success story spreads throughout a department. Research on Web 2.0 tools, mobile environments, and access issues confirmed our experience at our school (Bebell & Kay, 2010; Keengwe, Onchwari, & Wachira, 2008; Scheckelhoff & Murakami, 2010).

Pulling the Trigger

At this juncture, we had to decide either to go with a traditional 1:1 model of a uniform device purchased for every student, or explore the emerging approach of BYOT. The traditional model had proven examples and gave a universal method of implementation. BYOT was unproven and scary. Our "aha" moment was when we looked at our own technology preferences. J. D. Ferries-Rowe prefers his Windows7 desktop and his 7" Samsung Galaxy Tab. This combination allows him the mobility and high-end creation prowess needed for a chief information officer. Jen LaMaster has a dual-booted MacBook Pro and an iPad. She finds the iPad satisfies most of her mobility needs, and the MacBook Pro will suffice for larger-scale productivity. We considered how Blackberry users can't imagine a phone without a keyboard, and their thinking that everybody hates netbooks. With all the legitimate choices out there, why would we mandate one device for all our users?

Thus began our BYOT initiative. We chose the title "BYOT" as opposed to "Bring Your Own Device" deliberately. We encourage thinking beyond the device and letting students bring their own broad range of technologies into the building—from #2 pencils to cloud-based storage and collaboration resources. Brebeuf Jesuit IT focuses on the learning needs of the students, creating an environment where students, faculty, and staff:

- have *access* to all the resources necessary for teaching and learning;
- develop *evaluation* literacies (skills) to discern the appropriateness of their tools, their actions, and their behavior; and
- are supported in the *use* of technology tools personalized to the learner.

These goals support our school mission to provide an excellent college preparatory education for a lifetime of service by forming leaders who are intellectually competent, open to growth, loving, religious, and committed to promoting justice.

As technology drivers at the school, we felt that this concept might be an answer to some of the financial and access issues that we knew were floating around in the school. However, two people's opinions cannot force an educational revolution. In order to see how this concept would play out, it was necessary to take it to the classrooms and department centers throughout the building.

Details From the Grassroots: Developing the BYOT Strategic Plan

In creating a new technology strategic plan, we started with the students, the faculty, and the users (LaMaster, 2012b). It was important that we did not bias the conversation about 1:1, tablets, BYOT, etc. So we asked adults and students very general discussion starters: Of the students, we asked, "What would make you better able to learn at this school?" After hearing from the students, we went to each department individually and asked, "What do you need to be a successful teacher and facilitator?" and "What would your dream classroom look like next year? In 5 years?"

Students explained how technology impacted their learning experience. Their comments revolved around ease of communication in a 24/7 learning environment and preparation for their future. Remarkably, we heard the same things across disciplines. As one faculty member summarized, "My students and I need access to storage 24/7." Faculty asked to put their personal devices on the network and to use new mobile tools such as iPads and Galaxy tabs—open wireless, more access to Web 2.0 tools, 24/7 access; it all sounded familiar.

Several more meetings followed with various campus leaders, school administrators, and the Board of Trustees. We spent over 6 months talking to users and making idea maps on the whiteboard. We posted our idea maps on a large whiteboard in a teacher resource center to encourage more conversations over coffee. Because the goals that would eventually be met by BYOT were generated from the ground up, we were able to meet the challenges of implementation with the support of teachers and administrators, as well as parents and students. Including all voices in the implementation of BYOT proved key to our success.

Table 34.1 Results of Community Needs Assessment

General survey of students and faculty	Student face-to-face focus groups	Faculty face-to-face focus groups
Too many sites blocked (primary complaints were social media and collaborative sites)	Unblock Facebook	Increase student access to materials posted online by instructors (library is full; no computers available during student free times)
Increasing speed and stability of computers; wireless connections	Guest wireless/student access to the wireless network	The most advanced integration tools available in one place
Access student files from home	More Macintosh computers; more varieties of technology in general	Easier communication with students at any time
Student e-mail addresses	Ability for students to bring in their own computers	Student collaboration (papers, presentations, lab reports, etc.)
Computers in classrooms are difficult to use	Laptop borrowing systems (students "check out" a computer for a day, week, etc.)	Consistent stability: classrooms ready to go; network always up; laptops functioning
Student–IT communications should improve	Don't delete student work in cases of accidental log-off, etc.	Academic freedom for students and teachers to access materials, computers, tools, printers
Edline (other online tools) should be used by teachers more	Browser choices (something other than Internet Explorer)	Faster wireless

WHERE THE TECH PLAN MET THE ROAD

Under the Hood

Once the goals were set, the process turned to the technical implementation. Concerning hardware, the BYOT model mandates a change for most school IT departments. These changes are radical or part of the natural progression, depending on where a school sits technologically. The BYOT paradigm challenges assumptions about student vs. administrative control, access, and permissions. Ultimately, the question posed by BYOT is this: How do I create a network that maximizes choice while minimizing access to material that could harm students or that could threaten the network?

Drawing Lines in the Sand

Although we could not support a "Do anything you like with technology" policy, we wanted a balance between freedom and judiciousness. Our lines are as follows:

1. Students should be able to use a device from any major brand or operating system.
2. Because of the presumption that BYOT goes beyond the device that is in the student's hands, we wanted to operate off a premise that online resources are innocent until proven guilty.
3. Students cannot have access to pornographic or dangerous materials.
4. The school must have some way of tracking student activity, including monitoring specific access violations (see 3.).

When we reflected on what type of world we were creating, the IT department came to a stunning realization that has become a mantra in our BYOT environment. It is a variation of a Jesuit maxim: When possible, presume the good will of the user. The IT department works to keep every pipe as wide open as possible, while meeting the few restrictive guidelines stated above. The following describes our experience.

Setting the Foundation

We have four traditional lab spaces (science, publication/film and video, general-purpose open lab, and the media center), with desktop computers in a single-purposed classroom space. We have eight mobile carts in academic areas (social studies, English, math, science, computer applications, and the media center), with traditional laptops, and one Chromebook cart (religious studies). After conversations with departments, it became clear that, even after implementing BYOT, we would still need our high-end, specialty labs in science and publications. We would not expect students to have access to Adobe CS5 or Venier software on personal devices. Many mobile carts, on the other hand, would be reconfigured and repurposed.

Cloud Computing

In order to provide students and faculty 24/7 access to resources, we needed to identify a cloud-based solution. Traditional on-site server storage was not going to meet the need. We looked at both Microsoft Live Office (soon to be Office 360) and Google Apps for Education. Both would meet our need for solid cloud storage and mobile productivity. We chose Google Apps for Education for its proven track record in education and, more importantly, for its collaborative tools. The implementation was relatively smooth;

however, we were unprepared for the popularity and rapid adoption of the cloud-based system. This caused a strain on professional development and some frustration by users.

Opening up the Pipe

Bandwidth

As we began planning the BYOT network, we estimated high regarding the number of devices, assuming every student would have at least one, and some students would connect two devices. We immediately evaluated our content and usage and determined that we wanted to double the bandwidth pipe (from 25 MB to 50 MB), with an option to go higher if it was warranted.

Wireless

In evaluating the number of devices and internal network speeds, we determined that our wireless_G network was not sufficient. We planned for a wireless_N implementation, with increased access points (normally we had an access point covering a two- or three-classroom area) to cover 25 connections per access point (basically one per room).

Device Management

The BYOT model assumes that, if a student brings a device, that device will connect. Although there will always be an outdated or off-market device that may have issues, the IT department should make every effort to make the access possible. We ran all of our testing referring to the "big four": Windows, Mac, iOS, and Android. Recently, we added support for the Chromebooks running ChromiumOS from Google, owing to the popularity of the option.

Firewalls and Filtering

Brebeuf Jesuit has tried a number of firewalls and filtering solutions in the last 10 years. As we began to prepare for the BYOT environment, we quickly found out that ISA firewalls and proxy servers were not the best solution. Android devices, in particular, had a number of issues with proxies that operated well on PCs. Ultimately, we landed on a hardware firewall solution with a web-interface content-filter subscription that could be flexed based on categories and personal choices. We enabled transparent proxies in order to force all devices through our filtering solutions. Note: The first firewall that we purchased (based on the recommendations of vendor pre-sales support) was *tremendously* under-spec'd. Be sure to verify the number of simultaneous connections that you expect to be moving through the system. If you underestimate, you will drag the Internet to a halt, no matter how large the bandwidth pipe, as all requests will be queued up behind an overworked processor.

Student Tracking

There are many different ways to track student devices. One of the most common is to limit access to the student wireless network (in our environment, a separate SSID) to specifically allowed MAC addresses. Most firewalls and filters can give MAC-address reporting. Another method we considered implementing was to use each student's credentials for the school's network as the login for the wireless controller. Unfortunately, although this works well with school-based computers (using Windows network authentication), there is less success in using the login information as an identifier for filter tracking and notification purposes (the login credentials on wireless do not send to the filter's logs).

A third and our chosen method of implementation was to force all traffic logged into student wireless to authenticate to the firewall itself. This gave a credentialed login that could be tied to the logs generated by the firewall.

Power and Backstock

Finally, as our implementation begins to shift from voluntary to mandatory (see below), we focus on the impact of BYOT on classroom teaching. Two more issues surfaced that we had to address.

Batteries have come a long way in a short time, but few have the capacity to last a full school day. Although we work with the expectation that students will adapt, we needed to create charging stations in student public areas for a quick boost of juice.

The second issue has a direct impact on classroom integration. If a number of students have legitimate ("my computer is being repaired") or annoying ("I left my device at home") excuses, teachers will quickly adapt by checking out high-end labs or not using technology. To avoid these scenarios, the technology department had to devise a backstock program that gives students and teachers short-term and mid-term access to technology. Satellite mini-cabinets with a few older machines that could be borrowed on the fly and a number of check-out Chromebooks for students with temporary (repair, etc.) issues are the current plan to address this issue.

Equity of Access: Voluntary vs. Mandatory BYOT

There are two kinds of BYOT that, in practice, have different outcomes. Assuming one has a population that can afford technology, a voluntary program honors students' choices and offers teachers the flexibility to assign creative projects by eliminating single-platform access in the classroom. Reducing the number of computer labs that the school supports, however, will likely require mandatory BYOT. Brebeuf Jesuit adopted a mandatory 1:1 BYOT program in Fall 2012.

One of the major concerns is that BYOT may widen the digital divide. If students cannot afford the minimum expectations for student-owned technology, a program of financial support must be enacted and subsidized by the school. This is where grant-writing and fundraising comes into play. We brokered these discussions at two levels: educational and financial.

Educationally, we worked with teachers and students to determine our "minimum guidelines." Specifically, what is the minimum functionality of a device that could be used by most teachers, without the necessity of special hardware or software that may be out of the norm for most BYOT devices? We made a list of requirements (the ability to type out a multi-page paper, the ability to access Google Docs for productivity and collaboration) and options (some students, for example, supported a physical keyboard).

Financially, we began to design models of financial aid that would allow students a range of choices that met the minimum requirements. One model would be a sliding-scale stipend based on the amount of financial aid received. Another would be the setup of a vendor store through the school. We finally set a goal of providing a full $650 for any student on financial aid. This puts a number of full laptops and tablets, with warranty, into the price range. It is important to note that we prefer a stipend or credit to simply handing out decommissioned laptops to students. Choice and equal access are critical elements in our implementation, and we will ensure that all students enjoy those opportunities. Empowering students, after all, is at the heart of any BYOT program.

Policy Development

Innovation in education invites a flurry of policy issues. We revised acceptable-use policies (AUPs) for both students and adults. Previously, those policies took a decidedly "Thou-shalt-not" approach. Our most helpful resource for AUP writing was from the Consortium for School Networking Initiative. The primary change was a shift in focus from a litany of things not to do to a call for responsible student use. This included specific expectations for proper use of personal devices, but also a loosening of commonly excluded uses, such as "game playing." Other areas that were addressed included social-media interaction (e.g., adults may communicate with students through social media, but must be aware of the power relationships and the associated responsibility), context as an indicator of acceptable use (e.g., there is a difference in how a phone is used in the lobby, in the library, and in the classroom), and awareness of limited resources (e.g., including bandwidth while streaming; and even paper usage).

Professional Development

As a community, we knew the benefits of a technology-rich education. Klopfer, Osterweil, Groff, and Haas (2009) found that technology in the classroom encourages collaboration, facilitates real-world learning contexts, and creates opportunities for creative, higher-level thinking. Furthermore, the Office of Educational Research and Improvement for the U.S. Department of Education (n.d.) notes that, where technology is integrated into the classroom, students display increased motivation, higher technical skills, improved attendance, and a desire to work more collaboratively.

However, we also knew that we had to plan for professional development. Traditional, large, group, push-button training was not going to work in a BYOT school. Professional development would require a paradigm shift similar to the one that occurred with the IT staff. We encouraged teachers to look at teaching with technology, not from the standpoint of nouns (laptop, Blogger.com, PowerPoint), but from the standpoint of verbs (researching, writing, presenting) (Prensky, 2011). Although not a new idea, letting go of the nouns to encourage personal, creative illustrations of knowledge is a very different way of thinking about technology integration in the classroom. Examples of professional-development activities include:

- Monthly newsletters with tips, tricks, and tools for the classroom: For example, we promote Web-based tools such as paper.li.com as we become more mobile. Another good example from a neighboring school is the 30-Day Web 2.0 Challenge Blog, by Evansville Vanderburgh Schools, Integrating Curriculum and Technology Specialists (EVSC ICATS) (Wilhelmus, 2011).
- Workshops: Although the "training workshop" is not always popular or productive, we found the following practices helpful:
  - Offer workshops at multiple times of day.
  - Offer one-on-one and department-specific, small-group workshops when conducting push-button training to keep authentic to teaching experience.

- Offer larger, integrated round tables when thinking larger scale, such as assessment in BYOT environments.
- Bring in outside voices, either live or through webinars, to overcome the "you're not a prophet in your own backyard" environment. Make friends with other specialists from other schools and trade off workshops—no cost to anyone, builds positive relationships across schools, and reinforces conversations from another "expert".

One of the most productive workshops we have hosted included faculty and staff from four other local, private high schools. The interschool dialogue brought new ideas, new colleagues, and a sense of shared purpose in student learning.

In perhaps our most popular and productive strategy, we put every tool we could find out on tables for a "tech petting zoo." Teachers could put their hands on devices and play with them. We also served food and encouraged an atmosphere of playful discovery. Other "petting-zoo" events invited students and parents at open-house nights to dabble with the tools, igniting their sense of adventure. Title IIA grant money will even allow for the purchase of multiple devices to encourage professional growth and comfort with these devices.

To reach students and parents, we also messaged through social networks, from Twitter to our learning-management system (Edline), promoting all of the tools and resources available. We used Edline to upload video and print tutorials on Google Apps for Education. Of course, most importantly, we have an open-door policy in IT. Our offices are right across from the school media center. Students can ask questions and receive support just by walking in. Finally, for future students, we are considering a summer orientation for incoming freshman that includes a hands-on session with IT to explain BYOT, explore how their devices work at Brebeuf, and learn about our online learning resources prior to the first day of school.

GROWTH AND OUTCOMES

In terms of academic growth, we expect an increase in critical thinking. Students will be assessing learning objectives at a meta-level, asking not just, "What do I do to pass this assignment?" but "What technology will best aid me in fulfilling the requirements of the assignment?" Moreover, as technology is framed as a means to an end, teachers and students alike will focus their creative energy on achieving learning objectives. Simply put, our hope for the classroom is less time spent on how to make a PowerPoint slide transition and more emphasis on the discussion of the presentation.

Admittedly, our achievement goals are hard to measure within the traditional standardized testing model. Any reader looking at our state data will notice students performing at 100 percent pass rate on state tests. However, we do have hard data to work with—primarily through AP and college entrance-exam data. In tandem with the academic and student-life offices, we are watching trends in testing data support academic goals for score growth. But, how do you say BYOT increased any test score? In a small, collaborative learning environment, how do you isolate one initiative to say it worked? This is the challenge of sitting on the edge of a new initiative. As for other schools adapting BYOT, time will tell, and we'll be collecting as much quantitative and qualitative data as possible.

CONCLUSION

Initiating a BYOT program for any school requires considerable time for conversation, setting goals, and evaluating the objective achieved along the way. Our transition did not happen overnight. Additionally, it was a very collaborative process, including all building constituents: faculty, staff, administration, and students. If you are considering BYOT in your environment, we encourage you to take your time and discern if the environment is right for your students. BYOT is not for everyone, nor is it a quick, money-saving fix. The mission for your student population should be the driving force.

Our students love BYOT. Our Mac users were the first group we witnessed in the building. Mac users were thrilled to bring in their productivity device of choice to a previously all-PC school environment. Embracing a more mobile model of access has increased collaborative learning (almost two-thirds of our students have created a document that is shared with someone, and three-quarters of our students are collaborators on one or more documents in Google Docs) and increased communication between students and teachers. Students appreciate cloud storage options. Productivity and connectivity are now student-driven, empowering them to control how, when, and in what format they create.

Our faculty population is supportive. BYOT has allowed for a refocus on academic content and away from delivery systems. After a recent round table, the teachers reported freedom to teach again, as the technology resources are managed by students. Teachers can get back to the art of teaching.

Over time, technology expenditures for the school will decrease, but not immediately. Cost savings were not the primary objective of this initiative; it required some investment in our infrastructure. However, as costs shift from lab maintenance to stipends for technology, the budget sheets may start to shift.

Admittedly, this is not what we set out to do. Two years ago, we set out to improve access and use of technology. The process has developed into a whole new way of at looking how and why we make integration decisions.

REFERENCES

Bebell, D., & Kay, R. (2010). One to one computing: A summary of the quantitative results from the Berkshire Wireless Learning Initiative. *The Journal of Technology, Learning and Assessment, 9*(2), 5–59. Retrieved from: http://ejournals.bc.edu/ojs/index.php/jtla/article/view/1607/1462

International Society for Technology in Education. (2011). ISTE/NETS Standards. Retrieved from: www.iste.org/standards.aspx

Jesuit Secondary Education Association. (2005). Foundations. In *Profile of the graduate of a Jesuit high school at graduation* (pp. 1–6). Washington, DC: JSEA. Retrieved from: www.jesuitsmissouri.org/files/edu/The GraduateatGraduation.pdf

Keengwe, J., Onchwari, G., & Wachira, P. (2008). Computer technology integration and student learning barriers and promise. *Journal of Science Educational Technology, 17*, 560–565. DOI:10.1007/s10956–008–9123–5

Klopfer, E., Osterweil, S., Groff, J., & Haas, J. (2009). *The instructional power of digital games, social networks, simulations and how teachers can leverage them* (Report). Retrieved from The Education Arcade, MIT website: http://education.mit.edu/papers/GamesSimsSocNets_EdArcade.pdf

LaMaster, J. (2012a) Bringing home the NETS. *Learning and Leading with Technology, 35*(5), 22–27.

LaMaster, J. (2012b). Point/counterpoint: BYOT. *Learning and Leading with Technology, 35*(5), 6–7.

Office of Educational Research and Improvement: U.S. Department of Education. (n.d.). *Technology and educational reform* [Scholarly project]. In *Technology and Educational Reform*. Retrieved from: www2.ed.gov/pubs/EdReformStudies/EdTech/effectsstudents.html

Prensky, M. (2011). *Marc Prensky*. Retrieved from: www.marcprensky.com/

Scheckelhoff, T., & Murakami, C. (2010). 1 to 1 laptop program: Planning for success. *THE Journal*. Retrieved from: www.techlearning.com/article/1-to-1-laptop-program-planning-for-success/47208

Wilhelmus, T. (2011). EVSC ICATS 30-day challenge [Web-log post]. Retrieved from: http://icats30daychallenge.blogspot.com/

35

TOWARD A HOLISTIC FRAMEWORK FOR ETHICAL MOBILE LEARNING

Laurel E. Dyson, Trish Andrews, Robyn Smith, and Ruth Wallace

New technologies can be positive forces for stimulating change, as well as bringing with them new ethical challenges, and mobile technology is no exception. Ling and Donner (2009) note that the explosion of mobile devices in recent years has created a clash with accepted standards of behavior. One of the problems is the lag between the rapid development of the technology and the more gradual evolution of rules governing its use (Castells, Fernández-Ardèvol, Qiu, & Sey, 2007).

The wide diversity of contexts in which mobile learning (m-learning) can occur further complicates this issue (Farrow, 2011). As more universities, colleges, and schools adopt m-learning, concerns have emerged related to managing ethical risk. Certain ethical issues have arisen with the introduction of m-learning into pedagogic practice: these include knowledge-related issues as well as moral and legal ones. Other concerns represent teachers' and educational institutions' fears of what *might* happen if they were to embrace m-learning. Teachers often have a naïve or limited view of m-learning (Pachler, Bachmair, & Cook, 2011), with little recognition of its transformative potential in changing teaching practice, or of its role in the transition to a more mobile society (Traxler, 2009). In part, their worries stem from reports of the misuse of mobile technology in society more generally, in particular, incidents recounted in the media in sometimes sensational ways (Hartnell-Young, 2008). Indeed, some of their fears may be well founded, given that mobile technologies lend themselves to learning across multiple contexts, including outdoors and in the workplace: Control over social interaction or content acquisition in these conditions becomes greatly diminished compared with the more carefully supervised environment of the classroom and may lead to potentially inappropriate activities or data capture.

To dismiss such ethical concerns out of hand would be foolish, but it would be equally wrong to let these fears deter educators from adopting a form of learning that has enormous potential for both those students well served by the current education system, as well as for addressing the needs of disenfranchised groups of learners. A growing body of studies shows that m-learning has the power to support students from developing countries, indigenous learners, and people from socioeconomically disadvantaged backgrounds (Kim, 2009; Ragus et al., 2005; Wallace, 2009). Furthermore, the use of m-learning presents opportunities to engage with a range of knowledge sets, constructs, and contexts beyond those found in many formal educational settings. This might include multimedia-based representations of diverse lives and beliefs systems, or representations of knowledge as constructed by different social and cultural orientations, which can be potentially beneficial for learning. Thus, any consideration of the ethics of m-learning must acknowledge the need for a positive ethic of inclusion and personal responsibility, not just harm minimization. It must address the problems, but not limit the diffusion of this unique approach to learning.

This chapter discusses some of the ethical issues and concerns that can arise as a consequence of adopting m-learning, such as problems of privacy, data security, and the unauthorized use of images. It examines ethical considerations that might arise when students bring their own devices into the educational environment, such as distractions to learning, cyberbullying, and cheating, and puts forward theories of why these issues have arisen. It also examines ways in which stakeholders might respond negatively to the use of mobile devices for teaching and learning, and the possible impact on the successful adoption of m-learning. The authors then outline the need for, and key elements of, a framework for assessing and addressing ethical issues—both positive and negative—in integrating m-learning into educational contexts. The framework includes guidance for teachers and administrators in adopting m-learning into their pedagogic practice, as well as for educational institutions formulating m-learning policies. A strong case is made for the professional development of educators and other stakeholders to assist them in avoiding ethical problems when implementing m-learning. The conclusions discuss ethical behaviors in relation to the use of m-learning and the need for ethics to be considered from different perspectives.

ETHICAL ISSUES WITH M-LEARNING

In a study of educators' attitudes to m-learning, Aubusson, Schuck, and Burden (2009) recorded five ethical concerns about introducing m-learning into the classroom:

- cyberbullying;
- the potential for public dissemination of information originally intended for a limited audience;
- the ease and speed with which digital materials can be shared, compared with older, non-digital artifacts;
- the risk of unethical use of archived materials; and
- levels of parental and student consent to recording classroom activity.

Because m-learning lends itself readily to learning outside the classroom, many new ethical situations are likely to arise, enabled by the capabilities of the mobile devices. These are exacerbated by the lack of control over student behavior that occurs if the teacher is absent, for example, where students conduct unsupervised m-learning projects by themselves in the field or workplace. Gayeski (2002) points to the potential loss of privacy when mobile devices are equipped with GPS capability and the learner's location can be tracked. She also highlights the possibility of data interception when learners transmit information via wireless networks. Lonsdale, Baber, Sharples, and Arvanitis (2003) note that the gathering of contextual data in fieldwork, workplace training, and informal learning results in information that is often personal and private to the learners. This gives rise to considerations of informed consent and potential misuse of stored data by third parties. The area of clinical and practice-based education, in particular, raises many issues in relation to the ethical use of m-learning, which, while offering great benefits, including opportunities for reflective practice and just-in-time learning (Andrews, Davidson, Hill, Sloane, & Woodhouse, 2011), also creates considerable challenges in preserving individual privacy and ensuring any material is appropriately managed from a learning perspective.

The convergence of multiple functions in smartphones and other mobile devices has provided an affordance for the taking of photographs and multimedia recording, which has an enormous potential for infringements of privacy and misuse of data, both in classroom learning as well as in fieldwork and workplace training. For example, there is a very real possibility of photos, videos, or sound recordings of students in class or people in the field being taken without their permission and then used in an unauthorized manner—for instance, being uploaded to social-media sites such as YouTube or Flickr. This is what Hartnell-Young and Heym (2008, p. 17) describe as the "YouTube experience." They give an example where a video recording of an unruly class was posted to YouTube, who, when requested to take it down by the school, refused on the grounds that it was not illegal. These concerns are frequently associated with the use of photographs and video:

> There are particular concerns about how images are used, the ease of their capture and uploading to an online store and their usefulness in supporting learning and revision visually has meant that learner captured multimedia is part and parcel of nearly all the scenarios envisioned.
>
> (Wishart & Green, 2010, p. 27)

Aubusson et al. (2009, p. 243) highlight the much smaller size of mobile devices compared with traditional cameras and video cameras. This makes them "infinitely more portable and unobtrusive," allowing students to make surreptitious recordings much more easily than was possible with the older technology.

Ethical issues in relation to m-learning are not only associated with student behavior but can arise through the actions and beliefs of other stakeholders. Information and communications technology (ICT) departments can take very conservative views in relation to the use of mobile technologies and, in attempting to ensure security of data and information, can severely restrict educational activities. These restrictions can have a negative impact on the use of m-learning and the associated educational benefits. Individual educators, perplexed by the possible issues relating to the use of m-learning, can make a decision to ban such devices in the classroom, during work-based practicums or at students' research sites, a questionable approach in a world where mobility is increasingly influencing all aspects of work and life (Traxler, 2009). The banning of devices that might support m-learning can also impact negatively on disadvantaged groups, who may gain considerable advantages from m-learning not necessarily available to them through more traditional teaching and learning approaches (Dyson & Litchfield, 2011).

Furthermore, cultural differences can play a role, as different cultural groups have quite different understandings of what constitutes ethics (Traxler, 2012). Consequently, the use of m-learning for a whole range of teaching and learning activities in developing countries can easily and inadvertently contravene locally accepted norms (Traxler, 2012). Equally, cultural differences can be an issue with visiting academics, who might take and publish photos of students engaged in m-learning and so, inadvertently, contravene the students' privacy norms. Indigenous students, too, will be bound by protocols of ownership of intellectual property that might restrict the ways in which traditional knowledge can be captured using mobile devices or promulgated beyond their community using the Internet or Bluetooth.

On a completely different note, Engel and Green (2011) point to the ethical issue of accessibility when m-learning is introduced. If students lack a mobile device or have a disability that makes it difficult for them to use one, the educational institution must provide devices to these students, or put in place protocols to allow them to complete their tasks successfully without them and in ways that enable such students to be regarded as equally successful.

ETHICAL ISSUES WITH MOBILE DEVICES IN THE EDUCATIONAL SETTING

Equipping students with mobile technology or encouraging them to use their own devices to undertake m-learning activities obviously opens the way to various ethical abuses in educational settings across different contexts and educational levels. Moreover, there is a marked disparity between students' expectations arising from their use of mobile technologies in their private lives and academic expectations based on the traditional teacher-centered paradigm of the educational institution.

The smallness and portability of mobile devices mean that theft and loss can be quite common, compromising security of data and information (Wishart, 2009). Along with this, as Wishart (2009, p. 78) points out, technical systems relating to m-learning can be complex and "leaky," making it difficult to ensure privacy and confidentiality.

Remarking on disturbances to learning involving mobile devices, Burns and Lohenry (2010) found that more than 40 percent of students in a study used their mobile phones in class, to either send text messages or check incoming phone messages, and over 70 percent had their phones ring during class. Campbell (2006) described students' practice of playing video games in class on their mobiles or laptops for diversion from their studies. Furthermore, he surveyed students and academics and found that phones ringing in the classroom severely annoyed and distracted both groups, particularly older people. Looking at why mobile phones' ringing in the classroom is so frowned upon, when their use in other public spaces might well be tolerated, Campbell (2006) suggested that classroom behaviors are very strongly governed by accepted social norms: The classroom represents a public forum, with an important focus on learning. In addition, he notes the lack of competing background noises, which make a ringtone in class much more distracting than it might be on a bus or in a restaurant.

Ling and Donner (2009) explored cyberbullying and explained the ways bullies can hide behind the anonymity of mobile phones and send offensive messages, without the supervision normally provided by teachers or parents when students are using computers. Cyberbullies can reach their victims at anytime and in anyplace.

One of the greatest ethical concerns with mobile devices in the educational context has been their use in cheating and collusion. Ling (2000) noted the well-established use of text messaging by school students as a replacement for passing notes in class. Additionally, SMS has been used to ask peers questions in the middle of exams, and mobile-phone memory can store "cheat sheets" to be consulted during exams (Ling, 2000). Taking photos of exam papers for distribution to friends also occurs (Campbell, 2006). Ling and Donner (2009) quote a famous case where a University of Maryland professor posted bogus answers to an exam while it was in progress and caught a dozen students who had received the false answers via SMS from friends who were not sitting the exam at the time. Some authors have gone so far as to claim an "epidemic of cheating," facilitated by computer, online, and mobile technologies (Heyman et al., 2005). Ling (2000) suggests that such practice puts into question the whole concept of the educational institution as a place of control. Students engaged in cheating using mobile devices are subverting their teachers' role as judges of whether students have attained sufficient knowledge against some abstract standard determined by the teacher or other figure of authority (criterion-based assessment), or have succeeded in comparison with their peers (norm referencing). Although cheating is not new, mobile devices are viewed as exacerbating the problem. Avoiding cheating in assessment practices, in particular, has long been a challenge, and the use of mobile devices is facilitating new opportunities for students in this regard and, thus, creating new challenges for educators to productively control this issue. However, it should be noted that technology is equally providing the means to deter students, as there are now wireless devices that enable invigilators to detect when unauthorized devices are in use.

WHY ETHICAL ISSUES ARISE IN M-LEARNING

The affordances of mobile technology for particular types of activity and interactivity are a significant contributing factor to the potential increase of ethical issues related to the use of m-learning. The capture of digitized data about people without their permission—or the taking of embarrassing pictures, or violations of intellectual property, even without students being aware that they are doing so—followed by the rapid sharing of this material via the Internet, Bluetooth, or video calls can create enormous ethical challenges at all levels of education. It is, to a large extent, the convergence of multimedia functionality with the "always-on" nature of students' smartphones, laptops, or tablet PCs that has created the technical means to transgress acceptable standards of behavior. In addition, the high levels of ownership of smartphones among young people, their portability and pocket size, and the lack of security of wireless transmission are all important contributory aspects.

Building on the earlier work of Johnson on Internet ethics, one can propose the notion that mobile technology has certain unique characteristics that contribute to ethical issues which are "new species of generic moral problems" (Johnson, 1997, p. 61). For example, infringements of privacy are not novel, but m-learning in the field and workplace allows threats to privacy of a different nature and on a scale different from that seen before, when students were equipped solely with a clipboard and pen and paper. Speaking of mobile technology generally, Castells et al. (2007) note that technology does not eliminate social problems, but instead tends to amplify them, unless dealt with at their source.

From a human perspective, ethics can be a "slippery" concept, and, for many students, the notion of what is ethical in relation to the use of mobile devices in teaching and learning environments can be ill understood (Farrow, 2011). Consequently, as Farrow points out, "it's natural to lapse into . . . a kind of lazy ethical relativism ('follow your own path')" (p. 3). The general lack of training for students in how to ethically manage the use of their devices during their education allows the problem to continue.

Educators and institutions, too, when faced with ethical issues relating to the use of mobile devices, can take the path of least resistance and opt to ban or severely limit their use, as pointed out previously, rather than find a way to productively integrate them into teaching and learning practices. Further to this, Farrow (2011) suggests that making ethical judgments in relation to m-learning is complicated by both the diversity of the devices available and the contexts in which their mobility enables use. Although there are numerous acceptable-use policies (AUPs) relating to the use of technology in educational settings available in most institutions (e.g., Consortium of School Networking, 2011), these do not necessarily address the needs of m-learning and are often not enforced (Nagel, 2011). In many cases, individual educators may be unaware of their existence. In others, existing AUPs may be irrelevant or inappropriate to the contexts in which they teach.

PROFESSIONAL ETHICAL DEVELOPMENT

The need to research how systemic, attitudinal, and ethical issues may inhibit use of mobile technologies by teachers was raised by Aubusson et al. (2009) when they discussed the potential for m-learning as a tool for teachers' professional learning. In their view, mobile technologies are ideally suited to reflection-in-action and capturing learning moments particularly where this is part of collaborative practice, enabling "sharing, analysis and synthesis of classroom experiences by teachers and students" (2009, p. 233). Such sentiments align also with the movement toward using e-portfolios as more authentic means of providing evidence of learning (Abrami, et al., 2008; Pink, Cadbury, & Stanton, 2008; Sargent, Holland, & Frith, 2008; Savin-Baden, 2007).

Thus, the impetus for professional development comes from both technological and pedagogical innovation. The speed with which these movements are progressing raises the bar for rapid opening up of the debate about ethical use and, unfortunately, abuse. Developing appropriate frameworks and guidelines to assist teachers to manage m-learning commences this process. In medical education, as in other forms of professional development, the need for professional bodies to guide staff and student use of mobile devices in workplaces is emerging rapidly. For example, the Australian and New Zealand Medical Associations and their student affiliates have recently released a guide to online professionalism that intends "to assist doctors and students to continue to enjoy the online world, while maintaining professional standards" (AMA, NZMA, NZMSA, & AMSA, 2011, p. 2).

Additionally, there is a need for professional-development programs to raise awareness of the benefits of m-learning, which can minimize or eliminate the fear that can be associated with m-learning. Some studies demonstrate the potential for positive changes in teachers' attitudes once they have had success with m-learning. Actual experience overcomes the negative reports in the media of mobile phones as disruptive technologies (Hartnell-Young, 2008). Dyson, Litchfield, Raban, and Tyler (2009) quote an academic who stopped worrying about students being distracted through wireless access, once he discovered he could use a Web-based classroom response system operating from students' mobile devices to improve his students' learning:

> Wireless access in lectures is a controversial issue. Up to this point I have been concerned if access was available students would spend the lectures surfing the net (and I know some do this already). Now of course I would like to open it up.
>
> (Dyson et al., 2009)

A FRAMEWORK FOR AN ETHICAL APPROACH TO M-LEARNING

Much of the literature presented above focuses on harm minimization. It sees the potential dangers of implementing m-learning—or the dangers of allowing mobile devices to be used for personal reasons in educational institutions—and seeks to prevent the harm to students that might occur. Most AUPs also have this focus, protecting students from unethical uses of mobile devices or discouraging students' own unethical behavior with the technology.

However, for professionals working in the education arena, this is a simplistic approach and overlooks larger concerns. There are moral obligations additional to student protection at issue in the adoption of m-learning. One example for teachers, the "Code of Ethics for Educators" of the Association of American Educators (n.d.), notes the need "to create a learning environment that nurtures to fulfillment the potential of all students." For ICT professionals employed in educational institutions, there is similarly a higher level of ethical responsibility (Gotterbarn, 2001, p, 229): "The concern to maximize the positive effects for those affected by computing artifacts goes beyond mere 'duty care', mere avoidance of direct harm. . . . It incorporates moral responsibility and the ethically commendable."

The policies that ban mobile devices from educational premises and lead to the neglect of m-learning have a moral dimension that is hardly commendable. Such bans are unethical in that they prevent students from benefitting from m-learning, benefits that have been well documented in the literature for both disadvantaged and other learners. They further discourage students' critical reflection on the advantages and risks associated with their mobile-technology use in private life, or their learning how to analyze the rates charged for phone services in relation to their own usage patterns, both activities that can be enabled as part of an m-learning strategy (see examples in Pachler et al., 2010, p. 150). They thus overlook the role of m-learning in a mobile world, where mobile activities of all kinds are becoming increasingly commonplace.

Thus, any ethical framework must include a positive ethic of responsibility on the part of the teachers, administrators, and ICT personnel in our institutions who make decisions over the availability of mobile technology and m-learning. It must address the problems but not limit the implementation of this unique learning approach. It must recognize that our students now live in a mobile world, and their working lives will be part of that world: no better place to start equipping them to deal with the mobile-technology challenges that they will encounter through life than to acknowledge that our educational institutions belong to that world too. An overview of the framework is summarized in Figure 35.1.

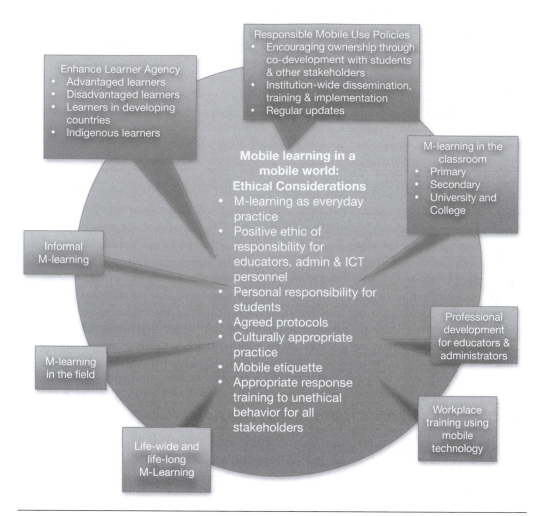

Figure 35.1 Considerations for a Holistic Framework for Ethical M-Learning

Formulating a Responsible Mobile-Use Policy

Adopting an ethical approach to m-learning might well begin with the formulation of an AUP for the educational institution, or what the authors of this chapter prefer to call a responsible mobile-use policy (RMUP). This term makes it clear that the policy deals with mobile technology use rather than desktop computers, and further emphasizes the essential role of both an ethic of positive responsibility on the part of educators, administrators, and ICT personnel, and the desirability of fostering an ethic of personal responsibility on the part of students.

There are many AUPs and much advice available online that provide some guidance on developing a policy suitable for mobile-technology use. It should be noted, however, that many existing AUPs are unnecessarily restrictive, with little or only passing recognition of the value of m-learning. Some of the more comprehensive documents include the following:

- The Australian Mobile Telecommunications Association (n.d.) offers a template for developing an AUP for school use, focusing on mobile technology, which could be adapted to other levels of education. It proposes the AUP should have sections on purpose, rationale, responsibility, acceptable uses, unacceptable uses, theft or damage, inappropriate conduct, and sanctions, as well as giving a parent-permission form.
- The Consortium of School Networking (2011) has published a guide for school districts on AUPs for Web 2.0 and mobile-technology use. It contains detailed information about U.S. federal and state laws relating to cybersafety, links to exemplary school AUPs, and other resources.
- Becta (2009) has compiled a comprehensive guide to developing an AUP for Internet use in UK schools that provides guidelines that could be adapted to developing an AUP for mobile-technology use. Most useful is a detailed list of what should be included in the AUP, the style in which it should be written, and who should be involved in developing it. It also includes notes on different levels of education and how ethical breaches should be dealt with.

Some of the more important principles for devising a RMUP are set out here:

1. *Enhanced learner agency.* The policy should recognize the key role that mobile technology can play in supporting all learners, whatever their background, and whether they are enrolled in the formal education system, engaged in workplace training, or as they continue learning through their lives. Furthermore, it should acknowledge the value of m-learning in supporting greater agency on the part of learners in participating actively in meaning-making rather than being passive consumers of information (Pachler et al., 2010).
2. *Responsibility.* If we as professionals believe in a positive ethic of responsibility to do good rather than merely avoid harm, then the policy should likewise encourage an ethic of personal responsibility in our students. For example, it should involve strategies for students to assist others who are victims of unethical practices, such as cyberbullying.
3. *Involvement of all stakeholders:* Those who will be affected by the policy as well as those who will enforce it should be involved in creating the RMUP (students, teachers, administrators, ICT personnel, and, if appropriate, parents), including the devising of sanctions. This will encourage ownership at all levels.
4. *Focus on ethical behavior.* In moving toward a more ethical approach to m-learning, Hartnell-Young and Heym (2008) note that we need to shift our focus away from the mobile device, away from the technology, and instead focus on the matter of real concern, which is how it is being used in learning. So, instead of banning devices, the policy should introduce steps to limit bad behavior and to equip students with effective tactics to deal with the inappropriate behavior of others.

Aspects of phone etiquette should be included, such as avoiding making calls and texting in the classroom unless they are related to the learning activity, and using soundless features in school grounds, such as sending text messages rather than making calls, setting the vibrate function as default, and letting calls go to voicemail.

Practical advice on responses for students to make when the targets of inappropriate behavior can also be included. Becta (2009) provides a good list of appropriate behaviors covering a number of situations: for example, protecting against theft; not responding to unwanted messages; the importance of seeking adult help; and noting the times, dates, caller ID, and contents of abusive messages to facilitate tracing.

Strategies for the Successful Implementation of an RMUP

In order to implement a policy successfully, various strategies are suggested in the literature:

1. *Education of stakeholders*: All the key stakeholders need to be aware of and understand the policy (Luscre, quoted in Nagel, 2011). In particular:
   - Teachers are often unaware of policies governing technology use and need to be given a copy of the RMUP and be allowed to discuss how it is being applied as part of their orientation when they begin teaching at an institution. In addition, professional development should focus on their acquisition of an attitude of professional responsibility with relation to m-learning, a recognition of the enhanced learner agency that m-learning can bring, and the building of competencies in implementing m-learning in their courses, so that all students gain from this learning approach.
   - Students need to be made aware of the contents of the RMUP as part of their induction into classroom rules at the beginning of the school year or, in higher education, at the start of their university studies. Aubusson et al. (2009) note that it is the responsibility of any teacher who implements m-learning in the classroom to educate students about the ethical behaviors expected of them. Luscre (quoted in Nagel, 2011) suggests translating the policy into sets of rules posted around the institution and written in a simple and concise manner. This provides visibility, allows for flexibility, in that the rules can be updated easily, and puts them in a language the students can understand, rather than the more formal language of the policy. One can go further and state that teachers should introduce their students to strategies for responding appropriately to irresponsible behavior, should they become victims themselves. Students also need to be introduced to the benefits of m-learning that can be realized if they take personal responsibility for their use of mobile devices.
   - If schoolchildren are involved, parents need to read the policy and sign an RMUP acceptance form. Luscre (quoted in Nagel, 2011) recommends creating a dialogue with parents by holding public meetings in which local experts, such as police or lawyers, come to educate parents about issues such as cyberbullying. He further suggests holding joint classes for parents and students to get parents involved in the policy-formulation process, while providing some valuable experiences for them. These classes could include understanding the affordances of mobile devices or editing multimedia content taken using a mobile device.
2. *Regular updating of the RMUP*: Given the rapid evolution of mobile technologies, the policy will need updating. Luscre (quoted in Nagel, 2011) notes that this provides a good opportunity to renew commitment from the various stakeholders by getting them involved in the updates.

CONCLUSIONS

This chapter has highlighted the need to develop a systematic approach to addressing the ethical use of mobile technologies to support learning for a range of learners and learning contexts. Apart from the disruptive potential of mobile-device misuse in the educational setting, perhaps the greatest ethical issue is fear of the technology. Fear has resulted in the underutilization of an approach to learning that has great potential both for students currently well served by educational institutions and for people from backgrounds where formal education has historically been neglected.

The authors propose an ethical framework as a necessary step to more effective management of m-learning. The framework advances the integration of m-learning into teaching and learning practices as a norm in which established protocols and behaviors are understood and adhered to. This is seen as vastly preferential to the banning of such devices, as proposed by Huss (2009) and practiced by some institutions. The framework is based on an ethic of responsible mobile-technology use that can contribute to informed decision-making by all stakeholders and promote a feeling that educators are able to manage the learning environment in a way that fits with their professional beliefs. This offers an approach that minimizes ethical issues around m-learning, while maximizing the potential educational benefits. As such, it takes a wider responsibility for education across society that is generally lacking in the existing m-learning ethics literature.

REFERENCES

Abrami, P. C., Wade, C. A., Pillay, V., Aslan, O., Bures, E. M., & Bentley, C. (2008). Encouraging self-regulated learning through electronic portfolios. *Canadian Journal of Learning and Technology /La revue canadienne de l'apprentissage et de la technologie, 34*(3), n.p.

AMA (Australian Medical Association), NZMA (New Zealand Medical Association), NZMSA (New Zealand Medical Students' Association), & AMSA (Australian Medical Students' Association). (2011). *Social media and the medical profession: A guide to online professionalism for medical practitioners and medical students.* Australian Medical Association. Retrieved from: http://ama.com.au/socialmedia

Andrews, T., Davidson, B., Hill, A., Sloane, D., & Woodhouse, L. (2011). Using students' own mobile technologies to support clinical competency development in speech pathology. In A. Kitchenham (Ed.), *Models for interdisciplinary mobile learning: Delivering information to students* (pp. 247–264). Hershey, PA: Information Science Reference.

Association of American Educators. (n.d.). *AAE code of ethics for educators.* Mission Viejo, CA. Retrieved from: http://aaeteachers.org/index.php/about-us/aae-code-of-ethics

Aubusson, P., Schuck, S., & Burden, K. (2009). Mobile learning for teacher professional learning: Benefits, obstacles and issues. *ALT-J Research in Learning and Teaching, 17*(3), 233–247.

Australian Mobile Telecommunications Association. (n.d.). *Developing an acceptable use policy for mobile phones in your school.* Manuka, Australia: AMTA. Retrieved from: www.amta.org.au/pages/Template.for.Mobile.use.in.Schools

Becta. (2009). *AUPs in context: Establishing safe and responsible online behaviours.* Coventry, UK: Becta. Retrieved from: http://education.qld.gov.au/studentservices/behaviour/qsaav/docs/establishing-safe-responsible-online-behaviours.pdf

Burns, S. M., & Lohenry, K. (2010). Cellular phone use in class: Implications for teaching and learning a pilot study. *College Student Journal, 44*(3).

Castells, M., Fernández-Ardèvol, M., Qiu, J. L., & Sey, A. (2007). *Mobile communication and society: A global perspective.* Cambridge, MA: MIT Press.

Campbell, S. W. (2006). Perceptions of mobile phones in college classrooms: Ringing, cheating, and classroom policies. *Communication Education, 55*(3), 280–294.

Consortium of School Networking. (2011). *Acceptable use policies in a Web 2.0 & mobile era: A guide for school districts.* Washington, DC: CoSN.

Dyson, L. E., & Litchfield, A. (2011). Advancing collaboration between m-learning researchers and practitioners through an online portal and Web 2.0 technologies. *International Journal of Mobile and Blended Learning, 3*(1), 64–72.

Dyson, L. E., Litchfield, A., Raban, R., & Tyler, J. (2009). Interactive classroom mLearning and the experiential transactions between students and lecturer. Same places, different spaces. In *Proceedings of Ascilite, Auckland 2009*, pp. 233–242.

Engel, G., & Green, T. (2011). Cell phones in the classroom: Are we dialing up disaster? *TechTrends, 55*(2), 39–45.

Farrow, R. (2011). Mobile learning: A meta-ethical taxonomy. In *Proceedings of IADIS International Conference on Mobile Learning 2011*, March 10–12, Avila, Spain.

Gayeski, D. (2002). *Learning unplugged: Using mobile technologies for organizational training and performance improvement.* New York: AMACOM.

Gotterbarn, D. (2001). Informatics and professional responsibility. *Science and Engineering Ethics, 7*(2), 221–230.

Hartnell-Young, E. (2008). Mobile phones for learning in mainstream schooling: Resistance and change. In *Proceedings of mLearn 2008*, Ironbridge, UK, October.

Hartnell-Young, E., & Heym, N. (2008). *How mobile phones help learning in secondary schools* (Report to Becta). Coventry, UK: Becta.

Heyman, J. D., Swertlow, F., Ballard, M., Barnes, S., Duffy, T., Gray, L., et al. (2005). Psssst . . . What's the answer? *People, 63*(3).

Huss, J. (2009). *The potential dangers of electromagnetic fields and their effect on the environment.* Parliamentary Assembly, Council of Europe, Committee on the Environment, Agriculture and Local and Regional Affairs. Retrieved from: www.avaate.org/IMG/pdf/Socialistas_asamblea_comision_europeaEDOC12608.pdf

Johnson, D. G. (1997). Ethics online: Shaping social behaviour online takes more than new laws and modified edicts. *Communications of the ACM, 40*(1), 60–65.

Kim, P. H. (2009). Action research approach on mobile learning design for the underserved. *Educational Technology Research Development, 57*, 415–435.

Lonsdale, P., Baber, C., Sharples, M., & Arvanitis, T. N. (2003). A context awareness architecture for facilitating mobile learning. In *Proceedings of mLearn*, 1–7.

Ling, R. (2000). The impact of the mobile telephone on four established social institutions. In *Proceedings of ISSEI2000 Conference of the International Society for the Study of European Ideas*, 1–23.

Ling, R., & Donner, J. (2009). *Mobile communication.* Cambridge, UK: Polity Press.

Nagel, D. (2011). A better approach to AUPs for mobile devices: 5 questions with Anthony Luscre. *THE Journal*, November–December.

Pachler, N., Bachmair, B., & Cook, J. (2010). *Mobile learning: Structures, agency, practices.* New York: Springer.

Pink, J., Cadbury, N., & Stanton, N. (2008). Enhancing student reflection: The development of an e-portfolio. *Medical Education, 42*(11), 1132–1133.

Ragus, M., Meredith, S., Dacey, D., Richter, C., Paterson, A., & Hayes, A. (2005). The Australian mobile learning network: Australian innovations. *Proceedings of mLearn 2005*, 1–21. Retrieved from: www.mlearn.org.za/papers-full.html

Sargent, V., Holland, T., & Frith, G. (2008). *Using mobile technologies to create ePortfolios and personalised learning environments for 16 health and social care professions.* Paper presented at the Conference on ePortfolios, Identity and Personalised Learning in Healthcare Education.

Savin-Baden, M. (2007). *A practical guide to problem-based learning online.* London & New York: Routledge.

Traxler, J. (2009). Learning in a mobile age. *International Journal of Mobile and Blended Learning, 1*(1), 1–12.

Traxler, J. (2012). *The ethics of mobile learning: Troubling and complex.* Retrieved from: http://mobileactive.org/ethics-mobile-learning

Wallace, R. (2009). Empowered learner identity through m-learning: Representations of disenfranchised students' perspectives. In *Proceedings of mLearn*, 13–17.

Wishart, J. (2009). Ethical considerations in implementing mobile learning in the workplace. *International Journal of Mobile and Blended Learning, 1*(2), 76–92.

Wishart, J., & Green, D. (2010). *Identifying emerging issues in mobile learning in further and higher education: A report to JISC.* Retrieved from: www.jiscdigitalmedia.ac.uk/blog/entry/resources-for-mobile-learning

36

COPYRIGHT AND FAIR USE IN M-LEARNING

Patricia Aufderheide

Copyright is today an ever-present concern for all media makers, for all teachers, and for all librarians and administrators. This is because digital platforms carry media and learning far beyond local venues, including those, such as classrooms, that are protected from copyright-infringement issues with educational exemptions. It is also because of the vast extension of copyright holders' monopoly rights since 1976, shrinking the public-domain materials available to create new culture with. Finally, it is a concern because of misinformation that has been spread, often inadvertently, not only by large media and software companies, but also by well-intentioned general counsels, institutional heads, and librarians.

This chapter will provide a basic grounding material for creators, students, and teachers on copyright and fair use for m-learning in a U.S. environment. (Such a background is relevant, although with conditions, to international actors as well, as will be discussed.) It will discuss:

- the basic premise of U.S. copyright policy, which is not to protect copyright holders but to encourage the ever-expanding pool of culture;
- the enacting of that policy in practice, including with the doctrine of fair use, a free-speech right as defined by the Supreme Court;
- features that keep people from employing fair use, including insecurity about its application and fear of penalties;
- the effect of creating codes of best practices in fair use on the practices of communities that have taken this measure;
- a discussion of how existing codes of best practices can be useful in an m-learning environment.

THE PURPOSE OF COPYRIGHT POLICY IN THE US

Ask any group of teachers or students the question, "What is the purpose of copyright?" and the answer will come with a minimum of delay: "To protect the rights of creators."

This answer, although correct, is a partial and tactical answer. In the US, the purpose of copyright policy is, as explicitly articulated in the Constitution, to encourage the creation of new culture ("to promote the Progress of Science [meaning knowledge in general] and useful Arts [meaning crafts and professions]"), with a variety of incentives.

One set of incentives provides the creators of new works a monopoly right to their works. This set of incentives, once a small feature of creative action—indeed, originally restricted only to books, and only to the original book and no derivative products, such as plays or translations or sequels, and only for 14 years—has increasingly grown until it touches virtually all aspects of culture. Since the passage of copyright reform in 1976, now part of the Copyright Act, all expressive work once caught in some tangible form (for instance, e-mail, back of envelope, napkin, phone message), is now copyrighted by default. Many "derivative" products—plays, translations, sequels, and more—are also under limited-monopoly protection. Copyright terms have been extended until they last longer than the life span of those who experience newly created culture (terms last, typically, for 70 years after the death of the author). This vast extension of the limited-monopoly rights of copyright holders now creates the threat of private censorship—the ability of rights holders to block future expression by barring access to their work.

That threat is mitigated by another set of incentives that provides creators of new works the right to access copyrighted material without permission or payment, under some circumstances. Sometimes, that is because exceptions have been carved out for particular situations. They include face-to-face teaching: Teachers have the right to use any copyrighted material not specifically designed for teaching their course material in the classroom. As well, librarians have specific exceptions to do their work, and disabled persons in certain categories also have special exceptions. Small bars can retransmit broadcast signals, and religious services can employ copyrighted materials such as songs, without permission or payment. There is a welter of smaller, highly specific exceptions as well.

The widest and most flexible exception is the doctrine of fair use. Everyone in the US, in any medium, has the right of fair use. Fair use is an exemption that applies to all of a copyright owner's monopoly rights, including the owner's right to control adaptation, distribution, and performance. Part of U.S. law for more than 150 years, in recent decades it has become a crucially important part of copyright policy. It is a core right, part of the basic package of freedom-of-speech rights available under the Constitution. The Supreme Court has recognized the fair-use doctrine as a key feature that protects copyright policy—even when heavily unbalanced in favor of monopoly rights holders—from unconstitutionality (Eldred v. Ashcroft, 537 U.S. 186 [2003]).

Most of this use, which occurs without getting approval from anyone, goes unquestioned. In copyright litigation, the first chance to formally invoke fair use comes only when someone accuses a user of infringement; in terms of court procedure, therefore, it is classified as an "affirmative defense." In everyday practice, however, fair use functions as a reliable, fully fledged right. It is similar to the doctrine of self-defense, which we do not claim until after we have resisted an attack and been sued for assault as a result.

The exceptions to limited-monopoly rights are critical to the core goal of copyright policy. That is because, to create new culture, all creators "stand on the shoulders of giants" (as Isaac Newton was not the first to say). All creators build new culture from existing culture—a fact that stands in stark contrast to a Romantic concept of the genius-artist as an entirely original creator (Woodmansee & Jaszi, 1994). Scientists have meticulously mapped the "emergent" quality of creativity as a product of social interaction; the most fundamental processes of brain development depend on collaboration and sociability (Csikszentmihalyi, 1996). Folk culture, from time immemorial, was a frankly collaborative process. Epic poetry survived by a process of transmission through repetition and subtle variation. At the beginnings of the novel form in the 18th century, as Elizabeth Judge has shown, novel readers felt entitled to re-imagine and project the lives of fictional characters in unauthorized sequels, the fan fiction of their day (Judge, 2009). Exceptions ensure that private censorship is avoided and, thus, within the US, that copyright policy is still constitutional, not violating the terms of the First Amendment. (The First Amendment, which prohibits government censorship, is involved because government policy sets the terms for copyright, and, if holders of copyright can act as private censors because of that policy, the government is implicated in their acts.)

THE PRACTICE OF FAIR USE

Fair use is used widely every day, sometimes in situations where those who rely on it do not even realize they are doing so. Its significance and frequency of use have grown with the extension of copyright terms and the amount of culture that is now copyrighted. Students and scholars, both independent and institution-related, regularly quote others' copyrighted work without permission or payment, in their pursuit of knowledge. Journalists do not think twice about quoting a local-government report or a think-tank document without asking permission. Broadcast newscasters routinely excerpt others' copyrighted material without permission or payment, and so do fake newscasters such as Jon Stewart and Stephen Colbert (whose shows, *nota bene*, are owned by Viacom, a major media corporation). Remix artists and vidders (artists who rework popular culture to make gender critiques) could not do their work without unlicensed access to the works they comment on.

Fair use is legitimately exercised when the use of copyrighted material adds value—new culture is created in some way—without significantly impairing the owner's private gain under his/her limited-monopoly rights. The law, under the Copyright Act's section 107, suggests four general questions to ask in order to make such a determination, about (1) the nature of the original work, (2) the nature of the new work, (3) the amount used, and (4) the effect on the market for the original work.

In practice, and as a result of judicial decisions since 1990, this boils down to two questions:

- Did the unlicensed use "transform" the material taken from the copyrighted work by using it for a different purpose than that of the original, or did it just repeat the work for the same intent and value as the original?
- Was the material taken appropriate in kind and amount, considering the nature of the copyrighted work and of the use?

In making judgments about fair use, judges have also, whether implicitly or explicitly, asked themselves another question: "What is the practice of the community in question?" They have, in short, asked how fair use applies to the needs of a particular community to create new culture.

The question of what is "transformative" is fairly simple in the case of someone making a new work—for instance, a documentary film that quotes a popular film to show how psychologists have been portrayed in the past, or a remix that uses an array of newscasters to demonstrate gender inequity on television news. It can be more complicated to understand in a teaching/learning context, where people may simply be reading a chapter of a book or watching a video. The Code of Best Practices in Fair Use for Academic and Research Libraries (discussed below) addresses this question, first generally and then specifically, in a discussion of e-reserves:

> In cases decided since the early 1990s, the courts have made it clear that in order for a use to be considered "transformative," it need not be one that modifies or literally revises copyrighted material. In fact, uses that recontextualize copyrighted content in order to present it to a new audience qualify as well. The courts also have taught that the more coherent an account the user can give of how and why the material was borrowed, the more likely the use is to be considered transformative . . .
>
> Most of the information objects made available to students, in whatever format, are not originally intended for educational use. Works intended for consumption as popular entertainment, for example, present a clear case of transformative re-purposing when an instructor uses them as the objects of commentary and criticism. Similarly, works written for consumption by a scholar's peers are transformed when instructors later assign them to illustrate particular movements in the history of ideas.
>
> (Adler, Aufderheide, Butler, & Jaszi, 2012, pp. 8, 13)

Fair use, like all free speech rights, is a case-by-case decision. Fair use is medium-agnostic: it applies to music, photographs, posters, film, video, and text equally. Fair use is also platform-agnostic: if something is fair use in print, it is also fair use on the Web, and on a mobile phone. Mobile technologies do not change fair-use logic.

WHY FAIR USE FRIGHTENS EDUCATORS AND STUDENTS

Despite its ubiquity and its centrality to the generation of culture, fair use has been labeled as a troubled area for many educators and students (Aufderheide, Hobbs, & Jaszi, 2007). This derives both from confusion—some of it enhanced by alarmist and hyper-cautionary guidance from institutions and school systems—and from well-intended attempts to facilitate decision-making.

Many educators stumble over the fact that fair use is designed to be flexible in its case-by-case determination; they seek rather a "bright line" to guide decision-making. For them, fair use is a "gray area," in which they may need approval for their decisions. They often believe, erroneously, that fair use is an arena in which litigation is rife. They may even have heard or read of "copyleft" critiques that inveigh against the consequences of unbalanced copyright, including that of Lawrence Lessig, who has called fair use "the right to hire a lawyer" (Lessig, 2001).

These concerns reflect an attempt to apply a reasonable approach—risk assessment—in the absence of an ability to judge risk accurately. There is risk in the application of any free-speech right, and copyright infringement carries potentially hefty fines. Copyright infringement can incur statutory penalties—fines above and beyond the damages done—up to $150,000 per infringement (even though such fines are almost never levied). Furthermore, even a lawsuit that is won involves time, money, and mental anguish. Finally, even a decision executed safely may incur the disapproval of a superior. A teacher may decide that a student's work violates copyright law, even if it does not. An administrator may perceive—correctly or not—a threat to the institution.

Hence, it is important in fair use, as in other free-speech rights, to understand where the normal practice of free speech lies. As judges implicitly or explicitly ask this question as well, knowing where that center is allows one to lower risk to the minimal level that exists in all exercise of free-speech rights. Knowing this also makes it possible to demonstrate to students, teachers, and administrators the level of responsibility taken in exercising one's rights.

This understanding has been made more difficult by a barrage of educational campaigns on the part of software and media companies, intended to discourage digital file-sharing. Often their attempts to do so have, in the process, swept fair use, a legitimate and legal practice, in with the practice of illegal file-sharing (Gillespie, 2009).

Ironically, many well-intentioned attempts of educators have also made the exercise of fair use more difficult (Hobbs, 2010). There is a plethora of fair-use "guidelines," some embedded into standards-and-practices documents of school systems, and some floating on websites, as Peter Jaszi and I discuss in *Reclaiming Fair Use*, on employing one's free-speech rights (Aufderheide & Jaszi, 2011). One set of guidelines was created during the 1976 revision of the Copyright Act, when Congressman Robert Kastenmeier brought together, with the best of intentions, publishers and educators to negotiate the *Agreement on Guidelines for Classroom Photocopying in Not-For-Profit Educational Institutions*. What emerged (and is now on educational websites everywhere) was drafted primarily by the publishers—a group that perceived, at the time, its own interests were opposed to educational applications of fair use. It was included in the legislative history, *despite* letters of protest from representatives of the American Association of University Professors and of the Association of American Law Schools.

These harshly limiting guidelines are not part of the Copyright Act and, thus, have no binding legal force. They are also not grounded in law. The photocopying guidelines, for example, spoke of making copies for class that included "not more than 1,000 words or 10% of the work, whichever is less." There is no basis whatever in the Copyright Act for such a numerical limitation. Indeed, it goes against the very logic of fair use, which is case by case and depends on the nature of the use and the nature of the copyrighted material to decide how much is appropriate.

However, because they are part of the record of congressional deliberation, they continue to carry some weight among educators, as does a sister document, *Guidelines for the Educational Use of Music*. They were followed by a third, *Guidelines for Off-Air Recording of Broadcast Programming for Educational Purposes* in 1981, also after negotiations called by Kastenmeier. (This third document was not even part of the legislative package.)

These guidelines have not been interpreted as they were designed, to indicate the safest of safe harbors. Rather, publishers pushed hard to promote a false interpretation of the guidelines as defining the outer limits of educational practice. And too often, as legal scholar Kenneth Crews has shown, they were treated that way within school systems across the country by administrators (and sometimes librarians) who had been charged with providing teachers clear instructions based on these documents (Crews, 2001). Professor Crews' analysis shows that the effect has been to limit educational practice.

Other "rule-of-thumb" guidelines circulate as folk wisdom in educational circles. Numerical catchphrases abound: 10 percent, 400 words, 30 seconds. These numerical guides are all myths, without a legal basis. They often have some grounding in a specific situation (for instance, many broadcast news programs used a "30-second rule" for copyrighted material included in 2-minute news segments), but they violate the fundamental purpose of fair use: to enable the making of new culture by the flexible application of fair use.

Another common myth in the educational community is that educational uses are fair, because they are non-profit. This is actually a dangerous myth, exposing educators to risk. Educators and librarians do have exceptions dedicated to specific practices, e.g., classroom use of copyrighted material, but much educational practice goes far beyond the four walls of a physical classroom, or the use of analog materials within the four walls of a library. Therefore, educators do need to apply fair use routinely, especially in a digital environment.

Rather than be bound by numerical limits that have no relationship to the purpose and needs of the work, or highly restrictive "guidelines" that do not acknowledge the range of legitimate fair use, educators and students would need to return to the two basic questions: the transformative nature of the work (am I just using this for free in order to not pay for the original use of the material, or am I adding value by reusing it in a different way?) and the appropriate amount (am I using just what I need?).

However, in an atmosphere of confusion and fear, with high statutory damages lurking in the wings and supervisor disapproval hovering over decision-making, it is entirely understandable that educators and students would look for some security.

HOW CODES OF BEST PRACTICES HAVE EXPANDED ACCESS TO FAIR-USE FREE-SPEECH RIGHTS

Some educators, as well as librarians, archivists, filmmakers, and poets, have addressed the challenge of employing fair use without confusion or anxiety, without losing the core flexibility permitted by the law. They have designed codes of best practices in fair use, providing help in the reasoning steps necessary to make case-by-case decisions within each community of practice. Eight of them were facilitated by the Center for Social Media and the Program on Information Justice and Intellectual Property (PIJIP) at American University. Two were executed with help from PIJIP, the Washington College of Law's legal clinic at American University. All are available at centerforsocialmedia.org/fair-use

These codes of best practices are structured around the practices of the community that require fair use, rather than providing rigid (and often abstract) rules for fair use, as many guidelines too. The codes, all of them the result of research and deliberation within the community of practice, identify the most common current practices that require fair use, and then describe (1) why fair use is applicable to this practice and (2) what the limits of fair use are. (In the case of the Code of Best Practices in Fair Use for Academic and Research Librarians, enhancements are also considered, which make it even easier for everyone to understand why fair use applies.)

Thus, documentary filmmakers isolated four of the most common situations they faced: critiquing/analyzing media; using copyrighted work to refer to something; incidental capture of copyrighted material; and referencing archival material within historical works. They articulated the reasons why fair use applied in each of these situations, and where a use would exceed fair use.

Media-literacy teachers identified five common situations that called for fair use—three of them involving teachers, and two involving students. They included: using copyrighted material in their teaching; putting copyrighted material into curriculum materials, including books and websites; distributing curriculum that incorporates unlicensed copyrighted material, both commercially and non-commercially; production of student assignments; and distribution of student assignments.

Academic and research librarians identified eight situations that required fair use, situations that extended beyond their existing exceptions: making teaching/learning materials available digitally (e.g., e-reserves); exhibitions, both virtual and physical; making copies (e.g., of aging VHS tapes where there is no distributor) to preserve and allow scholarly access to them; making archival and special collections available online; making versions of copyrighted work available for disabled patrons; making complete copies of scholarly work available in institutional repositories; giving patrons access to entire databases for "non-consumptive" research (e.g., when the goal is not to read the work within the database but to search for patterns in references or word use); and collecting digital ephemera, e.g., on the Web or mobile applications.

Scholars, including communication scholars, film scholars, and visual arts scholars, have all created codes of best practices for fair use in their research (in the case of the film scholars, both for teaching practices and for research). Common situations include critiquing/analyzing material, quoting for illustrative purposes, using copyrighted work in experimental settings, and archiving a collection of copyrighted work (e.g., advertisements on a particular topic over a particular period of time) used for research.

Creators of open courseware, free curriculum materials made available on a worldwide basis on the Web, also created a code of best practices in fair use. They discovered that they needed such a code in the following situations: incidental capture, analyzing/critiquing, illustrating, and demonstrating/explaining.

In a different approach, a blue-ribbon panel of experts—about half legal scholars and about half academic experts in participatory and online media—created a Code of Best Practices in Online Video. This code's situations echoed those of filmmakers and also included situations such as: triggering discussion online; preserving/memorializing an otherwise evanescent moment or cultural phenomenon that is otherwise inaccessible; and remix/mashup (i.e., collage in an audio-visual, digital form).

All of the codes structured by communities of practice around their needs as practitioners have been put into use without any legal or other challenge from copyright holders. They have all demonstrably changed habits within the communities of practice, and, in some cases, they changed industry practice.

U.S. documentary filmmakers, who once lived in a "clearance culture" in which all copyrighted material they excerpted was licensed, increasingly asserted their rights and employed fair use where appropriate. However, they still had to convince insurers, who had not insured against fair-use claims for two decades, to accept their claims. Documentary films without errors-and-omissions insurance cannot enter festivals, or be shown on television or in theaters, and garnering insurance is the filmmaker's responsibility. Once they read and employed the documentary-filmmakers' code, the insurers were able to assess risk more easily. They universally decided, within a year of the issuance of the code, to accept fair-use claims for uses that fell within the code.

The policy reversal was a direct result of the creation of the Documentary Filmmakers' Statement of Best Practices in Fair Use.

The professionals in charge of creating open courseware also saw dramatic changes, without challenges, after launching their code in late 2009. In 2011, Lindsey Weeramuni, intellectual property supervisor at MIT's OpenCourseWare project, reported:

> AT MIT OpenCourseWare we've made fair use claims quite a bit since the code was launched. It's now an integral part of our publication process. We've published thirty-one courses with instances of fair use content in them and another thirteen are in the pipeline. For context, we publish between 180 and 200 courses per year.
>
> Here are two examples of courses where fair use has made all the difference:
>
> - Music and Technology, Lecture Notes and Videos. The video for Lecture 13 is one file with many pieces of content being retained. Beginning at 64:18 you'll see a flurry of examples. If not for fair use, we most likely would not have published this course. Especially in the videos, there wouldn't have been enough material left with all of the proprietary pieces of content removed.
> - Microelectronic Devices and Circuits, Lecture notes. In Lecture 2, there is an image on slide 17 of the PDF that demonstrates the concept the professor is teaching. It relates directly to the adjacent diagram and graph. Without it, the concept may be more difficult to understand.
>
> You'll see that our approach has been to include a credit line that directs users to our fair use FAQ page. And, of course, we have not yet been challenged or questioned by anyone on this issue.[1]

Both teachers and students developing m-learning strategies can benefit from the principles and reasoning articulated in existing codes of best practices, some of which identify common learning and teaching situations across platforms. They can also benefit from the clear articulation of fair-use reasoning, which is part of the preface of all the codes. These codes of best practices have solidly demonstrated that they lower risk and improve decision-making, by making clear what is a normal and common application of fair use. They make it possible to do a far more rational risk assessment, in m-learning as in other teaching and learning situations.

THE INTERNATIONAL CHALLENGE

Mobile applications easily skip across national boundaries and provide opportunities, as well, for international collaboration. Thus, the grounding of copyright policy at a national level is worthy of consideration.

Fair use is a U.S. doctrine, shared internationally only by the governments of Israel and the Philippines. For work that originates in the US, fair use applies, no matter where the work may travel; consumers worldwide may use it freely without concern. (Anyone wanting to repurpose copyrighted material, however, will need to do so within the laws of their own country.) Fair use applies as well to material from anywhere in the world, harvested in any way, if it is applied in a work that originates in the US. In other nations, the logic grounding copyright policy in general and the specifics of exceptions and limitations to monopoly rights vary. However, all copyright policies have some kinds of exception and limitation to monopoly rights. In Commonwealth countries, the most common approach is called fair dealing. Fair-dealing clauses are typically lengthy and highly specific lists of exceptions for specific situations. Usually, scholarly and teaching activities are high on those lists. On the European continent, there is a wide variety in the amount and the range of exceptions, but usually there is a right-of-quotation clause, which can be scrutinized for its utility for m-learning.

In most countries outside the US, concern about the dangers of copyright infringement is usually far lower than in the US. This is because most other countries' policies do not include statutory damages, the high fines that make any risk seem overwhelming, particularly to users who do not know where the normal center of practice is.

CONCLUSION

M-learning shares with more traditional teaching and learning methods a range of situations within which the application of balancing features of copyright becomes essential to the learning process. Teachers need to share learning materials digitally with students; students need to create new works invoking older ones; scholars need to assemble ad hoc databases of copyrighted material to analyze them; they need to excerpt relevant copyrighted material in experimental situations; they want to critique and analyze the culture around them.

Teachers, students, and administrators can employ existing law successfully. In the process, they can do better educational work. They can also model appropriate, legal, and responsible copyright behaviors that will be applicable throughout the lifelong learning and cultural creation that good teaching enables.

For further information on fair use, its history, reasoning, and evolution, as well as discussion of myths and realities and pop quizzes, turn to *Reclaiming Fair Use* (Aufderheide, & Jaszi, 2011). For access to codes of best practices and monthly updates, turn to centerforsocialmedia.org

NOTE

1   Quoted in a blog post at the Center for Social Media: http://centerforsocialmedia.org/blog/fair-use/no-more-skeletons-or-swiss-cheese-fair-use-open-courseware-works

REFERENCES

Adler, P., Aufderheide, P., Butler, B., & Jaszi, P. (2012). *Code of best practices in fair use for academic and research libraries* (p. 29). Washington, DC: Association of Research Libraries.

Aufderheide, P., Hobbs, R., & Jaszi, P. (2007). *The cost of copyright confusion for media literacy* (p. 28): Center for Social Media, School of Communication, American University.

Aufderheide, P., & Jaszi, P. (2011). *Reclaiming fair use: How to put balance back in copyright.* Chicago, IL: University of Chicago Press.

Crews, K. (2001). The law of fair use and the illusion of fair-use guidelines. *Ohio State Law Journal, 62,* 98.

Csikszentmihalyi, M. (1996). *Creativity: Flow and the psychology of discovery and invention* (1st ed.). New York: HarperCollinsPublishers.

Gillespie, T. (2009). Characterizing copyright in the classroom: The cultural work of antipiracy campaigns. *Communication, Culture & Critique, 2*(3), 274–318.

Hobbs, R. (2010). *Conquering copyright confusion: How the doctrine of fair use supports 21st century learning.* Thousand Oaks, CA: Corwin.

Judge, E. (2009). Kidnapped and counterfeit characters: Eighteenth-century fan fiction, copyright law, and custody of fictional characters. In R. McGinnis (Ed.), *Originality and intellectual property in the French and English Enlightenment* (pp. 22–68). New York: Routledge.

Lessig, L. (2001). *The future of ideas: The fate of the commons in a connected world* (1st ed.). New York: Random House.

Woodmansee, M., & Jaszi, P. (1994). *The construction of authorship: Textual appropriation in law and literature.* Durham, UK: Duke University Press.

37

ACCESSIBILITY IN M-LEARNING

Ensuring Equal Access

Jodi B. Roberts

A shift is occurring in distance education in which learning can occur anytime and practically anywhere a learner has an Internet connection or telephone service. This new delivery method is known as mobile learning (m-learning). M-learning, as defined by Compton, Muilenburg, and Berge in Chapter 1, is "learning across multiple contexts, through social and content interactions, using personal electronic devices" (Crompton, 2013, p. 4). These personal electronic devices allow individuals to teach and learn at a distance in a manner that is digital, customizable, and real time, and incorporates the senses. Portable computing devices, such as smartphones, media players, personal digital assistants (PDAs), tablets, e-readers, and wireless laptop computers, to name a few, are considered examples of mobile technologies (EDUCAUSE Learning Initiative, 2010; Granic, Cukusic, & Walker, 2009; Quinn, 2008). What makes these technologies applicable to education is the ability for learners and instructors to access academic courses, learning materials, and textbooks, without having to log in from a fixed location. In addition, mobile technologies are able to assist in providing educational avenues "for populations of individuals who, for various reasons, have been unable to succeed in or are unable to participate in a traditional educational environment. One sub-group of this population includes [learners] with disabilities" (Roberts, Crittenden & Crittenden, 2011, p. 242). In order for learners with disabilities to actively participate in these educational opportunities, it is vital that the devices utilized have accessibility features that are compatible with, or act as assistive technology by accommodating, a learner's unique disability needs, as well as complying with current accessibility legislation.

This chapter will be broken into three sections: (1) accessibility laws in higher education, and why addressing accessibility is important; (2) accessibility and universal design principles to be considered when designing educational materials for m-learning applications; and (3) accessible m-learning recommendations that can be utilized to benefit all users. Although the intended audience is higher-education administrators and faculty who oversee, develop, and deliver educational materials through m-learning technologies, the information contained herein is generalized and, therefore, applicable to all educational levels and settings. The intended outcome is, therefore, to begin the discussion of accessibility and m-learning in a proactive manner.

What do disability and accessibility mean, and how do these this apply to m-learning? According to the IMS Global Learning Consortium (2004):

> The term disability has been re-defined as a mismatch between the needs of the learner and the education offered. It is therefore not a personal trait but an artifact of the relationship between the learner and the learning environment or education delivery. Accessibility, given this re-definition, is the ability of the learning environment to adjust to the needs of all learners. Accessibility is determined by the flexibility of the education environment . . . and the availability of adequate alternative-but-equivalent content and activities. The needs and preferences of a user may arise from the context or environment the user is in, the tools available (e.g., mobile devices, assistive technologies such as Braille devices, voice recognition systems, or alternative keyboards, etc.), their background, or a disability in the traditional sense. Accessible systems adjust the user interface of the learning environment, locate needed resources and adjust the properties of the resources to match the needs and preferences of the user.
> (Quote from www.imsglobal.org/accessibility/accmdv1p0/ imsaccmd_oviewv1p0.html, section 2; used with permission of IMS Global Learning Consortium)

In other words, the learner, instructor, and technologies implemented are all responsible for ensuring that materials are accessible to all individuals wishing to utilize them. This team approach is vital for a learner's educational success and, ultimately, makes the materials and devices available to all learners, regardless of whether a disability is present.

ACCESSIBILITY IN HIGHER EDUCATION

Federal laws exist that are associated with accessibility and higher education and have an impact on m-learning. These legislative mandates include the Americans with Disabilities Act (ADA) of 1990, amended in 2008, and Sections 504 and 508 of the Rehabilitation Act of 1973, amended in 2008, 1998, and 1999, respectively (Hermann & Rapple, 2011; Kolowich, 2011; Roberts et al., 2011; Utah State University, Center for Persons with Disabilities [USU], 2012; U.S. Department of Education [USDoE], 2004; USDoE, Office for Civil Rights, 2011).

Institutions of higher learning are required by the ADA of 1990, under Titles II and III, which cover private and public institutions of higher learning, to provide equal access to educational opportunities for all learners with disabilities (USDoE, 2009; USDoE, Office for Civil Rights, 2011). Equal access denotes that a learner is assured access to all educational opportunities, regardless of his/her disability. This access does not only apply to the physical classroom, but also to virtual classrooms, through use of course-management systems and other technologies, such as mobile devices, that may be utilized for course delivery. If not accessible, an equal alternative to the technology must be available as an accommodation. This legislation also requires that all educational materials be provided in an accessible format and/or alternate formats, and that accommodations implemented to address the disability are reasonable and do not present an undue burden for the institution (Danek et al., 1996).

Section 504 of the Rehabilitation Act of 1973, amended in 2008, requires that any institution of higher learning receiving federal financial assistance warrants that all learners be protected from discrimination, in addition to the ADA requirement, and further stipulates that Web-based programs including distance learning be accessible to all learners, regardless of whether or not a disability is present (Floyd & Santiago, 2007). This includes the mandate that programs, technologies such as mobile devices, and course materials are provided in an accessible format to learners with disabilities (USDoE, 2009; USDoE, Office for Civil Rights, 2011; USU, 2012) when used for educational purposes.

Finally, although Section 508, amended in 1998, was intended to ensure that all federal agencies provide accessible websites, products, and materials to all individuals, Section 508 has also come to have an influence on higher education in the following four ways: it (1) created the first accessibility standard for the Internet; (2) provided legislative language that can be enforced by all entities covered under Section 508; (3) developed legislation that holds state agencies, such as higher-education institutions, accountable to accessibility laws; and (4) established standards with which all businesses who work with the federal government must comply (USU, 2012). Although Section 508 is primarily directed at federal agencies, several states have adopted the 508 guidelines into their state laws, thus making them relevant to higher education (Hermann & Rapple, 2011). With recent litigation against institutions of higher learning for failure to provide adequate accessible technologies, technology-based services, as well as accessible websites, it is important that measures be taken from the onset of program and course development to implement universal design principles as a means of ensuring accessibility. Litigation, coupled with the USDoE's Office for Civil Rights' letter to college or university presidents regarding accessible mobile technology (USDoE, Office for Civil Rights, 2010), has placed institutions on notice that any lack of accessible technology, course materials, or Web access will not be tolerated (Joly, 2011; National Federation of the Blind, 2009, 2010, 2011; Seale & Cooper, 2010; USDoE, 2009; USDoE, Office for Civil Rights, 2011). In other words, steps must be taken to ensure all technologies, courses, and materials are accessible, regardless of whether a learner with a disability is enrolled in the program or course. This notice has placed the responsibility for compliance directly on the shoulders of the institution.

When researching accessibility, the terms accessibility, usability, and universal design have become more commonplace over the past several years. Oftentimes, they are used interchangeably, and this adds further to the confusion on how to comply with the law. Although all of the terms apply to accessibility of programs, courses, devices, and materials, they each have a unique meaning with regards to m-learning. In order to completely understand how they apply to m-learning and the issues at hand, it is helpful to define these terms.

ACCESSIBILITY AND UNIVERSAL DESIGN

Accessibility, with reference to m-learning, means that, during the course design process, the unique needs of learners with disabilities are considered from the onset, in order to guarantee that the majority of disabled users will be able to utilize the learning-management system, the course, and all course materials, including the Internet, as well as any mobile device utilized. For example, if a learner with a disability can access everything except the mobile device, then the institution is not in compliance.

Additionally, if the website that the instructor directs a learner to for information is not accessible, again the institution is not in compliance. Understanding how learners with disabilities use devices and access materials, whether it be done with keyboard modifications or assistive technologies such as screen readers or magnification, can determine if the mobile device is accessible. An example of an accessibility feature on mobile phones is the voice-over feature. When activated, this feature reads to the user the material that is presented on the screen. If the material has not been created with accessibility in mind, it may cause the device to not render the material properly or at all.

Usability, on the other hand, does not have the unique challenges of the disability community in mind during the course design process, but, rather, strives to provide technological tools, devices, and materials that are easy for the instructor to implement and can be used by everyone, whether a disability exists or not. The U.S. Department of Health and Human Services (DHHS) defines usability as "how well users can learn and use a product to achieve their goals and how satisfied they are with that process" (n.d.). DHHS further states that usability is multidimensional and encompasses the following five factors: (1) ease of learning, (2) efficiency of use, (3) memorability by the user, (4) error of frequency and severity, and (5) subjective satisfaction. All of these factors should be considered during the design, development, and implementation of learning programs, courses, and materials. An example of usability is the closed-captioning of video presentations (Burgstahler, DO-IT (Project), University of Washington, & Washington State Library, 2010). This captioning not only assists learners who are deaf in "hearing" the video presentation, but allows all learners the added value of being able to access the materials in another manner, thus making it more useable from a pedagogical standpoint.

Finally, universal design rests in the philosophy that the design should always include the needs of all potential learners, disabled or not, so that the technological tools, devices, and materials will not be adapted for any one group, but, instead, designed to be accessible/useable for all (Arrigo & Cipri, 2010; Burgstahler, 2011; Burgstahler, DO-IT (Project), University of Washington, & Washington State Library, 2009; DO-IT, 2011; Elias, 2011). The principles of universal design, first developed after the 1997 reauthorization of the Individuals with Disabilities Education Act (Edyburn, 2010), have been modified over the years for different applications, but have primarily been used for website design. However, in recent years, the principles have evolved to include distance-education instructional materials. The modified universal-design principles consist of the following:

1. equitable—can be used regardless of the learners' ability or device;
2. flexible—accommodates differing learner abilities and devices by offering choices in how the materials are used;
3. simple and intuitive—does not require advanced knowledge by the learner and is affordable;
4. perceptible information—information can be obtained regardless of the learners' sensory abilities, taking into account undisclosed disabilities;
5. tolerance for error—guides the user if wrong selection is made that is a good opportunity for scaffolding or situated learning;

6. low physical and technical effort—provides materials that can be accessed by learners in a variety of methods and can utilize assistive technologies designed for use with mobile devices;
7. community of learners and support—provides opportunities for learning by pairing learners by device for additional support and learning; and
8. instructional climate—frequent interactions between the instructor and learner to optimize the learning experience (Burgstahler, DO-IT (Project), University of Washington, & Washington State Library, 2009; Elias, 2011).

These principles are based on the idea of fairness, equity, and specialized support to all learners who may benefit from the use of the device or material (Edyburn, 2010). An example of a universal-design principle applied to m-learning would be to provide downloadable transcripts for video lectures that can be available to all learners.

ACCESSIBLE M-LEARNING RECOMMENDATIONS

It is outside the scope of this chapter to delve into all the possible devices that can be implemented in m-learning or to discuss their individual accessibility features. As previously stated, these devices, such as smartphones, media players, PDAs, tablets, e-readers, and wireless laptop computers, to name a few, are fluid in their technological advances and tend to change yearly at a minimum. The following are recommendations to consider at the beginning of the design process. These recommendations, which include (1) universal-design recommendations, (2) disability issues, (3) device selection, (4) Internet accessibility, and (5) testing for accessibility, can be looked to as guidelines in the process of designing and implementing m-learning courses and materials, while ensuring that accessibility standards are considered and implemented.

Universal-Design Recommendations

Elias (2011) expanded on these universal-design principles to include examples of flexible options for m-learning, which should be considered during the design of the course and/or materials to be utilized. Table 37.1 provides both online and m-learning suggestions for each of the principles discussed.

As Table 37.1 illustrates, not all accommodations need to be labor intensive, difficult, or expensive to implement. In fact, most accommodations cost nothing while assisting learners with varying degrees of abilities and technology experiences. With approximately 54 million persons who have disabilities in the United States alone, "universally designed mobile technologies enable people with disabilities ... to use technology to live independently, work competitively and fully participate in society as well as provide added functionality for many people without disabilities" (United Business Media, PRNewswire, 2011, para.3). With that said, the ultimate goal is to ensure that all m-learning devices and the materials accessed by those devices are accessible to all learners, regardless of whether a disability is present. Further, Wieder (2011) reported that, just because accessibility must be addressed, that does not mean that emerging technologies cannot be employed. Many administrators feel that it is too expensive to design for accessibility, and so the use of new technology is not feasible. This should not be the case; rather, these technologies can be used as long as "equally effective and equally integrated" (para. 4) alternatives are provided if the new technologies are not accessible.

Table 37.1 Universal Instructional Design (UID) Principles with Online and M-Learning Recommendations

UID principles	Online DE recommendations	M-learning recommendations
1. Equitable use	Put content online Provide translation	Deliver content in simplest possible format Use cloud-computing file storage and sharing sites
2. Flexible use	Present content and accept assignments in multiple formats Offer choice and additional information	Package content in small chunks Consider unconventional assignment options Leave it to learners to illustrate and animate courses
3. Simple and intuitive	Simplify interface Offer offline and text-only options	Keep code simple Use open-source software
4. Perceptible information	Add captions, descriptors, and transcriptions	
5. Tolerance for error	Allow learners to edit posts Issue warnings using sound and text	Scaffold and support situated learning methods
6. Low physical and technical effort	Incorporate assistive technologies Consider issues of physical effort Check browser capabilities	Use available SMS readers and other mobile-specific assistive technologies
7. Community of learners and support	Include study groups and tools Easy-to-find links to support services	Encourage multiple methods of communication Group learners according to technological access and/or preferences
8. Instructional climate	Make contact and stay involved	Push regular reminders, quizzes, and questions to learners Pull in learner-generated content

Note: Adapted from Elias (2011). Universal instructional design principles for mobile learning. *The International Review of Research in Open and Distance Learning, 12*(2), 143–156. © 2011 by the IRRODL.

Disability Issues

Although it is not reasonable for every course designer to have an in-depth background regarding disability, these issues must be considered when creating accessible m-learning materials. Burgstahler (2011) reported that approximately 6 percent of higher-education students reported having a disability, and that this number is increasing as veterans with disabilities are returning to school (p. 1). This, in addition to the reported 31 percent of all higher-education students who now take at least one course online (Allen & Seaman, 2011), further emphasized the importance of universal design. During the design process, it is recommended that a representative from the institution's disability support, as well as the instructional technology office, be included, as they have the expertise required to address any disability and/or technology considerations. Considerations should include, but are not limited to, the following: (1) attention, (2) communication, (3) hearing, (4) learning, (5) physical, and (6) visual (Burgstahler, 2011) with regard to all learning materials and devices. These disability and technology experts can also assist in the testing of materials and devices for accessibility, as well as providing information regarding accommodations.

Device Selection

A step that can be taken by administrators, faculty, and learners with regard to m-learning is to stress the importance of looking for devices with built-in accessibility features to accommodate the most people with the least amount of effort. This alone will not solve all of the accessibility issues, but will ensure that a learner with a disability will have access to these features from the beginning, thus not creating further exclusion to the learning activities (Freire, Linhalis, Bianchini, Fortes, & Pimentel, 2010). It is also recommended that the accessibility features be determined through the device website, as well as following up with the company if needed. This follow-up can often lead to features requested being created for use by all users. Two of the most common features include: (1) voice-over, which reads the screen to learners who are blind or who have low vision; and (2) hearing-aid mode, to cut down on interference between the device, the user's hearing aid, and whatever media they are trying to access. Kuzu (2011) conducted a study on learners with hearing impairments using PDAs to access their course materials. The greatest problem that the learners encountered was the interference between their hearing aids and the PDAs. Providing course materials in alternative formats would have alleviated the interference, thus making the course more accessible. Additionally, some of the software employed within the course was not compatible with the PDA (Kuzu, 2011). Therefore, it is important to test software compatibility with every device that a learner could potentially use.

Internet Accessibility

Another important aspect to consider is the Internet when designing m-learning courses and materials. Although it is believed that, today, everyone has Internet access, that access is not always equal. It is incumbent on the course designer, when using the Internet for instruction, to ensure that all Internet websites are accessible to learners with disabilities and compliant with federal regulations, as previously discussed. Vicente and Lopez (2010) conducted a study on the disability digital divide to determine the differences in Internet usage between individuals with and without disabilities. Their findings indicate that mobile technologies have become a more affordable way to access the Internet, especially for individuals with disabilities. Further, accessibility features for individuals with disabilities need to be built in to provide the greatest amount of access to the largest group of people. By not doing so, these devices become useless to many individuals with disabilities. Finally, Vicente and Lopez (2010) found that 45.9 percent of individuals with disabilities are looking for online courses, and 44.2 percent have downloaded learning materials. This is in comparison with 48 percent and 47 percent, respectively, of individuals without disabilities (p. 59).

Testing for Accessibility

Finally, one of the best ways to test course materials and devices for accessibility is to use staff and learners with varying disabilities. These learners typically have the expertise of what works best for their disability in the learning environment, as well as the assistive technology needed to determine if the materials or devices could be accessed using these technologies. Software used also must be compatible with devices, materials, and assistive technology used by learners with disabilities.

Additionally, these learners with disabilities can quickly provide feedback regarding accessibility, as well as suggestions for improvements. More often than not, the information provided includes suggestions that were not previously considered, thus making the improvements more valuable to the learner. Sheng, Siau, and Nah (2010) identified eight values that were fundamental for the use of mobile applications by both faculty and students. These eight values were maximizing: (1) convenience, (2) efficiency, (3) effectiveness, (4) usability, (5) security of information, and (6) individual privacy, while (7) minimizing cost, and (8) ensuring academic honesty (p. 36). These values, along with the belief that "accessibility is key for the application of mobile technology in education" (p. 37), will help to ensure compliance is the main objective of the design.

CONCLUSION

It has been the intent of this chapter to provide information regarding accessibility and m-learning to enable institutions of higher learning to begin the discussion toward becoming compliant with federal regulations. Although this topic seems overwhelming, expensive, and unattainable, those thoughts are far from the truth. Institutions of higher learning must step up and take accessibility seriously. Joly's (2011) interview with Daniel Goldstein, lead counsel for the National Federation for the Blind, states, "until colleges put procedures in place" and "stop offering grants to faculty to develop online courses without a plan to make those courses accessible . . . they will be at risk of further liability" (para. 18). It is incumbent on the administrators and faculty who oversee the design, development, and implementation of courses and materials to ensure that they are accessible and designed in a way that guarantees accessibility to all users.

REFERENCES

Allen, I. E., & Seaman, J. (2011). *Going the distance: Online education in the United States, 2011*. Boston, MA: Babson Survey Research Group. Retrieved from: www.onlinelearningsurvey.com/reports/goingthedistance.pdf

Arrigo, M., & Cipri, G. (2010). Mobile learning for all. *Journal of the Research Center for Educational Technology (RCET), 6*(1), 94–102.

Burgstahler, S. (2011). Universal design: Implications for computing education. *ACM Transactions on Computing Education, 11*(3). DOI:10.1145/ 2037276.2037283

Burgstahler, S., DO-IT (Project), University of Washington, & Washington State Library. (2009). *Universal design: Process, principles, and applications*. Seattle, WA: DO-IT, University of Washington.

Burgstahler, S., DO-IT (Project), University of Washington, & Washington State Library. (2010). *Web accessibility: Guidelines for administrators*. Seattle. WA: DO-IT, University of Washington.

Crompton, H. (2013). A historical overview of mobile learning: Toward learner-centered education (pp. 3–14). In Z. Berge, & L. Muilenburg (Eds.), *Handbook of mobile learning*. New York: Routledge.

Danek, M. M., Conyers, L. M., Enright, M. S., Munson, M., Brodwin, M., Hanley-Maxwell, C., et al. (1996). Legislation concerning career counseling and job placement for people with disabilities. In E.M. Szymanski & R. M. Parker (Eds.), *Work and disability: Issues and strategies in career development and job placement* (pp. 39–78). Austin, TX: Pro-Ed, Inc.

DO-IT. (2011). *What is the difference between accessible, usable, and universal design?* [Factsheet #337]. University of Washington. Retrieved from: www.washington.edu/accessit/print.html?ID=337

EDUCAUSE Learning Initiative. (2010). 7 things you should know about . . . mobile apps for learning. *Educause*. Retrieved from: http://net.educause.edu/ir/library/pdf/ELI7060.pdf

Edyburn, D. L. (2010). Would you recognize universal design for learning if you saw it? Ten propositions for new directions for the second decade of UDL. *Learning Disability Quarterly, 33*(1), 33–56.

Elias, T. (2011). Universal instructional design principles for mobile learning. *The International Review of Research in Open and Distance Learning, 12*(2), 143–156.

Floyd, K. S., & Santiago, J. (2007, March). The state of website accessibility in higher education. In H. R. Weistroffe (Ed.), *Proceedings of the 2007 Southern Association for Information Systems Conference* (pp. 109–113). Atlantic Beach, FL. March 9–10. Retrieved from: http://sais.aisnet.org/2007/SAIS07-25%20Floyd-Santiago.pdf

Freire, A. P., Linhalis, F., Bianchini, S. L., Fortes, R. P. M., & Pimentel, M. C. (2010). Revealing the whiteboard to blind learners: An inclusive approach to provide mediation in synchronous e-learning activities. *Computers & Education, 54*, 866–876. DOI:10.1016/j.compedu.2009.09.016

Granic, A., Cukusic, M., & Walker, R. (2009). mLearning in a Europe-wide network of schools. *Educational Media International, 46*(3), 167–184.

Hermann, K., & Rapple, L. (2011, November). *Universal design for educational technology: Usable learning environments for all learners.* Session conducted at the 17th Annual Sloan Consortium International Conference, Orlando, FL.

IMS Global Learning Consortium. (2004). *IMS accessforall meta-data overview.* Retrieved from: www.imsglobal.org/accessibility/accmdv1p0/imsaccmd_oviewv1p0.html

Joly, K. (2011). Web accessibility: Required, not optional. *University Business.* Retrieved from: www.universitybusiness.com/article/web-accessibility-required-not-optional

Kolowich, S. (2011). Elaborating on online accessibility. *Inside Higher Ed.* Retrieved from: www.insidehighered.com/news/2011/05/27/ education_department_elaborates_on_guidelines_against_discriminating_against_disabled_learners_with_technology

Kuzu, A. (2011). The factors that motivate and hinder the learners with hearing impairment to use mobile technology. *Turkish Online Journal of Educational Technology—TOJET, 10*(4), 336–348.

National Federation of the Blind. (2009). *National Federation of the Blind and American Council of the Blind file discrimination suit against Arizona State University* [Press release]. Retrieved from: www.prnewswire.com/news-releases/national-federation-of-the-blind-and-american-council-of-the-blind-file-discrimination-suit-against-arizona-state-university-61889957.html

National Federation of the Blind. (2010). *Penn State discriminates against blind learners and faculty* [Press release]. Retrieved from: www.prnewswire.com/news-releases/penn-state-discriminates-against-blind-students-and-faculty-107491993.html

National Federation of the Blind. (2011). *Adoption of Google apps program discriminates against the blind* [Press release]. Retrieved from: www.prnewswire.com/news-releases/adoption-of-google-apps-program-discriminates-against-the-blind-118015684.html

Quinn, C. N. (2008). *mLearning devices: Performance to go.* Retrieved from: www.quinnovation.com/Mobile Devices.pdf

Roberts, J. B., Crittenden, L. A., & Crittenden, J. C. (2011). Learners with disabilities and online learning: A cross-institutional study of perceived satisfaction with accessibility compliance and services. *Internet and Higher Education, 14*, 242–250.

Seale, J., & Cooper, M. (2010). E-learning and accessibility: An exploration of the potential role of generic pedagogical tools. *Computers & Education, 54*, 1107–1116.

Sheng, H., Siau, K., & Nah, F. F. (2010). Understanding the values of mobile technology in education: A value-focused thinking approach. *The DATA BASE for Advances in Information Systems, 41*(2), 25–44.

United Business Media, PRNewswire. (2011). *Accessibility: A new frontier for mobile technologies* [Press release]. Retrieved from: www.prnewswire.com/news-releases/accessibility-a-new-frontier-for-mobile-technologies-118008949.html

U.S. Department of Education (2004). *Disability discrimination: Overview of the laws.* Retrieved from: www2.ed.gov/policy/rights/guid/ocr/disabilityoverview.html

U.S. Department of Education (2009). *Disability discrimination: Overview of the laws.* Retrieved from: www2.ed.gov/policy/rights/guid/ocr/disabilityoverview.html

U.S. Department of Education, Office for Civil Rights. (2010). *Electronic book reader dear colleague letter: Questions and answers about the law, the technology, and the populations affected.* Retrieved from: www2.ed.gov/about/offices/list/ocr/docs/504-qa-20100629.pdf

U.S. Department of Education, Office for Civil Rights. (2011). *Frequently asked questions about the June 29, 2010, dear colleague letter.* Retrieved from: www2.ed.gov/print/about/offices/list/ocr/docs/dcl-ebook-faq-201105.html

U.S. Department of Health & Human Services. (n.d.). Usability basics. *Usability.gov.* Retrieved from: www.usability.gov/basics/index.html

Utah State University, Center for Persons with Disabilities. (2012). *Overview of the Rehabilitation Act of 1973 (Sections 504 and 508).* Retrieved from: http://webaim.org/articles/laws/usa/rehab#s504

Vicente, M. R., & Lopez, A. J. (2010). A multidimensional analysis of the disability digital divide: Some evidence for Internet use. *The Information Society, 26*(1), 48–64.

Wieder, B. (2011). Education department clarifies e-reader accessibility rules [Web log post]. *The Chronicle of Higher Education.* Retrieved from: http://chronicle.com/blogs/wiredcampus/education-deptartment-clarifies-e-reader-accessibility-rules/31507

38

THE ROLE OF ACADEMIC LIBRARIES IN THE DEVELOPMENT AND SUPPORT OF MOBILE-LEARNING ENVIRONMENTS

Rachel Wexelbaum and Plamen Miltenoff

Academic librarians have delivered resources and services in m-learning environments since the introduction of laptops and cell phones. As mobile devices become ubiquitous, and an increasing number of people can acquire Internet-based information through such devices, academic librarians reconsider their services and resources to fit into the m-learning environment. Academic librarians improve assistance for faculty and students in their learning and research endeavors by making online library catalogs, databases, subject guides, and e-book collections, and 24/7 reference services available for mobile devices will enable academic librarians to assist. Enabled by a collegial professional culture, academic librarians prepare the fertile ground for application of mobile devices in education.

Academic librarians deliver innovative content and services suited for mobile devices. Librarians are a major stakeholder in the m-learning process. Considering the arduous tasks of moving traditional services and educational practices to the realm of m-learning, it is an imperative for the administration to support academic library participation in m-learning.

A BRIEF HISTORY OF MOBILE DEVICES IN EDUCATION

The miniaturization of computing devices and their ubiquitous application have been the focus of discussion and research from the beginning of the computer age. The move from mainframes to personal computers heralded steady interest in making computing devices portable and communication-ready. As early as the mid 1990s, handheld devices were considered as a replacement for personal computers, including laptops. Gessler and Kotulla (1995) were researching the possibility of using PDAs as Web browsers, building on research started at Xerox PARC by Weiser (1993) on a future world of "ubiquitous computing." A variety of studies have been conducted about handheld or small-screen devices and their impact on library services. Several researchers have studied the use of library materials by handhelds. In response to their survey question, "Which of the following library materials would you like to be able to download to your PDA" (Carney, Koufogiannakis &, Ryan, 2004), 75 percent wanted databases available through PDA and 46 percent wanted the online catalog (Cummings, Merrill, and Borrelli, 2010).

Recently, mobile wireless devices have evolved at a rapid pace. This evolution of hardware is rivaled only by the pace of application development for these devices. In 2011, mobile devices surpassed computers in Wi-Fi usage (Lee, 2011). Mobile devices are steadily becoming prevalent with their potential to assist the end user in improving planning, efficiency in the work place, and the increase and improvement of communication and construction of knowledge. Mobile devices have been readily embraced by a growing number of industries, e.g., the medical professions. With the introduction of iPhone/iTouch, the educational world has shown interest in their pedagogical application. Academic librarians are at the forefront of adopting mobile devices in the educational process.

More than half of recent college graduates (57 percent) shared that at least some time during class they used a laptop, smartphone, or tablet computer. Most colleges and universities have not issued institutional guidelines for the use of these devices. Notably, almost half of the college presidents (41 percent) support the use of laptops and other portable devices in the classroom, whereas only 2 percent of college presidents spoke against the use of these devices (Pew Research Center, 2011). All stakeholders—students, administration, and faculty, including academic librarians—must be on the same page when it comes to the adoption of mobile devices and the respective transforming of the curricula.

ACADEMIC LIBRARY RESOURCES AND SERVICES AND M-LEARNING

Prior to the omnipresence of the Internet, academic librarians started gearing up their resources and services for distance and online learners. The earliest reference service offered online originated in the mid 1980s through e-mail (Janes, 2003). Academic librarians who pioneered those online reference services made library resources and services more convenient for patrons and explored the potential of campus-wide networks (Janes, 2003). In the early to mid 1990s, online reference services began to include chat and instant messaging (Anderson, 2005). By the 21st century, "virtual reference" was available to library patrons 24 hours a day, 7 days a week. As library patrons and academic librarians acquired Internet-capable mobile devices, academic librarians synchronized their online reference services for PDAs, laptops, cell phones, and other mobile devices.

In a series of articles, Joan Lippincott eloquently presented the strong connection between mobility and reference services at the academic library. While Millennials' fascination with mobile devices was still considered questionable, Lippincott (2008) urged library administration to consider the opportunities offered by mobile devices, as well as the necessity for reference services to change. Based on the evolution from stationary computing devices to mobile computing devices, Lippincott drew attention to the reconsideration of library physical spaces. Lippincott raised other important questions, such as the role of the library as a stakeholder in the entire educational process. Moreover, Lippincott asserted the necessity for librarians to assume a leadership role in these developments. Librarians, urged Lippincott, "should think creatively about the development of services for users of mobile devices, especially taking into account user needs and preferences and the relationship of services to the academic program of their institution" (Lippincott, 2010, p. 10).

Academic librarians actively share their observations, experience, and vision about the transition of practices and services to m-learning, and mobile devices in particular. West, Hafner, and Faust (2006) are a team of two library administrators and a computer analyst. Their 2006 study on the use of PDAs and smartphones as gateways to academic libraries established that a library website can be adapted to the "limited power, memory, small screen size, and bandwidth" (West et al., 2006). In the years following their research, mobile devices advanced into fully functional microcomputers. Moreover, the ability to display content on small screens has also been resolved, and contemporary mobile devices successfully replace laptops and personal computers for an increasing number of services and information access.

Cummings et al. (2010) and Hahn (2008) present an overview of the era of PDAs and, later on, iPods and smartphones, to be used as "e-book and web page readers" (Cummings et al., 2010, p. 23). This didactic application persisted through the evolution from PDA-like to iPad-like devices. However, the development of mobile applications led to conceptual changes in reformatting the content and services presented to patrons. Information about services and the information itself will increase as they are delivered through mobile devices. A parallel mobile interface for patrons, as described by Cummings et al. (2010) as a future trend, has become reality for an increasing number of academic libraries.

In the middle of the last decade, PDA use reflected a clear interest by patrons (faculty, staff, and students) to use their devices as "e-book and web page readers." Their desire to have PDAs as a referencing tool was clearly recognized. Students indicated that they would like "more general e-book availability," "using it for library research, like downloading database and catalog results," "saving searches so that every time you synch, the library catalogue is searched, and the list of articles or books are updated on your PDA" (Cummings et al., 2010). A survey of 766 librarians on their use of handhelds and their perceptions of use by library patrons indicated that demand was fairly limited. It was reported routine use of handhelds included electronic organizer functions, rather than accessing library-related content. Of library-related functions, those used with the greatest frequency were catalog access, reading documents, database access, and accessing ready reference material (Spires, 2008). Librarians surveyed in this study drew attention to the fact that handheld accessibility comes with substantial additional costs to the libraries. Whereas the demand for access to library resources was insignificant in 2007, the swift change in mobile devices' popularity is changing the landscape of services and demands libraries to prepare for changes in how information and services are delivered to patrons (Cummings et al., 2010).

The end of the "PDA" era was heralded by the arrival of iPhone-like devices. The latter supported both native applications and proper Web browsing. A single legacy technology that has a limited, but nevertheless relevant, future within libraries is short message service (SMS). Libraries can and already use SMS to provide loan and catalog information to mobile devices and to support texting. There are many ways of delivering content to mobile devices—probably as many as there are devices. Libraries need to determine which ones to choose and how to foster usage standards.

One of the most immediate library objectives was to create stand-alone applications for mobile devices. The applications serve the same role as software applications on a desktop computer. iPhone applications downloaded from Apple's App Store are some of the examples. Compared with Web-browsing for information and services, applications offer a more user-friendly and streamlined experience. Further, patrons can take advantage of built-in services, such as global positioning system (GPS), imaging, and motion sensing, that may compromise personal privacy and library security if used over the open Web on library computers. A high level of control over appearance and functionality for the user makes this a particularly attractive way of delivering content to mobile devices (Greenall, 2010). However, as noticed by Hahn (2008, p. 277) and Greenall (2010), mobile devices are not designed specifically for libraries, and that will further increase development costs. Today, the interoperability with other devices and across specification is taking the direction that Hahn expected in 2008.

Another trend, predicted in the middle of the last decade, is the students' ability to move freely through space–time constraints (Hill, 2006). Although not yet streamlined, an increasing number of students collaborate with peers through mobile devices in their effort to acquire information and build knowledge. Referred to as "georeferencing" (Hill, 2006), this process embodies the "yet unrealized potential of computing ubiquity and the library" (Hahn, 2008, p. 278). A common example of georeferencing in the academic library is use of QR codes to assist students in navigating the building and locating resources.

ATTITUDES OF ACADEMIC LIBRARIANS TOWARD TECHNOLOGY

The transition from the traditional "reference" style to "georeferencing" will require enormous effort by all stakeholders in the m-learning process. The challenge is most pronounced for librarians. Academic librarians need to understand new devices and the effect that they have on patrons. In addition, academic librarians must adapt resources and services to the environment created by the devices. For some librarians, such transition may be a challenging endeavor, as they are "digital immigrants" and were not taught these skills when becoming professionals (Bosque & Lampert, 2009). At the same time, diverse technical skills closely connected to user expectations are a significant requirement of academic librarianship. Librarians also perceive technical expertise as a way to connect with users (Bronstein, 2011).

In a survey of public and academic reference librarians, academic librarians were more likely to be regular online-service users than public librarians. Those librarians who most recently earned their Masters of Library and Information Science (MLIS) had the highest comfort level with online services and technology. They also had the most advanced knowledge of technology relevant to their position, even if they had worked in a degreed-librarian position for 2 years or less. Not all MLIS programs orient students with technology and online resources in the same way. New librarians from younger generations—or those librarians without entrenched ideas about library resources and services—relate better to their patrons in using online services and technologies (Bronstein, 2011; Murray, 2011).

With the increased variety of mobile devices, academic librarians must have technical skills and problem-solving capabilities to provide assistance to their patrons. They must use these same skills in order to acquaint themselves with changes in subscription-based online resources. According to three separate academic reference librarians who were interviewed about their attitudes toward technology on the job,

> Users expect us to have technical skills in order to help them solve networking problems, set proxy definitions, or just fix the printer.
>
> (Bronstein, 2011, p. 799)

> You need to be able to deal with constant technological change. You need to be able to get acquainted with new databases by yourself. Over the years I have learned to study a new database, compare it to other databases in my collection, and make a decision about whether to subscribe to it or not.
>
> (Bronstein, 2011, p. 799)

> Today we need to know the students' world of content: Facebook, Twitter, the cellular world. We need to know this world so that we can help them navigate through it.
>
> (Bronstein, 2011, p. 799)

Today's academic librarians are continually evaluating and using new technologies for professional and personal purposes. The bookish 19th-century librarian stereotype still persists; however, in the 21st century, librarians are likely to own and use mobile devices and apps for personal and professional use. College graduates aged 30–49, with earnings of $75,000/year, are most likely to own an e-reader or a tablet computer in addition to a laptop and cell phone (Pew Internet & American Life Project, 2013). Academic librarians continuously educate colleagues, instructors, and students about library resources and services. The newer generations of "wired" students, as well as patrons involved in online education, are of a particular focus. Academic librarians are utilizing Web 2.0 and social-media tools for their library instruction (Grassian & Trueman, 2007; Maness, 2006).

Academic librarians are strongly encouraged by peers and administrators to educate themselves about innovations in technology that would affect production, delivery, and access of library resources and services (Aharony, 2009). In the United States, all state and national professional library associations encourage presentations on the use of mobile technologies for reference and instruction. Further, professional exchange includes strategies to increase access to online and digital library resources through mobile devices. There are national conferences in the United States that focus specifically on the use of technology in libraries,[1] and the focus on mobile technologies is increasing. Librarians who attend these conferences are not strangers to mobile technologies. Based on observations in the field, 8 out of 10 librarians who attend these events bring at least one type of mobile device with them for note-taking, testing out new apps or library webpages presented at the conference, checking e-mail while out of the office, reading e-books or online periodicals using an e-reader app, or playing games.

The increasing ubiquity of mobile technologies among academic librarians leads one to question whether or not librarians view their gadgets as a necessity, or a display of "geek chic." It also stimulates internal peer pressure for low-tech librarians to at least dip their toe in the technological waters, which could lead to increasing personal interest in the devices and their applications (Martin, 2010; Rios, 2004). In the case of emerging technologies, it is difficult to tell where personal interest and professional development begin and end. Although academic libraries with decreasing budgets are less likely to invest in devices that may become obsolete, academic librarians will often buy gadgets out of personal curiosity, as well as to increase their professional knowledge.

Librarians have to function in a dynamic, multidimensional environment, where information transcends library walls, and the provision of information services to users through different media is constantly evolving (Bronstein, 2011; Tonhauser, 2009). Over time, librarians have become accustomed to working with resources in multiple formats, as well as different forms of online communication. As the nature of information retrieval and delivery continues to advance rapidly, academic librarians believe that mobile devices are essential to their professional development. They traditionally share gained expertise on m-learning and devices with colleagues in the workplace, as well as across the profession. Academic librarians who have personal and professional experience using mobile devices often assume the instructor's role in teaching students and faculty how to use the devices, as well as how to access content on mobile devices. For this reason, academic librarians often play a major role in the introduction of mobile devices and content to students and faculty, and can be the first point of contact (Rios, 2004).

M-LEARNING ENVIRONMENT AND LIBRARY SUPPORT FOR STUDENTS AND FACULTY

Academic librarians are spearheading technological advances in pedagogy (Fox, Carpenter, & Doshi, 2011). This is especially the case in colleges and universities with well-established online-education programs that require resources and services for faculty and students at a distance. Academic librarians with faculty status are more likely to be recognized as peers by the teaching faculty. College faculty are more likely to enjoy collaboration with faculty librarians in developing tools for teaching and research in the m-learning environment (Bhavnagri & Bielat, 2005; Owens & Bozeman, 2009; Rader, 1998; Wang, 2008).

Librarians and college faculty are in need of data to establish the effects of mobile technology on student information-seeking behaviors. Increasing numbers of academic librarians and college faculty collaborate on library instruction based on mobile technologies. Such collaboration may lead to a new research methodology on information-seeking behaviors. Such methodologies can be paired with research on m-learning in further understanding of how students engage in the research process using mobile devices (Hahn, 2008, p. 281).

Fozdar and Kumar (2007) consider mobile devices as an option to bridge the digital divide on campus. Students who cannot afford a personal computer do manage to purchase a mobile device. If content accessible on a PC can be delivered through mobile devices, students have a better chance to succeed in school. M-learning can be viewed as a retention tool during the first, most vulnerable year for new students and thereafter (Upcraft, Gardner &, Barefoot, 2005; Tobolowsky and Cox, 2007; Schreiner and Pattengale, 2000; Gardner and Van der Veer, 1998). M-learning as a bridge for the digital divide and as a retention tool is a rather large endeavor, difficult to frame, and challenging to execute. Testing m-learning at the academic library can be the starting point, which will provide the know-how on how to enable m-learning across campus.

Mobile devices, such as cell phones, smartphones, tablet computers, and laptops, situate students in constant connectivity. In the Pew Research Survey of the general public, more than half of recent college graduates and currently enrolled college students report that they have often (35 percent) or sometimes (22 percent) used these types of device during class time. One in five (19 percent) say they hardly ever used these devices in the classroom, and 22 percent say they never have (Pew Research Center, 2011). This dependency on connectivity and the invasion of mobile devices in the classroom did not escape the attention of instructors (Traxler, 2010; Young, 2006).

Further issues based on the prevalence of everlasting and ubiquitous connection reflect in issues such as plagiarism. A majority of college presidents surveyed have seen a rise in plagiarism over the past decade, and most believe that technology is a major factor behind that rise. Some 55 percent of college presidents say plagiarism has increased in college students' papers over the past 10 years. Of those who say plagiarism is on the rise, the overwhelming majority (89 percent) believe that computers and the Internet have played a major role in this trend (Pew Research Center, 2011). On the other hand, the *Chronicle of Higher Education* presents a myriad of reports on plagiarism. Plagiarism is an old and controversial issue, which is only exacerbated by the new communication technologies, including the Internet. Librarians have historically been an integral resource in educating the campus population on plagiarism and related issues.

As ubiquitous Internet access turns people to search engines, Internet-capable mobile devices force librarians to compete for relevance and authority in the research process. Multiple college surveys of the Web versus library resources confirm the faculty and librarian perceptions that students misuse the Web as a primary source for research, rather than searching the library website or catalog (Lippincott, n.d.). As librarians immerse themselves in the world of mobile devices, they will have opportunities to reformat content and services to reflect the activities expected by patrons (Hahn, 2008, p. 275).

According to a survey of 483 academic and public libraries conducted by *Library Journal*, the majority of academic libraries (65 percent) either "currently offer" or "plan to offer" resources and services for mobile devices (Thomas, 2010). Academic libraries consider "priority services" to be a mobile layout of the library website, a mobile catalog interface, SMS reference (reference assistance via text messaging), and SMS text-message notifications. Academic libraries are more likely to offer or plan to offer mobile library services to their patrons than public libraries. Academic-library patrons are more likely to use mobile devices to search for information owing to convenience or generational preference (Thomas, 2010).

DISCUSSION AND FUTURE RESEARCH

The proliferation of mobile apps among library patrons results in increasing connections to the Internet, yet less time conducting searches on the Web (Emery, 2010). If academic librarians create mobile apps for the library catalog, subject guides, databases, and e-book collections, it is possible that students will use the mobile apps for those resources on their mobile devices and bypass browsers and search engines completely.

While academic librarians can visualize, describe, evaluate, and promote mobile library resources and services, the majority of library staff is identified by a lack of technical expertise, either among their own ranks or within their institution. Such reality appears as a barrier to the development of instructional technologies for mobile devices (Thomas, 2010). As a result, campus leadership might ignore the library as the forerunner of mobile technologies and shift it to IT departments. Such a shift can result in frustration on the part of academic librarians, who feel constrained by "what the IT department will let [them] do" (Thomas, 2010). Such circumstances may limit opportunities for academic libraries to innovate and experiment with new technologies and, respectively, deprive faculty on campus of precious experience and knowledge in the didactical application of mobile technologies.

It is very important that academic librarians are not excluded or marginalized from the m-learning efforts on campus. Librarians must become an integral part of a team effort. They should serve as a conduit between the stakeholders in m-learning—faculty, students, and administration—and the enablers of m-learning—computer staff, educational information technologists, etc. As Hahn (2008) points out,

> Developing the infrastructure for m-learning need not be produced by librarians alone—researchers in engineering, computer science, education, psychology, and sociology may be investigating m-learning or may have similar interests in new technology. Researchers may not be aware that what they are investigating could serve a public service need and look for practical application for their hardware. Librarians are well suited to provide this practical viewpoint.
>
> (Hahn, 2008, pp. 279–280)

NOTE

1   Library Technology Conference (Macalester College, Minnesota); Computers in Libraries Conference (Information Today, Inc.); TechNet (Library Tech Network, Texas); Distance Library Services; Code4Lib; Handheld Librarian (online conference); Brick & Click Libraries Symposium (Northwest Missouri State University, Missouri).

REFERENCES

Aharony, M. (2009). Web 2.0 use by librarians. *Library & Information Science Research, 31*(1). Retrieved from: www.sciencedirect.com/science/article/pii/S0740818808001333

Anderson, R. (2005). IM me. *Library Journal, 130,* 34–35.

Bhavnagri, N. P., & Bielat, V. (2005). Faculty–librarian collaboration to teach research skills: Electronic symbiosis. *The Reference Librarian, 43*(89–90). Retrieved from: www.tandfonline.com/doi/pdf/10.1300/J120v43n89_09

Bosque, D. D., & Lampert, C. (2009). A chance of storms: New librarians navigating technological tempests. *Technical Services Quarterly, 26*(4), 261–286.

Bronstein, J. (2011). The role and work perceptions of academic reference librarians: A qualitative inquiry. *Libraries and the Academy, 11*(3), 791–811. Retrieved from: http://muse.jhu.edu/journals/portal_libraries_and_the_academy/v011/11.3.bronstein.pdf

Carney, S., Koufogiannakis, D., & Ryan, P. (2004). Library services for users of personal digital assistants: A needs assessment and program evaluation. *Portal: Libraries and the Academy, 4*(3), 393–406. DOI:10.1353/pla.2004.0043

Cummings, J., Merrill, A., & Borrelli, S. (2010). The use of handheld mobile devices: Their impact and implications for library services. *Library Hi Tech, 28*(1), 22–40.

Emery, J. (2010). Something so right. *Journal of Electronic Resources Librarianship, 22*(3/4), 88–92.

Fox, R., Carpenter, C., & Doshi, A. (2011). Cool collaborations: Designing a better library experience. *College & Undergraduate Libraries, 18*(2/3), 213–227.

Fozdar, B. I., & Kumar, L. S. (2007). Mobile learning and student retention. *International Review of Research in Open and Distance Learning, 8*(2), 1–18. Retrieved from: www.eric.ed.gov/PDFS/EJ800952.pdf

Gardner, J. N., & Van der Veer, G. (1998). The emerging movement to strengthen the senior experience. In J. N. Gardner & G. Van der Veer (Eds.), *The senior year exepreince. Facilitating integration, reflection, closure, and transition* (pp. 60–78). San Francisco, CA: Jossey-Bass, Inc.

Gessler, S., & Kotulla, A. (1995). PDAs as mobile WWW browsers. *Computer Networks and ISDN Systems, 28*(1–2), 53–59.

Grassian, E., & Trueman, R. B. (2007). Stumbling, bumbling, teleporting and flying . . . librarian avatars in Second Life. *Reference Services Review, 35*(1), 84–89. DOI:10.1108/00907320710729373

Greenall, R. T. (2010). Mobiles in libraries. *Online, 34*(2), 16–19.

Hahn, J. (2008). Mobile learning for the twenty-first century librarian. *Reference Services Review, 36*(3), 272–288.

Hill, L. L. (2006). *Georeferencing: The geographic associations of information.* Cambridge, MA: MIT Press.

Janes, J. (2003). Digital reference: Reference librarians' experiences and attitudes. *Journal of the American Society for Information Science and Technology, 53*(7), 549–566. Retrieved from: www.unc.edu/~bwilder/inls500/janes13.pdf

Janes, J. (2003). *Introduction to reference work in the digital age.* New York: Neal Schuman Publishers.

Lee, T. (2011). Mobile devices surpass PCs in WiFi usage. *Übergizmo.* Retrieved from: www.ubergizmo.com/2011/06/mobile-devices-surpass-pcs-in-wifi-usage/

Lippincott, J. K. (n.d.). *Net generation students and libraries.* EDUCAUSE. Retrieved from: www.educause.edu/Resources/EducatingtheNetGeneration/NetGenerationStudentsandLibrar/6067

Lippincott, J. K. (2008). *Mobile technologies, mobile users: Implications for academic libraries.* Retrieved from: www.arl.org/bm~doc/arl-br-261-mobile.pdf

Lippincott, J. K. (2010). Mobile reference: What are the questions? *Reference Librarian, 51*(1), 1–11. DOI: 10.1080/02763870903373016

Maness, J. M. (2006). Library 2.0 theory: Web 2.0 and its implications for libraries. *Webology, 3*(2). Retrieved from: www.webology.org/2006/v3n2/a25.html

Martin, M. (2010). Sharing our toys! Technology petting zoo @ BC Libraries Conference 2010. *BCLA Browser* [newsletter of the British Columbia Library Association], *2*(3). Retrieved from: http://journals.sfu.ca/bcla2/index.php/browser/article/viewArticle/189

Murray, A. (2011). Mind the gap: Technology, millennial leadership and the cross-generational workforce. *Australian Library Journal, 60*(1), 54–65.

Owens, R., & Bozeman, D. (2009). Toward a faculty-librarian collaboration: Enhancement of online teaching and learning. *Journal of Library & Information Services in Distance Learning.* DOI:10.1080/15332900902794898

Pew Internet & American Life Project. (2013). *Device ownership.* Retrieved from: http://pewInternet.org/Static-Pages/Trend-Data/Device-Ownership.aspx

Pew Research Center. (2011). *The digital revolution and higher education.* Retrieved from: www.pewsocialtrends.org/2011/08/28/the-digital-revolution-and-higher-education/1/

Rader, H. B. (1998, August). *Faculty–librarian collaboration in building the curriculum for the millennium: The US experience.* 64th IFLA General Conference, August 16–21. Retrieved from: http://ifla.queenslibrary.org/IV/ifla64/040-112e.htm

Rios, G. R. (2004). Technology and e-health advancements: PDA librarian. *Reference Services Review, 32*(1), 16–20. DOI:10.1108/00907320410519306

Schreiner, L. A., & Pattengale, J. (2000). *Visible solutions for invisible students: Helping sophomores succeed* [Monograph series No. 31]. Columbia, SC: National Resource Center for the First-Year Experience & Students in Transition, University of South Carolina.

Spires, T. (2008). Handheld librarians: A survey of librarian and library patron use of wireless handheld devices. *Internet Reference Services Quarterly, 13*(4), 287–309.

Thomas, L. C. (2010). Gone mobile? *LibraryJournal.com.* Retrieved from: www.libraryjournal.com/lj/ljinprintcurrentissue/886987-403/gone_mobile_mobile_libraries_survey.html.csp

Tobolowsky, B. F., & Cox, B. E. (2007). Shedding light on sophomores: An exploration of the second college year. *The first year experience monograph series, no. 47.* Columbia, SC: National Resource Center for the First-Year Experience & Students in Transition, University of South Carolina.

Tonhauser, C. (2009). *Teacher-librarians as technology leaders: The evolving role.* Graduate student paper, University of Alberta: Edmonton, Alberta, Canada. Retrieved from: http://tldl.pbworks.com/tonhauser.pdf

Traxler, J. (2010). Students and mobile devices. *Alt-J, 18*(2), 149–160. DOI:10:1080/09687769.2010.492847

Upcraft, L., Gardner, J. N., & Barefoot, B. O. (Eds.) (2005). *Challenging and supporting the first-year student: A handbook for improving the first year of college.* San Francisco, CA: Jossey Bass.

Wang, H. (2008). Wiki as a collaborative tool to support faculty in mobile teaching and learning. In K. McFerrin et al. (Eds.), *Proceedings of Society for Information Technology & Teacher Education International Conference 2008* (pp. 2865–2868). Chesapeake, VA: AACE.

Weiser, M. (1993). Hot topics—ubiquitous computing. *Computer, 26*(12), 71–72. DOI:10.1109/2.237456

West, M., Hafner, A. W., & Faust, B. D. (2006). Expanding access to library collections and services using small-screen devices. *Information Technology & Libraries, 25*(2), 103–107.

Young, J. (2006). The fight for classroom attention: Professor vs. laptop. *The Chronicle of Higher Education,* A27. Retrieved from: http://chronicle.com

Part V

Cases and Perspectives

39

MOBILE-LEARNING STRATEGIES FOR K–12 PROFESSIONAL DEVELOPMENT

Dustin C. Summey

M-learning provides a means by which to enable teacher professional development that is both meaningful and effective—that is differentiated and meets the unique and specific needs of teachers and their students within the context of diverse learning environments, curricular guidelines, and technology constraints. This chapter addresses m-learning as an integrated component of professional development. It identifies characteristics of effective programs, describes m-learning strategies being applied in the field, and makes connections with research-based models of K–12 professional development. In addition, guidance is given for avoiding common mistakes when planning and implementing professional development and making use of mobile technology.

PROFESSIONAL DEVELOPMENT TRAITS AND TENDENCIES

When exploring the integration of m-learning strategies within professional development, it is helpful to take a look at the traits that characterize well-planned and implemented professional development in general. K–12 educators are typically required by state licensure boards and school policies to complete a certain amount of professional development annually. Teachers meet such expectations by participating in in-house training programs and events provided by their school district and by pursuing outside opportunities such as conferences, seminars, and graduate coursework.

Rethinking the Approach

Teacher professional development is too often approached as a one-shot effort at disseminating information and skills, with little or no follow-up (Garet, Porter, Desimone, Birman, & Yoon, 2001). This is particularly true of that which is offered within the four walls of the local school. Teachers are often force-fed by disconnected administrators or outside consultants, who demonstrate little or no interest in actually understanding the professional growth needs of each individual teacher and instead arrive with their own agenda and dispositions. In reality, these individuals are merely mistargeting their well-intended efforts. The results, however, may fall short of rendering positive outcomes.

M-Learning-Enhanced Professional Development

A quick comparison of the characteristics of effective professional development and the advantages afforded by m-learning suggests that the two were naturally meant to be together. The portability of mobile devices allows professional development to take place in authentic environments—situated where instruction will occur—and just in time, that is, adjacent to, or even simultaneous with, instances of student instruction. Widespread availability of mobile phones among teachers and students and the increasing availability of tablets in schools mean that providers can incorporate much-needed modeling through collaborative, experiential learning within their training programs. Furthermore, personal ownership of mobile devices allows teachers to consistently use the same technology throughout all stages of professional development, an advantage that is likely to result in high satisfaction and greater transfer to the classroom.

Planning and Implementation

Needs Assessment

One of the critical factors in a successful professional-development effort is meeting the specific needs of the target audience. The most effective professional development starts with the end in mind. Planners use needs-assessment tools such as skill inventories, interest surveys, and feedback from prior training events in order to pinpoint the true needs of each constituent and align them with institutional and training-program goals.

Planners of professional development often make the mistake of creating a one-size-fits-all program in hopes of accomplishing all things in one unified effort. Evidence shows, however, that such an approach tends to result in lower participant morale, limited transfer to classroom instruction, and little if any impact on student-learning outcomes. On the other hand, a training event that is focused on one or two specific goals and accommodates the diverse learning needs and preferences of the participants will better equip teachers to make changes in their instruction that will, in turn, improve student learning (Kesson & Henderson, 2010; Mackenzie, 2007; Wlodkowski, 2003).

M-learning offers the ability to facilitate professional development that is differentiated based upon the unique needs of each teacher participant, in terms of technology proficiency, instructional context, and learning environment. A roundup of teacher-owned mobile devices would likely include a variety of feature phones, smartphones, and tablets. There is a place for each of these in the m-learning realm, and, although it is vital to consider device capabilities when planning for training events, the least common denominator still affords a wide range of possibilities in terms of teaching and learning. Professional development brings together teachers from many different content areas and grade levels—even within a single school. Mobile devices and the instructional strategies associated with them can be adapted within any instructional context. Teachers do not need to wonder whether elementary-school students have the technical skills necessary to use iPads within collaborative-learning activities. Similarly, a choir director and a science teacher can apply m-learning strategies in their own unique contexts after receiving training from the same event. Whereas whiteboards and flipcharts present environmental needs and location constraints, the mobility afforded by cell phones and tablets means that training can be situated in the chemistry lab, the band room, a field location, or any other venue deemed necessary, based upon the needs of time, space, and subject matter. The availability of Wi-Fi connectivity can certainly serve to expand the usefulness of non-cellular devices (e.g., Wi-Fi-only tablets) by providing access to a rapidly growing expanse of Web apps and services, but the lack thereof does not remove the potential for leveraging the numerous tools and functionalities that do not rely upon a constant connection to the Internet.

Mobile devices can be used to survey participants, prior to, or at the beginning of, a training session. There are a variety of online survey platforms, ranging from free to fee-based, which allow both open- and closed-response submission via mobile technologies such as text messaging (SMS), mobile Web, or even social-media apps such as Twitter. PollEverywhere.com is one such example. A multiple-choice survey used to gauge prior knowledge can assist leaders in providing the most relevant instruction for teachers. A poll at the end of a training segment checks for understanding. Still, an open-response survey invites participants to pose questions, rate satisfaction, or suggest future topics.

Leveraging Buy-In and Motivation

In addition to a targeted focus on actual needs, it is also essential to take time to leverage the buy-in of all stakeholders who will be participating in a training event. There is intriguing brain research that links interest and motivation to learning. An in-depth description of this connection is beyond the scope of this chapter. Fortunately, Sousa (2009) and Aguilar (2011) have provided plain-language explanations of this relationship, from which some insight can be gleaned.

In short, positive feelings stimulate the release of endorphins, which make a person feel good and consequently open to learning. At the same time, dopamine is released in the brain, which keeps a person attentive and increases the likelihood of retention of what is learned.

On the other hand, negative feelings—such as a dreaded after-school staff meeting—trigger the hormone cortisol to enter the blood stream, thereby kicking the brain into survival mode and pulling attention away from learning in order to focus on coping with stress. In this case, the stressor could be a poorly approached and delivered in-service presentation or perhaps an untimely topic.

Professional-development providers can leverage buy-in and stimulate motivation by considering some basic tenets of andragogy (Aguilar, 2011; Knowles, 1980)—the theory of adult learning. Teachers, as adult learners, want to know expressly the purpose of any activity in which they engage. They want it to be relevant to their specific needs, and they desire to be an active stakeholder in the formation of the instructional context. Job-embedded professional development is packed full of instant takeaways that teachers can use immediately in their classroom instruction. They value authenticity and crave the opportunity to exchange bidirectional feedback that actually makes a difference. Educational leaders would do well to invest time in developing and nurturing a positive sense of eagerness toward professional growth, instead of dropping mandates and using top-down approaches with regard to training and development.

The very use of mobile devices in professional development can serve to motivate teacher engagement. Observations across a variety of contexts seem to indicate that teacher participation and enthusiasm are significantly higher when m-learning strategies are incorporated, compared with lecture-only formats or even participant interaction via other means (Wishart, 2009). Although many teachers are still somewhat uneasy about turning their students loose with mobile devices in the classroom, the teachers themselves are, in fact, quite interested in exploring new uses of these personal devices inside and outside the classroom. Many of them would merely like to learn how to do more than make a call or send a text message. Regardless, this intrigue with regard to the deep penetration of mobile devices in today's society is an excellent source of motivation that can fuel participation and leverage positive attitudes toward new ideas and strategies being presented through professional development. Furthermore, the approaches described throughout this chapter for m-learning-infused professional development can serve to increase buy-in and motivation, which are viewed as critical factors in the success of any program.

Technology as a Tool

The ultimate goal of professional development is to improve student learning. Technology-skill acquisition should not be the sole purpose. Although it is almost always necessary to provide a certain degree of technical training when technology tools are involved in instruction, such training should not be the sole purpose of any emphasis. The fact that mobile devices are already an integrated part of life for most people in today's society means that educators can avoid adopting a new technology simply for its popularity or sensational appeal. Indeed, it is within the role of educators today to teach certain digital literacies, which include, among others, managing information and communication via cell phones, tablets, and other mobile devices.

Facilitating the Use of Mobile Devices

Professional-development providers who desire to incorporate mobile devices into programming can increase the likelihood of a successful experience by taking a few steps proactively in order to carefully usher faculty into this new and exciting frontier. These steps are not so different from the approach that should be taken for integrating m-learning strategies with students in the classroom. Figure 39.1 is a sample planning tool that can be used to integrate m-learning within any environment.

Any organization is compelled to maintain a healthy balance of *policies* and *people*. This means that policies should be established to guide safe and efficient operations, while giving consideration to the fact the people are involved, and, therefore, there are constantly changing needs and goals that must be addressed. Mobile-device policies (Anderson, 2012; Bosco, 2010) should address issues such as security, wireless access, and guidelines for bring your own technology (BYOT). Every environment will have different needs that warrant a unique set of policies. Although these policies can stand alone, some schools may integrate them into an overall acceptable-use policy (AUP) that encompasses the use of all technology systems and services by students and teachers alike.

Next, it is helpful to *market* the idea with a positive tone in order to generate excitement and *leverage buy-in* among all people involved. The idea of participant buy-in was referenced earlier in the context of motivation, but it certainly applies here too, with regard to the use of new technology. One way to make progress here is to involve a broad cross-section of individuals in developing the policies mentioned above. There is still a significant amount of skepticism, among teachers and administrators alike, as to whether mobile devices—especially cell phones—should be allowed in classrooms and hallways. It is only natural that this disposition might transfer to teacher-learning situations as well. As always, cultivating a widespread attitude of openness to new technologies and innovative methods of instruction will go a long way at achieving measurable results in the classroom.

	Implementation Timeframe	Stakeholders Involved	Description of Strategy
Policy Development			
Generating Excitement			
Leveraging Buy-In			
Ensuring Access			
Maintaining Simplicity			

Figure 39.1 M-Learning Device Implementation Plan

Source: D. Summey

Before the first meeting where m-learning strategies are to be implemented, it is vital to take an *inventory* of the types of mobile device that are available to each teacher. This can be dovetailed with the professional-development needs assessment. With regard to personal cellular devices, there will likely be a mix of smartphones (iPhones, Androids, etc.) and feature phones (devices with a camera, texting, and/or other functionalities). Although the personal ownership of tablets (iPads, etc.) is rapidly increasing, in most cases there may not be enough devices available to really take advantage of their potential, unless school-owned devices are available. Whereas some schools have taken steps to equip each and every teacher with an iPad, others have placed moratoriums on the very purchase of these devices, in order to allow the hype to dispel and further evaluate the potential benefits of iPads in the classroom. In any case, it is imperative that professional-development leaders align m-learning-enabled sessions with the technical capabilities of participants and their devices. Indeed, participants' inability to perform the tasks being demonstrated in a session can have a destructive impact on buy-in and motivation.

Finally, *simplicity* is essential when using technology within the context of teacher professional development. Start with instructional strategies involving simple tasks such as text messaging and taking pictures, before progressing to more advanced operations such as scanning QR codes or working with smartphone apps. When specific apps will be a core part of a training program, it can be helpful to distribute a list of required apps a few days prior to the first event where they will be used, so that participants can download the apps and set up any user accounts that might be necessary. Be sure to create separate app lists that correlate to each of the mobile-device platforms that will be in use (as learned through the device inventory and needs analysis).

Taking time to create and implement a deliberate implementation plan—and using a tool such as the one in Figure 39.1—will go a long way to ensuring the success of a professional-development program infused with m-learning.

Support

Ongoing support from teacher-experts is an essential—and often overlooked—element of professional development. Teachers need opportunities for job-embedded follow-up once they have had the chance to mentally process new concepts and make initial attempts at instructional integration. Because no single person can provide sufficient support to an entire faculty, teacher leaders should be identified and trained to support their peers. A train-the-trainer approach can be used prior to adopting the widespread use of mobile devices in order to establish a support structure.

Mobile devices are often used as a field reference for professionals who need access to manuals for a variety of equipment to be serviced, repaired, or operated (Ally, 2009). Similarly for teachers, instructional guides and tutorials can be converted into e-books and made available for download into the e-reader apps that are available for smartphones and tablets. Certainly, such resources can also be made available for native e-reader devices, too, such as the Kindle and the Nook. The cell phone makes just-in-time, live support a reality. Sometimes, a quick text message is all that is necessary, and it is much more timely and efficient than scheduling a face-to-face consultation or exchanging e-mails. A quick videoconference connection through Skype or Google+ allows a support-provider to assist a teacher and view the context of the problem through live video, made possible by using the built-in camera on a cell phone or tablet. Screen-sharing and virtual-network-computing apps for tablet devices allow remote desktop viewing and control, so that teachers can receive assistance with computer operations while geographically separated from the support personnel. Sound bytes recorded during presentations can also be referenced at the point of need. Even feature phones with relatively limited functions will typically include a sound recorder, which can be used for this purpose, among many others.

Program Evaluation

Feedback from all stakeholders is of vital importance for reflecting upon and improving a professional-development program. Soliciting such feedback involves engaging in formative and summative evaluation. Audience response systems such as polling tools (e.g., PollEverywhere.com) and digital bulletin boards (e.g., Wiffiti.com) allow teacher participants to submit open and closed responses before, during, and after professional-development events, using SMS text messaging, mobile Web interfaces, and even social-media apps. Audioblogging platforms and Web-based voice-messaging services such as Google Voice provide a means by which participants can convey feedback using the basic calling feature of their mobile phones.

One-shot training programs are much too common in K–12 school systems today. Effective professional-development initiatives—which lead to improved student learning—must be ongoing, with follow-up and an increasing degree of individualization as teachers progress through the program. Mobile technologies enable teachers to reflect upon their learning at the end of training sessions, as well as the successes and failures of their attempts at classroom implementation. Such reflection is often facilitated using a blog. Blog platforms such as Blogger and WordPress provide multiple ways for users to post entries using mobile phones and tablets—including device-compatible apps, mobile Web access, e-mail, and even text messaging. The ability to post to a blog via text message means that even the simplest feature phones can serve as a mobile blogging device. This is just another example of how m-learning narrows the digital divide and engages even the slowest technology adopters. These informal reflection activities not only lead to transformative learning on the part of the teacher participant, but also provide much-needed feedback to training providers, who can then make data-driven plans and revisions for future professional development.

PROFESSIONAL-DEVELOPMENT MODELS AND FORMATS

Conferences and Seminars

Professional development intended for broad dissemination of information often takes the form of a conference, seminar, or other large-scale event. Schools often send one or more delegates, who then return with the expectation of delivering on-site training that will empower a group of teachers, with new knowledge and skills for improving classroom instruction. This is a lofty feat to say the least, given the amount of information that is typically conveyed at educational conferences.

M-learning at this level of professional development might involve the conference attendees using mobile phones or tablets to take notes during breakout sessions, capturing audio and video clips for use in the on-campus workshops they will later facilitate, maintaining a blog for both personal reflection and sharing, and perhaps backchanneling with other conference participants using Twitter, Edmodo, or another social-media platform.

Conference-Wide Collaboration

Conference organizers are increasingly trying new, innovative methods to engage participants in collaboration at multiple levels. This often begins long before the actual conference date and spans infinitely beyond the closing keynote. A backchannel is a sidebar discussion that is often facilitated through Twitter, using a unique hashtag such as #TechConf2012 or something similar. Backchanneling was gaining in popularity long before conference organizers began endorsing an official hashtag. Attendees plan meet-ups in advance and maintain ongoing conversation using their cell phones and tablets while attending sessions and strolling exhibit halls. As Twitter is a public social network, a backchannel also allows those people who cannot attend a conference in person to get a glimpse into the transfer of knowledge and ideas that occurs at such events. Although many conferences establish one hashtag to be used for the entire event, others (such as EDUCAUSE) go as far as to associate a separate hashtag with each and every session. In addition to providing a venue for virtual conversation during a live event, a backchannel becomes a lasting transcript that can be referenced indefinitely.

Another avenue of conference-wide collaboration is to create a standalone, community-based social network using a platform such as Edmodo or Ning, which participants can access using their mobile devices during the conference and beyond. Organizers control access and privacy at multiple levels. They either establish exclusivity by requiring a passcode that is only available to registered conference attendees, or they make the online community open to the public in order to facilitate a wider dissemination of knowledge and even leverage increased participation in future events. This is also a place where presenters post slideshows, handouts, links, and other companion resources.

Session Participation

Skilled presenters adapt to their audience and increase participant engagement by projecting a poll or digital bulletin board on-screen prior to and during a breakout session. Web-based platforms such as PollEverywhere.com and Wiffiti.com allow participants to respond using text messaging, mobile Web, and even Twitter. Session facilitators might display on-screen a social-media aggregator such as TweetDeck or HootSuite in order to give participants a glimpse into the conference backchannel. It is rather exhilarating to submit a post and see it appear immediately on a screen in front of a large audience. Increasingly, conference attendees are expecting event organizers and presenters to incorporate a variety of social-media-driven modalities into the conference experience.

Collecting, Organizing, and Sharing

Mobile devices allow conference attendees to capture gems of information—perhaps audio or video clips, pictures, or text-based notes—that become instant takeaways that can be referred to at the point of need and disseminated to peers within professional learning communities and personal learning networks. Because the educators who attend conferences are typically delegates from a much larger faculty, there is often an expectation that these teacher leaders return to school ready to disseminate their newly acquired knowledge through presentations or workshops. A wiki is a type of collaborative website where a school's delegation might create a knowledge base by posting notes and resources from each session attended. The wiki serves as a sort of virtual home page, where team members organize their lists of sessions to attend so that they can obtain the widest possible range of information. Some examples of wiki platforms include Wikispaces, Google Sites, and PBWiki. Rather than having to wait until after the conference to get organized, a school's conference delegation can post to their wiki on the go, using their smartphones and tablets, and even begin to assemble a slideshow that will assist with school-wide presentations following their return from the event.

Virtual Conferences

Some organizations offer a virtual conference in addition to—or in place of—a face-to-face event. Some virtual conferences are free to paid attendees of the on-site event, whereas others require a separate registration. Florida Educational Technology Conference has offered virtual conferences at various points throughout the year, in addition to its annual event in Orlando. EDUCAUSE has held a virtual conference simultaneously with its convention-center gathering. Virtual conferences often involve the use of video-conferencing via Adobe Connect, Skype, and other platforms. Adobe Connect and Skype both offer iPad apps that make it possible for educators to actively participate in a virtual conference in any location of their choosing, provided that broadband Internet access is available.

Workshops and Presentations

Workshops and presentations offered within a school, district, or cooperative represent the most common method of professional development. Leaders can make use of a variety of m-learning strategies for leveraging participant engagement and motivation, facilitating collaboration, modeling innovative classroom instruction, and collecting participant feedback at multiple stages in the training.

Essential Components

The line that separates a workshop and a presentation seems to be somewhat fuzzy, especially in academia. The term *presentation* implies that one or more leaders will present some sort of information to an audience, while the very grammatical makeup of the word *workshop* points to an event involving the construction of something—perhaps knowledge! However, too often such sessions place a heavy emphasis on lecture and one-way communication and fail to engage faculty members as active participants in the learning process. Regardless of the terminology used to label this type of session, there are five elements that should be present in order to increase the likelihood of a meaningful learning experience.

1. *Direct instruction* is often accomplished with the help of a slideshow. Collaborative presentation tools such as Google Presentations and Prezi make it possible for participants to access and interact with a speaker's live presentation using their mobile devices, even as they sit in the same room. Presenters also share documents, notes, and other resources using tools such as Google Docs, DropBox, or iCloud, allowing participants to collaborate live on documents using smartphone and tablet apps and reducing the amount of paper that must be used to distribute session materials.

2. *Multimedia* elements such as slideshows, video clips, and interactive Web tools should be carefully selected and implemented using appropriate instructional strategies. Multimedia projected on a large screen in the front of a room offer limited options for interactivity. An alternative to this common approach is to provide a handout, with QR codes that participants can scan with barcode readers on their mobile devices. A QR code serves as a shortcut to access an informational website, a video on YouTube, or a simple string of text. Additionally, a QR code can be used to trigger a new text message that might be used for responding to a survey or perform other, more advanced operations, which vary between devices and platforms.

3. *Small-group discussion* is too often billed as extraneous when considering how to use limited professional-development time; however, it provides a much-needed initial opportunity for participants to consider how to apply their newly acquired knowledge, skills, and resources in their own teaching situations. Session facilitators should not assume or expect that teachers will take time to do this on their own in a future setting. Mobile devices allow for note-taking during these discussions, and groups can extend their conversation beyond the meeting room by taking advantage of group texting services such as Cel.ly and Pulse.to.

4. *Self-reflection* often takes the form of a blog, informal notes, voice recordings, or any other type of media. As mentioned earlier in the chapter, several of the major blogging platforms provide multiple ways by which mobile devices can be used for posting, commenting, and collaborating. Smartphone and tablet apps for note-taking abound, as do sound recorders and other apps for creating and managing media objects. Reflection is the critical process by which learning becomes

transformative, and learners (in this case, the teachers participating in professional development) make the connection between what was previously known to be true and what is now recognized as new understanding within the context of their applicable practice.

5. *Extension* involves the actual application in the classroom of what was learned in professional development, as well as bidirectional feedback from peers, teacher leaders, and administrators. As cited in Sousa (2009), teacher motivation is actually fueled by constructive feedback. This fact only serves to underscore the importance of ongoing follow-up related to professional-development initiatives. Mobile devices allow data collection during classroom walkthroughs, peer observations, and consultations. Mobile e-mail and text messaging provide means by which to transmit feedback and results from such activities.

Self-Directed

K–12 educators also engage in self-directed professional development, be it formal or informal in nature. Many schools require teachers to develop professional-growth plans, which may include activities such as book studies, online courses, or research. Teachers often unknowingly implement m-learning strategies as they access mobile versions of learning-management systems (LMSs), use mobile Web resources to perform research on the fly, use mobile RSS readers to follow blogs and other Web feeds, and share "aha moments" on Twitter or Google+ while reading a book on instructional improvement. Such activity is also the basis for establishing a personal learning network (PLN). A PLN leverages the power of the social Web and provides a means by which a teacher can contribute to the collective intelligence of the profession through active participation in niche professional communities, such as Classroom 2.0, blogging, tweeting, aggregating feeds, and curating information. All of these activities are greatly enhanced by the mobility of cell phones and tablets. PLN activity often happens on the go and becomes an embedded part of an educator's daily life.

Moodle is an open-source LMS that has a mobile-friendly portal that offers vast potential for learning and collaboration on the go. Although an LMS is most often associated with formal coursework, it is also used to deliver and facilitate professional-development modules and many other types of instruction.

Other Models and Formats

A variety of m-learning strategies have been described already within the chapter that are also applied within a variety of other professional-development models and formats. Mobile devices support field-based training initiatives through the use of instructional podcasts, digitized manuals and reference books, streaming media, and just-in-time support through text messaging, videoconferencing, chat, location-aware services, and other communication modalities. Professional-learning communities collaborate asynchronously via blogging and group texting. Peer mentors use mobile devices to video-record teaching examples and observations. They employ popular note-taking apps such as Evernote or proprietary apps when available to support observations and consultations. Data can then be transferred between teachers by being sent to their inbox, via SMS, through cloud-based file-management platforms, or using wireless protocols such as Bluetooth, infrared, or near-field communication (NFC). Within all of these contexts, mobile devices are useful for reflective blogging, note-taking, media capture, data collection, and providing immediate feedback.

COMMON PROBLEMS AND PITFALLS

Teachers who participate in technology-related professional development undoubtedly encounter technical, logistical, and affective concerns that should be addressed proactively in order to create the best possible conditions for instructional integration by each participant (Gaible & Burns, 2005). Carefully applying the strategies described in the first section of this chapter can go a long way toward eliminating such issues. Additionally, professional-development providers should avoid common mistakes such as:

- attempting a one-size-fits-all approach;
- incorporating too much of the lecture/presentation delivery format;
- placing too much emphasis on theory and not enough on practical applications;
- assuming that learning a new technology skill equates to knowing how to apply it within the context of classroom instruction (Lefoe, Olney, Wright, & Herrington, 2009).

Common issues when introducing m-learning include:

- participant buy-in;
- misperceptions of the technology;
- device availability and compatibility;
- wireless connectivity;
- technical support.

When approached correctly, each of these issues can be addressed successfully and potential barriers removed, making way for dynamic professional development that engages teachers as learners and makes a positive impact on student achievement.

CONCLUSION

Teacher professional development is an essential part of the continual effort to increase student-learning outcomes and equip 21st-century citizens for success in a constantly changing society. Mobile technologies have become increasingly pervasive as tools for managing information and communication in our highly digital world. Teachers are compelled to instill in students certain digital literacies—including those enabled by mobile technologies—and, as such, must be trained to do so by well-planned and implemented professional-development initiatives and ongoing support systems. By combining research-based strategies and best practices in both professional development and m-learning, educators can realize a paradigm shift in the way mobile devices are viewed and used in authentic contexts, both inside and outside of the classroom.

REFERENCES

Ally, M. (Ed.) (2009). *Mobile learning: Transforming the delivery of education and training.* Edmonton, AB: AU Press.

Anderson, S. (2012). *How to create social media guidelines for your school.* Edutopia. Retrieved from: www.edutopia.org/how-to-create-social-media-guidelines-school

Aguilar, E. (2011). *The science behind adult learning* [blog]. Retrieved from: www.edutopia.org/blog/adult-learning-pd-elena-aguilar

Bosco, J. (2010). *Acceptable use policies in a Web 2.0 & mobile era: A guide for school districts.* Washington, DC: Consortium for School Networking. Retrieved from: www.cosn.org/Portals/7/docs/Web%202.0/Acceptable %20Use%20Policies%20Web%2020%20Mobile%20Era.pdf

Gaible, E., & Burns, M. (2005). *Using technology to train teachers: Appropriate uses of ICT for teacher professional development in developing countries.* Washington, DC: infoDev/World Bank.

Garet, M. S., Porter, A. C., Desimone, L., Birman, B. F., & Yoon, K. S. (2001). What makes professional development effective? Results from a national sample of teachers. *American Educational Research Journal, 38*(4), 915–945.

Kesson, K. R., & Henderson, J. G. (2010). Reconceptualizing professional development for curriculum leadership: Inspired by John Dewey and informated by Alain Badiou. *Educational Philosophy & Theory, 42*(2), 213–229. doi:10.1111/j.1469–5812.2009.00533.x

Knowles, M. (1980). *The modern practice of adult education: From pedagogy to andragogy.* Wilton, CT: Association Press.

Lefoe, G., Olney, I., Wright, R., & Herrington, A. (2009). Faculty development for new technologies: Putting mobile learning in the hands of the teachers. In J. Herrington, A. Herrington, J. Mantei, I. W. Olney, & B. Ferry (Eds.), *New technologies, new pedagogies: Mobile learning in higher education* (pp. 15–27). Wollongong, Australia: University of Wollongong.

Mackenzie, N. (2007). Teacher morale: More complex than we think? *Australian Educational Researcher (Australian Association for Research in Education), 34*(1), 89–104.

Sousa, D. A. (2009, June). Brain-friendly learning for teachers. *Educational Leadership: Revisiting Teacher Learning, 66.* Retrieved from: www.ascd.org/publications/educational_leadership/summer09/vol66/num09/Brain-Friendly_Learning_for_Teachers.aspx

Wishart, J. (2009). Use of mobile technology for teacher training. In M. Ally (Ed.), *Mobile learning: Transforming the delivery of education and training* (pp. 265–278). Edmonton, AB: AU Press.

Wlodkowski, R. J. (2003). Fostering motivation in professional development programs. *New Directions for Adult & Continuing Education,* (98), 39.

40

AN EXPLORATION OF MOBILE LEARNING TO ENHANCE STUDENT PERFORMANCE IN HIGH-SCHOOL MATHEMATICS

Vani Kalloo and Permanand Mohan

Mathematics has always been a difficult subject for many students. In the last 6 years, 41 percent of high-school students in the Caribbean passed mathematics at the "ordinary" level (Caribexams, 2004). This chapter discusses an m-learning system, MobileMath, that was developed to address the high failure rates in mathematics in secondary schools in the Caribbean. Mobile technology was chosen to address this problem, given its attractiveness to high-school students and the readily available mobile infrastructure in the Caribbean. The design and implementation of the m-learning system are presented, and the results of several evaluation studies are discussed. The chapter wraps up with a mention of future plans for this project.

PROBLEM, BACKGROUND, AND JUSTIFICATION

Mathematics has proven to be a difficult subject throughout the world. Students in most Caribbean countries train for the Caribbean Examination Council (CXC) examinations. Table 40.1 shows the results for the CXC mathematics examination for the period 2004–2009. It shows that at most 28 percent of the students passed Paper 2. Paper 2 is the more comprehensive part of the examination and, thus, is a better indication of mathematics competence than Paper 1. The overall results show that at most 47 percent of the students passed CXC mathematics. This low pass rate is a major problem, as mathematics is one of the most important prerequisites for further education and employment.

Crompton, Muilenburg, and Berge's definition of m-learning is presented in Chapter 1 of this book (Crompton, 2013, p. 4). They define m-learning as "learning across multiple contexts, through social and content interactions, using personal electronic devices." M-learning was chosen as a potential solution to the low mathematics pass rates as it is popular, the mobile infrastructure is readily available, and mobile devices and connectivity rates are affordable.

Table 40.1 CXC Mathematics Results for 6 Years

Year	Total % passing Paper 1	Total % passing Paper 2	Total % of students scoring a pass grade overall
2009	62	26	45
2008	63	28	47
2007	60	15	34
2006	47	20	35
2005	71	20	39
2004	78	21	46

Source: Caribexams, 2009

M-learning was chosen to help tackle the problem of low pass rates in secondary schools in Trinidad and Tobago and perhaps the wider Caribbean. This study targets the following research questions:

1. Can m-learning help students improve their performance in mathematics?
2. Can m-learning motivate the students to work more on their mathematics skills?
3. At what time will the MobileMath application be most effective? Is it while the students are being taught the topics in the classroom or any time after?
4. Will personalization make navigation and selection of the topics and features easier?

LITERATURE REVIEW

As mathematics has been shown to be a challenging subject throughout the world, many e-learning solutions for learning mathematics have been investigated. Some of these experiences reported a positive outcome as a result of using technology for learning and have been a part of the justification for choosing to use m-learning for mathematics in the study discussed here. Cheng, Deng, Chang, and Chan (2007) described Edubingo, a computer-based game that is similar to regular Bingo. In Edubingo, the player is required to match the answers to the teacher's question to the possible answers on the screen of his or her computing device. The students enjoyed the game and preferred practicing mathematics this way. Shin, Sutherland, Norris, and Soloway (2011) investigated the effect of game technology on elementary students learning mathematics. Students who played technology-based arithmetic games outperformed students who played paper-based arithmetic games. The results of their studies provide evidence that game technology can have a positive impact on elementary students, regardless of their ability. Sedighian and Sedighian (1996) designed Super Tangram, a computer game designed to help sixth-graders with transformational geometry. The player has to slide, turn, or flip the shapes. The students found that this game brought a greater sense of relevance to the subject, and the feedback on the game was quite positive. These researchers have shown how students enjoy using game play for learning mathematics and how it had a positive impact on the students.

Kebritchi, Hirumi, and Bai (2010) examined the effects of computer games on students' mathematics achievements and motivation. Results of this study revealed that there was a significant improvement in mathematics achievement. The teachers verified that the students' skills and understanding improved. This study demonstrated evidence of how students not only had positive attitudes but also were able to show improvements, offering concrete evidence of its potential.

Ke (2008) presented a case study of using educational computer games to achieve a variety of mathematical skills and create positive attitudes toward mathematics. One example was the game called Cashier, which was used to develop arithmetic skills. The results indicated that using mathematical games significantly enhanced students' positive attitudes toward mathematics. In another study, Barkatsas, Kasimatis, and Gialamas (2009) found that high achievement in mathematics was associated with high confidence in mathematics, high confidence with using technology, and a strong positive attitude to learning mathematics with technology. These studies show that quite a number of successful mathematics games have been reported. Students' attitudes toward learning can greatly affect their performance, and researchers show here how the use of technology for learning mathematics seems to instill a positive attitude toward the subject, ultimately leading to improved performance.

M-learning studies have been used worldwide for assisting students with learning mathematics. MoMath (2010), for instance, is an m-learning project conducted in South Africa with a focus on low-end mobile phones. The project offered learning through theory, exercises, tutoring, peer-to-peer support, competition, tests, and self-assessments. Results revealed that the students used the learning activities outside the school's compound and on weekends, and it reached over 4,000 students. The students showed improvements in their end-of-term results. Project K-Nect (2008) is an m-learning study to help students focus on improving their mathematics using a smartphone. The students communicate with each other and with tutors using the smartphones to help master their skills. Franklin and Peng (2008) studied m-learning that employed iPods to help students learn algebra via videos outside the hours of the classroom. The results showed that the use of iPods was viable in middle school. These studies reveal that m-learning has potential benefits for learning and, hence, are part of the justification for using m-learning for the study discussed in this chapter.

Shin, Norris, and Soloway (2006) used Gameboys for mathematics learning, where the problem appeared on the screen, and the students had to solve it before if faded away. The results proved that gaming impacted positively on students learning mathematics. Busa, Greenop, and Volsoo (2008) discussed an innovative game for learning mathematics. Mathstermind was based on the well-known board game Mastermind and requires the player to solve mathematics puzzles using arithmetic and algebraic equations. This game was developed and tested in South Africa. The researchers have demonstrated the successes, such as creating positive attitudes and significantly improved performance. These results suggest that there is need for research in using these technologies for learning, especially for problematic topics such as mathematics. Therefore, these studies were part of the justification for using m-learning when learning mathematics.

Many studies have reported that personalization and adaptive educational content are needed for e-learning activities. It is thought that it can be beneficial to the learner, as each learner learns at a different pace and using different learning methods. Ketamo (2002) presented an adaptive geometry-learning game, another m-learning study, that adapted to the players' behavior. In this study, 6-year-olds used a Compaq PocketPC, which they found easy to use, and they were able to reach an average level of competence in the area. Based on their experiences with an intelligent tutoring system, Virvou and Tsiriga (2000) suggested that an intelligent tutoring system can help the teacher to provide individualized help for the students. These results highlight the advantages of using intelligent tutoring over traditional classroom teaching for mathematics. Kinshuk (2003) pointed out the need for frameworks to support adaptation of educational content and the individual preferences of learners. These studies highlight the need for personalization or adaptive learning and have influenced the study discussed here having personalized content available to the learner.

Parsons, Ryu, and Cranshaw (2007) presented a design framework for m-learning that was considered in the design of the MobileMath application. Parsons et al. (2007) suggested that the mobile content be in small nuggets, rather than large amounts of information. They further suggested that m-learning should use the game metaphor, meaning it should engage the learner, create excitement, have rules, goals, and objectives, and provide immediate feedback, conflict, challenge, opposition, and competition. These were all factors considered in the design of the m-learning study.

DESIGN AND IMPLEMENTATION

In order to determine if m-learning could motivate the students to spend more time working on algebra, an m-learning application was created, called MobileMath. Figure 40.1 shows the main components of the MobileMath system. The main components included a server, mobile phones, the Internet, a database, and the teacher.

The server is used to support communication between students and for storage of the usage data for all students, based on their use of the mobile application. The student is expected to log in to the application and use the learning activities. At the end of the sessions, the usage data and scores attained are sent to the server via the Internet. They are then stored on the database. The teacher analyzes the student-usage data on the server and uses this to give feedback and encouragement to the students.

Personalization is used to assist students in selecting an appropriate topic and learning activity. MobileMath was created based on algebra, more specifically subtopics such as finding factors, directed numbers, factorization, simplification of terms, and solving equations. Personalized recommendations are provided for each student, depending on their performance. The usage data and scores are used to provide feedback and suggestions to the user. Personalization was provided in two main ways: navigational personalization, so that students could navigate easily, and content personalization, which allowed the students to know which content was most suitable. The application used colored menus to recommend suitable learning activities, based on each student's performance. Green was used to represent recommended activities, and red was used to represent the activities that were not recommended.

MobileMath consists of several different learning activities for helping students with mathematics. These are text-based lessons, dynamic examples, tutorials, quizzes, fun facts about mathematics, and learning games. The learning games include games for practicing factors, directed numbers, simplification of expressions, factorization, and solving equations (Kalloo and Mohan, 2011a). The main objective of the games is to encourage students to practice algebraic skills, whereas the lessons, examples, and tutorials are resources for reviewing important concepts taught in the classroom. Different lessons,

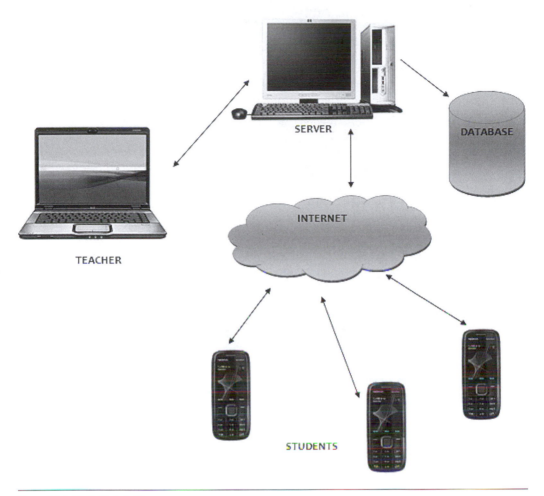

Figure 40.1 MobileMath System

examples, tutorials, and quizzes are provided for each topic. The fun facts demonstrate to the students that mathematics can be interesting and useful.

The lessons feature, shown in Figure 40.2, is a text-based explanation of a topic that was previously taught by the teacher in the classroom.

The example is a dynamic feature where the learner can change the numerical values in the worked example of a mathematics problem. A screenshot of an example is shown in Figure 40.3.

The tutorials feature was created as a quick way for the student to review concepts and attempt a problem. The student could review the topic, view an example, and then attempt a similar problem.

The quizzes feature was created for the students to assess themselves and be able to get immediate feedback on their progress. The quizzes provide a set of multiple-choice-type questions meant to assess the student on that particular topic. The fun-facts feature gives fun and interesting facts about mathematics and presents some mathematical

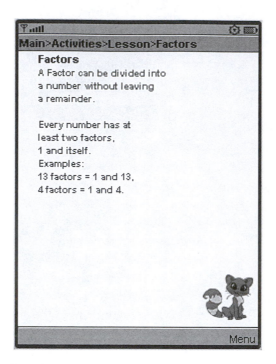

Figure 40.2 A Factors Lesson

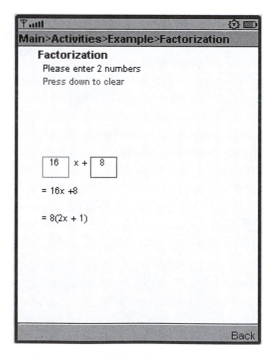

Figure 40.3 A Factorization Example

riddles and stories of famous mathematicians. There is a need for this, as students in secondary schools often complain that they do not see why they have to do mathematics, and that they will never use it in their life after high school.

The games were created with the intention that it would encourage the students to practice. Each game was based on one mathematics skill, where the player was required to use this skill in order to play the game. Therefore, as the student plays the game and is practicing the skill, the game and the skill in question are mastered (Kalloo, Kinshuk, & Mohan, 2010).

MobileMath offers seven games. There is a game for each topic targeted by this study. These include a finding-factors game, a directed-numbers game, a simplification-of-expressions game, a factorization game, and an equation-solving game. Each game's objective is to help the students improve a certain skill. There is also a Bluetooth game and a GPRS game. The Bluetooth game connects two players, and they play a game of snakes and ladders against each other. Each player has to answer an algebraic question correctly in order to move on in the game. Figure 40.4 shows a screenshot of the GPRS equation-solving game, and Figure 40.5 shows the equation-solving game.

MobileMath provides the student with feedback, depending on the feature. There are scores provided for the quizzes, tutorials, and games. MobileMath also offers a report of the last quiz scores, showing how the student is progressing.

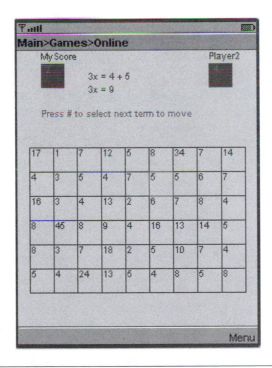

Figure 40.4 A GPRS Equation-Solving Game

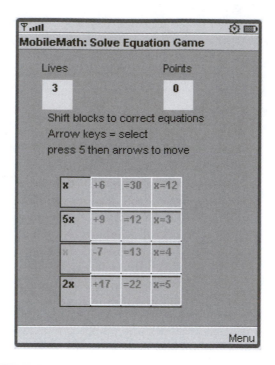

Figure 40.5 An Equation-Solving Game

EVALUATION STUDIES

This section of the chapter first identifies the target user group. Then it goes on to describe three evaluation studies that were conducted to evaluate the m-learning system in a real-world setting, with high-school students.

Limited resources and time constraints made it necessary to choose one topic from the mathematics curriculum. Algebra was chosen, as it is one of the more difficult topics in mathematics. The target group was students between the ages of 12 and 18 years, who were either learning algebra for the first time or had completed basic algebra in school and were having difficulty with it. Members of this target group often owned their own mobile phones and, therefore, were excellent candidates for m-learning.

A preliminary study was conducted with 11 students, in order to introduce them to an early version of the m-learning application. At this time, the application consisted of the learning activities and only one game. The preliminary study was intended to gauge the reactions of the students to MobileMath. The students' feedback revealed that they enjoyed using this method for learning mathematics. This positive feedback inspired the extension of the m-learning application to include more games, which was then evaluated in three other studies.

The goal of Study 1 was to determine whether the students would be motivated to use mobile phones for learning mathematics on their own, and, if they did, to determine whether it would improve their performance in mathematics. This study included students who had previously studied algebra in their secondary schools. The students were left on their own to use the mobile phones.

The goal of Study 2 was to explore whether teacher support can encourage students to use the mobile application for learning mathematics more than they would if left on their own. Therefore, even though they were not enrolled in an algebra class, there was a teacher assigned to encourage and support these students. This study was conducted with students who were exposed to algebra in their secondary schools in a previous class. It was different from Study 1, as the students received teacher support for using m-learning. During the study, the teacher would monitor the students' incoming data on the server and, depending on the data, would send messages to the students to encourage them to use the application.

The main goal of Study 3 was to investigate whether students, who were learning algebra for the first time, could perform better using the mobile devices than students who were not using them. Therefore, unlike in Studies 1 and 2, these students were enrolled in an algebra class during the evaluation. It attempted to verify the difference between two classes being taught by the same teacher, where one group used the MobileMath application for learning mathematics (experimental group), and the other group did not (control group).

During Studies 1–3, a total of 57 students used the mobile application for 3 weeks. Pre-test and post-tests were used to determine the changes in performance. They completed a questionnaire as part of the evaluation. The amount of time and frequency with which each feature was used by the students was accumulated.

RESULTS

The methods of evaluation were the pre-test, post-test, usage data, and the questionnaire responses. The students of Study 1 were able to increase their mathematics performance by 8.8 percent after using m-learning for learning mathematics. The students of Study 2 increased their mathematics performance by 10.2 percent after using m-learning. There was no difference in performance in Study 3 between the experimental group and the control group.

The results illustrated that 9 students passed the pre-test in Study 1, and 14 passed the post-test. In Study 2, 2 students passed the pre-test, and 7 passed the post-test.

A t-test was performed on the data to contribute further evidence that the students of Studies 1 and 2 improved performance. The t-test results revealed that there was a significant difference between the pre-test and the post-test scores for Studies 1 and 2. Therefore, this shows that the difference between the pre-test and the post-test scores is due to a change in performance after using MobileMath. There was an increase from the mean value of the pre-test to the mean value of the post-test, indicating that there was an increase in performance for both Studies 1 and 2 from the pre-test to the post-test. Therefore, the statistical data indicate that, after using MobileMath, students in Studies 1 and 2 improved their average performances. This statistical evidence implies that MobileMath had a positive impact on student performance in Studies 1 and 2.

The data demonstrated that the students in Study 2 used the mobile application the most frequently and for the longest time. Study 2 was the study that received teacher support.

Figure 40.6 shows the number of times that the students for all three studies used each feature of MobileMath. The graph shows that, for all three studies, the games feature was used the most. This information suggests that the games were the most preferred

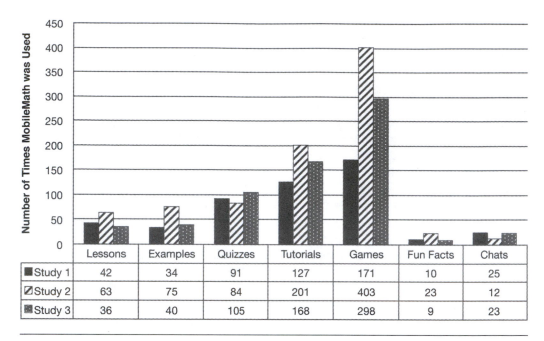

	Lessons	Examples	Quizzes	Tutorials	Games	Fun Facts	Chats
■ Study 1	42	34	91	127	171	10	25
▨ Study 2	63	75	84	201	403	23	12
▦ Study 3	36	40	105	168	298	9	23

Figure 40.6 Frequency of Use of Each Feature

feature. The next most used feature was the tutorial feature, followed by the quiz feature, suggesting that the tutorial and quiz were features also favored by the students. The graph shows that the students did not use the fun-facts and the chat features very much. It also demonstrates that the students of Study 2 used the lessons, examples, tutorials, games, and fun facts more than the students of Studies 1 and 3, suggesting that the teacher support that the students of Study 2 received caused them to use the application more than the other students.

Figure 40.7 gives a summary of the questionnaire responses of all the students who used the mobile application. Figure 40.7 shows that at least 80 percent of the students found the application easy to use and thought that m-learning helped them improve their skills, that it could help them in future if they used it for longer, and that it was useful to be able to learn anytime and anywhere.

Figure 40.8 illustrates that at least 50 percent of the students agreed that they preferred using mobile devices for learning rather than the PC. The students stated that they used the m-learning activities outside of home, implying that the mobility of learning was useful. Almost 70 percent stated that they preferred the learning games compared with the other learning activities. Data from the questionnaire revealed that 95 percent of the students stated that their parents thought that this method of learning was favorable, implying that this study would have parental support. Finally, 75 percent of the students agreed that the colored menus helped them to choose a learning activity.

DISCUSSION

The students of Studies 1 and 2 were able to improve their performance in mathematics after using m-learning. This was significant because the students were able to improve

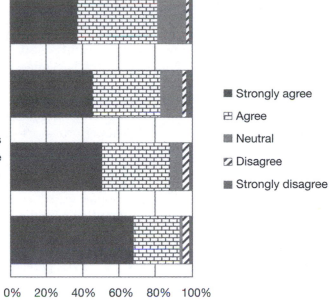

Figure 40.7 Questionnaire Data

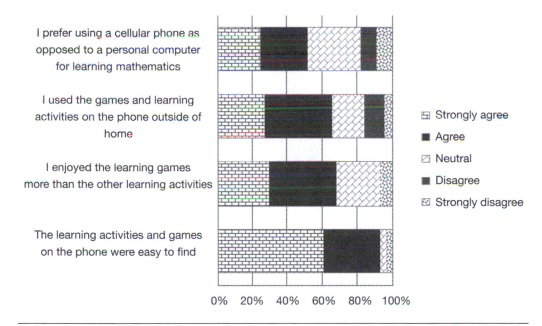

Figure 40.8 Questionnaire Data

their algebraic skill using m-learning in their own free time, and they chose to use the learning activities with no external motivating factors. They were intrinsically motivated to use the m-learning activities and, as a result, improve their performance. The usage information collected shows that the students of Study 2 used the mobile application the most. This can be attributed to the teacher support, which encouraged the students to use the mobile application. This suggests that teacher support can encourage students to use the mobile application more often than those without teacher support, and this can have a positive effect on learning outcomes. The evidence also demonstrated that the students in Study 2 improved their performance more than those in Study 1. Eighty-three percent of the students of Study 2 who received teacher support stated that both the mobile application and the teacher helped them to learn algebra. These results imply that this method of learning can help students improve their performance in mathematics, and that the teacher support was an essential aspect.

The results show that the game feature was the most used feature, and the tutorial was the second most used feature. The results show that the chat and fun-facts features were not used very much. The chat was not used because the GPRS connection was unreliable and slow. The fun-facts feature was perhaps not interactive enough to hold the students' attention.

The questionnaire data suggest that the students thought that the mobile application was easy to use, was beneficial in helping improve their performance in mathematics, and offered learning anytime and anywhere. The questionnaire data show that the most of the students responded favorably to learning with a mobile device.

Seventy-five percent of the students agreed that the personal recommendations helped them to choose an option. This information was derived from data collected on how many times a student chose to use the activity recommended by the system. These data were captured by the mobile application and sent to a server. However, there was no statistical evidence that demonstrated that the personalization affected their performance.

SUCCESSES AND CHALLENGES

Several challenges were encountered during this series of studies. The first major challenge met was the difficulty in the creation of mathematics learning games for a mobile phone. It was a challenge to create a fun game that included a mathematics topic and yet was suited to a limited device such as the mobile phone. This problem was solved by breaking up each topic into the smallest skills and basing each game on one skill.

Another problem encountered was the reluctance of secondary schools to allow mobile devices into the schools. Therefore, it was difficult to locate students to take part in the project. To solve this problem, most of the students took part in the study independently of their schools. Students were from a private school and took part in the study with the consent of their parents. In the third study, after much searching, a public secondary school finally allowed the use of the m-learning application with their students. It is expected that now that there is statistical evidence that this method of learning has some benefit it may be easier to convince principals to allow the mobile devices in the schools. It is hoped that, after schools see the tremendous influence it has on the students' learning, then perhaps they may be persuaded to change their thinking.

The GPRS connection was used to send data to the server and also to allow the students to communicate. However, the connect speeds were very slow, and this resulted in the students not being able to communicate via GPRS (Kalloo & Mohan, 2011b).

CONCLUSION AND FUTURE WORK

The results suggest that m-learning can be beneficial for students who learned algebra in a previous term and needed some help to improve their performance, such as the students of Studies 1 and 2. It suggests that teacher support was beneficial to the students' usage of the mobile application. However, it was not effective for students using the m-learning for the first time, such as the students in Study 3, who were enrolled in an algebra class during the evaluation. The next step for this study is to explore the reasons why it was not effective for students learning algebra for the first time.

The results will be analyzed, and the most successful factors will be identified from this study. These successful factors will be used to formulate a learning strategy to be used in the next stage of this study, to identify a method for learning algebra using e-learning. For instance, games were identified as the most effective and preferred feature by the students. Therefore, future research into learning games for mathematics is necessary.

REFERENCES

Barkatsas, A., Kasimatis, K., & Gialamas, V. (2009). Learning secondary mathematics with technology: Exploring the complex interrelationship between students' attitudes, engagement, gender and achievement. *Computers & Education, 52*(3), 562–570.

Busa, D., Greenop, K., & Volsoo, S. (2008, October). Guerrilla learning—Developing highly enjoyable, deeply engaging and professional looking educational games for the mobile phone. In J. Traxler, B. Riordan, & C. Dennett (Eds.), *Proceedings of mLearn 2008: The Bridge from text to Context*, October 7–10, Shropshire, UK. Retrieved from: www.scit.wlv.ac.uk/brendan/mLearn2008.pdf

Caribexams. (2004). *Caribbean Examination Council (CXC) mathematics pass rates assembled from data published by CXC annual school reports.* Retrieved from: www.caribcxams.org/m_pass_rates

Cheng, H. N. H., Deng, Y. C., Chang, S. B., & Chan, T. W. (2007, March). EduBingo: design of multi-level challenges of a digital classroom game. In T. W. Chan, A. Paiva, D. W. Shaffer, Kinshuk, & J. C. Yang (Eds.), *The First IEEE International Workshop on Digital Game and Intelligent Toy Enhanced Learning* (pp. 11–18). March 26–28. Jhongli, Taiwan: IEEE Publications.

Crompton, H. (2013). A historical overview of mobile learning: Toward learner-centered education (pp. 3–14). In Z. Berge, & L. Muilenburg (Eds.), *Handbook of mobile learning.* New York: Routledge.

Franklin, T., & Peng, L. (2008). Mobile math: math educators and students engage in mobile learning. *Journal of Computing in Higher Education, 20*(2), 69–80.

Kalloo, V., Kinshuk, & Mohan, P. (2010, July). Personalized game based mobile learning to assist high school students with mathematics. *Tenth IEEE International Conference on Advanced Learning Technologies (ICALT 2010)* (pp. 485–487). July 5–7, Sousse, Tunisia.

Kalloo, V., & Mohan, P. (2011a). An investigation into mobile learning for high school mathematics. *International Journal of Mobile and Blended Learning, 3*(3), 60–77.

Kalloo, V., & Mohan, P. (2011b, July). A mobile learning study in high school mathematics: Challenges, lessons learned and recommendations. *Eleventh IEEE International Conference on Advanced Learning Technologies (ICALT 2011)* (pp. 45–47), 6–8 July, Athens, Atlanta, USA.

Ke, F. (2008). A case study of computer gaming for math: Engaged learning from game play? *Computers & Education, 5*(4), 1609–1620.

Kebritchi, M., Hirumi, A., & Bai, H. (2010). The effects of modern mathematics computer games on mathematics achievement and class motivation. *Computers & Education, 55*(2), 427–443.

Ketamo, H. (2002, August). MLearning for kindergarten's mathematics teaching. In *Proceedings of IEEE International Workshop on Wireless and Mobile Technologies in Education (WMTE 2002)* (pp. 167–170). Växjö, Sweden.

Kinshuk. (2003). Adaptive mobile learning technologies, *Global Educator*. Department of Information Systems Massey University, New Zealand.

MoMath. (2010). Mobile learning for mathematics: Nokia project in South Africa. Symbian Tweet. Retrieved from: www.symbiantweet.com/mobile-learning-for-mathematics-in-south-africa

Parsons, D., Ryu, H., & Cranshaw, M. (2007). A design requirements framework for mobile learning environments. *Journal of Computers*, *2*(4), 1–8.

Project K-Nect. (2008). Retrieved from: www.projectknect.org/Project%20K-Nect/Home.html

Sedighian, K., & Sedighian, A. S. (1996). Can educational computer games help educators learn about the psychology of learning mathematics in children? In *18th Annual Meeting of the International Group for the Psychology of Mathematics Education* (pp. 573–578). Florida.

Shin, N., Norris, C., & Soloway, E. (2006, June–July). Effects of handheld games on students learning in mathematics. In *Proceedings of the 7th International Conference on Learning Sciences* (pp. 702–708). June 27–July 1. Indiana University, Bloomington.

Shin, N., Sutherland, L. M., Norris, C., & Soloway, E. (2011). Effects of game technology on elementary student learning in mathematics. *British Journal of Educational Technology*. DOI:10.1111/j.1467–8535.2011.01197.x

Virvou, M., & Tsiriga, V. (2000). Involving effectively teachers and students in the life cycle of an intelligent tutoring system. *Educational Technology & Society*, *3*(3), 511–521.

41

BECOMING A DIGITAL NOMAD[1]

Transforming Education Through Mobile Devices

Sharon Stoerger

Mobile technologies are evolving at an extraordinary rate. Along with these changes come new ways of thinking about how to do things. A smartphone, for example, can be used for activities beyond making telephone calls. These devices can be used to connect to the Internet, take pictures, and record videos, as well as send and receive information. With a mobile device, learning can become ubiquitous. Students with a mobile device have the ability to access information at their fingertips, which enables them to learn while standing in line at the store, taking a break at work, or waiting for the bus. The educational opportunities are endless.

This chapter will begin by examining the recent adoption figures associated with mobile devices. Following an overview of current and anticipated m-learning trends, a brief discussion about theoretical lenses through which to view this type of educational approach, such as George Siemens' concept of connectivism, will be presented. These segments will serve to frame an examination of the mobile initiatives that are taking place at one university located in the Midwest region of the United States. And, finally, this chapter will explore the potential of mobile devices for teaching and learning, as well as the challenges educators may face when undertaking mobile initiatives.

M-LEARNING: WHY IS IT IMPORTANT?

Young adults own a variety of gadgets, including mobile devices. According to recent figures, almost 90 percent of non-students in the 18–24 age cohort own mobile phones; the numbers for college students are even higher (Smith, Rainie, & Zickuhr, 2011). A recent EDUCAUSE Center for Applied Research (ECAR) report indicates that a large number of undergraduate students own approximately 12 digital devices (Grunwald Associates LLC, 2011). These devices range from laptop computers, to smartphones, to thumb drives, to webcams. At present, tablet ownership among students remains at the low end of the scale (Grunwald Associates LLC, 2011), but this is expected to change quickly. For instance, a survey conducted by the Pearson Foundation revealed that 70 percent of college-age students would like to own a tablet; 20 percent of those individuals planned to purchase one within 6 months (Finkel & Aspey, 2011, n.p.). If the adoption of mobile devices continues along this trajectory, reports suggest that, in 5 years, there will be more tablets than computers in schools (Hughs, 2011).

Currently, much of the use of mobile devices is for personal reasons. In these situations, many students are using mobile devices to create, communicate, and connect with others from around the world. The education community is beginning to recognize this development. For instance, the *Horizon Report*—a publication that has been produced annually since 2005—identifies emerging technologies that may impact education in the next 5 years. The 2011 report (New Media Consortium, 2011) in particular recognizes the adoption trends of mobile technologies and describes the impact these devices may have on the future of education. More specifically, this report lists mobile computing as a technology to watch and places it in its near-term adoption horizon, which is approximately 12 months.

Historically, however, change in education takes place slowly (e.g., Rainie & Hitlin, 2005). Although the students are bringing these devices to campus, the research also suggests that their use of these tools for academic purposes is often minimal (Smith, Caruso, & Kim, 2010). As the devices become increasingly integrated into the lives of students and their instructors, there are signs that these patterns are beginning to change. The focus is shifting from rote learning, which provided individuals with the knowledge needed for the Industrial Age, to the ability to create and understand (Pink, 2006). In an attempt to give students the skills needed to successfully compete in the 21st century, a greater number of instructors are beginning to investigate the use of mobile devices to enhance the teaching and learning processes.

M-LEARNING RESEARCH AND THEORETICAL FRAMEWORKS

Education Theories

Typically, schools have adopted a teacher-centered approach, with practices that adhere to behaviorist notions. Behaviorism, with its emphasis on behavior management, stresses lower-order thinking skills such as memorization and recall; higher-order thinking skills that involve the synthesis and analysis of content are difficult to teach using the behaviorism format. However, recent technological developments have generated renewed interest in more student-centered theories, such as constructivism. The constructivist epistemology suggests that the physical world contains no meaning per se; rather, individuals and cultures impose meaning on the world. Situated learning that takes place in authentic settings and guided discovery are examples of activities that support constructivist ideals.

Bonk and Cunningham (1998) argue that emerging technological developments make the concepts put forth by social constructivists such as Vygotsky now possible. However, other educational scholars assert that a new education theory is needed. Connectivism is one concept that has been put forth as a theory that might better frame discussions about educational uses of emerging technologies.

Connectivism: An Alternative Educational Epistemology

Some educational scholars have recognized that the technology is changing the ways in which information is disseminated and knowledge is acquired. As a result, the theories that were relevant in the past may be lacking and limited in these digitally enhanced spaces. It is also noted that the acquisition of knowledge is no longer a linear process. Moreover, scholars such as George Siemens believe that traditional educational models are not meeting the needs of today's students, and stress the need for new educational theories. Connectivism is one construct that emphasizes assessing the importance of information and linking it to the right people (Siemens, 2004). The idea behind connectivism is that the learner is at the center of the experience—not the instructor or the institution.

Technology is enabling students to connect to one another as a way to manage the glut of information and create knowledge (Siemens, 2008). The focus is no longer on rote learning or memorization. Instead, effectively navigating and filtering information are important. The ability to connect with information and resources at the point of need is essential, as well. With mobile devices, those learning connections can take place when students are in the classroom, at home, or on the go.

M-LEARNING: OPPORTUNITIES AND CHALLENGES

Opportunities

In the *Horizon Report* (New Media Consortium, 2011), social computing, digital storytelling, educational gaming, visualization, and simulation are described. These examples are meta-trends that work well via mobile devices. Through the use of mobile devices, instructors are also able to blend formal and informal learning opportunities. Although this remains a budding area of research and implementation for many educational outlets, Abilene Christian University (ACU) is an institution that has been investigating learning via mobile devices for several years. They first kicked off their m-learning initiative, Connected, in 2008. That project relies on the use of Apple mobile devices (i.e., iPads, iPods) and began with a focus on the consumption of data. As their instructors and students more readily used these devices, the activities expanded to include content creation, data collection, and transforming learning to be a mobile experience (e.g., Abilene Christian University, 2010–2011). Based on ACU's research findings, the devices have fostered favorable results. These include richer learning experiences—ones that have energized their students and faculty (Abilene Christian University, 2009–2010). These data suggest that mobile devices have the potential to enhance learning.

Mobile devices also provide educators a variety of options to rethink teaching and learning. In a sense, this technology can enable them to become "teacherprenueurs." These devices can support instruction that takes place inside the classroom, but they can also encourage learning activities that take place outside these four walls. With a mobile device, students can search and access information in real time, as well as share their findings with the class, often with the touch of a button. In addition, these students can access information in different locations—they can go outside to gather information from their physical environment.

Alternative-reality (i.e., augmented-reality) options that are accessible via a mobile device blur the lines between the physical world and the technology. One example is Harvard University's EcoMOBILE (Ecosystems Mobile Outdoor Blended Immersive Learning Environment; http://ecomobile.gse.harvard.edu/) project, which blends together science instruction, the physical world, and mobile devices. In the classroom, students learn about the scientists who study ecosystems. That knowledge is reinforced and extended when they collect data via a mobile device on a field trip to a pond ecosystem.

This example illustrates that the mobility of the device enabled students to engage in positive educational experiences. Attempting to complete this activity with a less portable device would have been difficult, if not impossible. However, there are challenges associated with the successful implementation of these and other m-learning opportunities, as well.

Challenges

Challenges some instructors may face include institutional bans on mobile devices, reliance upon the technology solely as a push-down communication tool, and "shovelware" dissemination of content, just to name a few. Currently, there are a number of structural issues and barriers that impede the adoption of mobile devices in educational settings. In this environment, pilot studies on the educational uses of mobile devices are important. Also, the m-learning products must be easy for instructors to use and integrate into their curricula. It is not the responsibility of the instructors and/or the students to make these products fit their lives; rather, the producers need to recognize that innovation does not always equal success, particularly if that means that the innovative product is unusable.

As has been noted, technology is popular with young people. More than 50 percent of undergraduate students who participated in a recent ECAR study own a smartphone (Grunwald Associates LLC, 2011). However, the numbers of students who own an e-reader or a tablet (e.g., iPad) are much lower, at 12 percent and 8 percent, respectively. Cost is one factor that can impact the ownership of these mobile devices—the lower the cost, the greater the number of individuals who can afford to buy them. Although the prices of some mobile devices, including smartphones, are dropping, the accompanying data plans offered by the service providers can be prohibitive. Students may have plans for unlimited talk and texting; however, they may not be able to afford similar data plans. There are signs that service providers are experimenting with innovative pricing structures. For example, "data snacking," or having 3G data services for a particular period of time for a set price is one idea that is proving to be successful in the UK and Malaysia (Panganiban, 2010). With this type of pricing option, a larger number of students may be able to afford to "snack" on data as they learn by doing.

Mobile devices enable students to readily access and collect information, as well as create and share content while they are navigating the physical-world environment. The computing power is lower on a mobile device than on a less portable device such as a laptop. However, the ability to use the technology to support and enhance anytime, anywhere learning opportunities can be powerful. As Wingkvist and Ericsson (2010) suggest, the focus should be on what mobile devices allow instructors to do with their students that they could not do otherwise. Stated another way, with pedagogically sound use, mobile devices can take the educational experience to a new level.

DIGITAL NOMADS: COLLEGE STUDENTS LEARNING ON THE MOVE

Devices advocated by technology enthusiasts do not always integrate well into the formal classroom structure. Typically, courses must be redesigned in order to accommodate emerging technologies. As part of these efforts, an examination of student activities and instructor roles when using technologies such as mobile devices is needed to determine best practices. The next section describes an m-learning curricular redesign initiative that is taking place at a university located in the Midwest region of the United States.

M-Learning Projects

In fall 2009, this institution of around 30,000 students began a pilot study on student response systems (i.e., clickers). The current figures suggest that approximately 15,000 of the students on campus own a clicker, and, at this institution, about 50 course sections a semester are using clickers. Although clicker devices are mobile, the information gleaned from them is very lean. A clicker can capture students' responses to comprehension questions and spark discussion, but there is little potential for qualitative feedback or an ongoing dialogue. This is true even as the campus moves to using smartphones as clickers.

To expand upon this work, as well as the educational opportunities for students, a curricular redesign project was launched to examine the use of mobile devices and related applications in the teaching and learning processes. For the purposes of this project, a device was considered mobile if it was portable, small, and light enough to be carried regularly in a pocket or a purse (see eLearning Guild, 2007). Although laptops and netbooks are portable, they are not as ubiquitous, intimate, or embedded in the lives of students as a smartphone, for example (e.g., Puentedura, 2011).

Instructors from across campus were invited to submit proposals outlining ways they would incorporate mobile devices into their courses. Nine instructors, from disciplines ranging from comparative literature to Japanese film to clinical laboratory studies were selected to participate in this project. In these courses, students are given the opportunity to complete a variety of assignments using mobile devices. For example, some instructors have asked students to identify and evaluate mobile apps that complement content presented in the required text. In courses such as Jewish studies, students are using mobile devices to make connections between the course content and items identified in the local community. Students involved in this project are also attending local events and "checking in" via tools such as Foursquare on their mobile devices. Examples of mobile assignments at this university also include capturing rich media such as audio, pictures, and videos with their mobile devices, to create digital stories. Not only are students creating stories, but they are enhancing them, as well. After watching students struggle with adding English subtitles to Japanese films, one instructor is convinced that tablets, in particular, have the capacity to simplify this process. He planned to test out this idea during the spring 2012 semester.

Student Mobile Device Ownership and Use

When this mobile initiative was launched, one unknown variable was the proliferation of these devices among the students on our campus. Of the students who have responded to the surveys thus far in the project, 98 percent own some type of mobile device. General cell phones and iPhones top the student-ownership list, at 30 percent each. Much lower figures are given for tablet devices, and only iPads have been mentioned by students. Android figures reported by students, in general, have been much lower compared with Apple products.

Given that a high percentage of students are bringing some type of mobile device to campus, what are they doing with them? The top mobile activities reported by the students have been text messaging and taking pictures. Sending photos and accessing the Internet are also very popular uses of mobile devices with students. Lower on the list, but still popular with students, are playing games and accessing social media.

Downloading apps is another activity that the majority of students have carried out using their mobile device. Many of these apps are for personal and recreational use. Although the students were typically using their mobile devices less frequently for social media and games, apps in these two categories were at the top of their download list. Interestingly, news and weather apps were also mentioned frequently by students. Not as surprising were the high numbers of downloaded apps related to music, entertainment, and movies. Downloading apps related to banking/finance and communication was somewhat popular with students as well, but these figures were lower compared with the recreational apps.

At this point, it appears that the students in this project are actively using their mobile devices. However, there are some types of task that have lower adoption rates. Students may be taking pictures while on the go, but fewer of them are posting those items online using their mobile device. Tagging pictures via a mobile device is also an "unpopular" mobile activity with students. They are also not frequently using their devices to capture and post videos or record audio. One of the least popular uses of mobile devices by students is sharing their location with others.

The M-Learning Experience: The Positives

As the earlier section suggests, students are frequent users of mobile devices and are using them for a wide range of activities. The assumption was that, because of this use, students would also enjoy having the ability to use their devices to learn, when and where it is convenient for them. For the most part, that assumption was validated by the students' responses to the survey. In general, the students in this project were happy with their m-learning experience. The majority of students claimed that the mobile devices were beneficial to the learning process and helped them understand concepts covered in the class. As one student in a language learning course remarked, "My mobile device was initially used to help me understand key concepts in class that I could not find from other resources, such as how to learn sounds."

A large number of students also asserted that the use of these devices helped them perform better in the course. Moreover, students noted that the integration of mobile activities into the curriculum was a good use of their time and supported their learning outside the classroom. As one student said, "Downloading apps helped me study in my free time at work. Something I would not have been able to do without mobile device." Another student indicated that successfully completing the course may have been difficult for her without the use of mobile devices: "Using the pinyin/ character app [Chinese language course] really helped me find a lot of extra time to study, which really helped me catch back up after I fell behind because of family matters." These findings are consistent with studies on mobile devices and learning (see Finkel & Aspey, 2011).

A point students mentioned repeatedly is that the use of the mobile devices made learning enjoyable and game-like. One student described the m-learning experience in the following manner: "I felt that it allowed us to better connect. We could study and it was more fun than actually studying with the text book. Using apps means the possibilities are endless." Not only did mobile devices make learning enjoyable for many students, but they also made classroom assignments feel less like work, even for students who were new to this concept:

> This is the first class I have had that introduced a mobile device as a new way to continue learning outside of class. I think that it made learning at home a lot more fun, and practicing a lot easier.

A student summarized the freedom and flexibility m-learning affords like this:

> Everything flowed smoothly for me, and I loved the fact that I could access all my course content at my fingertips, wherever I was. It helped stay up to date on the class and I didn't feel tied down to a computer all the time.

The M-Learning Experience: Areas for Improvement

Although the responses from the students using mobile devices in their courses were overwhelmingly positive, they did identify areas for improvement. In general, the students thought the instructors should increase the use of the mobile devices in the classroom. Students also wanted to use their devices more often for research activities and for presenting information to the class. Although a large number of apps are free or inexpensive, students, particularly in the medical courses, claimed that the costs of these mobile materials became a concern. In fact, they indicated that instructors should point them toward more free apps.

The instructors participating in this project were relying heavily on iPads to design and implement their course activities. However, not all students had access to an Apple mobile device, and this was problematic for students who owned Android devices. Even though a small number of students noted that they owned Android devices, they stated that instructors should identify apps that work on those devices, too. In addition, students recognized that the device determines the use. Stated another way, many indicated that a better device, such as a smartphone, would have enabled them to become more involved in the mobile activities. Another observation was that the costs associated with the data plans for the mobile devices were a deterrent, which has been an issue noted in the literature.

At this institution, almost all courses utilize the same course-management system (CMS). Although the CMS is not the focus of the projects mentioned in this paper, students voiced complaints about using it while on the go. On a mobile device, two different versions of the CMS can be accessed—the desktop version or the mobile version. Students who accessed the mobile CMS pointed out that it was difficult to use. They continued by stating that the CMS should be more user friendly.

Despite the issues that have surfaced, the students' responses thus far to the use of mobile devices have been favorable, and the experience has left them clamoring for more. As the following student remarked, the use of mobile devices should not be viewed as unique, but rather as tools that are part of everyday life:

> I think mobile technology in the classroom/university sphere is an asset. Mobile devices are with students all the time, and they are accessed probably more than computers. Making information readily available to students via mobile technology keeps the university up to date with the current student lifestyle.

The Instructor M-Learning Experience

The focus at this point in the mobile project has been on the student experience. However, mobile devices can also change the way instructors approach their teaching tasks. One instructor commented that tablets have changed the way he approaches tasks, as well as the way he uses other technologies. Even though he has a very portable laptop (i.e., a MacBook Air), he finds himself reaching more frequently for the mobile tablet.

Another instructor also observed that using mobile devices had a positive impact on her classes. In her classes, she focused on the use of apps to enhance the course content. Like the students, she noted that the apps enabled students to review challenging concepts in a game-like fashion. She also discovered that the mobile apps made the students more active in the course, encouraged them to communicate with each other, and allowed them to feel more in control of their learning of the course materials. According to this instructor, these activities helped students retain key course content and do better on assessments. Although this instructor indicated that students were typically excited about the use of mobile devices, she did observe that there were exceptions. In this case, she realized that the less enthusiastic mobile users were students who lacked an interest in technological advancement in general.

As was the case with the students, the instructors did not find it difficult to use the technology. Rather, the instructors remarked that time was their biggest challenge. More specifically, finding time to determine which apps would be most appropriate for their students was the main problem they encountered when using the mobile devices. Overall, however, the benefits associated with learning anytime, anywhere outweighed any negatives. As one instructor noted, "The main advantage was giving the students the opportunity to have knowledge at their fingertips."

DISCUSSION AND CONCLUSION: BECOMING DIGITAL NOMADS

We live in an information-rich world that is becoming increasingly connected. In this environment, individuals have to be continuous, lifelong learners. At present, however, many of our students view school as irrelevant and insignificant (Wesch, 2008). Reports suggest that young people go to school to meet people face to face and experience formal learning; they go home and use their mobile devices to connect with their social group and engage in informal learning activities (e.g., Becta, 2009). Because students are coming to class armed with technologies that support formal and informal learning, educators can capitalize on the affordances of these tools to create more meaningful educational experiences. Mobile devices may be the key to unlocking student capabilities in ways that transform the educational experience.

With mobile devices, students are able to become digital nomads who are truly able to learn anywhere, anytime, and with anyone. Based on student comments, mobile devices allow them to make the most of a few extra moments in their day. For some students, they did not feel tied down to the computer when learning. They were able to access course materials and complete activities while taking a break at work, for example, rather than waiting until they got home and had access to a computer to learn. Also, students indicated that learning via a mobile device did not feel like a chore; instead, the work they put into the class was fun and game-like. More work is needed to gain additional insight into the impact of mobile devices on education. However, at this point in this mobile initiative, the response from students and instructors participating has been overwhelmingly positive. In fact, both groups have placed requests for greater use of mobile devices for teaching and learning.

There are signs suggesting that we are on the path toward a mobile society. Thus, creating educational opportunities that capitalize on the affordances of mobile devices may enable students to become digital nomads—individuals who gather information and knowledge as they move from one learning location to another.

NOTE

1   The term "digital nomad" comes from the 1997 book *Digital Nomads*, by Tsugio Makimoto and David Manners.

REFERENCES

Abilene Christian University. (2009–2010). *ACU mobile learning report*. Retrieved from: www.acu.edu/technology/mobilelearning/documents/ACU2009-10MobileLearningReport.pdf

Abilene Christian University. (2010–2011). *ACU mobile learning report*. Retrieved from: www.acu.edu/technology/mobilelearning/documents/acu-mobile-learning-report-2010-11.pdf

Becta. (2009). *Narrowing the gap: An exploration of the ways technology can support approaches to narrowing the gap for underachieving and low-achieving learners in secondary schools*. Retrieved from: www.academia.edu/1578121/Narrowing_the_gap_An_exploration_of_the_ways_technology_can_support_approaches_to_narrowing_the_gap_for_underachieving_and_low-achieving_learners_in_

Bonk, C. J., & Cunningham, D. J. (1998). Searching for learner-centered, constructivist, and sociocultural components of collaborative educational learning tools. In C. J. Bonk & K. S. King (Eds.), *Electronic collaborators: Learner-centered technologies for literacy, apprenticeship, and discourse* (pp. 25–50). Mahwah, NJ: Erlbaum.

eLearning Guild. (2007). *Mobile learning 260 research report*. Santa Rosa, CA: eLearning Guild.

Finkel, S., & Aspey, S. (2011). New survey: Students who own tablets more likely to favor digital textbooks. *Pearson Foundation*. Retrieved from: www.pearsonfoundation.org/pr/new-survey-students-who-own-tablets-more-likely-to-favor-digital-textbooks.html

Grunwald Associates LLC. (2011). *ECAR national study of undergraduate students and information technology, 2011—Infographic (Infographic)*. Boulder, CO: EDUCAUSE Center for Applied Research. Retrieved from: www.educause.edu/ecar

Hughs, N. (2011). Schools expect to have more iPads than computers in the next 5 years. *Apple insider*. Retrieved from: www.appleinsider.com/articles/11/10/31/schools_expect_to_have_more_ipads_than_computers_in_next_5_years.html

Makimoto, T., & Manners, D. (1997). *Digital nomads*. Hoboken, NJ: Wiley.

New Media Consortium. (2011). *Horizon report 2011*. Retrieved from: http://net.educause.edu/ir/library/pdf/HR2011.pdf

Panganiban, M. (2010). A year of 3G in Vietnam: How attracting the young can accelerate growth. *NielsenWire*. Retrieved from: http://blog.nielsen.com/nielsenwire/global/a-year-of-3g-in-vietnam-how-attracting-the-young-can-accelerate-growth/

Pink, D. (2006). *A whole new mind: Why right-brainers will rule the future*. New York: Riverhead Books.

Puentedura, R. (2011, June). *The lively sketchbook tells a tale: Digital storytelling and mobile devices*. Paper presented at the 2011 NMC Summer Conference, June 14–18, Madison, WI. Retrieved from: http://hippasus.com/resources/nmc2011/Puentedura_LivelySketchbookTellsTale.pdf

Rainie, L., & Hitlin, P. (2005). The Internet at school. *Pew Internet & American Life Project*. Retrieved from: www.pewInternet.org/Reports/2005/The-Internet-at-School/Data-Memo/Findings.aspx?r=1

Siemens, G. (2004). Connectivism: A learning theory for the digital age. *Elearnspace everything elearning*. Retrieved from: www.elearnspace.org/Articles/connectivism.htm

Siemens, G. (2008). *Learning and knowing in networks: Changing roles for educators and designers*. Paper 105: University of Georgia IT Forum. Retrieved from: http://it.coe.uga.edu/itforum/Paper105/Siemens.pdf

Smith, A., Rainie, L., & Zickuhr, K. (2011). College students and technology. *Pew Internet and American Life Project*. Retrieved from: www.pewInternet.org/Reports/2011/College-students-and-technology/Report.aspx

Smith, S., Caruso, J. B., & Kim, J. (2010). ECAR study of undergraduate students and information technology, 2010. *EDUCAUSE*. Retrieved from: www.educause.edu/Resources/ECARStudyofUndergraduateStuden/217333

Wesch, M. (2008). Anti-teaching: Confronting the crisis of significance. *Education Canada, 48*(2), 4–7. Retrieved from: https://scholar.vt.edu/access/content/group/5deb92b5-10f3-49db-adeb-7294847f1ebc/Wesch_Anti_Teaching_Confronting%20the%20Crisis%20of%20Significance.pdf

Wingkvist, A., & Ericsson, M. (2010). A framework to guide and structure the development process of mobile learning initiatives. In M. Montebello et al., *mLearn 2010 Conference Proceedings.*

42

MOBILE-MEDICINE PRAXIS

Richard Brandt and Rich Rice

Telemedicine is an umbrella term that includes the use of electronic communication devices and networking, software, and protocols by health care professionals as a cost-effective means of providing high-quality health care and communication between patients and professionals at disparate locations. More specifically, "telemedicine" is translated from the Latin *medicus* and the Greek *tele*, and is defined as "healing at a distance" (Strehle & Shabde, 2006, p. 956). Telemedicine may also be referred to as "e-health" (Karkalis & Koutsouris, 2006), based on the popularized nomenclature of adding *e-* to all things electronically enhanced, such as e-mail, e-learning, e-portfolio, and e-filing. As technological devices have advanced, such as smartphones and tablets, polymorphic platforms such as video chats, wikis, and blogs have increasingly made use of Web 2.0 technologies; telemedical practitioners' creativity has also similarly evolved. Ease of use and increasingly affordable pricing have facilitated a near ubiquitous following within the general public and medical profession alike, and this ubiquity enables health care professionals to enhance patient care and health education in "diagnosis, consultation, treatment, and teaching" (Wurm, Hofmann-Wellenhof, Wurm, & Soyer, 2008, p. 106).

Although the exact origins of telemedicine are not clearly documented, telemedicine scholar Richard Wootton (2001) has popularized the example of deployed sea captains using ship-to-shore radios to seek medical advice from land-based physicians (p. 557). Where time and location distance exist between those who have medical knowledge and those who need it, so does the need for telemedicine. Just a few decades later than the use of ship-to-shore radios to facilitate telemedicine, the development of fax machines, cellular phones, webcams, databases, the Internet, mobile media tools, software, and networking have allowed clinicians, scholars, and researchers to advance dimensions and specialties of modern medicine. The increased mobility of Wi-Fi-enabled devices, for instance, as well as the use of retooled, real-time videoconferencing platforms, has more recently redefined collaborative medical consultation practices, and has done so within a variety of contexts. In particular, tablet-based *mobile-medicine* makes use of consumer-grade, portable devices equipped with Web 2.0 technologies, coupled with a directive to promote more divergent knowledge creation, embrace user-guided problem-based learning, provide real-time access to immediately relevant information, and increase health care benefits with untethered mobility. A potential benefit of divergent knowledge creation and user-guided problem-based learning (PBL), for instance, is that adult learners in particular have an interest in deciphering their own health ailments, and such awareness may result in discovering signs of personal health problems and seeking expertise earlier.

In this chapter, we review the origins of telemedicine, relevant mobile devices and technologies in connection with divergent knowledge creation and PBL, and real-world medical implementations and uses for these advancements in the delivery of medicine. Furthermore, we relate the use of mobile-medicine in clinical practice and implications that such a pedagogical platform may entail. Finally, we discuss ways in which such methodologies may come to impact global health care consumers.

INTRODUCTION: A SELECT HISTORY OF TELEMEDICINE

Telemedicine as "medicine at a distance" incorporates medical advice, collaboration, assessment, diagnosis, treatment, and education (Wootton, 1996, p. 1375). Such efforts are often categorized as store-and-forward (SAF), remote monitoring, or real-time interaction (LI: live interaction). One early, detailed and documented account of medicine at a distance, which begins to use all three categories, is that of a Dutch physiologist, Willem Einthoven, who developed the first electrocardiograph (ECG/EKG) in his Leiden laboratory. "With the use of galvanometer and telephone wires, he recorded the electrical cardiac [heart] signals of patients in a hospital 1½ km away" (Strehle & Shabde, 2006, p. 956). He further stated: "Where there is a link, actual and figurative, between laboratory and hospital, and collaboration between physiologist and clinician, each remaining in his territory, there one may fruitfully utilize these new electrical methods of research" (Strehle & Shabde, 2006, p. 956). Einthoven's results were published in 1906. Earlier, of course, African villagers used smoke signals, and people living in remote areas of Australia used two-way radios. Many other examples also point out the value of medicine at a distance. In each case, there are challenges related to cost and distance, lack of acceptance early on is common, and there are frequently cultural and experiential barriers.

Sometimes, the timing is right for new technology adaptation and implementation, however. In 1949, the founder of the Citizens Radio Corporation, Al Gross, adapted his 1938 two-way radio for "cordless remote telephonic signaling" (Lemelson-MIT Program, 2000, p. 1). Gross invented the mobile pager, in other words, and, from its inception, intended it to be used by physicians. In the same year, he attended a medical conference in Philadelphia to introduce his device to the profession, and, in the following year, the Jewish Hospital in New York implemented the technology (Lemelson-MIT Program, 2000). There is a long history of new devices changing the nature of practitioner research and patient care. Increasingly, technologies are adapted and implemented even more quickly, but legal implications require significant research study and testing, and even that testing can be done remotely.

Breen and Matusitz (2010), citing Turner (2003) and the work of Wittson and Benschoter (1972), conclude the "first telemedicine [research] study" was conducted in 1959 by the Nebraska Psychiatric Institute and the Norfolk State Hospital in Nebraska, whereby closed-circuit microwave television-like signals enabled bidirectional medical research and education at a distance (p. 62). Again, common themes in the study include issues related to cost and distance, and cultural acceptance. Also around this time, AT&T developed videoconferencing technology, basically as we know it today, which allowed for audio and video two-way communication, and AT&T presented the technology at the 1964 World's Fair in New York. Although official use of video-conferencing in medicine around this time is undocumented, multiple colleges and universities first adopted such technologies early, and wholesale in the 1980s for teaching and training purposes (Indiana Telehealth Network, 2009, p. 6).

Rollett, Lux, Strohmaier, Dosinger, and Tochterman (2007), as well as Licklider and Taylor (1968), identified the computer as a medical profession communication device as early as 1968, and, by the 1970s, the profession began using teleradiology programs that eventually led to picture archiving and communication systems (PACS). These technologies afforded practitioners at a distance access to X-rays, computed tomography scans, magnetic resonance imagery, and ultrasound scans (Strehle & Shabde, 2006, p. 956). Thus, in addition to specific technologies impacting practice, the distribution of the products of such advances plays a key role in telemedicine.

There is no greater distribution tool than the Internet. The Advanced Research Projects Agency Network project, based on the work of Lawrence Roberts at the Lincoln Laboratory (c. 1968), was the first operational packet switching network that has since come to represent global communication and connection capabilities as the Internet. In 1971, Ray Tomlinson of Bolt, Beranek, and Newman Technologies sent the first network e-mail. By 1982, the simple mail transfer protocol became the standard for sending and receiving packaged electronic messages. Local area networks and personal computers quickly enabled professionals and the public outside the military to communicate online.

Related, by the mid 1980s, fax machines were globally integrated and came to serve as a popular, relatively low-cost communication medium for hospital and medical personnel. Faxes are still commonplace and widely used today in medically advanced health care settings across the world. Electronic mail and faxes convey content in specific ways: The *ethos* of a hospital or medical professional's letterhead and signature may be retained, legal information can be presented as it must be explained to patients by medical professionals, and standardization for scalable record-keeping and quick referencing can also be maintained. Ubiquity, relative low cost, accuracy of presentation, and potential for storage and scalability are key traits of more recent mobile-medicine technologies as well.

In the 1990s, 2G digitalized mobile cellular phones were introduced, and as they quickly became ubiquitous in many countries, they quickly were used for professional peer-to-peer (P2P) medical consultation practices. Mobile phones are used today in telemedicine exchanges, but the emergence of mobile media tools has enhanced their effectiveness. CERN released the World Wide Web (WWW) in 1993 to the public, and Ward Cunningham first devised a collaborative wiki platform in 1995 (Rollett et al., 2007, p. 6). Although Web 1.0 and wikis both play an integral role in modern medical practice, with the use of mobile technology, Web 2.0 plays an even greater role. For instance, Eric Fossum and his team first developed the CMOS active pixel sensor in the early 1990s, and Philippe Kahn first shared real-time pictures of his newborn daughter around the world in 1997. By 2003, world purchases of camera-ready cellular phones

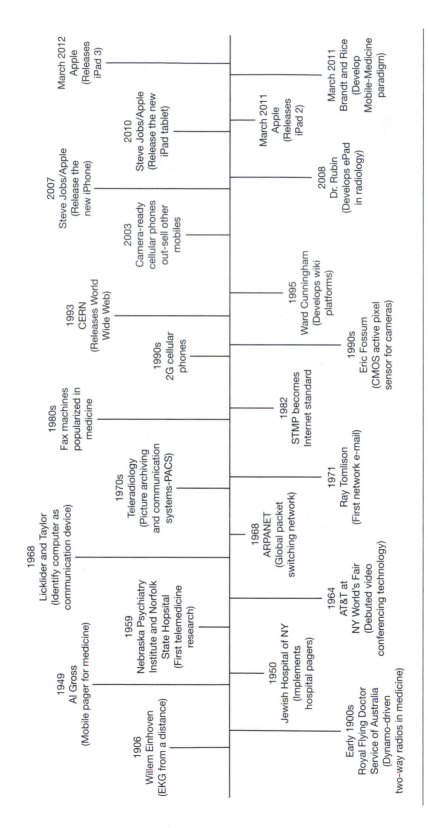

Figure 42.1 Telemedicine Timeline

outnumbered the sale of mobile phones without cameras. Figure 42.1 demonstrates the explosion of new technologies along this select telemedicine timeline. We are now at the beginning stages of the potential of mobile-medicine telemedicine technologies.

POPULATION SERVED: CURRENT USES OF MOBILE TELEMEDICINE

The incorporation of small, mobile, ubiquitous devices such as tablets and smartphones into modern medical practice has become widely accepted and commonly practiced across many specialties. One factor is the adoption rate of mobile Apple products among clinicians. A May 2011 poll revealed that "a whopping 75 percent of U.S. physicians own some form of Apple device" (Miliard, 2011, p. 42). Thirty percent of physician-owned Apple devices were iPads, and 28 percent of physicians surveyed were planning to purchase an iPad tablet by year's end (Manhattan Research Company, 2011, p. 1).

Telemedicine Examples Using Mobile Technologies
A sample of recent strides in mobile telemedicine follows. Each of these telecare solutions is integrated through specifically designed native mobile applications customized for specific devices and operating systems, or they are designed to work through standard Internet-based portals accessible on popular mobile smartphones and tablets.

Teleradiology and PACS in California
PACS, used for the transfer and accessing of radiology images, typically do not allow pertinent semantic data to be embedded or retrieved with a standardized interpretable format. In 2008, however, Stanford researchers and physicians presented a radiology "ePad," which allowed imagery data (e.g., average lesion size and links to comparable disease images) and non-imagery data (e.g., patient symptomatology and electronic medical records) to be easily accessed, compared, and analyzed by the physician radiologist (Rubin, Rodriguez, Shah, & Beaulieu, 2008).

Teleendocrinology and Diabetes in Spain
Since 2008, diabetes-management specialists in Spain have used computer supportive collaborative work (CSCW) to facilitate "supervised autonomy" for diabetic patient glucose monitoring and treatment. Under the direction of a physician-led diabetic nursing team, a mobile "shared care" suite functions to allow registered patients to: (1) access multichannel messaging services that allow electronic message exchange in any application format, (2) share information with disseminated group distribution, and (3) coordinate individual office visits and small-group meetings (Martinez-Sarriegui et al., 2008). The CSCW is a model for programs elsewhere.

Teledermatology and Eczema in Norway
Schopf, Bolle, and Solvoll (2010) have studied a secure, Web-based counseling system that is accessible by any personal computer or mobile Web browser, and affords physician feedback on patient-generated updates and photos (p. 4). Clinician responses were frequently sent to the database in SMS format. Their conclusion is that home-based follow-ups are "feasible" (Schopf et al., 2010, p. 3).

Teleemergency Medicine in Canada

In 2010, several Canadian Emergency Department physicians and trauma care professionals implemented an asynchronous wiki-based discussion board that served as a collaborative repository for updating medical education materials, as well as a reminder protocol for promoting policy improvements and health care delivery best practices. Benefits may include updating new knowledge, softening information overload, homogenizing departmental standards, training students, disseminating ideas across rotating work schedules, and improving cost effectiveness (Archambault et al., 2010, p. 1). Of course, similar Web-based content is also readily available on current smartphone platforms.

Telemedicine in Laboratory Sciences in Italy

In 2009, computer scientist Aldo Franco Dragoni revealed "MIRO ON RAILS" a broker-based Internet architecture for medical telereporting to serve as an international repository for laboratory, diagnostic, and health maintenance results. In his words, this was a "step towards our vision of a worldwide Virtual Health Care Agency" (Dragoni, 2009, p. 162).

Teledermatology in Texas

In March 2011, within weeks of the Apple iPad2 release, we began to develop the concept of mobile medicine. One of the authors of this chapter studied and implemented the dual-camera iPad2 mobile tablet in clinical practice for provider-based collaboration during the delivery of patient care. The theory and praxis of mobile-medicine, including outcomes and design, are discussed further below.

OUTCOMES DESIRED: MOBILE-MEDICINE PRAXIS

Mobile-Medicine Defined

Mobile-medicine, thus, is a new, tablet-based, collaborative learning paradigm that engenders mobile, affordable, customizable, and self-directed health care consultation and other andragogical efforts between medical professionals in disparate locations. The protocol is simple and easily implemented, even by less technologically savvy clinicians. As if placing a cellular phone call, any two physicians or health care professionals with camera-ready, mobile devices such as an iPad2, videoconference technologies such as Apple FaceTime, and Wi-Fi connectivity to Web 2.0 connections or content may open a live, real-time video link while examining a patient. The patient may be at a routine visit in a medical center, at a hospital bedside, in an emergency vehicle en route, or even at home. Once secure Wi-Fi access is preconfigured and saved within the mobile device, such a video consultation call requires just three to four finger swipes across the tablet's face (On > FaceTime > select contact > initiate call). Figure 42.2 offers a simulated example of such an interaction. Although the concept is simple, the collaborative clinical implications are dynamic.

Traditional Medical Education

First, it is important to understand how this mobile protocol augments traditional medical learning and professional collaboration, without introducing time-consuming learning processes or impeding the bidirectional transfer of knowledge with cumbersome

Wi-Fi

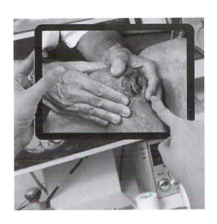

Figure 42.2 Medical Cases Presented Between Clinicians

technology. In the simplest of parlance, most medical-school training is bifurcated into two main learning models: social-constructivism in the early didactic years, and problem-based learning (PBL) in the later, clinically based training. Allied health professionals such as physician assistants (PA) and nurse practitioners (NP) experience similar, although shorter, biphasic-learning models. Regardless of the career path chosen, health care professionals in the world's most medically advanced societies generally complete a rigorous and structured didactic phase, an extended supervised PBL clinical phase, and lifelong continuing medical education efforts to learn of medical improvements and advancements.

Post-graduate, professional practice-based learning and PBL for health care professionals is important because these models: (1) can keep health care providers up to date with newly discovered and advancing medical knowledge, (2) can teach and enhance new procedural skill sets, (3) might facilitate intra-specialty collaboration such as specialist-to-specialist, (4) could foster interdepartmental consultation or specialist-to-generalist, and (5) might improve patient-care outcomes by increasing pertinent and useable knowledge. The culmination of, and the benefits from, such pedagogical efforts will likely affect each of us as patients some day; thus, it should be of paramount importance to us, as educators, technical communicators, practitioners, patients, and scholars, to understand, appreciate, and develop learning models to assist health care professionals and their communication efforts.

Our mobile-medicine paradigm was developed to allow newer mobile technologies to facilitate established and time-honored learning methodologies. Traditional, medically based PBL has been limited by time and space, where a junior clinician could only collaborate with a senior colleague who was in the same building or general vicinity at that time. SAF protocols for taking digital photographs and later forwarding them to a colleague were not timely, and a delay of hours to days impeded the process. LI techniques, which established a live audio–video link between two physicians, required costly and stationary equipment that only slightly remedied the space discrepancy between practitioners. The praxis of mobile-medicine rectifies both concerns, time and space, and allows for immediate, self-directed PBL and collaboration between medical professionals in disparate locations.

For example, my medical group operates two centers, approximately 10 miles apart, that are staffed by two dermatologists (MDs) and two dermatologic PAs. Electronic communication and capabilities must be available and accessible at all times. Traditionally, a clinician seeking consultation with a colleague would be required to discuss the case verbally via telephone or transfer laboratory results via fax technologies. Through the mobile-medicine praxis, Clinician A may place an iPad-based FaceTime call to Clinician B at a different office and facilitate a clear, mobile, and fully interactive collaborative discussion. Our pilot testing revealed high patient acceptance levels, and, unexpectedly, many patients wanted to, and did, interact directly with the consulting dermatologist. HIPAA guidelines, verbal and written informed consent, and patient education are provided to each participant, but an in-depth discussion of such nuances is beyond the scope of this chapter. Ultimately, the praxis of mobile-medicine serves as a self-guided PBL tool that advances both post-graduate physician training and P2P collaboration at the exact point of patient care.

Andragogical Teaching and Learning

Pedagogy is the general study of teaching and learning; andragogy is the more specific study of teaching adult learners. Adult learners have specific needs, according to educational psychologists, such as the need to: (1) know why one is studying a specific subject, (2) access a foundation of knowledge, (3) privilege a self-concept, (4) draw on ready content, (5) establish an immediately relevant orientation, and (6) personally motivate their own learning (Knowles, Holton, & Swanson, 2005). One primary purpose of mobile-medicine is to meet utilitarian needs of medically based, post-graduate teaching and learning andragogical activities, and to further advance the use of ubiquitous technologies to complement such efforts. Underlying learning principles of social–constructivist and PBL models, thus, are directly related.

For instance, social–constructivist models rely on "knowledge that is socially situated and is constructed through reflection on one's own thoughts and experiences, as well as other learners' ideas" (Shieh, 2008, p. 707). This bifurcated model blends knowledge acquisition through authentic cultural and social-based interactions with an active and self-constructed individual educational framework that each learner customizes. The selection of learning methodology and the inherent ownership of the content gathered are fundamental to the success of the mobile-medicine platform; selection further enhances motivation, critical thinking, and collaboration (Zhu, Valcke, & Schellens, 2009, p. 167).

PBL is a student-centered learning model that was initially implemented with medical students so they could learn diagnostic skill sets, develop problem-solving abilities, and enhance critical thinking and decision-making capabilities (Nelson, 2010, p. 99). Although designed for face-to-face (F2F) interactions, PBL researcher Nelson (2010) acknowledges, "courses are being redesigned for delivery online" (p. 100). Mobile technologies enable learners studying to become medical practitioners to interact with patients in more scaffolded environments, connecting instantly to repositories of purposeful content and leading experts. Further, mobile tablet displays can facilitate simulated but clear F2F interaction.

Although not a substitute for F2F communication, mobile-medicine praxis does fulfill human propensity to prefer communication in a "co-located and synchronous manner" in order to mitigate ambiguity (Kock, 2005, p. 119). Kock's media naturalness theory implies that an increase in the naturalness of a communication interaction will: (1) lessen cognitive effort, (2) reduce ambiguity, and (3) increase physiological stimulation (p. 117). According to the theory, our human evolutionary natural-selection processes have served as a catalyst for species-wide genetic enhancements that have improved survival by allowing us to nonverbally communicate with over "6,000 communicative expressions" (p. 120). When time and distance or other social constructs interfere, approximating F2F communication as closely as possible maximizes communication effectiveness.

Enhanced communication between peers, in any profession, leads to better productivity, more robust idea exchange, and more effective development of skill sets. If collaboration between peers laboring to solve a patient's mysterious medical ailment is clearer and more informative, and ultimately more productive, then such media-rich divergent thinking processes are warranted. Robinson, a leader in educational theory, describes divergent thinking as an essential capacity for creativity that increases one's ability to formulate different answers and interpretations for a given question (RSA Animate & Robinson, 2010). The ramifications for patient care and clinical outcomes cannot be overstated; divergent thinking lends itself to identifying a particular ailment's etiology among a potential list of many possibilities more readily.

IMPLICATIONS FOR M-HEALTH

The applications of mobile-medicine and m-health are many. In rural locations in some countries, for instance, where transportation to regional medical services is limited or too slow or even unavailable, but where mobile technology is readily accessible, bridging time and distance through media-rich mobile devices using Web 2.0 technologies is critical. Patients might use mobile-medicine to avoid high-traffic commutes and therefore seek medical advice more frequently. According to a leading research firm on m-health: "Nearly 90 percent of doctors want patients to monitor health indicators such as weight, blood sugar levels, vital signs, etc., via mobile devices" (Jackson, 2012, para 3). Hume describes this "brave new world" through examples such as the Mobisante MobiUS SP1 Ultrasound System, machine-to-machine monitoring trials, the SIMAP (Intelligent Personal Alert Monitoring System), and the Dexcom Seven Plus Continuous Glucose Monitoring System (Hume, 2012).

Ongoing practical training for medical consultants can be scaffolded and more immersive in some cases. Patients en route to a hospital in emergency situations could be connected to the medical practitioner, while in an ambulance, many crucial minutes before arriving. These are all scenarios medical practitioners are currently engaged in, but there are specific areas of consideration worth noting, including: patient satisfaction, legal considerations, and factors related to early implementation. For instance, in 2012, Palomar Pomerado Health in San Diego, California, improved its workflow and culture by developing its own Android medical apps to provide physicians real-time patient information. This mobile-medicine practice enables the specialist and the primary care physician to have access to the same information when consulting live with the patient (O'Neill, 2012, p. 1).

Patient Satisfaction

Warshaw et al. (2011), in a literature review of 78 teledermatology studies, conclude that teledermatology practices have received "relatively high" levels of patient satisfaction over the last 20 years (p. 769). These findings, however, are for LI methods using expensive and cumbersome video-camera equipment, as well as the SAF method of e-mailing digital still photographs to colleagues for collaboration and consultation. A study recently completed by one author of this chapter—including a patient survey reporting patient acceptance of P2P, tablet-based collaboration—found that patients were overwhelmingly accepting of such technologies.

Medical Legal Considerations

As medical practitioners and academicians, we are not attorneys, nor do we claim to offer legal advice. It is comforting to know that the Apple FaceTime brand of tablet-based videoconferencing has been studied and was found to be sufficiently encrypted and HIPAA compliant (Chan & Misra, 2011), which conforms to regulatory and privacy expectations and requirements. No doubt other mobile tablets and their operating systems will work to achieve HIPAA compliancy as well. Furthermore, it is appropriate to receive informed, written consent from each participating individual. Currently, more often than not, the lack of recording and archived imagery does seem reassuring to many patient participants.

Early Implementation Examples

Such archiving and medical report updating will take more time to negotiate culturally and legally. However, the benefits of mobile-medicine are clear. Again, in the ongoing work of one of the authors of this chapter, the Apple iPad2 was used just weeks after its release in March 2011 in a dermatological clinic setting. Research is still being collected at the time of writing this chapter; however, patient and practitioner results are reporting very positively. Similarly, telehealth services provider, Teladoc, which has traditionally offered consumer-to-physician telephone consultation for routine medical concerns, announced plans to incorporate Apple FaceTime technology into its service repertoire in May 2011 (Dolan, 2011, p. 1). Shortly thereafter, in October 2011, Boston radiologist Henry Feldman was featured in a *MacLife* magazine vignette for using FaceTime to "bring a team of doctors right to the [patient's] bedside" (Crythoys, Hayward, Simon, & Vargus, 2011, p. 24).

THE FUTURE OF TABLET-BASED TELEMEDICINE

Although some popular telemedicine protocols and studies—such as *Eczema in Norway* (Schopf et al., 2010)—have been discussed, it is imperative to know that most tablet programs and platforms are either Internet-based or embedded in a device as a "native app." The former allows a tablet's Internet browser to connect to and access a given program's Web-based features; Schopf et al. could easily enact their eczema protocols on a tablet through this process. In contrast, a "native app" is specifically customized to utilize and maximize features of the device or mobile operating system on which it is used. "iPhone apps, for example, can include the ability to notice the tilt angle or motion of the device and adjust accordingly—consider a pinball machine video game or the practical level tool app available for many touch screen phones" (Heise, 2011, p. 1).

Additionally, it is noteworthy that many electronic medical record (EMR) systems are being designed and customized with native app programs. An EMR platform is a stand-alone, computerized, medical charting and health information system utilized within hospitals and physician offices to assist in treatment and care. One example is NexTech Systems, which has produced an industry-leading EMR and practice-management platform, and has enabled "links to photo imaging, CareCredit, Smart Phones, tablet PCs and barcode scanners" (NexTech Systems, Inc., 2012).

Related, the U.S. Health Information Technology for Economic and Clinical Health (HITECH) Act, enacted as part of the American Recovery and Reinvestment Act of 2009 (H.R. 408), was designed to promote the adoption of health information technologies such as EMR systems (HHS.gov, 2012). The goal of this legislation is to induce a complete nationwide acceptance and utilization of electronic medical records. Practitioners will no doubt use mobile-medicine, in large part, to do so.

It is in the convergence of the technological, corporate, and legislative initiatives that mobile-medicine, and other like protocols, can be meaningfully and directly integrated. Imagine a tablet-based videoconferencing platform coupled with real-time, mobile-medicine collaboration paradigms to enhance patient care within an established EMR system that is mandated and incentivized by U.S. Federal law within current, clinical medical practices.

One example of such tablet-based integrated functionality is the PrimeMOBILE native iPad app within the PrimeSUITE 2011, by Greenway Medical Technologies in Carrollton, Georgia. The PrimeMOBILE app provides a clinician remote, password-protected access to a patient's medical records, semantic data, clinical documents, laboratory values, diagnostic imagery, billing information, and prescription history. As illustrated in Figure 42.2, a Wi-Fi-enabled tablet weighing just 1.33lbs can provide and combine many aspects of health care delivery into a single, portable device for use and dissemination. Vascular surgeon Dr. F. John Senkowsky of Arlington, Texas, is an early adopter of PrimeMOBILE technology and has used this platform since its inception, on both iPhone and iPad devices. Senkowsky notes its success and convenience of use (Healthcare IT News, 2011). Many similar support services are being developed every few months across the US and the world.

CONCLUSIONS

The history of telemedicine is wide and varied, but depends directly on the use and implementation of new technologies, access to those technologies, and the ability to use those technologies to teach and disseminate. With wide adoption of Apple devices by U.S. physicians, and with the recent push to enhance mobile telemedicine by medical providers around the globe, it is clear that mobile-medicine is on the rise. The andragogical benefits afforded to health care professionals through inexpensive, P2P, tablet-based, mobile-medicine protocols is also of great interest. While more technology-savvy clinicians are currently utilizing mobile tablet-based devices and platforms, more clinicians are following suit.

Implications for global health are also significant. Many technologically under-developed and medically underserved countries and communities are experiencing a health care crisis in disease treatment and management. "According to the World Health Organization, among 57 countries, mostly in the developing world, there is a critical shortfall in health care workers, representing a total deficit of 2.4 million health care workers worldwide" (Vital Wave Consulting, 2009). As such, the United Nations Foundation maintains a growing list of m-health initiatives focusing on applications and benefits, including remote monitoring, health care training, and treatment support (http://unfoundation.org).

Communications infrastructures in developing communities around the world continue to grow. While conducting field research in the rural farming village of Ragihalli, India, for instance, Levy (2011) noted a local villager who had a cellular phone with "four bars," and he compared this with significant patches in the US "where one can barely pull in a signal" (p. 2). Such advancing global circuitry and communication infrastructure, the invention of improved mobile devices, benefits of videoconferencing platforms, the ease of Internet and cost-effective access, and collaborative andragogical medical protocols such as mobile-medicine stand poised to flatten global health care and help provide more equitable access to medical communication, information, and care.

REFERENCES

Archambault, P. M., Légaré, F., Lavoie, A., Gagnon, M.-P., Lapointe, J., St-Jacques, S., et al. (2010). Healthcare professionals' intentions to use wiki-based reminders to promote best practices in trauma care: a survey protocol. *Implementation Science, 5*(45), 1–9.

Breen, G.-M., & Matusitz, J. (2010). An evolutionary examination of telemedicine: A health and computer-mediated communication perspective. *Social Work in Public Health, 25,* 59–71. DOI:10.1080/19371910902911206

Chan, B., & Misra, S. (2011). *FaceTime is HIPAA compliant and encrypted, could change the way physicians and patients communicate* [Web log post]. Retrieved from: www.imedicalapps.com/2011/09/facetime-hipaacompliant-encrypted-avenue-telemedicine

Crythoys, P., Hayward, A., Simon, M., & Vargus, N. (2011, October). Go all iPad, all the time. *Mac Life, 57,* 18–24.

Dolan, P. L. (2011). Health care embraces the iPad: Doctors jump on new technology. *America Medical News.* Retrieved from: www.amednews.com

Dragoni, A. F. (2009). Stable communications and social networking for the netmedicine of tomorrow (or today). *AIM-Abridged Index Medicus, 17*(3), 161–164.

Healthcare IT News. (2011). *Greenway's PrimeMOBILE available on iPad.* Retrieved from: www.mhimss.org/press-release/greenways-primemobile-available-ipad

Heise, D. (2011). The mobile application: Browser vs. native. *CMS Wire Magazine.* Retrieved from: www.cmswire.com/cms/web-engagement/the-mobile-application-browser-vs-native-010223.php

Hume, T. (2012). Mobiles and medicine: The brave new world of mHealth. *CNN Tech*. Retrieved from: www.cnn.com/2012/02/29/tech/mobile-health

Indiana Telehealth Network. (2009). *Video conferencing eseentials: Telehealth technology—executive summary*. Retrieved from: www.indianaruralhealth.org/clientuploads/ITN/Video.Conferencing.Essentials.ITN.Executive. Summary.Final.%2001052010.pdf

Jackson, S. (2012). Docs want patients to use mHealth apps. *Fierce Mobile Healthcare*. Retrieved from: www.fierce mobilehealthcare.com/story/docs-want-patients-use-mhealth-apps/2012-03-19

Karkalis, G. I., & Koutsouris, D. D. (2006). *E-health and the Web 2.0*. Retrieved from: http://medlab.cs.uoi.gr/ itab2006/proceedings/ehealth/124.pdf

Knowles, M., Holton, E. F., & Swanson, R. A. (2005). *The adult learner: The definitive classic in adult education and human resource development* (6th ed.). Burlington, MA: Elsevier.

Kock, N. (2005). Media richness or media naturalness? The evolution of our biological communication apparatus and its influence on our behavior toward e-communication tools. *IEEE Transactions on Professional Communication, 48*(2), 117–130.

Lemelson–MIT Program. (2000). *Inventor of the week archive: Al Gross*. Retrieved from: http://web.mit.edu/invent/ iow/gross.html

Levy, S. (2011). *In the plex: How Google thinks, works, and shapes our lives*. New York: Simon & Schuster.

Licklider, J., & Taylor, R. (1968). The computer as a communication device. *Science and Technology*. Retrieved from: http://memex.org/licklider.pdf

Manhattan Research Company. (2011). *75 Percent of U.S. physicians own some form of Apple device* (U.S. v11.0 Study). New York: Manhattan Research.

Martinez-Sarriegui, I., Garcia Saez, G., Hernando, M. E., Rigla, M., Brugues, E., de Leiva, A., & Gomez, E. J. (2008). Chapter 8: Mobile telemedicine for diabetes care. In Y. Xiao & H. Chen (Eds.), *Mobile telemedicine* (pp. 143–160). Boca Raton, FL: Auerbach Publications.

Miliard, M., (2011). Smart mobile users tempted by Apple. *Healthcare IT News, July*(42). Retrieved from: Healthcare IT News App for iPad.

Nelson, E. (2010). Elements of problem-based learning: Suggestions for implementation in the asynchronous environment. *International Journal on E-Learning, 9*(1), 99–114.

NexTech Systems, Inc. (2012). *Products and services—NexTech practice 2011* [Data on web page]. Retrieved from: www.nextech.com/Products.aspx

O'Neill, S. (2012). Android on call: Hospital builds custom mobile app for patient data. *Network World*. Retrieved from: www.networkworld.com/news/2012/022412-android-on-call-hospital-builds-256571.html

Rollett, H., Lux, M., Strohmaier, M., Dosinger, G., & Tochterman, K. (2007). The Web 2.0 way of learning with technologies. *International Journal of Learning Technology, 3*(1), 87–108.

RSA Animate (Producer), & Robinson, K. (Author) (2010). RSA Animate—Changing educational paradigms [Video file]. Retrieved from: http://www.youtube.cpm/watch?v=zDZFcDGpL4U

Rubin, D. L., Rodriguez, C., Shah, P., & Beaulieu, C. (2008). iPad: Semantic annotation and markup of radiological images. *Proceedings of AMIA 2008 Symposium*. Washington, DC: AMIA.

Schopf, T., Bolle, R., & Solvoll, T. (2010). The workload of web-based consultations with atopic eczema at home. *BMC Research Notes, 3*(71), 1–4.

Shieh, R. (2008). A case study of constructivist instructional strategies for adult online learning. *British Journal of Educational Technology, 41*(5), 706–720.

Strehle, E. M., & Shabde, N. (2006). One hundred years of telemedicine: Does this new technology have a place in paediatrics? *Archives of Disease in Childhood, 91*, 956–959. DOI:10.1136/adc.2006.099622

Turner J. W. (2003). Telemedicine: Expanding healthcare into virtual environments. In T. L. Thompson, A. M. Dorsey, K. I. Miller, & R. Parrott (Eds.), *Handbook of health communication* (pp. 515–535).

United States Department of Health and Human Services (2012). *HITECH act enforcement interim final rule* [Data on web page]. Retrieved from: www.hhs.gov/ocr/privacy/_hipaa/administrative/enforcementrule/hitech enforcementifr.html

Vital Wave Consulting. (2009). *mHealth for development: The opportunity of mobile technology for healthcare in the developing world*. United Nations Foundation. Retrieved from: http://unpan1.un.org/intradoc/groups/ public/documents/unpan/unpan037268.pdf

Warshaw, E. M., Hillman, Y. J., Greer, N. L., Hagel, E. M., MacDonald, R., Rutks, I. R., & Wilt, T. J. (2011). Teledermatology for diagnosis and management of skin conditions: A systemic review. *Journal of the American Academy of Dermatology, 64*(4), 759–772. DOI: 10.1016/j.jaad.2010.08.026

Wittson, C. L., & Benschoter, R. (1972). Two-way television: Helping the medical center reach out. *American Journal of Psychiatry, 129*, 624–627.

Wootton, R. (1996). Telemedicine: A cautious welcome. *British Medical Journal, 313*, 1375–1377.

Wootton, R. (2001). Recent advances: Telemedicine. *British Medical Journal, 323*, 557–560.

Wurm, E. M. T., Hofmann-Wellenhof, R., Wurm, R., & Soyer, H. P. (2008). Telemedicine and teledermatology: Past, present and future. *JDDG: Journal Der Deutschen Dermatologischen Gesellschaft, 6*(2), 106–112.

Zhu, C., Valcke, M., & Schellens, T. (2009). Cultural differences in the perception of a social-constructivist e-learning environment. *British Journal of Educational Technology, 40*(1), 164–168. DOI:10.1111/j.1467–8535. 2008.00879.x

43

A MOBILE KNOWLEDGE MANAGEMENT SYSTEM FOR MILITARY EDUCATION

Ioana A. Stănescu and Antoniu Ştefan

Technology has become a necessary and everyday part of people's lives, being employed in education, work, and leisure. Advances in the information and communication landscape facilitate the development of new strategies, the optimization of knowledge creation, teaching with new methods, and implementation of technology-rich projects. The rapid expansion of social media, the ubiquity of smartphones and new devices such as tablets, as well as the growth of wireless communications are a few of the factors that generate change in learners' expectations. Educators have the responsibility to engage learners without sacrificing good pedagogy, and to somehow teach them and learn from them at the same time.

Technology-enhanced learning has entered a new era characterized as m-learning (Botzer & Yerushalmy, 2007; Guy, 2009; Sharples, Taylor, & Vavoula, 2005), seamless learning (Seow, Zhang, Chen, Looi, & Tan, 2009), and ubiquitous learning (Rogers et al., 2005). Central to these notions is the idea that mobile technologies can be designed to enable the development of a new dimension of the learning environment, where learners can move in and out of overlapping physical, digital, and communicative spaces. This mobility can be achieved individually, in groups, or as a whole classroom, together with teachers, mentors, experts, professionals, and others (Guy, 2009).

It is assumed that mobile technologies provide continuity across various learning journeys, enabling learners to make connections between what they are observing, collecting, accessing, and thinking about over time, place, and people. Several researchers suggest that m-learning can encourage new forms of social interaction, thinking, or reflection (Carliner & Shank; 2008; Sharples et al., 2005; Stănescu & Ştefan, 2009).

There are several definitions of m-learning. For the purpose of this chapter the authors adopt a broad definition—the exploitation of ubiquitous handheld technologies, together with wireless and mobile-phone networks, to facilitate, support, enhance, and extend the reach of teaching and learning. Learners involved may or may not be mobile. Learning can take place in any location, and at any time, including in traditional learning environments, such as classrooms, as well as other locations, including the workplace, at home, in community locations, and in transit.

Core benefits of m-learning for adult learners include:

- increased engagement, motivation, and enthusiasm for learning;
- improved independent learning;
- improved punctuality and attendance;
- increased participation in extracurricular activities.

The rationale behind this chapter consists of employing the strengths and opportunities of mobile technologies in knowledge-management (KM) settings. In a society dependent on information, but also dominated by information overload generated by the complexity of the communication processes and of social relationships, knowledge is an everlasting power that ensures socioeconomic and democratic progress and that does not erode in time.

Within educational and organizational contexts, KM aims to provide an intelligent response to the requirement, *I need to know what I need to know when I need to know it; even when I don't know what I need to know*. KM-enabling tools constitute a solution that addresses the information overload that is plaguing an educational institution that use an intranet, an enterprise resource planning or business intelligence system. Technology enabled new knowledge behavior. Information and communication technology tools amplify the existing knowledge processes and also create new kinds of knowledge experience, particularly among generations of users who grow up in IT-pervasive environments.

The provision of knowledge is essential in any domain of activity, and the emerging mobile technologies bring forth new opportunities for development. The initiatives in the field of mobile KM have grown to include the P2P knowledge-sharing paradigm (Matuszewski & Balandin, 2007), product life-cycle design (Spiteri & Borg, 2008), aircraft engine repair and overhaul (Thiele, Knapp, Schader, & Prat, 2008), and supernetwork models of KM in paroxysmal public crisis (Li & Wang, 2009). These approaches do not consider standardization opportunities—such as the sharable content object reference model (SCORM)—or the semantic web at the basis of their development, restricting accessibility and reusability of content.

Under these premises, the authors of this chapter explore the development settings of a mobile knowledge management system (mKMS) and detail the main functionalities of this system, which aims to support accessibility, user-friendliness, and adaptation of knowledge capture, storage, and acquisition in the mobile arena. The mKMS has been developed within a research project funded under the Romanian "Partnerships" program and implemented between 2008 and 2011. The project is entitled the MOBNET: "Research regarding the design of an experimental model of a mobile learning-type virtual network with real time access to knowledge and learning, using communication technologies and wireless terminal devices." The development process was based on the findings of the main analyses carried out within the MOBNET project that refer to fundamental research on m-learning and net-centric concepts, and also on their applications in education and KM; research on the virtual educational network based on mobile technologies; scientific research on standardized digital content for multi-usage; the report between learning object and learning management system; study on the current state of mobile Web services development; the European market of services based on mobile technologies; study of the domain of applicability of mobile services in an information and knowledge society; and restrictions and perspectives. The mKMS enables smart access to content and knowledge in mobile settings, represents a novel, practice-driven approach in the Romanian research area, and aims to become a significant contribution to the implementation of mobile KM in both m-learning and training. The system is an innovation both in terms of KM technology and in the field of m-learning.

THE USE OF MOBILE TECHNOLOGIES IN MILITARY EDUCATION

Mobile technology has emerged as an enabler of timely information, as well as a capturer of context-generated knowledge, changing the perspective on learning and opening up new possibilities for education. Moreover, adult learning with mobility technologies could be claimed to be a revolutionary mode of knowledge distribution and skills development. Under certain circumstances, it can be used in almost all types of teaching and learning process.

Specific Requirements of Military Education

The military is one of the most important services provided by the state, and the education of this body is, or should be, one of the highest priorities of governments (Kennedy & Neilson, 2006). As armed forces are entrusted with the protection of the state, its wealth, and its citizens, they are required to achieve the highest level of education possible (Watson, 2007).

In this context, military education stands out as a particular field of applicability. Military education and training aim to better the performance of soldiers and officers by providing access to both military and civilian qualifications, from education on operations to skills for life. The army represents a domain of high expertise that imposes special availability and security requirements on information and knowledge. One of the targets of military education is to improve knowledge in order to form units capable of meeting the most effective military requirements of the future.

Challenges and Opportunities in Mobile KM

Information and communication technologies play a significant role in facilitating KM practices in today's globalized world, which operates in a complex web of partnerships and alliances. Wide access to KM architecture, Web-based applications, data mining tools, mobile devices, worldwide access, high performance, user friendliness, a standardized structure, and an easily administered controlling system represent key requirements of the supporting KM infrastructure. However, it is important to keep in mind that technology is not a panacea for a KM practice, though an easy-to-use knowledge-sharing infrastructure is an important enabler.

The KM initiatives have to be, in essence, people-centric, even if technology represents a significant dimension in the effort to demonstrate the multiple possibilities of KM. If people are not able to see and experience the direct benefits of KM, no amount of incentives, rewards, or recognition is likely to elicit sustained enthusiasm, participation, and involvement.

KM has always been a challenge, as knowledge usually results from experiences, which are rarely captured, and, even if they are, they reside in unstructured formats that make them difficult to reuse. In this context, mobile KM brings both new challenges and opportunities. Challenges, in terms of supporting participation and knowledge sharing in mobile settings and in terms of the inherent limitations of mobile devices. Opportunities, in terms of real-time knowledge acquisition, storage, and retrieval (Rabin, 2008; Stănescu, Hamza-Lup, & Tuncay, 2009; Stănescu & Ştefan, 2009).

Knowledge capture and assimilation manifested within educational institutions confirm a functional maturity that is consistent with the essence of the information society to which they are connected. The integration of KM tools within the learning environments answers the need to enhance the learning processes by engaging innovative dimensions and facilitating fast updating of learning objects according to military requirements and realities. However, this approach considers the current technological developments and the skills of the future generations, and generates sustainable practices that support lifelong learning processes.

Classical KM systems were desktop solutions that hindered users' activities and did not allow them to explore the full potential of such systems, nor did they enable learners to perform successfully in future careers. Mobile contextual learning requires specific knowledge and, at the same time, generates valuable input data, which generally are lost owing to the lack of adequate input collection systems. The mKMS aims to capture tacit knowledge generated in mobile environments.

Implicit or tacit knowledge incorporates the experiences of each individual, and it is very difficult to express and transmit. Explicit knowledge takes methodical, systematic, and articulated forms; it is stored, and used by various means of communication. For many decades, the transition from implicit to explicit knowledge has represented one of the key challenges in KM. Mobile technologies support the transformation of knowledge from default to explicit by facilitating socialization (implicit knowledge exchange), combination (explicit knowledge), and internalization (from explicit to implicit).

LEARNING EXPERIENCES WITH MKMS

The mKMS Mission

An important goal of the MOBNET project has been the development of a knowledge acquisition and retrieval system that operated as an m-learning assistant, allowing users to access and capture KM when they need it. The mKMS helps mobile learners to fulfill their tasks more efficiently, as it exploits the learner's context in order to filter information that is of special interest in a specific circumstance. The system is currently implemented within the Advanced Distributed Learning Partnership Lab at the Carol I National Defence University in Bucharest, as a supplement and improvement tool of formal or informal military learning activities.

The mKMS integrates actions such as organizing, filtering, blocking, collecting, storing, sharing, dissemination, and use of knowledge objects, identified as information, data, experiences, evaluations, analyses, and initiatives. The system allows the capture of knowledge in the location it is created and its real-time sharing, in order for it to be effectively embedded, for example, within decision-making processes.

The content of the mKMS is referred to as objects. The aim of the developers was to create knowledge objects that are highly structured, interrelated sets of data, information, knowledge, and wisdom, concerning some organizational, management, or leadership situation, which provides a viable approach for dealing with a situation. These objects can provide the users with *information* (What? When? Where? Who?), *knowledge*

(How?—a foundation for viable action), or *wisdom* (Why?—with implications of action) because of its consistency and lack of ambiguity. The mKMS aims to become an effective vehicle that enables people to develop and improve their abilities and performance by contributing to their education, their future, their organization's future, and society's future.

The System Architecture

The core of the system is composed of a Web service that centralizes knowledge base data and other external data sources. This Web service implements all the search logic and data networking, as well as the security policies.

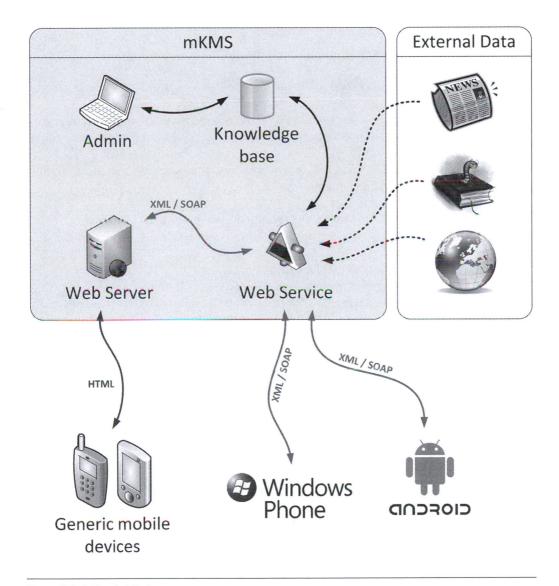

Figure 43.1 System Architecture

The users interact with this service via a GUI implemented using open Web standards, or an interface developed specifically for a particular mobile device. Thus, the system can be accessed by a wide range of mobile devices using the standard GUI, and for those devices for which a dedicated user interface can be financially justified, additional functionality can be implemented in order to allow the users to utilize the maximum capabilities of their devices. This architecture reduces the costs of device-centric development, because most functions are already implemented in the Web service.

The Development Platform

Choosing the development platform is the first step that needs to be taken when developing an application. Each platform has advantages and disadvantages that concern the technical features and the number of potential users. The technical solution chosen for the development of the mKMS combines Web-based development with device-oriented development to achieve the best functionality, efficiency, and compatibility with mobile devices, at a low cost.

The system uses a common database for both the KM system and the learning-management system. This improves the results of the search and allows easy administration of knowledge and learning objects and unified access from the users' standpoint. The knowledge is accessed via a mobile GUI that follows the above-mentioned recommendations. The mobile website is developed based on the Microsoft .NET Framework, using ASP.NET and C#. For the backend, the developers used Microsoft SQL Server 2008 as the database engine.

Performance in M-Learning Development

A Web-based approach translates into the following benefits:

- It is easy to deploy, manage, and update.
- A single solution can target multiple platforms.
- The use of a document-style interface makes it more adaptable to different screen sizes and resolutions.
- It does not suffer from platform fragmentation.
- It does not require expensive validation and certification.
- It is not limited by handset and operator distribution agreements.
- It is more cost efficient to maintain for end-of-life platforms.
- The developers can take the one-size-fits-all approach.

The main advantages of device-centric development are:

- It provides an optimal experience for each device type.
- The user experience can be fully integrated with the mobile platform (home screen tiles, shortcuts, intents, etc.).
- It provides faster loading times and a fluid user interface through accelerated graphics support.
- It can access device-specific hardware such as GPS, camera, and microphone.
- It can operate in the background and automatically notify users when new items of interest are added.

mKMS Essentials

The start page allows users to access the login option, to create a new account by registering as a user in the system, and to access the first chapter of the User's Guide that provides information about what steps are to be taken in order to register in the system (see Figures 43.2 and 43.3).

The main page of the application integrates the basic tools and components of the mKMS, enabling the user to access the latest information uploaded in the system and also the knowledge database.

The mKMS provides advanced search options: by keyword, by full text search, by topic, and by similar articles, to target the preferences of a larger group of mobile users. For a better user experience, the mKMS allows the users to further refine search results by applying search criteria progressively, against the current result set (i.e., a search within a search).

For example, users could do a search for the term "engine" and, if they are not satisfied with the results, they could further narrow down the list by searching for "boat." This

Figure 43.2 Authentication in the System

Figure 43.3 The Search Window

would be the equivalent of searching "boat engine" from the very beginning, and would prevent the user from writing extra keywords. To achieve this functionality, the system temporarily stores search results in the database and performs further searches based on this list rather than on the whole database.

The system displays the messages received by a user, the latest articles uploaded in the mKMS, and new comments added to articles that the user is following. Each of these options can be accessed within dedicated sections of the applications.

The "News" section displays the last ten articles collected automatically from news sites or sites that make their information public in an RSS format. This enables users to collect information that is of interest to them, without redundantly creating costly mobile content and uploading it in the system. The articles uploaded in the mKMS can be accessed by clicking on the "Articles" section in the footer of the application or by using shortcut key 3. The articles are grouped in alphabetical order, by publication date, or by user name. The mobile interface was developed in accordance with standards and recommendations of the World Wide Web Consortium (W3C), in order to maximize positive mobile user experience and support to motivate them to contribute actively to the development of mobile KM.

The mKMS integrates connections with social networks such as Facebook, Twitter, MySpace, and many others, with the purpose of supporting participation and knowledge sharing. Social networks have become a real-time environment that produces many valuable resources, many of which are not used at their full potential. The system aims to capture specific knowledge generated within social networks through a friendly approach that does not burden the mobile user. The mKMS allows registered users to include links to their social-network profiles, to blogs and other types of personal resource that support knowledge sharing, and to increase the rate of participation within knowledge-driven communities.

These are a few of the key features of the mKMS that have been developed within the MOBNET project. The system builds adaptive-learning resources that are reconfigurable based on the device attributes and users' preferences, and provides mobile learners with knowledge in the Romanian language, becoming a start-up project in this domain.

INNOVATION IN MOBILE KNOWLEDGE-BASED LEARNING

The mobile revolution enables new learning experiences in various contexts. To support user participation in the knowledge-collection processes, the system developers have implemented the Mobile SCORM Module, which allows users to download an article as a SCORM package. This feature implements the interoperability of learning resources, contributing to their efficiency and reducing the implementation costs of IT solutions in education.

To enhance the mobile experience, the application integrates flexible formatting options for mobile content (Wikitext Markup), and it enables users to upload resources in the system using various multimedia formats.

M-Learning and Standardization: SCORM Compliance

The key role of standards has long been implicitly recognized in education settings. However, the increased awareness of educational institutions all over the world of the importance of implementing standardization activities is a more recent trend. Implementation of SCORM on mobile Web applications represents a new challenge in the learning environment. Mobile devices have limitations related to screen size, availability of required technology/software, browser compatibility, and availability of a consistent Internet connection.

The mKMS content is SCORM-compliant, and the SCORM implementation method that was used is JavaScript (JS). Mobile browsers now almost fully support JavaScript, and this makes it possible to implement SCORM using JS support. Each mobile device has different configurations, and it is always better to identify the device requesting content before rendering the HTML content. To identify devices, the developers have used the information in request headers. There is some variation in each mobile-device browser. The developers have used the following variables from the headers to get the device type:

- user-agent (most widely used)
- x-operamini-phone-ua

Figure 43.4 Mobile SCORM-Compliant Content

- x-wap-profile
- x-skyfire-phone.

Users can download the mobile content as SCORM packages that can be accessed offline or loaded into SCORM-compliant platforms, such as learning-management systems. This represents a significant innovation in the mobile arena. The mKMS not only builds the bridge between tacit and explicit knowledge, but it also enables content reusability.

Ideally, when new content is launched, it is opened in a new pop-up window, so that the content gets its own desirable window size. However, while implementing such on mobile devices, the developers have discovered that some of the well-known mobile-device browsers don't support pop-up windows—the Blackberry is an example. This is a recommendation included in the best practices of the W3C. Therefore, the new content is displayed in the base window.

Accordingly, the developers made changes in the SCORM implementation to accommodate both conditions. Some of the low-level mobile-device browsers don't support either pop-up windows or frame structures. If that is the case, then users just can't run SCORM content on them. SCORM has provisions to track time spent by the user in session. Normally, the setTimeOut() function is used to track time, but some browsers do not support it.

The Web/browser-based solution chosen for the mKMS has a wide reach, as every basic mobile handset has a browser, but it also has one drawback—it requires a continuous Internet connection. This is not a problem on desktop PCs, as normally they have continuous Internet connections. On a mobile device, however, there is no guarantee of continuous connectivity, and this may lead to issues with SCORM tracking.

Rich Text Formatting Using Wikitext Markup

To increase user-friendliness and also content readability, the mKMS enables the following basic formatting of text items added by users:

- Mark text as: bold, italic, underline, or strikethrough.
- Format article's headline sizes.
- Add links to images that are previously stored in another Web location.
- Use external links and refer to any external URL that underpins the content that is published, leading the user directly to the additional resources outside the application.
- Create simple table templates within the published articles.
- Align the text of an article using standard formatting options.
- Create and integrate various types of list within the text published in the system, facilitating the accessibility of the information provided to the mobile user.
- Use macros for Silverlight that allow users to insert Silverlight applications within the wiki page.
- Insert the media files within the mobile wiki page.

Secure Mobile Connections

Security is a major concern in military settings. The main security objectives concern access control, authentication, integrity, accountability, and privacy. Mobile users expect to be able to access data securely, no matter where they are. Mobile-content developers have to take into account the wide variety of mobile browsers and operating systems that are available on the market. Although high-end devices with operating systems such as iPhone OS, Windows Mobile, Android, and Symbian are better equipped to handle rich Internet applications, they only comprise a small number of the mobile-device market, mostly owing to the high costs of such devices. In order to make the content accessible to as many users as possible, designers of mobile Web applications need to maintain a delicate balance between the features that they provide to end users and the features that they require from the device.

In order to access data using a mobile Web interface, the developers have used an encryption data connection. In this way, no third party is able to intercept the communication between the client and the server. Hypertext Transfer Protocol Secure is a protocol that encrypts and encapsulates normal Hypertext Transfer Protocol (HTTP) traffic using Secure Sockets Layer. Data encryption and client authentication are done

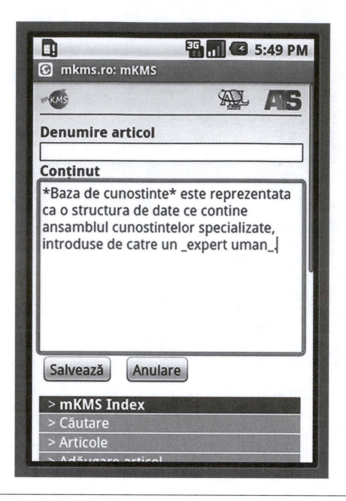

Figure 43.5 Adding an Article Using Wikitext Markup

through the use of Public-Key Infrastructure certificates issued to each client and installed in the subscriber identity module (SIM) card of the mobile device. Besides the normal data-encryption application, issuing self-owned client certificates allows developers to embed them into the SIM cards and, therefore, they can prevent any attempts to copy the private key, and this allows them to easily revoke client certificates in case a mobile device is stolen or lost.

CONCLUSIONS

Online and mobile technologies have opened up new possibilities in military education. Technology has become a necessary and everyday part of studying. Although some learners follow a course that is completely online, most of them make use of online and mobile technologies, alongside their attendance at classes or tutorials, the use of text books, or the discussion of project work. Some learners study part time, and others study at a distance. There are also people who undertake continuous professional development

Figure 43.6 The Result of Wikitext Formatting

or work-based training. No matter in what context learners may be, mobile technologies have a significant impact upon their learning environment in terms of access to information and knowledge. They constitute a source of change in abilities, behaviors, attitudes, values, and social dimensions.

This chapter highlights the valuable opportunities brought by mobile technologies in the military learning environment and the associated knowledge communities by presenting a mobile knowledge management system developed by Advanced Technology Systems (Romania).

In this chapter, the authors explore and analyze the impact of mobile technologies corroborated with KM on the learning environment, as well as the opportunities and the challenges of developing mobile systems based on the activity carried out within the MOBNET-Learning Project entitled, "Research regarding the design of an experimental model of a mobile learning-type virtual network with real time access to knowledge and learning, using communication technologies and wireless terminal devices," funded under the Romanian "Partnerships" Program and implemented between 2008 and 2011.

The mKMS is used by teachers/trainers and students/trainees at Carol I National Defence University in Bucharest, to supplement and improve formal or informal learning activities.

The project represents an innovative practice-driven approach in the Romanian research area and aims to become an innovative contribution to the implementation of KM tools within m-learning. The system promotes new concept-based learning tools for synthesis of knowledge and real-time assistance in the learning process, and supports real-time capture of both explicit and tacit knowledge of users. The technical solution used significantly reduces the development costs—as it eliminates the need to support custom development projects by type of mobile device—and running costs—as the system is accessible from a wide range of mobile devices.

The mKMS introduces innovative developments in the mobile environment that support content reuse and user-friendliness through SCORM-compliant modules and wiki formatting.

REFERENCES

Botzer, G., & Yerushalmy, M. (2007). Mobile application for mobile learning. *Proceedings from CELDA '07: The IADIS International Conference on Cognition and Exploratory Learning in Digital Age*, Algarve, Portugal.

Carliner, S., & Shank, P. (2008). *The e-learning handbook: A comprehensive guide to online learning*. San Francisco, CA: Pfeiffer.

Guy, R. (2009). *The evolution of mobile teaching and learning, informing science*. Santa Rosa, CA: Informing Science Press.

Kennedy, G. C., & Neilson, K. (Eds.) (2006). *Military education: Past, present, and future*. Westport, CT: IAP LLC.

Li, Z., & Wang, H. (2009). Supernetwork model of knowledge management in paroxysmal public crisis. *Proceedings from ICMECG '09: International Conference on Management of e-Commerce and e-Government*. Nanchang, China.

Matuszewski, M., & Balandin, S. (2007). Peer-to-peer knowledge sharing in the mobile environment. *Proceedings from C5 '07: The Fifth International Conference on Creating, Connecting and Collaborating through Computing*. Kyoto, Japan.

Rabin, J. C. (2008). *Mobile web best practices 1.0*. Retrieved from: www.w3.org/TR/mobile-bp/

Rogers, Y., Price, S., Randell, C., Fraser, D. S., Weal, M., & Fitzpatrick, G. (2005). Ubi-learning integrates indoor and outdoor experiences. *Communications of the ACM, 48*(1), 55–59.

Seow, P., Zhang, B., Chen, W., Looi, C. K., & Tan, N. (2009). Designing a seamless learning environment to learn reduce, reuse and recycle in environmental education. *International Journal of Mobile Learning and Organisation, 3*(1), 60–83.

Sharples, M., Taylor, J., & Vavoula, G. (2005). *Towards a theory of mobile learning*. Retrieved from: http://www.mlearn.org/mlearn2005/CD/papers/Sharples-%20Theory%20of%20Mobile.pdf

Spiteri, C. L., & Borg, C. B. (2008), Mobile knowledge management for product life-cycle design. In *Global design to gain a competitive edge* (pp. 137–146). DOI:10.1007/978–1–84800–239–5_14

Stănescu, I. A., Hamza-Lup, F., & Tuncay, N. (2009). Designing the transition into the mobile arena for enriched user experience. *Proceedings from eLSE '09: eLearning and Software for Education Conference*. Bucharest, Romania.

Stănescu, I. A., & Ştefan, A. (2009). Mobile knowledge management toolkit. *Proceedings from ECEL '09: The 8th European Conference on eLearning*. Bari, Italy.

Thiele, O., Knapp, H., Schader, M., & Prat, N. (2008). MobileAERO: Using tag clouds for mobile knowledge management. *Proceedings from ICN '08: Seventh International Conference on Networking*. Cancun, Mexico.

Watson, C. A. (2007). *Military education: A reference handbook (Contemporary military, strategic, and security issues)*. Westport, CT: Praeger.

44

M-LEARNING DURING EMERGENCIES, DISASTERS, AND CATASTROPHES

An Australian Story

Julie A. Willems

It was Saturday 7 February 2009. The bushland in the southerly state of Victoria, Australia, was tinder-dry following an extended drought. As the day progressed, the mercury quickly reached the predicted extreme of 47° Celsius (117° Fahrenheit) – hot even by Australian-summer standards – accompanied by gale-force winds from the north west. Of the 316 grass and bushfires reported to be burning across the state that day, 15 were noted as fires of concern: fires that had either caused, or had the potential to cause, the greatest damage (Parliament of Victoria, 2010). Some of these fires were caused by natural events such as lightning strikes (Australian Broadcasting Commission, 2009), and others were considered to be brought about by human inactions or actions, such as failure to fix faults in power lines, or arson (Parliament of Victoria, 2010). This was the day that was later to become known historically as the national catastrophe, 'Black Saturday': a day in and around which – along with wildlife and stock losses, property damage and business and community decimation – 173 people were to lose their lives (News Limited, 2009).

Armed with a mobile phone, I joined a group of neighbours at the end of our street to watch the cloud of smoke rising beyond the pastoral valley on the outskirts of our town. The fire that had been steadily growing in the nearby Bunyip State Forest was gathering momentum. By lunchtime, the now vast smoke plume was 'raining' live embers overhead, causing personal injuries and spotting new fires ahead of the main fire front.

Official sources of information on the day, such as emergency-services websites, were unable to deal with the high volumes of traffic, and, when one was able to get through, localized information was difficult to find. Sutton, Palen and Shklovski (2008) report a similar situation in the 2007 Southern California wildfires. Similarly, television and radio broadcasts were unable to provide up-to-date information about our local situation. However, via mobile phone, my brother – some 1,800 km to our north – kept us posted with current fire details and even the location of our nearest fire crews. This was used,

Figure 44.1 Bunyip State Fire from Drouin, Victoria, Australia ('Black Saturday', 7 February 2009)

in turn, to advise our neighbours and friends. It became the basis for decision-making in person, via telecommunications and virtually, via the social network Facebook.

Two years later (Saturday 5 February 2011) I was involved in another crisis, brought about by the swiftly rising flood waters engulfing parts of Victoria. Owing to water inundation, the east-bound lanes of the main highway from Melbourne to the east of the state had already been closed, and police and emergency services were closely monitoring the west-bound lanes. Although official communication channels were beginning to raise public awareness of the emergency, there was a lag in up-to-date information getting to those affected. In the midst of the flooding, with my smartphone connected to mobile social media, I was able to instantly upload warnings and photos to friends in my social network who, in turn, shared the information with others. When used alongside other sources of crisis informatics, these actions helped inform effective decision-making processes. As one friend travelling with her children replied: 'Thanks for that update – we [had] just turned onto the freeway when I read this so we turned around and went home.'

In emergencies, disasters and catastrophes, the saving of lives and livestock and the limiting of social, environmental and economic consequences become paramount. Often, the only means to communicate in these situations, to obtain vital and necessary information and/or to participate in training or learning in the field, is via mobile devices. Mobile technologies enable learning opportunities (m-learning) that are 'just enough, just in time, just for me' (Rosenberg, 2001) for the multiple stakeholder

Figure 44.2 West Gippsland Flooding Near Pakenham, Victoria, Australia (5 February 2011)

groups involved. These include civilians, researchers, emergency-services personnel, the broadcast media, business owners and government-service employees. This chapter explores m-learning in and around emergencies, disasters, and catastrophes. It views m-learning in such situations as encompassing both formal (official) and informal ('backchannel') mobile communications (m-communications), and formal and informal education and training.

IN CRISIS: EMERGENCIES, DISASTERS AND CATASTROPHES

In Australia, for operational purposes, a crisis includes such types of situations as war, acts of terrorism, civil disturbances, and natural disasters (including fires, storms, floods, earthquakes, cyclones and other events), whether these have been caused by natural factors or are the result of the actions or inactions of humans (Department of Broadband, Communication and the Digital Economy, 2011). Crisis is an umbrella term describing both the type of the event and the scale of the situation. Emergencies, disasters and catastrophes are all examples of crises; however, they are quantitatively and qualitatively different events that fall on a 'continuum of magnitude' (Oliver, 2010), and so need to be clearly differentiated (Britton, 1986).

As a precedent, an accident is a localized disruption affecting a relatively small group of people and tends to be of short-term duration. An emergency is on a larger scale than an accident and/or covers a broader geographic area. It involves many more people, its effects are more widely felt, and there is a broader time element between the actual emergency and its resolution (Britton, 1986). The West Gippsland flooding, noted previously, is an example of a state emergency.

Disasters are distinguishable from emergencies by the 'quantity' and 'quality' of destruction and experiences (Britton, 1986). Although different countries have localized definitions of what constitutes a disaster, there is general acknowledgement that, in disasters, three facets operate: the event is sudden or unpredictable; it causes human, material, economic or environmental losses; and it exceeds the ability of the affected community to cope in the situation (European Commission, 2008). As such, disasters are defined as 'a serious disruption of the functioning of a community or a society involving widespread human, material, economic or environmental losses and impacts, which exceeds the ability of the affected community or society to cope using its own resources' (United Nations International Strategy for Disaster Reduction, 2009, p. 9).

The United Nations adds the category of 'catastrophe' to events that can be classified as a crisis (United Nations International Strategy for Disaster Reduction, 2009). Quarantelli (2006) argues that catastrophes can be distinguished from disasters in terms of organizational, community and societal effects: in a catastrophe, most, if not all, of the community's built structure and facilities are impacted; local emergency personnel are unable to perform their usual roles owing to losses of staff, facilities or equipment, both during the event and the recovery period; assistance from neighbouring communities cannot be gained, as they are also affected; most of the everyday community functions are sharply and concurrently interrupted; national government becomes directly involved in the situation; and, finally, the mass media socially 'constructs' the catastrophe and reports it over a long period of time. Further, the economic recovery following a catastrophe may be felt across the entire nation, for months or even years following the disaster event. Using Quarantelli's guidelines, Victoria's 'Black Saturday' is an example of a national catastrophe.

M-LEARNING AND CRISES

Mobile Technologies

Mobile technologies are personal mobile electronic devices. They span the spectrum of technology from 'cell phones, PDAs (personal digital assistants), MP3 players . . . tablets and laptops' (Wagner, 2005, p. 40), in addition to 'smart-phones, game consoles, digital cameras, media players, netbooks, in-car sat-nav [satellite navigators], and handheld computers' (Traxler, 2010, p. 3). According to Johnson, Smith, Willis, Levine, and Haywood (2011, p. 5), the benefits of mobile technologies are that they enable 'ubiquitous access to information, social networks, tools for learning and productivity, and much more'.

M-Learning Defined

As an umbrella term, m-learning means different things, dependent on the context of use (Laouris & Eteokleous, 2005). Accordingly, there are a number of subsets of m-learning: technology-driven m-learning; miniature but portable e-learning; connected classroom learning; informal, personalized, situated m-learning; mobile training and performance support; and remote, rural or development m-learning (Traxler, 2007). In emergencies, disasters and catastrophes, all the listed subsets may potentially be involved in the provision of risk communications (crisis informatics), ongoing planning, evaluations, and education and training for the various stakeholder groups. M-learning, therefore, can be defined as 'learning across multiple contexts, through social and content interactions, using personal electronic devices' (Crompton, 2013, p. 4). Further, m-learning provides opportunities that are 'just enough, just in time, just for me' (Rosenberg, 2001).

Crisis M-Learning Framework

In crisis situations, the boundaries between formal and informal communication and informatics, and between learning and training are blurred. Adapting Stuckey and Arkell's (2006) flexible e-learning model, Figure 44.3 provides a useful means to graphically represent the blurring of these boundaries in a crisis m-learning framework.

Mobile Phones

Nielsen (2010) lists three types of mobile phone: non-Internet-capable mobile phones; Internet-capable mobile phones; and Internet-capable smartphones. As Johnson et al. (2011) have noted, with the continued evolution and increased access to affordable and reliable networks, mobile phones are becoming capable computing devices in their own right. In many poorer communities and regions of the world, Internet-enabled mobile-phone technologies are more readily available to the public than other means, and are

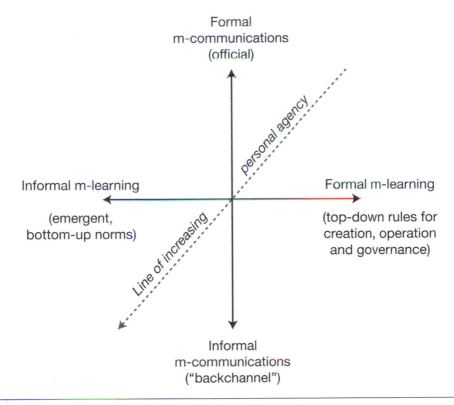

Figure 44.3 M-Learning Framework in Emergencies, Disasters and Catastrophes

Source: Based on Stuckey & Arkell, 2006

increasingly the first choice of Internet access for users, as is the case in Kenya, where 99 percent of the population who access broadband do so from their mobile phones (Verma, 2011). Recent Australian analytics suggest that, whereas numbers of fixed landlines are decreasing (Australian Communications & Media Authority [ACMA], 2009), 92 percent of the population own a mobile phone (Sensis, 2011), and, of these, ownership of smartphones was at 65 percent in 2010 (Nielsen, 2010).

In this chapter, the mobile technology of interest for m-learning in crises is the smartphone. Providing battery life and connectivity are available, the smartphone has multiple benefits over other mobile technologies for the delivery of m-learning in emergencies, disasters and catastrophes. In addition to their portable, lightweight nature and relatively long battery life if fully charged before any incident (or if portable or 'wind-up' energy supplies can be sourced), the virtue of smartphones is that they 'support the myriad forms of communications – voice text, database access, images, and streaming video – that [are necessary] for situational awareness and effective response during emergencies' (Palm Inc., 2006, p. 2). The wireless connectivity (mobile broadband) of the smartphone helps to enable greater call reliability and access to high bandwidth for the user (including the possibility of making video calls). This can be of benefit for those living in rural areas, where landline operations, static ICT access or electricity failure in times of crisis may be obstacles. Further, in terms of m-learning during crises, civilians do not need additional training to operate this everyday technology (Hiltz, Diaz & Mark, 2011).

Mobile Social Media

Social media are defined by Kaplan and Haenlein (2010, p. 61) as 'Internet-based applications that build on the ideological and technological foundations of Web 2.0, and that allow the creation and exchange of User Generated Content'. The user-created content of social media enables civilians to be actively involved in the learning opportunity. It can be self-policed for errors (Sutton et al., 2008) and provide localized information that might not be easily accessible elsewhere. As such, social media can be seen as a means towards the democratization of the Internet and the reduction of the digital divide (Kaplan & Haenlein, 2010). Via the creation of public or semi-public profiles (Boyd & Ellison, 2007), members can send asynchronous messages, e-mails and synchronous instant messages (IM), and share other Web links and digital artefacts, such as photos and audio and video files, with other 'friends' within the system. Whitelaw (2010) refers to the use of social media during crises as 'Emergency 2.0' and argues that its benefit is that it places information at people's fingertips.

Social media are being increasingly accessed via mobile technologies (Lundin, Lymer, Holmquist, Brown & Rost, 2010) through downloaded mobile applications (apps) or via the mobile Web (J.D. Power Assoc., 2011). Research suggests that the two major uses of smartphones are 'social networking on the go' (Nielsen, 2011) and e-mail (ACMA, 2011). Indeed, some phone companies now incorporate access to social media such as Facebook as part of their mobile-phone plans.

Mobile Communications

In emergencies, disasters and catastrophes, communications take on an urgency. In terms of communications processes, Perry and Lindell (2003) note that the associated risk communication, or crisis informatics, is oriented towards educational exchanges to guide stakeholders involved within the crisis. Crisis informatics is defined as 'a social system where information is disseminated within and between official and public [informal] channels and entities' (Palen et al., 2010, p. 3).

Formal mobile communications in times of crisis are known as 'front-channel' communications. These are considered to be credible, official sources of information. There are two major types of formal m-communications. The first is the official responses and updates from national agencies, such as the police and emergency-service organizations, and include SMS alerts, Web updates or information via apps. The second type of formal communication comes from official media outlets. In Australia, these include public broadcasting through the Australian Broadcasting Commission's television and radio stations (both national and regional), plus the commercial television and radio channels.

However, there are a number of issues in relying on formal communications during emergencies, disasters and catastrophes. First, front-channel m-communications are traditionally 'unidirectional, official-to-public information dissemination' (Sutton et al., 2008) and, as such, offer little opportunity for civilian involvement. Second, power-supply stability and ICT disruptions can be a frequent consequence in crises (Country Fire Authority [CFA], 2012a) and prevent official communications getting through. Third, emergency services might be reliant on the stability of public telecommunications carriers' stability during the height of a crisis. This has been the situation in Australia, and, as a response, the Police Federation of Australia has called for changes in telecommunications access during crises, stating that currently, 'a 16-year old with a Smartphone has a more advanced communications capability than many first responder police officers or emergency services personnel' (Police Federation of Australia, 2011, p. 3).

Fourth, there may be delays in the community receiving formal m-communications. As an example, during the recent Cyclone Yasi, which bore down on the coast of Far North Queensland on Thursday 3 February 2011, the national SMS and voicemail alert system – 'Emergency Alert' (www.emergencyalert.gov.au) – was relied upon to advise the local civilian population on the basis of the home billing address. However, in some reported instances, alerts were not received by civilians until hours after the messages had been sent and the crisis was over (Barry, 2011). Further, there is a greater danger in relying on dissemination on the basis of the home billing address for visitors in the region. As an exemplar, the seaside resort of Lorne in southern Victoria is ringed by the Otway ranges and was affected by the 1983 bushfire, on 'Ash Wednesday'. Lorne's usual population of 900 residents can swell to over 20,000 during the summer months (Brown, 2012), and so plans are currently underway to have mobile alerts sent to all in the area, irrespective of the home billing address.

Fifth, as previously noted, there can be a lag in localized information getting to official communications sources and then back out to the affected public. In research by Palm Inc. for government-service employees in the field, smartphones were promoted as a means of more rapidly sending or receiving critical messages to those affected (Palm Inc., 2006). M-communications in crises can result in crucial time savings that can impact by 'saving lives, minimizing property loss, and protecting the environment' (Palm Inc., 2006, p. 6).

Finally, one often overlooked issue in formal m-communications in and around accidents, emergencies and disasters is the fact that there is great diversity both between and within the various stakeholder groups. This encompasses, not only their ability to understand the information, but also how an individual might choose to respond. Lachlan and Spence (2007) argue that government agencies and crisis practitioners continue to produce generalized messages that do not adequately address these diverse needs and call for the customization of crisis informatics. The authors recommend the consideration of 'multiple publics', who come from different demographic and economic backgrounds; have differing interests to protect; have varying needs for learning, communication and information; are linguistically diverse; may respond better to images than text; and may be suspicious of crisis informatics emanating from dominant cultural groups. Furthermore, this diversity can affect the responses within the crisis situation itself. In the 'Black Saturday' fires, for example, the 2009 Victorian Bushfires Royal Commission Australia (Parliament of Victoria, 2010, p. 5) noted that: 'nearly half of the people who died were classed as "vulnerable" because they were aged less than 12 years or more than 70 years or because they were suffering from an acute or chronic illness or disability'.

Although formal and official communications have their place, informal m-communications enable peer-to-peer opportunities. Referred to as 'backchannel' communications, the term implies 'an unofficial, unwanted, illicit quality' (Griswold, 2004, p. 3). However, for many in the height of crises, backchannel communications may be the only source of up-to-the-minute local information. Palen et al. (2010) argue that, although civilians' participation in crises is not new, their use of ICT both widens and foregrounds their participation. New technologies provide the perfect conduit for backchannel communications and learning opportunities in crises through the affordances of mobile phones, ICT, and particularly through the increased use of social networks. Sutton et al. (2008) write that:

> With each new disaster, peer-to-peer communications through social media such as social networking sites, text and instant messaging applications, blogs, wikis and other web forums, are growing as a means for supporting additional, often critical and accurate, dissemination of information within the public sphere.
>
> (p. 2)

Further, in crises, civilians are often the first on the scene. As Fischer (2003) notes, the community has both the capacity and the resources to activate a response. Through such means, rather than being passive recipients, the civilian population becomes actively engaged (Lawley, 2004), fostering increased personal agency (Evans & Larri, 2007), as 'a powerful, self-organizing, and collectively intelligent force [which] has the potential to play a remarkable and transformational role in the way society responds to mass emergencies and disasters' (Palen et al., 2010, p. 1). This is of note, as Dynes (1998) argues that the community should be the locus of analysis in emergencies, disasters and catastrophes, as the findings have cross-national and cross-cultural applicability.

However, the danger of relying on informal communications in crises lies in the authenticity of the message. This was highlighted in the statements of lay witnesses during the 2009 Victorian Bushfires Royal Commission Australia, in which some commented on the confusion caused by a number of false reports on 'backchannel' communications via mobile phone and social media, in the absence of formal communications (Parliament of Victoria, 2009).

In summary, official channels of communication in the field are traditionally formal and designed to push information from an authoritative source to the civilian masses. They have often been given legitimacy over backchannel communications, which are informal and participatory sources of local knowledge and conditions in the field. However, through mobile technologies and social media, formal and informal m-communications in and around crises are becoming blurred. Although social media have been among the chosen vehicles for backchannel communications, we are now witnessing official networks such as the broadcast media sourcing their material from these so-called 'informal' sources for the purposes of 'formal' communications. Palen et al. (2010) refer to this as the changing of information pathways.

In emergencies, disasters and catastrophes, news sells, and there is often a race between television channels and radio stations to be first with the breaking news. During the Category 5 tropical storm Cyclone Yasi on the coast of Far North Queensland (Thursday 3 February 2011), broadcast media were making regular pleas to the civilian population to send in their stories, photos and videos of the crisis, so that they could broadcast rolling news updates. In this process, national and international media outlets were gathering civilian digital resources shared in various forms of social media. As one exemplar, uploaded videoclips on YouTube of Cyclone Yasi were used by the global media outlet Russia Today. Formal communications channels crossed over to informal channels in other ways too. For example, in the immediate aftermath of Cyclone Yasi, Channel 7's weather man, Grant Denyer, was travelling with emergency-service crews at the time. His portable mobile-reporting solution was to use his smartphone connected to the social network Skype. This enabled Denyer to get swiftly into affected areas and go live to air without the need for an accompanying sound and film crew (Dodd, 2011).

Blurring of Formal and Informal Learning

In times of crisis, the boundaries between formal and informal learning blur. Formal learning is structured learning under the auspices of an educational body. In crises, Perry and Lindell (2003) distinguish between two types of learning: education, which is aimed at the civilian population and other key stakeholder groups who do not hold an official function in the crisis situation, and training, which is specifically targeted for the civilian population that is at risk, in addition to the emergency-services personnel who work in these situations. As an added benefit, the associated learning can also become an important source of feedback regarding potential problems with plans in place for dealing with future events (Perry & Lindell, 2003).

By contrast, Facer (2004, p. 1) describes informal learning as 'the sort of learning that goes on as part of our normal day-to-day activities when we don't even think we are learning'. Informal learning is the least recognized (Siemens, 2004) form of learning and often considered inferior to formal learning (Coffield, 2000). Informal learning is often learner-driven and encourages exploration and play, and the development of skills.

In the mobile environment, apps are one means of providing flexible learning opportunities that are 'just enough, just in time, just for me' (Rosenberg, 2001). The Country Fire Authority (CFA) of Victoria has recently released its FireReady app for smartphones (CFA, 2012b), which contains key aspects from the organization's official website (www.cfa.vic.gov.au/). The official website itself is linked to social-media sites such as Digg it, Facebook and Twitter. To address the diversity within and between the various stakeholder groups, a PDF on fire information is available on the CFA website, accessible via a button on the FireReady app, with the information contained available in different languages. It also includes a crisis educational program entitled 'Are you ready?' as a fire-risk assessment program that can be used to assess one's own knowledge of fires. Other aspects of the FireReady app include tutorials and a checklist to complete; incident reporting (by oneself or with others); the ability to upload video or photographs or view those shared by others; location maps; the ability to locate oneself in relation to the incident via the mobile's GPS; being able to set personal alerts; and get directions (Figure 44.4). Through such programs, some of the challenges of learning in and around crises such as fires can be overcome.

CONCLUSION

Emergencies, disasters and catastrophes, either from natural causes or resulting from human actions or inactions, occur around the globe on a daily basis. Surviving such crisis situations is paramount for civilians and emergency-services personnel alike. Understanding local conditions, receiving warnings and guidance, and learning and training may help reduce human losses.

Mobile phones and the social media of Web 2.0 are becoming the means by which the dissemination of information and educational offerings can be more swiftly achieved than by traditional means. M-learning is thus a means for rapid response and the provision of learning opportunities that are 'just enough, just in time, just for me'.

However, to be fully effective, the preparation and implementation of m-learning in and around crises need to factor in three fundamental aspects. These are the diversity of the stakeholders, their access to the mobile technology and social networks, and the subsequent mobile connectivity. To understand not only the potentials of m-learning in crises, but also the challenges, can help in the creation of a powerful means to minimize losses.

Figure 44.4 CFA Victoria's FireReady 2.0 App

ACKNOWLEDGEMENTS

Julie Willems wishes to gratefully acknowledge permission from the CFA Victoria for the use of the image in Figure 44.4. She also wishes to acknowledge the auDA Foundation (http://audafoundation.org.au) 2011 funding for the i-Survive Project – a pilot project on the use of smartphones and social networks during Australian emergencies and disasters. Two of the images in this chapter form the i-Survive Project logo (http://isurviveproject.wikispaces.com/i-Survive+Project).

REFERENCES

Australian Broadcasting Commission. (2009). *Lightning starts new bushfires in the Grampians.* Retrieved from: www.abc.net.au/news/2009–02–08/lightning-starts-new-bushfires-in-grampians/287662

Australian Communications & Media Authority. (2009). *Convergence and Communications: Report 1: Australian household consumers' take-up and use of voice communications services.* Retrieved from: www.acma.gov.au/webwr/_assets/main/lib100068/convergence_%20comms_rep-1_household_consumers.doc

Australian Communications & Media Authority. (2011). *Australians hunger for choice in communications* [Media release]. Retrieved from: www.acma.gov.au/WEB/STANDARD/pc=PC_410252

Barry, S. (2011). The eye of the storm: Authorities looking at ways to improve SMS texting of warnings for natural disasters. *ABC News.* Retrieved from: www.abc.net.au/news/video/2011/09/30/3330099.htm?site=canberra

Boyd, D. M., & Ellison, N. B. (2007). Social network sites: Definition, history, and scholarship. *Journal of Computer-Mediated Communication, 13*(1), article 11. Retrieved from: http://jcmc.indiana.edu/vol13/issue1/boyd.ellison.html

Britton, N. (1986). Developing an understanding of disasters. *Australian and New Zealand Journal of Sociology, 22*(20), 254–272.

Brown, M. (2012). Victoria gets location-based emergency warnings. *ABC News.* Retrieved from: www.abc.net.au/news/2012–01–13/victoria-gets-new-location-based-emergency-warnings/3770884

Country Fire Authority. (2012a). FireReadyKit. Retrieved from: www.test.cfa.vic.gov.au/fm_files/attachments/plan_and_prepare/frk/fire-ready-kit-complete.docx

Country Fire Authority. (2012b). FireReady app. Retrieved from: www.cfa.vic.gov.au/plan-prepare/fireready-app/

Coffield, F. (2000). *The necessity of informal learning.* Bristol, UK: The Policy Press.

Crompton, H. (2013). A historical overview of mobile learning: Toward learner-centered education (pp. 3–14). In Z. Berge, & L. Muilenburg (Eds.), *Handbook of mobile learning.* New York: Routledge.

Department of Broadband, Communication and the Digital Economy. (2011). *Natural disasters.* Retrieved from: www.dbcde.gov.au/policy_and_legislation/responsibilities_under_the_telecommunications_act/natural_disasters

Dodd, A. (2011). *iPhones in hand, they rushed to the scene of Yasi devastation.* Retrieved from: www.crikey.com.au/2011/02/03/iphones-in-hand-they-rushed-to-the-scene-of-yasi-devastation/

Dynes, R. R. (1998). *Dealing with disasters in the 21st Century.* Newark, NJ: Disaster Research Center, University of Delaware.

European Commission. (2008). Agricultural insurance schemes. *Agricultural and Rural Development.* Retrieved from: http://ec.europa.eu/agriculture/analysis/external/insurance/index_en.htm

Evans, V., & Larri, L. J. (2007). Social software and its possible future uses. *Australian Flexible Learning Framework: Supporting e-learning opportunities (Part III).* Retrieved from: www.masternewmedia.org/online_collaboration/social-software/future-of-social-software-for-learning-and.-education-20070531.htm

Facer, K. (2004). Forward. In J. Sefton-Green (Ed.), *Literature review in informal learning with technology outside school.* Report 7. FutureLab. Retrieved from: www.futurelab.org.uk/resources/documents/lit_reviews/Informal_Learning_Review.pdf

Fischer, H. (2003). The sociology of disaster: Definitions, research questions, and measurements in a post-September 11, 2001 environment. *International Journal of Mass Emergencies and Disasters, 21*(1), 91–107. Retrieved from: www.ijmed.org/articles/82/download/

Griswold, W. G. (2004). Position statement. In J. McCarthy, D. Boyd, E. F. Churchill, W. G. Griswold, E. Lawley & M. Zaner (2005). Digital backchannels in shared physical spaces: Attention, intention and contention. *Proceedings of the 2004 ACM Conference on Computer Supported Cooperative Work (Chicago, November 6–10, 2004)* (pp. 550–553). New York: ACM Press. Retrieved from: http://www.danah.org/papers/CSCW2004Panel.pdf

Hiltz, S. R., Diaz, P., & Mark, G. (2011). Introduction: Social media and collaborative systems for crisis management. *ACM Transactions on Computer-Human Interaction, 18*(4), article 18.

J.D. Power Assoc. (2011). *Social media use drives higher satisfaction among owners of smartphones and traditional mobile phones* [Press release]. Retrieved from: http://businesscenter.jdpower.com/JDPAContent/CorpComm/News/content/Releases/pdf/2011030-wrhs.pdf

Johnson, L., Smith, R., Willis, H., Levine, A., & Haywood, K. (2011). *The 2011 horizon report*. Austin, TX: New Media Consortium. Retrieved from: http://net.educause.edu/ir/library/pdf/HR2011.pdf

Kaplan, A. M., & Haenlein, M. (2010). Users of the world, unite! The challenges and opportunities of social media. *Business Horizons, 53*(1), 59–68.

Lachlan, K. A., & Spence, P. R. (2007). Audience responses and informational needs: Considering diversity in crisis communication. In A. Ferguson & A.R. Narro (Eds.), *Diversity & mass communication: Evidence of impact*. Southlake, TX: Fountainhead Press.

Laouris, Y., & Eteokleous, N. (2005). *We need an educationally relevant definition of mobile learning*. Paper presented at the mLearn2005: 4th World Conference on mLearning, Cape Town, South Africa. Retrieved from: www.mlearn.org.za/CD/papers/Laouris%20%26%20Eteokleous.pdf

Lawley, E. (2004). Position statement. In J. McCarthy, D. Boyd, E. F. Churchill, W. G. Griswold, E. Lawley & M. Zaner (2005). Digital backchannels in shared physical spaces: Attention, intention and contention. *Proceedings of the 2004 ACM Conference on Computer Supported Cooperative Work (Chicago, November 6–10, 2004)* (pp. 550–553). New York: ACM Press. Retrieved from: www.danah.org/papers/CSCW2004Panel.pdf

Lundin, J., Lymer, G., Holmquist, L. E., Brown, B., & Rost, M. (2010). Integrating students' mobile technology in higher education. *International Journal of Mobile Learning and Organisation, 4*(1), 1–14. Retrieved from: www.inderscience.com/storage/f123671110152948.pdf

Nielsen. (2010). *Nielsen's state of the online market: Evolution or revolution?* [Media release]. Retrieved from: http://au.nielsen.com/site/documents/AustralianOnlineConsumersReportMediaRelease.pdf

Nielsen. (2011). *State of the media: The social media report, Q3 2011*. Retrieved from: www.befirstinc.com/nielsen-social-media-report.pdf

News Limited. (2009). *Bushfire death toll revised down*. Retrieved from: www.news.com.au/national/bushfire-death-toll-revised-down/story-e6frfkvr-1225697246725

Oliver, C. E. (2010). *Catastrophic disaster planning and response*. Boca Raton, FL: CRC Press.

Palen, L., Anderson, K. M., Mark, G., Martin, J., Sicker, D., Palmer, M., & Grunwald, D. (2010). A vision for technology-mediated support for public participation & assistance in mass emergencies & disasters. *Proceedings of ACM-BCS Visions of Computer Science 2010*. Retrieved from: www.bcs.org/upload/pdf/ewic_vs10_s4 paper2.pdf

Palm Inc. (2006). *The value of smartphones and handheld devices for government Continuity of Operations (COOP) and emergency response* [White Paper]. Retrieved from: www.hpwebos.com/asia/assets/pdf/COOP Whitepaper.pdf

Parliament of Victoria. (2009). *2009 Victorian Bushfires Royal Commission Australia: Final Report Volume IV: The statements of lay witnesses*. Retrieved from: http://vol4.royalcommission.vic.gov.au/index.php?pid=155

Parliament of Victoria. (2010). *2009 Victorian Bushfires Royal Commission Australia: Final Report Summary*. Retrieved from: www.royalcommission.vic.gov.au/finaldocuments/summary/PF/VBRC_Summary_PF.pdf

Perry, R. W., & Lindell, M. K. (2003). Understanding citizen response to disasters and implications for terrorism. *Journal of Contingencies and Crisis Management, 11*, 49–60.

Police Federation of Australia. (2011). *Police federation of Australia submission to the Environment and Communications References Committee: Inquiry into emergency communications*. Retrieved from: www.pfa.org.au/files/uploads/PFA_Submission_Emergency_Communications_0.pdf

Quarantelli, E. L. (2006). Catastrophes are different from disasters: Some implications for crisis planning and managing drawn from Katrina. In *Understanding Katrina: Perspectives from the social sciences*. Brooklyn, NY: Social Science Research Council (SSRC). Retrieved from: http://understandingkatrina.ssrc.org/Quarantelli/

Rosenberg, M. J. (2001). *E-learning: Strategies for delivering knowledge in the digital age*. New York: MacGraw-Hill.

Sensis. (2011). *E-business report: The online experience of small and medium enterprises 2011*. Retrieved from: http://about.sensis.com.au/IgnitionSuite/uploads/docs/2011%20Sensis%20e-Business%20Report%20FINAL.pdf

Siemens, G. (2004). *Categories of e-learning*. Retrieved from: www.elearnspace.org/Articles/elearningcategories.htm

Stuckey, B., & Arkell, R. (2006). *Development of an e-learning knowledge sharing model: 2005 Knowledge sharing services project* [Australian Flexible Learning Framework Project Report]. Canberra: Commonwealth of Australia.

Sutton, J., Palen, L., & Shklovski, I. (2008). Backchannels on the front lines: Emergent uses of social media in the 2007 Southern California wildfires. In F. Fiedrich & B. Van de Walle (Eds), *Proceedings of the 5th International ISCRAM Conference, Washington, DC, May 2008* (pp. 624–631). Retrieved from: www.iscram.org/dm documents/ISCRAM2008/papers/ISCRAM2008_Sutton_etal.pdf

Traxler, J. (2007). Defining, discussing and evaluating mobile learning. *The International Review Of Research In Open And Distance Learning, 8*(2). Retrieved from: www.irrodl.org/index.php/irrodl/article/view/346/875

Traxler, J. (2010). Will student devices deliver innovation, inclusion, and transformation? *Journal Of The Research Center For Educational Technology, 6*(1), 3–15. Retrieved from: www.rcetj.org/index.php/rcetj/article/view/56

United Nations International Strategy for Disaster Reduction. (2009). *UNDISR 2009 terminology on disaster risk reduction.* Geneva: United Nations. Retrieved from: www.unisdr.org/files/7817_UNISDRTerminology English.pdf

Verma, S. (2011). *Smartphones to redraw the African mobile phone map.* Retrieved from: http://tilt.ft.com/ #!posts/2011-09/30696/rise-of-smartphones-africa

Wagner, E. D. (2005). Enabling mobile learning. *EDUCAUSE Review, 40*(3), 40–53.

Whitelaw, D. (2010). *Social media and crisis (Emergency 2.0).* Retrieved from: www.slideshare.net/Digitaldarren/ social-media-and-emergencies

45

IMPROVING STUDENTS' MODERN LANGUAGE SPEAKING SKILLS THROUGH MOBILE LEARNING

Harry Grover Tuttle

The American Council for the Teaching of Foreign Languages (ACTFL) (1999) identifies five learning goals of language: communication, cultures, connections, comparisons, and communities. However, most students and their parents focus on the *speaking* dimension of communication: parents ask their children, "Can you speak the language?" (Bailey, 2005). Of all these five ACTFL language areas, students develop least in their speaking skills, and their inability to express themselves has a negative impact on their confidence and enthusiasm (Office for Standards in Education, Children's Services and Skills, 2008).

PROBLEM

How can students develop their spontaneous speaking in the target language? Most student speaking in the modern-language class focuses on textbook grammar and vocabulary exercises, not on conversing in the language (Tuttle, 2011b). As modern-language teachers realize that their students use mobile devices to communicate in their native language, these teachers can begin to use those mobile devices in the classroom to enable students to converse in the target language. When students use their phones or other m-learning devices in the target language as a basis for talking about topics that interest them, they develop their speaking ability. In general, "when students use their phones for learning, they engage in m-learning learning which is learning across multiple contexts, through social and content interactions, using personal electronic devices." (Crompton, 2013, p. 4). When learners use m-learning in modern languages, it is called mobile-assisted language learning (MALL). In MALL, language learning is assisted or enhanced through the use of a handheld mobile device such as a cell phone or smartphone, tablets and MP players (Valarmathi, 2011).

Although some modern-language teachers have their students use mobile technology in their classes, the students most often do lower-level learning for vocabulary, grammar, pronunciation, or reading activities. These MALL programs develop memorization learning through repetition and drills (Bahrani, 2011; Tuttle, 2011a). For example, the students use their m-learning device to hear and then repeat a French word for pronunciation (Demouy & Kukulska-Hulme, 2010). Also, m-learning programs (apps) focus on learning the discrete parts of language, but not on using the language in spontaneous speaking. For example, the apps merely provide lists of words such as in dictionary apps, certain phrases such as traveling apps, or verb conjugations as in verb-conjugation apps, but these apps do not develop conversational skills (Tuttle, 2011b).

Likewise, Chih-Ming and Yi-Lun (2010) argue that students' m-learning should be within a meaningful context. Usually, m-learning activities lack context; for example, students study restaurant words in the classroom, not in a restaurant. Wong, Chin, Tan, and Liu (2010) and Tuttle (2011c) urge that m-learning devices can help the students bring the world into the classroom through students taking pictures of real things such as restaurants and then talking about those pictures in the classroom.

As seen from the research, most present-day m-learning activities concentrate on lower-level basic skills, not on speaking proficiency. Modern-language teachers can use m-learning devices to promote the communication skill of spontaneous speaking through contextual learning.

POPULATION SERVED/TARGETED

I use m-learning activities in my first- and second-level Spanish courses at a community college in central New York, with students from diverse ethnic backgrounds and from the ages of 16 to 55 years old. M-learning has been successfully implemented on both the main campus and the satellite campus, which is in a shopping mall. Depending on the learning goals for the class, I use from one to three m-learning activities during each class meeting. These m-learning activities last 3–10 minutes. Modern-language middle- or high-school teachers or college professors can apply these mobile language learning techniques to their classes.

DESCRIPTION OF MANAGEMENT PROCESSES

Some educators may hesitate to use m-learning, because they worry about the equity issue. When students work in pairs, only half the class needs to have smartphones. Through surveys, I have learned that more than half of my students have smartphones. Also, students can do many of my classroom m-learning activities with a regular feature phone, which has the ability to take pictures and record video. Furthermore, when the students have a low battery or connectivity problem with their own smartphones, they use the teacher's computer or even his/her smartphone.

The use of m-learning with smartphones has some minor logistical issues. Students need to have charged phones. Students can plug in their phones at the beginning of class if they need more battery power. In the satellite mall campus, students have discovered that certain parts of the room have a stronger signal, so they grab the signal and then move back to their usual area. Some students, about half of those with smartphones in my classes, have a minimal data plan. However, when those students put their m-learning devices on the school's network, they do not use up any minutes during classroom use.

M-learning with smartphones has overcome some classroom issues. When students look at a projected image, not all students, particularly those in the back of the room, can easily read the text or see the image. As students can make the font or image bigger on their m-learning devices, all students can clearly see the words or image. Often, in pair work, students do not face or look at each other. In contrast, as students generally share a smartphone, they focus on the smartphone and each other. Likewise, if students have class in a computer lab, the students cannot see other students owing to the large computer monitor. Most students put the smartphone on the desk or hold it in their lap, so they can easily see their partner.

QR codes speed up classroom interaction. The teacher shows the students a QR-code reader and identifies QR-code readers for various types of phone. Furthermore, he/she demonstrates how to click on the QR-code-reader app, focus the camera on the QR code, see the link(s) appear, and click on the link. During the time that a student takes to turn on the computer in a computer lab, log in, and access the website, three students can use the QR-code reader on the same m-learning device to do a short Internet activity. Additionally, students do not waste time in retyping a mistyped Web address, even a shortened one, when they use QR codes. Furthermore, the learners can jump from one website to another just by reclicking on the QR code, which contains more than one website. More importantly, the classroom instructor does not have to print out a QR code for the students; the instructor simply projects the code on a PowerPoint screen. The students walk up toward the screen, focus their phones on the QR code, click on the link, and begin the activity.

Teachers can learn some tips to better utilize QR codes. Before creating a QR code, teachers can shorten the website address (URL) by using a URL shortener such as bt.ly. Therefore, the teacher can include four to six different websites in the same QR code. When educators use a QR code, they will want to label each QR code with a title, such as "German weather map," for future quick reference. When QR codes contain numerous websites, each code becomes a rich resource, as opposed to a single website QR code. Moreover, teachers can link the QR code to a fixed location, such as a website page, wiki page, or blog page, so that they can change the information on that Web location without having to physically modify the QR code. For example, a teacher may have two pictures of restaurants on a Web page and a QR code for that link. The teacher can change one or both of the restaurant pictures on the Web page, while the QR code stays the same (Tuttle, 2011c).

SPEAKING ACTIVITIES WITH M-LEARNING

Language learners improve in their speaking by using m-learning devices, as indicated in the following activities (Tuttle, 2011c).

Speaking

Picture

Students open a teacher-provided QR code and select a picture of their choice to talk about with their speaking partners. For example, students choose a link to a sport picture or to a hobby picture. They compare what is in the picture with what they normally do in their lives for that sport or hobby. They share with their partner sentences such as "He plays soccer in a stadium. I play soccer in a field. He has a team shirt. I wear my blue shirt."

Series of Pictures

Students use their mobile devices to take a series of three to five pictures that tell a story. In class, they tell their partner the story as the partner looks at the pictures. The partner asks questions for more information. For example, a student takes pictures of herself getting ready for, going to, and leaving a party. Her partner asks about the location, the type of music, the number of people, and the food.

Videos

Students use their phone's movie-recording feature to record a minute or two of any daily life event, such as the family eating, friends playing basketball, their little sister playing in a park, etc., without any sound. In class, the partner views the movie once and then replays it as he/she narrates it to the student who recorded it. The two students can collectively comment on the event, such as saying how much the little sister enjoys the park, or making up a conversation she has with her older brother or sister.

Voice Recording

Students use their m-learning device's voice-recorder app to record their conversation with a native speaker of the language who lives in the area. Even beginning language students can have a basic communication exchange (What is your name? How are you? Where are you from? What sport do you like?) with a target-language speaker. More advanced students converse in detail about one topic, such as food or school, with sentences such as, "What is your favorite food? How do you make it? Is it a favorite food of many people in your country? What do you like about USA food?" In class, students who have recorded the same topic, such as food, form pairs and listen to each other's recording. They identify what similar and different ideas each conversation had.

Flickr Speaking

Students take pictures of 10 topical vocabulary items, such as pictures of sports items; then, they individually e-mail one picture at a time to the teacher's Flickr e-mail account, such as samp88bab@photos.flickr.com. The students write the name of the individual sport in the subject line, such as *béisbol* and write the tag in the message box, such as tag:sport (tag:*deportes*). In class, the teacher selects a tag such as sports (*deportes*) and uses the slideshow mode to show each picture, as the students orally identify all the picture vocabulary in that topic. Next, the teacher has the students, in groups of two, say a short sentence about each vocabulary slideshow item, before the slideshow moves to the next picture, and, then, the partner says the next sentence. For example, for baseball, a student might say, "My brother plays baseball," "I do not like baseball," or "My favorite baseball team is The Yankees," and the partner may say, for the next sport, basketball, "I play basketball in June," "I play in a park," and "I make many points." If students are going to put up about 200 pictures in total in a month, then teachers will need to pay for professional membership of Flickr, which costs $24.95 a year.

Translation and Conjugation Apps

As students speak using a specific language function (describing something, requesting information, etc.) about a common topic such as school, their partners monitor them and tell them specific speaking problems. Next, the students use an m-learning device's instant translator app or a dictionary app to find the vocabulary word that they were struggling to think of, or one that they misused. Likewise, they can verify a verb form that they forgot or were confused about by checking a verb-conjugation app. Finally, they practice with the corrected vocabulary and/or grammar to improve their speaking.

Phone Conversation

Students use their m-learning device to talk to a person of the language area. A French person who is in the USA has a short, 5-minute phone conversation with the whole class or a small group of students about the class's current topic of celebrations. That person, or another French-speaking person, can call the class once a week. The teacher can hold a computer microphone next to the phone and use the higher volume of the computer's speakers to allow the whole class to hear the person. Likewise, student teams can prepare topical questions for the French-speaker. For example, for the celebration topic, the students might ask how that person celebrates a birthday, Christmas, or a wedding. If the m-learning device has a videoconferencing capability, then the students see the person. That person can show the students items such as a French birthday card or a picture of a birthday party.

Interest-Survey Reaction

Learners use a QR code to access an interest survey in Google Forms, such as "What sport do you play?" or "What sport do you watch the most?" As soon as they finish the multiple-choice interest survey on their m-learning device, the teacher opens up that Google Form on the class computer, goes to Form—Show summary of responses, and projects the results, which do not have any individual students listed. The students discuss the results. A beginning student may say, "I like to play American football because I am strong."

App Conversation

Students, in pairs, listen to a language app that speaks the basic phrases for a topic, such as shopping, and, then, these students create a meaningful conversation from those phrases. For example, they hear phrases such as "Do you have this in a large?" "How much does it cost?" and "I do not like the color." They combine these listened-to phrases into a logical conversation about someone wanting to buy a red shirt in a clothing store.

Image Reaction

Students, in pairs, use their m-learning device's Internet search engine to find a target-language search engine such as www.google.es for Google Spain. They click on Images. Next, they type in a word from their current unit of study in the target language to find pictures. For example, they type in the Spanish word *ropa* for clothing and, then, they look at the various items of clothing being shown/advertised. Additionally, they discuss the various items of clothing, the prices, decide if they want to buy the product or not, and say why or why not. At beginning levels, they can say, "I like the dress. It is red. It is long," whereas, at a more advanced level, they might say, "The dress has long sleeves and is made of silk. I would wear it to a dance."

Target-Language Songs

Language learners listen to two songs in the target language on their m-learning device, using a site such as www.live365.com. They search for their target country and select from one of the many stations that broadcasting music in the target language. After each song, they identify the message, story line, key words, main metaphors, emotions, or instruments and then compare the two songs. Beginning students might say sentences such as, "I like the song. I hear guitars. It repeats 'Love' many times. It is sad," whereas advanced students might say sentences such as, "This is a sad love song. The singer compares a break up to a fire. Her heart no longer burns for her boyfriend."

Video House Tour

Students can individually use their m-learning device to create a tour of their house. They take pictures of their house and upload those pictures to a program such as Yodio. If their m-learning device does not send pictures, then they take the pictures with a digital camera, upload to their computer, and send the picture from their computer. Next, they record a target-language narration for each room in Yodio using their phone. Then, they move the picture and the audio for the first room into the first track, the next room's picture and audio into the second track, etc. Finally, they publish their media tour of their house.

Online Recordings with Voki

Modern-language learners can record their conversation with their partners, such as a conversation about an athlete event, in a program such as Voki. They go to Voki.com, find the call-in number, call it, and record their conversation on their phone. For example, one student might try to convince another student to go to the school's baseball game. Later on, they move this recording to their wiki page, where other students or the teacher can give them feedback. They can create an audio e-portfolio of their speaking.

Narrate Partner's Pictures

Students take a series of eight or more phone pictures showing the actions for a specific topic. For example, students may take pictures of classroom actions, such as to enter, to sit down, to study, to write, etc. Then, the students show their pictures to their partners, who narrate a story using those topical actions. A student might say, "Mary enters the German classroom. She sits down in a chair. She opens her book." The partner provides additional information to the information already said; he/she might add, "Mary enters the German classroom at nine o'clock. She likes German. She sits down in a wooden chair and puts her books under the chair."

Speaking and Culture

Contrast and Compare

Learners, in pairs, click on the teacher-provided QR code to see links to two different pictures of the same topic. They carefully look at the first picture before looking at the second picture. The students contrast the two pictures, such as two houses, two beaches, two universities, or two restaurants from the target-language area, to decide which is better and why. For example, they look at a map of the University of Mexico and then look at a map of the University of Madrid and contrast the two universities; they say which university they think is better and why.

Sports Analysis

Students can analyze culture with their m-learning devices. A Spanish teacher has his/her students get into pairs and gives each pair the name of a different country of the target language. For example, student pairs may have Mexico, Puerto Rico, Dominican Republic, Venezuela, etc. Then, the students look up their country plus the word for sports in the Spanish Google image search engine, such as Puerto Rico + *deportes*. In their pair grouping, they take turns in identifying the various sports in the first 30 pictures. Then, they determine which sport has the most pictures by counting the number of pictures per sport. Next, they make up a story involving the various pictures of the most popular sport.

Daily Culture with Webcams

The students describe what they see in teacher-provided QR codes of various webcams from a webcam site (such as www.liveworldwebcam.net/country/Italy/1_page.html) from a country of the target language. For example, Italian students can pick a location in Italy from the choices on the left, or a category such as cathedrals from the center. In pairs, the students describe one location in detail, go to another location in Italy, talk about it, and, next, they say the similarities and differences between the first location and the second one in terms of geography, weather, homes, streets, activities, etc. As students do this activity, they may search the Google map of the target-language country for the specific city, as often these webcam sites do not have maps that show the city's specific location within the country.

Weather Discussions

Students bring up the weather from a target-language country such as China, where the terms are in Chinese. The students, in pairs, identify the major weather and temperature in different parts of the country. Next, they say where they want to be in that country and why, based on weather and temperature. A beginning student might say, "Harbin is very cold. I like the cold," whereas a more advanced student might state, "I prefer the warm climate of Haikou. Also, it is near the ocean so I can watch boats."

Assessment of Speaking

QR in Class Assessment

Learners take a quick in-class assessment on their m-learning device. For example, they use a QR code to access a Google Form five-question quiz on topical vocabulary, such as places to get food, with sentences such as "I buy food in . . ." with four multiple-choice answers. As soon as they complete the quiz, the teacher shows the class's responses using the Form > Show summary-of-responses feature. The program shows the results in pie charts or bar graphs, without any student's name. Then, the teacher can immediately go over any learning gaps and provide new learning strategies for the students. Such in-class formative assessments enable students to have critical vocabulary for their speaking.

Teacher Record of Student Data

Teachers can use any online form such as a Google Forms to create a teachers' assessment of their students' speaking progress. The teachers can have a form for a particular speaking function, such as describing a photo in 10 sentences in 1 minute. The form lists the students (going down the form) and the dates of each class when students do this speaking exercise (going across the form). The teachers walk around the classroom and click on that form's date when a student has been successful. For example, Rowan may say 10 sentences in the third day of doing this activity, and so the teacher clicks on the third date. The teacher can look at the list to see who has already mastered this skill and who needs additional support. In a slight variation, the teacher has the students listed down the left side and the rubric score going across (0–10, with each number in its own column). As soon as a student finishes speaking, the teacher records the data in the form. As students improve, the teacher changes the number to the higher number. As an illustration, the first time Lily scores a 3, the teacher clicks on the 3 button. However, when she improves and scores a 5, the teacher clicks on the 5, which removes the 3 score. At any given moment, the teachers know the exact speaking level of the students and can provide necessary feedback for their improvement.

Students' Progress

Students use Google Docs, specifically the spreadsheet, to keep track of their own progress. For each speaking function, such as asking and answering questions, they record their own score after each in-class exercise. They try to increase their score. They often want to check their mobile device to see what they scored last time on the Google spreadsheet, before doing the present day's speaking exercise.

RESULTS

Outcomes

Through the use of MALL, students speak about authentic situations by accessing a picture of a real restaurant, a family at a party, etc., or by talking with people of the target language. Students not only learn daily culture through seeing pictures of modern-day people and places, but they use this culture in their speaking. As the classroom interaction comes to more closely resemble the outside world, the students learn to speak using real language. Students go from learning about a language to speaking it spontaneously.

Successes

Students enjoy the interactivity of using the smartphone in class. They like seeing what life (culture) is like in the target area and they like talking about it. More importantly, they increase in their ability to speak spontaneously, as their speaking becomes more based on talking about real situations and real people.

Failures

Students do become very impatient if the school's network is not fast enough to instantly bring up images and information; some give up on an activity. Sometimes, smartphone-enabled websites become overloaded, and the students cannot get through. A student might try once or twice, but they will not usually try more times. Also, students want to go to mobile-enabled Web pages instead of having to scroll all over a Web page to find the image or information that they want. Some students have a low tolerance for not immediately finding the designated image or information.

Likewise, although students want to talk about a real-world photo, they may have forgotten the vocabulary. Some students experience a high degree of frustration when not remembering the words. When a teacher does a preliminary review of critical vocabulary, then students feel more comfortable about their talking.

Advice

Teachers will want to:

- do any m-learning activity themselves before having the students do it. If the activity has multiple steps, the teachers will write out the steps for the students. Also, they will demonstrate it in class or make a short video using a screen-capture program on how to do a particular new m-learning activity.
- take time to find higher-level thinking and culturally relevant Internet resources for QR codes.
- structure the m-learning to guide students from the lower levels of speaking to the higher levels of speaking. As an illustration, teachers will have students move from just simple vocabulary identification to using that vocabulary in real-life conversations about the shown situation.
- keep activities to short and meaningful ones. For example, most of my Web-based speaking activities last about 3 minutes.
- ask students to act responsibly when they encounter any objectionable material. In an image search for France + waiter to get ready for a restaurant conversation, the students might encounter a waitress with very little or no clothing. They simply skip that image and go on to the next.

DISCUSSION AND CONCLUSION REGARDING M-LEARNING AND EDUCATION

As more students have Web-enabled m-learning devices, then teachers can alternate between pair work and individual work. However, teachers will want to retain a large amount of students talking in pairs or small groups, as such intrapersonal communication is the essence of modern-language conversation.

As more schools' networks get faster and more reliable for Web-enabled m-learning devices, then students can do their work more effectively. When students have to wait 3 or 4 minutes for their short audio file from their m-learning device to be transferred to the cloud, they lose interest in the activity.

As modern-language apps move from just text-based vocabulary drills and grammar drills to simulations and visually interactive sites, students can become more active in authentic language use.

If modern-language m-learning turns into learning from the textbook on your phone with traditional drill-and-kill activities, then students will quickly become disengaged. Textbook companies will have to create interactive media-rich activities.

As teachers create higher-level thinking communication activities for m-learning, students will become better able to speak spontaneously.

WEBSITES

bit.ly: www.bit.ly.com
Flickr: www.flickr.com
Google Spain: www.google.es
Live365: www.live365.com
Live world webcams: www.liveworldwebcam.net/country/Italy/1_page.html
Voki for Education: www.voki.com/

REFERENCES

American Council for the Teaching of Foreign Languages. (1999). *ACTFL revised proficiency guidelines—Speaking.* Yonkers, NY: American Council on the Teaching of Foreign Languages. Retrieved from: www.sil.org/lingualinks/languagelearning/OtherResources/ACTFLProficiencyGuidelines/contents.htm

Bahrani, T. (2011). Mobile phones: Just a phone or a language learning device? *Cross-Cultural Communication, 7*(2), 244–248. DOI:10.3968/j.ccc.1923670020110702.028

Bailey, K. M. (2005). *"Washback": Practical English language teaching speaking.* New York: McGraw-Hill.

Chih-Ming, C., & Yi-Lun, L. (2010). Personalised context-aware ubiquitous learning system for supporting effective English vocabulary learning. *Interactive Learning Environments, 18*(4), 341–364. DOI:10.1080/10494820802602329

Crompton, H. (2013). A historical overview of mobile learning: Toward learner-centered education (pp. 3–14). In Z. Berge, & L. Muilenburg (Eds.), *Handbook of mobile learning.* New York: Routledge.

Demouy, V., & Kukulska-Hulme, A. (2010). On the spot: Using mobile devices for listening and speaking practice on a French language programme. *Open Learning, 25*(3), 217–232. DOI:10.1080/02680513.2010.511955

Office for Standards in Education, Children's Services and Skills. (2008). Speaking is the weak link in language teaching. *Education* (14637073). Retrieved from Academic Search Premier database.

Tuttle, H. G. (2011a). Modern language mobile learning apps. In R. Goldberg & W. White (Eds.), *People, practices, and programs that inspire.* Buffalo, NY: NYSAFLT.

Tuttle, H. G. (2011b). Smartphone apps for Spanish. *Language Connections, 6*(6), 15.

Tuttle, H. G. (2011c). *Improving students' speaking through Smartphones.* New York Association of Foreign Language Teachers Conference, Rochester, NY.

Valarmathi, K. E. (2011). Mobile assisted language learning. *Journal of Technology for ELT, 1*(2). Retrieved from: https://sites.google.com/site/journaloftechnologyforelt/archive/april2011/mobileassistedlanguagelearning

Wong, L. H., Chin, C. K., Tan, C. L., & Liu, M. (2010). Students' personal and social meaning making in a Chinese idiom mobile learning environment. *Educational Technology & Society, 13*(4), 15–26.

46

HOW MOBILE LEARNING FACILITATES STUDENT ENGAGEMENT

A Case Study from the Teaching of Spanish

Elizabeth A. Beckmann and M. Daniel Martìn

M-learning is not a new phenomenon. Ever since human societies began to record their achievements, philosophies, histories, and ideas in resources that were portable—whether stone tablets, printed books, wax cylinders, or cassette tapes—people have taken advantage of that portability to learn what they want, where they want. The difference today is the increasing plethora of mobile electronic devices that have seemingly few limits on what they can access from across the whole world of human knowledge. As Chapter 1 explains, m-learning can be defined as a process whereby personal electronic devices are used to facilitate "learning across multiple contexts, through social and content interactions" (Crompton, 2013, p. 4). This chapter explores these contexts and interactions as contributors to higher-quality, and more authentic, learning outcomes when m-learning is encouraged. For example, during 6 years (2005–2011) of action research into diverse innovations in teaching Spanish to undergraduates at the Australian National University (ANU), we have found that facilitating m-learning is an effective way for teachers to maximize students' exposure to, and engagement with, language resources as both listeners and speakers. Using evidence primarily from this case study, we explain why and how those of us who wish to emphasize student-centered teaching must support—perhaps even insist on—increasing use of mobile technologies.

In this chapter, we first outline the case study, explaining why and how the Spanish program at ANU, like many language programs, adopted an educational design that focused especially on audio and audio-visual resources, and how this led to the recognition that students with mobile devices had better learning outcomes than those who did not. Then, we detail the incorporation of m-learning into the teaching strategies, and—as an adjunct to a more detailed analysis of educational outcomes previously presented (Martìn & Beckmann, 2011)—we consider some key issues such as copyright, technological support, and the provision of mobile devices. Finally, in the context of some current attempts to conceptualize and theorize m-learning, we discuss why our experiences encourage us to support m-learning as an effective tool in student-centered learning.

PROBLEM STATEMENT

As Laurillard (2007) explains, "The mobility of digital technologies creates intriguing opportunities for new forms of learning because they change the nature of the physical relations between teachers, learners, and the objects of learning" (p. 153). In language learning, as in many other educational contexts, a key question at present is how to imagine mobile technology, not just as another way of delivering traditional content, but rather as an opportunity to develop new kinds of activity specifically aimed at utilizing the affordances of mobile devices and the new contexts in which learning can occur (Kukulska-Hulme, 2010; Kukulska-Hulme & Shield, 2008). Our problem as tertiary educators, therefore, is to discover what benefits can accrue for our learners if we redesign our teaching specifically to embrace the possibilities and peculiarities of today's m-learning devices, and to be better prepared for what tomorrow will bring. In this chapter, we consider these issues through a case study of m-learning used in university-level language teaching.

THE CASE STUDY

Teaching Spanish to Undergraduates Through Simulated Immersion

The ANU—based in Australia's capital, Canberra—has had a Spanish program since 2005, with an average 450–500 students enrolled at any one time. Students come from across the university, as language proficiency is targeted by many disciplines, and so no background in language or culture is assumed, especially as Australia provides few natural opportunities to hear or speak Spanish outside the learning environment. Typically, students take 3 years to complete the language major, working through beginner, continuing, intermediate, and advanced language levels.

Although the approach to teaching has elements of both audio–lingual and social–communicative teaching styles (Richards & Renandya, 2002), it has evolved into a model of "simulated immersion" (Martìn & Beckmann, 2011) that seeks to create sufficient levels of proficiency in the communication skills of students that they can feel linguistically confident and spontaneous in Spanish-speaking environments. Classes are conducted only in Spanish, spoken by native-language tutors originally from different Spanish-speaking areas. Students thus quickly become acquainted with a diversity of accents and begin to understand the linguistic impacts of the Spanish diaspora.

As Nunan (2002) noted, limited class time at university level can unintentionally direct students' focus toward reading literacy, with speaking and listening skills often falling behind. We certainly saw a need to provide more engagement with listening and speaking skills, especially in intermediate-level courses. Two thematically based courses, *Current Affairs in the Spanish-Speaking World* and *The Spanish Speaking World through its Songs*, were therefore developed to provide additional pathways for students to engage intellectually with the Spanish language and the many Hispanic cultures. However, after these courses were implemented in 2006 through teacher-controlled, text-based learning environments, it became clear that there were opportunities to enhance students' aural and oral competencies still further by adopting a more flexible, audio-focused approach.

Audio Resources as a Central Focus

Along with others, Nunan (2002) argued for the recognition of listening as a crucial element in language acquisition. Although audio resources were used in the Spanish thematic courses in 2006, we needed to focus students' attention on these resources by enhancing their motivation to listen. In 2007, therefore, both thematic courses were restructured in a way that emphasized self-directed learning using audio resources, in ways that met the key design criteria for an effective listening program suggested by Nunan (2002; Table 46.1) and encouraged critical reflection, collaboration, and accountability (Martin & Beckmann, 2011). Importantly, we found it was becoming easier to acquire authentic listening material—defined by Nunan (1989) as "material . . . not specifically produced for the purpose of language teaching"—because of the increasing availability of podcasts of broadcast and Internet-based radio programs from across the world. Initially, we provided these audio resources as audio and text (song lyrics) files in a language-laboratory setting on campus, as well as in formats for students to copy onto their own CD media. Subsequently, the audio resources were presented as downloadable or streamed files in a range of formats, accessible on- and off-campus through the university's virtual learning environment (VLE).

Students with Mobile Devices Had Better Learning Outcomes

From the beginning, we followed an action-research approach, that is, we were "thinking systematically about what happens in teaching practice, implementing action where improvements are considered possible and monitoring and evaluating the effects of the action for continuing future improvement" (Zuber-Skerritt, 1992, p. 16). We were,

Table 46.1 Teaching Listening Skills Through M-Learning

Key design criteria of an effective listening course (Nunan, 2002, p. 241)	How the use of m-learning in two thematic Spanish courses addresses these criteria
Use of authentic material, including both monologues and dialogues	Students are provided with access to an extensive database of authentic material, including single-narrator and interview formats with different Spanish accents, in the form of radio programs and podcasts sourced from authentic Spanish-language contexts
	"I loved the iPods, the emphasis on discussion and getting to learn about real issues!" (student feedback, 2010)
Strategies for effective listening built into the materials themselves	The resources are selected specifically to provide a diversity of lengths and themes to allow for personal engagement with topics
	Each resource has a playlist description identifying its relevance as core or support material
	The materials are "professional broadcast" quality, which facilitates effective listening
	Key resources are preloaded on the mobile device. Additional resources are available to be downloaded from database on VLE
Learners being able to listen to a resource several times	By providing students with a mobile device (MP3 player) for the duration of the course, not only are students able to listen multiple times at will, but the portability and freedom of use encouraged listening in "natural" and "downtime" contexts, as well as in scheduled study time

therefore, able to identify two clear outcomes in our early experiences of emphasizing the use of audio resources in the thematic courses. First, the students' overall learning surpassed expectations, with listening and speaking skills showing a marked improvement compared with previous years. Second, even though we had made the audio resources available in diverse formats specifically to offer flexibility, a clear divide in the student cohort became obvious between those who owned, and used, an MP3 portable listening device (such as an iPod) in their course studies, and those who did not.

We explored the reasons for this second finding. The audio resources for the two thematic courses comprised authentic songs (3–6 minutes) or radio programs (20–60+ mins) that generally needed repeated listening to ensure good comprehension by students at this level. Thus, to prepare themselves adequately for classwork and presentations, all students needed to accomplish 3–5 hours of listening, ostensibly at a language laboratory (requiring physical attendance on campus) or via a home computer and Internet through the university VLE. In 2006, there was no wireless network on campus and relatively few local homes with wireless networks, and so this kind of commitment was quite difficult for students faced with other diverse demands in their lives (e.g., other courses, commuting, part- or even full-time work, family life). Students without MP3 players had been physically constrained to listen to the resources through the streaming server or the language labs, although some students had asked for CD formats so that they could play resources through offline computers or domestic audio systems when it suited them. In contrast, the students with MP3 players had been able to download material directly onto their mobile device and listen repeatedly, when and where it suited them. They reported that this freedom of having resources on a mobile device had allowed them to create "listening time" in many otherwise uncommitted intervals (e.g., short gaps between classes on campus, commuting time on public transport, housework, and certain kinds of paid work).

Clearly, the learning opportunities offered by repeated listening through an already available and easily portable mobile device were extensive. It became apparent in the classes that the MP3-player owners were better prepared and keener to participate, apparently because they had been able to access the audio resources more easily and more often, and thus felt a higher degree of familiarity and confidence with the material than their device-less peers.

M-Learning for All

This experience not only demonstrated to us very clearly that mobility and accessibility were crucial factors in learning options and outcomes for today's students, but it also coincided with recognition in the literature of the huge potential of portable MP3 and video devices in language teaching (e.g., Lafford, Lafford, & Sykes, 2007; Thomas, 2008). Our interest in encompassing m-learning more directly was also influenced by considerations of equity, as, obviously quite unintentionally, we were essentially disadvantaging students who did not own MP3 players. So, from 2007, we sought funding to provide class sets of MP3 players—specifically 2GB iPod Nano devices—in both thematic courses.

Before being loaned to a student for the duration of the course, each iPod was preloaded with a database of carefully selected resources (e.g., songs, current-affairs podcasts). Students were also able to upload additional resources during the semester, either from the course database on the VLE or syndicated from public podcasts on the

Internet. In this way, the iPod essentially became that student's personal portable learning space for the duration of the course. In a subsequent year, additional funding allowed us to upgrade to 8GB iPod Nano players, which allowed the introduction of video files.

OUTCOMES

We have previously given a detailed analysis, including quantitative and qualitative data focusing on the *Songs* course, of the positive learning outcomes of introducing the use of mobile devices into the thematic courses (Martin & Beckmann, 2011). Students were engaged throughout the teaching period, demonstrated improved levels of language skills in assessment tasks, and rated the courses highly in terms of satisfaction and learning in standardized university evaluations (Figure 46.1), valuing the "contemporary focus, breadth of topics, and use of iPods" (student feedback, 2010).

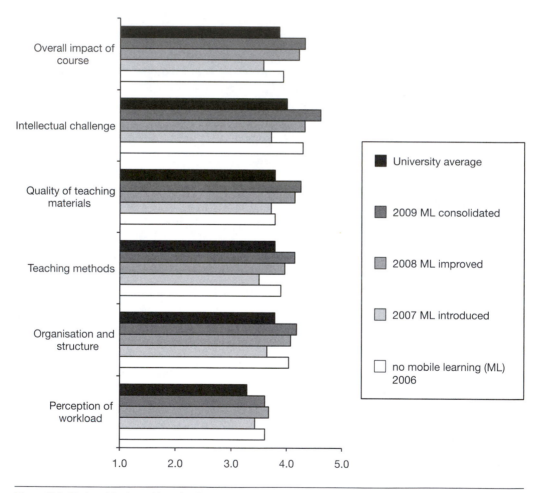

Figure 46.1 Students' Ratings of Learning Parameters During Evolution of M-Learning Project (Averages Across Both Thematic Courses; Standardized University Evaluations With 5 Point Scale, 1 = Poor, 5 = Excellent)

Note: The 2007 data reflect the common decrease in ratings that can occur when an innovation is introduced, both because of teething problems with the innovation itself, or because students' original expectations and assumptions about the courses are challenged. However, the overall trend is of increasing satisfaction, as procedures became fine-tuned and expectations changed.

Overall, we found that using and creating podcasts had made students "fully aware of the opportunities for mobile technologies, especially MP3 players such as iPods, to act as personal and portable language laboratories presenting audio and text resources in highly individualized playlists" (Martìn & Beckmann, 2011, p. 126).

However, although the educational benefits have been clear, for teachers there was undoubtedly a great deal of work, and a steep learning curve, involved in incorporating the mobile devices effectively into the teaching strategies. Apart from the increased workload required in creating and maintaining the databases of audio resources, key areas of additional activity were related to copyright issues, technological support, and the provision of technology to students.

Copyright Issues

Although it was technically easy to create the database of hundreds of audio/video resources from which each iPod would be loaded, we needed to comply with Australian and international copyright legislation, such as obligations under the Screenrights Agreement.[1] We chose materials that were either free of copyright restriction or useable under the university's usual copyright procedures, or entered into direct agreements with radio and television agencies that broadcast in Spanish to allow use of those materials. Fortunately, doing this is much less onerous than it may appear to be, with many resources freely available, with attribution, through appropriate Creative Commons and similar licenses.[2]

Technological Support

Our experiences showed us two ends of the technical-support spectrum, both of which provide traps for the unwary teacher. First, there was the mistaken belief that if a little of something is good, more is better. In the first year that we received funding for a class set of iPods, we were provided with extensive student access to an educational technologist. The temptation for this person was to give the students a great deal of information about the mobile technology they were using, and especially about programs such as Garageband that were being used to create podcasts. Although most students relished these extra insights, a few did not adapt well to this "invasion" of technology, and told us so: "It's a Spanish course, not an IT course" (student feedback, 2007). In subsequent years, we ensured that the need to acquire skills in the technology was pared down to a minimum, but that interested students were able to access more information about the technology or software if they chose.

However, if assuming that students want to know everything about technology is one end of the spectrum of potential pitfalls, assuming that students today are completely familiar with mobile technologies is the other end. For example, one student did not know how to recharge the loaned iPod, but (being of a generation supposedly very tech-savvy) was too embarrassed to ask, until "found out" during a class assessment task (Martìn & Beckmann, 2011). This led to a rewriting of technological support material to include the absolute basics.

Our findings related to students' needs for, and experience of, support in using the mobile technology are consistent with research on the use of iPods in teaching by Caron and Caronia (2008). Rather than make assumptions about the capabilities of students as potential mobile learners, these authors argue that we should engage more carefully with the cultural contexts and recognize that "successful adoption of technologies in education depends . . . on their integration into the specific cultural frames by which students live their academic life" (Caron & Caronia, 2008, p. 25).

Providing Students With Mobile Devices

Once it became clear in 2006 that, in the now audio-focused thematic courses, students with MP3 players were achieving better learning outcomes than those without, it became a matter of equity to explore the possibilities of providing mobile devices to all students. Through an innovation grant in 2007, a set of 35 2GB iPod Nano devices (with charger and ear buds) was purchased for loan to enrolled students for the duration of each course (one semester, 3 months). In subsequent years, these were replaced with 25 video-capable 8GB devices. In addition, a "portable recording studio" backpack (laptop computer, professional-standard microphone, and digital recorder) was provided on short-term loan.

Protection of university equipment was important, and so, after consultation with the university's legal office, a contract was drawn up for students to sign, whereby they were responsible for replacing any device only if it was not returned, was maliciously damaged, or was lost through carelessness. Our experience with this aspect of our m-learning strategy has been positive: in the 5 years of operation (i.e., 9 sets of loans to about 150 students), only one student lost a mobile device (< 1 percent), although a small number were returned without earbud headphones or with minor damage. Indeed, the original devices were more likely to fail internally, or to become obsolete technically, than they were to be damaged or lost. The overall cost of the 5 years of implementation of the m-learning project has been less than A$300 per student, which included two semesters of intensive support from an educational technologist (no longer considered necessary), creation of the original database, and the replacement of 2GB with 8GB devices.

DISCUSSION

One way to think about m-learning as an aspect of educational design is to understand the motivation for its inclusion in a teaching strategy: in other words, what are the benefits? Traxler (2007) identified six categories of m-learning based on the primary motivation and context. However, our experience in this case study indicates several areas of overlap, both in motivation and usage (Table 46.2). From our perspective, it appears that those designing educational activities for m-learning instinctively seek to meet multiple objectives and, therefore, to achieve multiple benefits.

Another way to think about the different elements of m-learning relevant to this case study is through Koole's Framework for the Rational Analysis of Mobile Education (FRAME). Koole (2009) argues that effective m-learning "provides an enhanced cognitive environment in which distance learners can interact with their instructors, their course materials, their physical and virtual environments, and each other" (p. 38): In other words, m-learning results from the integration of key aspects of the mobile device (D), the learner (L), and the social context (S). Apart from what we believe is an unnecessary emphasis on distance learners, this view coincides well with the Crompton et al. (Crompton, 2013, p. 4) definition of m-learning as occurring "across multiple contexts, through social and content interactions, using personal electronic devices," as presented in chapter 1. In our case study, students' interactions with the content and with one another were strongly conditioned by the availability and use of the mobile devices.

Table 46.2 Motivations for M-Learning

Categories identified by Traxler (2007) as diverse motivations for introduction of m-learning	Relevance to this case study
Technology-driven m-learning—specific technological innovation deployed in academic setting to demonstrate technical feasibility and pedagogic possibility	Highly relevant—the initiation of this teaching approach was based on an innovation grant specifically to examine the benefits of m-learning in language learning
Miniature but portable e-learning—mobile, wireless, and handheld technologies used to re-enact approaches and solutions already used in "conventional" e-learning (e.g., porting VLE to these technologies or using mobile technologies as flexible replacements for desktop technologies)	Highly relevant—the use of audio-visual resources is by no means new in language learning, but this approach focused on the portability enabled by mobile listening devices
Connected classroom learning—same technologies used in classroom settings to support collaborative learning	Highly relevant—with all students using the same mobile technologies, collaborative learning could be made a focus for the key assessment task
Informal, personalized, situated m-learning—same technologies enhanced with additional functionality and deployed to deliver educational experiences that would otherwise be difficult or impossible	Highly relevant—especially with the introduction of the 8 GB video-enabled devices, students were able to forge their own paths, as individuals and groups, through the resource database, allowing previously impossible individualized explorations of topics and themes
Mobile training/ performance support—technologies used to improve productivity and efficiency of mobile workers by delivering information and support just in time and in context for immediate priorities	Not relevant
Remote/rural/development m-learning—to deliver education where "conventional" e-learning technologies would fail	Not relevant

Of particular relevance are Koole's (2009) FRAME concepts of mediation, relative use of knowledge, and selection of information, which are all aspects of the m-learning teaching strategy evident in this case study (see Table 46.3) that encourage and support the development of desirable graduate attributes, such as critical analysis and reflection.

CONCLUSION

Through a case study of the Spanish thematic courses at our university, we have shown how the introduction of m-learning can be used to diversify and enhance learning opportunities in a model that simulates immersion in language learning. Although we used MP3 (audio) players as the original mobile device of choice, and augmented these with MP4 (video) players as our budget and technology permitted, these are, of course, no longer the only mobile technologies relevant to learning—netbooks, portable DVD players, digital dictionaries, PDAs, multimedia cell phones, e-readers, and tablets are similarly prime contenders for adjuncts to teaching strategies. In particular, current versions of the multimedia iOS (iPhone 4S and third-generation iPad) and Android (4.0) platforms are crying out for examples of ways in which they can be used to innovate, stimulate, and excite in a diversity of learning contexts.

Table 46.3 Case-study Connections to the FRAME Model

FRAME component	Description (from Koole, 2009, p. 39)	Specific relevance to m-learning in this case study of Spanish thematic courses
Mediation (between learner and task, learner and environment, learner and tools, etc.)	As learners diversify their interactions with other learners, learning environments and tools, and the available information, the nature of these interactions themselves change	Compared with Spanish courses without m-learning, students in the thematic courses developed much deeper relationships with their peers as co-learners through a greater process of engagement, communication, and collaboration
Selection of information	As the amount of available information increases, learners must become better at evaluating its accuracy and relevance	As they had to explore the large range of resources to present group-selected themes, students became more skilled at selecting, understanding, and using audio resources to build their own presentation and argue their own perspective on individually or group-selected themes
Relative use of knowledge: production (KP) versus navigation (KN)	In KP, teachers determine what and how information should be learned. In KN, learners acquire skills to appropriately select, manipulate, and apply information to their unique situations and needs	Course design moved from a teacher-focused model to a student-focused model, with students using the opportunities afforded by m-learning to navigate their way through acquiring the knowledge that they needed to apply *de novo* in assessment tasks

With the significant decrease in cost and increase in reliability of MP3/MP4 players and similar mobile devices, and the greater likelihood of students having their own device (so that only some students will require loaned devices), the necessary financial investment in an m-learning approach continues to decrease in real terms. In our context, a recently implemented campus-wide wireless network and growing ownership of personal mobile devices supported by widespread 3G networks are increasing the opportunities for mobile access almost on a daily basis. Although cost is thus obviously a potentially significant issue in implementing an m-learning strategy, it should no longer be considered a limiting factor, especially when a more realistic cost-effectiveness measure takes into account the enhancement of learning outcomes and student satisfaction demonstrated consistently in our case study.

However, based on our experience and the lessons learned along the way, we remain convinced that m-learning initiatives must be driven by a student-centered pedagogical imperative. Without a clear understanding about how the use of mobile devices will enhance the flexibility and interactivity of individual and social learning choices, outcomes are unlikely to improve simply by introducing or allowing the use of such devices. Thus, the key questions to consider in a mobile-favored teaching context are not only "Will students have more flexibility to study when and where they want or need to if we embrace the use of mobile technology in our teaching strategy?" but also "How will the use of this technology enhance the learning opportunities for these students?"

Reporting on a mobile language learning project at the University of Wisconsin–Madison, Gilgen (2005) concluded, "When students get a chance to hold the world in their hands, language learning becomes more exciting, more interesting, and more relevant" (p. 39). This is certainly our experience with the integration of mobile devices into our teaching strategies and, hence, into our students' learning strategies. In 5 years of action research on the use of m-learning, we have found that the ready availability of text, audio, and video resources on MP3/MP4 players such as the iPod Nano, easily accessed and re-accessed, helps the students move with natural ease from being language learners to language users. The success we have had so far in a limited number of courses has encouraged us to extend m-learning opportunities and strategies into other courses in the program, and across the university, not least because students who have enjoyed the benefits of m-learning have told us they expect, and look forward to, this as a component of their future study.

NOTES

1 The non-profit society Screenrights is appointed by the Australian Government to administer the provision of the Copyright Act 1968 with regard to radio, television, and film.
2 Apart from the numerous podcasts in Spanish freely distributed over the Internet, most international broadcasters, such as Spanish External Radio or the Spanish Team of Radio Netherlands, not only allow rebroadcasting of their programs but actively seek local rebroadcasters through sophisticated distribution networks via satellite or through the diplomatic missions of their countries.

REFERENCES

Caron, A., & Caronia, L. (2008). *Mobile instruction technologies and the culture of education: An empirical study on the appropriation of iPods.* Paper presented at the Annual Meeting of the International Communication Association, Montreal, Quebec, Canada. Retrieved from: www.allacademic.com/meta/p232087_index.html

Crompton, H. (2013). A historical overview of mobile learning: Toward learner-centered education (pp. 3–14). In Z. Berge, & L. Muilenburg (Eds.), *Handbook of mobile learning.* New York: Routledge.

Gilgen, R. (2005) *Holding the world in your hand: Creating a mobile language learning environment.* EDUCAUSE. Retrieved from: www.educause.edu/ir/library/pdf/EQM0535.pdf

Koole, M. L. (2009). A model for framing mobile learning. In M. Ally (Ed.), *Mobile learning: Transforming the delivery of education and training* (pp. 25–47). Edmonton, AB: AU Press, Athabasca University.

Kukulska-Hulme, A. (2010). Charting unknown territory: Models of participation in mobile language learning. *International Journal of Mobile Learning and Organisation, 4*(2), 16–129. DOI:10.1504/IJMLO.2010.032632

Kukulska-Hulme, A., & Shield, L. (2008). An overview of mobile assisted language learning: From content delivery to supported collaboration and interaction. *ReCALL, 20*(3), 271–289.

Lafford, B. A., Lafford, P. A., & Sykes, J. (2007). Entre dicho y hecho . . . [Between what is said and done]: An assessment of the application of research from second language acquisition and related fields to the creation of Spanish CALL materials for lexical acquisition. *CALICO Journal, 24*(3), 497–529. Retrieved from: https://calico.org/html/article_658.pdf

Laurillard, D. (2007). Pedagogical forms of mobile learning: Framing research questions. In N. Pachler (Ed.), *Mobile learning—towards a research agenda* (pp. 153–175). London: WLE Centre, Institute of Education, University of London.

Martìn, M. D., & Beckmann, E. A. (2011). Simulating immersion: Podcasting in Spanish teaching. In B. R. Facer and M. Abdous (Eds), *Academic podcasting and mobile assisted language learning: Applications and outcomes* (pp. 111–131). Hershey, PA: IGI Global.

Nunan, D. (1989). *Designing tasks for the communicative classroom.* Cambridge, UK: Cambridge University Press.

Nunan, D. (2002). Listening in language learning. In J. C. Richards & W. A. Renandya (Eds.), *Methodology in language teaching: An anthology of current practice* (pp. 238–241). Cambridge, UK: Cambridge University Press.

Richards, J. C., & Renandya, W. A. (2002). *Methodology in language teaching: An anthology of current practice.* Cambridge, UK: Cambridge University Press.

Thomas, M. (2008). *Handbook of research on Web 2.0 and second language learning.* Hershey, PA: Information Science Reference [IGI-Global].

Traxler, J. (2007). Defining, discussing, and evaluating mobile learning: The moving finger writes and having writ . . . *International Review of Research in Open and Distance Learning, 8*(2), 1–12.

Zuber-Skerritt, O. (1992). *Action research in higher education.* London: Kogan Page.

47

ARCHITECTURE OF A DEVICE-INDEPENDENT COLLABORATIVE LANGUAGE LEARNING GAME

Andreas Christ, Patrick Meyrueis, and Razia Sultana

M-learning, through the use of mobile technology, will allow citizens of the world to access learning materials and information from anywhere and at anytime. This idea will come true only after a worldwide successful implementation of presentation of device-independent learning content. There are three identified barriers that have to be taken care of to support device-independent m-learning. First, various kinds of device used by different users, or by the same user at different times, have to be recognized by the system in order for device capabilities to be known (Gaedke, Beigl, Gellersen, & Segor, 1998). In a stable place such as at home or at the office, it is more convenient to use a PC. While on the move, it is obvious that a user would like to access the same content with the same outlook and feel using a mobile device. So, a system is necessary that is device-dependent from the point of communication functionality, interactivity, 3D capabilities, and information presentation and information depth. At the same time, however, it must be device-independent from the point of view of information access and (a)synchronous communication possibilities (Christ & Feisst, 2010). Second, the overall number of users of specialized content or interactive applications for learning issues is too low to adapt the application/content to all possible devices manually. Third, content and user interfaces could include different kinds of data format, such as text, image, audio, video, 3D virtual-reality data, and other upcoming formats (Meawad & Stubbs, 2008). The architecture should be able to deal with all the existing and upcoming formats of data, without requiring any huge enhancement.

For a successful implementation of m-learning, it is important to support different user devices, and language acquisition is one of the most important sectors of m-learning. The Language Learning Game (LLG), developed at the University of Applied Sciences Offenburg, is a helping tool that provides users with an easy and efficient way to improve their knowledge level of a desired language by using their own device exclusively, their mobile phone. LLG is an example of a suitable tool for adult learners because it is a device-independent application, where different kinds of device and data format are presented for collaborative learning.

The need for more and more people to learn different languages has never been higher. As globalization increases, the old boundaries that separated language groups are becoming increasingly blurred by the relative ease of travel, advances in technology, the pursuit of higher studies, and internationally focused economic systems. As a result, foreign-language benefits have never been more valuable.

According to the Critical Period Hypothesis (CPH), after a certain age it is not easy for most people to learn a new language. Moreover, language acquisition needs interaction with others to practice it often, which is very difficult for adults owing to other responsibilities in their social and professional lives. In this regard, an adult learner needs a helping tool that is always available for him/her to learn and interact with others, anytime, anywhere. Nobody carries a high-end device such as a laptop all the time, nor would someone be motivated to open it somewhere for learning purposes just for couple of minutes. The only device that appears to be a potential solution to these problems is a small mobile device, such as a mobile phone, that is always switched on and that people carry everywhere.

The main idea of the LLG is to create a short story in a foreign language by exploiting mobile devices. The story is developed by a group of participants exchanging sentences/data. In this way, the participants can learn from each other by sharing their individual knowledge, without the need for constant support from a tutor and without the fear of making mistakes, because the group members are anonymous.

PEDAGOGICAL CONCEPT

To learn a foreign language interactively with others in a way that facilitates practice of the desired language is very important, because learners acquire fluency by using whatever skills they have. They should be presented with activity-based approaches that engage them in interactive experiences and support the development of intrapersonal and interpersonal skills. As the learners develop their ability to understand, appreciate, and relate positively to others using the target language, they learn to demonstrate constructive attitudes and values through participation in challenging, real-life situations.

Collaborative-learning theory has exerted great influence on language teaching and learning. For mathematical sense-making, Schoenfeld (1992) found that students socially construct knowledge through their participation in collaborative activities. They can elaborate on their existing knowledge and build new knowledge when they articulate their reasoning (Ploetzner, Dillenbourg, Preier, & Traum, 1999), integrate other group members' reasoning (Stahl, 2000), reflect on misconceptions, and work toward a shared understanding (Van den Bossche, Gijselaers, Segers, & Kirschner, 2006). In LLG, students are not talking to each other, but the idea of collaborative learning could be equally true, because they are also sharing knowledge, by writing, correcting, and voting for the best proposed sentence of a story. Their improvement is depending upon knowledge sharing, and this is possible by collaborating with each other. However, in order to collaborate effectively during the process, the students need to display positive collaborative behaviors (Johnson & Johnson, 1990), and it has been observed that they generally do not do so without assistance (Lou, Abrami, & d'Apollonia, 2001). Small-group collaboration can be supported in several ways: through the use of human facilitation to guide the interaction (Hmelo-Silver, 2004), through precollaboration training (Prichard, Stratford, & Bizo, 2006), or through scripting of the collaborative interaction by giving students designated roles and activities to follow (Fischer, Mandl, Haake, & Kollar, 2007; Kollar, Fischer, & Hesse, 2006). Especially for writing, previous studies have shown that all the participants in a collaborative-learning process obtain satisfactory results, but the students with lower writing ability make more progress than those with higher ability. However, higher-ability students will also benefit from the experience of tutoring (Ge, 2011).

In spite of the benefits of collaborative-language learning, a lack of peer engagement and intercultural communication persists, because of religion, political views, or personal feelings (Hannon & D'Netto, 2007). Other studies show that, in the area of collaborative learning, the cultural differences of the participants in a group do have an impact on participants' satisfaction, interest, and motivation. For example, people tend to avoid finding fault with each other so as to save face. Moreover, a lot of people do not participate actively in teamwork because of the fear of making mistakes (Carducci, 2009). They feel shy and confused about their level of knowledge. This is a great barrier to knowledge sharing in collaborative learning. Besides, it is established that competition fosters a win–lose situation, where superior students reap all the rewards and draw all the recognition, and mediocre or low-achieving students reap none. In contrast, everyone benefits from a collaborative-learning environment. In the learning process, emotions and a comfortable environment play very important roles, because emotions do not merely facilitate, filter, or hinder an individual's inner cognitive functioning; rather, they can, in any forms, mediate development, especially when learning is embedded in an interpersonal transaction (Imai, 2010).

Errors are a natural part of language learning. This is observed from the development of a child's first language, as well as in second-language learning by both children and adults. A very common phenomenon for a learner is that he learns more from his mistakes (Helbig, Götze, Henrici, & Krumm, 2001). Formerly, a child's speech was seen as just a faulty version of an adult's. Now, it is instead recognized as having its own underlying system, which can be described in its own terms, and later the system develops toward that of adults (Littlewood, 1998). Researchers have realized the importance of focusing on learners' errors, especially for adult learners' process of language learning. According to error analysis, the errors made by learners are usually systematic rather than random. Many researchers, such as Zha and Hong (2007), began to realize that, "learners' errors need not be seen as signs of failure. On the contrary they are the clearest evidence for the learner's developing system" (pp. 34–38).

Availability of a supportive tool (for example, LLG), collaborative corrections, digital resources (for example, mobile phones), and peer assistance could become important resources in formulating a space for learners' creative engagement (Cekaite, 2009).

DESCRIPTION OF THE GAME

The LLG was developed to allow language learners to practice the target language using a mobile device. It is not designed for beginning language learners, but rather for people with a basic knowledge of the desired foreign language. The game requires a supervisor who has very good knowledge of the foreign language to perform an overall check at the very end. If a new device or technology is required to provide a service, it is never possible to reach a lot of people within a short time. The game requires neither new technology nor a new device, it requires only a device that supports Java applications and can access the Internet. The reason behind focusing on the mobile phone is to reach a huge number of people, anytime, anywhere. Nowadays, the mobile phone as a device has become almost a part of the human body, because, most of the time, everybody carries a mobile phone. New language learning needs a lot of interaction with other people. LLG can meet this entire requirement by implementing the proposed system on a mobile phone, without needing a physical presence in a certain place and without keeping the participant actively waiting for an action (Newport, 1991).

The instructor or supervisor will create the game, provide instructions, and decide about the total number of group members in each group, and the game end condition. Group members should be selected randomly, with no more than three to five members. Slavin showed that groups with two or three members would usually do better than groups with four or more members (Slavin, 1987). In LLG, as the participants are improving by knowledge sharing, it makes more sense to build a group with at least three students. Participants will write sentences, and the aim is to build a short story in the desired language. When a group member writes and sends a sentence, the other members of the group will have a chance to dispute by proposing another version of the sentence, or they can simply agree with it. They are only allowed, by the rules of the game, to change spelling or grammatical mistakes in their proposed version. Afterwards, all group members will receive the proposed sentence and possible corrected versions. At this stage, every group member has to vote for the version the individual prefers. The sentence with the most votes gets selected. In case of equal votes, the first one submitted wins. Each group member has to create one sentence per round. Typically, the game is finished after 15–20 rounds. The final short story is sent to all group members, as well as to a supervisor, who will perform overall corrections. After that, all the participants will receive the supervisor's corrections of all the mistakes that occurred during the game. This overall correction is necessary, because there might be a situation where the majority of group members agree with an incorrect sentence. At the end, the corrections made by the supervisor will help them to learn correctly. This process could be depicted as Figure 47.1.

Description of the Game States

LLG is designed in such a way that all the participants need to communicate with each other frequently. The reason behind this communication is that their improvement will depend upon knowledge sharing among the group members and, at the end, among all the participants, including the teacher. So the game requires different activities from the participants during the various game states (see Figure 47.2 and Table 47.1). Each of these game states and the user actions required are explicated in the following sections of this chapter.

Login

First of all, participants need to log in to the system (Figure 47.3). The first screen that is displayed to the player is the login, where the users can write their corresponding credentials (User ID and password, provided by the university and saved in the LDAP server). The login is one of the most important parts of this total procedure, because of data security and access rights over the system, and, more specifically, to assign a participant to a group. The server is in charge of connecting to the LDAP server, retrieving the user's information, and verifying that the user exists and that the password introduced is the correct one. Some user information, such as e-mail and mobile number, needs to be stored in a local table in order to allow quick access to these data.

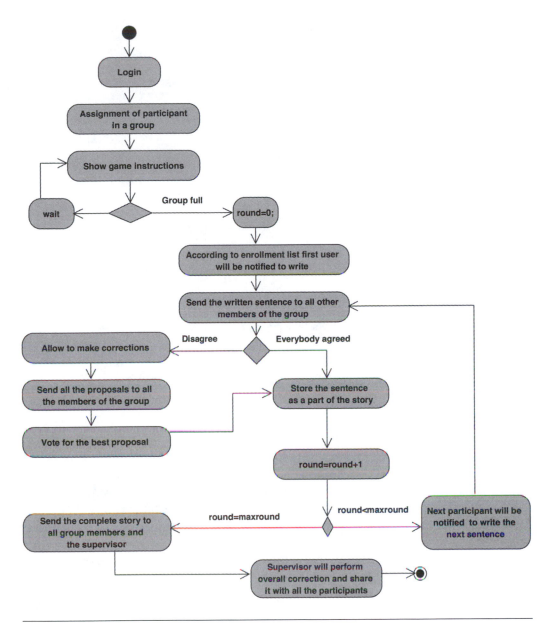

Figure 47.1 Game Logic—Simplified Version

Table 47.1 Different States with Correspondence Between Game and User

Current user	Other users in the group	Game
Wait	Wait	Wait
Write	Wait	Write
Wait	Dispute	Dispute
Vote	Vote	Vote

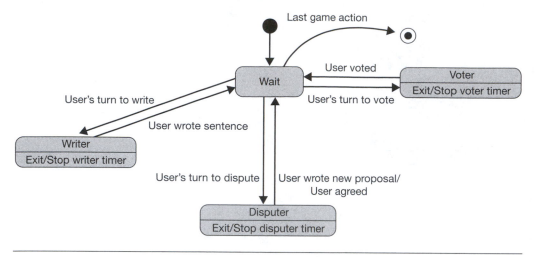

Figure 47.2 Different Game States of the LLG

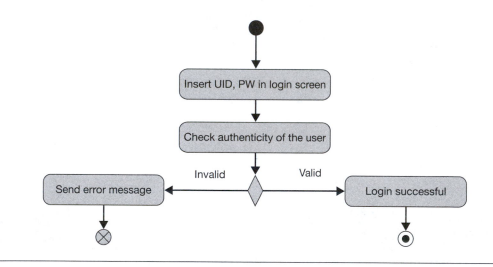

Figure 47.3 Login—Simplified Version

After a successful log-in, a selection procedure of the courses takes place, if it is the first log-in. After the user has selected the game (course) to play, his state information and the state of the selected game are retrieved. Using that information, the server can decide which actions the user is allowed to do and how the game should behave.

The use of timers is important in order to control that the game is not blocked by a player. The only state that does not start a timer is the state in which the user is waiting for an action by a team member. For the other states, a timer should run each time the player is given a new action to complete.

It is also important to send a message to the player notifying that the state has changed and an action is needed. The correspondence between game states and user actions is shown in Table 47.1.

Wait/Idle State

After a successful log-in procedure, all the participants are in the wait state until the group has the required number of participants (Figure 47.4). This is also considered the default state of this system. Whenever either the game or any one of the participants is waiting for the next required activity, their current state is wait/idle. This is the only state where there is no time-out period.

Write State

When the group is full, the writer timer is immediately started; the game and the first participant who enrolled in the game are in the write state. The first player is notified of his/her action to write the first sentence of the story (Figure 47.5). Apart from the game itself and the first participant, all the others are still in the wait state, until a written sentence is submitted. After submission, the writer timer is stopped, and the game goes to the dispute state; the writer of that submitted sentence goes to the wait state; all the other participants of the group go to the dispute state, along with the game, and receive notification about their state and action.

Dispute State

The disputer timer is started as soon as the game is in dispute state, and the sentence submitted by the writer is presented to all participants of the group except the writer (Figure 47.6). They should check for grammatical and spelling mistakes. After checking, an individual participant may agree if s/he thinks the written sentence is correct. If the individual found any mistakes, s/he has the chance to make another proposal. After disputing, the timer is stopped.

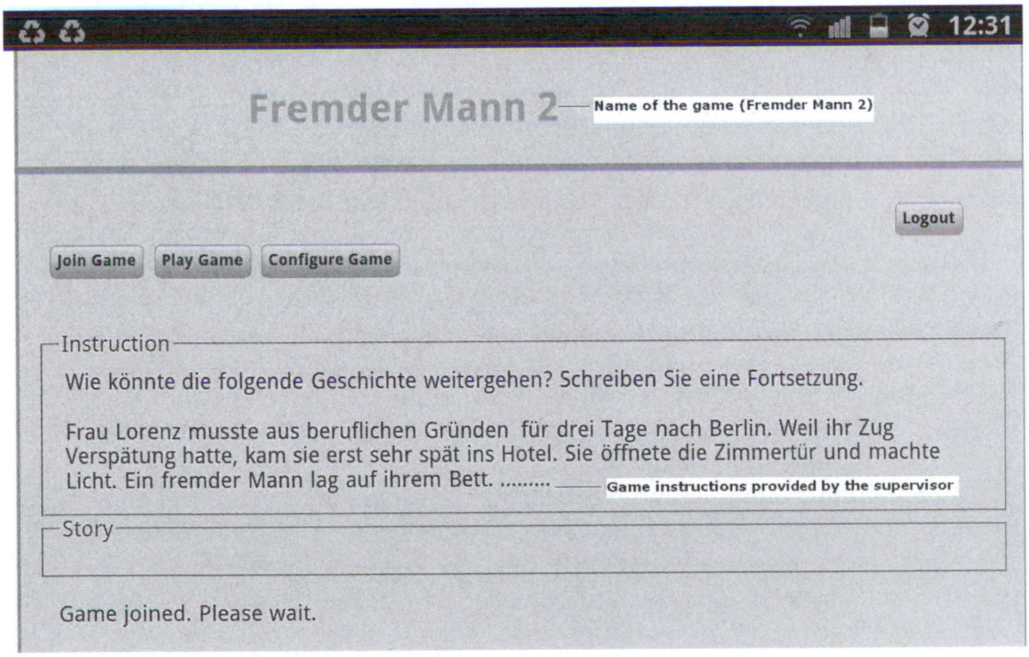

Figure 47.4 User Interface of Wait State

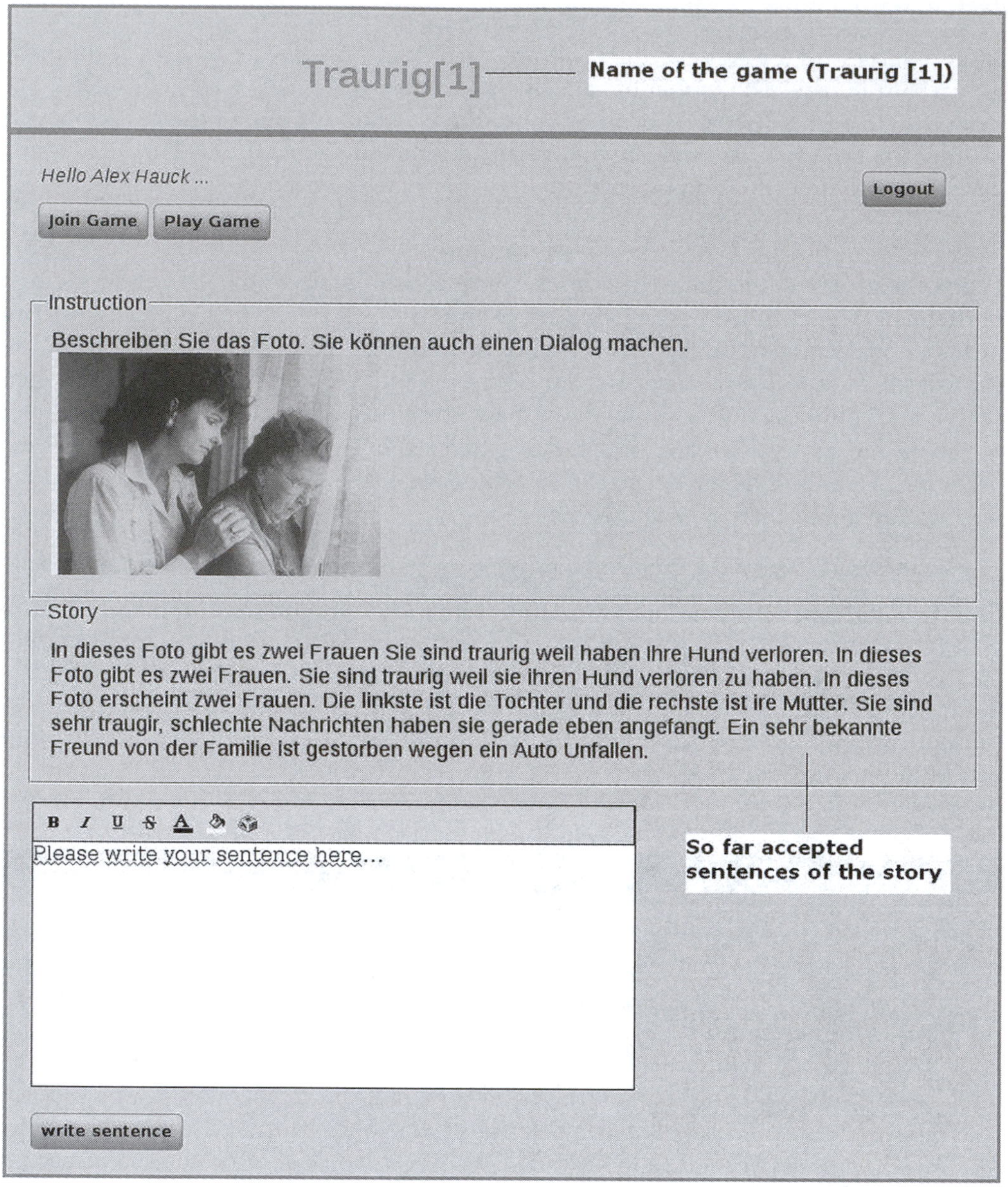

Figure 47.5 User Interface of Write State

Vote State

Apart from the written sentence, if any new proposal is made in the dispute state, then all the participants of the group and the game go to the vote state. The voter timer is started, and everybody receives notification. All the proposals are presented to the participants for them to select the best one (Figure 47.7). The sentence with the most votes is accepted as a part of the story. In case of an equal vote, the first one submitted is accepted. Afterwards, the voter timer is stopped. Then, the next member of the group

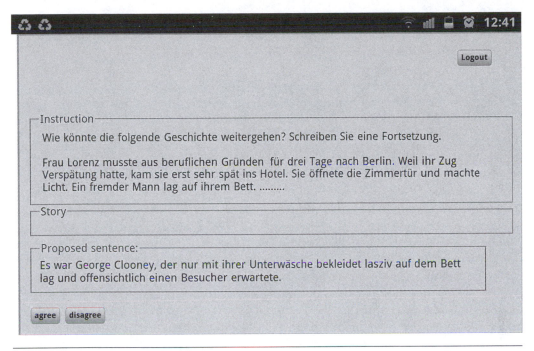

Figure 47.6 User Interface of Dispute State

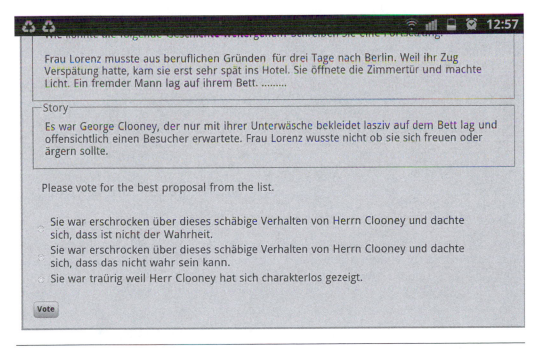

Figure 47.7 User Interface of Vote State

is in the write state, to write the next sentence, and the writer timer is restarted. This is how the game proceeds, until it reaches the game-end condition, which was decided by the supervisor at the very beginning when creating the game.

End of the Game and Reward Procedure

When the game reaches the ending condition, the system shows all participants a game-over page containing the complete story (Figure 47.8). The completed story is sent to the corresponding supervisor for evaluation of individual and group performances. Then, all the participants receive the corrections of all the mistakes made while building the story. From this, participants can see if they made the same common mistakes as other members of the group. Individual rewards are important, because individual performances could be better than the group performance. It is possible that a correctly written sentence was not chosen during voting, owing to the group's lack of knowledge, but the writer's effort should be appreciated.

IDENTIFICATION OF THE CONNECTED DEVICE

LLG is an m-learning game that can be played using any kind of computing device, such as a desktop computer or mobile phone. Therefore, the very first responsibility of the system is to identify the end user's device, along with device capabilities, as soon as a participant logs in to the system. It is a basic right of the user to be able to see the instructions of the game on their chosen device to enable game play. There might be a necessity to translate the instructions, based on the end user's device capabilities.

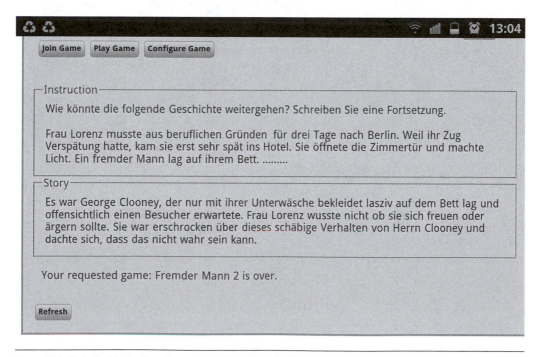

Figure 47.8 Outlook of Game-Over Page—A Very Short Example, With Only Three Rounds

Wireless Universal Resource File (WURFL) (WURFL, 2012) was selected for the description of the features of mobile devices and browsers, because the WURFL model is an XML configuration file that contains information about the capabilities and features of many mobile devices in the wireless world. Also, the repository of devices listed in WURFL is updated every day by contributors in the world. Therefore, it is an up-to-date specification that brings reliability in device data manipulation. Our system works with a combination of WURFL and a local database. Figure 47.9 shows a simplified version of the whole process.

First, it is detected whether the user is connecting to the system via mobile device or by desktop device, by analysis of the user-agent parameter of the HTTP header. The parameter of the HTTP header named Accept shows what can be supported or rendered by this client. Table 47.2 shows examples of message headers from different devices and the response of the server.

In the case of mobile devices, the local database is checked to determine whether the device is listed, and if the available information is up to date. Outdated device information is determined by using the WURFL.

Generalized Content

A device-independent system is able to deliver content to any device in such a way that the received content can be presented. This task can be approached in the two following

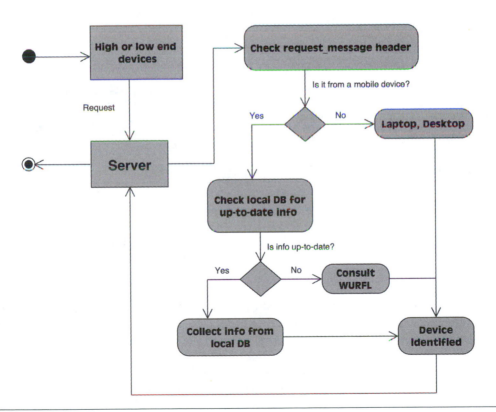

Figure 47.9 Process of Device Detection—Simplified Version

Source: Based on Christ & Feisst, 2010

Table 47.2 Example of Message Headers from Different Devices

Request from laptop browser	Response from the server
GET / HTTP/1.1 Host: www.xxx.de **User-Agent:** Mozilla/5.0 (X11; U; Linux i686; en-US; rv:1.7.12) Gecko/20050920 **Accept:**text/xml,application/xml,application/ xhtml+xml,text/ html;q=0.9,text/plain;q=0.8,image/png,*/*;q=0.5 Accept-Language: en-us,en;q=0.5 Accept-Encoding: gzip,deflate Accept-Charset: utf-8,* Keep-Alive: 300 Connection: keep-alive	HTTP/1.1 200 OK Date: Mon, 29 Aug 2011 07:41:16 GMT Expires: -1 Cache-Control: private, max-age=0 Content-Type: text/html; charset=UTF-8 Set-Cookie: PREF=ID=1a8c277baf1f8905:FF=0:TM=1314603676: LM=1314603676:S=ZlEHjAj6ssqLt1vx; expires=Wed, 28-Aug-2013 07:41:16 GMT; path=/; domain=.xxx.de Set-Cookie: NID=50=ewkG8txoy4- nLjYZFnGtsUne8VcVYZh6V3WK 8JAdWyMV7qRtCGYgbRYzPYFkFKKGJSdW8Bspy MWoDw8ewU2 uUN2D39myvEQYKQB9PbDRt3cpj2jfD3o_mYryyO xorE9Q; expires=Tue, 28-Feb-2012 07:41:16 GMT; path=/; domain=.xxx.de; HttpOnly Content-Encoding: gzip, Server: gws, Content-Length: 10285
Request from a mobile device (iPhone)	**Response from the server**
GET / HTTP/1.1 Host: www.xxx.de **Accept:**text/css,*/*;q=0.1,application/xml, application/xhtml+xml, text/html;q=0.9,text/plain;q=0.8,image/png Accept-Encoding: gzip, deflate Accept-Language: en-us Connection: keep-alive **User-Agent:** Mozilla/5.0 (iPhone; U; CPU iPhone OS 3_1 like Mac OS X; en-us) AppleWebKit/528.18 (KHTML, like Gecko) Version/4.0 Mobile/7C144 Safari/528.16	HTTP/1.0 301 Moved Permanently Date: Mon, 29 Aug 2011 07:39:44 GMT Server: Apache Location: http://www.xxx.de/ Content-Length: 230 Content-Type: text/html; charset=iso-8859–1 X-Cache: MISS from lnxp-3954.srv.mediaxxx.net X-Cache-Lookup: MISS from lnxp- 3954.srv.mediaxxx.net:101 Via: 1.0 lnxp-3954.srv.mediaxxx.net (squid/3.1.4) Connection: close

ways: Either content for every device exists in the system, which is very expensive, time consuming, and labor intensive, or the system is able to adapt content for each device. In case the system is capable of adapting content to a device-dependent presentation, the content has to be available in the system in a generalized form. Additionally, such a system should support a device-independent authoring process, where the author can focus on the content generation and not on device-dependent content adaptation, for example, while creating the game and providing instruction in LLG. XML was chosen for generation, structuring, and storage of generalized content.

Content Adaptation

In order to optimize the content presentation on different devices, the generalized content has to be adapted or translated in a device-dependent manner. W3C in W3C–MBP (2008) has categorized three approaches where the adaptation is taking place: (1) client-side, (2) server-side, and (3) proxy-side. It is intended to use both the server- and proxy-side approaches, based on necessity. For example, for a 3D picture or a virtual-reality scene as an instruction in a game, it is advantageous to use a proxy-based approach (Feisst, 2006). When a mobile device requests a specific 3D virtual-reality file, the device has to inform the proxy about the device capabilities, such as processing power, screen resolution, supported sound formats, and so on. On the proxy side, the specific file is requested from a target server. By parsing this file, the proxy creates an object-oriented representation of that scene. Additional resources (e.g., links to other files) can be detected and preloaded. The proxy will remove unneeded and unsupported content, according to the mobile device specification. If the identified device has lower processing power, then additional content, such as fog, texture, and light source, could be excluded from a 3D virtual-reality scene. If the mobile device does not have the required capabilities to provide this information, it does not make sense to transmit the data over the wireless network. This information can be removed at the proxy without any loss at the client side. The 3D virtual-reality scene is transformed into the correct modeling language, while the mentioned methods are taken into account to reduce the content. The idea of the process could be pictured as shown in Figure 47.10.

ANALYSIS OF THE TEST RESULTS

Three prototype tests were done, for three different languages, with 13 groups of three members on average in each group. In the fourth field test, all the participants had complete freedom to choose a high-end and/or low-end device, according to their convenience. What kind of device, what kind of communication medium, the personal context or situation (for example, a classroom, meeting room, or supermarket) cannot be predicted of participants, nor when the system (LLG) will be used. So, all sorts of notifications and alerts are sent as SMS and e-mail.

Participants' and language-course professors' opinions were collected using a questionnaire that included both closed- and open-ended questions. Using a prototype, all the important functions and features of the mobile game were tested. Findings based on the

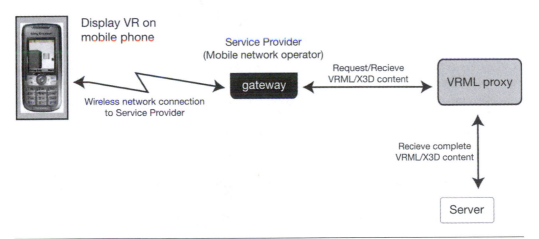

Figure 47.10 Process of Displaying VR Data on Mobile Device

Source: Based on Feisst, 2006

overall statistics of the game are very positive. Among all the users, 89 percent liked the game, 92 percent thought the tool was very helpful when learning a new language, and 82 percent could imagine playing the game using their mobile phone. Both the participants and the teachers were very interested in accepting this game as part of their course.

CONCLUSION AND CONSIDERATIONS FOR THE FUTURE

In LLG, students/participants help each other and, in doing so, build a supportive community that raises the performance level of each member. Their critical-thinking skills increase, and their retention of information and interest in the subject matter improve. This, in turn, leads to higher self-esteem of all the participants, which is the ultimate goal of LLG. In other words, the goal of this project is to provide a language learning tool as a game where all the participants will be able to improve their language level by knowledge sharing, using a mobile device such as a mobile phone that we all carry everywhere, all the time. It facilitates the participants' accessing the system at their convenience, without time and place constraints. The collaborative story-building process of LLG makes each participant bound to interact with team members every now and then, to deal with a real-life situation that is not predictable. For example, it is not possible to guess what sentence is going to be written by a team member, which of the proposals will be accepted as part of the story, and what kinds of data format the supervisor will use as instructions in the game. Even though LLG requires very active participation, none of the participants has to wait or feel stressed, because participants will be notified of all sorts of required activity. LLG provides a comfortable environment that is sensitive to participants' emotions, to ensure participants' maximum level of benefit. As the game is played anonymously, there is no possibility of problems regarding cultural differences or knowledge-level differences or personal feeling. Various research results show that learners learn from their mistakes too. It is a way of analyzing personal improvement. Even if a proposal made by a participant was not accepted as part of the story, it will remain saved in the database. At any time, a participant can compare his/her proposal with the accepted sentence and, eventually, with the supervisor's correction.

From questionnaire responses, we know that participants think LLG is a creative way to learn a new language, because:

- Learners can practice grammar and learn new vocabulary.
- Participants can evaluate themselves by comparing with the other group members.
- This game is highly interactive, which is very important when learning a new language.
- Everyone is simultaneously a teacher and a student.
- Participants can write without fear of making mistakes or feeling shy, because play is anonymous.
- In the vote state, everybody can compare and then select the correct sentence.

This evaluation shows that participants were provided with a comfortable learning environment, where their affective state was taken into account; LLG was a supportive tool; this tool did not require any new or unknown digital-device assistance, because the students were able to use either their own mobile phone or their own computer or

PDA; and anonymity was a factor that gave participants the freedom to give their best effort, which enhanced peer assistance and, as a result, collaborative performance.

The aim of this research was to establish anytime, anywhere learning, independent of place, time, device, data format of the learning content, or end user's status. To achieve this goal, the first step was to identify the connected device to know its capabilities, the second step was to prepare generalized content from the learning material provided by the author, and the third was to translate and transfer generalized content according to the capability of the end user's device. To make the process more realistic, it was also a necessity to support different devices owned by the same user, used in parallel or at different times. Primarily, the idea was tested with text and a .jpg data format in platform-type Connected Limited Device Configuration (CLDC)/Mobile Information Device Profile (MIDP). CLDC–1.1 and MIDP–2.0 was used with some optional packages such as Mobile 3D Graphics 1.1, Wireless Messaging 2.0, etc. So far, device detection, generation, structure and storage of generalized content, and translation and transfer of the generalized content according to the detected devices' capabilities with the above-mentioned data and device profile are working.

Moving forward, LLG has to be tested with other possible devices with different operating systems, such as Android, iOS, Windows Mobile OS, and Linux, and different data formats, especially with 3D data and VR scene. Regarding 3D data as learning content, we will consider polygonal data instead of Non-Uniform Rational B-Spline to avoid data-rendering complexity. The experimental validation could be conducted between two or three virtual-reality systems, including 3D images, by polarization separation on large size and cellular phones including 3D capacities, with micro lens filter or other technology.

REFERENCES

Christ, A., & Feisst, M., (2010). SWArchitecture for device independent mobile learning. In S. Caballe, F. Xhafa, T. Daradoumis, & A. A. Juan (Eds.), *Architectures for distributed and complex m-learning systems: Applying intelligent technologies* (pp. 72–93). Hershey, PA: IGI Global.

Carducci, B. J. (2009). *The psychology of personality* (2nd ed.). Malden, MA: Wiley-Blackwell.

Cekaite, A. (2009). Collaborative corrections with spelling control: Digital resources and peer assistance. *International Journal of Computer-Supported Collaborative Learning*, 4(3), 319–341.

Feisst, M. (2006). *Etude de protocole et réalisation d'un système de réalité augmentée mobile.* Unpublished doctoral dissertation, University of Strasbourg, France.

Fischer, F., Mandl, H., Haake, J., & Kollar, I. (2007). *Scripting computer-supported collaborative learning cognitive, computational, and educational perspectives. Computer-supported collaborative learning series.* New York: Springer.

Gaedke, M., Beigl M., Gellersen, H., & Segor, C. (1998). Web content delivery to heterogeneous mobile platforms. *Workshops on Data Warehousing and Data Mining: Advances in Database Technologies,* vol. 1552, pp. 205–217.

Ge, Z. (2011). Exploring e-learners' perceptions of net-based peer-reviewed English writing. *Computer Supported Collaborative Learning,* 6, 75–91. DOI:org/10.1007/s11412–010–9103–7

Hannon, J., & D'Netto, B. (2007). Cultural diversity online: Student engagement with learning technologies. *International Journal of Educational Management,* 21(5), 418–432.

Helbig, G., Götze, L., Henrici, G., & Krumm, H. G. (2001). *Deutsch als Fremdsprache.* Germany: WB-Druck, Rieden/Allgäu.

Hmelo-Silver, C. E. (2004). Problem-based learning: What and how do students learn? *Educational Psychology Review,* 16(3), 235–266.

Imai, Y. (2010). Emotions in SLA: New insights from collaborative learning for an EFL classroom. *The Modern Language Journal,* 94(2), 278–292.

Johnson, D. W., & Johnson, R. T. (1990). Cooperative learning and achievement. In S. Sharan (Ed.), *Cooperative learning: Theory and research* (pp. 23–37). New York: Praeger.

Kollar, I., Fischer, F., & Hesse, F. W. (2006). Collaboration scripts—A conceptual analysis. *Educational Psychology Review, 18*(2), 159–185.

Littlewood, W. (1998). *Foreign and second language learning.* Cambridge, UK: Cambridge University Press.

Lou, Y., Abrami, P. C., & d'Apollonia, S. (2001). Small group and individual learning with technology: A meta-analysis. *Review of Educational Research, 71*(3), 449–521.

Meawad, F., & Stubbs, G. (2008). A framework for enabling on-demand personalised mobile learning. *International Journal of Mobile Learning and Organisation, 2*(2), 133–148.

Newport, E. (1991). Contrasting concepts of the critical period for language. In S. Carey & R. Gelman (Eds.), *The epigenesis of mind: Essays on biology and cognition.* Hillsdale, NJ: Lawrence Erlbaum Associates.

Ploetzner, R., Dillenbourg, P., Preier, M., & Traum, D. (1999). Learning by explaining to oneself and to others. In P. Dillenbourg (Ed.), *Collaborative learning: Cognitive and computational approaches* (pp. 103–121). Oxford, UK: Elsevier.

Prichard, J. S., Stratford, R. J., & Bizo, L. A. (2006). Team-skills training enhances collaborative learning. *Learning and Instruction, 16*(3), 256–265.

Schoenfeld, A. H. (1992). Learning to think mathematically: Problem-solving, metacognition, and sense making in mathematics. In D. Grouws (Ed.), *Handbook for research on mathematics teaching and learning.* New York: Macmillan.

Slavin, R. E. (1987). Ability grouping and student achievement in elementary schools: A best-evidence synthesis. *Review of Educational Research, 57*(3), 293–336.

Stahl, G. (2000). A model of collaborative knowledge building. In B. Fishman & S. O'Connor-Divelbiss (Eds.), *Fourth International Conference of the Learning Science* (pp. 70–77). Mahwah, NJ: Erlbaum.

Van den Bossche, P., Gijselaers, W., Segers, M., & Kirschner, P. (2006). Social and cognitive factors driving teamwork in collaborative learning environments. *Small Group Research, 37,* 490–521.

W3C–MBP (2008). *Mobile Web Best Practices 1.0.* Retrieved from: www.w3.org/TR/mobile-bp/

WURFL (2012). Retrieved from: http://dbapi.scientiamobile.com/wiki/index.php/Main_Page

Zha, Y., & Hong, Y. (2007). Errors in language learning. *Sino-US English Teaching, 4*(2), 34–38.

48

AN INTERNATIONAL PERSPECTIVE
ON MOBILE LEARNING

Diana J. Muir

When considering m-learning in the international arena, the definition of m-learning takes on broader meaning. Developed countries have advantages such as infrastructure, connectivity, and technology that make m-learning readily available. In developing countries, cost, connectivity, availability of mobile devices, bandwidth, and technology-transfer restrictions become major issues. All can be overcome if a few adjustments in curriculum development and delivery method are made. Local culture, needs, and resources must be considered, language barriers can be overcome, and cost can be mediated.

You might ask, "Why do we even have to worry about these things? Why can't we just discuss what devices and applications work best?" The answer to that question is simple. Without understanding how m-learning is used internationally and what your students' needs and resources are, you have no way of knowing what will work best for them. That's why it's important to think about m-learning in a broader context. Instead of simply using mobile devices for instruction and assessment "inside" the traditional classroom, the mobile device often "becomes" the classroom, when students use them at home, work, or in the field.

The first thing to establish when creating an international educational program is the goal of the school. This doesn't necessarily affect the types of mobile device you might use, but will help define how you "use" those devices.

Does the school want its programs to become self-sustaining in the local community after a period of years, or does the school want to continue to support the program indefinitely? Does the school want to be a for-profit or non-profit school? Both questions are important, as they determine how to structure your program. A well-defined mission statement should also reflect the aims and goals of UNESCO's education and humanitarian efforts, in order to gain the most support from the local community and country in which you are operating (UNESCO Institute of Statistics, 2011).

MAJOR ISSUES IN INTERNATIONAL M-LEARNING

Although issues in international m-learning might seem insurmountable and costly, they really are not. They simply take a little pre-planning and innovation.

The World Virtual School (WVS) now has more than 540,000 students in 117 countries around the world and has learned, over the past 15 years, that nothing can stop the desire to learn except a reluctance to try and find solutions. With each new challenge, we have had to adjust our thinking, learning sometimes by trial and error, and other times by allowing our students to lead the way and teach us. As we progress through this chapter, we will look at some of the different obstacles that have come forward, such as:

1. local culture, resources, and needs;
2. connectivity;
3. cost of connecting to the Internet;
4. availability of mobile devices (and what works best);
5. bandwidth issues for different topics;
6. technology-transfer restrictions, including the problem of using hard-copy books;
7. learning barriers (such as a low percentage of high-school graduates in the area);
8. local teachers;
9. language barriers;
10. local commitment and support.

You might notice that local culture, resources, and needs are first on the list, and language barriers are near the bottom. You might think this is backwards, but language barriers are actually the least of our worries, as you will see moving forward. Let's look at each issue, one by one.

Local Culture, Resources, and Needs

The first and most important issue that needs to be overcome is the assumption that foreign students want to learn the same things that we want to learn, and in the same manner. This just isn't so.

We typically think that international students have the same needs as we do; a middle-school or high-school diploma, or even vocational technical training. Although this is true of students in developed and former communist countries, or even students with a higher than average income, the average international student simply wants to learn how to make their life, and their families' lives, better.

The WVS recently conducted an International Needs Survey, where more than 178,000 students in 56 countries responded to a variety of questions concerning how they accessed the Internet, what courses they wished to take, and what were their educational and economic backgrounds. This was approximately a 38 percent response rate, and the survey was conducted online and through e-mail. The WVS found the following (please note that we surveyed students who were already connected to the Internet—either at school or at home—or were connected to local agencies and NGOs within their home countries for training): The majority of students taking online or distance-learning courses were in the 18–30-year-old age group. Of all the respondents, 67.74 percent were men, and 32.26 percent were women.

When asked what they would like to study through distance learning (assuming that these courses will be delivered through mobile devices), the following list was generated (Muir, 2010):

a   world languages = 3.7 percent;
b   sustainable development = 3.7 percent;
c   PhD courses = 3.7 percent;
d   peace and conflict = 3.7 percent;
e   online-course development = 3.7 percent;
f   office management = 7.41 percent;
g   nursing, pharmacology = 3.7 percent;
h   MBA = 7.41 percent;
i   IBO programs = 3.7 percent;
j   hospitality and tourism = 3.7 percent;
k   government and politics = 3.7 percent;
l   ESL = 7.41 percent;
m   eco business = 11.11 percent;
n   disaster preparedness = 11.11 percent;
o   conflict transformation = 3.7 percent;
p   business management = 3.7 percent;
q   automotive sciences = 3.7 percent;
r   agricultural sciences = 3.7 percent;
s   accounting and finance = 3.7 percent.

The most telling of all situations was a recent request by the new head of the Uganda Virtual School (a division of the WVS) relating to what programs he would like to offer to his students. He responded with the following list: computer studies, graphic design, Web design, tailoring and garment design, knitting, carpentry, building technology, business management, entrepreneurship, catering and cake baking, event management, art and design, and pottery. As you can see, the list of courses are specifically what the young people in war-torn Uganda need to make a living and to change their lives. They aren't necessarily what we might expect, which is why it is always important to ask first. Another good example is the Mongolia Virtual School. Students there wish to take construction, welding, masonry, and English classes, whereas students in Jamaica are more interested in hospitality and tourism courses.

Another thing to consider is the actual culture, even the religion and ethnic makeup, of the country. For instance, in Saudi Arabia, we were invited to offer courses in international business, computer studies, and media, but were told that the Saudis would supply their own teachers and control the enrollment. This is because, in some countries in the Middle East, women are not allowed to take courses in the same environment as men, if at all. They also did not want our teachers to accidentally teach Western ideals or concepts that typically pervade our curriculum, sometimes called "*the hidden curriculum.*" By using their own teachers, they could more easily control what they truly wanted their students to learn.

Connectivity

One of the most important issues for foreign students is the ability to connect to the Internet. Although connectivity and infrastructure have greatly improved over the past

10 years, local corporations, universities, and schools are usually the only way students have of connecting to the Internet, unless they buy a private plan or visit a telecenter.

When carrying out the International Needs Survey, WVS found that only 12 percent of respondents had access to the Internet at home, 43 percent had access to the Internet at school or work, and 80 percent could find access at a local telecenter (Internet café) if needed.

When we asked how the majority of those who were already taking distance-learning courses only were accessing the Internet, they responded as follows:

- tablet or iPad = 2 percent;
- laptop = 11 percent;
- desktop = 13 percent;
- cell phone = 74 percent.

The fact that so many used a cell phone was illuminating, so we asked what type of phone they were using. They responded as follows:

- smartphone = 22 percent;
- "dumb phone" = 20 percent;
- Web-enabled phone = 58 percent.

As you can see, the majority of students use their cell phones to connect to their courses (making m-learning a natural way of learning for them), but only about 22 percent of them have "smart" phones. The survey showed that 58 percent have Web-enabled phones, but 20 percent are still using "dumb" phones and are unable to connect to the Internet at all over their cell phones. Only 2 percent of the surveyed population own or use tablets or an iPad to access the Internet, indicating that they are connecting to a private network somewhere in their area.

Because of the way that students are accessing the Internet, and the availability of Internet access at home, curriculum developers need to determine how best to deliver content through a Web-enabled cell phone—the device most used for m-learning. Although this may change over time, content can always be improved as accessibility improves.

Cost of Connecting to the Internet

The most difficult obstacle for international students to overcome for m-learning is the cost of connecting to the Internet. The following is an example of cost for Internet service around the world, per month. Although the data are old (2010), they show the average cost is outrageous for students who might not have a job, or whose family only makes less than US$50 per month to live on. See Table 48.1 (Africa Bandwidth Maps, 2005) for a sample of the cost of Internet by country, along with the bandwidth provided.

Another cost to consider is the cost of the course itself. There is not only a cost at the school's end to pay instructors, overhead costs, and fees for e-books and technology, but there is a cost at the student's end for the course and the loss of income he/she might experience while in school.

WVS offers its courses for free, in order to mediate these costs for students who might not necessarily be able to afford it, through government grants and private donations.

Table 48.1 Example Costs of Monthly Internet Access by Country, with Download Speeds

Country	Cost of Internet per month, US$	Bandwidth download speed, Mbps
Australia	22.82	5.55
Brazil	25.98	2.53
Bulgaria	7.32	14.36
Cameroon	44.56	0.45
Canada	8.90	6.59
China	9.75	2.70
Egypt	4.97	0.95
Germany	7.40	9.95
Guatemala	54.34	1.14
Haiti	70.99	1.13
Hong Kong	0.86	11.53
India	6.78	1.46
Iran	2.26	0.61
Korea, South	32.62	22.46
Latvia	12.48	18.03
Lithuania	7.20	15.81
Maldives	51.24	1.37
Mali	28.42	0.48
Netherlands	12.37	14.51
New Caledonia	80.34	1.55
Nigeria	50.42	0.55
Philippines	1.81	2.68
Romania	16.96	16.10
South Africa	63.21	1.95
Sudan	65.51	0.84
Switzerland	7.95	9.61
Tanzania	93.60	1.18
Uganda	99.59	2.39
United Kingdom	27.25	5.85
United States	14.95	7.78
Venezuela	42.61	1.05

Source: Information retrieved from: www.nationmaster.com/

Not all schools will be able to do this, but they should consider both the benefits and drawbacks when setting their prices for international students. The average cost of an online course in the K–12 arena in the United States is $250 per semester per course. International students often can only pay $1–10 per course. Institutions should take into account individual country GDPs when setting course prices.

Availability of Mobile Devices (and What Works Best)

Although foreign students tend to use whatever is available to them—usually a Web-enabled cell phone—there are still other devices to consider, such as iPads, Android tablets, or other educational devices. The most effective device that the WVS has found is an Android tablet that has applications that can store online textbooks, illustrations, RSS feeds, and video/audio feeds, and that can be used out in the field—away from an Internet connection—yet has the ability to connect to a Wi-Fi or Internet connection when back at school, home, local college or university, or telecenter.

According to MobiThinking (2012), the Android operating system will soon be the predominant OS for smartphone mobile devices. It is important to note that the "type" of Android tablet isn't specific, although you should try to use one that has at least a 7.5-inch screen instead of a small Android smartphone. It simply needs to be able to use the mobile applications necessary for the job.

The cost of an Android tablet is still an issue for foreign students, and schools operating overseas should consider bearing the cost of the tablets themselves. A company in India (Bharat Electronics) recently announced a new Android tablet that will be very useful for m-learning outside the classroom, for only US$35 (Kell, 2011). As new technologies develop, the cost of Android tablets will undoubtedly go down. As long as the tablet can provide e-book storage capabilities, the appropriate apps, and Internet connectivity, it can be used for m-learning in the international classroom.

Bandwidth Issues for Different Topics

Online content, video and audio, illustrations for vocational technical courses, and interactive quizzes, models, and activities often take up excessive bandwidth and are time consuming for students to download, especially with high Internet costs.

Because of the wide variation in download speeds, it is strongly recommended that curriculum developers consider the download speeds of the country they are writing curriculum for. Instead of including highly interactive demonstrations, they should consider other methods of content delivery, as discussed later in the chapter.

Technology-Transfer Restrictions, Including the Problem of Using Hard-Copy Books

One of the most difficult things about running any type of an online school or distance-learning program, regardless of whether you are using mobile devices, is the ability to get the book to the student in time to start the course. When working within a typical school-year calendar, hard-copy books often take up to 2 weeks to arrive at their destination, or might even be backordered. With the new trends toward using e-books, this is quickly being solved. However, for international use, e-books are not always an option, because of language barriers, technology-transfer restrictions, costs, and problems with downloading the e-book to a tablet. Some e-books are only available for use online, whereas others can be downloaded.

The best option for providing instructional materials to international students is to either write the curriculum from scratch yourself (not always the best and most efficient option), or to find a publication company such as Pearson Education, McDougal Littel, or Glencoe McGraw that allow you to use the textbook overseas in an e-book format. CourseSmart, eChapters, and other online book stores are most often the best solution, as they carry books from several publishers. Even then, they might only be available in English, or not available to international students.

For instance, although CourseSmart and eChapters are excellent resources, overseas students cannot access the textbooks without having a credit card or other method of payment. Therefore, it is better for the school to acquire the rights to the e-book itself, on behalf of its students. This often requires a memo of understanding for international use with the publisher and website. Even then, parts of the book might need to be translated into the local language in order to be of use to students. Online translators can be used, but are often inadequate and do not translate educational content correctly.

The best way to utilize online e-books for effective instruction is as follows:

- acquire the right to use a particular e-book and upload it to student tablets, or to your school's Internet. Be certain to follow all rules concerning copyright and use for educational uses only;
- hire in-house (or online) translators who will translate each chapter for you and then upload it the school website; or
- hire local instructors for on-site instruction who speak and read English, as well as the local language, who can translate on-site for students with limited English;
- teach English at the same time as teaching the actual course content.

The latter option might seem a convoluted way to get around the problem, but most students who want to learn, also want to learn English. By teaching English at the same time, through a local instructor, you actually address two needs at once: learning English and delivering the content. It might not be as efficient as teaching English students with an English textbook, but this is one way of solving the problem of language barriers.

Another important thing to remember is that, although the students might not have a hard copy of the textbook, instructors should always have their own hard copy for reference, when needed. This is especially useful when illustrations are difficult to see on a small tablet screen, or need to be enhanced.

It is also necessary to consider technology-transfer issues before buying and sending computer equipment such as PCs, laptops, ancillary materials, and tablets to another country. It is best to check with the software manufacturer's legal department to find out any restrictions on what can be sent to different countries.

The next thing to remember is that, when something is sent to a foreign country, the receiver must pay import taxes. When sending expensive equipment, it should be sent as a "gift," or with a special business permit. Otherwise, the receiver might end up spending US$200–300 for a cell phone or tablet that only cost US$150 at the sending end. Some countries' mail officials also add surcharges (whether legal or illegal), and you should always send materials to a reputable receiver or corporation, instead of an individual, if possible.

Learning Barriers (Such as a Low Percentage of High-School Graduates in the Area)

Most students in foreign countries have limited education, but are passionate about extending their education. In a typical African village of 50 children, only 10 students might get to go to middle school; only 1 to high school; and only 1 student in 10 villages is able to attend college. This means that the average students who enroll in online courses have only a middle-school education. They are considered "literate," but have only completed 6 or 7 years of school. Few of them know English, and almost all will need remediation in mathematics and science when considering taking vocational technical courses.

Educators should always consider the prerequisites for a course, but should never allow it to be an obstacle for a potential student. Often, a student can learn English, complete his high-school diploma, and learn a career or technical skill at the same time. It may take 2 or 3 years to complete the program, as opposed to 1, but students who want to succeed will gladly put in the effort.

Utilizing Local Teachers

The most important factor in creating a successful international program is to have local "buy-in" and participation in the program. The best way—and by far the most important aspect of any program—is to use local teachers, who can assist in on-site translation and instruction of students.

On-site instructors can not only explain concepts to students with learning barriers, but can translate and explain content, as well as teach students English. By using local instructors, schools will be supporting the local economy and will learn more about the challenges faced each day by the village, school, and students. Local instructors also provide valuable insight to local issues, political and cultural barriers, and learning obstacles that you might not be aware of. Local colleges and universities have lists of students searching for jobs who make wonderful instructors, and it is easy to seek them out.

Language Barriers

The easiest way to conquer language barriers is to utilize local teachers who speak and write English and the local language. Although it is important to remember that there are several online programs that teach English, educators should also remember that many developing-world countries were once colonies of countries such as France, Italy, England, Portugal, and Spain. Local students may also know French, Italian, Spanish, or some other major language that can be used to instruct students.

Arabic, Chinese, and Korean are also widely used languages that can be used to deliver curriculum content. Although many Mideast countries use a different version or dialect of Arabic, "all" Arabic speaking countries use something called "high Arabic" in their religious ceremonies, which all Arabic speakers use and understand. The same is true for Mandarin Chinese, which is widely used in Mongolia, as well as in mainland China and Hong Kong.

Local Commitment and Support

In order to have a successful international education program, it is important to have local commitment and support. This can be achieved in several ways, such as hiring local teachers; committing to local, on-the-job (OJT) projects that will enhance the community; establishing local Internet centers at telecenters, local colleges, or universities, where students can log in once a week; and working with local UN and NGO groups (such as Teachers Without Borders) or other international organizations that function within the countries. Without local support, programs often melt away or never get off the ground, because of low enrollment and participation.

One way to guarantee local support is to offer incentives to local companies or corporations. If local corporations are offered remediation classes, English, or business courses for free or at a reduced price, they will often allow students to visit their computer labs to participate in their own programs. Local companies will recognize the benefit of having better employees, while at the same time building their consumer base in the surrounding community.

An excellent program should be sustainable by local teachers and staff after 5 years, with minimal support from the school. Once again, it depends upon the goals of the school: to help the local community to become self-sustaining, or to keep making money for the school. Both goals need not be exclusive of each other, just well planned.

CURRICULUM DEVELOPMENT NECESSITIES

We have discussed the 10 major obstacles to m-learning that we've identified for international students, and will now talk about how to surmount these obstacles by adjusting curriculum-development techniques.

Creating Content in Deliverable Bites

Mobile devices are an excellent method by which to deliver content to international students, particularly by smartphone or tablet. As discussed previously, e-books can be utilized and downloaded through Kindle and other e-book applications for access in the local classroom, as well as at an OJT site or at home. The issue then becomes the instruction, or lessons, itself.

Lessons or individual instruction bites should be small and compact enough to be delivered on one screen on the mobile device. The lessons can refer to e-book content and URLs where interactive activities and illustrations are available. The same applies for exams or quizzes. Quizzes should be a small number of questions at the end of each small, deliverable bite of instruction, if relying solely on the smartphone or tablet. If other quiz-taking devices or assessment methods are used on site, on-site instructors can relay the results each week when they log in at their main Internet site.

Since the advent of the iPad, several technology companies have begun to develop course infrastructures that work specifically with tablets and iPads. Other hosting companies also offer Web-page templates that emulate the larger website that is available on a laptop screen and will fit on a mobile-device screen. Many of these can be found online by searching for "tablet course template." Others can be located by contacting traditional infrastructure providers such as Desire2Learn, Moodle, and Blackboard.

The main thing to remember in developing m-learning content is that, whatever is asked of the student needs to be in a small enough "bite" that students with limited English or learning skills can feel successful by completing small steps at one time. The "bites" also need to be downloadable by local bandwidth standards in a small amount of time, so that students don't get frustrated or distracted. Scaffolding instruction and project-based learning are perfect methods for delivering content in this way.

ADJUSTING DELIVERY METHODS

Students with a learning or language barrier, or limited connectivity, may need adaptable delivery methods. Instead of delivering an entire chapter in one large bite, it might need to be broken down into steps. Instructors who typically use a lot of interactive activities, audio, or video, may have to restructure the content into a different format in order for it to be delivered over a smartphone or tablet.

Instructors will also need to take into consideration that not all cultures learn in the same manner. Students in some areas are much more tactile–kinesthetic-oriented than American students. Creating a project for them to complete that applies to their real-world situation and that teaches them the same concepts as a chapter of mathematics might be better than having them read a chapter in a language they don't always understand.

CONCLUSION

Teaching and delivering courses through m-learning devices, or even online in a distance-learning platform, require a lot of thought and preparation at the international level. Local needs, resources, and customs need to be considered in all aspects of education, because they will affect what is offered, how it is offered, by whom it is offered, and how it is accessed. Clear goals should be established before beginning an international program of any type, because they will greatly affect the way the program is developed. Some of the same principles that apply in teaching students face to face also apply when using m-learning. For instance, learning styles need to be addressed, and appropriate methodology must be applied. Techniques such as scaffolded learning, project-based learning, and real-world applications (to a student's home country) should also be considered when developing the curriculum content.

It is important to listen to our students, because they will always tell us what they want or need, and what is working, and what is not. It is our job as educators to find a way of fulfilling those needs, so that all students, worldwide, can participate more fully in the global social and economic community. We may never know what talent and knowledge are lost in that small village, where no child goes beyond primary education. Basic education is a human right, according to the United Nations. Let us do our best to fulfill that.

REFERENCES

Africa Bandwidth Maps. (2005). *Mapping Africa's ICT growth*. Retrieved from: http://www.africabandwidthmaps.com/?page_id=10

Kell, C. (2011). *India's new $35 Aakash table computer designed in Canada*. Retrieved from: http://ca.news.yahoo.com/blogs/right-click/india-35-aakash-tablet-computer-designed-canada-194516502.html

MobiThinking.com. (2012). *Mobile marketing tools*. Retrieved from: http://mobithinking.com/mobile-marketing-tools/latest-mobile-stats

Muir, D. (2010). *International schools needs assessment survey*. Retrieved from: www.scribd.com/doc/27063906/International-School-Needs-Assessment-Survey

Nation Master. (2012). *Country Internet profiles*. Retrieved from: www.nationmaster.com/

UNESCO Institute of Statistics. (2011). Retrieved from: www.uis.unesco.org/Pages/default.aspx/

FURTHER READING

Barbour, M., Brown, R., Waters, L., Hoey, R., Hunt, J., Kennedy, K., & Ounsworth, C. (2010). *Online and blended learning: A survey of policy and practice of K–12 schools around the world*. Retrieved from: www.inacol.org/research/docs/iNACOL_IntnlReport2011.pdf

InternetWorld Stats. (2011). Retrieved from: www.Internetworldstats.com/

Muir, D. (2000). *The case for introducing Internet education into Africa*. Retrieved from: www.icte.org/T00_Library/ID167.pdf

Muir, D. (2007). *Connecting Russia to the world through Internet education*. Retrieved from: http://plci.academia.edu/DianaMuir/Papers/186231/Connecting_Russia_to_the_World_Through_Internet_Education

Muir, D. (2008). *Ten years of online data*. Retrieved from: http://wvs.us.com/papers/tenyears.ppt

Muir, D. (2008). *The virtual school and the hidden agenda*. Retrieved from: http://wvs.us.com/papers//VS_and_hidden_curriculum.ppt

49

M-POWERING THE POOR THROUGH MOBILE LEARNING

Sheila Jagannathan

Imagine a world where you can pay school or health fees, open a savings account and earn interest, withdraw money from an ATM machine (no ATM card necessary), and conduct a host of other transactions just with your mobile phone. While this may seem like a vision from the future, it is already a reality in Kenya, a low-income country with a population of 40 million and a nascent telecom industry.

(World Bank News, 2010)

INTRODUCTION

According to Wayan Vota (2009), from UNESCO,

There is a mobile phone revolution in the developing world today. From the rural Maasai to the slum dwellers of Mumbai, poor people are acquiring mobile phones by themselves—without the government subsidies of the telecenter era. In fact, mobiles represent a huge shift in the technology deployment burden from the state to private companies and individual consumers.

(para. 3)

The saturation level of mobile devices is already nearing one-to-one in the developed world, and gaining momentum quickly in the developing world across Africa, Asia, the Middle East, and Latin America. According to Cellular-news (2008), global mobile-phone subscriptions reached annual growth rates of 7.9 percent during the period 2007–2012, boosting the number of global mobile-phone subscribers to 4.5 billion in 2012, with a penetration rate hitting 64.7 percent, up from 46.8 percent in 2007. Much of this increase is happening in developing countries, where there is a huge transformative effect and potential for information delivered over mobile phones to catalyze poverty alleviation.

The major driver for the mobile innovation is the fact that 75 percent of the world's population now lives within range of a cell-phone tower. In addition, high-end smartphones are starting to outnumber and outperform personal computers, and some of this functionality is available in low-end mobile phones as well. Rapidly declining costs and increasing ubiquity have, therefore, given users in even very poor communities of the developing world the opportunity to benefit from the availability of mobile applications to facilitate "anytime, anywhere" learning, especially outside formal educational settings.

This chapter focuses on the innovative uses of m-learning (blended with social media, crowdsourcing, and geospatial tools) to achieve mobile transformation (m-transformation) around the world, and it illustrates the important role pedagogical techniques play in making this happen. It examines m-transformation as an emerging trend and a new frontier in international development.

The first section presents interesting cases illustrating how mobile blends have made a difference to the lives of the world's poor by:

- enabling better service delivery (e.g., in health, education, and water);
- eliminating gender violence;
- improving good governance and accountability through citizen feedback (using mobiles with geospatial tools);
- promoting citizen media and freedom of information;
- encouraging democratic decision-making through polls, m-voting, and other forms of real-time communication between citizens and the government;
- law enforcement (using SMS to report crimes or request emergency services).

The second section discusses the role innovative pedagogies can play in developing sustainable learning interventions that can greatly expand the reach and impact of these learning opportunities. Notably, one needs to think differently about learning design when dealing with mobile environments for informal learning, and consider the distinctive characteristics of the media. The key point is that the challenge is not about disseminating dense content (modules) via mobile devices, but rather about leveraging the reflective, collaborative, and constructive opportunities for just-in-time learning that mobile allows users to access. Relevant active and collaborative pedagogical techniques are discussed in this context.

MOBILE PHONES ENCOURAGE CITIZEN PARTICIPATION

Challenge

Many countries in Africa have been struggling with building a voice for their citizens and strengthening the accountability of public officials to the communities they serve. The two following illustrations from the Democratic Republic of Congo (DRC) and Nigeria provide some useful insights into the potentials for m-learning.

DRC is located in the heart of Africa, with nearly 70 million people, trying to recover from serious conflict that has been happening since the 1990s. As a result, infrastructure in DRC is still weak, and most of the country has very poor access to electricity. As the country rebuilds itself, citizens need to have increased participation in helping the government provide the necessary services such as roads, electricity, and water.

Mobile-centric Approach

Although many citizens in DRC do not have access to water or electricity, most have cell phones. The World Bank Institute's ICT4Gov initiative is introducing mobile technology to enhance participatory budgeting processes in DRC's South Kivu province (New Media and Development Communication, 2007). Using mobile technology, citizens vote on the priorities that are crucial for their communities, and then the local government devotes a percentage of the local investment budget to the projects selected by the citizens.

The program uses mobile phones for four purposes. The first is to invite citizens to the participatory budgeting assemblies through geo-targeted SMS messages that broadcast details (date, time, location) of the assemblies to all phones receiving signals from a particular tower. Second, citizens use text messages to vote on the priorities for the community. Third, mobile phones are used to announce the decisions based on the voting patterns, thereby ensuring transparency and inclusion. Finally, mobile phones are used by citizens to monitor progress on their selected projects and also to provide feedback via text messages.

Results

Beyond empowering citizens to have a voice in the budgetary decisions that affect their families and communities, one tangible result is that more public funds have been mobilized for the poor. Through the use of mobile phones, citizens in the DRC are

Figure 49.1 Ismail on Mobile Telephone

Source: Arne Hoel/World Bank. Photo ID: Hoel_100913_232. World Bank Photo Collection. Retrieved from: www.flickr.com/photos/worldbank/7826373720

changing the way they engage with their governments, their communities, and one another.

The example from Nigeria is equally interesting. A network of mobile election monitors of Nigeria is using mobile phones and SMS to monitor the Nigerian presidential election to ensure impartial elections (mobilemonitors.org, 2007). With millions of active subscribers, even in rural and conflict areas of Nigeria, mobile phones have proven to be the most useful communication tool to engage with and inform citizens directly and immediately, and report back cases of electoral fraud and ballot box tampering.

MOBILES FACILITATE QUICK RESPONSE TO MEDICAL CRISIS

Challenge

Maternal health care continues to be a concern to policymakers in Pakistan as, for every 100,000 babies born, some 260 women die during childbirth. Global statistics indicate that Pakistan is one of 11 countries worldwide that account for 65 percent of global maternal deaths in 2008; yet these deaths could have been prevented, if qualified medical care was provided during childbirth. As women find it difficult to travel to health clinics and hospitals on their own because of social restrictions, the Pakistan government has established a cadre of health workers who visit the homes and advise women on various health issues (UNICEF, 2010).

Mobile-Centric Approach

Women health workers are facing a number of institutional, cultural, and political challenges, but, in the near term, mobile devices are being used innovatively to address the problem. Women health workers who visit village homes as a part of their work in

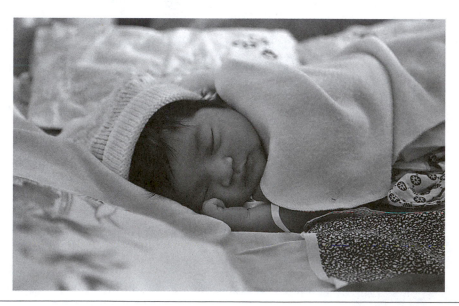

Figure 49.2 Newborn in Hospital

Source: © Ray Witlin/World Bank. Photo ID: IN053S18 World Bank. World Bank Photo Collection. Retrieved from: www.flickr.com/photos/worldbank/2182854617/in/photostream/

Pakistan are being equipped with mobile devices (with a data-collection server at the back end), with the objectives of (1) providing an immediate response to a medical crisis and (2) collecting data for future policy action.

Results

Although the mobile-centric approach by itself may not provide a lasting solution, it is a start in the process of providing timely health care to women in remote areas, where medical care may not be available, and helping improve birthing outcomes, as the health worker is able to prioritize her visits based on the needs. It also allows women to attend to women, especially in families where seeing a male medical specialist may be considered taboo. Another related benefit is that equipping women health workers with mobile phones reduces male domination in the technology arena and empowers women to take a lead in improving service delivery via technology innovations.

Let me illustrate with another example here. Grameen Foundation (a global nonprofit dedicated to fighting poverty) and BabyCenter (global pregnancy and parenting initiative), in collaboration with Columbia University, are using mobile services to provide health education to pregnant woman in rural Ghana (Grameen Foundation, 2010). This initiative has a potential to reach more than 20 million underserved mothers worldwide.

The objective of this free service, called "Mobile Midwife" (Gremeen Foundation, 2010), is to educate pregnant women and empower them to take control of their own health by providing timely advice and tips on topics such as delivery, breastfeeding, immunization, and good nutrition. The hidden objective of the initiative is also to dispel deeply held cultural taboos and superstitions about pregnancy and childbirth that often exist in traditional societies. For example, many Asian societies believe that the mother must stay indoors for at least 6 weeks after a baby is born, be on a restricted diet, and limit physical activities to prevent further muscle weakening. The lack of exercise and dietary restrictions actually end up weakening the mother.

USING CELL PHONES, CROWDSOURCING TO GET WATER TO THE THIRSTY

Challenge—Will I Get Water Today?

An unreliable water supply is a major problem for citizens in many cities in South Asia, Africa, and Latin America. Although residents in these developing countries may have access to a piped water supply, the actual availability of water is limited to just a few hours per day! Moreover, owing to inefficiencies in service delivery, residents have no idea when water will be provided, and, hence, families (generally women and the poor), waste several hours each day simply waiting for precious water to arrive.

Mobile-Centric Approach

NextDrop (http://nextdrop.org/), which started in 2009 as a project in a competition in a University of California, Berkeley, civil-engineering class, is funded today by the Knight News Challenge. It provides households with timely information about water delivery via cell phones. The flow of information is illustrated below:

- Utility workers in the field use their cell phones to call NextDrop's interactive voice response system when they manually open neighborhood water valves.

Figure 49.3 Ismail Drinks Water

Source: Arne Hoel/World Bank. Photo ID: Hoel_100913_274-2. World Bank Photo Collection. Retrieved from: www.flickr.com/photos/worldbank/7826374734

- The system automatically generates text-message updates for local residents, 30–60 minutes before water delivery starts.
- Updates from the utility team are converted into Google Map-based streaming visual data, so that engineers and residents can track the status of the delivery network in real time using a live updating dashboard.
- Finally, crowdsourcing via mobile phones is used to verify the accuracy of utility reports and create a feedback loop between citizens and service providers.

Results

The pilot initiative served 1,000 families in Hubli, India. Starting July 2013, NextDrop hopes to serve the entire city population of approximately 1 million. This innovation has also resulted in enhancing the accountability of the water utility staff in terms of serving the low-income customers better.

In addition to mobile phones, SMS texting, and GPS-enabled mapping, applications have the potential to improve the day-to-day lives of the poor. These tools can be used to empower citizens to fight crime and violence, and help provide feedback on the delivery of services and get timely information on jobs, markets, and hazard conditions.

CAN ACCESSIBILITY THROUGH MOBILE APPLICATIONS BE COMBINED WITH PEDAGOGY TO BUILD NEW APPROACHES FOR LEARNING?

Build Learning Around What We Know About How People Use Mobiles

With almost all adults in developing countries having access to mobile telephones, the potentials of using these as capacity-building tools are intuitively obvious. In particular, the millions who continue to be without the basic "3R" skills and are socially disempowered (notably women and ethnic-minority groups), have an opportunity to learn and apply this learning to enhance the quality of their lives and livelihoods.

In this section, I will pull out and build on lessons from existing adult-learning principles and pedagogical frameworks to develop effective design principles to produce quality programs for mobile dissemination for this audience.

Use Existing Frameworks for Effective Learning Design

The well-known Bloom's taxonomy (Bloom, 1956, as cited in JISC TechDis, 2012) provides a framework for developing effective m-learning solutions. A recent article in JISC TechDis (2012) discusses these opportunities at length, and I have adapted this further to show how Bloom's taxonomy can be relevant to design learning for the poor and disadvantaged via mobile devices.

This framework suggests that any learner passes through five levels to achieve mastery. As the learner moves from a surface level (comprehension) to a deeper level (evaluation) of understanding of the concepts, the quality of the learning experience improves. Well-crafted pedagogical design along Bloom's taxonomy could enable even illiterate or

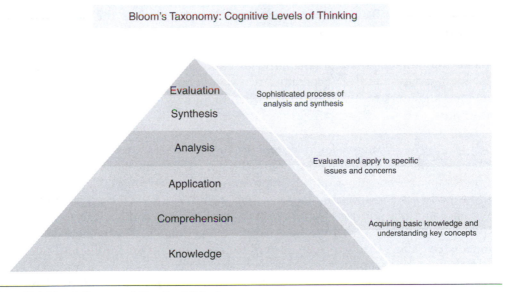

Figure 49.4 Bloom's Taxonomy of Educational Objectives

Source: Adapted from Bloom, 1956, as cited in JISC TechDis, 2012

semi-literate individuals to move up the learning triangle. The higher-level tasks require the development of new insights and critique of available information and are a lot more challenging to design than sharing basic information (as the stories in the earlier section illustrated).

Examples of Lower Levels of Bloom's Taxonomy

The lower levels of Bloom's taxonomy (Bloom, 1956, as cited in JISC TechDis, 2012), describe a learner acquiring basic knowledge and understanding key concepts. For example, a radio program broadcast over the Sahelian countries could be immensely useful in giving farmers information on how to protect their crops from locust infestations, which occur on a regular basis. The connections established through this medium also enable knowledge to be transmitted on relatively "new" topics, such as climate change, so that the farmers begin to mobilize themselves to protect the crops and livestock from prolonged droughts caused by climate change or from global economic events, such as the increase in the price of foodgrains and other commodities because of an ongoing civil war in a neighboring country, which is an important trans-shipment center for essential supplies.

With the diffusion of mobile telephones, the ability to customize information and knowledge has expanded greatly. In many of the least-developed countries, for example, diarrhea has been an avoidable cause of death of infants because mothers were not aware that the dehydration that accompanies diarrhea could be easily prevented by ensuring that the child had plenty of fluids. A text message from the mobile phone could inform the mother of the key actions she needs to take for an oral rehydration therapy, and she could seek further guidance from the physician on the symptoms and when she should take the child to a hospital. This access to information also empowers the poor to understand and appreciate their economic and political rights. For example, many countries have laws on minimum wages, but these laws are not enforced. When information is made available through the mobile texting service, the landless farmer or sharecropper is in a position to demand that he receives the minimum wage. More generally, brief text-based information can serve as a powerful instrument for ensuring accountability among civil servants and utility providers by (1) disclosing data on the reliability (or unreliability) of basic water, electricity, health care, and education services, and (2) generating two-way communication between the service providers and users, so that both groups begin to understand each others' concerns and constraints.

Example for Medium Levels of Bloom's Taxonomy

At the medium level of Bloom's taxonomy (Bloom, 1956, as cited in JISC TechDis, 2012), learners move beyond just acquiring information and are able to evaluate and apply this to specific issues and concerns they face. For example, taking the example of sharing data on commodity prices discussed in the earlier paragraph, farmers evaluate the experiences of peers on what should be their strategy (on whether to sell and cash in by immediately selling their crops, or instead to take a mortgage to build a silo in which they can store their crop when commodity prices are low, and sell when prices are high). With advances in mobile technology, many more exciting opportunities have now arisen. For example, a farmer facing a virus threat to his crops texts a message, along with photo clips, to the local agricultural university and to other farmers who are similarly affected. Based on group discussions on the issue, and advice from agricultural researchers, they are able to figure out a strategy on how to tackle the problem.

Example for Higher Levels of Bloom's Taxonomy

The higher level of Bloom's taxonomy (Bloom, 1956, as cited in JISC TechDis, 2012), describes a more sophisticated process of analysis and synthesis. In the minimum-wages example in the first section, a civil activist or community leader listens to audio or text messages from peers and assesses them (i.e. exercises judgment) for bias or discriminatory practices based on religion, gender, or service access by local officials or elites. The group collectively launches, through social media, actions (such as prosecution of employers who are paying less than the minimum wage) that lead to the landless farmer or sharecropper receiving a legal wage. There are other incidents of communities sharing text messages and audio clips to "crowdsource" strategies to raise awareness in the media of their specific concerns. For example, a village community gets together, analyzes, and articulates the reasons why the construction of an all-weather road is important for improving farm-to-market access for their farm products, and is able to successfully lobby for its construction.

In general, the higher the learner travels up Bloom's taxonomy triangle, the greater the interactivity, engagement, and overall learning effectiveness in terms of achieving desired outcomes.

Design Learning at the Intersection of Learner, Device, and Social Aspects

Another useful framework for m-learning is Koole's (2009) FRAME model, which describes m-learning as a "convergence of mobile technologies, human learning capacities, and social interaction" (p. 25).

Learning is defined by all three aspects—the learner needs to be motivated to learn, get stimulated by interactions with peers, and utilize technology applications via mobile devices. The more the capabilities of the device, the greater the potentials for interactivity; the greater the interest of the learner, the greater the potential of utilizing social norms and existing technology; the greater the density of social norms promoting interaction, the better the opportunities for using technology to foster interactive learning.

Effective m-learning tools empower learners to assess and select relevant information, redefine their goals, and reconsider the way they see themselves tackling the economic and social challenges they face.

In summary, an m-learning application tailored to meet the learning needs of hundreds of millions of literate and semi-literate adults needs to adapt to the enhanced capabilities of newer generations of mobile devices, while being fully cognizant of:

- learner characteristics and specific interests;
- local social norms and conventions that shape the way interactivity is promoted and deepened;
- cultural characteristics that facilitate the communication and receptivity of "bite-sized" learning modules; and
- the need for just-in-time feedback loops that strengthen and reinforce the key learning objectives through complementary media (such as radio, television, laptop computers etc.).

Creatively Blend Learning Methods and Tools

Blending learning methods (such as role play, lecture, or games) and tools (e.g, mobile phone, SMS, polls, etc.) based on the clear understanding of the target audience as well as learning objectives has worked well to create sustainable learning interventions in face-to-face environments. In designing m-learning environments also, innovative blends should be considered.

For example, in the uReport (2011) initiative in Uganda, UNICEF uses a blend of mobile phones and broadcast media such as radio to get immediate feedback from citizens on everything from access to medication to youth employment or water and sanitation. Mobile users can add their voice to the discussions by sending text messages (via a toll-free shortcode) or participate in SMS polls. Citizen responses are collated and relayed in weekly radio talk shows to raise awareness and reach out to the broader community on its rights to basic services and other community-related issues. For wider visibility, the results of polls are also posted on the website as maps or charts. An added benefit is that the data gathered from citizens are shared among the donor community and used to track results, including what is working well and what does not.

Provide Opportunities for Learners to Generate Content

Design learning activities that encourage learners to generate content by taking photographs and, if possible, by recording video and audio in the field. A rural health care worker can send photos of a patient's skin condition and ask for help with a diagnosis from the city's medical team. An agricultural expert can create a photo album for farmers, showing conditions that indicate soil erosion. Rather than take notes, a trainer can voice record his or her thoughts on how to improve water and sanitation.

Seize the Moment—Do Not Wait for the Latest Technology

With the fast pace of innovations and advances in mobile technology, there is a danger that learning solutions that are designed today may not be relevant in the future. It is important that the products designed are flexible enough to operate on a number of technologies and devices in the developing world. There is also the temptation to design for smartphones or even wait for the latest technology. It is best to seize the moment and design informal learning for the mobile devices that are prevalent among the learners. Ideally, the applications should be device-agnostic, in order to reach as many people as possible. For example, designing programs or preparing content for smartphones may exclude the majority of people who live in extreme poverty and are in the greatest need of such content and learning.

To sum up, learning does not happen automatically: it needs to be carefully structured, with the objectives and the target audience kept in mind.

Know the needs of the community; before investing in the design of an m-learning program, invest the time required to know the needs of the community. Some key considerations are as follows:

- M-learning works well with smaller chunks of learning material in the form of the "review–refresh–reinforce" model of learning (Mobl21, 2010).
- Structure both individual as well as group activities using the built-in features of mobile devices.
- Provide facilitation and support.

CONCLUSION

Is the potential of m-learning hype or reality? There is clearly a good potential for bite-sized learning through mobile telephony. However, successes have been so far mainly in the form of informing the users. More research is needed to understand how this ubiquitous technology can provide educational resources to those most in need, while also developing a sustainable and robust business case.

Perhaps the next step could involve convening thought leaders and experts in order to work toward growing the m-learning industry in a structured way. Best practice and learning design could be shared among key players in order to determine what an m-learning industry should look like for the people at the bottom of the pyramid and to determine the value chain.

REFERENCES

Cellular-news. (2008). *Global mobile phone subscribers to reach 4.5 billion by 2012*. Retrieved from: www.cellular-news.com/story/29824.php?source=newsletter

Grameen Foundation. (2010). *Grameen Foundation and BabyCenter join forces to support mobile healthcare initiatives in developing countries*. Retrieved from: www.grameenfoundation.org/press-releases/grameen-foundation-and-babycenter-join-forces-support-mobile-healthcare-initiatives-d

JISC TechDis. (2012). *Technology matters: Pedagogy, practice and accessibility potential*. Retrieved from: www.jisctechdis.ac.uk/techdis/technologymatters/mobilelearning/exploringopportunities/pedagogypractice andaccessibilitypotential

Koole, M. L. (2009). A model for framing mobile learning. In M. Ally (Ed.), *Mobile learning: Transforming the delivery of education and training* (pp. 25–47). Edmonton, AB: Athabasca Press.

mobilemonitors.org. (2007). *Key facts for mobile phone election monitoring*. Retrieved from: www.mobile monitors.org/

mobiThinking. (June 2012). *Global mobile statistics 2012*. Retrieved from: http://mobithinking.mobi/mobile-marketing-tools/latest-mobile-stats

Mobl21. (2010). *3-Rs of mobile learning: Review–refresh–reinforce*. Retrieved from: www.mobl21.com/blog/19/3-r%E2%80%99s-of-mobile-learning-review-refresh-reinforce/

New Media and Development Communication. (2007). *Monitoring elections with mobile phones*. Retrieved from: www.columbia.edu/itc/sipa/nelson/newmediadev/Public%20participation.html

UNICEF. (2010). *UNICEF's support of midwives in Pakistan preventing maternal deaths*. Retrieved from: www.unicef usa.org/news/news-from-the-field/unicefs-support-of-midwives.html

uReport. (2011). Retrieved from: http://ureport.ug/about_ureport/

Vota, W. (2009). *Mobile phones: Better learning tools than computers?* Retrieved from: https://edutechdebate.org/mobile-phones-and-computers/mobile-phones-better-learning-tools-than-computers/

World Bank News. (2010). *Mobile banking goes viral: M-Pesa and Kenya's telecom revolution*. Retrieved from: http://web.worldbank.org/WBSITE/EXTERNAL/NEWS/0,,contentMDK:22770800~pagePK:34370~piPK:34424~theSitePK:4607,00.html?cid=ISG_E_WBWeeklyUpdate_NL

50

ACCEPTANCE OF TABLET DEVICES FOR LEARNING AND TEACHING IN INSTITUTIONS OF HIGHER LEARNING

The Malaysian Perspective

Zoraini Wati Abas and Raja Maznah Raja Hussain

The wide availability of mobile devices such as smartphones (e.g., iPhones and Blackberries) and tablet devices (e.g., iPads and Galaxy tablets) in the Malaysian market has driven Malaysians to own either a smartphone or tablet or both. The devices are being used, not only for communication and gaining information, but also to increase one's daily productivity, such as in managing daily personal, work, and family-related activities. The fact that mobile-service subscriptions coupled with broadband wireless or 3G and 4G Internet-access subscriptions are affordable means such devices have attracted the interest of most Malaysians, including academics in institutions of higher learning (IHLs). Likewise, an increasing number of students are seen to have these devices.

ICT AND THE DEVELOPMENT OF M-LEARNING IN MALAYSIA

In the last decade, the rapid development of the Malaysian information communication and technology (ICT) industry was contributed to, in part, by the aspiration of the government to establish a knowledge-based economy. For example, the Malaysian Super Corridor (MSC) and its seven flagship applications were launched in 1997. The MSC initiative aimed to strategically position Malaysia in the international ICT arena. Chaired by the prime minister of Malaysia, the International Advisory Panel (IAP) of the MSC comprises a group of over 30 personalities and renowned figures in the ICT world. This includes heads of corporations such as Microsoft, Sun Microsystems, Sony Corporation, Motorola, Oracle, Acer, Apple Computers, British Telecom, Fujitsu, Ericsson, DHL, and so on. As such, Bill Gates, Larry Ellison, and Alvin Toffler, to name a few, are members of the IAP and have attended meetings held locally.

As reported by the local news (www.mysinchew.com/node/67681), 17.5 million Malaysians are on the Internet. Among the 30.38 million people in Malaysia, 110.6 percent (30.7 million) are mobile-phone subscribers, indicating multiple subscriptions among some individuals. As published on the Socialbakers website (www.socialbakers.com/facebook-statistics/malaysia), more than 12.3 million Malaysians (72.58 percent of Internet users) are on Facebook, representing 46.89 percent of the Malaysian population. In order to provide Malaysians with greater access to the Internet, the National Broadband Initiative and high-speed broadband were launched by the prime minister in March 2011. The initiative, implemented by the Malaysian Communications and Multimedia Commission, aims to have 75 percent of the country's mobile-phone subscribers on broadband Internet by 2015, from the current 53.5 percent (www.theborneopost.com/2011/11/11/mcmc-on-right-track-to-achieve-national-broadband-penetration-target/).

With these recent developments, the infrastructure for e-learning and m-learning is being put in place. Although many, if not all, universities have had their own learning-management system for the past several years, m-learning is relatively new. It has, however, been successfully implemented with distance learners in two local institutions, namely, the Open University Malaysia (OUM) and, on a smaller scale, the University of Science Malaysia (USM). Whereas OUM launched m-learning in January 2009 and has since benefited over 20,000 students, USM started m-learning in 2008 and has since benefited a few hundred students. Another distance-learning university, the Asia e-University, gave away iPads to its new batch of students in 2011. OUM also recently announced that academic staff's purchase of tablet devices would be subsidized.

These developments and the success of the m-learning efforts in OUM reported by Abas, Lim, and Ramly (2011) and Peng, Abas, Goolamally, Yusof, and Singh (2011), as well as m-learning experiments at USM (Baharum, Ismail, & Idrus, 2010), are expected to lead to more interesting m-learning initiatives. Given the aspiration of the government to have Malaysia become an education hub and to further internationalize its education overseas, a study of the current state of the art, particularly in the use of tablet devices among Malaysian academicians, is timely. At the same time, the authors obtained feedback from academicians who are using tablet devices to determine the potential implementation of m-learning using tablet devices.

USAGE OF TABLET DEVICES IN INSTITUTIONS OF HIGHER LEARNING

The literature review examines the current usage of tablet devices and the benefits and challenges, as reported from around the world, as publications on the usage of tablet devices are lacking in Malaysia.

Tablet devices fall in the growing number of mobile devices being used to power education today. Goundar (2011) states that mobile devices offer a number of advantages in education in comparison with laptops or notebooks, as they are generally lighter, more interactive, and more mobile. This ease of use, combined with a growing suite of educational applications for tablets, makes tablets an ideal choice for developing technology-based learning.

However, the usage of tablets in IHLs is still lagging behind their usage in K–12 schools. As pointed out by Hodge, Welch, and Woodcock (2011), schools are much further ahead of the game when it comes to iPad (tablet) adoption. Academic institutions have a tendency to ban tablets, as, according to university administrators, they can take up university bandwidth, thereby slowing the campus network. However, it should be noted that universities such as Cornell and Princeton, which once instituted bans on iPads, have reversed their decisions.

In IHLs, usage of iPads tends to revolve around their ability to deliver multimedia content (Davis, 2011; Hodge et al., 2011; Marmarelli & Ringle, 2011), record lessons (Hodge et. al, 2011), and their general ease of use (Marmarelli & Ringle, 2011; Ward, 2012). Tablets and iPads also have brought into focus the usage of e-textbooks (Bailey, 2012; Barber, 2012; Magrath, Nihalani, & Perkins, 2011). E-textbooks are digitalized textbooks that can be stored in tablets, thus allowing a student to carry several textbooks on a single mobile device. E-textbooks, according to Magrath et al. (2011), allow students to interact with the textbook, thus having the potential to promote creative thinking. Digital textbooks ideally should contain video and audio files and links to external sites, thus creating a more interactive learning environment for the student.

Research regarding the usage of tablets in the university setting has been conducted by researchers such as Wieder (2011), Ward (2012), and Magrath et al. (2011) regarding the usage of iPads by students in their respective institutions. Research into faculty's usage of the iPad and tablets has been conducted by Marmarelli and Ringle (2011). All of the research above found that, in general, iPads and tablets are well accepted by students but still face many logistical and practical issues that may hamper their usage in universities. Next, the benefits of using tablet devices in the academic classrooms are reviewed, and the current challenges in implementation of the devices are highlighted.

THE BENEFITS OF TABLET-DEVICE USAGE IN M-LEARNING

The benefits of tablet devices can be seen from both the faculty and student points of view. From the faculty's point of view, the iPad and tablet are generally seen as a boost to students' learning. Davis (2011) has found that the usage of iPads lead to strong conceptual understanding among students. Barber (2012) has noted the increased use of learning analytics (via iPad) to better personalize the learning environment. Bailey (2012) found that students have better study habits and performance with tablets. He attributes this to digital textbooks accessible via tablets, which are richer study materials compared with their print counterparts. In his study, Bailey (2012) primarily encourages his students to utilize tablets to access and search for information on the Internet. Bailey (2012) views the recent tablet developments as something very positive, as the interactive content that the tablet enables can boost learning among students. Furthermore, the increase in use of the tablets creates a bigger market for digital publishing, which will allow subject-matter experts to publish their own materials online for use in tablet-powered classrooms. This view is shared by Goundar (2011), who mentioned the importance of free software (iBook Author) that will allow authors to publish e-books direct to market. The iBook Author, recently launched, is a powerful and simple application for authors to publish their own interactive e-books for the iPad.

According to Ward (2012), the iPad excelled for reading and viewing textbooks and course materials. However, he questioned its overall benefit to the classroom and pointed out that the goals for using iPads in the classroom must be carefully considered before implementation. Fahey and Sebastian (2010) found that students' learning process is deepened and their memory and comprehension are enhanced through the use of tablets in their education.

Marmarelli and Ringle (2011) found that faculty members found the iPads to be extremely useful as portable repositories for storing text and their own notes. In their research, it was also found that the iPad tends to be more useful in settings that require a great deal of movement (such as the lab, or dance classes), and they were found to be superior to laptops in active classroom environments.

From the students' point of view, iPad and tablet usage is seen as a positive addition to their learning experience. In research conducted by Magrath et al. (2011), they found that students reported a heightened ease of use and motivation to study, owing to the increased mobility and convenience afforded by the use of tablets. Students, in their research, also reported increased engagement in the lesson and a greater general understanding when tablets were assigned to students for them to use to complete their class assignments. Students have also found certain aspects of the tablet to be very conducive to their learning. Hodge et al. (2011) have described the iPad as the perfect device for dealing with student life, as it is small and portable. In their research, they noted that students utilize the iPad to record lessons and take notes, and as a collaborative tool for producing media (for group work).

ISSUES AND CHALLENGES WITH USAGE OF TABLET DEVICES

Surprisingly, the most prominent group that expressed disappointment with iPad usage was the students themselves. Faculty members, as pointed out in research by Marmarelli and Ringle (2011), find tablet devices very favorable to teaching. Students, on the other hand, according to Ward (2012), found that their laptops were far more functional than an iPad, and their smartphones can perform similar functions to an iPad. In his research, Ward (2012) pointed out that students were not completely impressed by the technology of tablet computing.

Although the iPad and tablet may be good platforms for reading and viewing material, they are poor platforms for word-processing, spreadsheet calculation, and creating presentations. Ward (2012) mentioned a need to train students to utilize the new technology in order to benefit from it. Wieder (2011) claims that the tablet is a passive device that has limited use in higher education. He further adds that tablets, in their current form, cannot be used to mark up materials on the fly or show changes to students in response to their questions, issues that are at the forefront of technology usage in the classroom. In his research, Wieder also found that students did not use the iPad to complete their coursework, concerned that they were unable to save their work in a transferrable and readable format on the iPad. Wieder also pointed out the current lack of content for e-textbooks. Magrath et al. (2011) support this point by stating that the large majority of applications produced and marketed for educational use displayed poor multimedia learning principles. Marmarelli and Ringle (2011) share similar views. Nyaggah (2011) calls it the content and curator problem—content for m-learning can be difficult to access, and, when it can be accessed, teachers are often challenged in utilizing it to teach their students. Magrath et al. (2011) also pointed out that most e-textbooks are just digitalized prints of the conventional textbook, conferring no additional educational advantage, apart from the obvious benefit of carrying all of your textbooks on a single device.

From a practical point of view, tablets have a poor input method, as the keyboard input was found to be slow and unresponsive (Marmarelli & Ringle, 2011; Wieder, 2011).

Furthermore, iPads in particular were found to be difficult to use, owing to the lack of USB support and a proper file-management system (Marmarelli & Ringle, 2011; Ward, 2012). This can make organizing and sharing student work more complicated (Goundar, 2011). It should be noted that competing tablets (Android-based) have USB support and file-management systems, thereby making this an iPad-only problem.

Adding to the list of iPad-only problems is the lack of support for Flash-based applications, a Web software used to power many Web-based applications and, in particular, educational Web-based applications (Marmarelli & Ringle, 2011). Therefore, iPad users cannot access these websites for use in interactive classroom activities. It should be noted that such websites can be accessed on competing tablets (Android-based) or by downloading an alternative browser software for the iPad (not Safari).

Cost-wise, tablet PCs and iPads are quite expensive, creating a significant hurdle to organizations that wish to utilize them in their programs. Kim (2010) describes the use of iPads in education as a sustaining innovation, that is an innovation that generally benefits education as a whole, but drives up its cost in the long term. Kim also mentions that the iPad will not lower the cost of education as a whole; instead, it will drive up its price. This is because, with greater iPad proliferation, costs will be spent on training and the development of educational applications. Wieder (2011) also shares a similar view that iPads and tablet PCs are high-priced items.

Another new issue that surfaced is that of e-book publishing. As mentioned in the previous sections, the ability to publish directly via e-book authoring programs such as iBooks Author is touted as one of the benefits of using iPads in academia. However, Bott (2012) has pointed out that iBooks Author has an unfavorable end-user license agreement that essentially restricts the user of the software to distribute any material created by the user using the iBooks Author software to the Apple distribution network. Furthermore, Apple can bar any material from being distributed on its network at its discretion. Barred material, then, cannot be hosted on any other network, owing to the conditions present in the license agreement. This means that paid material will be subject to Apple's approval, with the author paying a royalty of 30 percent to Apple for utilizing its software and distribution. Such a license agreement can be detrimental to the academic profession, which takes pride of ownership very seriously, and can limit access to educational material and e-textbooks in the future. However, free material can be distributed as seen fit. It should be noted that this is an iPad-only problem, but, until a similarly powerful alternative to the iBook Author emerges, it still remains a concern for academia.

Adoption of tablets as facilitators of education has been experimented with in several institutions. In terms of fulfilling the goals of m-learning, namely the ability to learn from anyplace at anytime, the tablet fares as well as the standard laptop or netbook, although, in some cases, perhaps not as well, owing to restrictions placed on Flash websites (which is present on many educational websites) on tablets such as the iPad. The tablet, however, has been useful in facilitating classroom lessons and as devices to promote greater interaction between student and teacher.

The literature has shown how using tablet devices in the classroom, for lesson purposes, yields greater student attention, interaction, and participation in the lesson. On the other hand, assigning tablets to students to complete assignments or as a laptop replacement has generated largely negative responses from students.

Academics who have used tablets for their personal use have expressed great appreciation of its ability to facilitate interaction with educational objects and help them prepare interactive lessons for their students. Students, on the other hand, seem less impressed by tablet technology, perhaps owing to the generational gap and their being digital citizens, as opposed to digital immigrants, which most of the older members of academia are.

Universities need to carefully consider their learning objectives before executing learning policies for tablet devices. The tablet device is primarily a tool that can facilitate greater interaction with educational content. It is by no means a laptop replacer in its current form, nor is it necessarily the best platform to utilize for m-learning, owing to the cumbersome input method and application limitations (conversely, netbooks offer a more efficient input method and application support for assignment and writing purposes). However, as a platform to access information online, they are more interactive than netbooks.

Overall, the use of tablets in education needs to be done with careful consideration and not be driven by a "me-first" mentality. Newer technology does not necessarily result in better learning outcomes. Until the tablet can perform laptop functions as well, it should be primarily used as an interactive learning tool.

A STUDY OF iPAD USE IN MALAYSIAN INSTITUTES OF HIGHER LEARNING

Given the potential of tablets and the interest of the Malaysian Ministry of Higher Education (MOHE) in e-learning and in turning Malaysia into an education hub for both conventional and distance learning, an initial study on the current use of tablet devices among Malaysian academics and their interest in adopting them for teaching and learning in the near future is of value to the academic community as a whole. E-learning is a focus and one of the Critical Agenda Projects led by the MOHE. It was believed that a study to ascertain how iPads are being used by academics and what their perceptions are of the device for teaching and learning would be useful to assist MOHE in its planning for e-learning.

A survey was conducted to examine current tablet-usage patterns among Malaysian academicians. The first survey was conducted in December 2011 among 38 academicians from two universities, during a workshop on the iPad for academicians. Academicians from two universities who were already using tablets were invited to the workshop. The objective of the survey was primarily to determine what the tablets were being used for, what the participants would like to learn more of in future workshops, and what their thoughts were on using tablets for teaching and learning. A second survey, similar to the first, was conducted online in early 2012. The latter had responses from 44 academics in 17 IHLs. The findings are highlighted and discussed in the next section.

Findings

Reason for Purchase of Tablet Devices

One interesting revelation was how the iPad was the choice of the majority, as stated by 64 percent of those surveyed the first time and 82 percent the second time. The rest who owned tablets purchased the Samsung Galaxy Tab, Asus EEE Pad, Acer Iconia Tab, and HTC Flyer. Most of them were new to tablets, having purchased them less than

6 months prior to the time the survey was conducted. Their primary reasons for purchasing tablet devices were to experiment with new technology and to fulfill the desire of having a mobile device.

Use of Tablet Devices Among Academicians

The results of the survey indicated that the top two uses of the tablets were for Web surfing and e-mailing. They also used tablets for self-learning, entertainment, and research. Only 40 percent used the tablets in the classroom when they taught. Several academicians also listed using the tablet devices to look up dictionaries, make online purchases, develop apps, and to tweet. In general, when asked, more than 90 percent of the respondents felt that tablets would be useful for teaching and learning, but were not sure how exactly. They expressed interest in attending future workshops on using iPads for teaching and learning so that they could learn the various ways of doing so. For example, they suggested that future workshops should focus on:

- how to maximize the use of iPads in the classroom;
- how students can benefit from iPads;
- examples of how various faculties have used iPads;
- how to connect with students without encroaching on their privacy;
- how to use iPads for research;
- hands-on activities on various iPad applications.

Opinions on Introducing Tablet Devices for Learning and Teaching in Universities

Respondents generally agreed that these devices should be introduced in universities. They felt that tablets would be excellent devices to help transform learning and will help drive m-learning. It was also believed that tablets would lead to ubiquitous learning and encourage collaborative learning and sharing of ideas, opinions, and resources. Tablets would make it easier for students to access information, conduct discussions, and communicate with course mates and lecturers. It was thought that tablets are appropriate tools in today's learning environment and more so when the new generation of students on campus today are digital natives. In addition, students would have greater access to their lecturers and, in turn, will create more opportunities for in-class interactions. Respondents cautioned that the focus should be on the pedagogical elements rather than the technology itself. Strategies had to be thought of prior to implementation, for use of tablet devices to succeed in supporting learning and teaching. It was also mentioned that infrastructure, in terms of network capacity or broadband availability, was important. The university should also provide the necessary resources, technical and financial, to ensure successful implementation.

One particular respondent stated:

The importance of iPads in education is that it allows the students and educators to easily access lessons and learning materials, effectively learning and at the same time as fun taking it easy using their iPads. Some of the functions of the iPads in education that will definitely provide convenience to students and educators are: Internet and research capability, easy notetaking, instant calculator, voice recorder, photo organizer, video and movie watching, educational and useful applications that will be useful in finding facts and research for lessons.

How Should Institutions Support Purchase of Tablet Devices?

Respondents were asked to respond to this question in relation to support for academic purchase as well as student purchase of tablet devices. About 35 percent of the respondents believed that institutions should provide all academicians with a tablet device, some 44 percent of those surveyed stated institutions should subsidize the purchase of a tablet, and a minority said faculty members should buy their own tablets. Hence, the majority felt institutions should be supportive of academicians by either providing (similar to what is done with PCs) or contributing to the purchase of a tablet.

Respondents felt that institutions should support students' purchase of tablet devices, either by fully sponsoring the purchase by students or subsidizing the cost of purchase by half. Some of the respondents suggested that universities should buy tablet devices in bulk and pass on the savings to students, provide easy payment schemes, and provide some form of technology allowance for students.

Reasons for Introducing Tablet Devices in Institutions

Based on responses to an open-ended question on why IHLs should introduce tablet devices, respondents said that "it was trendy," "to help the Net Geners learn best," "as an alternative to curriculum delivery," and "embracing the idea of providing 24/7 access to learning in the 21st century." Many respondents believed that the iPad in particular was easy to use, convenient, and suitable for m-learning and had numerous apps for a variety of purposes to support learning and teaching. Many agreed that tablets were more mobile than any other ICT device, such as notebooks. On the other hand, there was some disagreement. One particular respondent thought that laptops can be cheaper and more powerful than tablet devices. Another thought that the tablets were more useful for academicians than students. One respondent asked whether tablets were necessary to be introduced to students, because we will first need to identify the need or learning problem that is to be solved, prior to embarking on their use.

One respondent summarized,

> It's mobile. Students can keep their notes, contact lecturers (have online discussions), look up references, send assignments (without having to print, thus helping the environment) and lecturers can look at the assignments via iPad . . . but it's important to note that the institution must give good wireless connection! Otherwise, the benefits of iPads/tablets would not be fully realized.

DISCUSSION

It appears that academicians who have adopted tablet devices in their daily lives are excited with the potential of these tablets to enhance learning and teaching. The tablets offer greater mobility, yet are useful for gaining information and communication, and these academicians believe that students should be provided opportunities to own or use a tablet for their own learning. However, the same group of academicians is concerned with implementation issues, if users were dependent on the campus wireless networks. It is expected that, in due course, users would be able to afford their own personal broadband facilities and not depend on campus networks. The strategy to have students "pull" the learning materials and activities to their devices will then soon materialize. Nevertheless, Malaysian academics are still at the exploratory stage. Less than half of those surveyed have started using tablets for teaching, typically to show their presentation slides or as a presentation tool. Based on informal discussions outside the survey, some lecturers use tablets as a convenient device to stay in touch with their students via e-mail or through forums in social-learning platforms, or the learning-management system, especially when they are traveling. The next stage is to further support each other to determine other possibilities for the tablet devices to support learning and teaching. One of the activities that the authors have started is the establishment of a Facebook group to enable members to share and learn from each other's experience. Another activity is a face-to-face workshop to enable the champions to share their knowledge and experience using the devices for learning and teaching with their counterparts.

CONCLUSION

The findings of the study show that academicians tend to prefer iPads over other models of tablet device, and, although the exact reasons why this preference is given have not been thoroughly discussed, it can be put down to the wide availability of learning applications available for the iPad, compared with other competing tablets.

Academicians find tablets in general useful for information and communication, mainly to enhance their own personal productivity. In addition, they believe in the potential of the tablets for learning and teaching. These findings seem to be in line with the work done by Davis (2011), Barber (2012), and Bailey (2012), who all found that academic staff have positive experiences with the use of tablets.

Most academics surveyed are at the exploratory stage and willing to learn and experiment with apps for learning and teaching. However, a lack of content and limiting ideas on how to use them in the classroom, as discussed and elaborated by Ward (2012) and Wieder (2011), may lead to confusion on how to implement the tablet usage in the classroom and align it with learning objectives.

Based on interactions with fellow colleagues, iPads in particular have definitely created excitement among academicians and are a favorite topic of conversation among those who have a passion for learning technologies. Based on a quick poll in 2012 of a Facebook group on iPad (& Tablets) for Academicians, respondents indicated that more than half of the academicians in their own institutions have bought or own tablet devices. In some of the institutions, iPads have been given out, or their purchase subsidized. Hence, many academicians can be seen with their tablets at meetings and conferences. This newfound passion for tablet devices among the faculty is mentioned in Marmarelli and Ringle's (2011) work, showing how academicians value the ability to store texts and carry their notes on their tablets.

Academicians need to be cautioned as well. The idea of, or interest in, introducing tablet devices should not be because the technology is available, but because tablet technology still has issues to be worked out, primarily its input methods and development of education applications (Magrath et al., 2011; Marmarelli and Ringle, 2011; Nyaggah, 2011; Wieder, 2011). Rather, it should be what the technology can provide to learners or how learners can benefit compared with other devices, as pointed out by Ward (2012). They should be implemented as learning and teaching devices if they can be leveraged to produce the desired learning.

REFERENCES

Abas, Z. W., Lim, T., & Ramly, R. (2011). Unleashing the potential of mobile learning through SMS for open and distance learners. In A. Kitchenham (Ed.), *Models for interdisciplinary mobile learning: Delivering information to students* (pp. 154–174). Hershey, PA: IGI Global.

Baharum, H., Ismail, I., & Idrus, R. M. (2010). Simplistic is the ingredient for mobile learning. *International Journal of Interactive Mobile Technologies, 4*(3), 4–8.

Bailey, T. (2012). Why tablet publishing is poised to revolutionise higher education. *Mashable Tech.* Retrieved from: http://mashable.com/2012/01/06/tablet-publishing-education/

Barber, D. A. (2012). 5 higher ed tech trends for 2012. *Campus Technology.* Retrieved from: http://campustechnology.com/articles/2012/01/09/5-higher-ed-tech-trends-for-2012.aspx

Bott, E. (2012). *Closing thoughts on Apple's greedy, "crazy evil" iBooks license.* Retrieved from: http://m.zdnet.com/blog/bott/closing-thoughts-on-apples-greedy-crazy-evil-ibooks-license/4414

Davis, H. (2011). *The iPad in education: The professor's perspective, academic technology @ Palomar College.* Retrieved from: www2.palomar.edu/pages/atrc/2011/07/04/the-ipad-in-education-the-professors-perspective/

Fahey, S., & Sebastian, E. (2010). Universities web squared: How universities are rethinking approaches to international education, research and global Engagement. *AFG Venture Group Dispatches.* Retrieved from: www.afgventuregroup.com/dispatches/afg-venture-group-newsletter/universities-web-squared-how-are-universities-rethinking-approaches-to-international-education-research-and-global-engagement/

Goundar, S. (2011).What is the potential impact of using mobile devices in education? *Proceedings of SIG Glob Dev Fourth Annual Workshop*, Shanghai, China.

Hodge, K., Welch, J. C., & Woodcock, R. (2011). Train your brain. *Macworld AU.* Retrieved from: www.macworld.com.au/features/train-your-brain-38008/

Kim, J. (2010). iPad and the risk of "sustaining innovations." *Inside Higher Ed.* Retrieved from: www.insidehighered.com/blogs/technology_and_learning/ipad_and_the_risk_of_sustaining_innovations

Magrath, M., Nihalani, P., & Perkins, S. (2011). Digital texts and the future of education: Why books? *EDUCAUSE Quarterly.* Retrieved from: http://www.educause.edu/EDUCAUSE+Quarterly/EDUCAUSEQuarterlyMagazineVolum/DigitalTextsandtheFutureofEduc/225855

Marmarelli, T., & Ringle, M. (2011). *The Reed College iPad Study, Summary of Faculty Evaluation Reports, Reed College.* Retrieved from: www.reed.edu/cis/about/ipad_pilot/Reed_ipad_report.pdf

Nyaggah, M. (2011). *Tablets are good, content is better, and teachers are the best educational ICT investment.* Retrieved from: https://edutechdebate.org/tablet-computers-in-education/tablets-are-good-content-is-better-and-teachers-are-the-best-educational-ict-investment/

Peng, C. L., Abas, Z. W., Goolamally , N. T., Yusof, Y., & Singh, H. K. D. (2011). Implementation of mobile learning at the Open University Malaysia. In W. Ng (Ed.), *Mobile technologies and handheld devices for ubiquitous learning: Research and pedagogy* (pp. 170–186). Hershey, PA: IGI Global. DOI:10.4018/978-1-61692-849-0.ch010

Ward, D. (2012). What I've learned from teaching with iPads. *The Chronicle of Higher Education—Prof Hacker.* Retrieved from: http://chronicle.com/blogs/profhacker/what-ive-learned-from-teaching-with-ipads/37877

Wieder, B. (2011). *iPads could hinder teaching, professors say.* Retrieved from: http://chronicle.com/article/iPads-for-College-Classrooms-/126681/

51

TEACHERS AS LEARNERS

Concerns and Perceptions About Using Cell Phones in South African Rural Communities

Mpine Makoe

The potential for using mobile technologies in education is enormous in a country of limited access to electricity and telephone networks, poor roads and postal services, and fewer people who have expertise in using computers. The lack of infrastructure for information and communication technologies (ICT) in Africa has lead to the rapid growth of a wireless infrastructure. Over the past 10 years, the number of cell-phone users in Africa has increased at an annual rate of 65 percent—twice the global average (Rao, 2011). By 2010, there were more than 600 million cell-phone subscribers in Africa, second only to Asia (Reed, 2011). In South Africa alone, the cell-phone penetration is estimated at 98 percent. The multimedia functionality and their simpler and user-friendly interface make cell phones easier to use for people who may be uncomfortable with using other technologies, such as computers.

A recent survey found that 39 percent of urban South Africans and 27 percent of rural residents are now browsing the Internet from their cell phones (Rao, 2011). Cell phones are more accessible to most rural communities in terms of cost, geographic coverage, and ease to use. Farmers use them to compare market prices; rural health workers utilize them to send text messages to patients; migrant laborers use them to send money to their families; and banks utilize them to alert customers about financial transactions (Aker & Mbiti, 2011). "Interestingly in Africa, consumers might not have shoes, but they have cell phones," remarked Brian Richardson, a founder of a mobile service company (Rao, 2011). Despite evidence that shows that cell phones have occupied every facet of our lives, they are still not viewed as a viable tool for providing education in Africa.

CONTEXT

Several studies have shown evidence that cell phones, even the low-cost ones, can be used successfully in education (Hendrikz, 2006; Makoe, 2009; Nonyongo, Mabusela, &

Monene, 2005; Traxler & Dearden, 2005). Cell phones' software features, such as pictures, video, music, games, instant messaging, and the Internet, can be used in education for collaboration, tutoring, research, reading, and writing (Prensky, 2001). However, many teachers in rural South Africa have not fully explored the pedagogical affordances of cell phones. The purpose of this study is to look at how practicing teachers educating students perceive cell phones as a teaching and a learning tool. "The why and how teachers use ICT (cell phones) and what prevents its use," is central to understanding factors that influence teachers' use of a tool (Hennesy, Harrison, & Wamakote, 2010, p. 41) These practicing teachers, who are also distance-education students, were selected because they have a number of challenges that make teaching and learning particularly difficult in their rural environments. They teach in schools that are among the poorest in financial resources, physical structure, and management and support (Department of Education [DoE], 2006). However, a majority of them reported that they personally own or have access to a cell phone, and yet they do not use it for teaching and learning.

By and large, teachers are not convinced about the cell phone's potential because they have never seen it being used before for education. This is what makes "the shift towards the sophisticated usage of mobile devices for purposes other than personal communication be a generation of teachers away" (Aubusson, Schuck, & Burden, 2009, p. 238). Most students who were born after the 1980s, popularly known as the "net generation" (Barnes, Marateo, & Ferris, 2007) or the "digital natives" (Prensky, 2001), use these technologies with ease. Prensky (2001) describes them as the native speakers of the digital language, who consider ICT devices as a natural part of their environment. The integration of cell phones into educational processes has the power to radically change pedagogy as it is currently known, necessitating different skills for teaching. Adapting to these changes brought on by new technologies is no longer an option but a necessity, if teachers are to unleash the innate potential of their students (Beyers, 2009). Despite this, teachers' own beliefs and attitudes toward the use of cell phones contribute to their reluctance in adopting this technology.

The Concerns-Based Adoption Model (CBAM) will be utilized to outline the stages that people have to move through when they are involved in the process of adopting innovations (Hall, 1975; Hall & Hord, 1987; Hall & Loucks, 1978). What stands out about this model is that it looks at change from the perspective of the person who needs to adopt a particular technology to enhance his or her practice. People are more likely to adopt new technologies if their concerns are addressed at each specific stage of development.

THEORETICAL FRAMEWORK

The starting point of successful implementation of any innovation, such as using cell phones in education, is to involve people who are affected by change. To help understand stages of change that teachers have to go through in considering using cell phones for teaching and learning, the CBAM will be used as a theoretical framework. The primary focus of this model, which was developed by Hall and his colleagues, is to look at a person who is involved in the change process. It is based "on the belief that people respond to change in uniquely personal ways" (McCarthy, 1982, p. 20). The key assumptions of the CBAM model are that:

1. change is a process, not an event;
2. change is accomplished by individuals;
3. change is a highly personalized experience;
4. change involves developmental growth in feelings and skills;
5. change can be facilitated by interventions directed toward the individual's innovations.

The CBAM is based on the premise that concerns are part of the change process, as experienced by individuals who are involved in implementing the change. To examine how users go through change, the model uses three diagnostic dimensions, namely the "stages of concern," the "levels of use," and the "innovation configuration." The stages-of-concern dimension focuses on describing the feelings, motivations, and concerns of people as they progress though the adoptions process. The levels-of-use diagnostic dimension is concerned with the "general patterns of teacher behavior as they prepare to use, begin to use, and gain experience implementing a classroom change" (Anderson, 1997, p. 335). The difference between the two dimensions is that the stages of concern describe attitudes and concerns, whereas the levels of use involve the behavior of a person as he/she uses the technology. The third diagnostic dimension, the innovation configuration, is concerned with "how the innovation is being implemented by an individual teacher" (Anderson, 1997, p. 336).

The CBAM is useful in this study because it attaches great importance to the role of context in shaping teachers concerns, use, and change-facilitator interventions (Anderson, 1997). Human behavior is situated within a social context that influences human actions. Straub (2009) argues that technology adoption is a complex, inherently social, developmental process, and, therefore, there is a need to address a variety of concerns, such as social, emotional, and contextual issues that impact on the adoption or the lack of use of a particular technology. M-learning, by nature, is more strongly mediated by its context than by the content of the study material (Sharples, Taylor, & Vavoula, 2005). Therefore, it is important to deal with local contextual factors that affect the adoption and implementation of change (Hall & Loucks, 1978).

Although the CBAM has three diagnostic dimensions, this study will focus on the stages-of-concern dimension, which posits the existence of a sequence in addressing specific concerns (Hall & Hord, 1987; Hosman & Cvetanoska, 2010). This diagnostic dimension has been used in a number of studies to chart the process that teachers follow before they adopt a particular innovation. "It hypothesizes that as individuals move from unawareness and nonuse of an innovation to ultimate, highly sophisticated use of the innovation, their 'concerns' move through identifiable stages as well" (Hall, 1975, p. 5). "If the lower stages of concern are not resolved or addressed," according to Hosman and Cvetanoska (2010), "then the higher stages are not likely to materialize."

METHODS

The purpose of this study was to find out, from practicing teachers who are enrolled in distance-education institutions, about their concerns toward adapting cell phones into their classrooms and in their own learning environment. The characteristics of users and their concerns and perceptions are equally important in understanding the use and nonuse of the technological device.

Data Collection

Participants in this study were selected because of their dual role of both being teachers and distance-education students, who live and work in remote rural areas in South Africa. Distance education plays a pivotal role in providing educational opportunities to people who, either because of work commitments, personal, social circumstances, or geographical distance, would not have had the opportunity to access higher education. More than 36 percent of all higher-education students in South Africa are studying through distance learning. Data were collected from practicing teachers who have a basic qualification in education and who are also registered in distance-education programs in three South African universities.

Institution A is a dedicated distance-education institution offering formal teacher-education programs. More than 85 percent of all students who are enrolled in distance-education programs study though this university, which has an enrollment of over 300,000 students.

Institution B is a contact institution with a unit that offers distance-education programs for practicing teachers. Although the number of students in this university is over 50,000, a very small number of those are enrolled in distance-education program.

Institution C is also a contact institution, with a school devoted to offering teacher-education and professional-development programs through distance mode to practicing teachers. It has about 45,000 students dispersed in three different campuses.

In choosing the data-collection process, I had to weigh the tradeoffs between risking low response rate by mailing the questionnaire or using a classroom setting to maximize the response rates. Relying on colleagues to distribute the questionnaire was the only way to ensure higher response rates, even though there may be some ethical concerns if participants feel that they may be under pressure to participate. A sample was drawn from teacher-education students who were attending face-to-face contact sessions in three out of nine provinces in South Africa. Questionnaires were distributed at the end of each contact session.

The 40-item questionnaire was divided into three sections. The first section focused on biographical data of participants, the second section focused on statements addressing teachers' perceptions of using cell phones in their own classrooms, and the third section addressed the use of cell phones by teachers as distance learners. Of the 300 questionnaires that were given to colleagues, 187 were returned, and 86 of those were partly completed. The analysis was therefore based on 101 completed questionnaires. The demographic information of the students who participated in this study is summarized in Table 51.1.

Teachers' Profile

The biggest challenge in most developing countries, including South Africa, is the issue of teachers who are either unqualified or under-qualified to teach. The 2011–2025 technical report on teacher education revealed that 89 percent of all practicing teachers have a low-level professional teaching qualification. Only 18 percent of teachers have a 4-year Bachelor of Education or a Bachelors degree with a post-graduate certificate in education (Department of Basic Education [DoBE] & Department of Higher Education and Training [DoHT], 2011). Up until 2001, most teacher-training programs were offered by teacher-education colleges, which operated essentially as secondary schools rather than tertiary institutions. As a result, the quality of their teaching qualification is quite low for most teachers. To address this problem, the government decided to

Table 51.1 Demographic Profile of Participants in Percentages

		Institute A (N = 34)	Institute B (N = 38)	Institute C (N = 29)
1. Profile				
Gender	Male	22	23	31
	Female	78	77	69
Born	1961–1970	14	30	17
	1971–1980	33	36	56
	1981–1990	31	31	13
	1991–2000	22	4	14
2. Do you own or have access to:				
A desktop computer		25	36	37
A desktop computer with Internet connection		14	19	13
A cell phone		90	98	81
A cell phone with Internet access through Wi-Fi		26	23	25
A telephone		26	24	21
A laptop		24	19	17
A television		86	81	88
A radio		89	77	83
3. Do you have access to:				
Electricity connection		70	72	74
Landline telephone network		58	51	46
Road infrastructure		42	40	28
Internet connection		38	28	32

introduce continuous professional development programs that are geared toward reskilling practicing teachers with knowledge and skills underpinned by theory and research (DoBE & DoHT, 2011). The aim was to ensure that all teachers have proper post-diploma qualifications that will assist in raising the standard of teacher education and, by extension, the quality of education.

The problem of quality is even more acute in rural areas, where the education department has difficulties in recruiting and retaining qualified teachers. The student-to-teacher ratio in most rural areas is between 60 and 80 students per teacher, and this puts a large number of students at risk of dropping out (DoE, 2006). Poverty, high illiteracy rates, poor infrastructure, and transport problems exacerbate the problem. More than 70 percent of the participants reported that they have access to an electricity connection. However, a majority of them have limited access to infrastructure and basic amenities to support networked technologies. This makes teaching extremely difficult in rural communities. Most teachers who have an option to work elsewhere choose to leave the rural communities for better-resourced urban schools. Those who are left behind are mostly older females, born before the technological era.

Teachers were asked to indicate whether they have used any of the technologies listed in Table 51.2 for education purposes.

Although most of the teachers reported that they have access to a number of ICT tools, very few teachers use them for teaching and learning purposes. Over 90 percent of participants have cell phones, and yet less than 35 percent from two institutions

Table 51.2 Use of Technological Devices for Teaching and Learning

	Institute A ($N = 34$)	Institute B ($N = 38$)	Institute C ($N = 29$)
Which of the following devices do you use for teaching and learning:			
A desktop computer	26	32	25
A desktop computer with Internet connection	20	19	15
A cell phone	29	65	28
A cell phone with Internet access through Wi-Fi	10	12	9
A telephone	8	13	13
A laptop	14	19	15
A television	22	47	33
A radio	26	34	21

reported that they used them for teaching and learning. About 65 percent of participants from Institution B use cell phones for education. This is because the institution has a bulk SMS messaging system that it uses for administrative and academic purposes. Two of these institutions have experimented with using SMS text-messaging systems to send information to students (Hendrikz, 2006: Nonyongo et al., 2005). Like most distance-education institutions, they teach through print-based, prepackaged study material. Some have computer-based learning-management systems that students can access to download study material. In addition, they offer limited face-to-face contact sessions to support their students, who are geographically dispersed throughout the country.

USE OF CELL PHONES

To understand teachers' concerns about using cell phones, the next section of the questionnaire listed a number of statements relating to stages of concern, as outlined by Hall and Hord (1987), Hall and Loucks (1978), and Hosman and Cvetanoska (2010). Statements were further refined, and the items used were those that were deemed relevant to the use of cell phones in the South African context. Participants were asked to indicate which statement is true or false in terms of expressing an individual concern. Table 51.3 illustrates the stages of concern, including the clusters and examples of statements used relating to each stage. The statements were further divided into those that dealt specifically with teachers' concerns about using cell phones in their classrooms, and those that focused on their concerns as distance learners (in italic).

Participants were asked to indicate whether they had used cell phones for teaching and learning. Those who responded yes to this question were further asked to explain, in an open-ended question, how they used the cell phones for teaching and learning purposes. The concerns exhibited in their responses illustrated that 68 percent of teachers had never used cell phones for education purposes (awareness stage). Even those who indicated that they had used them, a very small number reported that they used cell phones to call their lecturers to find out about their classes or study material or to ask for an extension in their assignments.

In fact, a majority of them have not moved beyond using cell phones for social purposes (92 percent). Very few of them use them for business purposes (23 percent).

Table 51.3 Stages of Concern

Clusters	Stages and key concern	Example of expressions of concern by teachers and students
Self-concerns	0. Awareness – What it is?	I don't know anything about using cell phones for teaching *I would like to know in what ways I can use for education*
	1. Informational – How does it work?	I have explored using different tools in my cell phone *I have used cell phones to contact my lecturers for assistance*
	2. Personal – How does it affect me?	I do not feel comfortable in using cell phones in my classrooms *I would be willing to buy a new cell phone if it would assist me with my studies*
Task concerns	3. Management – How can I master the skills? – Where will I find time to do this?	I am concerned about the time I need to learn how to use cell phones for teaching *I am concerned about people bothering me if they have my number*
Impact concerns	4. Consequence – Is this worth it or is it working? – How would it affect my students?	I find cell phones disturbing and disruptive *I do not see the value of using cell phone in my studies*
	5. Collaboration – How do other people do it? – What are my colleagues doing?	I would be willing to use it if I have seen it work elsewhere *I am concerned about contacting my classmates through Mxit*
	6. Refocusing – Is there anything else that is better? – What don't we consider doing?	I don't see how cell phones will improve my teaching. *I may consider investing my personal time if I am convinced that it will make my life easier*

Source: Adapted from Hall, 1975; Hall and Hord, 1987; Hall and Loucks, 1979; Hosman and Cvetanoska, 2010.

Their concerns in terms of using cell phones for education purposes were more in the nonuser stage. This means that teachers in this study had little knowledge or no interest in using cell phones for teaching and learning.

Concerns About Use of Cell Phones in Classrooms

Following this open-ended question, participants were asked to indicate which statements were true or false in relation to their own concerns about using cell phones in the classroom. The findings suggest that 63 percent of teachers had never thought of using cell phones in their classrooms (awareness stage). This finding is similar to what they reported in the open-ended question. About 78 percent reported that they would not allow their students to use cell phones in their classrooms. They were concerned about how teaching would be affected by the use of cell phones (consequence stage). At this stage, teachers were concerned about how the introduction of an innovation in the classroom would affect their everyday practice.

Lack of expertise in using cell phones for teaching was one of the prominent concerns raised by 86 percent of teachers. They were concerned about the knowledge and skills required to confidently use cell phones and the time needed for training (personal stage). About 73 percent raised concerns about increased workload, which is often associated with learning new technologies. It is at this stage that teachers were concerned about their own inadequacies and the changes that they were expected to go through to address their own inadequacies.

Although teachers had indicated their concerns throughout the different stages, most of the teachers' concerns were highest around the self cluster. They were more concerned about their comfort level with using cell phones in the classrooms. Lau and Shiu (2008) also found that nonuser profiles typically show highest concerns in stages 0, 1, and 2 (awareness, information, and personal). It is at this stage that they begin to know and learn about some of the benefits of using technologies, and it is also where they question their ability to use the proposed technology for their teaching.

Concerns About Use of Cell Phones as Students

Even when teachers were asked to respond on their use of cell phones as students, their concerns clustered around the self (awareness, information, and personal stages). More than 75 percent of participants had never explored the different applications in their cell phones. In fact, a great majority of teachers used their cell phones only for making calls (96 percent) and text messaging (88 percent). Most participants were at the awareness stage where they were not even aware of the potential of using cell phones to enhance interaction with their peers and their lecturers.

One of the main barriers to learning in distance education is lack of interaction. In the absence of lecture-based instruction, where the teacher's role is to motivate students to learn, distance learners tend to rely on their peers for motivation and lecturers for support. However, 63 percent of them had never contacted their lecturers, and 87 percent had not used cell phones to communicate with their peers. The incorporation of cell phones as a teaching device can enable interaction between a student and the lecturer, as well as between a student and her or his peers. The strength of using cell phones is that they offer learning that is intimate, spontaneous, situated, and versatile.

About 85 percent indicated that they were willing to buy new cell phones with the necessary applications, if it would assist them with their studies (refocusing stage). Out of the 20 statements, this was the only statement that expressed the highest concern. The refocusing-stage concern deals with considering using cell phones to assist them with their studies. Most teachers thought that a sophisticated cell phone, which was different from what they already owned, might help them with their studies. However, a great a number of low-cost cell phones have a variety of applications that can be used in education.

Makoe (2009) found that a majority of younger distance-education students are already using a cell-phone social network, Mxit, to form peer-support study groups to assist each other with study. Mxit is a cell-phone instant-messaging software application that is freely downloadable and affordable to use, making it very attractive to young people. Despite its popularity among 12–25-year-olds, more than 75 percent of teachers in this study reported that they do not have this system on their cell phones. This shows that older people—68 percent of participants in this study were born before 1981—are, therefore, not technologically savvy. This generation, which Prensky (2001) refers to as digital immigrants, usually has negative perceptions toward these social networks. Teachers are particularly skeptical about the use of Mxit among young people. They perceive cell phones as destructive tools that hinder students' academic performance.

IMPLICATIONS FOR PRACTICE

The findings from statements on participants' use of cell phones, both as teachers and distance-education students, revealed that teachers in this study have not used cell phones in both roles. Their conceptual understanding of both teaching and learning is influenced by the beliefs they accumulated through personal experience, and sociocultural influences lead to their reluctance in embracing this technology (Straub, 2009). The concerns raised by teachers were highest on the first three stages, which dealt with awareness, information, and personal concerns.

The success of using cell phones in education depends on the attitudes and concerns teachers' exhibit. It is, therefore, important that training programs geared toward teacher development should be grounded in educational and pedagogic principles that teachers are familiar with (Hennesy et al., 2010). Teachers should not perceive the innovation as a threat to their everyday practice. In fact, they should see it as something that will enhance their practice.

One of their biggest concerns was how this technology would impact on pedagogical beliefs and values (consequence stage). Even when 70 percent of the participants indicated that they were willing to spend their own personal time in learning how to use cell phones for learning, 63 percent of them were against using them in their own classrooms. When teachers are uncomfortable with using a device, because they have never used it before, or seen it being used, they will not allow their students to use it either. "Teachers remain the gatekeepers for students' access to educational opportunities afforded by technology" (Carlson & Gadio, 2002, p. 119). It is therefore important that change to, and adoption of, any technology must begin with the teacher (Zulkafly, Koo, Shariman, & Zainuddin, 2011).

The starting point of a teacher-training initiative aimed at equipping teachers with the necessary skills should address teachers' concerns. The CBAM provides guidance in matching interventions to the needs of the teachers and lecturers (Evans & Chauvin, 1993). Teachers in this study raised concerns about their limited knowledge and skills regarding how to use cell phones for both teaching and learning. Therefore, the teacher-training intervention should start with raising awareness. Once people are aware of the possibility of using cell phones, intervention should focus on information and support "and letting 'teachers' know that it's okay to have personal concerns—we all do" (Evans & Chauvin, 1993, p. 172). It is, therefore, important that intervention at this stage is introduced gently, so that teachers are familiar with the technology. However, Evans and Chauvin (1993) warn that change facilitators should not prolong this stage; they should recognize personal concerns and move on quickly, so that they can progress to other stages.

The CBAM is helpful in assisting lecturers, policymakers, and course developers to assess individual concerns before identifying actions that need to be taken to facilitate the change process. By acknowledging teachers' concerns, training will be meaningful, and innovation adoption will be sustained, because it will be relevant to the teachers' needs (Donovan, Hartley, & Strudler, 2007). The concerns of teachers and their use of technology can provide a foundation for a bottom-up approach to effect systemic change in education (Dirksen & Tharp, 1997). Sustainable change in teaching practice can only occur if teacher development programs require practitioners to engage in dialogue about practical theories of teaching and learning. Each theory of learning leads to adoption of specific teaching and learning processes. Therefore, teachers themselves need to be sufficiently technologically literate in order to analyze the pedagogy needed to support the technology.

Despite several studies that proved that m-learning can be used to enhance learning, the use of cell phones should not be seen as a panacea for the social-interaction problem associated with the correspondence nature of distance education. The success of using this technology should be based on its ability to enhance social interaction.

CONCLUSION

The stages-of-concern dimension provided an important insight into understanding the stages individuals have to go through before they are convinced about the innovation. It is through this framework that concerns about the adoption of an innovation can be addressed, so that teachers can be convinced to use it in their own practice. The greater the understanding of the change process, the greater the likelihood that the innovation will be effectively implemented in a sustainable manner. This model is also helpful because it gives an indication of where an intervention should be targeted.

Although studies have shown that technology use in schools has not been as effective as it should be, Hosman and Cvetanoska (2010) argue that change requires time; teachers need ongoing support, and they need to be treated as part of the plan. There is no doubt that cell-phone use in education is even more appropriate in rural communities, because of its availability and accessibility. Other members of rural communities are already using it with success. There is need for rural teachers and their lecturers to learn how to integrate cell phones into teaching and learning using contemporary pedagogical approaches. The use of cell phones in teaching and learning is no longer a luxury, but a necessity in most under-resourced rural communities.

REFERENCES

Aker, J. C., & Mbiti, I. M. (2010). Mobile phones and economic development in Africa. *Journal of Economic Perspectives, 24*(3), 207–232.

Anderson, S. E. (1997). Understanding teacher change: Revisiting the concerns based adoption model. *Curriculum Inquiry, 27*(3), 331–336.

Aubusson, P., Schuck, S., & Burden, K. (2009). Mobile learning for teacher professional learning: Benefits, obstacles and issues. *ALT-J, Research in Learning Technology, 17*(3), 233–247.

Barnes, K., Marateo, R., & Ferris, S. (2007). Teaching and learning with the net generation. *Innovate Journal of Online Education, 3*(4). Retrieved from: http://innovateonline.info/?view=article&id=382

Beyers, R. N. (2009). A five dimensional model for educating the net generation. *Educational Technology and Society, 12*(4), 218–227.

Carlson, S., & Gadio, C. T. (2002). Teacher professional development in the use of technology. In W. D. Haddad and A. Draxler (Eds.), *Technologies for education: Potentials, parameters, and prospects.* Paris and Washington, DC: UNESCO and the Academy for Educational Development. Retrieved from: http://portal.unesco.org/ci/en/ev.php-URL_ID=22984&URL_DO=DO_ PRINTPAGE&URL_SECTION=201.html

Department of Basic Education and Department of Higher Education and Training. (2011). *Integrated strategic planning framework for teacher education and development in South Africa, 2011–2025 Technical Report.* Retrieved from: www.education.gov.za/LinkClick.aspx?fileticket=lXfDtQxRz3M%3D&

Department of Education. (2006). *The national policy framework for teacher education and development in South Africa: "More teachers; better teachers."* Pretoria: DoE.

Dirksen, D. J., & Tharp, D. (1997). Utilising the Concerns-Based Adoption Model to facilitate systemic change. *Technology and Teacher Education Annual* (pp. 1064–1067). Retrieved from: www.loyola.edu/edudept/facstaff/marcovitz/AD682/DirksenTharpSITE97.pdf

Donovan, L., Hartley, K., & Strudler, N. (2007). Teacher concerns during initial implementation of a one-to-one laptop initiative at the middle school level. *Journal of Research on Technology in Education, 39*(2), 263–286.

Evans, L., & Chauvin, S. (1993). Faculty developers as change facilitators: The concerns based adoption model. *To Improve The Academy.* Paper 278. Retrieved from: http://digitalcommons.unl.edu/podimproveacad/278/

Hall, G. E. (1975). *The effects of change on teachers and professors: Theory, research and implications for decision makers.* Paper presented at the National Invitational Conference on Research on Teacher Effects: An examination by policy-makers and researcher, Novermber 3–5. Retrieved from: http://eric.ed.gov/ERICWeb Portal/search/detailmini.jsp?_nfpb=true&_&ERICExtSearch_SearchValue_0=ED128338&ERICExt Search_SearchType_0=no&accno=ED128338

Hall, G. E., & Hord, S. M. (1987). *Change in schools facilitating the process.* New York: State University of New York Press.

Hall, G., & Loucks, S. (1978). Teacher concerns as a basis for facilitating and personalizing staff development. *Teachers College Record, 80*(1), 36–53.

Hendrikz, J. (2006, October–November). *Mobile phone technology as an instrument for student support in Africa.* Paper presented at the Fourth Pan-Commonwealth Forum on Open Learning, Jamaica, 30 October–3 November.

Hennesy, S., Harrison, D., & Wamakote, L. (2010). Teachers factors influencing classroom use of ICT in Sub-Saharan Africa. *Itupale Online Journal of African Studies, 2,* 39–54.

Hosman, L., & Cvetanoska, M. (2010). *Technology, teacher and training: Combining theory with Macedonia's experience.* Retrieved from: www.gg.rhul.ac.uk/ict4d/ictd2010/papers/ICTD2010%20Hosman%20et%20al.pdf

Lau, J., & Shiu, J. (2008). *Teachers' perceptions of impending innovation: The use of pair work in large-scale oral assessment in Hong Kong.* Paper presented at the 34th International Association for Educational Assessment (IAEA) Annual Conference, Cambridge, UK.

Makoe, M. (2009, June). *Exploring the potential for using Mxit—A cellphone instant messaging system in supporting distance learners.* Paper presented at the Mlearn 2009 Conference, Maastricht, Netherlands, June 7–10. Retrieved from: www.ou.nl/Docs/Campagnes/ICDE2009/Papers/Final_Paper_290Makoe.pdf

McCarthy, B. (1982). Improving staff development through CBAM and 4MAT. *Educational Leadership, 40,* 20–25. Retrieved from: http://eric.ed.gov/ERICWebPortal/custom/portlets/recordDetails/detailmini.jsp?_nfpb=true&_&ERICExtSearch_SearchValue_0=EJ269892&ERICExtSearch_SearchType_0=no&accno=EJ269892

Nonyongo, E., Mabusela, K., & Monene, V. (2005). *Effectiveness of SMS Communication between university and students.* Retrieved from: www.mlearn.org.za/CD/papers/Nonyongo&%20Mabusela.pdf

Prensky, M. (2001). Digital natives, digital immigrants. In *On the Horizon.* MCB University Press. Retrieved from: http://www.marcprensky.com/writing/prensky%20–20digital%20natives,%20digital%20immigrants%20-%20part1.pdf

Rao, M. (2011). *Mobile Africa report: Regional hubs of excellence and innovation, mobile Monday.* Retrieved from: www.mobilemonday.net/reports/MobileAfrica_2011.pdf

Reed, M. (2011). *Africa is world's second connected region by mobile subscription* [Press release]. Informa telecoms and media, November 3. Retrieved from: http://blogs.informatandm.com/3485/press-release-africa-is-world%E2%80%99s-second-most-connected-region-by-mobile-subscriptions/

Sharples, M., Taylor, J., & Vavoula, G. (2005). *Towards a theory of mobile learning.* Retrieved from: www.mlearn.org.za/CD/papers/Sharples-%20Theory%20of%20Mobile.pdf

Straub, E. T. (2009). Understanding technology adoption: Theory and future directions for informal learning. *Review of Educational Research, 79*(2), 625–649.

Traxler, J., & Dearden, P. (2005, September). *The potential for using SMS to support learning in organizations in Sub-Saharan Africa.* Proceedings of the Development Studies Association Conference, Milton Keynes, September. Retrieved from: www.wlv.ac.uk/PDF/cidt-article20.pdf

Zulkafly, N. A., Koo, A., Shariman, T. P. N., & Zainuddin, M. N. (2011, July). *Educators' perceptions towards mobile learning.* Paper presented at the Artificial Intelligence Workshop (AIW) at UNITEN Putrajaya Campus, Malaysia, July 18–19. Retrieved from: http://ktw.mimos.my/aiw2011/paper_id_16/paper.pdf

52

FROM MXIT TO DR MATH

Adele Botha and Laurie Butgereit

In 2007, Laurie Butgereit, a researcher at the CSIR Meraka Institute, started to use Mxit as a communication channel to tutor her son in mathematics. Her son and a number of his friends logged in, and Dr Math was born. At the inception of Dr Math, Mxit freely communicated with numerous Jabber servers around the world. Butgereit (2011a) simply created a chat account (http://jabber.org) using an open-source chat client, such as Gaim or Pidgin, and, within minutes, the author was chatting to the handful of high-school friends about their mathematics homework.

Mxit is one of South Africa's largest social-networking platforms and currently has over 50 million users registered (Mxit, 2012). The original concept for Mxit started in 2000, with research into a massively multiplayer mobile game. The original game was SMS based and, alas, because of the high cost of SMS, the original game was not successful. With the advent of cheaper Internet connectivity over cell phones, such as general packet radio service (GPRS), however, this mobile game was successfully transformed into a mobile instant-messaging service (Knott-Craig and Silber, 2012). The popularity is partly due to the cost-effective solution it provides to Web-enabled phone users to participate in a social network, either free or at a marginal cost, depending on the network used. This has enabled Dr Math to provide the service free, or virtually free, to the learner as end user.

RAPID EXPANSION

After seeing the positive interaction through Mxit, Butgereit approached the CSIR Meraka Institute and the management of the senior secondary school where the learners were, in order to formalize the assistance that Dr Math would provide to the learners at that high school.

CSIR Meraka Institute facilitated the tutoring to assist the learners after school hours, and the management of the high school consented to advertising of the Dr Math service as providing online assistance with mathematics homework for a few hours after school, using Mxit as a communication medium. Initially, there was no intention to scale the service or to formally embark on a research initiative, and the initial expectation was that there would be about 20–30 learners logging on. However, the popularity of the service grew beyond all expectation, and, when there were in excess of 50 learners logging on, processes were initiated to formalize research pertaining to the phenomenon.

The Dr Math service was initiated in the beginning of the academic year in 2007. As the Easter holidays approached, an announcement was posted that the service would not be available during the holidays. However, the viral growth of the service was not anticipated. Schools in different provinces in South Africa have different school terms, and there was an outcry from learners who were using the system, as they were as far away as the Kwa-Zulu Natal coast, approximately 600 km from where the service was initiated. The learners indicated that they had heard from friends about the service, and the number of users was growing throughout the country via virtual, "word-of-mouth" viral advertising over Mxit. As a result, the popularity of the user-initiated services was growing, and additional tutors had to be sourced.

With only viral advertising, the Dr Math service has grown from a single school and about 25 learners, to, currently, 37,000 registered users.

TUTORS

As it became more difficult for a single person to cope with the increasing number of users and demand for longer hours, the University of Pretoria Faculty of Engineering, Built Environment, and Information Technology was approached. The university's Faculty of Engineering, Built Environment and Information Technology has a required module that students must pass in order to obtain a Bachelors degree from the department. The module requires that the students do a number of hours of community service (University of Pretoria, 2008). The students involved in this module are demonstrating meaningful engagement in the community. Students were recruited who would act as "Dr Math." As the service ran on a centralized system, volunteer tutors were required to physically log on from the CSIR Meraka. This created logistical stress, as office space and equipment needed to be provided to the students.

During the next 3 years, numerous enhancements were added to the Dr Math software platform. It developed from an implementation that used an available, open-source chat client program, allowing only one tutor to answer questions at a time, to facilitating numerous tutors at distributed locations. All interactions are logged, and the log files are checked by the CSIR Meraka. Relevant feedback is given to the students regarding their handling of situations and questions, and to the institution as to the hours and conduct of the students.

All tutors are required to sign a code of conduct outlining the expectations regarding their interactions with the learners. The code of conduct stipulates that the tutors are restricted from physically meeting up or arranging to meet learners who they meet virtually while in the persona of Dr Math. In addition, tutors agree to limit the conversations to mathematics, science, and other educational topics. On average, it was found that each interaction takes about 20 minutes, and a single tutor can support in the region of 50 individual learners per hour, depending on the nature of the interaction. A typical session is outlined in Figure 52.1.

Although emotional feedback (Anghileri, 2006) is not intrinsic in the direct inter-actions, it is facilitated through tutoring in the friendly, safe, and open environment

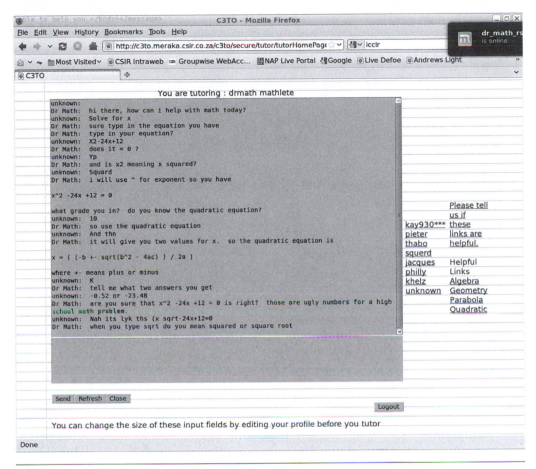

Figure 52.1 Typical Dr Math Tutoring Session
Source: Butgereit, 2011a

created. This type of environment is planned and facilitated. Tutors have to sign a code of conduct when they start tutoring, and they are presented with a list of characteristics that embody Dr Math. When acting as Dr Math, tutors are expected to have the following personality traits (Butgereit, 2010):

- have a sense of humor—always have a few math jokes ready to share;
- be intelligent—if a tutor doesn't know the answer, then look it up on Wikipedia and tell the learner you will cut and paste something for them;
- be genderless—Dr Math does not identify him/herself as either male or female;
- be friendly and helpful—tutors should be willing to look up other information via the Web for learners and cut and paste it for them if it is appropriate—for example, information about science or university entrance exams; and
- be encouraging: encourage learners to go to university—Dr Math always encourages people to study further.

Some of the things that Dr Math does not do include (Butgereit, 2010):

- correcting spelling errors;
- talking down to learners; and
- counseling, but Dr Math can refer people to Childline, Life Line, or Family Life Centre.

SCHEDULING

Tutors and learners need to link up, and, as such, scheduling is important. Initial attempts to organize volunteers to cover all time slots when learners may need assistance caused tremendous stress and unnecessary friction between the administration and volunteer tutors. This top–down scheduling was abandoned in favor of a bottom–up, tutor-initiated availability. Subsequently, the tutors advertise their expected availability. When they register, tutors are invited to indicate when they are able to tutor. These times are automatically broadcast to the learners on their cell phones. For example, one tutor may be available Mondays from 14:00 until 16:00, and another available Tuesdays from 15:00 until 18:00. The platform generates an overall schedule of tutors that learners can access on demand.

When a learner asks a question, he/she is assigned to a tutor who is the least *busy* according to a *busy-ness* model, which is a formula taking into account the number of learners a tutor is already chatting with, the number of messages that are going back and forth, and the number of outstanding messages in a tutor's queue (Butgereit, 2011a). Once a learner is connected to a specific tutor, the conversation is sustained until either the learner or the tutor logs off. If the tutor logs off first, the learner will be automatically swapped to another tutor who is logged in. Additionally, the system allocates multiple conversations to an individual tutor to facilitate. As learners initiate conversations, their pseudonyms appear. This indicates that a learner has a query, and selecting a name brings up the entire chat history of the tutor and the learner.

SENSE OF COMMUNITY

Dr Math tutors are a virtual team working towards a common end, and, as a result, many of the same social issues that arise in telecommuting situations are mirrored (Butgereit, 2011b). Identified social concerns in virtual teams include (Kirkman, Rosen, Gibson, Tesluk, & McPherson, 2002):

- building trust among team members;
- overcoming perceptions of isolation;
- interpersonal relationships between team members; and
- recognition of performance.

As a result, Dr Math administrators maintain an active mailing list and encourage tutors to communicate with the administrator and each other. The mailing list additionally serves as a platform to disseminate interesting interactions on difficult topics that tutors had encountered.

NATURE OF THE INTERACTIONS

The nature of the interactions between tutor and learner ranges beyond just helping with mathematics homework problems. Although tutors are extremely busy answering questions, they are encouraged to promote further study. As a result, the tutors often look up university requirements for learners and refer learners to additional websites that have educational materials.

The interactions often emulate interactions in a classroom. As such, many of the strategies that apply in the classroom are also relevant. Dr Math endeavors to create a sympathetic, accepting audience by maintaining a sense of fun and approachability. A typical interaction of this kind would be as illustrated in the following excerpt:

> *Dr Math:* Is your teacher tired of the excuse "The dog ate my homework?" Well, try this one "I divided by zero and my paper burst into flames" hahaha (I'll be here until 15:00 to help with math homework)

As the interaction is learner-initiated, the onus is on the learner to explain his/her problem. As the medium is limited to text, and very little specific affordances are available in terms of mathematics symbols, it is imperative that the learner and the tutor create and negotiate common understanding in relation to the meaning of symbols. The Dr Math persona does not give answers to questions, but aims to facilitate understanding. An example of this is the following exchange:

> *Learner:* need help with factorising.
> *Dr Math:* numbers or polynoms?
> *Learner:* quadratic trinomials
> *Dr Math:* sure type one in we do it tog.
> *Learner:* 5x square + 80x + 300
> *Dr Math:* i use ^ for exponent 5x ^2 + 80x + 300 so first i would factor out the 5 giving 5(x^2 + 16x + 60) right?
> *Learner:* yes

Answering a question such as "How do you find the area of a circle?" would require chatting back and forth with the learner to establish common meaning about:

- what data he or she might have ("do you have the radius, diameter, or circumference?");
- negotiating the use of the symbol ^ to represent an exponent ("I will use ^ to mean exponent");
- negotiating the use of the symbol * to represent multiply ("I will use * to mean multiply");
- discussing the value of pi ("pi is approximately 3.14 or 22/7"); and
- providing the correct formula "area = pi * radius ^ 2."

Some additional examples of this negotiated meaning are given below.

> *Dr Math:* can you type it in
> *Learner:* thats the prob.my frnd is tryin it on his phone for the symbols that my phone doesnt have
> *Dr Math:* oh, simbols like theta and phi? just write them out

And:

> *Learner:*   hw 2 complete squares?
> *Dr Math:*   do you have a polynom to solve we can do it tog
> *Learner:*   cn u pls cum up wth it so dat we cn solve it 2geda bcouz mi fone does nt hv maths symbols
> *Dr Math:*   i will use ∧ for exponent. how about $x^2 + 4x - 6 = 0$ so you add the 6 to the other side so you have $x^2 + 4x = 6$ are we together?

Through the interaction, the tutor gains insight into the learners' thinking and where their level of understanding is at, often making explicit the learners' conveyed understanding and aiming to direct the learners to construct their own understanding. An example is given below:

> *Learner:*   i wanted to say the signaficant figure
> *Dr Math:*   like in 12.34 to 3 significant digis?
> *Learner:*   yes
> *Dr Math:*   so did you cover rounding?
> *Learner:*   no
> *Dr Math:*   so 12.34 to 3 sig digits is 12.3
> *Learner:*   ok
> *Dr Math:*   but if it was 12.36 then it would be 12.4
> *Learner:*   ohk thank you. tomorrow am writing my maths test am nervous
> *Dr Math:*   so what did your teacher say about 12.35 which way must it go up or down
> *Learner:*   up
> *Dr Math:*   ok
> *Learner:*   thank 1 more tym

An additional example is outlined below:

> *Learner:*   simplification of fractions
> *Dr Math:*   okay. which grade are you in? can you give me an example of a fraction you are having trouble with?
> *Learner:*   gr11$(x - 2)(x + 1) + 3(x - 2)/(x - 2)$
> *Dr Math:*   is the question: $((x - 2)(x + 1) + 3(x - 2))/(x - 2)$? in other words are both parts of the expression divided by $(x - 2)$?
> *Learner:*   yes
> *Dr Math:*   let's begin with this simpler expression. what is x/x?
> *Learner:*   how
> *Dr Math:*   how about this? $4/4 = ?$
> *Learner:*   1
> *Dr Math:*   so now replace 4 by any other number. Say $7/7 = ?$
> *Learner:*   1
> *Dr Math:*   right. now consider "x" to mean any number (4 or 7 or anything else). now what do you think $x/x = ?$
> *Learner:*   x
> *Dr Math:*   if i divide any number by itself what will i get?

Learner: 1
Dr Math: let us pretend that the letter "x" means a number. x can be equal to 1 or 2 or 3 or any number we choose. does that make sense?
Learner: yes
Dr Math: so what happens if i divide any number (we call it "x") by itself (again call it "x")?
Learner: 1 myb
Dr Math: that's right! if you divide x/x you get 1. x stands for any number. if you divide any number by itself you get 1.
Learner: k so how do i attempt that q
Dr Math: consider this. if x/x = 1, what do you think $(x-2)/(x-2) = ?$
Learner: 1 or cancel each other
Dr Math: yes. that's right, $(x-2)/(x-2) = 1$. this is because you have the something $(x-2)$ divided by itself. this will always be
Learner: 1. so then what is $(2x-1)/(2x-1) = ?$
Dr Math: perfect! now what do you think $3x/x = ?$
Learner: 3
Dr Math: that's right. well done. now what do you think $3(x-2)/(x-2) = ?$
Learner: 3
Dr Math: correct again. let's try something a little harder

A tutor occasionally has to create and solve a particular problem that shares some of the characteristics of the student's problem to model a concept without solving the learner's example. In addition, the need to change the contextual setting to what might be more familiar to learners is illustrated below:

Dr Math: how can i help with matht doay?
Learner: probability
Dr Math: sure what is your question about probability
Learner: wt iz the meaning of probability
Dr Math: it's like "chances" in gambling. so if you want to know the probability of getting an even number when rollaing a dice to
Learner: ohk example pls
Dr Math: so how many possible chances are there on a dice
Learner: 4
Dr Math: no there are 6 a

Where a student is unsuccessful in constructing meaning, the tutor has the opportunity to simplify a task so that understanding can be built in progressive steps toward the larger problem. The tutor often has to unpick the essence of the learner's interaction and rephrase it where necessary to make ideas clearer, without losing the intended meaning.

Learner: how do i send you an math problem?
Dr Math: you just type it in
Learner: 1 on cos x − cosx on 1 + sinx = tanx
Dr Math: did you mean $(1/\cos(x)) - (\cos(x)/1) + \sin(x) = \tan(x)$?

Despite our best efforts, there were times when there were no tutors available. In addition, learners started asking tutors wasteful questions such as "What is sin(90)?" or "Who was Pythagoras?" These questions, although being foremost for the learner, took up valuable tutor time. What the learners really needed was simply a scientific calculator or an encyclopedia. To address these issues, the tutoring service was expanded.

MORE THAN JUST TUTORING

Additional functionalities have been incorporated into the tutor service over time. One of the most successful has been the mathematical competitions, ranging from addition to finding polynomials. In addition to the competitions, there is a Wikipedia lookup service (Web scrape), access to a scientific calculator (as many learners indicated that they do not own one), several static lookups for math terms, a text game, a space for learner feedback, and a leader board that lists the *TopScores* in the competitions (these are additionally sent to Twitter). Figure 52.2 illustrates these functionalities in addition to the tutoring service.

These functionalities, which are in addition to the tutoring service, and their impact are briefly outlined below.

Competitions

The competitions are a number of self-correcting games in the form of multiple-choice quizzes that have proven to be extremely popular. There are 14 of these games that are generated from a function. The format of all the competitions is similar: When a learner starts a competition, the current *TopScore* (or current winner) is displayed with his or

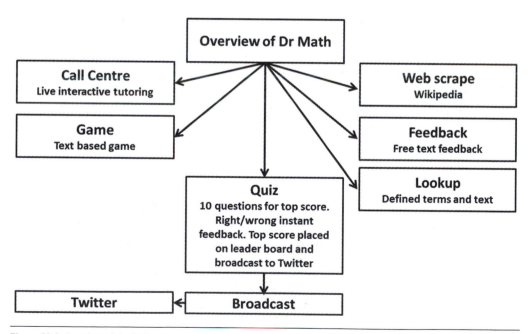

Figure 52.2 Overview of the Dr Math Service and Additional Functionalities

Source: Botha, 2010

her percentage correct. The new competitor is given a calculation and must reply with an answer. These calculations are generated from a function. The answer is evaluated, and the competitor is given his or her running score and percentage. The competitor must do 10 calculations. If the new competitor ties or betters the score of the *TopScore*, then this new competitor becomes the new *TopScore*. In order to drum up enthusiasm and competition, a message is sent to the previous *TopScore* that he or she has been deposed as *TopScore* and invites that competitor to return to defend his or her title. All scores above 80 percent are broadcast on Twitter. The number of times a learner achieves *TopScore* is shown in brackets next to the learner's Mxit pseudonym on the leader board. The competitions that are available are:

- Addition: Addition of two positive integers from 1 + 1 up through 14 + 14.
- Subtraction: Subtraction of two positive integers, where the difference remains positive, ranging from 2 − 1 to 28 − 14.
- Multiplication: Multiplication of two positive integers, from 2 * 2 up through 14 * 14.
- Division: Division of two positive integers, where the quotient remains an integer, ranging from 2/1 up through 196/14.
- Times tables: Multiplication as described above, but one operand is fixed. For example, 2 times table, or 3 times table.
- BODMAS: Order of operations where results will be positive integers. For example (8 + 4)/6.
- Addition and subtraction of positives and negatives: Simple addition and subtraction calculations, with both positive and negative integers.
- Multiplication and division of positives and negatives: Simple multiplication and division calculations, with both positive and negatives integers, with the results remaining integers.
- X intercept: Finding the X intercept of a straight line, where the intercept is a positive or negative integer, and the slope is also a positive or negative integer, with all integers ranging between -14 and +14.
- Roots of a 2nd-degree polynomial: Finding the 2 real roots of a 2nd-degree polynomial where the roots are positive or negative integers and all coefficients are also positive or negative integers, with all roots ranging between -14 and +14.
- Factors of a 2nd-degree polynomial: Find the factors of a 2nd-degree polynomial where the roots are positive or negative integers and all coefficients are also positive or negative integers, with all roots ranging between -14 and +14.
- Simultaneous equations: Find the intersection of two straight lines where all coefficients are positive or negative integers and all intersection points have integer coordinates, with all integers ranging between -14 and +14.
- Prime factors: Find the prime factors of a number.
- Simple interest: Find the interest, interest rate, original principal, original term, or resulting total value of a loan using simple interest calculations, where all values are integers between -14 and 14 or multiples of 100.

The following text extract shows the interaction of a learner with one of the competitions. A user called PIMP(*)STAR logged on at 17:28:12 (5.28 p.m.) and started competing in the "factor a polynomial" competition.

17:28:12   PIMP(*)STAR:

17:28:12   Bot -> PIMP(*)STAR: The current *TopScore* is einstein's mother with 100%. To clear your score and start over send .z with nothing after it. *TopScores* are updated after 10 questions. What are the FACTORS of the polynomial x^2 + 10x + 24 Write the factors in the form .z x + 3x − 7 with one space between the factors.

PIMP(*)STAR played on and off for 5 hours, getting better and better and eventually becoming the *TopScore*.

22:51:23   Bot -> PIMP(*)STAR: Correct. Your score is 10 correct out of 10 or 100%.

Bot -> Congratulations. You are the new TopScore. What are the FACTORS of the polynomial x^2 − 7x − 44. Write the factors in the form .z x + 3x − 7 with one space between the factors.

Dr Math allows users to change their aliases. Once PIMP(*)STAR was the *TopScore* and her name was going to be displayed for all to see (even though they don't publish telephone numbers or any identifying comments), the user tried out a few other aliases such as "*Qun of Maths*" and eventually settled on "*smartyCAT.*"

22:52:43   Bot -> PIMP(*)STAR: We currently know you as PIMP(*)STAR. Send us a .n followed by the new name you want on our system.

22:54:23   PIMP(*)STAR: Qun of maths

22:54:23   Bot -> Qun of maths: We have changed your name to Qun of maths on our system.

22:55:23   Qun of maths:

22:55:23   Bot -> Qun of maths: We currently know you as Qun of maths. Send us a .n followed by the new name you want on our system.

22:56:03   Qun of maths: smartyCAT

22:56:03   Bot -> smartyCAT: We have changed your name to smartyCAT on our system.

Lookup

The *Lookup* function allows learners access to relevant math definitions. Currently, there are 191 definitions. Figure 52.3 illustrates the lookup of the definition for absolute value.

By providing this large collection of definitions and formulae as static lookups, tutors could refer learners with relevant queries to the static lookups, thereby freeing themselves up for more important tutoring and enabling learners to search for the information in future. As this functionality was always available (and tutors were only available during specific times), learners were empowered and able to access information whenever they needed it.

Encyclopedia

It was noted that tutors were often asked "off-topic questions." In accordance with the Dr Math persona, the tutors would search online encyclopedias for the information and then "cut and paste" the information and send it to the learners. Although this was useful

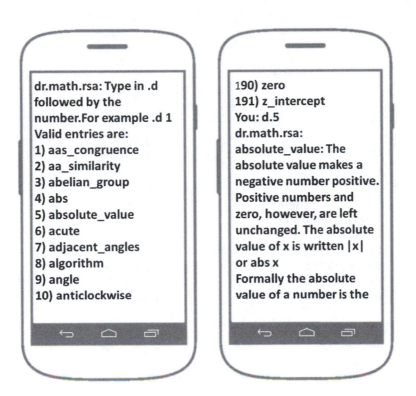

Figure 52.3 Lookup of Math Definitions

to the learners, it often kept the tutor busy with things that were not specifically tutoring. Learners who use Mxit on their cell phones often do not realize that, if they can use Mxit, then they have full access to the Internet on their cell phones using their phone browser (Donner, Gitau, & Marsden, 2009). To facilitate access to an encyclopedia, the Wikipedia wiki was made accessible through the platform. The graphic images are removed, and articles plus their relevant subsections are available. The learner is able to drill down to the information he/she is looking for, as shown in the search for *cat* as an example (see Figure 52.4).

Scientific Calculator

A functionality provided is a scientific calculator, as it became obvious that many learners do not have access to one (see Figure 52.5).

Peer Collaboration

Anghileri (2006) identifies peer collaboration as an additional environmental provision. In classrooms, this is achieved by grouping learners in order to co-construct understanding. The nature of the Mxit social-networking environment where Dr Math space is located fosters peer collaboration. Learners are able to have multiple conversations simultaneously. These conversations include face-to-face, as well as virtual, conversations with peers.

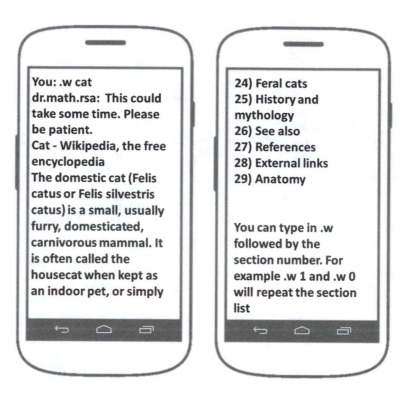

Figure 52.4 Searching Wikipedia Through Dr Math

CONCLUSION

Dr Math is a pragmatic solution to a real need for assistance in mathematics among learners as end users. It is partially motivated by the belief that mobile cellular technology has the potential to provide alternative access and participation mechanisms in ways that are beneficial and relevant to both the educational community and the learners. As such, the meaningful integration of this appropriate technology into the teaching and learning interaction has been empowering learners to engage in significant interactions with information and tutors, enhancing mathematics skills motivation, and ultimately equipping some of today's learners for full participation in tomorrow's world. Dr Math has proved a sustainable solution in the m-learning domain, where many small pilots have failed to scale or be sustainable. It can truly be viewed as a community initiative, with support from the Department of Basic Education, the Department of Science and Technology, and the invaluable institutionalization of community service and support of the University of Pretoria. Various volunteer tutors have been logging in and investing their time in the youth of South Africa. Dr Math has additionally been a forerunner in introducing mobile phones to formal education and providing practice-based evidence of a successful educational service. The final word thus belongs to the learners as end users (Butgereit, 2011a):

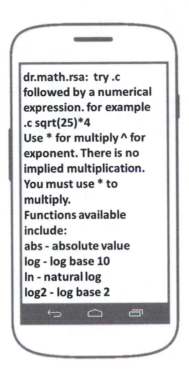

dr.math.rsa: try .c
followed by a numerical
expression. for example
.c sqrt(25)*4
Use * for multiply ^ for
exponent. There is no
implied multiplication.
You must use * to
multiply.
Functions available
include:
abs - absolute value
log - log base 10
ln - natural log
log2 - log base 2

Figure 52.5 Scientific Calculator

0k thx! I realy admire y0u pe0pl . . . Thanx again!
thx dis is a gud srvc u hv g2g
n thx 4 hlping me lst wk.
kwl thank u
kwl,thank y0u l0ts.
thank 4 yo patience.
Hey thank gudnes ur here
Oh ur realy doing a gr8 job thank u!
Ja i knw bt i reali thank god 4 tat finding u on my mixtq
Aaah thank u hihi
K thnx becovse ure gud hlp 2 us
Wow thnx alot
K thnx 4 evrythng
K,thnx
G2g thnx alot
this doctor maths thing is such a great thing cos you got me 20 Mark's, i did'nt
understand a day b4 my exam and u saved me thanks!!

REFERENCES

Anghileri, J. (2006). Scaffolding practices that enhance mathematics learning. *Journal of Mathematics Teacher Education, 9*(1), 33–52. DOI:10.1007/s10857–006–9005–9

Botha, A. (2010). *AxS*. Pretoria: CSIR Meraka Institute.

Butgereit, L. (2010). *How to tutor for Dr Math*. Pretoria, South Africa: CSIR Meraka Institute.

Butgereit, L. (2011a). *C_TO: A scalable architecture for mobile chat based tutoring*. Magister Technologiae: Information Technology, Nelson Mandela Metropolitan University, Port Elizabeth.

Butgereit, L. (2011b). *Seven characteristics of a successful virtual volunteering platform*. Paper presented at the IST Africa, Botswana.

Donner, J., Gitau, S., & Marsden, G. (2009). *"i-Internet? Intle" (beautiful): Exploring first-time Internet use via mobile phones in a South African women's collective*. Paper presented at the 3rd International Development Informatics Association Conference, Berg-en-Dal, Kruger National Park, South Africa.

Kirkman, B. L., Rosen, B., Gibson, C. B., Tesluk, P. E., & McPherson, S. O. (2002). Five challenges to virtual team success: Lessons from Sabre, Inc. *The Academy of Management Executive, 16*(3), 67–79.

Knott-Craig, A., & Silber, G. (2012). *Mobinomics, Mxit and Africa's Mobile Revolution*. Johannesburg, South Africa: Bookstorm.

Mxit. (2012, October). Mxit statistic. Retrieved from: http://site.mxit.com/files/MxitStatistics.pdf

University of Pretoria. (2008). *Community engagement at the University of Pretoria*. Retrieved from: http://web.up.ac.za/

53

MOBILE LEARNING GAMES FOR LOW-INCOME CHILDREN IN INDIA

Lessons from 2004–2009

Matthew Kam

The cell phone's ubiquity in developing countries has made it widely hyped as a highly appropriate e-learning device in these regions. It is relatively affordable, can run without constant access to reliable electricity, and can be used by low-income populations who do not possess high levels of literacy or schooling. However, according to the World Bank, "there are still precious few widespread examples of the use of [mobile] phones for education purposes inside or outside of classrooms in developing countries that have been well documented, and fewer still that have been evaluated with any sort of rigor" (2009).

In this chapter, I seek to address the above gap by sharing the key results from the Mobile and Immersive Learning for Literacy in Emerging Economies (MILLEE) project from mid 2004, when I started it, until mid 2009.[1] During this period, my research team and I conducted ten rounds of field research, spanning more than 10 months on the ground, with poor children living in the urban slums and villages in both North and South India. This period included numerous rounds of field testing and iterations of our educational-games prototypes that target literacy in English as a second language (ESL), as well as two semester-length summative evaluations. Although the results have been reported in earlier peer-reviewed publications (Kam, Ramachandran, Sahni, & Canny, 2005; Kam et al., 2006; Kam, Ramachandran, Devanathan, Tewari, & Canny, 2007a; Kam, Rudraraju, Tewari, & Canny, 2007b; Kam et al., 2008; Kam, Mathur, Kumar, & Canny, 2009a; Kam, Kumar, Jain, Mathur, & Canny, 2009b; Kumar et al., 2010), I have not previously sought to synthesize and make them accessible in a single publication for a broad audience. That is the intent of this chapter.

PROBLEM STATEMENT

According to the *BBC News*,

> eight . . . states [in India] account for more poor people than . . . the 26 poorest African countries combined. . . . The Indian states, including Bihar, Uttar Pradesh and West Bengal, have 421 million "poor" people . . . This is more than the 410 million poor in the poorest African countries.
>
> (*BBC News*, 2010)

For the poor in developing countries, gaining access to high-quality education remains a huge challenge. Among fifth-grade children in rural India, for example, more than 40 percent of them are lagging by at least three grade levels in terms of their ability to read in their local languages, and only a quarter of them are able to read simple sentences in English (Pratham, 2010). Worse, teachers in rural schools who are responsible for teaching ESL struggle themselves to communicate in the language. However, the English language is widely perceived to be a socioeconomic enabler: "[Indians] secretly believe, if not openly say, that competence in English makes a considerable difference in their career prospects. . . . Politicians and bureaucrats denounce the elitism of [English-medium] schools but surreptitiously send their children to them" (Gupta, 1995, p. 76).

POPULATION TARGETED

In the context of the above problem about acquiring English-language skills in environments where rural children do not receive adequate exposure to the language everyday, the MILLEE project aims to leverage the increasing ubiquity of the cell phone in developing countries as a channel for educational delivery. The goal is to make high-quality ESL instruction accessible to the vast number of low-income children in the developing world who are either out of school, or who attend public schools where the quality of instruction is widely perceived to be poor. In particular, the cell phone was selected as the educational technology platform because it has the potential to allow children to access high-quality digital learning resources at places and times more convenient than schools, thereby increasing the amount of time spent on learning. Although the project has focused on India, and, more recently, China to a smaller extent, I expect the approach and results to be applicable to other geographic regions, as well as other subjects, such as mathematics and science.

RESEARCH GOALS AND OUTCOMES DESIRED

At a high level, my research goals were twofold. First, I sought to evaluate the extent to which m-learning can improve English literacy among children in the developing world. However, I wanted to take a perspective that does not view educational technology as a "black box," which simplistic questions such as "*does* technology succeed in improving learning?" reflect. Instead, I took the position that (1) the social context in which the technology is embedded mattered, and that (2) this black box could be opened, i.e., the technology is highly *malleable* and could be designed so as to consciously account for this social context. When seen from the latter perspective, my second and more important research goal arose, namely: *how* can m-learning experiences be designed to enhance English learning among poor children in India? This perspective, which emphasized the role of design in educational technology, was crucial. It implied that, although intervention evaluation (i.e., the first research goal) was important, intervention *design* (i.e., the second research goal) was even more important. An educational technology intervention that was not thoughtfully designed to account for its intended social context was doomed to fail from the outset, such that the poor learning outcomes observed from its evaluation were likely attributable to the intervention design process that was poorly carried out, as opposed to technology being inherently non-beneficial or counter-productive to learning.

I addressed the second research goal through more than three rounds of formative testing (from summer 2006 to summer 2007), in which the team field-tested and iterated on the m-learning software prototypes until children found the instructional designs to be adequately intuitive and free from usability problems. It was only after these iterations that the prototypes were sufficiently polished to be piloted and assessed in subsequent summative studies. However, the research outcomes from the formative assessments not only were the final software designs and prototypes that evolved from multiple iterations, but also encompassed the broader lessons, design guidelines, and design tools for designing English learning games that targeted low-income Indian children. In particular, these design tools included more than 50 design patterns that captured the best practices reflected in state-of-the-art commercial software for language learning (Kam et al., 2007a), as well as a list of 74 differences between traditional village games and con-temporary Western videogames (Kam et al., 2009a). As I will elaborate in the next section, these guidelines and design tools took into consideration the social context, such as the target learners' familiarity with (1) games, (2) teacher-centered instruction, and (3) inexpensive technologies.

Subsequently, to investigate the first research goal, I led two summative assessments, which took place in a semester-long after-school program (spring 2008) and everyday rural environments for 26 weeks (spring 2009), respectively. Performing a summative evaluation in an after-school program that was run by adult facilitators enabled us to assess the extent to which the technology supported child participants to acquire English, when adults were present to supervise and ensure that participants actually used the cell phones for educational purposes.

At the same time, however, interviews with participants and their parents revealed that the former spent significantly more time outside school than in school, in everyday rural environments such as the home, playground, and temple. Out-of-school environ-ments, therefore, constituted the largest opportunity that m-learning should target. As such, it was necessary to evaluate the extent to which children would use the prototypes *voluntarily* to learn English in these everyday environments, *when close adult supervision was normally absent.* For this reason, game-like elements were incorporated into the software prototypes so as to encourage children to replay the educational games, i.e., to return to the instructional software again and again. In other words, I hypothesized that it is possible to dramatically increase the reach of English language and literacy learning in the developing world by using portable mobile devices, such as the cell phone, as the delivery platform (which can be easily taken around outside the school), and by designing e-learning experiences mediated by these devices that take the form of educational games.

PROCESS DESCRIPTION

In this section, I first describe the results of our needs analysis, which pointed to the opportunity for m-learning, after which I describe the design methodologies behind the English learning games. Regarding the latter, briefly, the design of our educational games drew on the latest research by education researchers in second-language acquisition and the psychology of reading, as well as the principles of videogame design and cross-cultural design. Following that, I report the key results from the formative assessments, as well as the summative assessments in the after-school program and everyday rural environments. Whereas the first summative assessment focused on the extent of English learning in the after-school program as measured via post-test gains, the second summative assessment examined the social ecology around the games in the everyday lives of rural Indian children. The latter enabled me to go one step beyond merely assessing learning, in order to identify the broader cultural and technical issues that affected the adoption of m-learning.

Needs Analysis (2004–2005)

When I began the MILLEE project in 2004, the thinking was that, instead of starting with preconceived ideas about what the project should be, I needed to begin by gaining a first-hand understanding of the ground-level conditions in poor schools in India. Only then is it possible to identify opportunities for technology-enhanced learning that are appropriate for these local contexts (Kam et al., 2005). That summer, with the help of local interpreters, I performed qualitative interviews in India with teachers, low-income students, and their parents, at five rural schools and an afternoon school program for girls living in the slums. In those interviews, my goal was to understand the everyday obstacles that my respondents faced in obtaining access to high-quality education, as well as their attitudes toward technology-enhanced learning. Respondents consistently cited English as a second (or even third) language as one of the three most difficult subjects for teachers in poor schools to teach. This difficulty was illustrated by the limited ability of rural teachers to communicate in English with me, to the extent that much of my interactions with them were facilitated by interpreters. Most importantly, I gained a deeper appreciation of how infrastructural constraints—not only irregular electricity, but more significantly, insufficient classroom buildings in rural schools with doors that could actually be padlocked, so that they could house desktop computers securely—made it challenging for technology-enhanced learning on computers to scale.

During winter that year, I carried out an exploratory study involving multimedia storytelling at the above afternoon school program for urban slums girls (Kam et al., 2005). The goal was to examine the feasibility of some emerging ideas for technology-enhanced learning that developed from my fieldwork that summer, in order to identify a subset of those ideas that were promising enough to proceed further with. Some of my ideas included helping children to learn by scaffolding them to create multimedia stories that communicate academic concepts to their peers. However, attendance at the digital story creation sessions that I ran was lower than expected. This salient lesson suggested that it was difficult for participants to find time to attend educational sessions and underscored the potential for m-learning to facilitate learning in everyday settings such as the home that were more convenient for low-income children to access compared with school.

In the following summer in 2005, I led a similar exploratory study at a government rural school (Kam et al., 2006), with 12 fifth-graders (10 girls and 2 boys) between the ages of 10 and 16. We experimented with digital cameras, authoring software, and ESL educational games meant for desktop computers. We found that a vocabulary learning game was well received by the children and demonstrated positive learning outcomes in terms of short-term retention. This finding supported the viability of designing educational games as a major thrust in the project, which we began to undertake from this point onwards, on cell phones.

In contrast, we found that it was much more challenging, at least in the short term, to engage in constructionist learning (Papert, 1993), i.e., having students learn through the process of creating digital artifacts on topics that they find personally meaningful. One primary constraint was that this approach required the presence of adult facilitators who possessed both the pedagogical and technological knowledge (about the authoring software) to coach the child learners effectively. Furthermore, we observed that the brightest students at the above rural school had already taken 3 years of ESL classes, yet struggled to read every letter in the English alphabet. This experience made us realize that it was essential to return to the basics in English teaching, as opposed to assuming that children were ready to engage in constructionist learning, which requires reasonable mastery of foundational skills and knowledge such as grammar and the ability to read extended passages.

More importantly, the needs analysis suggested that, whereas poor electricity and building infrastructure made desktop computers less than ideal for low-income schools and communities in India, m-learning on cell phones appeared promising and deserved further consideration. Furthermore, educational games appeared to be a promising m-learning application in the rural Indian context.

Formative Assessments and Emergent Design Methodologies (2006–2007)

Beginning in the summer of 2006, I built on the success of the above vocabulary learning game, which was meant for the desktop computer, by leading the design and implementation of a similar set of vocabulary learning games specifically for the cell phone (Kam et al., 2007a). The goal was to examine the feasibility of delivering ESL instruction using the cell phone, in terms of user acceptance, usability, and learning benefits. Conducting user studies with rural children—compared with their urban slum counterparts—is more challenging, given the former's lower levels of familiarity with technology, in addition to logistical obstacles in traveling to the villages. In large part, I overcame the difficulties of conducting formative studies in this complex cross-cultural design project by running every field study with children in the urban slums, before I attempted every study in a similar manner with rural children. This systematic and cautious approach not only enabled the team to iron out initial kinks in the research designs and prototype designs with children in the urban slums, but also provided us with a base of sound experience, in preparation for the subsequent studies with rural children.

The first formative assessment was carried out in August 2006 at the above afternoon school for urban slum students (Kam et al., 2007a). For the study, I led the design and prototyping of six games based on the best practices found in successful language learning applications on the commercial market. I do not claim that commercial software products for language learning are perfect, but, nevertheless, note that their success on the commercial market constitutes some indirect evidence for their pedagogical effectiveness. In total, I reviewed a sample of more than 35 state-of-the-art commercial language learning software applications and other digital materials, which include bestsellers such as Pimsleur and Rosetta Stone. Applications in this sample were selected based on factors such as glowing reviews on home-schooling, e-commerce, etc. websites, and that the overall sample reflected a balance between listening, reading, speaking, and writing skills.

In examining the above commercial applications, I applied task-based language teaching (Ellis, 2003; Nunan, 2004; Prabhu, 1987; Skehan, 1998) as my analytical lens. The task-based language-teaching framework for curriculum development has shown successes with children in India (Prabhu, 1987). In this framework, tasks are goal-directed learning activities in which the learner focuses on communicating meaning (vs. manipulating language forms). Tasks can be composed with other tasks to form larger instructional sequences. As such, digital activities such as word–picture matching activities and conversations with non-player characters in digital games can be designed as pre-task activities that prepare learners to engage in the communicative task proper, and other digital activities can involve posing questions to help learners to reflect on what the task has just covered, or provide high-level feedback, as part of the post-task activities. In other words, in applying this framework, technology-enhanced learning can take the form of digital activities during the pre- and post-task stages that, respectively, scaffold the learner in building foundational linguistic skills and reviewing the target linguistic units.

In total, I identified more than 50 design patterns that captured the best practices in those commercial products for teaching listening, speaking, reading, and writing skills. Examples of these patterns include tasks that involve the learner associating letters with their sounds, word–picture matching tasks for vocabulary learning, and dictation tasks in which some letters of the word to be spelled are displayed, so as to reduce the difficulty of recalling the word's spelling. The design pattern is increasingly popular in domains such as building architecture (Alexander, 1977) and videogame design (Björk and Holopainen, 2005) as an abstraction for representing solutions to design problems that are frequently encountered. The benefit of a design pattern is to facilitate the reuse of solutions that have been found to work, so as to minimize the need to reinvent the wheel. My work is the first to apply design patterns to the domain of language and literacy learning. The design pattern enables the educational-computing community to capture the best practices in the instructional design of state-of-the-art commercial language learning software, as a starting point that researchers and practitioners can revise and iterate on, based on a combination of (1) education theory, (2) practical experiences in classroom language teaching and (3) empirical experience with the patterns resulting from field-testing.

The six games that we piloted in the first formative assessment in August 2006 incorporated a subset of the above 50 design patterns in their instructional designs (Kam et al., 2007a). The participants included 11 sixth-graders between the ages of 11 and 15 who had attended school regularly for 3–6 years. We found that this group of learners exhibited significant post-test gains of 4.3 out of 12 points ($p < 0.001$, $\sigma = 3.7$) in terms of short-term vocabulary retention.

In January 2007, I led a second feasibility study (Kam et al., 2007b). Unlike the above study in August 2006, this study took place at a village school in South India. It enabled us to observe learning and usage dynamics among rural children, as opposed to children from the urban slums (as well as children from a different state in India, to understand the generalizability of our work). Similarly, unlike the study in August 2006, which focused on learning, this study focused on gameplay enjoyment. As such, the games that we designed and piloted drew on game design patterns such as those found in Björk and Holopainen (2005), as opposed to the above patterns for language pedagogy. We learned that there were aspects of the games that participants did not understand, and that there were contextual factors that we should have considered when applying the game design patterns, so as to design mobile games that were more intuitive and/or appealing to participants.

In particular, whereas the initial game designs were fairly successful with urban slum children, the same designs needed numerous iterations before we ironed out usability issues with rural children. Over 13 weeks in the summer of 2007, three of the game designs underwent three iterations in the field, with nearly 50 children between second and fifth grades (Kam et al., 2008). It appeared that rural children faced more usability problems than their urban slum counterparts, because the former were less familiar with high technology and videogames. For instance, we learned that the educational goals in our e-learning games became more obvious to rural learners when we maintained a distinction between pleasure and learning in the software designs. In particular, when we redesigned our earlier designs to de-emphasize the game's fantasy setting, and instead reoriented the user interface around a blackboard, with a teacher character who explained vocabulary words on the blackboard, we observed that such classroom-based visual elements cued rural children to focus their attention on what the games were trying to teach them. It appeared that these user-interface elements reflected the rote-based, teacher-centered educational experiences that children in rural Indian schools understand learning to be.

The more pressing challenge is that some of the game mechanics in our game designs continued to elude rural children, whose understanding and expectations about games differed from our Western notion about games (Kam et al., 2009a). This prompted us to take a step back to understand what rural children knew about games during the same summer. Specifically, I studied the characteristics of 28 traditional village games that children play in the villages in both North and South India. After that, I analyzed how these traditional village games contrasted with contemporary Western videogames, and distilled a list of 74 qualitative differences between the two families of games.

Tree-Tree was the first educational game that we designed based on insights from the above cross-cultural analysis. Tree-Tree was mirrored after the "tag" family of traditional games. It aimed to help the player acquire an English vocabulary of everyday fruits in India. The screen would show three different trees, such that each tree was associated with a different fruit. The computer-controlled opponent would call out one of these fruits, after which the player was tested on his/her knowledge of what the word meant and had to move his/her character to touch the corresponding tree. While moving, the player needed to evade capture by the opponent. Designing digital games such as Tree-Tree that accounted for the distinctions between traditional and contemporary Western games appeared to result in games with rules and elements that rural children could understand more easily. Since then, this design methodology has been replicated with equally promising results in the context of traditional Chinese games for rural children in China (Tian et al., 2010), as well as traditional Mexican games for Hispanic immigrant children in California (Tewari et al., 2010).

Summative Assessments (2008–2009)

Following the above formative assessments, I proceeded with the first summative assessment throughout the spring of 2008 (Kam et al., 2009b). This assessment took the form of a pilot in an after-school program at a village school in North India with 27 children, and spanned 38 two-hour sessions over 5 months. On average, three sessions were held every week in the afternoon, when regular classes at the school were over. Participants were recruited from the community living in the school's vicinity. The participants were aged 7–14 years (mean = 11.5 years) and ranged from second to ninth graders (mean = sixth grade). The average participant had a good knowledge of the English alphabet and a fair vocabulary of written words that he or she could read. On the other hand, the average participant was weaker in recalling and spelling every-day nouns, and even weaker in constructing complete sentences with these words. Twenty-five participants came from families who owned at least one cell phone. The after-school sessions were supervised by adult facilitators who provided technical support for the cell-phone devices, as well as supervised the participants to ensure they were devoting their attention to learning from the mobile games. I explicitly instructed the facilitators not to teach English, so that our games were the only source of English instruction.

The mobile games introduced in this pilot targeted a set of common nouns, verbs for actions that can be performed with these nouns, sentence structures for constructing sentences out of these nouns and verbs, as well as sentence structures for phrasing question-and-answer sequences with the same nouns and verbs. The designs of these games drew on the above (1) design patterns for language pedagogy, (2) analysis of how the elements in traditional village games are unique compared with those in contemporary Western games, and (3) formative assessments and iterations with rural children elsewhere in India. On the pre- and post-tests, test-takers were awarded one point for each common noun in the syllabus that was spelled correctly. On average, participants exhibited statistically significant post-test gains on a one-tailed t-test with an effect size of 0.71 ($p = 0.007$). I also observed that, among possible covariates, post-test gains exhibited high correlation with the grade level at which the learner was currently enrolled in school ($r = 0.61$) and medium correlation with age ($r = 0.45$). Similarly, participants' post-test gains exhibited a high degree of correlation with their qualifying test scores ($r = 0.57$) and their scores on the spelling section on the qualifying test ($r = 0.70$).[2]

Even though the first summative assessment had demonstrated the efficacy of m-learning within an after-school setting, the learning benefits were restricted to learners who were able to incur the opportunity costs of attending the after-school sessions. On the other hand, the "learn anywhere, anytime" promise of m-learning argues that the greatest impact is in out-of-school settings, where learners could conveniently engage in m-learning when they have time, such as when they are taking a rest in the middle of agricultural work. However, it was unclear what rural children would do every day with cell phones, and, more importantly, the extent to which they would actually engage in m-learning voluntarily when adults were not always present to supervise them to use the devices for educational purposes. This led us to carry out a second summative assessment (Kumar et al., 2010), which took the form of preparatory fieldwork (two weeks in the summer of 2008), leading up to an *in situ* study proper (26 weeks in the spring and summer of 2009).

A total of 18 children (2 upper-caste girls, 6 upper-caste boys, 7 lower-caste girls, and 3 lower-caste boys) between 10 and 14 years old participated in the in situ study (Kumar et al., 2010). For the 26-week duration of the study, I led the design and implementation of a new set of m-learning games that targeted a total of 180 word families in the English language, and preloaded these games on the cell phones that were loaned to each participant. Besides using data logging to track the extent of vocabulary learning, we performed interviews and observations that are ethnographic in spirit (e.g., "thick descriptions"). We observed that rural children voluntarily played these games without adult supervision, to the extent that the average learner covered three vocabulary words per week under "steady-state" everyday conditions, after the novelty factor has worn off (i.e., after the first 8 weeks). Most importantly, the average participant was restricted to using his or her phone for 2 hours and 23 minutes per week, owing to irregular electricity, which made it impossible to keep his or her cell-phone battery fully charged. However, children with better access to electricity at home played our games over a longer duration. Participants also reported that 75 percent of the time that they spent playing the games actually took place in the home.

In terms of our qualitative findings, we identified eight scenarios in which m-learning could be integrated into the fabric of everyday rural Indian life (Kumar et al., 2010). For instance, girls could engage in m-learning when there is downtime between household chores. Similarly, lower-caste girls could engage in m-learning when they take their goats out to graze. (Upper-caste families' households do not rear goats.) Furthermore, upper-caste boys could engage in m-learning when supervising lower-caste boys who are working as hired laborers in the agricultural fields, or when performing watch duty at night in the fields. Although lower-caste boys cannot engage in m-learning when working in the fields, they nevertheless have other opportunities, such as after dinner and before bedtime. On the other hand, although their sisters can engage in m-learning after dinner, the girls are first required to wash the dishes and finish other housework. As a result, the above scenarios illustrate how caste and gender are important "social fault lines" that affect adoption and learning around the games in everyday rural Indian life.

DISCUSSION AND CONCLUSION

In the first summative assessment, I found that the English-literacy learning games that we had designed for the cell phone were associated with as much as one standard deviation pre- to post-improvement on tests of English spelling knowledge, in the case of learners with a high base level of English knowledge. More importantly, the fact that post-test gains were greater for students with a stronger academic foundation (as measured by, for instance, spelling performance on the qualifying test and grade level enrolled in school) reiterates the importance of designing a curriculum for the games that is appropriate and in line with what the learner already knows.[3]

Furthermore, the number of words that participants voluntarily covered in the games in the second summative assessment is substantial. This volume of out-of-school learning alone is close to one-third of the ideal vocabulary that children in industrialized countries, with excellent school infrastructures and well-trained teachers, should learn. Furthermore, given how it was observed that irregular electricity was a significant obstacle, should participants have more regular electricity to recharge their phone batteries, they are likely to cover more words. That is, at the observed levels of gameplay, the volume of vocabulary learning was restricted by infrastructural constraints and not learner motivation. In underdeveloped regions, where rural children do not have alternative access to quality instruction, the above learning outcomes support the case for m-learning among underserved learner communities in the so-called developing world, and call for further research in this area.

Despite the hype that m-learning allows "learning anywhere, anytime," our preliminary findings suggest that m-learning, at least in rural Indian communities, is more likely to take place indoors, vis-à-vis the outdoor settings that are conventionally claimed to be where m-learning could occur. If our finding holds true elsewhere, the ramifications are significant. At the least, they imply that future research on m-learning needs to focus on the social dynamics in the home and other indoor environments where m-learning actually takes place. This social context, which may include gender attitudes and caste differences, would in turn need to be accounted for in the design of future m-learning initiatives and software.

ACKNOWLEDGMENTS

The author led the work described in this chapter when he was a doctoral candidate at the University of California, Berkeley, and, later, an Assistant Professor at Carnegie Mellon University. This research was supported by the MacArthur Foundation, Microsoft, National Science Foundation (Grant No. 0326582), Qualcomm, and Verizon. The author thanks Mehnaaz Abidi, Aishvarya Agarwal, Aman Anand, Pratim Basu, Siddharth Bhagwani, John Canny, Jatin Chaudhary, Anshul Chaurasia, Deepti Chittamuru, Jane Chiu, Varun Devanathan, Lv Fei, Denny George, Sonal Gupta, Ashwin Jain, Shirley Jain, Anjali Koppal, Anuj Kumar, Siddhartha Lal, Babu Mathew, Shalini Mathur, David Nguyen, Alok Prakash, Neelima Purwar, Anand Raghavan, N. S. Soundara Rajan, M. L. Ramanarasimha, Divya Ramachandran, Vijay Rudraraju, Urvashi Sahni, Rolly Seth, Geeta Shroff, Gautam Singh, Kartikey Singh, Kavish Sinha, Satyajit Swain, Anuj Tewari, Feng Tian, Pallav Vyas, and Jingtao Wang for their contributions as collaborators or team members on this research.

NOTES

1   At the time of writing, we have just wound down a comparative study that took place with 250 children in four low-fee private schools in Hyderabad, India, over the entire 2011–2012 academic year, based on a second generation of educational games that we designed and developed between 2009 and 2011. The data from this recent pilot study will be analyzed and reported in future publications.

2   A qualifying test was administered prior to the pilot to ensure that every participant had the basic numeracy and English literacy to benefit from the English curriculum targeted by the mobile games in the after-school program. The test included a section in which the participant was asked to spell the English words for everyday objects.

3   The reader may recall that Indian children from high-poverty backgrounds typically lag 3 years academically behind their urban, middle-class counterparts. For our recent pilot conducted over the 2011–2012 academic year, we had designed a "bridge curriculum" that targets the prerequisite remedial knowledge that such disadvantaged children need to know, in order to successfully learn the official government curriculum that urban, middle-class learners are better prepared to master. More details will be forthcoming in future publications.

REFERENCES

Alexander, C. (1977). *A pattern language: Towns, buildings, constructions.* Oxford, UK: Oxford University Press.

BBC News. (2010). *"More poor" in India than Africa.* July 13.

Björk, S., & Holopainen, J. (2005). *Patterns in game design.* Independence, KY: Charles River Media.

Ellis, R. (2003). *Task-based language teaching and learning.* Oxford, UK: Oxford University Press.

Gupta, R. K. (1995). English in a postcolonial situation: The example of India. *Profession 95, 18,* 73–78.

Kam, M., Ramachandran, D., Sahni, U., & Canny, J. (2005, July). Designing educational technology for developing regions: Some preliminary hypotheses. IEEE 3rd International Workshop on Technology for Education in Developing Countries. In *Proceedings of IEEE International Conference on Advanced Learning Technologies* (pp. 968–972). Kaohsiung, Taiwan, July 5–8.

Kam, M., Ramachandran, D., Raghavan, A., Chiu, J., Sahni, U., & Canny, J. (2006, June). Practical considerations for participatory design with rural school children in underdeveloped regions: Early reflections from the field. In *Proceedings of ACM Conference on Interaction Design and Children* (pp. 25–32). Tampere, Finland, June 7–9.

Kam, M., Ramachandran, D., Devanathan, V., Tewari, A., & Canny, J. (2007a, April–May). Localized iterative design for language learning in underdeveloped regions: The PACE framework. In *Proceedings of ACM Conference on Human Factors in Computing Systems* (pp. 1097–1106). San Jose, CA, April 28–May 3.

Kam, M., Rudraraju, V., Tewari, A., & Canny, J. (2007b, September). Mobile gaming with children in rural India: Contextual factors in the use of game design patterns. In *Proceedings of 3rd Digital Games Research Association International Conference.* Tokyo, Japan, September 24–28.

Kam, M., Agarwal, A., Kumar, A., Lal, S., Mathur, A., Tewari, A., et al. (2008, February). Designing e-learning games for rural children in India: A format for balancing learning with fun. In *Proceedings of ACM Conference on Designing Interactive Systems.* Cape Town, South Africa, February 25–27.

Kam, M., Mathur, A., Kumar, A., & Canny, J. (2009a, April). Designing digital games for rural children: A study of traditional village games in India. In *Proceedings of ACM Conference on Human Factors in Computing Systems.* Boston, MT, April 4–9.

Kam, M., Kumar, A., Jain, S., Mathur, A., & Canny, J. (2009b, April). Improving literacy in rural India: Cellphone games in an after-school program. In *Proceedings of IEEE/ACM Conference on Information and Communication Technology and Development.* Doha, Qatar, April 17–19.

Kumar, A., Tewari, A., Shroff, G., Chittamuru, D., Kam, M., & Canny, J. (2010, April). An exploratory study of unsupervised mobile learning in rural India. In *Proceedings of ACM Conference on Human Factors in Computing Systems.* Atlanta, GA, April 10–15.

Nunan, D. (2004). *Task-based language teaching.* Cambridge, UK: Cambridge University Press.

Papert, S. (1993). *Mindstorms: Children, computers, and powerful ideas.* New York: Basic Books.

Prabhu, N. S. (1987). *Second language pedagogy.* Oxford, UK: Oxford University Press.

Pratham. (2010). *Annual status of education report (rural) 2009 (Provisional).* Retrieved from: http://econpapers.repec.org/scripts/redir.pf?u=http%3A%2F%2Fwww.esocialsciences.org%2FDownload%2FrepecDownload.aspx%3Ffname%3DDocument1211201070.1138117.pdf%26fcategory%3DArticles%26AId%3D2373%26fref%3Drepec;h=repec:ess:wpaper:id:2373

Skehan, P. (1998). Task-based instruction. *Annual Review of Applied Linguistics, 18,* 268–286.

Tewari, A., Goyal, N., Chan, M., Yau, T., Canny, J., & Schroeder, U. (2010, December). SPRING: Speech and pronunciation improvement through games, for Hispanic children. In *Proceedings of IEEE/ACM International Conference on Information and Communication Technologies and Development.* London, United Kingdom, December 13–16.

Tian, F., Lv, F., Wang, J., Wang, H., Luo, W., Kam, M., et al. (2010, April). Let's play Chinese characters—Mobile learning approaches via culturally inspired group games. In *Proceedings of ACM Conference on Human Factors in Computing Systems.* Atlanta, GA, April 10–15.

World Bank. (2009). *Surveying the use of mobile phones in education worldwide.* Retrieved from: http://blogs.worldbank.org/edutech/surveying-the-use-of-mobile-phones-in-education-worldwide

INDEX